Public Finance of the Dutch Republic in Comparative Perspective

Library of Economic History

VOLUME 9

The titles published in this series are listed at *brill.com/lehi*

Public Finance of the Dutch Republic in Comparative Perspective

The Viability of an Early Modern Federal State (1570s–1795)

By

Wantje Fritschy

BRILL

LEIDEN | BOSTON

Cover illustration: "*Ereprent Liberale Gifte*". Engraving made by J. Smit in 1747 to commemorate the so-called 'Liberal Gift', an exceptional – and very successful – national wealth tax of two percent, levied after the restoration of the 'stadholderate' in the 'stadholderless' provinces of the Dutch Republic, in order to allow the new stadholder to resist a French invasion. Printed by Steven van Esveldt, Amsterdam, the Netherlands. (Courtesy of the *Belasting en Douane Museum* in Rotterdam, the Netherlands.)

The Library of Congress Cataloging-in-Publication Data is available online at http://catalog.loc.gov
LC record available at http://lccn.loc.gov/2017003789

Typeface for the Latin, Greek, and Cyrillic scripts: "Brill". See and download: brill.com/brill-typeface.

ISSN 1877-3206
ISBN 978-90-04-34127-2 (hardback)
ISBN 978-90-04-34128-9 (e-book)

This book is printed on acid-free paper and produced in a sustainable manner.

Contents

Preface

This book is the result of a long-term research project that started in the early 1990s with the construction of a database on the public finance of the provinces of the Dutch Republic at the Institute of Dutch History – now Huygens-ING – which was completed in 2009.[1] It brings together insights to be found already in earlier publications related to the project in various scholarly journals and contributions to books. As these earlier research results are partly only available in Dutch, one aim of this book was to offer a coherent overview of the public finance of the Dutch Republic in English. Another aim was to make a comprehensive book available for readers new to the subject. The book contains also much new work and new insights, however, especially in its comparative aspects, which may interest specialists as well.

I am very grateful to the historians Leendert van der Ent, Victor Enthoven, Ruud Liesker, Wybren Verstegen, Cor Trompetter and Wietse Veenstra for the thorough groundwork they accomplished by their participation in the collection of the data, and the publication of seven volumes accompanying the database, without which this book would not have been possible.[2] I am grateful to the Huygens Institute of Dutch History for its hospitality during two years and for hosting on its web site the database as well as the spreadsheets of tables containing the totals for the main data on the public finance of the Dutch Republic – with added estimates for missing data – that were constructed when I prepared the writing of this book.

I owe thanks to the Netherlands Institute of Advanced Studies in Wassenaar for accepting me as a NIAS-fellow during the academic year 2010/2011 which allowed me to start the process of writing. I am grateful to the Faculty of Arts of VU University in Amsterdam for releasing me two times from my teaching obligations to do research for a period of a year, and for allowing me guest status after my retirement, to facilitate its completion.

I am much obliged to two anonymous referees for stimulating comments on an earlier version of this book, and to a great number of friends, former colleagues, NIAS-fellows, and participants in several scholarly conferences on fiscal history where parts of this research-project could be presented (Colchester, Ghent, Madrid, Utrecht, Prato, New York) for stimulating discussions, for their reading of, and comments on, parts of this book, and for other

1 http://resources.huygens.knaw.nl/gewestelijkefinancien/en.

2 Electronically accessible on http://resources.huygens.knaw.nl/retroboeken/gewestelijke_financien/.

forms of support, especially Michael Braddick, Murat Čizakča, Petra van Dam (special thanks!), Oscar Gelderblom, Patrick Glenn, Jane Glenn, Marjolein 't Hart, Manon van der Heijden, Joost Jonker, Kamil Kivanç Karaman, John Lindsay, Patrick O'Brien, Luciano Pezzolo, Els van der Ree, Paul Rusman, Peer Vries, Bartholomé Yun Casalilla, Jan Luiten van Zanden (special thanks!), and last – and most – my husband Gied ten Berge.

Maarssen, August 2016

List of Illustrations

NB If not indicated otherwise, all Dutch fiscal data in the Tables and Figures in this book originate from the database and spreadsheets to be found on http://resources.huygens.knaw.nl/gewestelijkefinancien/en.

Tables

Figures

Abbreviations

ESFDB	European State Finance Database http://esfdb.websites.bta.com/Database.aspx/
GDP	Gross Domestic Product
GFD	L. van der Ent and W. Fritschy, *Gewestelijke financiën ten tijde van de Republiek der Verenigde Nederlanden. Deel 2 Drenthe, 1602–1795* (The Hague 1998); http://www.historici.nl/retroboeken/gewestelijke_financien
GFF	C. Trompetter, *Gewestelijke financiën ten tijde van de Republiek der Verenigde Nederlanden. Deel 6 Friesland (1587–1795)* (Den Haag 2007); http://www.historici.nl/retroboeken/gewestelijke_financien
GFG	L. van der Ent, and V. Enthoven, *Gewestelijke financiën ten tijde van de Republiek der Verenigde Nederlanden. Deel 3 Groningen (1594–1795)* (The Hague, 2001); http://www.historici.nl/retroboeken/gewestelijke_financien
GFH	R. Liesker and W. Fritschy, *Gewestelijke financiën ten tijde van de Republiek der Verenigde Nederlanden. Deel 4 Holland (1572–1795)* (Den Haag, ING, 2004); http://www.historici.nl/retroboeken/gewestelijke_financien
GFO	W. Fritschy, *Gewestelijke financien ten tijde van de Republiek. Deel 1 Overijssel, 1604–1795* (Den Haag 1996); http://www.historici.nl/retroboeken/gewestelijke_financien
GFU	S.W. Verstegen, *Gewestelijke financiën ten tijde van de Republiek der Verenigde Nederlanden. Deel 5 Utrecht (1579–1798)* (Den Haag 2006); http://www.historici.nl/retroboeken/gewestelijke_financien
GFZ	W. Veenstra, *Gewestelijke financien ten tijde van de Republiek der Verenigde Nederlanden. Deel 7 Zeeland, 1573–1795* (Den Haag, 2009); http://www.historici.nl/retroboeken/gewestelijke_financien
gld(s)	guilder(s)
HZFGO	Holland, Zeeland, Friesland, Groningen and Overijssel
JEH	Journal of Economic History
'Memorie 1755'	*'Memorie ofte Verhandeling van het geene omtrent het stuk van de finantie van de provincie van Holland en Westvriesland van tijd tot tijd is voorgevallen, en in wat toestand dezelve zig bijzonderlijk in 1755 bevindt, om daar uijt op te maaken het vermoogen waarna de maatregulen van staat genomen kunnen worden'* (NA, arch. nr. 3.01.29 *Financie van Holland*, in nr. 797); http://www.historici.nl/Onderzoek/Projecten/GewestelijkeFinancien/memorie

NA	*Nationaal Archief* (=National Archives in The Hague) http://www.gahetna.nl/en/collectie/archief
RSG	*Resoluties Staten Generaal* (=Resolutions of the States General); www.inghist.nl/retroboeken/statengeneraal
VOC	*Verenigde Oost-Indische Compagnie* (= Dutch East India Company)
WIC	*West-Indische Compagnie* (= Dutch West Indies Company)
ZFGO	Zeeland, Friesland, Groningen and Overijssel

Map

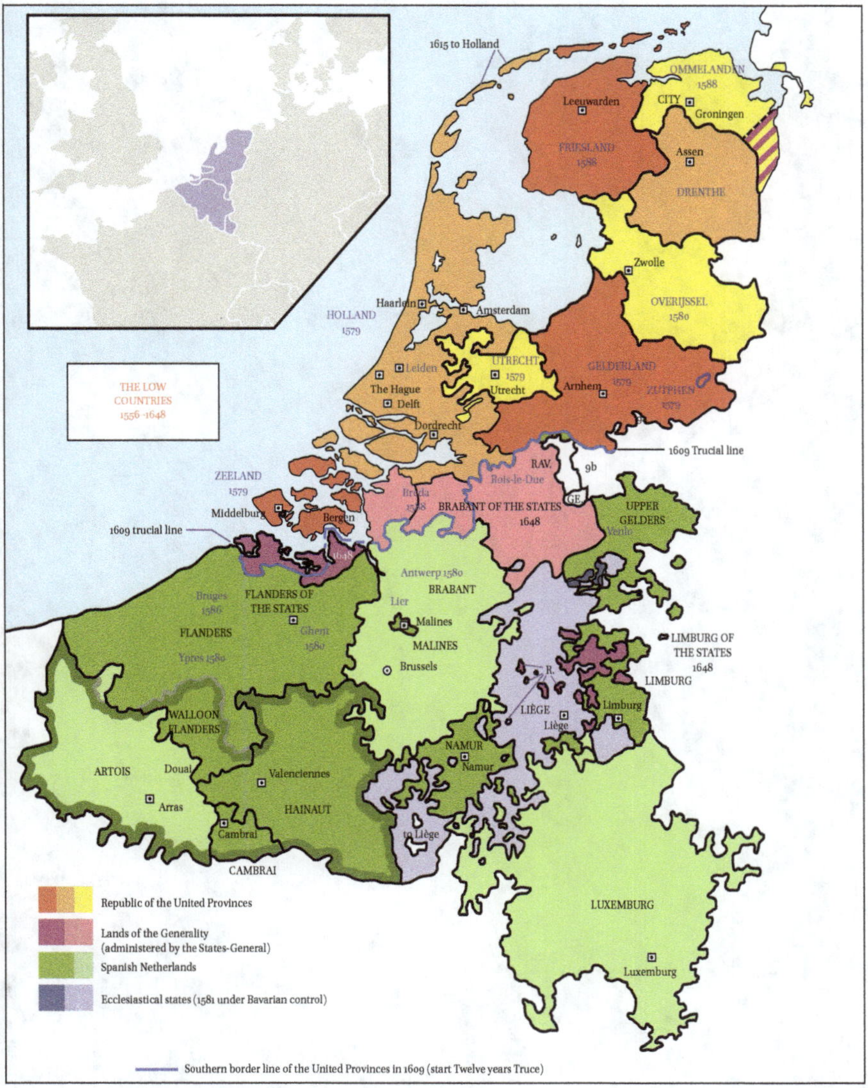

MAP *The Low Countries in the Early Modern Period*

General Introduction

The emergence of the Dutch Republic was part of the general process of the formation of states in the world since the end of the Middle Ages.[1] The rise of new territorial states in the Western world alongside empires, remnants of empires, and remaining city-states, was largely determined by military competition. Technical and organizational innovations in war faring and the large increases in the use of mercenary foot soldiers led to rising state expenditure, for land wars as well as for naval wars.[2] In modern historiography processes of increasing fiscal centralization are generally supposed to have been indispensable in order to obtain the required increase in state revenues.[3] States in the Western world developing since the sixteenth century are often characterized as '*fiscal*-military' states.[4]

---

1 For excellent summaries of the historiography of 'state formation' since the 1960s see: Th. Ertman, 'State Formation and State Building in Europe', in: *The Handbook of Political Sociology*, eds. T. Janoski a.o. (Cambridge 2005) pp. 367–383 and Tuong Vu, 'Studying the State through State Formation', *World Politics* 62, 1 (2010) pp. 148–175.

2 C.J. Rogers, ed., *The Military Revolution Debate. Readings on the Military Transformation of Early Modern Europe*, (Boulder, CO and Oxford, 1995); J. Glete, *Navies and nations. Warships, navies and statebuilding in Europe and America, 1500–1860* (Stockholm 1993).

3 B. Yun-Casalilla, 'Introduction: the rise of the fiscal state in Eurasia', in *The rise of fiscal states. A global history, 1500–1914*, eds. P. O'Brien and B. Yun Casalilla, (Cambridge, CUP, 2012) p. 14: 'centralization (…) appears to be a sine qua non of the very concept of a fiscal state'; A. Harding, *Medieval law and the foundations of the state*, (Oxford, 2002) p. V: '(…) France and England were both large enough to demand and small enough to make possible the centralized administration from which the notion of the state could develop'; for S.R. Epstein, *Freedom and growth. The rise of states and markets in Europe, 1300–1750* (London and New York 2000) p. 169 'centralization of government' belonged to the main contributions by European states to pre-modern growth; for an overview of older literature emphasizing the importance of centralization in state formation see M.C. 't Hart, *The making of a bourgeois state. War politics and finance during The Dutch Revolt*, Manchester, Manchester UP, 1993, pp. 2–6; M. Dincecco, *Political transformations and public finances: Europe, 1650–1913*, (Cambridge, 2011) emphasizes in contrast how fragmented the revenue systems of many European still remained in the sixteenth century and situates the start of centralization in the period after 1650; J. Tracy, *The founding of the Dutch Republic*, Oxford, 2008, p. 4 also doubts 'whether a state in which power and authority are concentrated is, in all historical circumstances, necessarily stronger or more effective than one in which power is decentralized'.

4 J. Brewer, *The sinews of power. War, money and the English state, 1688–1783* (London 1989) p. XVII was the first to use the term; see also J. Glete, *War and the state in early modern Europe. Spain, the Dutch Republic and Sweden as fiscal-military states, 1500–1660* (London 2002); M. Braddick, *State formation in early modern England, 1550–1700* (Cambridge 2000); S. Finer,

 | DOI 10.1163/9789004341289_002

The Dutch Republic was heavily involved in nearly all the wars of, what is called, the 'early modern period' (c. 1500–1800). Nonetheless it was a federal republic without strong central institutions, from its start in the latter decades of the sixteenth century until its downfall at the end of the eighteenth century. In 1787, not long after the Republic's disastrous defeat in its last naval war with Britain,[5] American 'Federalists' thought of 'the United Netherlands' as a mere 'confederacy', comparable to the weak confederation formed at the start of the American Revolution of 1776.[6] During the debate on the constitution of the thirteen 'United States of America' the state structure of the Dutch Republic was depicted by the Federalists Alexander Hamilton and James Madison as an 'imbecility', an 'Awful Example'.[7] Hamilton and Madison successfully advocated for the USA a federal constitution with much stronger central institutions. However, the famous American political scientist and historian William Riker argued already long ago that the American Federalists were poorly informed on the real character of the Dutch Republic which had been one of the 'Great Powers' of Europe during the seventeenth century.[8] Riker had become convinced that the Dutch Republic should be characterized as 'by far the most successful of modern federal republics'.[9]

It was the French philosopher Jean Bodin who presented the first contemporary theoretical reflections on state formation in the sixteenth century in his *Les six livres de la république*, published in 1576, when the Dutch Republic did not yet exist. He emphasized the desirability of a strong central power in

---

The history of government (Oxford 1997) p. 16; *The fiscal-military state in eighteenth-century Europe. Essays in honour of P.G.M. Dickson*, ed. C. Storrs, Ashgate publishers, Farnham, 2009, focuses on the seventeenth and eighteenth century but mentions the origins in the sixteenth century (ibidem, pp. 2–3 and note 15 for older literature).

5 The term 'Britain' will be used when only 'England and Wales' are meant; when 'England, Wales and Scotland' are meant 'Great Britain' will be used.

6 *Federalist* no. 20, 11. December 1787: http://www.foundingfathers.info/federalistpapers/fed20.htm.

7 *Federalist* no. 20, 11. December 1787: http://www.foundingfathers.info/federalistpapers/fed20.htm.

8 W. Riker, 'Dutch and American Federalism', *Journal of the History of Ideas* 18 (1957) pp. 495–518, p. 513–514; or even until 1748 according to O. van Nimwegen, *De Republiek der Verenigde Nederlanden als grote mogendheid* [= *The Republic of the United Netherlands as a Great Power*] (Amsterdam 2002).

9 Riker, 'Dutch and American Federalism', p. 495; for a theoretical instead of an historical approach of especially fiscal federalism see W. Oates, 'On the evolution of fiscal federalism: theory and institutions', *National Tax Journal* 61, 2 (2008) pp. 313–334.

a much more radical way than the much later American Federalists, and he is often seen as the first theorist of the concept of 'absolutism'.[10] By '*république*' he just meant 'state', not a republic as opposed to a monarchy. He was even convinced that sovereignty in states could best be embodied in a prince who was only accountable to God.[11] A '*république*' was for him 'a territorial unit ruled by a single sovereign' with a community enjoying 'a unity of sentiment as a consequence of living under a common sovereign'.[12] Its finances were for him the 'nerves of the republic'.[13]

The German Calvinist scholar Johannes Althusius published his *Politica Methodice Digesta*, which explicitly disagreed with Bodin's concept of supreme central power as the primary characteristic of a state in 1603. For Althusius a state is an association ('consociation') in which 'many cities and provinces obligate themselves to hold, organize, use, and defend, through their common energies and expenditures, the right of the realm'.[14] He is seen as the first theorist of federalism.[15] He added a special chapter on 'The Province' as an entity 'which contains within its territory many villages, towns, outposts, and cities united under the communion and administration of one right' in the second edition of his book of 1604. Provinces could also have 'rights of sovereignty in their territory' in his conception, even although they 'recognize the supreme magistrate of the realm as their superior'.[16]

Already in the same year as Bodin's 'Six Books on the Republic', the Swiss scholar Josias Simler had published *De Republica Helvetiorum*, designating the

10 J. Franklin, 'Bodin's doctrine and its limitations', *The Cambridge History of Political Thought, 1450–1700*, (Cambridge, CUP, 1991), pp. 299–309 and J.P. Sommerville, 'The meaning of absolutism', in: *idem*, pp. 347–350.

11 *Bodin. On Sovereignty* ed. J.H. Franklin, Cambridge, CUP, 1992, p. 2 (orig.: Book I. Chapter VIII, 346); http://classiques.uqac.ca/classiques/bodin_jean/six_livres_republique/bodin_six_livres_republique.pdf, p. 74 [111].

12 H. Dyson, *The state tradition in Western Europe. A study of an idea and institution* (Oxford, 1980) p. 27.

13 It is the opening sentence of Chapter 2: '*Les finances sont les nerfs de la République*' http://classiques.uqac.ca/classiques/bodin_jean/six_livres_republique/bodin_six_livres_republique.pdf [last access 01-02-2016].

14 *The Politics of Johannes Althusius. An abridged translation of the third edition of Politica Methodice Digesta, atque Exemplis Sacris et Profanis Illustrata*, ed. ed. F.S. Carney (Boston 1964) accessible on http://www.constitution.org/alth/alth_01.htm.

15 Th. Hueglin and A. Fenna, *Comparative Federalism. A Systematic Inquiry* (Peterborough, Broadview Press, 2015^2; 2006^1) 78.

16 Althusius, *Politica Methodice*, Chapter 7; http://www.constitution.org/alth/alth_07-08.htm.

Swiss confederacy as a 'republic', too, despite its lack of a sovereign.[17] The Swiss republic was much older than the Dutch. Its oldest preserved charter – signed by three rural Swiss communes – dates from 1291. Other Swiss cantons had joined the confederacy in the course of time. It successfully fought the dukes of Burgundy and the Habsburgs during the fifteenth and early sixteenth century. No wonder that, like the Dutch Republic, also the Swiss Republic has been characterized by modern political theorists as a successful federal state.[18]

However, in contrast to the Dutch Republic, the Swiss republic was hardly involved in the large European wars between 1515 and 1798. For the Swiss war faring became not a cause of increasing public expenditure, but a source of revenue, as its famous soldiers were hired by war faring states.[19] The saying 'no money, no Swiss'[20] was a sixteenth century variation on the classical phrase *pecunia nervus belli* ('money is the nerve of war').[21] In contrast to the Swiss Republic the Dutch Republic belonged to the European states which were confronted by large increases in military expenditure on mercenaries. In contrast to the Swiss Republic, it was involved, besides, in naval competition and the defence of colonial trade routes, requiring an expensive navy. Although the Swiss Republic survived during a much longer timespan than the Dutch, it is an especially intriguing question, therefore, how the small Dutch union of seven autonomous provinces, with a population of less than a quarter of that of its main enemies,[22] and without a powerful sovereign or other strong central

17 T. Maissen, 'Inventing the sovereign republic: imperial structure, French challenges, Dutch models and the early modern Swiss Confederation', in: *The Republican Alternative* eds. A. Holenstein, T. Maissen and M. Prak (Amsterdam 2008) 125–151, 126; although it became never as famous as Bodin's study, also Simler's book was several times reprinted (and translated into Dutch in 1613).

18 A. Wuergler, '"The League of Discordant members" or how the old Swiss confederation operated and how it managed to survive for so long', in: *The Republican Alternative. The Netherlands and Switzerland compared,* eds. A. Holenstein, T. Maissen, M. Prak (Amsterdam 2008) 29–51, 29; M. Forsyth, *Unions of state. The theory and practice of confederation* (Leicester 1981) p. XI, mentions the Netherlands, together with Switzerland, as the main historical examples of successful federal unions of states in the early modern period, followed by America and Germany in modern times.

19 The Dutch were the first to break the French monopoly on Swiss mercenaries in 1693; Maissen, 'Inventing the sovereign republic', p. 139.

20 As was said by the commander of the Swiss mercenaries to the French king in 1521 when he was no longer able to pay him during his defense of Milan against Charles V; the saying became well known in Dutch (*'Geen geld, geen Zwitsers'*).

21 Marcus Tullius Cicero, *Philippicae* 5,5: ... *primum nervos belli, pecuniam infinitam* (='first of all the sinews of war, infinite money); http://www.thelatinlibrary.com/cicero/phil5.shtml#5.

22 See Table 3.3 below.

institutions, was able to realize the increasing military expenditure needed to survive.

The Question at Stake

This book on the public finance of the Dutch Republic is not restricted to the question of how its wars were financed, but studies its fiscal system as a whole.[23] Without any doubt military expenditure was the all-important driving force explaining the large increases in public revenue resulting in the formation of 'national states' in Europe in the early modern period. 'War made the state, and the state made war', as Charles Tilly formulated it long ago.[24] States are, however, not only 'a by-product of ruler's efforts to acquire the means of war'.[25] Discussions in the early Middle Ages on the concept of the 'public good' in the newly discovered Roman law have been observed as important, too, for the development of European states.[26] The history of European states is not just the history of strong centralizing governments and princely power driven by military competition.[27] It is also a history of tax payers and investors in public debt, and of societies interested in internal rest and order, the maintenance of common values and a smooth functioning of the economy. In the opening sentence of her theoretical study *Of Rule and Revenue*, Margaret Levi preferred to present 'the history of the evolution of the state', as 'the history of state revenue production' not as that of 'war'.[28]

Recent studies leave no doubt at all as to the comparatively extremely high level of public expenditure and revenue realized in the Dutch Republic.[29] It is this extremely high level of Dutch public finance that forms the focus of this

23 For Dutch readers of this book it may be useful to note that the English word 'fiscal' differs from the Dutch word *'fiscaal'* in that it not only refers to taxation, but to all aspects of public finance, also public expenditure and public loans; the term 'fiscal system' will be used in this book as a synonym of 'system of public finance'.

24 *The formation of national states in Western Europe*, Ch. Tilly ed. (Princeton 1975), 'Introduction'.

25 Ch. Tilly, *Coercion, capital and European states. AD 990–1992* (Oxford Blackwell 1992) p. 14.

26 Dyson, *The State Tradition in Western Europe*, p. 26; for an overview of this discussion see S. Gunn, D. Grummitt, and H. Cools, 'War and the State in Early Modern Europe: Widening the Debate', *War in history* 15, 4 (2008) pp. 371–388.

27 A. Harding, *Medieval law and the foundations of the state* (Oxford, 2002) p. v.

28 M. Levi, *Of Rule and revenue* (Berkeley 1988) p. 1.

29 A nice illustration is offered by a comparison of ten states by K. Kivanç Karaman and Ş. Pamuk, 'Ottoman state finances in European perspective', *Journal of Economic History* 70, 3 (2010) pp. 593–629 fig. 5 p. 611 and fig. 6 p. 615.

book. How and why was it realized? And how and why was this possible? The question 'how' refers on the one hand to the formation of a new fiscal system as part of the emergence of the Dutch state during its 'Eighty Years War' against Spain: how did it come into existence? It refers on the other hand to the question of the relative importance of the constituting elements of public revenue during the course of its existence: how, by what specific means, had it been possible to raise it? The question 'why' refers on the one hand to the expenditure for which public revenue was considered to be necessary: why was it raised, to what specific aims? On the other hand to the historical circumstances that made possible the raising of such large amounts: why was it possible to reach this high level?

It is a fascinating question how the small federal Dutch Republic was able to survive military competition with much larger states during more than two centuries, but money was not the only factor in its survival. This book will not discuss, however, the role of the international political situation, that of alliances, and that of international balance-of-power politics for the survival of the Dutch Republic. Important as these were, 'money' is considered in this book as 'the nerve' of the state, – and as the nerve of the state in its totality, not only of war.[30]

On the expenditure side, not only the size of army and navy expenditure in different periods is at stake, also their relative importance in comparison to the amounts spent on general administration and on debt service. Debt service is treated as a separate item of public expenditure, despite the fact that public loans in the early modern period were mainly negotiated for wars, because interest payments, indispensable to maintain the credit of the state, could very well conflict with priorities of war finance.

On the revenue side not only the relative importance of taxes, customs and of different types of taxes is discussed. Since Dickson's study on what he called 'the Financial Revolution in England', the ability to sustain a public debt consisting of long-term voluntary loans at low rates of interest – that *could* be, but did not *have to* be redeemed – is generally seen as the most important cause of the fiscal superiority of the British vis-à-vis the French state during

30 An often found alternative for the phrase *pecunia nervus belli*, was *pecunia nervus rerum*; G. Parker called it '...the favorite Latin tag [of the mid-16th century]' in his *The army of Flanders*; see also M. Stolleis, *Pecunia nervus rerum: Zur Staatsfinanzierung in der frühen Neuzeit*, Frankfurt am Main, Klostermann, 1983; John Brewer, *Sinews of power: war, money and the English state, 1688–1788*,(London, Unwin Hyman, 1989).

the eighteenth century.[31] A taxonomy of changes in European fiscal history from 1130 to 1830 by Bonney and Ormrod distinguished a 'fiscal state' from a 'tax state' by its 'capacity to borrow sums on a scale unthinkable in earlier eras, without any significant debt reduction'.[32] Long-term loans, either voluntarily supplied or forced ones, are therefore considered as elements of public revenue in this book, despite the fact that loans do not figure as sources of public revenue in, for instance, Levi's theoretical study on public revenue.[33]

The capacity to borrow on a voluntary basis remains however, always dependent on the reliability of interest payments, and thus on the reliability of sufficient tax revenues to this end. The question if, and how, *tax* revenues could be raised remains, therefore, the crucial element in the question how increasing levels of public revenue could be attained. In his important study on 'war, money and the English state' Brewer emphasized already that Dickson underestimated the importance of taxes to the so-called financial revolution.[34] The relative importance of loans and debt service in the fiscal system will receive due attention in this book, but the primary focus is on the question how taxation contributed to the high level of Dutch public finance.

The main historical question is, of course, *why* the small federal Dutch Republic was able to attain its remarkably high level of public finance – so crucial for its viability during about two centuries – before it succumbed to British naval power and French troops at the end of the eighteenth century. This raises inevitably the additional question if it could have avoided its downfall by means of an earlier centralization of its state structure.

Possible Answers

The main theoretical reason why centralization seems indispensable to maximize public finance is the risk of 'free-riding' by members of a federation.[35]

31 P.G.M. Dickson, *The financial revolution in England: a study in the development of public credit, 1688–1756* (London 1967).

32 R. Bonney and W.M. Ormrod, 'Introduction', in: *Crises, Revolutions and Self-Sustained growth. Essays in European Fiscal History, 1130–1830*, eds. W.M. Ormrod, M. Bonney and R. Bonney (Stamford 1999) pp. 1–21, 6.

33 See also P. O'Brien and Ph. Hunt,'The Rise of the Fiscal State in England 1485–1815', *Historical Research* (1993) 129–176, p. 134: 'as a statistical indicator designed to measure changes in the fiscal capacity of the state for effective action, tax revenues include borrowing'.

34 Brewer, *Sinews of Power*, p. 88.

35 The concept of 'free riding' was first applied to the history of the Dutch Republic in J.L. van Zanden and A. van Riel, *Nederland 1780–1914. Staat, instituties en economische ontwikkeling*

A reason why centralization may be in practice not always efficient, is its dependency on monitoring revenue-raising in bureaucratic systems that may be susceptible to corruption and venality, and its dependency on the possibilities of communication with regions outside the administrative centre, and on the viability and efficacy of sanctions. No wonder that the degree to which early modern states can be really seen as efficiently centralized states has come to be doubted.[36] A historical situation of intensive mutual contacts, and a strongly felt mutual interest and interdependence between the members of a federation may in fact contribute to restrain tendencies to 'free-riding' and result in a relatively high level of public revenue.

Two factors may be supposed to be of primary importance to explain a high level of public revenue: economic conditions resulting from historical developments and political institutions resulting from historical developments. The idea that, additionally, differences in the 'mentality' of a tax paying population might be an important independent factor is less convincing as will be shown. This book will focus on the concept 'urban system' to understand how and why the very high level of public finance in the decentralized Dutch Republic turned out to be possible, this in order to emphasize that it is neither sufficient to have institutions that facilitate increases in public revenue, nor to have an economic structure that generates enough wealth to this end. The term 'urban system' refers to the existence of a collectivity of cities, characterized by some degree of political-institutional and economic integration resulting from long-term historical developments, involving the abandoning of elements of urban autonomy. It will be argued that the use of this concept allows a more adequate understanding of the high level of early modern Dutch fiscal performance than isolated references to the presence of 'representative institutions', or a 'citizenship-mentality', or 'wealth'.

The following short historiographical overview of the possible role of political institutions, mentality and economic factors, on the one hand, and of the role of urbanization in processes of state formation, on the other hand, will provide the explanatory framework within which Dutch public finance will be discussed in this book.

(Amsterdam 2000) p. 52; translated as *The strictures of inheritance. The Dutch economy in the nineteenth century* (Princeton 2004) see Ch. I.3; for a more general argument see H. Spruyt, 'Institutional selection in international relations: state anarchy as order', *International organization* 48, 4 (1994) pp. 527–557, p. 531.

36 Dincecco, *Political transformations and public finances*.

(1) *Political Institutions*

Brian Downing's *The Military Revolution and Political Change* (1992) is often seen as the most important alternative to the geopolitical approach of state formation, as it started at the beginning of the twentieth century with the early work of the famous German historian of public administration Otto Hintze (1861–1940) that influenced many 'military revolution'-historians.[37] Downing emphasized that not only 'war' made the state, but that also 'medieval government' should be seen as an important building block for the modern world.[38] Hintze, like later 'military revolution'-historians, had emphasized the absolutist and centralistic-bureaucratic outcomes of the state building processes resulting from the geopolitical ambitions of early modern war faring. Institutionally most European states remained *'Ständestaaten'*, between 1500 and 1800, however, implying that revenue-increases for war often remained more or less dependent on the consent of meetings of representatives of the society from which the revenue had to be raised, even in states with 'absolutist' tendencies like Spain and France.[39] Downing emphasized, that absolutism also *impaired* the possibilities for rulers to increase public revenue, as was evident in France at the end of the eighteenth century. He pointed to the fact that Britain's high level of military expenditure during the eighteenth century resulted from *parliamentary* power to realize increases in national revenue by means of a centralized bureaucracy, instead of from absolutist monarchical power.[40]

He assumed, moreover, that representative government had been more able to persist 'where war was light or where military modernization was achieved without relying on substantial amounts of domestic resources',[41] as had been the case in Britain before the eighteenth century. However, not only Britain, also the Dutch Republic belonged to the states where representative institutions continued to be very influential after the Middle Ages. Remarkably enough Downing was convinced for that reason, that 'domestic resource mobilization' for military expenditure could not have been 'high' in the Dutch Republic, and decided to characterize it as of only 'medium' height.[42]

---

37 Praised as such by Ertman, 'State Formation and State Building', p. 378.

38 B. Downing, *The Military Revolution and Political Change. Origins of Democracy and Autocracy in Early Modern Europe* (Princeton 1992), p. 251.

39 Dyson, *The state tradition in Western Europe*, 26; F. Tallett, *War and society in Early Modern Europe, 1495–1715* (London 1992) p. 196; D. Stasavage, *States of credit. Size, Power and the Development of European Polities* (Princeton, Princeton UP, 2011), p. 22.

40 Also Brewer, *The sinews of power*.

41 Downing, *The Military Revolution*, p. XI.

42 Downing, *The Military Revolution*, p. 242.

He argued that the Dutch received military assistance from other countries for land wars, and that the high costs of its naval wars could be covered by loans, thanks to its wealth.[43] It is known by now that the Dutch level of public expenditure financed by domestic resources and taxation was extremely high, however, in comparison to that in other states,[44] and Downing's other assumptions on the Dutch republic as just mentioned, are questionable as well, as we will see. The question how and why the federal Dutch Republic had been able to combine an in fact extremely high level of 'domestic resource mobilization' with a lack of absolutist centralizing tendencies, remains pertinent, therefore.

That 'absolutism' as such was not necessarily an effective way to increase public revenue was emphasized by Margaret Levi as well. Her approach was influenced by the 'institutional economics' of Douglas North. She saw rulers as being always confronted by three 'constraints' in their 'predatory' attempts to maximize tax revenue: (1) 'their relative bargaining power' vis à vis social groups, (2) their 'discount rate',[45] and (3) the 'transaction costs' of tax systems. These three constraints she sees determined in their turn by respectively 'forms of government', 'the international context', and 'productive forces and economic structures'.[46]

Since the emergence of 'institutional economics', and especially since Douglas North's and Barry Weingast's influential publication on 'constitutions and commitment',[47] not only political history, but also economic history displays an increasing tendency to explain 'fiscal efficiency' primarily from the specific institutional characteristics of a state. In this way representative institutions originating in the Middle Ages came increasingly to be seen as possibly more important for the realization of the increasing expenditure related to war, than increases in absolutist centralization or even than economic developments.

If loans to finance sudden increases in public expenditure due to wars that were felt as necessary, were negotiated by a parliament with the power and the willingness to introduce new taxation to service the debt, this guaranteed a 'credible commitment', that tended to be missing in the case of rulers with military ambitions believing in the desirability of 'absolute' power. It was

43 Ibidem, pp. 238, 241, 224–226.

44 Karaman and Pamuk, 'Ottoman state finances in European perspective', fig. 5 p. 611 and fig. 6 p. 615.

45 Levi, *Of Rule and revenue*, p. 13, she added that military conflict is 'the most important cause of a high discount rate' and that 'low discount rates accompany security of rule'.

46 Levi, *Of Rule and revenue*, 13.

47 D. North and B. Weingast, 'Constitutions and commitment: the evolution of institutions governing public choice in seventeenth-century England', *Journal of Economic History* 49 (1989) 803–832.

a 'credible commitment' to debt service that enabled the realization of decreasing rates of interest. Economic historians nowadays tend to emphasize the superiority of representative institutions, not only in explaining the high level of public finance in for instance the Dutch Republic, but also the low level of public revenue in the 'despotic' alternative of 'autocracies' like for instance the Ottoman Empire.[48]

More recently Philip Hoffman referred similarly – in looking for an answer to the question *Why did Europe conquer the world?* – to, on the one hand, military competition in Europe, which spurred innovations in military technology, but on the other hand, and even more strongly, to 'political conditions in Europe' that allowed states to finance high levels of military expenditure. European political conditions forced rulers everywhere to negotiate, which lowered what he calls the 'variable costs', or the 'political costs', of heavy taxation: the discontent of different social groups (called the 'transaction costs' of taxation by Levi).[49] This explains, he says, why in Europe even small states could spend generously for wars they thought important, as their representative institutions allowed them to tax heavily and borrow at low costs.[50] It is rather implausible, nevertheless, to deny the importance of what Levi called 'productive forces and economic structures' as, at least, an underlying condition for the possibility 'to spend generously for wars'.

(2) *Mentality*

It has been argued by the Dutch historians Maarten Prak and Jan Luiten van Zanden that the high level of public expenditure and revenue in the Dutch Republic might have been made possible mainly by the development of a 'citizenship-mentality', as a result of the great number of cities and their large political influence in representative institutions.[51] Tax payers were expected to be more ready to accept tax increases, if they had a say in the way taxes are spent, they argued. Yet, the question remains, firstly, to what extent the majority of Dutch tax payers felt themselves represented by the elites in power in

48 J.L. van Zanden, E. Buringh and M. Bosker, 'The rise and decline of European parliaments, 1188–1789', *Economic History Review* 65, 3 (2012) 835–861, p. 851.

49 Ph.T. Hoffman, *Why did Europe conquer the world?* (Princeton 2015) pp. 14–15, 23.

50 Hoffman, *Why did Europe conquer the world?*, p. 141.

51 M. Prak and J.L. van Zanden, 'Tax morale and citizenship in the Dutch Republic, in; *The political economy of the Dutch Republic* ed. O. Gelderblom (Farnham 2009) 143–167; also in J.L. van Zanden, *The long road to the Industrial Revolution. The European Economy in a global perspective, 1000–1800* (Leiden 2009), Chapter 7'. State formation and citizenship: the Dutch Republic between medieval communes and modern nation states', pp. 205–233.

the cities, and, secondly, to what extent early modern 'citizenship', limited as it was before the advent of political nationalism to belonging to one particular city, can convincingly explain tremendous increases in public finance on the much larger level of a state.[52] The concept of an 'urban system' allowing the perception of common – alongside particularistic – economic interests among the ruling elites of a collectivity of cities, may be more promising, therefore, to explain the high level of Dutch public finance than that of an urban citizenship mentality.

If 'tax morale' was indeed higher in the Dutch Republic than elsewhere, one may, in addition, even wonder if not the influence of Bible-texts referring to taxation[53] may have been more influential than a 'citizenship-mentality', in a country where Calvinism became the dominant religion. Philip Gorski published a study titled *The Disciplinary Revolution. Calvinism and the Rise of the State in Early Modern Europe* (2003). According to the standard theory of state formation 'the Dutch state should have been weak because it was not centralized, but in fact it was quite strong', he wrote.[54] He added – with good arguments – that the amount paid in taxes was high, even when we control for income, and that the claim that the financial strength of the Dutch state was due to its access to capital markets 'is clearly overblown' (for which there are more arguments indeed than he put forward, as will be shown).[55] Gorski then suggests that the fiscal strength of the Dutch Republic had more to do with 'state infrastructure' than with 'state structure', that this infrastructure was 'in no small part the product of the Calvinist disciplinary revolution', and that 'the impact of disciplining from below is almost invariably greater than that from above'.[56]

His focus was not on the behaviour of tax payers, however, but on that of public servants in the emerging bureaucracies of early modern states. Nor does he claim that the influence of Calvinism among Dutch civil servants should be

52 Despite their emphasis on 'citizenship' to explain the character of state formation in the Dutch Republic Prak and Van Zanden concede 'that citizenship was still largely an urban phenomenon in this period' (Van Zanden and Prak, 'Economic interpretation of citizenship', p, 112).

53 Romans, 13, 6–7: 'This is also why you pay taxes, for the authorities are God's servants (…). Give to everyone what you owe them: If you owe taxes, pay taxes (…)' https://www.biblegateway.com.

54 Ph. Gorski, *The Disciplinary Revolution. Calvinism and the Rise of the State in Early Modern* Europe (Chicago 2003) p. 40.

55 Gorski, *The Disciplinary Revolution*, pp. 9–50.

56 Gorski, *The Disciplinary Revolution*, pp. 75, 33.

seen as really crucial for an understanding of the high level of Dutch public finance, but only as a factor that deserves additional attention. It may be true that Dutch civil servants were less prone to corruption than, for instance, those in France – although incidental examples of malversation among Dutch tax receivers exist as well. It may be true as well, however, that the system gave them perhaps less chances than in France, because of the smaller size and the more integrated character of Dutch society.

As we will see in the course of this book, there are good reasons to doubt that either Calvinism or a 'citizenship-mentality' made (rich) Dutch tax payers less prone to the evasion of direct taxes than other people. It can, moreover, be doubted – as we will see in the course of this book as well – that the relatively small number of tax riots against the price increasing effects of indirect taxes in the Netherlands, was related to a Calvinist or to a 'citizenship- mentality' of the Dutch population, and might not rather be explained from economic developments.

It has been argued correctly by others that the development of religious diversity was no doubt an important general factor in sixteenth-century processes of state formation.[57] The Peace of Augsburg of 1555 put a seal on the process of fragmentation of the Holy Roman Empire from the principle that internal order and safety, and the viability of states, were served by religious unity in a state. The 'unity of sentiment' within a community, which according to Bodin was realized 'as a consequence of living under a common sovereign', came often to consist of the dominance of one religion in states in Early Modern Europe.[58] It is as a rule not easy, however, to disentangle religious and economic motives in for instance the voting behaviour of Dutch Calvinists and this will not be attempted in this book.[59]

---

57 W.T. Cavanaugh, *The Myth of Religious Violence. Secular Ideology and the Roots of Modern Conflict* (Oxford 2009) p. 141 argues that the concept of 'religious wars' is a 'myth' disguising the role of secular factors in war faring and that 'the state building process was not simply the solution, but a contributing cause of the violence of the sixteenth and seventeenth centuries'.

58 Although religion was not part of Bodin's state concept; see http://classiques.uqac.ca/classiques/bodin_jean/six_livres_republique/bodin_six_livres_republique.pdf, Introduction by G. Mairet (1993) p. 20.

59 One explicit example of the influence of religion on an increase in Dutch public revenue was a decision of the States General of 4. March 1688 to negotiate a loan of four million guilders to pay for stadholder William III's expedition to England after he had been invited by English protestants to replace his catholic father-in-law James as king of England. The loan became a success – despite an interest rate of only two percent – mainly thanks to the subscriptions of the many Huguenots in Amsterdam, who had fled from France

(3) *Economic Factors*

Economically the 'tax base' of a state can be said to consist primarily of its population size and its level of wealth per capita. It may be argued that it consists additionally in the size of its foreign trade. The population size of the Dutch Republic cannot have caused its comparatively high level of *total* public revenue, of course, as it was comparatively very small. It would be surprising, however, if the level of Dutch *per capita* wealth would not have been offered as a likely explanation in the existing literature.[60]

Three historical developments in particular can be seen as possibly relevant economic factors for public finance: (a) the Dutch role in the development of world trade after the discovery of ocean routes to the Indies, (b) the development of capital markets, and of the financial institutions required to the functioning of these markets, and (c) internal economic developments, more in particular the preceding processes of commercialization and urbanization since the later Middle Ages. Although the three are strongly interrelated, and although all three are related to wealth per capita, they could have different possible effects on fiscal systems.

Developing external trade could in theory increase revenues from customs as well as from direct taxes on personal wealth. The development of capital markets and financial institutions could enlarge the opportunity to finance warfare by means of long-term public loans at low rates of interest, and increasing urbanization could facilitate a tendency to invest in public loans instead of in land, if people trusted that the state would give priority to debt service. Preceding internal commercialization and urbanization could especially facilitate trends in the fiscal system directed towards more domestic indirect taxes: on production, transport, distribution and consumption, and on direct taxes on services, like legal deeds, and on transfers of property instead of on land or other types of property or sources of income. The role of these three factors in the historiography will be shortly discussed in this order.

a) *The Development of Foreign Trade*

It is evident that European state formation between 1500 and 1800 was not only connected to territorial competition, the continuity of medieval

---

to the Netherlands after the cancellation of the Edict of Nantes that had allowed them religious freedom in 1685; Dormans, *Het tekort*, p. 142.

60 The prosperity of the Dutch Republic was also stimulated by its involvement in war faring; see M. 't Hart, *The Dutch Wars of Independence and the Republic's Golden Age, c. 1580-c. 1680* (London 2014).

representative institutions, and religious divergence, but also to colonial expansion overseas and to naval power as a powerful means to enrichment. In his introduction to *The rise of fiscal states. A global history, 1500–1914* (2012) Bartolomé Yun-Casalilla even assumed that it was the opportunity to shift the composition of revenue towards foreign trade that distinguished the most efficient fiscal regimes both in Europe and Asia. Similarly Timur Kuran supposed that the remarkable 'fiscal fecundity' especially of 'maritime' states like the Dutch Republic and Britain, that sharply contrasted with the fiscal performance in the Islamic world of the early modern period, was directly connected to the large profits of their chartered overseas trading companies.[61]

It seems logical to assume that customs revenues might have become increasingly important for governments during these ages, or to assume that a state in which part of the population was enriched as a result from the development of foreign trade was able to raise higher amounts in direct taxes than others. The question remains, of course, if what seems logical is confirmed by quantitative data on public expenditure and public revenue. In Britain the East India Company was a source of increases in customs revenue, as well as a possible credit facility, indeed. But was this also the case for the VOC, the Dutch East India Company?[62] What was the relative importance of this very influential company for Dutch public finance for total public expenditure and revenue? And to what extent was the Dutch fiscal system really able to tax wealth resulting from foreign trade?

b) *The Development of Capital Markets and Financial Institutions*

Charles Tilly's impressive monograph *Coercion, Capital and European States, 990–1992* (1992) showed in an admirable way how the development of a market for voluntary long-term public loans at low rates of interest could offer a powerful alternative for fiscal 'coercion' in order to achieve high levels of military expenditure.[63] An abundance of flourishing cities with a large capital supply as well as possibilities for indirect taxation for debt service – in combination with a large demand for safe investment possibilities other than land or commercial enterprises – were preconditions for the successful development of this alternative. These conditions seemed largely fulfilled in the case of especially

61 T. Kuran, *The long divergence. How Islamic law held back the Middle East* (Princeton 2011) pp. 32, 55, 119, 132.

62 V.O.C. = *Verenigde Oostindische Compagnie* = United East Indian Company.

63 Ch. Tilly, *Coercion, capital and European states, 990–1992* (Cambridge, CUP, 1992);. 't Hart, *The making of a bourgeois state.*

the Republic's main province, Holland. This raises the question if quantitative data confirm that the high level of Dutch public revenue can mainly be explained by the high 'capital-intensity' of Dutch society and that its fiscal system was characterized by a relatively small dependence on the 'coercion' of direct taxation.

David Stasavage (2011) argued that the Republic's 'oligarchic' representativeness, dominated by rich merchants, was fiscally more efficient than more 'democratic' forms of representation, especially to obtain large amounts in loan revenue. This did 'not automatically imply that representative institutions did not matter', he added, but it was just easier to convince investors in public debt of a 'credible commitment' to give priority to servicing the public debt, when those in power were from families which could be supposed to have invested largely in public debt paper themselves. Although Stasavage focused in his book on the role of institutional factors, he also noted that, among the hypotheses he tested, the one that access to credit depended mainly on commercial and economic development, yielded, nevertheless, in fact the strongest statistical support.[64]

Also Pepijn Brandon explained the Republic's 'sustained involvement in war fare' despite its federal structure from 'the close connections between capitalists and bureaucrats' that 'allowed state-makers to draw much more successfully on the resources of their subjects than their more centralized counterparts'.[65] The question remains, however, to which extent public revenue in the Dutch republic consisted of voluntary loans on the capital market and to which extent of just extracting taxes (or *forced* loans) from the population.

As to the role of financial institutions there is no doubt that the existence of the institution of an adequate banking system could facilitate a successful issue of state loans, as for instance the Venetian *Banco del Giro* did. In England it was the Bank of England that played a well-known crucial role in the so-called 'Financial Revolution' between 1688 and 1756, which was such an important factor in the increasing level of its public finance in the eighteenth century. Similarly, the late development of a national debt in the Ottoman Empire is often linked to the lack of a large bank to facilitate state loans. This may on the one hand raise the question whether the declining position of the Dutch Republic in the course of the eighteenth century was related to the lack of a central bank, but on the other hand even more why permanent public debts

64 Stasavage, *States of credit*, p. 17.

65 P. Brandon, *War, capital and the Dutch state (1588–1795)* (Leiden 2015), pp. 3, 11.

could play a significant role in financing wars during the earlier period *without* a similar institution.

c) *Internal Economic Integration*

The wealth-increasing effect of internal economic integration may have been, in fact, the most important economic factor explaining the high level of public revenue in the Dutch Republic. Processes of urbanization, induced by population growth, economic specialization and commercialization, offered new fiscal possibilities for states everywhere in Europe. Based on an analysis of the work of contemporary political and economic theorists – like for instance the Italian political theorist Giambattista Vico (1668–1744) who was especially convinced of the 'strength, wealth and wisdom of republics' in contrast to monarchies – the economist Albert Hirschman suggested already long ago, that it was the expansion of domestic trade that created more cohesive communities and furthered the development of territorial states.[66] His aim was to shed light 'on the political consequences of economic development in the early modern period'. He even described the seventeenth and eighteenth century as the era in which the heroic pursuits of glory and power of earlier periods started to be more or less 'tamed' by the pursuit of economic interests. The fact that the Napoleonic wars seemed to contradict this analysis does not preclude the possibility, however, that he was right in supposing a link between state formation and economic integration by means of the expansion of *domestic* trade.

(4) *'Urban systems'*

The emphasis on the increase in the cohesion of communities by means of the expansion of domestic trade as an aspect of state formation is supported – albeit along very different lines – by Jan de Vries' important study of European urbanization between 1500 and 1800. De Vries concluded on the basis of an analysis of population developments in ca. 400 European cities, that in this period – in which Europe's total population almost doubled – urbanization was surprisingly enough not characterized primarily by an increase in the percentage of people living in cities, but rather by the coming into existence of 'urban systems', gradually replacing the isolation of the walled cities of the Middle Ages, the existence of which had been mostly primarily dependent on the directly surrounding countryside. The emergence of 'urban systems' was a development occurring parallel to

66 A.O. Hirschman, *The passions and the interests, Political arguments for capitalism before its triumph* (Princeton, Princeton UP, 1977) p. 52.

the development of nation states, the control of colonial empires and the expansion of global trade. In a later collection of studies on the history of urbanization De Vries speaks of 'a national or regional set of urban units that are interdependent, or bound together by economic interactions'.[67] In the same book C.A. Smith emphasized – in a theoretical article on types of city-size-distribution – that urbanization implies more than quantitative developments in urban population: it is also about the 'reorganization of the urban system'.[68]

Stasavage pointed to the possible importance of small geographical scale as an explanatory factor in realizing high amounts in public revenue within a context of representative institutions. Large travelling distances not only reduced the number of meetings of representatives, which obstructed their adequate functioning in large countries like France, he wrote. Large geographic distances impeded also the development of a wide spread system of state loans that was attractive for investors, as well as not too burdening for the state.[69] This made the interconnectedness of cities in a territory with relatively many cities more conducive to a high level of public revenue.

The question how the density and organization of cities in a region may affect the character of states was also addressed by Charles Tilly in his study on coercion and capital as factors in state formation. He noted, likewise, that the word 'cities' in his book was actually 'a metonymy for regional networks of production and trade' and that 'the presence or absence of urban clusters significantly changed the possibilities for state formation'.[70] The question was posed once again in a number of studies edited by Tilly and Wim Blockmans some years later. They argued 'that (…) the character of urban networks systematically affected the path of state formation because urban merchants and financiers wielded considerable influence in the organization of state facilities'. States in densely urbanized regions are different, therefore, from states with few cities, they concluded.[71]

---

67 Jan de Vries, *European urbanization 1500–1800* (London, 1984) pp. 254–255, 263, idem, 'Problems in the measurement, description and analysis of historical urbanization', in: *Urbanization in history. A process of dynamic interactions*, eds. A. van der Woude, A. Hayami and J. de Vries, (Oxford 1990) p. 82.

68 C.A. Smith, 'Types of City-Size Distribution. A Comparative Analysis', in: *Urbanization in History*, pp. 20–42, 20.

69 Stasavage, *States of credit*.

70 Tilly, *Coercion, capital and European states*, p. 34.

71 *Cities and the rise of states in Europe*, eds. Ch. Tilly and W. Blockmans, (Boulder: Westview Press, 1994) p. 2 and p. 242.

Margaret Levi mentioned 'transaction costs', another main concept of 'institutional economics', as one of the three factors influencing the realization of public revenue, as we saw. She defined it as the costs of bargaining and implementing a common policy, assuming the omnipresence of contractual relations between parties with different interests.[72] In the Dutch Republic it were cities with diverging particularistic interests that had to negotiate common taxation, and to device mechanisms preventing particularistic tax avoidance among each other. A smoothly interconnected urban system within a rather small territory, with an institutional infrastructure facilitating urban contacts, will certainly have diminished 'transaction costs', thus making it easier than in large states to realize relatively high amounts of public revenue for a common objective.

Anyhow, communities consisting of strong webs of interdependent relationships may be better aware of common needs for public goods – like 'internal rest and order', 'safety against external aggression' and 'effective protection of international commercial routes' – than single cities focusing on particularistic urban needs. Such an awareness facilitated decisions to increase public expenditure by means of common taxes to serve economic interests. Clé Lesger described the 'spatial and organizational development of the network of interregional trade and shipping' in the Dutch Republic between 1400 and 1700, and visualized the connections between regional nodal points across its territory, from Groningen in the north to Middelburg in the south-west and Nijmegen in the south-east, by means of two beautiful maps.[73] For Jan de Vries the common carrier system of the '*beurtveren*', as analysed by Lesger, was an indication of the relatively high degree of economic integration in the Republic, which he saw further confirmed by consistently high correlations in price fluctuations.[74] Much earlier the same author wrote a nice study on the remarkable, 'inter-urban' initiative of digging and exploiting '*trekvaarten*' (canals) between cities meeting the increasing need for smooth passenger transportation in the Dutch Republic.[75]

The existence of urban systems not only facilitated the raising of large amounts in public loans, as Stasavage argued, it also enabled provincial

72 Levi, *Of Rule and revenue*, p. 23.

73 C. Lesger, 'Intraregional trade and the port system in Holland, 1400–1700', *Economic and Social History in the Netherlands* 4 (1992) 185–217, pp. 207, 200, 201.

74 J. de Vries, and A. van der Woude, *The first modern economy: success, failure and perseverance of the Dutch economy, 1500–1815* (Cambridge, 1997) pp. 180–182 and p. 176.

75 J. de Vries, 'Barges and capitalism. Passenger transportation in the Dutch economy, 1632–1839', AAG *Bijdragen* 21 (1978), pp. 33–398.

governments to the introduction of special types of indirect, price-increasing, taxes on production, transport, distribution and consumption of goods and services, that were as a rule less hated by the population than 'coercive' direct taxes, especially when the resulting price-increases were offset by increasing general wealth and wages. All this might increase public revenue without the necessity of a powerful 'absolute' sovereign.

Whereas the fragmented state structure of the federal Dutch Republic has sometimes been characterized as the result of a 'failed transition' to a modern national state,[76] it might perhaps – in line with these approaches – be seen more adequately as the early result of an important 'modern' process of state formation, more driven by economic interests than by lust for power, and made possible by special economic and institutional conditions, related to the specific character of the trajectory of urbanization in its territory. 'War drove the formation of all European states, but it did not drive them all into the same direction', as Marjolein 't Hart concluded in the first study on the relations between public finance and state formation in the early Dutch Republic.[77]

This book will not deny that the character of the political institutions of a state may contribute to high levels of public finance, especially when a comparatively strong collective interest is felt among elites to realize a high expenditure level. It is evidently not enough, however, to have the right political institutions to be able to obtain a high level of public revenue. Having supportive economic conditions is at least as important. As an alternative for approaches that tend to isolate either political conditions, or mentality, or economic conditions as the main explanatory factor for the level of public finance, this book will argue that the concept of an 'urban system', resulting from long-term historical developments, characterized by a certain degree of economic integration and political coordination, is especially helpful in understanding the ability of the small federal state of the Dutch Republic to realize comparatively extremely high levels of public finance in the early modern period. It does not claim that it is unique in emphasizing the importance of urbanization to understand the fiscal performance of the Dutch Republic. It claims, however, that a comparative historical approach on a quantitative basis allows a better understanding of the specific ways in which newly developing 'urban systems' in the early modern period could influence the fiscal performance of a state than the works published on this subject until now.

---

76 Van Zanden and van Riel, *The strictures of inheritance*, Introductory chapter.

77 't Hart, *The making of a bourgeois state*, p. 226.

The Approach of This Book

This is the first study of public finance in the Dutch Republic based on an extensive quantitative dataset of the public finance of the Dutch provinces, covering the whole period of the Dutch Republic.[78] To construct the necessary relevant tables and graphs the often incomplete data found in the archives were complemented for this book with estimates for missing data as far as this was reasonably possible. Besides, data had to be collected for other institutions in the Dutch Republic involved in its 'state'-finance than only the provinces. Data on the 'admiralties', that collected the customs duties to be spent on the maintenance of the navy, and on the so-called 'Generality' of the Republic, which coordinated war expenditure, were collected mainly from the existing literature and incidentally additional archival research. As these data were very defective as well, they were complemented, too, as far as possible by means of estimates.

The resulting tables allowed, for the first time, general answers on a number of basic factual questions; on the one hand general questions like: how did the level and the structure of the public expenditure and public revenue of the Dutch Republic develop in the course of time? on the other hand, more specific questions – resulting from the historiographic-theoretical framework offered above – like: how was the proportion between expenditure on land wars and on naval wars? How important was customs revenue and the part played by the VOC in Dutch public finance? How much was paid by the province of Holland, how much by the other provinces of the Republic? Did 'free-riding' occur? How important was the 'capital-intensity' of the Dutch Republic, or in other words, how much of state expenditure was paid from taxes, how much from loans? And how much from direct taxes, hitting the more well to do, how much from indirect price-increasing taxes mostly hitting the poor? What happened to the interest burden on public debts in the course of time, which was a source of income for debt holders, and what happened to the tax burden on the common man, one of the sources of state revenue from which the interest burden had to be paid? How was this in Holland, how in other provinces?

The collected quantitative material also allowed comparisons with other states of a more detailed and more integrated character than was possible in earlier collections of studies comparing developments in state finance. The three states, the fiscal systems of which are compared to that of the Dutch Republic in this book were partly chosen, because quantitative data regarding their public finance were available to at least a certain extent, although

78 Accessible on http://resources.huygens.knaw.nl/gewestelijkefinancien/en.

often with large lacunas without estimates for missing years.[79] Earlier publications on the public finance of more than one state often consisted of separate contributions by region-specialists, incidentally referring to comparable data mentioned by other region-specialists, with an introduction and a conclusion by the editor(s) attempting to connect the available threads.[80] Important comparative monographs on the history of public finance either lacked a satisfying quantitative foundation, like Tilly's admirable study on 'Coercion' and 'Capital', or remained restricted either to naval expenditure, or to state finance until 1660 (Glete (1993) and Glete (2002)), or chose a primarily econometric approach (Dincecco (2011) and Karaman and Pamuk (2011) and (2013)) not very accessible for 'ordinary' historians.

This book has been written by a historian, not by an economist. The results of the long-term quantitative comparisons in this book are presented in the form of descriptive graphs and tables. No attempts have been made to present arguments within the rigorous – for many historically interested readers however rather deterring – methodological framework of econometric-statistical analysis.[81] By using only the methods of historical description and descriptive historical comparison, supported wherever possible by quantitative data, and by restricting theoretical inspiration to the existing historiography, the book rather aspires to offer a bridge between the fascinating approaches of specialist econometric-statistical historical comparative research and a more easily accessible descriptive historical comparative approach. Despite a conviction that the use of available quantitative data is indispensable for the reliability of historical argumentation, the approach in this book is in fact more inspired by an ambition to *understand* the 'why' of a remarkable historical fiscal

---

79 The first initiatives to collect quantitative data on state finance were taken in the 1980s by Richard Bonney; they resulted in the European State Finance Data-Base http://esfdb.websites.bta.com/ [last access 26-08-2016] and his important *Economic systems and state finance*, ed. R. Bonney (Oxford 1995).

80 *The formation of national states; Cities and the rise of states; Fiscal crises, liberty, and representative government, 1450–1789*, eds. Ph. Hoffman and K. Norberg, Stanford, Stanford UP, 1994; *Economic systems and state finance*; *The rise of the fiscal state in Europe, 1200–1815*, ed. R. Bonney (Oxford 1999); *Crises, revolutions and self-sustained growth. Essays in European fiscal history, 1130–1830*.

81 See Dincecco, *Political transformations and public finances: Europe, 1650–1913*, K. Karaman and Ş. Pamuk, 'Different Paths to the Modern State in Europe: The interaction between domestic political economy and interstate competition', *LEQS Paper* 37 (London: London School of Economics and Political Science, 2011); a new version published in *American Political Science Review* (2013) 1–24; Stasavage, *States of credit*; Van Zanden, Bosker, and Buringh, 'The rise and decline of European parliaments, 1188–1789'.

phenomenon, than by an ambition to rigorously *prove* statements on the relation between historical developments and fiscal phenomena.

This book does not aim, therefore, at reaching generalizing conclusions on the efficiency of federal versus centralized states. It offers primarily a historical comparative, not a theoretical study. It does not deny, for instance, that centralization may be efficient to realize higher levels of revenue under specific historical circumstances. Its main ambition is to understand in what ways, and as a result of which historical circumstances, the small federal Dutch Republic was capable to realize its remarkable high level of fiscal performance. It aims to achieve this by means of, on the one hand, an analysis of the formation and structure of its public finance and, on the other hand, by means of international comparisons.

The Structure of This Book

The book consists of two parts. The first part argues the importance of the concept 'urban system' for an understanding of the fiscal performance of the Republic by means of a description of the rise and the development of its fiscal system and its resulting structure. The second part further explores this argument by means of comparisons with the public finance of three contemporary early modern states in a long-term perspective. The two parts are structured as follows.

Part 1 starts with an Introduction that offers a brief discussion of the character of the early modern Dutch 'state' and of the new ways in which late medieval institutions functioned in this emerging early modern political entity. This introduction ends with a short discussion of the concept 'the public finance of the Dutch Republic' and a discussion of data and estimates.

Chapter 1 offers a description of the toilsome attempts by prince William of Orange to find money for what would become an 'Eighty Years War' against Spain in order to highlight the crucial importance of the decision of a great number of cities in the province of Holland to offer him financial support.

The long Chapter 2 describes the formation of the new Dutch fiscal system made necessary by this decision, which was completed by the start of the so-called Twelve Years' Truce (1609–1621). It contains short comparisons: with Holland's fiscal system in the two decades before the Revolt, with that of Castile, the most important urbanized part of the Spanish Empire, and between Holland and the other provinces. It emphasizes the importance of the '*tax* revolution' starting in Holland and Zeeland in 1574 and argues that Holland experienced its 'real' *financial* revolution only during the first decade of the seventeenth century.[82] Lastly it compares the role of provincial and central sources of revenue in the emerging Dutch fiscal system until the Twelve Years' Truce and it summarizes weaknesses that seemed to become apparent.

Chapter 3 shows the main characteristics of the development and structure of public expenditure and public revenue since then until the end of the Dutch Republic. It shows how the small federal Dutch Republic realized an even more remarkable fiscal performance during the much more expensive wars since then, despite such apparent weaknesses. It discusses the relative importance of 'coercion' and 'capital' in its public finance. Lastly it will argue that the failure of the old Republic to win its last naval war with Britain (1780–1784) and its failure to stop the French invasion of January 1795 which led to its collapse were not caused by the federal character of its fiscal system.

Part 2 offers the international comparisons and argues that they largely support the conclusion of the importance, for an understanding of fiscal performance, of the character of 'urban systems' resulting from preceding historical developments. It consists of three chapters each containing a comparison with the public finance of one of three contemporary states in a long-term historical perspective. The Introduction explains the choice for the Venetian Republic, Britain and the Ottoman Empire and offers a general discussion of their comparability with the Dutch Republic.

Chapter 4 contains the comparison with the Venetian Republic, a state of about the same size as the Dutch Republic and often characterized like the Dutch state as an urbanized, commercial, 'maritime' state; a state, however, where fiscal power, in contrast to the Dutch Republic, was strongly centralized in one city.

Chapter 5 offers the comparison with Britain, a much larger much more centralized state developing into a parliamentary monarchy; an agrarian commercial state, as well as a 'maritime' colonial empire, like the Dutch Republic, but with a national instead of a federal parliament and with an 'urbanization trajectory' very different from that in the Dutch Republic.

Chapter 6 offers the comparison with the Ottoman Empire, a very different and very large agrarian autocracy, characterized by an overall comparatively modest level of commercial development. It was involved, like the powers of the preceding chapters, in territorial and naval competition with European powers, but had a fiscal system determined by a 'state-driven' 'urbanization

82 J. Tracy, *A financial revolution in the Habsburg Netherlands. Renten and Renteniers in the County of Holland, 1515–1565* (Berkeley 1985) offers arguments for a financial revolution already during the 1540s and 1550s.

trajectory' very different from the much more 'economy-driven' urbanization trajectories in large parts of Europe.

The General Conclusion summarizes the main results of the quantitative research on the questions how and why the Dutch Republic realized its high level of public finance and how and why this had been possible. It ends with an Epilogue offering a very short reflection on the old Union of the Seven Provinces and the present European Union in comparative perspective.

PART 1

The Development of the Fiscal System of the Dutch Republic

Introduction to Part 1

The title of this book uses the term *public* finance, not the term *state* finance and for good reasons. This Introduction will open with the question, if the so-called 'Union of Utrecht' of 1579 from which the Dutch Republic originated, can in fact be considered as the start of a new state, comparable to other early modern states.[1] One may wonder if it was not rather just an alliance of provinces comparable to the North Atlantic Treaty Organisation, or the European Union nowadays. The initial intention of the Union of Utrecht to become a state with a centralized fiscal system did never materialize. This did not preclude, however, that the new union of the seven provinces came to be acknowledged as a state by other states in the course of time and was able to function as such.

This Introduction will, secondly, offer, to readers not familiar with the general history of the Dutch Republic, some basic historical information on the Dutch revolt against Spain from which the 'Union of Utrecht' originated, and on the main institutional characteristics of the emerging Dutch Republic by means of which its public finance system would have to function. On the one hand, the institutions relevant for Dutch public finance were largely inherited from the late medieval Habsburg period. On the other hand, the new intensity and the new aims of their use implied a fundamental change.

Lastly this Introduction offers a discussion of the concept 'public finance *of* the Dutch Republic' as opposed to 'public finance *in* the Dutch Republic' and a discussion of the reliability of the data and estimates used for its analysis.

The Union of Utrecht: The Start of a New State?

In January 1579, a number of provinces, regions and cities in the Low Countries[2] convening in the city of Utrecht decided to 'confederate and unite (…) as if they were only one province'.[3] They promised to help each other to defend valued liberties and traditional rights and habits against whomsoever would

1 The Dutch Republic is sometimes even described as an 'anti-state': D. Ormrod, *The Rise of Commercial Empires: England and the Netherlands in the Age of Mercantilism, 1650–1770* (Cambridge 2003) p. 350.

2 The terms 'Low Countries' and 'the Netherlands' refer in this book to the territory of seventeen provinces. The Dutch Republic would remain confined to the about eight and a half of them, that form the main part of the Netherlands nowadays.

3 Art. I of the Union-treaty; the complete text can be found on http://nl.wikisource.org/wiki/Unie_van_Utrecht.

 | DOI 10.1163/9789004341289_003

dare to encroach on them. The signatories promised moreover not to interfere in each other's affairs unless this was desirable to reach mutual agreement. The treaty which sealed the decision came to be known as the Union of Utrecht. Its primary aim was mutual assistance against the violence to which the Netherlands were subjected 'under the pretence of being used in the name of the Royal Majesty'.[4] Can such a treaty be considered as the birth of a state?

The twenty six articles of the treaty left no doubt that the Union intended to be more than just a temporary coalition to end the violence from troops of the king of Spain to whose empire the territories of the rebelling provinces belonged. Already the third article stated that it was also meant to counter jointly attempts by other princes to make war against them. Moreover, the intention was proclaimed that the union would have to be a monetary union.[5] It was considered as self-evident, too, that it would have to be a customs union.[6] In addition to these defensive and economic objectives the treaty stipulated that each province would take care that religious differences among individuals would be tolerated. All provinces and cities in the Netherlands would be accepted as members, if only they promised to accept its articles like 'good patriots'.[7] Conflicts among them would have to be submitted to arbitrage of their lords, the 'stadholders'.[8] Foreign policy would have to be the result of joint decisions. Decisions on how much to spend on the defence of the Union and on the maritime interests of its members would be taken jointly.[9] Consequently the signatories agreed to provide jointly for the financial means necessary for the defence of their territory.[10]

According to a famous definition by Max Weber a state is an institution that successfully claims a legitimate monopoly of violence in order to maintain internal order and safety within a certain territory.[11] This definition can be

---

4 Preamble: '*malcanderen met lijff, goet ende bloet bij te staen*' (to support each other with their bodies, property and blood) and Art. II; the 'Royal Majesty' is the Spanish king Philip II.

5 Art. XII: '*de provincien sullen gehouden zyn sich metten anderen te conformeeren int stuk vander munte te weeten inden cours vanden gelde*' (the provinces have to conform to each other in monetary matters).

6 Art. XVIII (the United Provinces would not be allowed to levy customs without joint consent, or tax each other's inhabitants more heavily than their own).

7 Art. XIII, and the explanatory official addition to this article dated 1 February 1579.

8 Art. XVI and XXI; 'stadholder' means 'substitute' and is used for the noblemen who served as the substitute of the Spanish king in the provinces of the Netherlands; despite its meaning the title remained in use after the Revolt.

9 Art. III and IX–XI.

10 Art. V.

11 M. Weber, *Politik als Beruf* (München 1919) p. 3: '*Staat ist diejenige menschliche Gemeinschaft, welche innerhalb eines bestimmten Gebietes – dies: das „Gebiet", gehört*

considered as a sophisticated version of Bodin's state concept of sovereignty in a territorial unit. According to more recent definitions, however, a state can also be seen as an institution that has to be the 'agent' of its inhabitants in order to provide them with 'public goods' like internal safety and protection against foreign enemies, and with the means to facilitate the acquirement of wealth and happiness.[12] Common protection against foreign aggression was evidently the primary concern of the Union of Utrecht, not the realization of an internal monopoly of violence. The realization of 'public goods' was an important aim as well, but the signatories do not seem to have felt, that this required an undivided 'agent'.

More detailed discussions of the concept 'state' and its historiography will be avoided here. The premise of this book is, that the Union of Utrecht may be said to have signalled the start of a state, if one accepts that a state can be seen as the result of a mutual agreement of landed and urban elites claiming successfully to be the representatives of certain territories in order to (1) protect the population against foreign aggression, (2) to conduct a common foreign policy, (3) to care for (a) internal order, (b) the maintenance of shared values and (c) the means to economic prosperity of the population, (4) to accept existing institutions and regulations to these ends, and (5) to realize these purposes by means of sustainable procedures to get the required financial means.

Historical Backgrounds and Institutional Characteristics

From Revolt to Republic

The developments leading to the Union of Utrecht had started in 1568 with a military revolt under the leadership of prince William of Orange (1533–1584) against the Spanish governor of the seventeen provinces of the Netherlands, the Duke of Alva (1507–1582). As a young man the Prince of Orange[13] had been one of the most important and esteemed young nobles at the court of the Habsburg emperor Charles V (1500–1558), ruler of the Netherlands and king of

zum Merkmal – das Monopol legitimer physischer Gewaltsamkeit für sich (mit Erfolg) beansprucht.'

12 As used in J.L. van Zanden and M. Prak, 'Towards an economic interpretation of citizenship: the Dutch Republic between medieval communes and modern nation-states', *European Review of Economic History* 10 (2006) pp. 111–145, p. 113.

13 Inheriting the princedom of Orange in Southern France from a childless brother of his mother had made him a 'prince';, but his rich properties in the Netherlands were economically much more important. The princedom became part of the kingdom of France in 1713 after the childless death of his great-grandson William III; the Frisian branch of the family – the ancestors of the present Dutch king – was allowed to maintain the title.

Spain. Since 1559 William of Orange was the 'stadholder' (= substitute) of the new Spanish king Philip II (1527–1598), in the provinces of Holland, Zeeland and Utrecht.

The Revolt was originally directed against the fierce anti-protestant religious policy of Philip II, who had succeeded his father emperor Charles V as sovereign of the Netherlands in 1555. The revolt under Orange's leadership would gain real momentum only since April 1572, when cities in the urbanized and commercialized provinces Holland and Zeeland started to support the Prince. This support was at least partly triggered by the threat of the introduction of a new centralized tax by Alva, a 'tenth penny' (ten percent) on all sales of merchandise, to be levied on the same footing in all provinces, modelled on the *alcabala*-taxes in Spanish cities, and comparable to the modern Value Added Tax.[14]

The Union of Utrecht of January 1579 was signed at its start by representatives from four provinces and from some other regions and cities of the Netherlands, and got gradually more members during the next months.[15] The initiative had been taken by the stadholder of the province of Gelre (=Gelderland), a younger brother of the Prince of Orange. Holland, Zeeland and Utrecht, the provinces of the Prince, were the other provinces that were involved from the start. The stadholder of four other northern provinces, Friesland, Groningen, Overijssel and Drenthe (not related to the Prince), sent a letter of adhesion in June, but decided to return to the Spanish side already less than a year later. Friesland disagreed with its stadholder and decided to remain in the Union, but elites in Groningen, Overijssel and Drenthe did not take the same decision as Friesland. These three provinces would be conquered by Union-troops during the 1590s.[16]

Groningen and Overijssel were accepted again in the Union as autonomous provinces with voting rights since then. The very small and poor province of Drenthe became a fiscally autonomous member of the Union without voting rights. Other territories conquered later by troops of the Union, of which the

---

14 F. Grapperhaus, *Alva en de tiende penning* (Zutphen, Walburg Pers, 1984) pp. 317–340 contains a detailed comparison of the announcement of 31. July 1571 regulating the conditions and implementation of the tenth penny and that of the V.A.T. in Europe nowadays.

15 At the start: Gelderland, Holland, Zeeland and Utrecht; in February 1579: the city of Gand; March 1579: the city and countryside of Nijmegen and of Arnhem, and several cities and counties in Friesland; April 1579: the city of Venlo; June 1579: the city of Amersfoort; July 1579:, the cities of Ypers, Antwerp, Breda, Brughes, Lier and the small province of Drenthe.

16 Overijssel en Drenthe would continue to pay contributions to Spain as well as to the Union well into the seventeenth century to buy off pillaging by troops. Overijssel paid about 200,000 guilders per year to the Union and about 50,000 guilders per year to Spain in the years around 1600; in 1635 resp. 600,000 and 80,000 guilders; *GFO*, p. 64, p. 187.

northern half of the large province of Brabant was the most important part, would no longer be granted autonomy, but be centrally administered by the 'Generality', the term for the States General and its executive organization. The conquered part of Brabant came to be called *Staats-Brabant* (='Brabant of the States (General)'), this in contrast to its southern part that remained part of the royal Spanish Netherlands in the South.

Already in 1579 the Union had also been signed by a number of cities in the Southern Netherlands, not only by Ghent, Ypres, Bruges and Lier, but also by Antwerp, until then by far the largest city and the economic heart of the Low Countries with a population of about 90,000 people in 1550. These cities would *not* become part of the Dutch Republic, as Flanders would gradually be reconquered by Spain, culminating in the conquest of Antwerp in 1585.[17] The Dutch navy that began to develop since the start of the Revolt, succeeded, however, in permanently blockading the river Scheldt, by means of ships forming a dam flanked by two forts on both sides of the river. This put a drastic sudden end to Antwerp's position as the main international port of North-Western Europe, and caused about half of its population to leave the city.

Many merchants went to Amsterdam that succeeded – and soon largely exceeded – Antwerp's position in world trade and became the economic heart of the Dutch Republic.[18] It should be noted, however, that Holland's urbanized territory was characterized in addition by a general underlying trend of economic growth already since the middle of the fourteenth century, despite fluctuations and a period of decreasing wealth in the years before the Revolt.[19] Its economic strength, the fundamental precondition for its later fiscal strength, was certainly not only a result of the external shock of the fall of Antwerp, but also of long-term internal developments.

Only in 1581 the Spanish king would be formally abjured by the rebellious provinces as their sovereign. A decisive event in the development from Revolt to Republic was that the Prince of Orange was murdered in 1584, before discussions whether he should become the sovereign of the new state had finished.

17 J. de Vries, *European Urbanization,, 1500–1800* (London, Methuen & Co., 1984) p. 272; by 1600 this number would have decreased to 47,000 due to emigration after the closure of the Scheldt.

18 C. Lesger, *The rise of the Amsterdam market and information exchange. Merchants, commercial expansion and change in the spatial economy of the Low Countries, c.1550–1630* (Ashgate, Aldershot, 2006).

19 J.L. van Zanden and B. van Leeuwen, 'Persistent but not Consistent: The Growth of National Income in Holland 1347–1807', *Explorations in Economic History*, 49 (2) 2012, pp. 119–130; http://www.cgeh.nl/reconstruction-national-accounts-holland-1500-1800-0 [last access 28-08-2016].

Attempts to find another European prince to assume the sovereignty over this territory ended in disappointments. In 1587, fifteen years after the start of the Revolt, a States General assembly of the revolting northern provinces of the Netherlands decided to assume the sovereignty itself. The 'Republic of the Seven United Provinces' then consisted of: Gelderland (= Gelre), Holland, Zeeland, Utrecht, Friesland, Groningen (= 'Stad en (Omme)Lande(n)' = 'City and (Surrounding) Countryside of Groningen') and Overijssel.

The Republic came soon to be seen as an independent political entity by French and British monarchs, and the States General started to receive English loans and French subsidies for their struggle against the common enemy Spain. In 1596 France and Britain even concluded the so-called Triple Alliance with the 'United Provinces' against Spain.[20] The king of Spain would acknowledge the Dutch Republic *de facto* as a state, when the two concluded in 1609 a Twelve Years' Truce interrupting the long war that had started in 1568. Formal international recognition as a state, also by Spain, had to await, the peace treaties of Westphalia of 1648.

The Institutional Legacy of the Habsburgs

The Union of Utrecht contained no articles about the institutions by means of which it would function and be financed. In this sense the treaty was not what we would call nowadays a 'constitution'. The new state did not have to be built up from scratch, however. Institutionally it was unmistakably the offspring of the seventeen provinces of the Netherlands, which had been formally acknowledged as a separate political entity within the empire of Charles V by an Imperial Diet of the German Holy Roman Empire already in 1548.

The unity of these 'seventeen Netherlands' was embodied in the institution of the assembly of the so called 'States General', summoned for the first time already in 1464 by the duke of Burgundy, at the time when a large part of the territory of the medieval Netherlands, including the northern provinces Holland and Zeeland, was part of the late medieval Burgundian state. The meetings of this institution consisted of representatives of 'Provincial States'-assemblies, in which representatives of the three 'states' that were seen as the main composite parts of societies in this part of the world – nobility, clergy and citizens – were, already before 1464, convened by their lord.[21] The most

20 The States of Holland argued in 1587 that the foreign recognition of the Republic as a state dated already from the Treaty of Nonsuch in 1585 between Britain and the States General; Parker, *The Dutch Revolt*, p. 243; *A General Collection of Treaties, manifestos* (…) *from the Year 1495 to the Year 1712*, London, 1732, pp. 83–88; http://books.google.co.uk/books?id=U8nYFSTQhXcC&pg=PA83#v=onepage&q&f=false.

21 In Holland for instance since 1428, in Gelre since 1423.

important reason to convene States General assemblies from time to time was the recurring need for the ruler of these territories to raise more money for war faring.

The Burgundian Netherlands were inherited in 1515 by the later Habsburg emperor Charles V from his father Philip the Fair of Burgundy. Four years later, in 1519, Charles was elected emperor as the successor of his grandfather Maximilian of Habsburg. He had become king of Castile, Aragon, Naples, Sicily and Milan as well, through his mother Joanna of Castile. He was able to annex the northern provinces of the Netherlands, Friesland, Utrecht, Overijssel, Drenthe, Groningen, and the duchy of Gelre to his empire between 1524 and 1543. Since then all seventeen provinces, constituting the territory called 'the Netherlands', were under his rule.

In order to obtain money for wars, first the Burgundian dukes, and subsequently the Habsburg monarchs, addressed requests – *beden*[22] – to the 'States' of the Netherlands. The States had to weigh the possible advantages of the military ambitions of a powerful sovereign, and the risks of arousing his displeasure, against the burden of increased taxation. In practice the *ordinaris bede* (= the ordinary request) was always granted without problems for a large number of years. When more money was needed the States General had to be convinced of the desirability of such ad hoc *extra-ordinaris beden*.

The royal government made a division of the needed sum across the provinces. The real negotiations were carried on with the provincial states separately, and even separately with the wealthiest of the individual cities, which allowed a policy of 'divide and rule' by allowing special privileges if required. The availability of this institutional situation, which guaranteed a ruler the cooperation of local elites in raising revenue for his war after they had consented in a *bede*, and which guaranteed these elites and the territory in which they lived protection and privileges for themselves, will have made it easier to realize a high level of revenues for wars than its absence would have been, although the negotiations with the States could be toilsome.

Economically – and therefore fiscally – by far the most important provinces of the Netherlands under the Habsburgs were Flanders with a population of c. 620,000 people around 1550, and Brabant with then c. 420,000 people, each with a great number of flourishing cities.[23] They contributed in the 1540s respectively 34 percent and 29 percent of the tax revenues from the

22 Pronounce 'baiden' like in 'maiden'(to pronounce the singular '*bede*' just omit the 'n').

23 33 in Flanders in 1515, 25 in Holland; Lesger, *The rise of the Amsterdam market and information exchange*, p. 134 with a map of the spatial distribution of population in the Low Countries on p. 18 fig. 1.1.

Netherlands to its government in Brussels.[24] Holland, which would become the fiscally most important province of the later Dutch Republic, came next in importance with a population in 1550 of c. 330,000.[25] It contributed 13 percent to the tax revenues of the Netherlands in the 1540s, when Antwerp was still the centre of world trade, and Brussels still the capital of the Netherlands. The other fourteen provinces of the Netherlands contributed each less than 6 percent.

Holland counted twenty-five cities in its small territory in 1515. Urban political power was already comparatively strong: the landowning nobility had one vote in Holland's Provincial States assembly, the six largest cities had in Holland each one vote; the economic power of the clergy was not large enough to grant it a seat in the States of Holland. The internal division of the sum to be paid by Holland for the *bede* was centrally determined under the Habsburgs and based upon an extensive inquiry into the wealth of the cities and the surrounding countryside executed by the central royal government in 1514.[26] Separate negotiations with cities gave the sovereign the possibility to promise cities individual rebates (*'gratiën'*) on their part in the *bede*. This made the division of the contributions less fair, but helped to forestall resistance of cities with voting right to the consent of their province in the proposed total sum.[27]

So, apart from provincial states assemblies and the States General, also the decentralized negotiations by a central government with separate provinces and even with individual cities were important institutional 'building blocks' of the fiscal system of the Netherlands before the Revolt. The lack of the central power of a sovereign that would result from the Revolt, would force the provinces in the States General, and the cities in the provincial states assemblies, to

24 W. Blockmans, 'De vorming van een politieke unie (veertiende-zestiende eeuw)', in: *Geschiedenis van de Nederlanden*, eds. J.C.H. Blom and E. Lamberts (Rijswijk, s.a.) pp. 45–117, p. 98.

25 This figure results from the estimate of 274,810 for 1514 and a growth rate of 0.5% on average per year; J. de Vries, *The Dutch rural economy in the Golden Age, 1500–1700* (London, 1978) pp. 86, 90, 93 assumes for the five biggest cities a growth rate of on average 0.37% per year and a higher growth rate in the countryside.

26 Nationaal Archief, Archief van de Grafelijkheidsrekenkamer of Rekenkamer der Domeinen van Holland, toegangsnummer 3.01.27.01, inventarisnummer 648A; the printed edition made in 1866 is accessible on http://socialhistory.org/sites/default/files/uploads/informacie.pdf.

27 By the 1550s these rebates had increased to about 35% of the total amount of Holland's *bede*. In the case of the privileged six cities with a seat in the States the rebates could increase to half or even two thirds the amount they originally had to pay; Tracy, *Financial Revolution*, p. 53.

act as a collectivity, and to become more aware of common, instead of primarily particularistic interests.

A major difference between the functioning of these institutions before and after the Revolt was, moreover, that during the Habsburg period the States General met only when summoned by the king. The States General met in Brussels, the governmental centre of the late medieval Netherlands, with a population of about 40,000 people in 1550 in the rich province of Brabant,[28] not in much larger Antwerp, its economically most powerful city, similar to the difference in Spain between government centre Madrid and economic centre Sevilla, and, after the Revolt, between The Hague and Amsterdam in the Dutch Republic; even in the Dutch Republic economic power and political power were kept separate.

The last meeting of the States General in Brussels before the Duke of Alva became governor of the Netherlands in 1567 had been held in 1559. It had granted King Philip II a *bede* for a period of nine years. In consenting to this *bede* the provinces had stipulated that they would have a say in the collection and administration of the money and to be allowed to be present when the troops to be paid from it, were mustered.[29] This implied, of course, a decentralizing tendency, which tended to make the provinces into more autonomous 'political bodies'. The increasing financial autonomy of the provinces in the Netherlands before the Revolt may have contributed to the efficiency of state formation in this part of the Habsburg Empire.[30]

On its next meeting in 1568 Alva would present a plan that counteracted these decentralizing tendencies. It amounted to a change from the old *beden*-system – which kept him fiscally dependent on the consent of the States General and negotiations with Provincial States assemblies – towards a centralized fiscal system based on taxes collected by a central royal bureaucracy. He intended to raise in this way enough tax revenue to make the Seventeen Netherlands independent from military subsidies from Spain. These subsidies to what was called 'the army in Flanders' had become increasingly necessary in the preceding years to contain religious riots and political resistance against the royal religious policy to maintain Catholicism and to crush Protestantism. His fiscal plans, in combination with the aversion stirred by the intolerant royal religious policy, led to the start of the Revolt.

---

28 De Vries, *European Urbanization*, p. 272.

29 Grapperhaus, *Alva en de tiende penning*, p. 66.

30 H. de Schepper, 'Beleid en bestuur inzake de hoge overheidsfinancien in eht Bourgondisch-Habsburgse Nederland', in: *Van Tresorier tot Thesaurier-Generaal*, ed. J.Th. de Smidt a.o. (Hilversum 1996) 17–52, 31–32.

The States General, Holland, the Council of State and the Stadholder

The States General assembly of the seventeen Netherlands, convened by Alva in 1568, had been its first meeting since nine years and it was attended by no less than a few hundred deputies.[31] This States General assembly decided to convene on its own authority for the first time in 1576, on the initiative of the province of Brabant, this in order to discuss how to find the money to put an end to the increasing disorder in society resulting from the presence of unpaid Spanish troops. This is not the place for a detailed history of the institution of the Dutch States General,[32] but some explanations on the differences between its character before and since the Revolt – and on its relations to the powerful province Holland, and to its executive organ the *Raad van State* (=Council of State) and the 'stadholders' – are necessary to understand its role in the process of the formation of the Dutch state and its fiscal system.

After the start of the Union of Utrecht gradually a split came about between a States General of the Northern and one of the Southern Netherlands. The most characteristic difference between the two would become that the States General of the Southern Netherlands was hardly ever convened any more after 1585. That of the Northern Netherlands, in contrast, became a permanent institution. It convened in principle at least once a year to discuss the amounts needed for 'ordinary' war finance. Additional meetings were necessary to discuss petitions for 'extraordinary' war finance, and other 'Generality' affairs. A characteristic element of the new process of state formation since the start of the Revolt was therefore the large increase in the frequency of States General meetings and also the much lower number of representatives attending the States General. New developments in the way it functioned became apparent, too.

In 1600 on average about 45 deputies were present at meetings of the States General of the seven united provinces, in 1650 on average about 80, no longer the hundreds of 1559 and 1568, therefore. Since 1625 the meetings were attended by a core group of about fifteen members that attended at least 40 percent of c. 320 meetings until 1650.[33] To prepare details of points to be discussed, small temporary committees were appointed from the representatives, in 1600 about 50 per year in 1650 already about 350 per year, some of which

31 Grapperhaus, *Alva en de tiende penning*, p. 108.

32 This history is summarized in the Introduction to the published decisions of the States General: *Resolutien der Staten Generaal Part 1 1576–1609* electronically accessible on http://resources.huygens.knaw.nl/retroboeken/statengeneraal.

33 S. Groenveld, 'De institutionele en politieke context', in: *Van Tresorier tot Thesaurier-generaal* (Hilversum, Verloren, 1996) pp. 55–89, p. 61, 64.

became rather permanent. Although the States General was as a legacy of the Habsburg period, and although much of the terminology used for its functioning remembered of the time of the Habsburgs, its functioning as a permanent sovereign institution at the centre of the new Dutch state became really very different, therefore, from that of the States General before the Revolt.

The Hague, a small town in Holland near the coast, of then less than 10,000 inhabitants, became the place where the States General of the Northern Netherlands established its permanent seat since 1593. It had been the residence of the feudal counts of Holland during the thirteenth century. Before 1593 the States General had, during some years, met in Utrecht, the geographic heart of the Republic and the largest city after Amsterdam. The choice of The Hague, after the States General had decided to assume the sovereignty themselves, was very convenient for the representatives of the 'States of Holland' which had its meetings in this former centre of Holland's 'sovereignty', too.[34] The choice can be seen as symbolic for the fact that Holland was right from the start the most powerful part of the federal republic, due to its much larger fiscal importance than that of the other provinces.

It may, on the other hand, also be seen as symbolic for the fact that Amsterdam's power in Holland was less overwhelming than that of Holland in the Republic, and that Holland's fiscal power would mainly come to consist in that of the collectivity of its cities, not, for instance, in mainly that of Amsterdam. The fiscal contribution of Holland to the Union would soon become about sixty percent of the Union as a whole. Amsterdam was at the time about two times as large as the next largest city in Holland (Haarlem), but – due to the large number of cities in Holland – Amsterdam's contribution to Holland's main taxes would never become more than about one third. The functioning of Holland's Provincial States was largely intensified as well, of course, even much more so than that of the States General. A board of about ten so-called 'commissioned deputies' (*Gecommitteerde Raden*) would come to function as a kind of daily board of the States, meeting in fact nearly daily.[35]

The petitions of the States General to the provinces for money, with specified proposals for (changes in) army expenditure – or for more navy expenditure than could be paid from the customs revenues earmarked to this end – were prepared by a Council of State (*Raad van State*) consisting of twelve members, three representatives for Holland, and two or one for each of the other provinces. It decided by majority vote. The Council was advised by the

34 Thomassen, *Instrumenten van de macht*, p. 76.

35 J.W. Koopmans, *De Staten van Holland en de Opstand : de ontwikkeling van hun functies en organisatie in de periode 1544–1588* (Den Haag 1990).

stadholder of the most important provinces, who was at the same time the commander-in-chief of army and navy.[36] Each of the seven provinces had one vote in the States General-assembly, and unanimity was required for important decisions. In the meetings of the States General the provincial representatives were urged to obtain the consent of their Provincial States, and they were provided with the arguments that made it desirable to do so. The Council of State and the stadholder, both lacking any sovereign power, could subsequently do not much more than just hope the best of it.

'Consents' were given by provinces individually after the proposals were discussed in the Provincial States assemblies, and the consents often contained conditions and restrictions.[37] As the army-companies, that had to be paid by the provinces outside Holland, were mostly garrisoned in these provinces in peace time, they had, however, a strong interest, of course, in not leaving these troops unpaid. It was less easy to obtain all the money thought necessary by the Council of State for the navy, especially from the inland provinces. However, products entering the Netherlands by means of the foreign trade that had to be protected by the navy were also appreciated by elites in the other provinces. An awareness that their level of consumption was partly dependent on Holland's foreign trade will have mitigated a trend to abstain from contributions to navy expenditure.

As long as Holland was convinced of the necessity of increases in war expenditure, and as long as the other provinces remained convinced of the desirability of defence of their territory by Generality troops, the Council of State did not need to despair completely as to the acceptance of its fiscal wishes, therefore, although complaints about slow consents and about payments arrears in given consents were a common characteristic of the text of the petitions. In practice, the fiscal system of the Republic was prevented from getting jammed by simply putting off voting as long as possible, to increase the chance of acceptance, and by just keeping payments going, if necessary by means of 'Generality'-loans.

The *de facto* hegemonic position of Holland, resulting from a much larger economic strength than in the other provinces, was the most important point

---

36 A number of provinces used to have the same 'stadholder', only since 1747 all provinces had the same stadholder. There were two periods when a number of provinces, including Holland, choose not to appoint a new stadholder after the death of the former: the years 1650–1672 and 1702–1747 are known in Dutch history as the 'stadholderless' periods.

37 't Hart, M., *The making of a bourgeois state*, pp. 83–84 gives an example of the proposal for changes in the former war budget in 1624 and the decisions taken as the result of discussions in the provincial assemblies.

in which the Republic of the Seven United Provinces of the Netherlands differed from the Confederacy of the Thirteen United States of America nearly two hundred years later.[38] It was mainly Holland's hegemonic position and the perceived interest of the other provinces in remaining part of the Union, which would make the functioning of the federal Dutch Republic in practice less 'imbecile' than the famous American federalists Hamilton and Madison thought it must have been.[39]

The Fiscal Articles of the Union of Utrecht

The treaty of 1579 had envisaged a new uniform tax system for all the provinces, proposing in its fifth article an integrated system of new taxes, on urban as well as on agrarian commercial products, activities, and assets, under the name of 'general means', consisting for a large part of price-increasing indirect taxes on primary necessities. This article constituted a clear attempt at fiscal centralization to strengthen the Union, comparable to Alva's plan for a centralized sales tax of the 'tenth penny'. 'General means' would indeed be introduced in all provinces in the course of time.[40] However, each province would decide itself which 'general means' – and at which tax rates – would best fit its economy to enable it to pay its share in the amounts for 'general' expenditure, as well as for its own internal provincial expenditure. Neither would the 'general means' be specifically destined, in practice, for 'general' expenditure, consisting mainly of war expenditure. Often a preference would develop to destine them primarily for interest payments on provincial loans negotiated for war financing.

A unified centralized tax system would never be realized during the existence of the Dutch Republic. A fixed distributive key developed instead, for the share each province had to take in 'general expenditure', a key that was reminiscent of the way the *bede*-amounts had been distributed across the provinces under the Habsburgs. The various expenditure-items themselves – army companies, fortifications, magazines etc. – came to be partitioned across the provinces. The payments for this so-called 'general' expenditure (*'generale lasten'*) were primarily done and administered by the provinces themselves.

---

38 In the early United States of America, the three largest states each contributed between 14% and 19% to the Confederacy during the years 1777–1781; K.L. Dougherty, 'An empirical test of Federalist and Anti-Federalist theories of state contributions, 1775–1783', *Social Science History* 33, 1 (2009) 47–74; Table 1; in the Dutch Republic the contribution next in size after the about 60% from Holland was the about 12% from Friesland.

39 See the General Introduction here above.

40 In most provinces the first general means were those on wines, beers, milling of grains, salt, cloth – woolen as well as gold and silver brocades and silk –, horned cattle and sown lands, slaughtering of cattle, sale of horses and oxen and on weighing of merchandise.

At the central level of the Generality data about what had been paid for the common cause were collected, and compared to what had been agreed to, and delegates of the States General were sometimes sent to provinces with important payment arrears to convince them to pay. Tax receipts, however, were only administered on the provincial level, and the provincial accounts were audited by a provincial accounting chamber or by deputies of the Provincial States not by the Accounting Chamber of the Generality.

Although no centralized system of domestic 'general means' would come into being, a customs union would be realized in the next years in conformity to article XVIII of the Union of Utrecht. The number and rates of the taxes to be levied on foreign trade and shipping came to be decided centrally. Apart from the hegemonic position of Holland this was another important point in which the federal republic of the United Provinces was different from the early Confederacy of the United States of America of 1776 two centuries later. Here a customs union would have to await the more centralized federalist constitution of 1789.

A last feature of the financial structure of the new state was, that the revenues from later conquered territories, that did no longer become autonomous parts of the Republic and would have no vote in the States General, became central revenues. It was the States General that decided which taxes at which rates were levied in these 'Generality-territories' and what expenditure would be paid from them. These tax revenues would allow the Generality the debt service on 'Generality-loans' that were negotiated in addition to the public loans by each of the fiscally autonomous provinces, in order to enable more war expenditure than could be paid for from tax revenues.

The Concept 'Public Finance of the Dutch Republic', the Data and the Estimates

Public Finance of *and* in *the Dutch Republic*

This book uses the concept 'public finance *of* the Dutch Republic' as to be distinguished from 'public finance *in* the Dutch Republic'. The first concept comprises the public revenue and expenditure of the main institutional elements of the Republic: the fiscally autonomous provinces, the so-called Generality and the admiralties that maintained the navy. These were the elements of public finance on which the fiscal functioning of the new state, as it would develop between 1572 and 1609, would be mainly based.

The concept 'public finance *in* the Dutch Republic' refers in addition to social and economic tasks, which may be seen as typically public tasks, like water management, poor relief, public education and the provision of public urban facilities, that were not financed by the provincial governments. Decisions to these ends were taken by water boards and urban governments autonomously and were financed from their own tax revenues (in as far as not financed by churches or private initiative). It may even be argued that, especially for comparisons with public finance in other states, the military expenditure by the VOC, the East Indian Company, that had to be realized for the protection and expansion of its trade from its own revenues, should also be included in the concept 'public finance *in* the Dutch Republic'.

Not enough was known on the finance of urban governments and water boards to incorporate them systematically into this book. Data for Amsterdam, Leiden, Haarlem, Dordrecht, Zwolle and Groningen in the period between about 1650 and 1675 show an average of about 6 guilders for annual urban revenue per capita.[41] At an urban population of about 800,000 people at that time,[42] public expenditure by all urban governments in the Dutch Republic may then have been roughly about 4.8 million guilders per year.

A beautiful study on Holland's most important water board, 'Rhineland', responsible for the major seventeen km long sea dike between Amsterdam and Haarlem along the IJ, which was in fact an arm of the Zuyder Zee, mentions an average expenditure of about 100,000 guilders per year between 1650 and 1750. Although a very important water board, it was only one of many regional and local water boards, however. A rough total estimate for Holland, mainly based on the length of dikes to be maintained, may amount to between 1 and 2 million guilders around 1700, which would imply an addition of 6 to 12 percent to Holland's total public expenditure around 1700. The percentage for the whole Republic will have been lower, because water control in the 'land provinces' required much less than in the 'sea-provinces'. A rough estimate for total expenditure on water management may amount, therefore, to perhaps on average about 1.5 to 2.5 million guilders per year for the whole Republic for the period around 1700.[43]

---

41 Lowest in Leiden: c. fl. 5.37, highest in Groningen: c. fl. 7.33: L. Nagtegaal, 'Stadsfinanciën en stedelijke economie. Invloed van de conjunctuur op de Leidse stadsfinanci:en, 1620–1720', *Economisch- en Sociaal-Historisch Jaarboek*, 52 (1989) pp. 96–148, p. 140; M. van der Heijden, *Geldschieters van de stad. Financiële relaties tussen stad, burgers en overheden, 1550–1650* (Amsterdam, Bert Bakker, 2006) pp. 270–274; M. Schroor, *Rurale metropool: Bevolking, migratie en financiën van de stad Groningen ten tijde van de Republiek (1595–1795)* (Groningen, 2014) pp. 61, 255.

42 De Vries and Van der Woude, *The first modern economy*, p. 61.

43 P.J.E.M. van Dam and M. van Tielhof, 'Losing land, gaining water. Ecological and financial aspects of regional water management in Rhineland, 1200–1800', in: *Water management,*

As to the East and West Indian Companies: VOC-specialist Gaastra estimated that about 30% of all expenditure of the VOC between 1613 and 1792 was spent on war, amounting to on average about 1.4 million guilders per year. The WIC in contrast was for military expenditure completely dependent on state support.[44]

Total public expenditure of the Dutch Republic between 1621 and 1794 was, in non-war years, on average about 30 million guilders per year. If the estimates for the East India Company, the water boards and urban public expenditure as just mentioned would be added, this would raise total public expenditure to on average perhaps nearly 38 or 39 million guilders between 1621 and 1795. This would mean that public expenditure *of* the Dutch Republic amounted in peace years to more than 75 to 80 percent of that *in* the Republic, and a much higher percentage, of course, in its many war years. Urban public life, water management in the countryside and the protection of colonial trade were vital elements in the functioning of the Dutch Republic, but as regards its public finance it was evidently predominantly a federation of provinces. The rest of this book will remain restricted to the public finance *of* the Dutch Republic consisting in that of the provinces, the Generality and the admiralties, with that of the provinces as by far the most important element.

The Reliability of the Data and the Estimates

Archives on Dutch public finance in the seventeenth and eighteenth century are not only far from completely preserved. The preserved sources are also different in character for each of the provinces and for different periods within a province.[45] The character of public finance data implies, moreover, that they are never reliable on a year to year basis, because of differences in accounting practices. Table 0.1 offers a striking example for Holland, the most important of

communities and environment. The Low Countries in Comparative Perspective, c. 1000–1800; *Jaarboek voor Ecologische Geschiedenis* 10 (2006) 63–94, 81; *Man-made Lowlands, History of water management and land reclamation in the Netherlands*, G.P. van de Ven ed. (Utrecht, Matrijs, 2004) p. 114; A. Fransen, *Een kleine dijk met een groot doel. De financiering van de Diemerdijk, 1591–1864* (diss. Amsterdam 2009); I am indebted to Petra van Dam for a discussion on the estimate.

44 Brandon, *War, capital and the Dutch state*, pp. 98–114.

45 Exact information on the sources used for all preserved data, and on the years and the revenue- and expenditure items for which estimates had to be used, can be found in the database on http://resources.huygens.knaw.nl/gewestelijkefinancien/en under 'Sources' and in the electronically accessible printed volumes (under 'Go to the digital version' on the left side of this web page).

TABLE 0.1 *Generality expenditure paid by Holland from different archival sources, 1586–1599.*

	a	b	a minus b
1586	1,943,291	1,863,739	79,552
1587	2,220,760	3,490,956	-1,270,196
1588	1,927,542	1,944,141	-16,599
1589	1,927,542	890,504	1,037,038
1590	1,863,291	2,048,531	-185,240
1591	2,056,045	1,992,497	63,548
1592	2,120,297	1,963,984	156,313
1593	2,184,548	2,195,719	-11,171
1594	3,580,081	2,605,852	974,229
1595	1,300,989	2,167,610	-866,621
1596	2,813,091	2,810,299	2,792
1597	3,131,388	3,018,830	112,558
1598	2,714,871	2,939,941	-225,070
1599	4,610,032	4,285,079	324,953
Average	*2,456,698*	*2,444,120*	
Average difference in %			*0.5%*

(a) NA 1.10.42, Van der Hoop, inv.nr. 93, *'Balance van Betalingen bij de provincie van Hollandt en Westvriesland op de volgende jaren gedaan',* made in or shortly after 1724, and offering an overview of what Holland had paid 'too much' (*'t'over'*) or 'too little' (*'te weijnigh'*) on its quota in Generality expenditure in the years 1587–1724.
(b) NA 3.01.14, Van Oldenbarnevelt, inv.nr. 187, *'Rekeningen van de Staten van Holland en West-Friesland ten gunste van de Generaliteit over de jaren 1586–1599 aan ordinaris en extraordinaris quoten in de consenten'* (one document written about 1600).

the provinces, and at the same time a province in which large parts of the fiscal archives were destroyed already in the eighteenth century.[46]

It shows amounts for 'general expenditure' paid by the province of Holland according to different primary sources. The first column comes from a detailed contemporary list of the total amounts in payments actually done per year found in the archives of the famous Dutch statesman and very capable financier Van Oldenbarnevelt. The second column results from a list of what Holland had to pay according to the 'Statements of War' or 'War-lists' (*Staten van Oorlog*) and the 'Petitions', and a later overview of what was paid 'too much'

46 W. Fritschy, 'A "financial revolution" reconsidered: public finance in Holland during the Dutch Revolt, 1568–1648', *Economic History Review* (2003) pp. 57–89, p. 63.

and what was paid 'too little' in each of these years. Although the two columns vary widely on a year to year basis, the difference between the totals is only 0.5% for the whole period of 14 years.

As figures for revenue and expenditure that were intended to be realized in a certain year were, of course, not necessarily identical to the ones realized in fact during that year, sometimes nine years averages were used for graphs. Graphs on a year to year basis have mostly been preferred, however, to maintain a visible link with the primary source material that was used and to avoid the 'flattening' out of historically remarkable sudden peaks, especially the wars in which the Republic was involved.

Estimates for missing data on *expenditure* for certain periods in one of the provinces were often based on available data for *other* provinces in the same period, and on the assumption that the 'payment-behaviour' (the extent to which a province paid in fact what was expected according to the quotas), and the general characteristics of expenditure-patterns in the 'land-provinces' and to some extent Friesland (as opposed to the 'sea-provinces' Holland and Zeeland and to some extent Utrecht) were more or less similar. Estimates for missing data on public *revenue* were rather based on what seemed likely in view of other data on the *same* province, as for instance data about decisions on taxation or decisions to negotiate a certain amount in loans, and data on interest payments and interest rates.

As the accumulated totals for expenditure and revenue – incl. long-term loans! – were often based on different estimating procedures, the difference between them offers a rough test of the overall reliability of the estimates. The difference between the results for total public expenditure and total public revenue was 2.8 percent of total revenue for the period from 1621–1794, 5.2 percent for the period from 1621–1713 and about 0.6 percent for the period from 1714–1794. For shorter periods, and especially for early periods, these percentages could be (much) higher, however, although the average margins are only seldom higher than about ten percent for time-periods of nine years. The two least reliable periods appeared to be 1628–1648 and 1702–1713, most probably partly because of lower estimates for extraordinary revenues, partly because of higher estimates for war expenditure than realized in fact (see the spreadsheets on http://resources.huygens.knaw.nl/gewestelijkefinancien/en).

CHAPTER 1

Financing the First Phase of the Revolt against Spain (1566–1572)

It was a collectivity of cities in the provinces of Holland and Zeeland that would start the process of state formation without which a war against Spain could not have been financed. It was the Prince of Orange, however, who started the war. This first chapter describes his toilsome efforts to get the money required for the war during the years preceding the formation of the fiscal system of the Dutch Republic. It highlights the crucial importance of the – initially rather reluctant – support of this collectivity of cities.

1.1 Calvinist Donations and the Credit of the Prince of Orange

On 10 August 1566, 'a wave of popular violence against the old Church and its images started an iconoclastic frenzy spreading over Flanders, Hainault, Brabant, Zeeland, Holland, Utrecht, Gelderland, Friesland and Groningen', wrote Jonathan Israel in his impressive history of the Dutch Republic.[1] As a result city councils were forced to permit Protestant worship in Roman Catholic churches, thus violating the 'anti-heresy laws' issued by their Roman Catholic Spanish king Philip II. Geoffrey Parker, the most important historiographer of the Dutch Revolt, could show that this 'wave' of violence was better prepared than the word 'wave' suggests: the iconoclasts received payments from the financial reserves of Calvinist consistories.[2] Calvinist donations would subsequently become a source of finance for the first military confrontations between the Spanish troops and those who started the resistance against their oppression of Protestantism.

The possibility of resistance against the religious policy of Philip II had already been discussed in other layers of society than that of Calvinist ministers and iconoclasts, too. A number of nobles had met to this end in the castle of the count of Brederode in Vianen in September 1565. Among those present,

1 J. Israel, *The Dutch Republic: its rise, greatness and fall 1477–1806* (Oxford: Clarendon Press, 1995) pp. 147–148.

2 Parker, *The Dutch Revolt*, p. 93.

 | DOI 10.1163/9789004341289_004

was the prince of Orange,[3] 'stadholder' for the Spanish king in the provinces Holland, Zeeland and Utrecht, and the most esteemed among the Dutch nobles. He had publicly rejected the royal religious policy of persecution of Protestantism, for the first time in a long speech in the Council of State, the king's advisory board in the Netherlands, on New Year's eve 1564/5.

First attempts to try to raise troops were made in December 1565. This was done on the one hand by soliciting support from German princes who favoured the Protestant cause. On the other hand there were initiatives to secure aid from French relatives of the Prince of Orange, who were the leaders of the French Protestant Huguenots.[4] On 25 January 1566, William of Orange wrote his brother Louis of Nassau to ask him about the possibilities of recruiting troops and raising a loan in Antwerp.[5] On 31 January 1566 he gave orders to muster 200 harquebusiers in Holland. He had started recruiting troops in German countries in March 1566 already before the iconoclastic 'wave'.

Since the iconoclastic disturbances in the Netherlands also the royal government of the Netherlands in Brussels was aware of the necessity to have more troops available. Having received worried messages on the situation in the Netherlands from his half-sister Margaret of Parma, who was at the time his governor in the Low Countries, her brother king Philip II told her to try to raise troops in Germany. He sent her 300,000 crowns (about 450,000 guilders) from Spain on 9 August 1566, not only to enlist 5,000 new recruits and but also to pay arrears to veteran troops garrisoned on the southern frontier.[6] As this was not enough Margaret of Parma asked the king's stadholder William of Orange to help her to get loans in Antwerp, Holland, Zeeland and Utrecht to pay the soldiers. Orange wrote her a reassuring letter on the recruitment of troops in Hessen and Brunswick,[7] just the day after his brother Louis had written him about the increased need to recruit troops to counteract the rigorous measures expected from Philip II. Less than two months later, on 26 October 1566, the Prince informed Henry of Brunswick of his great displeasure at Brunswick's brother's attempts to recruit soldiers on behalf of the Spanish king.

At the same time a Calvinist consistory in Ghent in Flanders took the remarkable initiative to announce to the Spanish king that it was ready to collect and pay him three million guilders, in exchange for freedom of religion.

---

3 Parker, *The Dutch Revolt*, p. 69.

4 Parker, *The Dutch Revolt*, pp. 68–69, 91.

5 http://www.inghist.nl/Onderzoek/Projecten/WVO; all letters to and from William of Orange mentioned in the text can easily be retrieved on this website by means of the dates.

6 Parker, *The Dutch Revolt*, p. 92.

7 Letter of 3 September 1566; http://www.inghist.nl/Onderzoek/Projecten/WVO.

It was added that – if he did not accept – the money would instead be used to pay troops held ready in German countries. Pamphlets were printed informing the people of the plan. The central collector got arrested with the money, however, when yet only a small part of the three million had been collected.[8] In fact the only choice was that between submission to the Catholic Spanish king or military resistance.[9] In Flanders' Westerkwartier Calvinists effectively succeeded in raising about 1500 men in troops, that were financed through another Calvinist treasury administered by two parsons. These troops were attacked and defeated by the royal army. The Calvinist leader Brederode succeeded in raising even 3,000 men in troops in Antwerp, which were also paid for by Calvinist consistories. They too were attacked and most of them killed by government troops. Subsequently cities were forced by government troops one after another to expel Calvinist preachers. By the middle of 1567 the start of the initial phase of the armed revolt, financed by means of funds collected by Flemish Calvinists, was exhausted and over.[10]

The second, and much more important, source of money for armed resistance was the credit of the prince of Orange. As count of Nassau he had inherited rich properties in the Holy Roman Empire after the death of his father in 1559 and he also became the owner of important family-properties in the Netherlands. Several attempts of the Prince to secure loans on his personal credit in Germany, that were obviously not related to Margaret of Parma's request that he secure loans for her, are visible in his correspondence in 1566 and 1567.[11]

The Prince even asked the States of Holland for a loan of 20,000 guilders on 21 April 1567, 'at 5 percent or at any other rate that they may think reasonable', 'to assist him and to help him pay his debts' during the time that he would be travelling through Germany 'for his personal affairs' (*pour 'mes négoces particuliers'*). It was very hard to get money in Germany during these troubled times, he explained. To convince the States of Holland to give him this personal loan he referred in his letter to the 'affection' that they had always shown

8 R. van Roosbroeck, *Willem van Oranje* (Den Haag, Kruseman, 1974) p. 182; Parker, *The Dutch Revolt*, p. 93.

9 Israel, *The Dutch Republic*, p. 152.

10 Parker, *The Dutch Revolt*, pp. 94, 96–98.

11 On 11 November 1566, one for 4000 *thaler*, 24 January 1567 10,000 goldguilders, on 14 March 1567 a request to postpone repayment of a personal loan of 6,000 *thaler*. In a letter of March 1563 he had mentioned an amount of 300,000 Frankfort guilders in family debts, with an interest burden of no less than 14,000 guilders per year; http://www.inghist.nl/Onderzoek/Projecten/WVO.

him.[12] Orange received a message from his Chamber of Account in Breda, at the end of May, that his request had been granted indeed.[13] Although personal financial problems of a different character may perhaps not be excluded,[14] it may be noticed that in the same period a letter to the count of Holstein Schaumburg, dated of 13 March, had contained another attempt to recruit troops.

King Philip II had decided, in the meantime, to replace his half-sister Margaret as governor of the Netherlands by the Duke of Alva. He expected the Duke to act more ruthlessly in suppressing Protestantism and to introduce a new tax system to pay for the increasing numbers of troops needed in this part of his empire. In August 1567 Alva arrived at the head of an army of 10,000 men in Brussels. The prince of Orange had already left the city in April. Although he had until then operated secretly and had not yet directly participated in the armed revolt, he rightly feared for his life. Two of his fellow members of the high nobility of the Netherlands, the counts of Egmond and Hoorne, were arrested in September 1567 and executed in June 1568, despite the fact that Egmond had not hesitated to provide Margaret with military assistance during the troubles in Flanders. Orange himself would be outlawed by Philip II in 1580 and be murdered in 1584 after a price had been put on his head.

As soon as Alva had understood that Orange would refuse to come to Brussels, he appointed a new stadholder in Holland, Zeeland and Utrecht. He moreover confiscated all the Prince's possessions in the Netherlands, thus depriving him of personal revenue sources worth about 150,000 guilders a year.[15] Since then it was doubtless an even harder job for the Prince to find enough money for an armed revolt than before.[16]

When Calvinist merchants in Antwerp heard in April 1568 that the prince was ready to sell gold and silver crockery from his personal possessions up to an amount of 125,000 guilders to finance armed resistance to Alva, they decided to promise him double this amount on the condition that he would start his offensive in Antwerp. They explained him that their idea was to pay him on a 'no win no fee'-basis. He would be paid only after having succeeded in

12 Earlier during his 'stadholderate' William had refused the offer of the States to pay him a salary.

13 Letter dated 31 May 1567; http://www.inghist.nl/Onderzoek/Projecten/WVO.

14 The correspondence with his brothers shows that in 1563 the family was heavily in debt: it mentions an amount of 300,000 Frankfort guilders with an interest burden of 14,000 guilders per year (letter 5588 10-3-1563).

15 Parker, *The Dutch Revolt*, p. 48.

16 See the letter dd. 5 September 1568 to Hans von Heydelbach; a letter to Hilmar von Münchausen dated 15 October 1567 yet mentions a German loan of about 50,000 guilders; http://www.inghist.nl/Onderzoek/Projecten/WVO.

securing freedom of religion for their city. The prince answered them dryly, that he was ready to service the cause of religion and liberty, if they would promise him a guarantee of 600,000 guilders.[17] In the event, no more than about 12,000 guilders seems to have come forward from these merchants.[18]

In the course of 1568 the prince appeared to enjoy still enough personal credit, however, to be able to raise money to recruit no less than about 30,000 troops. His plan was to attack the Netherlands simultaneously from four sides. He himself would enter Brabant from the east; his brother Louis would invade Groningen in the north, while additional support would come from French troops under Huguenot leadership in the south. Protestant refugee churches in Britain had financed ships with soldiers that were to invade Flanders from the west. The scale of the military initiatives had thus increased considerably in comparison to the modest Calvinist initiatives of earlier years. No wonder that the Revolt is often said to have started in 1568.

However, the master plan of the Prince of Orange to conquer the Netherlands failed. Although in the north the rather small army of Louis of Nassau won the battle of Heiligerlee in May 1568, it was defeated in Jemmingen two months later. The planned attack by sea on Flanders had not remained secret and the soldiers were captured immediately upon landing. The French king moreover blocked the advance of the Huguenot troops. Letters of the Prince in June and July mention attempts to recruit yet more troops, while letters of August and September mention a loan of about 100,000 guilders from August of Saxony.[19]

The vicissitudes of the huge army of the Prince in the important province of Brabant are described in a line in the *Wilhelmus*, a sixteenth century song, which is nowadays the Dutch national anthem. It stages William of Orange as addressing himself to the Dutch people saying: 'My horsemen could be seen galloping courageously through the fields'.[20] This was, in fact, exactly the problem. Alva avoided a battle, and the cities in Brabant did not open their gates for the Prince, refusing to lodge his soldiers. By February 1569 the Prince was forced to disband his army because there was no money left to pay them any longer.

---

17 Letter nr.11006, 24 April 1568 to ten Protestant merchants in Antwerp; http://www.inghist.nl/Onderzoek/Projecten/WVO.

18 Van Roosbroeck, *Willem van* Oranje, p. 216.

19 23 June and 3 July 1568 to Fredrick III of the Palts, and 30 June 1568 to William of Hessen; August of Saxony letters 30 August and 16 September 1568; http://www.inghist.nl/Onderzoek/Projecten/WVO.

20 *'Mijn ruyters sach men draven/Seer moedich door dat Velt'.*

The Prince now had to flee his creditors.[21] It is known that in January 1571 an auction had to take place to satisfy them. Lists of all the prince's personal belongings made for this auction have been preserved: seventy-six pages in total, carpets, crockery, paintings etc.[22] Friends had been approached and asked to buy certain family items to save them. Details on the financial results are not known. It is likely, however, that, between 1566 and 1569, William of Orange invested probably at least about a million guilders, on the credit of his personal possessions, in order to combat Alva.[23] His brothers had invested 350,000 guilders to the same cause.[24] The sums were really substantial, exceeding even the total annual tax revenue from the seventeen provinces of the Netherlands then received by the king's treasury in Brussels.[25] 'Neither life nor property/ Did I spare for you/My brothers of high reputation/ Did the same for you',[26] says another – rather unknown – part of the national anthem, and obviously rightly so.

Nevertheless, the invested sums were by far not enough. The king's governor Alva could not only dispose of the tax revenues of the Netherlands for his war expenditure, but also received no less than about 3.2 million guilders in subsidies

---

21 K.W. Swart, *William of Orange and the Revolt of the Netherlands, 1572–1584* (Ashgate 2003) p. 33.

22 The list is published in A.J.M. Brouwer Anchor, 'Lijsten van door prins Willem I verpande goederen', *Oud Holland* (1899), pp. 9–32.

23 This estimate is based on the following data: the annual wages of 25,000 men amounted to 2,400,000 guilders, not counting officers' pay (Tracy, *The founding of the Dutch Republic*, p. 105) i.e. 0.263 per man per day; also according to p. 6 the lowest paid soldiers got 0.262 per day (cavalerymen, however, earned 0.60 per day); in October 1568 (according to Israel, according to Swart, *William of Orange*, p. 23 however already 27 August) the prince invaded Brabant with 30,000 men; in February 1569 he paid them off 'as best he could' (Parker, *The Dutch Revolt*, p. 110); which means that he had to pay his army during at least four months; 30,000 soldiers for 4 months required therefore at least 960,000 guilders; as captains earned 3.57 guilders per day and a company was 150 men, the additional total amount to be paid for captains for four months must have been about 85,680 guilders. In 1576 members of the States General promised Orange even payment for some 2 million guilders in debt he had contracted during the war (Tracy, *The Founding of the Dutch Republic*, p. 136).

24 Parker, *The Dutch Revolt*, p. 149; R. Glawischnig, *Niederlande, Kalvinismus und Reichsgrafenstand, 1559–1584* (Marburg, 1973) p. 94: 1564–1574 about 350,000, including interest payments (5%) during the next decade in total about 600,000 guilders.

25 About 850,000 guilders in 1567, less than 620,000 guilders in 1566; Parker, *The Dutch Revolt*, p. 250.

26 *'Lyf en goed al te samen / Heb ick u niet verschoont / Mijn broeders hooch van namen / Hebbent u oock vertoont'.*

from Spain in 1567 and even more per year over the next two years.[27] In order to continue the war, much more was evidently needed than Calvinist donations, generous brothers, and the Prince's personal readiness to contribute large sums – and plunge himself deep into debts – could supply.

1.2 A Prince in Search of New Sources of Finance

A remarkable new attempt of the Prince to acquire funds consisted of using his princely rights to issue 'letters of marque' (*kaperbrieven*). He used them for the first time in February 1569, as payment for the ships that had been hired from a local pirate by Louis of Nassau for his invasion in the north. In doing so, he acted in conformity with general practices of war of monarchs in the sixteenth century. Even the government of the huge Habsburg Empire tried to gain better control of the sea by issuing 'letters of marque'. Such 'letters of marque' legitimated the capture of enemy ships and other sea-bound forms of harming the enemy, such as raiding the coasts of enemy territory.[28] Dutch privateers possessing the letters could claim the protection of the Prince against being arrested for their deeds, when arriving in harbours of states recognizing the legitimacy of his title. In exchange, the privateers were expected to hand over a percentage of their booty to him. Parker found sources showing that the British Privy Council recognized, indeed, the entitlement of the prince of Orange, as a sovereign ruler, to issue letters of marque.[29]

Orange went to Britain himself later that year, with a dual purpose. Firstly, he wished to try to get financial support from the British Queen Elizabeth by exploiting her well known resentment of Spain. She proved ready indeed to grant him loans probably up to an amount of about 300,000 guilders in total during the years 1568–1573.[30] Secondly, he wanted to form a real fleet of privateers with the help of Calvinist merchants living in exile in Britain, in order to continue attempts to harm the Spanish enemy at sea in an organized way.

27 Parker, *The Dutch Revolt*, p. 250 Appendix G: nearly 3.7 million in 1568, nearly 3.5 million in 1569.

28 Louis Sicking, *Neptune and the Netherlands : state, economy, and war at sea in the Renaissance* (Leiden: Brill, 2004), pp. 426–427.

29 Parker, *The Dutch Revolt*, p. 122; it was not always that easy to obtain recognition of this right everywhere: V. Enthoven, *Zeeland en de opkomst van de Republiek: handel en strijd in de Scheldedelta, c. 1550–1621* (Leiden 1996), p. 59.

30 Parker, *The Dutch Revolt*, p. 148 mentions 0.6 million guilders, but according to Glawischnig, *Niederlande*, p. 94 the original amount was more than doubled due to unpaid interests.

The consistories of the Dutch Calvinist refugees in Britain, among whom many merchants, were indeed willing to realize a privateer fleet of thirty vessels by the spring of 1570. They were not only eager to support the Calvinist cause, but also attracted by the possibility of buying the booty taken by the pirates at relatively low prices and subsequently sell it at attractive profits.[31] Their support diminished however when it proved hard to prevent the new privateers from hijacking Dutch and British merchantmen as well.

The Prince's next attempt to secure finance for the Revolt dates from February 1570. He then instructed Diederik Sonoy, a member of the lower Dutch nobility in Holland and a Calvinist military leader, to inform the Provincial States of Holland and Utrecht that the Prince of Orange was ready to come to protect religion and liberty in their provinces, on the condition that they would no longer hand over their tax revenues to the Spanish government but to him.[32] To no avail, however. Financial support for the prince and his supporters in Holland and Utrecht would still remain restricted during the next two years to the revenues from collections among the population organized by Calvinist ministers as had been the case earlier in Flanders.

In the meantime, his opponent Alva had much more financial success. Although Alva had not been able to convince the States of the desirability to introduce his uniform 'tenth penny' in the Netherlands, all provinces had at least accepted a 'hundredth penny' (1 percent) tax on the value of all property and they had agreed to contribute two million guilders for two years to enable Alva to pay his troops to restore order in the Netherlands. Even the States of Holland had agreed, at last, to pay a contribution of 271,000 guilders annually for two years, until May 1572, as Holland's part in these two million guilders. The States even approved the collection of a supplementary 15,000 guilders in taxes for the king, on 25 April 1572, to pay for extra defence measures against Orange's privateers which by then had arrived from Britain on the coasts of the Netherlands.

In addition, however, Holland's States urged Bossu, Orange's successor as the royal 'stadholder' in Holland, Zeeland and Utrecht, to try to convince Alva to refrain from his decision to start the imposition of the 'tenth penny' in May 1572, arguing once more that the introduction of this tax would damage the country economically. Most likely they also feared the ensuing loss of autonomy and financial control that this centralized form of taxation would entail. Bossu had to tell them, however, that Alva did not intend to give in,

---

31 Parker, *The Dutch Revolt*, p. 121.

32 P. Bor, *Oorsprongk, begin en vervolgh der Nederlandsceh oorlogen etc.* 4 vols. (Amsterdam 1679) Vol I p. 312.

and that the tenth penny tax would no longer be postponed: it was to start in May 1572.

From then on the rebels had a much better chance of winning cities for the prince. The propaganda offensive against the tenth penny, which they started, coincided with an extremely miserable economic situation during that year, which had started in fact already in 1569 and would continue to 1574.[33] On top of this, indignation was widespread over the intolerant religious policy of the king and his governor, who had installed a special 'Council of Troubles' that by then had inflicted many death penalties on those involved in the iconoclastic 'wave'. In Holland now occurred what had failed to happen in Brabant in 1568. One after another the governments of cities and small townships in Holland started to let troops of Calvinist rebels enter their cities, despite the fact that the Calvinist Church did not yet have many members in Holland by that time.[34] This implied that they had to feed and lodge them, and thus to finance, partly, the army for the Revolt.

The new development started with the small city of Brielle in Holland on 1 April 1572. Queen Elizabeth had decided to expel Orange's pirating privateers from her shores because their actions harmed British trade. Thereupon the group had decided to set course for Brielle, familiar to one of them, to try to establish a new naval base for their ships in the Netherlands. They succeeded indeed in taking Brielle on 1 April 1572 'in the name of the prince of Orange and liberty'. This 'naval victory' would prove to be the first lasting success of the Dutch military revolt against Spain, and the start of the Dutch navy.[35] Some days later, they also took Vlissingen in the province of Zeeland and one month later Veere that formerly had been for some time the seat of the admiralty of the Habsburgs in the Netherlands.

The small city of Enkhuizen in Holland went over to the prince in May, followed by Oudewater and Gouda. More important cities like Dordrecht, Leiden and Haarlem and Delft could be included in June and July. By then Alva informed the States that he agreed to definitively abandon the idea of a tenth penny tax and that for the future a yearly contribution, as usual, would do.

---

33 Parker, *The Dutch Revolt,* p. 128; Grapperhaus, *Alva*, pp. 243–244. According to recent estimates of the real value of GDP in Holland it dropped to a level of on average 56 during 1569–1573 (if the average of 1564–1568 is set at 100; during the next five years it would be restored to a level of 84, and the same level in 1579–1583; during the remainder of the period unit 1609 it was on average 95 (with a peak of 102 in 1595–99)) (Van Leeuwen and Van Zanden, http://www.cgeh.nl/reconstruction-national-accounts-holland-1500-1800-0).

34 Parker, *The Dutch Revolt,* p. 153.

35 Parker, *The Dutch Revolt,* pp. 117, 134.

By then, however, it was too late to stop the revolt in Holland and Zeeland.[36] Soon the number of cities and small townships in revolt in Holland had risen to twenty-six. Some cities in Flanders also joined the movement. However, Holland's largest city Amsterdam would only join the Revolt in 1578 and was not yet among their number at that time.

A meeting of revolting cities in Holland was prepared in the city of Dordrecht, which would enable them to jointly discuss a letter by the Prince of 7 July with an urgent request for money to enable him 'to free them of Spanish tyranny and to restore their privileges and liberties'.[37] The letter informed the rebellious cities that a number of army leaders were willing to remain in his service in exchange for a one-off payment of 100,000 crowns at once, plus a guarantee by Holland's cities that they would collect 500,000 guilders for army payments within two months.[38]

1.3 The First Financial Decisions of the 'Free' States of Holland

The first 'free' meeting of the States of Holland on 19 July 1572 decided to support the Prince of Orange in his struggle against the Duke of Alva, indeed, and to recognize him again as the stadholder of the king in Holland, instead of Bossu who had been appointed by Alva to replace him.[39] Holland's provincial tax receiver was replaced by someone loyal to the Prince, and the governments of the cities participating in the Revolt were instructed to secure that the revenues from taxes in their districts were from now on put towards the cause of the Revolt. The result of Orange's letter was that on 4 August 1572 an *'obligatie'* of the very large amount of 500,000 guilders was sealed by the separate seals of thirteen cities plus one seal of Holland's nobility, that contained their promise to raise this money in Holland's cities and countryside during the following months.[40]

36 The city of Vlissingen had already refused to admit Spanish troop on 6 April 1572and shortly thereafter announced its support for the Prince; Parker, *The Dutch Revolt*, p. 139 offers a map of towns in revolt.

37 *'totter verlossinge der Nederlanden van der Hispanischer Tyrannye, om die te brengen tot haere oude privilegien ende vrijheden';* www.inghist.nl/Onderzoek/Projecten/WVO/brief/10439 letter to the States of Holland 7-7-1572.

38 Letter 10439 7 July 1572.

39 http://www.dutchrevolt.leiden.edu/english/sources/Pages/15720819Dordt.aspx.

40 Alkmaar, Brill, Delft, Dordrecht, Edam, Enkhuizen, Gouda, Haarlem, Hoorn, Leiden, Medemblik, Monnikendam and Oudewater; the document with most of the seals still attached to it is preserved in a flat silver box in the National Archives in The Hague; Tracy, *The Founding of the Dutch Republic, pp.* 84–85 has a photograph.

The story goes that the confidence of army leaders in the prince's creditworthiness had re-emerged already in May 1572, when an administrator of royal domains in Veere, that had fallen into the hands or the rebels that month, brought the prince, during his talks with some German army leaders, an amount of 10,000 guilders from his cash reserves.[41] Still on 25 July, however, Orange had not been able to prevent his troops from plundering the city of Roermond in the south, because he had not been able to pay them, and from brutally murdering a number of monks, in blatant contradiction to his belief in the importance of religious tolerance.[42]

The huge obligation of 500,000 guilders sealed by thirteen cities will have inspired the army leaders with much more confidence than the financial support of a domain administrator. This decision can be seen as the real start of the Revolt in Holland. In a thorough study on the founding of the Dutch Republic during 1572 to 1588, which pays abundant attention to financial aspects, Jim Tracy has rightly underlined the remarkable size of this obligation in a comparative fiscal perspective. The old States of Holland before the Revolt had never previously issued an *'obligatie'* for anything close to 500,000 guilders for earlier rulers in their territory.[43]

It is moreover remarkable that the sum, which the States had promised the Prince to collect, would not even be used for the defence of Holland, but to relieve the Protestant city of Mons in Hainault from the Spanish siege, that had followed its earlier conquest by one of the Prince's brothers.[44] The attitude of these city representatives had become much more broad-minded and politically determined than the 'no win, no fee'-approach of the ten individual Antwerp merchants in the first phase of the Revolt. Soon it would become clear, however, not only that the attempt to relieve Mons had failed, but also that this one grand gesture would be by far not enough to win the war.

The 500,000 guilders obligation may seem to have announced the start of the importance of the use of the credit of Holland's cities for war, but it would not be as easy as that. The cities in the States of Holland appeared to be much slower in devising sufficient new taxes to honour the large obligation, than in

---

41 The actions of this administrator, Arend van Dorp, were probably inspired by his fear of legal action against him for malversations; see the introduction to *Brieven en onuitgegeven stukken van Jonkheer Arend van* Dorp, ed. J.B. van der Schueren (Utrecht 1887–8).

42 Thanks to Wilbert Dekker in Roermond for showing me the Carolus-chapel where the relics of the bodies of the twelve monks are still preserved.

43 Tracy, *The Founding of the Dutch Republic*; J. Tracy, 'The taxation system of the county of Holland', in: *Economisch- en Sociaal Historisch Jaarboek* 48 (1985) pp. 71–118, pp. 108–109.

44 Despite this, the city nevertheless had to surrender to Alva on 21 September 1572.

sealing it. In August 1572 Holland's new States-assembly had decided to levy a land tax, but at a rate of only 8.3 percent of rental value, lower than the 10 percent rate on revenue from all property that had been levied several times in the 1560s. The collection of the provincial taxes on urban and agrarian commercial products, assets and activities, that had been introduced in 1570 as part of compensation package for the postponement of Alva's 'tenth penny', was suspended in February 1573 in view of the war circumstances.[45] Its revenue had not yet been very impressive until then anyhow.[46] Only the older provincial excises on beer and wine continued to be levied, now at doubled rates to compensate for the revenue loss of the abolished taxes.

By that time the war had really begun to be waged in the territory of Holland. Alva had decided to reconquer the rebellious cities one by one, starting in December 1572 with a siege of Haarlem, which had to surrender to him in June (and would be reconquered by the Prince not earlier than in 1577). The successful siege of Haarlem was followed immediately by months-long Spanish sieges of Alkmaar and Leiden. These sieges failed, however, a failure still celebrated each year in both cities until today. Cities were forced to pay part of the war costs themselves from extraordinary direct levies or forced loans on their burghers during these early years. It is known that for instance the important city of Delft, one of the six large cities of Holland at the time, spent more than 200,000 guilders 'for the common interest' from its urban revenues between 1572 and 1576.[47]

In 1573 the States decided to devalue the currency to allow the prince to continue paying troops, as an emergency measure to compensate for failing tax revenues. All coins were to be handed in to the mints, where they were marked to increase their token value by 15 percent, after which 15 percent less was returned to the owners. This measure is reported to have produced an amount of c. 250,000 guilders for the war.[48] A similar move was made in 1575, when Holland started to issue its own coins without the portrait of the king. They were given an official value about 10 percent above their intrinsic value, the profit of which has been estimated at about one million guilders.[49] Disruptive

45 Revenues are known for those on beer, wine, the milling of grain, slaughtering animals and peat during the first half of 1572 totaling 35.238 guilders; *GFH*, 165.

46 The preserved accounts of Jacob Bol, loyal to the king and his successor Franchoys Valckesteyn, loyal to the prince, over 1571 and 1572 contain amounts totaling 128,883 and 44,834 guilders, exclusive the land tax; *GFH*, 165.

47 J.H. van Dijk, 'De geldelijke druk op de Delftsche burgerij in de jaren 1572–1576', *Bijdragen voor Vaderlandsche Geschiedenis and Oudheidkunde*, 7, V (1935) pp. 169–186.

48 H.E. van Gelder, *De Nederlandse munten* (Utrecht, Spectrum, 2002) p. 90.

49 *Ibidem*, p. 91.

social-economic effects of rising prices and problems in foreign trade resulting from this coin debasement may have contributed to article XII in the Union of Utrecht of 1579 expressing the wish to become a monetary union with a stable uniform monetary policy.[50]

In January 1574 the collection of provincial excises like the taxes on milling of grain and on slaughtering, that Holland had started already under Alva in 1570 on top of older excises on beer and wine and peat, was at last resumed, and new taxes were added in May 1574, like a provincial tax on the old urban tax of the weighing of merchandise and taxes on horned cattle, sown lands, woollen cloth. It should be noticed that this new range of taxes not only taxed urban commercial products and activities, but also horned cattle, the main capital asset of a countryside specializing in commercial dairy farming. The character of Holland's new fiscal system can be seen as an expression of the commercial integration of the province.

A preserved account of the receiver of these taxes shows, that the total revenue of these taxes from – probably – June 1573 to July 1574 was less than 200,000 guilders at the end of July. It was not much more than the receipt from *urban* excises during the same period, made available to the provincial receiver for the war as well, but still levied on the authority of city governments, which had been about 180,000 guilders according to the same account.[51]

In view of these modest amounts it is not surprising, that the 500,000-guilders 'obligation' sealed in the States of Holland in August 1572, turned out to be not a very reliable security. A large part of this amount was owed to army commander Ernst van Mandersloo. Preserved archival documents show that he had to wait for a first meagre repayment of only 10,000 guilders until 1579 and was then promised that the rest of the sum would be paid to him in four yearly instalments, which were not forthcoming either. Part of this debt was redeemed in 1583 by handing over confiscated real estate in Holland to the Mandersloo

50 Attempts at introducing uniform coins in 1585 and 1681 would not be completely successful however, as also other provinces had started to mint their own coins and were not eager to give up this privilege. In 1681 only three other provinces agreed with a new proposal by Holland to issue silver coins with an identical intrinsic value, and only with different provincial coats of arms. Holland was able to interfere with the silver supply to mints outside this area, which restricted possibilities of other mints to issue similar coins with a lower intrinsic value. Zeeland, however, continued to be able to issue two-and-a-half guilder-pieces at 52 stiver instead of 50 stivers.

51 *GFH*, p. 165; Gelderbom and Jonker, 'Public finance and economic growth', p. 5 suggest that 'an administrative change transformed the patchwork of local excises into a uniform tax system', which was not the case; urban excises continue to exist beside provincial excises.

family.[52] In 1585 the family accepted a settlement for the remaining 104,800 guilders of the debt by means of a conversion into an annuity of 6,240 guilders per year. It must have been a serious blow to Holland's credit that the seals of thirteen cities had not been trustworthy.

The addition of new provincial taxes in the list of May 1574 followed the decision of the States in the same month to promise the Prince a regular amount of 30,000 guilders per month for the war during the next half year. To this end also the rate of the land tax was now doubled from the twelfth penny (8.3 percent) to the sixth penny (16.7 percent) of the land rents, and a tax on the value of houses was added of which the rate came down to 2 percent per year (1/6 of the hundredth penny per month). So here, at last, we witness the start of a new tax system consisting of much more taxes and much higher rates than before. The cities in the States gradually became aware that more taxation was the only way to continue the war.

The real breakthrough can be said to have dated from November 1574. Then the Prince announced that he needed henceforth 45,000 guilders per month. When, initially, the States decided to refuse, the Prince threatened to lay down all his offices immediately, adding cynically that this would save them his salary as well. The States assured him that they really did not want to do without a 'head and high authority' (*'Hooft ende Overigheid'*).[53] So in December they introduced a new list of provincial taxes at such rates as seemed necessary to produce the required 540,000 guilders per year. The important taxes on wine and beer, that had produced less than 65,000 guilders in 1573, would now have to yield no less than 240,000 guilders per year. Additionally, the rates of the taxes on milling of grain, weighing of merchandise, on woollen textiles, and on horned cattle would be doubled, and taxes on soap producing, on fish and a new tax on grains per weight were added (see Table 2.3 below).

To this end a completely new tax apparatus was now, moreover, created. A number of provincial district receivers were appointed in addition to Holland's provincial receiver in Delft called, from then on, Holland's General

52 A number of estates of Anna van Barnicourt Lathienloyę, who had fled to Spain; all the financial documents regarding the 500,000 guilders-obligation are to be found in the National Archives in The Hague, arch. *Financie van Holland*, inv.no. 884.

53 Fritschy, W., 'Willem van Oranje en de overheidsfinanciën', in: W. Fritschy en G. Zalm, Willem van Oranje en de overheidsfinanciën (Delft, Museum Prinsenhof, 2006) noot 38; A. Kluit, *Historie der Hollandsche Staatsregering. 5vols.* (Amsterdam 1802–1805), vol. I, p. 401, res. SH, 1, 12, 13, 25 Nov. 1574; J.W. Koopmans, *De Staten van Holland en de Opstand : de ontwikkeling van hun functies en organisatie in de periode 1544–1588* (Den Haag 1990) p. 120.

Receiver. Five receivers were appointed in Holland's Southern Quarter, and seven in Holland's Northern Quarter, each tax district consisting of a city with its surrounding countryside containing other towns and villages, all receiving the same kind of provincial taxes and all at the same rate. In the end all eighteen cities that would come to be represented in the States of Holland would house a district receiver.[54] The receivers remained officials of the province not of the city. They were not allowed to take orders from city governments in their tax districts. The collection of the taxes would be leased, and the auctions of the tax leases had to be supervised by two representatives from other districts to prevent fraudulent practices serving particular local interests.[55] Not individual cities, but Holland's 'urban system' was the crucial fundament for its new fiscal system.

The States also decided that the cities would no longer be allowed to keep more than one third of the revenues from urban excises on beer and wine for their own urban expenditure.[56] In December 1572 the magistrates of the city of Delft, at that time the most important and wealthiest of the cities in revolt, had yet opposed a proposal for a massive expansion of taxes levied by the province, because it feared the expected damage to the revenues of urban taxes, but in 1574 the city felt forced to comply. Delfts urban accounts show that the decline in urban revenues from the beer tax made the payment of interest on urban loans no more possible for a period of four years. Similar problems will have been experienced by other cities. So the massive increase in indirect provincial taxes meant a very serious curtailment in the fiscal autonomy, which cities until then had *de facto* enjoyed.

To convince the Prince of their good intentions the States of Holland promised him (1) that war expenditure would enjoy first priority the next months, (2) that no salaries to officials would be paid, except that for himself, and (3) – very remarkable – that no interest would be paid on provincial public debts for the time being.[57] This implied that the States of Holland judged that it was useless to try to maintain public credit to obtain loans on the free market, and that, for the time being, they saw their only solace in either taxation, or *forced* loans, to obtain the money for the war.

54 Between 1796 and 1764 there were sixteen tax receivers for the common means, in 1764 Schiedam and surroudings was separated from the district of Delft, in 1788 Schoonhoven and surrounding countryside was separated from the district of Dordrecht.

55 Fritschy, 'A "financial revolution" reconsidered', p. 69n60.

56 Tracy, *Founding*, p. 103.

57 *Memorie 1755,* 17r-v; http://www.historici.nl/Onderzoek/Projecten/Gewestelijke Financien/memorie.

1.4 Conclusion

The formation of the Dutch Republic was preceded by war efforts of the Prince of Orange against Spain between 1566 and July 1572. He received money from dispersed groups of Calvinists, was backed by family members, and able to secure the help of privateers. He was even able to obtain the support of some foreign monarchs. He invested also personally large sums in the Revolt and he was able to arrange loans to pay soldiers, during some time, by mortgaging personal possessions. Impressive as his efforts were, they could never have sufficed to finance a long war against the Spanish Empire, however. The crucial importance of the first meeting of a great number of cities, designating themselves as the 'free States of Holland', was, that it gave the Prince access to the joint taxing power of a great number of increasingly wealthy cities, or, in other words, to the fiscal possibilities of an early modern 'urban system'.

They gave him this access slowly and reluctantly, starting by issuing a large obligation to Orange's army leaders, in April 1572, on the urban credit of each of the cities involved separately, a debt which Holland would not feel able to redeem for many years to come. Only in November 1574 a remunerative new 'tax system' started to appear in Holland, consisting of 'common means': provincial taxes based upon the fiscal potential of an urbanized region with a commercialized agriculture and with an already relatively large degree of economic integration.

Increases in direct taxes and forced loans were needed in addition to the amounts in public revenue that could be realized from the 'common means'. The extreme financial exigencies of the war required nevertheless that the cities had to resign in the suspension of interest payments on existing urban debts in which their own burghers had largely invested as well. The 'tax state' that started to emerge in 1574 was certainly not yet a 'fiscal state', capable to use the capital market in addition to taxation and to increase public revenue also by means of voluntary public loans. This 'tax-state' was however an indispensable precondition for the later development of a 'fiscal state'.[58]

58 Elaborate definitions of the different characteristics of the 'tribute state', the 'domain state', the 'tax state' and the 'fiscal state', can be found in: M. Ormrod, M. Bonney and R. Bonney, 'Introduction', in: *Crises, revolutions and self-sustained growth. Essays in European fiscal history, 1130–1830*, pp. 4–8.

CHAPTER 2

From Under-taxed Part of an Empire to Heavily Taxed Republic (1550s–1609)

Three examples of fiscal systems in the Habsburg Empire are especially relevant for a comparative understanding of the character of the fiscal system that emerged in Holland: Holland's old fiscal system under the Habsburgs that had experienced a first form of a 'financial revolution',[1] Alva's failed plans for a new centralized fiscal system for the Netherlands, and the fiscal system resulting from Castile's 'urban system' in the Spanish empire.

The analysis of these three systems of public finance in the first section of this chapter forms the background for its core: an analysis of the development and the character of Holland's fiscal system until the start of a Twelve Years' Truce. How much revenue did Orange need for the revolt of the provinces of the Netherlands during these years in comparison to Holland's war expenditure before the Revolt? How did this compare to what Alva would have needed to keep military expenditure in the Netherlands independent from Spanish subsidies for the army? Why was the enormous tax increase, needed to support the Prince, accepted, whereas Alva's much more modest 'tenth penny' inspired on the 'alcabala' of Castile's cities, failed? The first two sections show that fiscal developments in Holland remained restricted to a '*tax* revolution' until the first decade of the seventeenth century, despite serious attempts to restore provincial credit. Holland experienced what might be called its 'second' – or in fact perhaps even its 'real' – *financial* revolution only during the first decade of the seventeenth century.

The third section describes how – like Alva's plan for centralization – also the attempts of the States General to introduce uniform 'general means' in all the provinces of the Netherlands failed. It will be shown to what extent the other provinces in the northern Netherlands contributed financially to the Revolt in the period until 1609, with special attention for Zeeland, Holland's first ally in the Revolt. Like in Holland the Revolt would lead to an increased political importance of cities also in the other provinces that would come to belong to the Union of Utrecht. It would take until the first decade of the seventeenth

1 Tracy, *A financial revolution in the Habsburg Netherlands.*

 | DOI 10.1163/9789004341289_005

century, however, before the other five provinces in the Northern Netherlands had all accepted the necessity to exploit the fiscal potential of their cities to realize the necessary increases in their public revenue.

The last section examines the modest role of the central sources of revenue of the new republic, the importance of which declined further when foreign subsidies and loans ended with the start of the Twelve Years' Truce.

2.1 Holland and the Spanish Empire

Before the Revolt, Holland was a fiscally very insignificant part of an empire consisting not only of Spain and the Netherlands, but also of a large part of Italy, and parts of North-Africa and of Central and South America. Even the Netherlands as a whole were certainly not the most important part of this Empire. Spain in the 1550s had a population of about 7.4 million; the Habsburg dominions in Italy of about 6.7 million, the entire area of the Habsburg Netherlands had a population of about 3 million. Of these 3 million people about 1.25 million are said to have lived at that time in what later would become the Dutch Republic.[2] Holland's population in c. 1550 cannot have been more than about 350,000 people.[3]

The seventeen Netherlands together were good for not more than about 9 percent of the empire's total public revenue in c. 1530, and Holland contributed about 13 percent of what the Netherlands paid together in the 1540s. Castile, including the American dominions, contributed at that time about 63 percent, the other Iberian estates about 5 percent, the Italian estates of the Spanish king about 24 percent.[4] The Spanish Empire had no unified treasury.[5] The Netherlands, like Spain and Italy, had their own financial administrations. The *beden*-system, implying separate negotiations with the provinces on how they would realize their contribution, allowed a separate analysis of Holland's fiscal system before the Revolt. This allows a comparison, therefore of Holland's old system with the performance of the new system developing since the start of the Revolt.

2 Parker, *The Dutch Revolt,* p. 47; De Vries and Van der Woude, *The first modern economy,* p. 50.

3 Same estimate in Lesger, *The rise of the Amsterdam market,* p. 134.

4 F. Comín Comín and B. Yun-Casalilla, 'Spain: from composite monarchy to nation-state, 1492–1914. An exceptional case?', in *The rise of fiscal states. A global history,* pp. 233–267, p. 235.

5 G. Muto, 'The Spanish system: centre and periphery', in: *Economic systems and state finance,* pp. 231–253, p. 232.

Holland's Fiscal System under the Habsburgs

The most remarkable aspect of Holland's fiscal system during the decades before the Revolt was that public revenue for wars of the Habsburgs ruler in which the States of Holland had consented was largely realized by means of loans based on the *common* credit of the six cities with voting right in the States, not on that of individual cities.[6] The interest on the annuities that were sold to the public to this end was paid from *common* urban taxes, received by the *provincial* tax receiver. This receiver was controlled by the Provincial States and his financial importance tended to increase in the course of time compared to Holland's *royal* tax receiver. It was the emergence of this fiscal system since the 1540s that was designated by Tracy as 'a financial revolution in the Habsburg Netherlands'.

Tables 2.1 and 2.2 offer an impression of the size of the amounts of all elements involved in the structure of public finance in Holland during the two decades preceding the Revolt. They summarize data published by James Tracy from the accounts of, firstly, Holland's royal receiver of the *ordinaris and extraordinaris beden* whose receipts were mainly destined for royal military expenditure, but also some civil expenditure and some debt service, and, secondly, the accounts of Holland's own provincial receiver, whose main expenditure consisted by then of the debt service of annuities sold to pay for the *extraordinaris beden* and also some other expenditure.

Table 2.1 offers an attempt to summarize the level and structure of Holland's public expenditure, firstly, during the wars between the Habsburg monarchs and the king of France (1552–59), and, secondly, during peace-years in the 1560s (the most relevant figures in bold font; see rows 4, 8 and 11). Table 2.2 has a similar function for public revenue. Both tables show this changing relative financial importance of the two receivers in Holland.

Row 1 of Table 2.1 shows, firstly, the large degree to which expenditure especially for the army had to be advanced by Antwerp bankers on the security of expected *bede*-receipts. These advances were necessary because the cities were often slow in delivering their part in the *bede*; advances by bankers could even occur on the security of *beden*-amounts for years yet to come. This access to Antwerp's banking system, important to keep payments going during wars despite arrears in tax receipts, would be not possible any more after the start of the Revolt. Section 2 of this chapter will explain how and why Holland would become independent of the services of such bankers after the Revolt.

6 Tracy, *A financial revolution.*

TABLE 2.1 *Holland's public expenditure under the Habsburgs, 1552–1559 and 1560–1565/6; annual averages (pounds(=guilders)).*[7]

		1552–1559		1560–1565/6		Source
						Tracy (1985):
1	[*paid by the royal treasurer out of loans from Antwerp bankers on the security of (future) bede-revenues (mainly military expenditure*)]	[*289,999*]		[*60,812*]		Table I col 14
2	paid out of extraordinaris bede for the war by the royal receiver of the *beden* (mainly to Antwerp bankers see row 1)	292,750		59,694		Table I col 10
3	paid for warships by the provincial receiver to protect fisheries during the war	3,188				Table IV col 8
4	**sum military expenditure** (and/or debt service on short term war loans plus some civil salaries)		**295,938** (68%)		**59,694** (19%)	
5	paid in interest on annuities by the royal *beden*-receiver	16,622		16,303		Table I col 12
6	paid in interest on annuities (long term debt) by the provincial receiver	52,026		81,874		Table IV col 5
7	paid in redemption of annuities by the provincial receiver	35,457		117,655		Table IV col 6
8	**sum debt service on annuities**		**104,105** (24%)		**215,832** (67%)	

7 The old 'Dutch pound' was an equivalent of the guilder; in the rest of this book only the term 'guilder' will be used.

		1552–1559		**1560–1565/6**		**Source**
						Tracy (1985):
9	paid from ordinaris *bede* by the *beden* receiver (after deduction of the interest payments in row 5)	36,384		45,148		Table I col 9 minus col 12
10	**sum other expenditure**		**36,384** (8%)		**45,148** (14%)	
11	*Total bedenreceiver (ords + extrords)*	345,756		*121,145*		rows 2 + 5 + 9
12	*Total provincial receiver*	*90,671*		*199,529*		rows 3 + 6 + 7
13	**TOTAL ANNUAL EXPENDITURE**		**436,427** (100%)		**320,674** (100%)	

Source: J. Tracy, 'The taxation system of the county of Holland', in: *Economisch- en Sociaal Historisch Jaarboek* 48 (1985) pp. 71–118; Tables I and IV.

Tracy noted that in the earliest years of the reign of Charles V the bankers had been satisfied with guarantees by great lords in Holland, like the stadholder, to continue their loans, and subsequently came to prefer assurances from revenue-collectors like the royal *beden*-receiver in Holland personally. By 1553 the guarantee of the States of Holland was needed to continue the advances from bankers.[8] This guarantee allowed bankers to take hostage citizens of any city in Holland if their debts were not honoured. It charged the States of Holland with the responsibility to prevent this from happening.[9]

A remarkable feature of the 500,000 guilders *obligatie* of August 1572, the first *obligatie* issued by the 'free' States of Holland discussed at the end of Chapter 1, was that it was sealed by a number of Holland's cities each separately.[10] In the circumstances of the time the seals of the separate 'corporate bodies' of cities were apparently expected to make this obligation more reliable than just one seal of the collective body of a rebellious States-assembly, that did not yet even consist of all important cities in Holland. In fact, however, the cities failed

8 Tracy, 'The taxation system of the County of Holland', pp. 76–77.

9 Tracy, 'The taxation system of the County of Holland', p. 100.

10 There were 14 seals, 13 of cities, one of the nobility, 13 of which are still attached to the document as it is now preserved in the National Archives.

in honouring this obligation, as we saw, and Holland compensated its main owner only many years later, by changing the remaining debt into an interest bearing long-term annuity. As we will see, it would take about three decades after the start of the Revolt before the States of Holland regained the credit that it had enjoyed during the last years before the Revolt.

In row 2 of Table 2.1 an unknown part of 'military expenditure' must have consisted of interests on the advances of bankers in Antwerp. Tracy found that *obligaties* issued by the States of Holland were accepted by major bankers at 12 percent annual interest before 1572 (and that the king's receiver had to pay a rate of even 22–24 percent during the 1520s).[11] High renting short-term loans were probably as soon as possible converted into much lower renting long-term loan formats by means of the sale of '*renten*' (=annuities).

Row 8 of the table shows that debt service on such long-term loans was already an important element in Holland's public finance in Habsburg times, during war years. Initially an interest rate of 'the twelfth penny' (8.3 percent) had to be offered to persuade investors to buy so-called '*losrenten*' (=redeemable annuities), which the government intended to redeem as soon as possible after the war. In addition, life-annuities at an interest rate of 'the sixth penny' (16.67 percent), were offered, which could not be redeemed, but would just end at the dead of the holder. By 1559 redeemable annuities could already be sold at an interest rate of only 'the sixteenth penny' (6.25 percent). Obviously interest payments had been reliable during the foregoing years, thus increasing the confidence of investors in the attractiveness of this investment possibility, which made them ready to accept lower interests. This aspect of Holland's public finance under the Habsburgs form stood in sharp important contrast to the province's lack of credit during the first decades after the Revolt.

The much larger amount in debt service during the peace years in the 1560s visible in row 8 of Table 2.1 was due to debt redemption in addition to interest payments. This debt redemption can be seen as a first indication that the financial developments during the decades before the Revolt cannot really be seen as a 'financial revolution'. Only after the restoration of Holland's credit debt redemption would no longer play a large role in debt service any more. Credit would then become possible without redemption, despite the fact that the importance of life-annuities in loans would decrease, as long as the interests were punctually paid.

---

11 J. Tracy, 'Holland's New Fiscal Regime, 1572–1576', *The Political Economy of the Dutch Republic*, ed. O. Gelderblom (Ashgate, Surrey, 2009) pp. 41–55, p. 42; Tracy, 'The taxation system of the County of Holland', p. 100 n51.

Rows 5–7 in Table 2.1 show that the provincial receiver was more important than the king's *beden*-receiver for the service of long-term debt, and increasingly so. This had the result that the total amounts in public expenditure of the provincial receiver became much larger than that of the royal *beden*-receiver during the 1560s, as rows 11–12 also show. The new situation after the Revolt would be that the Provincial States would have to combine the two tasks of army payments and interest payments, which were before the Revolt divided between the royal and the provincial administration.

Table 2.2 shows how the increased debt service necessitated an increase in public revenue for Holland's provincial receiver, changing the relative financial importance of the two receivers as soon as the war was over, as can be seen especially in rows 13–14.

This table offers, moreover, an attempt to categorize Holland's public revenue before the Revolt into direct and indirect tax revenues on the one hand, and long-term loans on the other hand, which was again made visible by means of a bold letter type (in rows 3, 6, 9 and 12). Rows 1–3 show that this subdivision was not possible for about a quarter of Holland's revenue, because the degree is not known to which villages and cities paid their part in the *bede*-amounts by means of direct or indirect local taxes or by sales of urban annuities. It is only known that the apportioning of the amount to be paid by Holland's cities and villages, the so-called *schiltal*, was mainly based on the detailed royal enquiry in Holland's wealth of 1514, which showed that Holland's twenty five cities were then good for nearly 60 percent of its assessed wealth, which indicates the fiscal importance of Holland's cities already long before the Revolt.[12]

Rows 4–5 show that an increasing part of the direct tax called the '*morgental*' went to the provincial receiver to be used for debt service. Originally this was a land tax, but sometimes it was levied in the form of a tenth penny on the income from all real property. This occurred five times in total between 1543 and 1564. Tracy found that in 1553 and in 1561 about 30 percent of the immovable wealth then assessed in the *morgental*, was urban wealth, a remarkable difference with the 60 percent in 1515. This was probably largely due to the fact that in 1514 the assessment had been done by royal officials, whereas the assessments for the 10 percent-*morgental* were made on the authority of the Provincial States, dominated by cities who had of course an interest in minimizing their part in taxable wealth. Row 6 shows the increase in the average of the total receipts of the *morgental*. The old yearly flat-rate *morgental* had yielded much smaller amounts per year than the 10 percent-levies. The one in 1553

12 http://socialhistory.org/sites/default/files/uploads/informacie.pdf.

TABLE 2.2 *Holland's public revenue under the Habsburgs, 1552–1559 and 1560–1565; annual averages (guilders).*

		1552–1559		1560–1565		source
						Tracy (1985):
1	from 'schiltal' by the *beden*-receiver (after deduction of 'gratien')	116,015		74,387		Table I (col 1 minus 7) + (2 minus 8)
2	from 'schiltal' by provincial receiver	2,438		1,286		Table IV col 1
3	**total schiltal** (apportioning of *bede* to villages and cities according to wealth as assessed in 1515; probably mainly direct taxation)		**118,453** (27%)		**75,673** (22%)	
4	from 'morgental' by *beden*-receiver	71,500		2,668		Table I col 5
5	from 'morgental' by provincial receiver	30,437		113,996		Table IV col 4
6	**direct taxation** (morgental: mainly 10% on income from real property)		**101,937** (23%)		**116,664** (34%)	
7	from 'imposten' (excises on beer and wine) received by the *beden*-receiver [only in 1559: 76,691 and in 1560: 90,256]	9,586		15,043		Table I col 4
8	from 'imposten' (or 'common means') received by provincial receiver	27,993		52,974		Table IV col 3
9	**indirect taxation**		**37,579** (8%)		**68,017** (20%)	
10	from sold annuities received by the *beden*-receiver	145,014		30,616		Table I col 3

		1552–1559		1560–1565		source
						Tracy (1985):
11	from sold annuities by provincial receiver [in 1557: 320,437 and in 1562: 374,548]	40,054		53,507		Table IV col 2
12	**long term loans**		185,068 (42%)		84,123 (24%)	
13	*Total bedenreceiver (ords + extrords) av pyr*	*342,115*		*122,714*		rows 1 + 3 + 6 + 9
14	*Total provincial receiver*	*100,922*		*221,763*		rows 2 + 4 + 7 + 10
15	TOTAL ANNUAL REVENUE		443,037 (100%)		344,477 (100%)	

Source see Table 2.1.

produced 185,204 guilders, that in 1564 228,499 guilders, most probably an indication for the increased wealth in Holland.[13]

Row 8 shows the role of the indirect, price-increasing, 'common' taxes on beer and wine in Holland's fiscal system before the Revolt. Although this role was obviously not yet very large, it was clearly increasing: from 8 percent in the 1550s to 20 percent in the 1560s. In view of later developments in Holland's fiscal system it is noteworthy, that in this category of indirect taxation, customs were not yet levied, whereas customs would become part of the Dutch fiscal system since the Revolt. The only exception under the Habsburgs had been the temporary introduction in 1543 of 1 percent on the value of export, levied in the whole Netherlands during two years, despite strong resistance.

The imposition of customs duties was seen by the royal government, at the time, as belonging to the sovereign rights of the Emperor not needing the consent of the States. Holland's foreign commerce was already important in the northern part of Europe, because of its need to import grain: in 1540 Holland's merchant fleet was already larger than that of Britain and France combined, and more than half of the ships passing the Sound Tolls were based

13 Tracy, 'The taxation system of the county of Holland', p. 90; *'Memorie 1755'*, f13v mentions that in 1560 new commissions for the assessments were installed.

in Holland.[14] However, of the about 0.2 million guilders this export tax would come to yield, only 12,682 guilders – about 7 percent – was collected in Holland. By far the largest part (72 percent) was the result of the rich international trade of the important city of Antwerp. After this export tax had been abolished again, no similar tax was reintroduced in the Dutch provinces before the Revolt. [15]

Rows 10–12 show the importance of long-term loans by means of the sale of annuities as a revenue source for war financing in Holland during the two decades before the Revolt.[16] These figures illustrate, in combination with the increase in interests paid by the Provincial Receiver (row 6 in Table 2.1) and the increase in his receipts in *common* taxes on beer and wine (rows 7–9 in Table 2.2) and in the *morgental* (line 5) the developments characterized by Tracy as a 'financial revolution'.[17] Until the 1540s annuities had only been sold on the credit of individual cities secured by their own *urban* beer excise.[18] By introducing annuities on the *common* credit of cities, on the security of *common* means received by the same *provincial* receiver who was charged with the interest payments and redemption on these annuities, it would become possible to realize much larger sums at once, and much more easily than by granting individual cities the right to issue annuities to pay their part in the *bede*.[19] Because the provincial receiver acted under the authority of the States, and because the States consisted mainly of representatives of cities, investors could safely expect that enough taxes would be voted to pay their interests and that interest payments would enjoy high priority. Foreign investors could appeal to the governments of their own city to take hostage citizens from cities who failed to pay the interest on annuities. The chance that a States assembly

14 Tracy, *Founding of the Dutch Republic*, p. 33.

15 Tracy, 'The taxation system of the county of Holland', 86; Lesger, C., 'De wereld als horizon: de economie tussen 1578 en 1650' in: *Geschiedenis van Amsterdam. Deel 2 Centrum van de wereld*, eds. W. Frijhoff, M. Prak and B. Bakker (Amsterdam, SUN, 2004) pp. 103–187.

16 The seemingly still large amount in annuities sold in 1562 were used to redeem annuities at a higher rate of interest.

17 Tracy, *A financial revolution*.

18 Tracy, 'The taxation system of the county of Holland', p. 90 Figure F, summarizing the receipts of the urban beer excise and the amounts in urban interest payments for four cities in Holland between 1531 and 1543.

19 Zuijderduijn, *Medieval Capital Markets*, p. 89 has argued that even already since the end of the thirteenth century forms of collective, instead of urban, taxation were used as securities for urban loans.

would do the utmost to avoid this was much larger than in the case of annuities sold by a royal bureaucracy.

In summary: the two tables show how financial requirements resulting from war, in the Habsburg Empire, contributed to the rise of a *provincial* fiscal system, the strength of which consisted in the collectivity of its six main cities. Its citizens, although loath to pay a fair share of taxes and trying to transfer the tax load as much as possible to the countryside, were ready to invest in public loans and to consent in taxes needed to service this debt. They could be confident that the control over taxation by their own representatives, in combination with the increasing population and wealth of their cities, would guarantee sufficient revenue for interest payments and redemption. This taxation consisted on the one hand of the receipt of a direct tax on wealth, the 10 percent-*morgental*, burdening the countryside as well as the cities, on the other hand, and increasingly so, of indirect taxes on domestic consumption taxing all consumers, initially mainly consisting of the common beer-excise.

The importance of Holland's urban system for its fiscal system became visible, therefore, already before the Revolt. The differences with its functioning after the Revolt will be further discussed in Section 2 of this Chapter after an analysis of the attempt to reform the old system by Alva and of the system in Castile by which this reform was said to have been inspired.

Alva's Attempt at Centralization

Alva's intention when he came to the Netherlands in 1567 was a centralization of taxation in *all* the seventeen provinces at once, in order to realize a system of reliable military payments. Already soon after his arrival in the Netherlands in 1567 he convened a meeting of the States General, because the nine-year *ordinaris bede* of 1.2 million guilders per year, granted in 1559, came to an end in March 1568. In this meeting he announced his plans to introduce uniform taxes in all seventeen provinces: a hundredth penny (1 percent) on the value of property, once only, to be used to pay arrears to the army, and a 'twentieth penny' (5 percent) of all transfers of immovable property, plus a 'tenth penny' (10 percent) of the sales of all other goods, as permanent taxes, to be collected by royal instead of by provincial officials. The most controversial element of Alva's plans was the 'tenth penny', that was more or less comparable to the modern Value-Added-Tax nowadays.[20]

This new permanent tax would create a continuously flowing stream of revenues that would moreover increase automatically with demographic and economic growth and would make the royal government much less dependent on

20 Grapperhaus, *Alva*, pp. 317–340.

the cumbersome system of the *beden*. Cities would, moreover, no longer have to be allowed to finance their share in the *bede* by means of loans through the sale of annuities instead of by means of taxes. In Holland it would thus put an end to the privilege to collect and administer an increasing part of the received taxes themselves in order to secure priority for the service of the public debt above military expenditure for this revenue source. An important advantage in comparison to the *beden*-system would be moreover, according to Alva, that the realized amounts would only be known to the royal administration, not the provinces themselves.[21] This in contrast to the situation that would develop in Holland after the Revolt, where widespread knowledge on the increasing amounts of the revenue of its 'common means' may have contributed to the restoration of its credit since c. 1600.

From the perspective of the central government it could reasonably be argued that the Netherlands were 'under-taxed' as long as they were not able to finance themselves the troops deemed necessary for the maintenance of internal order and for protection against foreign aggression. The receipts from Spain for what was called 'the army in Flanders' amounted to on average about three million guilders per year in the years 1567–1569. Alva had asked a paymaster of the army in Flanders to estimate the total value of sold industrial goods in 1570 in the Netherlands. His estimate came down to about 47 million guilders for thirteen of the seventeen provinces.[22] A successful introduction of the 'tenth penny' might, therefore, have yielded revenue with an order of magnitude of more than four million guilders. The 'tenth penny' seemed an excellent means, therefore, to make an end to this 'under-taxation' and to end the necessity of Spanish subsidies. A detailed study (in Dutch) is available of the negotiation process by which Alva tried to realize his plans. It shows the remarkable fiscal potentialities of a combination of 'absolutism' and the necessity of bargaining with representative institutions, despite the final failure of the 'tenth penny'.

The meeting of the States General was not meant to discuss the new proposals collectively. During the next days Alva started immediately separate talks with the representatives of each of the provinces in order to avoid such general discussions and to be able to send them home as soon as possible, with the task to convince their provincial States of the necessity of his plans.[23] Alva's own advisors became convinced, however, that the economic arguments against the tenth penny, put forward during the separate negotiations, had to be taken

21 Grapperhaus, *Alva*, p. 119.

22 Grapperhaus, *Alva*, p. 119.

23 Grapperhaus, *Alva*, p. 108.

seriously. It was decided, therefore, to postpone its introduction two years, and to be satisfied for the moment with the 'hundredth penny' on real property at once, and a contribution of two million per year from the Netherlands according to the old *beden*system, albeit for only two, instead of for nine years.[24]

Alva intended Flanders to pay 650,000 guilders in the two million (33 percent), Brabant 'a sixth less than Flanders' (27 percent), Holland 'half the amount of Brabant' (14 percent), Artois 'a quarter of Brabant' (7 percent), Hainault the same (7 percent), Zeeland 'a quarter of Holland' (3 percent), Utrecht 'a tenth of Holland' (1 percent), Namen '4 percent of Brabant' (1 percent). The contributions of the nine remaining provinces would be good for the remaining 7 percent, a distribution which shows that at that time the provinces of the future Dutch Republic were thought to be good for about 20 to 25 percent of tax revenue in the Netherlands. The taxes by means of which each of the provinces would be allowed to collect the required sum were negotiated with each of the provinces separately. By the end of August 1569 Alva had succeeded in forcing a majority in the most important provinces for the acceptation of his proposals, by threatening them with the billeting of unpaid soldiers in their cities if they would not comply.[25]

The contribution of 14 percent that he asked from Holland amounted to 271,000 guilders, whereas Holland's contribution had been 100,000 guilders per year under the former *ordinaris bede* during the years 1559–1568, then being only 8 percent of the total *bede*-amount of 1.2 million guilders. The increased percentage may have been the result of the observation that the increasing receipts from the 10 percent-*morgental* tax on revenues from real property showed that wealth in Holland was increasing. Holland's first reaction on Alva's revised proposals was that it accepted the 'hundredth penny' on real property meant to pay the arrears on payments to the troops, but that it did not want to pay 271,00 guilders on top of this, but only 100,000 guilders as had been paid during the former *bede*. However, when it was threatened with the billeting of troops, like Flanders and Brabant, it submitted.

Holland's States proposed to realize the increased *bede*-amount partly by more land taxes and partly by a loan by means of the sale of annuities on the

24 Grapperhaus, *Alva*, 27 published the original document; De Vries and Van der Woude, *The first modern economy: success, failure and perseverance of the Dutch economy, 1500–1815* (Cambridge, 1997) p. 99 suppose that the list in Grapperhaus was made in 1515, which is not the case as there was no *bede* for an amount of 2 million in 1515; moreover Friesland and Groningen are not in Grapperhaus' list.

25 Grapperhaus, *Alva*, p. 140; the negotiations are described in detail on pp. 125–149.

security of a number of new provincial excises and increased rates on the existing 'common excises' on wine and beer and peat, to which Alva agreed.[26] The new common provincial excises in Holland, consisting in taxes on the milling of grain, the slaughtering of cattle, on butter, cloth, foreign beer and herring were authorized on 12 July 1570. The collection was leased by the province at an auction to 'tax farmers' as used to be done in the case of urban excises.[27] In such auctions bids were made on the amounts in tax revenues to be transferred to the government, when having the right to collect a tax at the tax rate determined by the States. The highest bidders, who got this right for one or more taxes in one of the tax districts, were allowed to keep any surplus as their profit, if they had been able to find two people to stand surety for their reliability.

The States of Holland agreed, therefore, to an increase in *provincial* indirect domestic taxes increasing the prices of first necessities like bread, meat, butter, cloth and fish, already before they had decided to support the military revolt of the Prince of Orange. Also Brabant, like Holland in 1570, introduced several provincial excises instead of Alva's tenth penny, although not identical to those in Holland: on wine, honey, mead, beer, vinegar, wheat, cattle, meat, birds, game and candles, also to be leased by the province as provincial taxes, instead of by the cities as urban taxes.[28] In Friesland a list mentioning 'all merchandise, wines, beer, butter, grains, fat wares, quadrupeds etc.' was proposed. Here however in the end just the provincial tax on land was increased.[29]

Alva did not yet succeed immediately in replacing the *beden*-system by a system of uniform permanent taxes. He succeeded pretty well, however, for these two years, in fulfilling his orders to make the Netherlands financially more self-sufficient by means of these negotiations. The total amount received *de facto* by the central royal treasury in Brussels from the whole territory of the *Netherlands* had been on average only about 0.7 million guilders per year in 1566 and 1567, the years before he had become governor of the Netherlands. The subsidies from *Spain* for 'the army in Flanders' rose to nearly 3 million guilders on average per year, in the years 1567–1569.[30] During the years 1570/71–1571/72 the

26 Grapperhaus, *Alva,* pp. 132–136, 154–169 offers a detailed analysis of the negotiations.

27 Tracy found the ordnance announcing the farming of these seven excises for the period 1. May 1571 to 30. April 1572, *Founding*, p. 44; see also *'Memorie 1755'*, f15v; http://www.historici.nl/Onderzoek/Projecten/GewestelijkeFinancien/memorie; *GFH*, pp. 31 n121.

28 E.H. Korvezee, 'Belastingen in Noord-Brabant vóór 1648', Varia Historica Brabantica (Den Bosch 1975) pp. 97–164, p. 109.

29 *GFF*, p. 14.

30 Grapperhaus, *Alva*, p. 120; G. Parker, *The army of Flanders and the Spanish Road, 1567–1659: the logistics of Spanish victory and defeat in the Low Countries' wars* (Cambridge, CUP, 2004) p. 250; no data are available on receipts from the Netherlands in 1568.

combination of the 'hundredth penny' and the largely increased *beden*-receipts from the Netherlands yielded the enormous sum of nearly 3.7 million on average per year, making subsidies from Spain, therefore, superfluous during these years.[31]

Alva's remarkable achievement is nicely mirrored in Spanish military expenditure. Figure 2.1 shows the large part spent since 1566 on what is called 'the Flanders campaigns' of the Spanish king.[32] It shows also the exceptionality of the years 1570 and 1571, when nearly nothing had to be spent by Spain on the amounts necessary for the army in Flanders as a result of Alva's tax measures (which may have contributed therefore to the successful battle of Lepanto against the Ottoman Empire in 1571).

The early 1570s provide us, therefore, on the one hand, with a remarkable example of the success of the combination of an attempt at centralization,

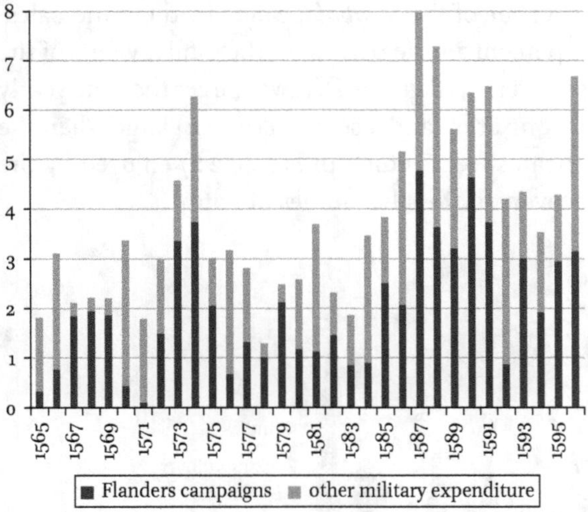

FIGURE 2.1 *Estimates of Castile's military expenditure, 1565–1596 (real value; millions of 1565 ducats).*
Source: M. Drelichman and H.J. Voth, 'The Sustainable Debts of Philip II: A Reconstruction of Castile's Fiscal Position, 1566–1596', *JEH* 70, 4 (2010) pp. 813–842, p. 824, Figure 4 [with kind permission of Cambridge University Press; I am obliged to Mauricio Drelichman for sending me the data].

31 Grapperhaus, *Alva*, p. 123.

32 M. Drelichman and H.-J. Voth, 'The Sustainable Debts of Philip II: A Reconstruction of Castile's Fiscal Position, 1566–1596', *Journal of Economic History* 70,4 (2010) 813–842, p. 824 fig. 4.

with a willingness to negotiate with representative institutions. On the other hand they also offer us a famous example of a failing attempt to increase public revenue by means of forceful centralization: it was to a certain extent Alva's failure to renew negotiations for a *bede* at the end of the two years period of the former, and his determination to rush into an enforced introduction of the 'tenth penny', that brought the lucrative fiscal possibilities of Holland's 'urban system' into the hands of his enemy, the Prince of Orange.

Castile's Fiscal System

Although Alva's plans are often thought to have been inspired by the Castilian *alcabala*-tax in the Spanish part of the Habsburg Empire, the Castilian fiscal system based upon the Castilian 'urban system' was in an important aspect rather similar to Holland's old fiscal system under the Habsburgs.

The alcabala – tax was levied in Castile already since the fourteenth century and it was an important source of revenue. Research by Drelichman and Voth shows that the share of the revenue of the *alcabala*, called by them the 'sales-tax', varied between about 20 percent and 30 percent of the total revenue of the Castilian crown between 1555 and 1575 (Figure 2.2). It was larger than the yearly amount in revenue from direct taxation and also often (much) larger than the volatile revenues from American silver ('Indies' in Figure 2.2) enjoyed by the Spanish Crown since the discovery of the silver mines of Potosí.

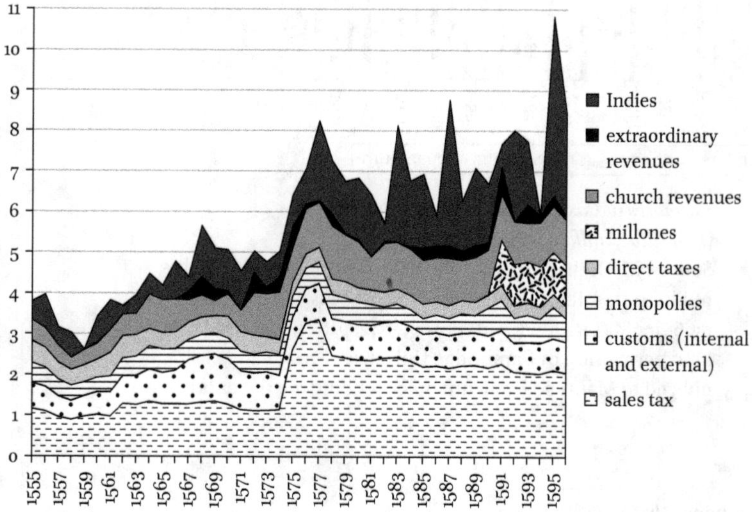

FIGURE 2.2 *Castile's crown revenues, 1555–1596 (real value; millions of 1565 ducats).* Source: same as Figure 2.1 (p. 824, Figure 1) and same acknowledgments.

Why was this tax, that caused Holland's cities to revolt, apparently accepted in the cities of Castile? The somewhat surprising explanation is that, at least since 1494, the fiscal system within which the *alcabala* functioned was in fact very different from what Alva intended to realize in the Netherlands, and was in fact much more similar to the old *beden*-system in Holland during the two decades before the Revolt.

In the Castilian *Cortes* eighteen cities were represented. This assembly was comparable to Holland's States-assembly, in which six cities were represented before the Revolt. The Castilian cities were on average larger than Holland's cities, but not completely incomparable in size. In Holland their average population was c. 12,000 in 1550, which would increase to c. 20,000 in 1600. In Castile their average population did hardly increase and was c. 25,000 in both these years. The two largest cities in Castile, Valladolid and Madrid had nearly 50,000 inhabitants; Amsterdam in Holland grew from about 30,000 to 65,000 people between 1550 and 1600. The two main differences between these two urban systems were that the cities in Castile were spread over a much larger territory than those in Holland, and that they displayed much less growth than in Holland in this period. They convened exclusively for taxation with intervening periods of mostly several years, this in sharp contrast therefore to the permanent meeting of the States of Holland after the Revolt.

In 1494 the royal government had accepted *encabeziamento* for the collection of the Castilian *alcabala* during a meeting of the Cortes.[33] This meant that a fixed sum was divided across the cities and the countryside, and that the cities could negotiate individual exemptions with the royal government, as was the case with the *bede* in Holland under the Habsburgs. And, comparable to Holland's 'common means' of the 1550s, it was accepted by the royal government that Castile's cities would organize the collection of the sum apportioned to them themselves. When Charles V tried to return to a centralized leasing and collection of the *alcabala* in 1519, a revolt of the cities forced him to maintain *encabeziamento*.

The effect of *encabeziamento* was, as contemporary investigations showed, that by 1574, instead of the intended 10 percent, an amount equivalent to only 2 to 3 percent of the total value of sales was paid in the *alcabala*, in fact.[34]

---

33 J.I.A. Ucendo, 'Castile's Tax System in the Seventeenth Century', *The Journal of European Economic History* 30, 3 (2001) pp. 597–617, p. 598; M. Ulloa, *La Hacienda Real de Castilla en el Reinado de Felipe II* (Madrid 1977) p. 181 gives the revenues for the *encabeziamentos* in 1547–56, 1562–74, 1575, 1576–7, 1578–87 and 1588–1610.

34 Gelabert, 'Castile', 210; Ulloa, *La Hacienda real*, p. 173.

Until 1574 the Castilian cities never consented in increases in the amount to be paid by them in *alcabala*. They only consented in *servicios,* direct taxes on land, burdening the surrounding countryside. Like in the case of Holland's *morgental*-tax before the Revolt the tax revenue paid by the countryside increased relative to that of the cities as soon as royal control of the organization of taxation was replaced by urban control. Like in Holland the Castilian cities transferred the tax burden as much as possible to the countryside.

Another similarity between Holland's fiscal system under the Habsburgs and the Castilian system, that explains the acceptance of the *alcabala,* was that these taxes – like the 'common means' in Holland before the Revolt – were used as the security for the interest payments on long-term debts, annuities, called *renten* in Holland and *juros* in Spain. Most of these *juros* were held by the Castilian nobility and bourgeoisie.

The much more volatile revenues from the import of American silver were the revenues that were used as the main security for short-term loans from foreign (mostly Genoese) bankers, necessary to ensure regular payments to the army in Flanders, that had to maintain order in the Netherlands. Voth and Drelichman studied hundreds of *asientos,* the complicated contracts which enabled the Spanish Crown to obtain these short-term advances at high interest rates of about 14 percent on average per year. Their article emphasizes that, although Spain four times failed to sustain interest payments on these short-term *asientos* – in 1557, 1560, 1575 and 1596 – it never had to fail on its long-term *juros,* which bore an interest rate of only about 7 percent, and that were paid from the *alcabala* collected in Castilian cities, administered by urban instead of royal officials.[35]

Only two times between 1555 and 1596 the government acquired the consent of the *Cortes* for a substantial increase in the sum to be collected by the cities in indirect taxation, the first time in 1575. Then the Cortes agreed to double the existing sum for the *alcabala,* in addition to a onetime levy of 1 percent on real property. Secondly in 1590: after the loss of the large new war fleet, the Armada, they agreed to a substantial increase in the form of the *servicio de millones,* consisting in about one million ducats per year in new excise taxes on wine, meat, olive oil, and vinegar on top of the about two million ducats per year in *alcabala*. In both cases the explanation was that this was the only way to secure the continuation of the interest payments on *juros.* The increase in *juros* resulted from the conversion of high renting short-term debts to bankers into much lower renting long-term loans in the form of *juros,* in which wealthy

35 Drelichman and Voth, 'The Sustainable Debts of Philip II', p. 822.

Castilians were eager to invest to obtain a rentier's income. The investment was reliable because city governments administered the taxes from which the interests were paid, not the royal government.[36]

Voth and Drelichman concluded that Castile's fiscal system provided enough 'breathing room' to cope with high debts,[37] as Castile's success in raising new tax revenues underpinned the ability to service debts, which kept them attractive as an investment opportunity for the Castilians. It may be noted in addition that is not likely that the Cortes would ever have consented in the much larger amounts of money needed to pay an army in Flanders. The bloody mutiny in Antwerp of the unpaid soldiers of the Spanish army in 1576 did not jeopardize the 'breathing room' of Castilian citizens.

In short: a centralized ten percent sales tax as envisaged by Alva for the Netherlands did not exist in Castile at that time, because the *alcabala* had become in 1494 a fixed sum partitioned across the cities, levied by those cities as a sales tax of ten percent in name, but at a much lower percentage in fact. So, the *alcabala* were raised in a way much more comparable to the old *beden*-system of Holland than to Alva's fiscal plans for the Netherlands. Increases in tax revenue in Spain remained as dependent on slow cumbersome negotiations with the Cortes as they were dependent on the States assemblies in the Netherlands.

This calls for the question what changes in Holland's fiscal system would enable it to increase its tax revenues sufficiently to continue to pay the troops necessary to wage the war. Spain was at that moment a state which, despite sizeable reductions in military expenditure after its financial default in 1575,[38] could still afford to send, on average, no less than nearly 3 million guilders per year to its army in Flanders during the next years. Holland's old fiscal system produced less than 0.5 million guilders per year before the Revolt.

2.2 The Development of Holland's Fiscal System until 1609[39]

The Increasing Amounts Needed for the War

The request of the Prince of Orange in May 1574 to the States of Holland to provide him with a monthly sum for the war equivalent to 360,000 guilders per

---

36 I owe thanks to Bartolomé Yun Casalilla for his comments.

37 Drelichman and Voth, 'The Sustainable Debts of Philip II', pp. 836–837.

38 According to Parker, *The army of Flanders*, p. 250 the receipts in Brussels from Spain were during 1572–74 on average about 4.8 million guilders.

39 This section is an extended, and sometimes slightly revised, adaptation of Fritschy, 'A "financial revolution" reconsidered'.

TABLE 2.3 *Taxation in Holland before and after the Revolt, 1571–1608 (guilders).*

	1571/72	1572/73	1573/74	1575	1578	1586	1590	1599	1608
	a	b	c	d	e	f	g	h	i
beer(&wine)	84,071	24,669	64,242	240,000			494,175		1,536,001
wine							63,216		281,874
grain per weight				108,000					
milling of grain	29,153	5,811		24,000			75,492		698,084
slaughtered cattle		3,187					91,781		415,496
horned beasts	9,421			72,000					363,366
peat	6,238	1,571		24,000					205,035
weighage				18,000			85,490		200,655
cloth				7,200			4,436		112,893
herring				10,800					
soap				36,000			20,507		76,063
salt							29,772		207,504
other									247,230
total 'common means'	**(128,883)**	**?**	**111,498**	**288,000****	**818,397**	**1,498,424**	**(1,800,000)**	**2,700,000**	**(4,344,201)**
urban taxes	44,205		105,038						
on land (after 1575 land&houses)	50,669	*43,000*	*43,000*	?	*105,000*	*500,000*	*1,100,000*	*1,300,000*	*1,300,000*

repartitions/ (forced) loans		*200,000*	*200,000*	*200,000*				*600,000*	*500,000*
40. penny on transfers								*200,000*	*200,000*
Total revenue	223,757*	?	*460,000*	*488,000*	*925,000*	*2,000,000*	*2,900,000*	*4,800,000*	*6,300,000*

NB Between brackets: subtotals; italics: my estimates (see *GFH* pp. 164–183).

* My addition (Tracy's source had a total of only 202,801 guilders).

** The total of the preceding figures from a contemporary budget is 540,000; Tracy found that the revenue for 'total common means' in 1575 was in fact only about 24,000 guilders on average per month, which would be 288,000 guilders for a year; a comparison with the receipts of the common means in Zeeland at the time made this amount more likely indeed.

Sources: Tracy, *The founding of the Dutch Republic*, 102–107; 'Memorie 1755', f17r; *GFH*, 496, 499–502, 160, 164–169, 171–174, 177–185, 246, 252, 505, 507.

year was more ambitious than Alva's controversial *bede* to Holland of 271,000 guilders per year in 1570. Further increases would follow soon. The Prince's request of November 1574 amounted to 540,000 guilders per year, that of April 1575 even to 930,000 guilders (excl. 270,000 guilders from Zeeland), much more, therefore, than Holland had ever to bring in under the Habsburgs in war years. Nevertheless it was a small amount in comparison to the five million guilders received from Spain in Brussels for the army in Flanders that had to combat the Prince, in 1575, and even than the only 1.7 million guilders sent by Spain to Brussels after the Spanish financial debacle of that year in 1576.[40]

There was a difference, moreover, between the amounts asked and the amounts actually realized for the Prince. Data for the amounts in taxes that were received *de facto* are extremely scarce and very incomplete for the first decades after the Revolt. Table 2.3 summarizes data available for some years from 1571/2 to 1608, with estimates added where this seemed reasonably possible.

The difference between the amounts asked by the Prince and the totals for the 'common means' of the columns a-d show that it was not easy for the States of Holland to realize the money promised to the Prince during the first years after 1572. Total provincial revenue probably more than doubled since 1572 to about 500,000 guilders in 1575, but by that time the States' promises to the Prince amounted already to 930,000 guilders per year. Columns e-i show that the main breakthrough came from the decision in 1574 to reintroduce and expand the 'common means', that increased since then from perhaps less than 300,000 guilders in 1575 to nearly two million in 1590 and more than four million guilders in 1608.

Since 1570 the 'common means' can be characterized as 'provincial taxes on domestic commercial products, activities and assets in the cities as well as in the countryside'. They were no longer just mainly excises on beer and wine jointly levied in a number of cities, as earlier in the Habsburg period. The increase in their number had started already in 1570 as part of the compensations for the postponed 'tenth penny', then, however, still earmarked as the security for an annuity-loan.[41] The levying of these 'common means' had been stopped in 1573 because of the war. After their reintroduction in 1574 an important difference with the earlier practice was that they had now to become the primary means to finance the war, instead of being the security for interest payments on loans.

---

40 Parker, *The army of Flanders*, p. 250; Grapperhaus, *Alva*, p. 120.

41 Tracy, *The founding*, p. 44.

Holland's 'Tax Revolution'

The amounts in taxes realized by the 'common means' soon became a multiple of the amount with which Alva's 'tenth' penny might have burdened Holland's economy. At the contemporary estimate of 47 million guilders for the value of industrial production in the Netherlands the revenue of the tenth penny would have been maximally 4.7 million guilders. If Holland would have been good for 14 percent, as was its part in the *bede*, it would have been good for maximally about 650,000 guilders in the tenth penny. Table 2.3 shows that the amount realized by means of the 'common means' was twofold already in 1586. Three factors may be considered in an attempt to explain the acceptance and the revolutionary increase of this revenue: the characteristics of these taxes, the political conditions under which they were raised, and demographic and economic developments.

The main difference between the common means and the tenth penny was that the tenth penny had originally been intended to be levied as a cumulative turnover tax of ten percent of the value of each sale of all products. In the revised version before its intended start in 1572 it was even reduced to a tax only on the value of the last sale of products to the consumer.[42] The common means were levied in a largely varying number of ways, not only on the last sale of products to consumers, but also on wholesale transactions, on transport, weighing etc. or directly on producers.

For example: in 1583 the taxes on beer and wine had to be paid per ton by consumers as well as by publicans, wholesale traders, brewers and producers of brandy, and at differing rates according to the quality. Grains were taxed per last when they were milled and at different rates for different kinds of grain – high rates for high quality wheat, low rates for low quality rye – and for a certain period of time there was even a tax on the domestic transport of grains, and later one on measuring its quantities was added. The peat tax was paid per ton where it was cut, but in 1605 taxes on its transport and consumption were added. Meat and fish were taxed as a percentage of their value (5 percent, since 1605 14 percent), meat when cattle was slaughtered, fish by 'the first buyer'. Soap producers as well as its 'first buyers' (whole sale traders) paid a tax rate per 240 pound. There was a salt tax per 100 pound on the wholesale trader. There was also a direct tax on salt by means of a fixed amount per family, for farmer-families according to the number of cows,[43] for other families dependent on the number of persons.

---

42 Grapperhaus, *Alva*, p. 160; pp. 317–340 offers the complete text of the revised version of 31. July 1571.

43 Salt was an important addition to cow fodder.

All products were moreover taxed differently according weight, when they were weighed in a public weigh house. The tax to be paid on horned cattle was a direct tax on what can be considered as a 'capital good' in commercial husbandry levied at different rates per beast according to the kind of beast and its age. Horses were originally taxed when sold (at 5 percent of their value since 1605 14 percent), later by means of a direct tax similar to that on horned cattle. So, the 'common means' consisted partly of direct taxes on commercial assets and activities, but mainly of indirect taxes on consumer goods, with the same kind of price-increasing effects as could have been expected from the 'tenth penny'.

It is hard to say if this bewildering conglomerate of taxes was perhaps better fine-tuned to prevent economic damage than the 'tenth penny' would have been. A general difference was that most of the common means were taxed according to quantities, the tenth penny according to values. Was there a fear among traders for the red tape of having to show accounting books to the tax man, whereas most common means only required the control of stocks? However, if particular characteristics or economic drawbacks of the tenth penny were important to explain the start of the Revolt, why then did Amsterdam not participate before 1578? The fact that the tenth penny would in its revised version be mainly restricted to 'the last sale', thus to the retail-trade, may have been felt as an important concession, but there were of course many retail-traders in Amsterdam as well. At this time, when Antwerp was still by far the main commercial city of the Netherlands, the importance of Amsterdam's foreign trade was not yet as dominant as it would become. Most probably the main explanation is that the strength of Catholicism and fear of Calvinism and chaos were greater in Amsterdam than in the smaller cities.

The degree to which trade and commerce in Holland were already more or less accustomed to important elements of the common means will have contributed their acceptance. Taxes on beer and wine were already known in the thirteenth century as important sources of public revenue in cities.[44] As infrastructural facilities financed by urban public revenue were used not only by citizens, but also by traders and visitors from the countryside and other cities, it had been a logical step for urban governments to devise taxes by means of which also outsiders contributed indirectly to these facilities by means of the price they paid for urban consumption. In a densely urbanized territory as

44 W. Dirksen, 'Stedelijke heffingen in Middelburg', in: *Steden en dorpen in tal en last*, eds. T. Pfeil a.o., (Amsterdam, NEHA, 1999) p. 21 mentions excises in Liège 1230, Haarlem 1274, Zierikzee, 1303, Middelburg 1325.

Holland, this may have made the step easier to *common,* province-wide, excise taxation.

It seems most likely, however, that the acceptance of the revolutionary increases in the common means has to a large extent to be explained simply by support for the war. The extremely cruel treatment, ordered by Spanish commanders-in-chief, of the populations of the small revolting cities of Zutphen in November 1572 and of Naarden in December 1572 on the one hand, and the victories of Alkmaar and Leiden in 1573 and 1574 on the other hand, may have contributed to the determination of Holland's cities to continue the war. Once the Revolt had started, a way back became hardly conceivable any longer. Accepting the necessity of war meant the acceptance of the necessity of large tax increases.

The revenue increase was certainly also the result, however, of economic and demographic development, especially between 1586 and 1600. We know that there were important increases in the number and the tariffs of 'common means' between 1574 and 1586, especially in 1583 and 1585,[45] and between 1600 and 1607, especially in 1605.[46] We also know however that the real value of GDP per capita had increased to a level of on average 148 in the years 1574–1578, if the average level of the economic crisis years 1569–1573 is set at 100.[47] No indications were found for increases in the number or tariffs of taxes between 1586 and 1600, except for the introduction of a tax on unfunded lawsuits in 1595 that yielded only about 5,000 guilders in 1608, and that was probably mainly introduced to discourage lawsuits, not to increase public revenue. This implies that the impressive increase in the total revenue of the 'common means' between 1586 and 1600 from about 1.5 million to about 2.7 million guilders, which amounts to a growth of on average 4.6 percent per year, must have been mainly due to population growth and economic development in Holland during those years.[48] According to estimates of the real value of GDP per capita in Holland it

---

45 Holland promised in 1583 to increase its contribution to the war from (then) nearly 60,000 to 92,000 guilders per month; the revenue of the common means in increased in 1583 from about 74,000 to about 84,000 on guilders average per month. In 1585 they promised to increase it from (then) 80,000 to 124,000 guilders per month, the common means revenue then increased from about 82,000 to about 92,000 guilders on average per month. See the detailed overview in Van Oldenbarnevelt's personal archives, published in *GFH*, pp. 497–503, p. 498 and p. 500.

46 Details are to be found in *GFH*, pp. 304–336.

47 Van Leeuwen and Van Zanden, http://www.cgeh.nl/reconstruction-national-accounts-holland-1500-1800-0.

48 Holland's population was in 1514 about 275,000 people, in 1622 about 672,000; De Vries and Vander Woude, *First Modern Economy*, p. 52.

had increased to a level of 181 in the period 1595–1600, if the level of 1569–1573 is set at 100.[49]

The immigration by many thousands of protestant textile workers from the Flemish countryside to the city of Leiden since 1574 – especially in 1582 when the main textile centre of Hondschoote had been destroyed by the Spanish troops – must have been one important cause of the revenue increase of taxes consisting in large part of indirect taxes on primary consumption. The number of Leiden's inhabitants more than doubled from about 12,000 in 1582 to about 25,000 in 1600.[50] The population of Haarlem, too, increased explosively: in 1550 it was about 14,000 and in 1600 about 30,000, mainly due to immigration from the Southern Netherlands.[51]

The successful closure of the Scheldt after Antwerp's seizure by Spain in 1585, and Amsterdam's subsequent rise as the centre of world trade offers another important part of the explanation.[52] This had of course a very favourable effect on employment opportunities. Amsterdam's population increased from about 30,000 in 1550 to about 65,000 in 1600. The population in cities in Holland with more than 10,000 inhabitants increased from c. 139,000 to c. 247,000 people.

Summarizing: during the 1570s so-called 'common means' became a major source of direct war financing, whereas they had been used only as a security for debt service before the Revolt. A shared conviction that war was necessary stimulated political decisions for huge additional tax increases. It was helpful for their acceptance that a modest version of the 'common means' existed already since the 1540s. After a hesitant start, and some pressure by the prince of Orange, Holland's 'urban system' – as it was embodied in the interdependence of the cities and the countryside of its commercial economy, as well as in the necessary collective decisions of cities in the States of Holland –, made possible the decisions to increase the 'common means' in a revolutionary way.

Determination to persevere in the Revolt was no doubt the most important part of the explanation of the acceptance of the more than six-fold increase in the revenue of the common means which not only must have increased prices, but also largely diminished the fiscal autonomy of the individual cities.

---

49 Van Leeuwen and Van Zanden, http://www.cgeh.nl/reconstruction-national-accounts-holland-1500-1800-0.

50 De Vries, *European Urbanization*, p. 271; 45,000 in 1622; J.K.S. Moes, 'Speciale en economische facetten uit de geschiedenis van de Leidse textielnijverheid', in Stof uit het Leidse verleden, eds. J.K.S. Moes and B.M.A. de Vries, Leiden, 1991, 7–31, 15.

51 De Vries, *European Urbanization*, p. 271.

52 Lesger, *The Rise of the Amsterdam Market and Information Exchange*.

However, apart from drastic political fiscal decisions, also demographic and economic developments contributed noticeably to the success of the new tax system.

Direct and Indirect Taxes

Despite their revolutionary increase the receipts of the common means were not sufficient for the war. As Table 2.3 shows, additional taxes, in the form of direct taxes on property, were levied as well. In characterizing fiscal systems it is usual to make a distinction between direct and indirect taxes, although the dividing line between the two is not watertight. An indirect tax differs from a direct tax in that its burden is mostly shifted unto the consumer of the taxed product or service by means of the price. Indirect taxes are price-increasing taxes. Because they are 'hidden' in the price of taxed goods and services, they are less directly noticeable for the tax payer than taxes to be paid directly in cash to a tax collector.

Producers or sellers who have to pay such taxes may choose, however, not to pass the burden of a tax – or not completely – unto consumers. In their turn consumers can also (more or less) choose either or not to diminish their purchase of taxed goods or services. Because of this possibility to choose, indirect taxes may, on the one hand, be seen as taxes that leave more 'freedom', and direct ones as more 'tyrannical' or 'coercive' taxes. This 'freedom' implies, however, that indirect taxes on primary necessities, have to be preferred by governments to avoid disappointing revenue results. This meant that they often left people not very much of a choice in fact. It implies that indirect taxes can also be seen as taxes that burden the poor disproportionately, as poor people have to spend a much larger part of their income on primary consumption. Direct taxes, in contrast, can be seen as taxes burdening social classes who own property.

In the fiscal practice before the nineteenth century direct taxes were often levied in the form of a lump sum to be divided across tax districts according to a distributive key, mostly resulting from an inquiry in relative capacity, similar to the *beden*-system. The distribution across the tax districts was often called a 'repartition' or 'quotisation' and, in the case of the land and house tax in Holland, the '*verponding*'. The tax districts had to divide their share across the taxpayers in their districts by means of assessments. In the case of taxes on real property, houses and pieces of land had to be assessed according to their value in local registers of land and houses (*reële kohieren*). In the case of taxes on total wealth people were assessed and listed in registers of persons (*personele kohieren*) with the tax amount to be paid by each of them assessed by local commissions appointed to this end. The intermediary role of local governments in this type of taxation made their collection much more cumbersome and slow than that of the 'common means' that were leased to tax farmers from whom the provincial tax receivers just received the agreed lease price after they had been collected by them. They were not necessarily very fair either, as tax registers tended to become obsolete when they were not renewed each year.

A last important difference between the common means and the direct taxes on property was that their revenue per year did not change with economic and demographic developments, but only as a result of political decisions to demand its collection more than once a year (or to ask an addition of a half or a quarter etc. of the original amount). This made them different not only from price increasing indirect taxes, but also for instance from the direct tax on cattle that was part of the 'common means', the revenues of which did not only change as a result of political decisions, but also of demographic and economic fluctuations, although the introduction of a transfer tax of 2.5 percent, in 1598, on inheritances and sales of property made it possible to profit somewhat from increases in the value of real property.

Direct taxation started in Holland immediately in August 1572 with a twelfth penny (8.3 percent) on land rents which was increased to the sixth penny (16.7 percent) in 1574, as was mentioned. In 1575 a register of houses was made, in addition to already existing land registers. Since 1576 each month one sixth of 1 percent of the value of lands and houses was levied, i.e. 2 percent per year. Its receipt can be estimated at initially about 105,000 guilders per year.[53] In 1580 the rate was doubled. In 1584 a *'verponding'*-register based on lands and houses was brought into use, which was intended to yield about 220,000 guilders per year for each *'verponding'*. The total receipt from *'verpondingen'* was probably already since 1586 more than 1 million guilders per year, because there were often as much as six *verpondingen* in one year. In 1599 the *'verponding'* was valued at 1.3 million guilders per year according to a contemporary source, and this valuation remained unchanged until 1621.

Anyhow, the existence and expansion of direct taxation hitting the more well to do, alongside indirect price-increasing taxes affecting the whole population, may have contributed to the social acceptance of the emerging tax system in Holland. To determine the relative importance of direct and indirect taxes in Holland's new tax system the revenue of the direct taxes on horned cattle and horses had to be added to the amount in direct taxes on real estate and to be subtracted from the common means. The same is true for that part of the revenue of the salt tax that was levied from families: from urban families

---

53 *GFH*, p. 171.

according to their size and from farmer's families according to the number of dairy cows. Then the outcome would be that in 1608 taxes on the middle class and the rich were good for about 40 percent of all tax revenue, whereas about 60 percent of all taxes were on primary necessities used by everybody, also poor people: beer, fuel, grains, meat, soap, fish, building materials, woollen cloth, candles and grease, and weighing of merchandise.

This may have made the tax system rather 'regressive'. It should be added however that the rates on expensive kinds of beer and were higher than on the cheaper kinds, and that the lowest quality beer was even tax free.[54] Similarly the tax rates on cheap grains like rye were lower than those on wheat, which must have made the tax system somewhat less 'regressive' than suggested by the mentioned percentage. Moreover, to the degree that indirect taxes just pushed up wages,[55] the effect of increases on the living standard of the poor may have been mitigated. Anyhow no tax riots are reported in Holland before the Twelve Years' Truce.[56]

The Tax Burden before and after the Revolt

What were the consequences of the Revolt for the tax burden? Provincial tax revenues in Holland during the two years before the Revolt may be estimated at about 550,000 guilders per year.[57] Holland's population in 1570 may be estimated at about 365,000 people.,[58] This would imply a tax burden of about 1.5 guilder on average per person. The wage of a day labourer in the Western Netherlands at the time was about 0.28 guilders per day, resp. that of a journey man about 0.40 guilders per day.[59] This implies a tax burden on average of about five (resp. four) daily wages per year shortly before the Revolt.

54 The so called *'dunne, scheyn, of scherte-bieren'*; GFH, p. 308.

55 De Vries and Van der Woude, *The first modern economy*, p. 631 fig. 12.6 shows the real wage increases in the Western Netherlands between 1575 and 1620.

56 Table 3.5 in the next chapter examines the relation between tax burden and tax riots in the Dutch Republic.

57 The total *beden*-revenue by the royal central treasury in Brussels had been about 3.6 million guilders, Holland's part was supposed to be 14%, which comes down to 504,000 guilders, of which probably 150,000 guilders was realized by means of an annuity-loan, which leaves 354,000 guilders for taxes; to this should yet be added the amount received in taxes by Holland's provincial receiver of about 200,000 guilders per year; the data in Tracy, *Founding*, pp. 44 and 102.

58 This figure results from the estimate of 274,810 for 1514 and a growth rate of 0.5% on average per year; Vries, *Rural Economy*, pp. 86, 90, 93 suggests for the five biggest cities a growth rate of on average 0.37% per year and a higher growth rate in the countryside.

59 De Vries and Van der Woude, *The first modern economy*, pp. 610–611.

By 1608 total tax revenue had increased to about 6,345,000 guilders. Holland's population by then may be estimated at about 550,000.[60] The daily wages of a day labourer and a journeyman in the western Netherlands were now on average about 0.74 guilders (resp. 0.90 guilders). This would make the tax burden on average nearly sixteen (resp. thirteen) daily wages. On the eve of the Twelve Years' Truce the real tax burden in Holland had become therefore on average about threefold the one on the eve of the Revolt.

It is hard to say with any precision what this may have meant for individual people. Day labourers will not have shared in the payment of all of Holland's taxes, as they will not have owned property, or have drunk wine. As the revenue in taxes on primary necessities in 1608 was estimated at about 60 percent of total revenue, the tax burden due to primary necessities may be said to have come down to 9.4 (resp. 7.7) daily wages per capita of a day labourer (journeyman). It is not known how many persons on average lived on the wage of a journeyman, but women will on average have earned less, if they did paid work.[61] If one wage did on average feed for instance three persons then perhaps about 28 (23) daily wages of day labourers' (journeymen's) income went to taxes on primary necessities. If the number of working days was 300 per year, the tax burden due to provincial indirect taxes on primary necessities would have been in this case nearly 9 (8) percent of a day labourer's (journeyman's) income. If one wage fed four persons and the number of working days was only 250 days, it would have been 15 percent (12 percent).

This part of the 'tax burden' was hidden, however, in the prices of primary necessities. It is important therefore to notice that not only nominal, but even real wages rose significantly between 1570 and 1610 – although strongly fluctuating from year to year.[62] An economic development, in which nominal wages rose on average faster than prices, as occurred in the Western Netherlands between 1570 and 1610, was no doubt an important part of the explanation for the social acceptance of the fiscal system in Holland before 1610.

---

60 An increase of 0.5% on average per year since De Vries' estimate of 274,810 in 1514 and of 1.45% on average per year after 1585 results in in figure about equal to De Vries' estimate for 1622 of 670,661; De Vries, *Rural Economy*, pp. 86, 90, 93.

61 E. van Nederveen Meerkerk, *De draad in eigen handen, Vrouwen en loonarbeid in de Nederlandse textielnijverheid 1581–1810* (Amsterdam, Aksant, 2007) p. 290 found that, at least later in the 1670s, male and female spinning wages did not differ in Leiden's textile industry, but that the percentage of women in the lower paid spinning jobs was always larger.

62 De Vries and Van der Woude, *The first modern economy*, fig. 12a-b, p. 629: the thirteen year moving average for the real wage index for hod-carriers stood at 70 around 1570 and at around 95 in 1610 (1451–1475 = 100).

Loans as a Source of Revenue: 'Short'-Term Obligations and Long-term Annuities

The decision of the States of Holland in November 1574 to use the 'common means' primarily to provide the Prince with the money needed for the war, precluded for the time being interest payments on the existing provincial debt in annuities. This made the marketing of new issues of annuity-loans impossible.[63] The last element to be discussed in the emergence of Holland's new fiscal system is the restoration of the possibility to raise public revenue by negotiating long-term loans at low rates of interest as had been possible since the 1550s. This would actually remain rather difficult during most of the first three decades after the Revolt.

How did the States handle deficits in public finance in this period? Firstly, army-leaders had evidently to provide credit willy-nilly much longer than they had most likely intended to. Tracy found that a number of German, Dutch and British army-leaders and some other persons were, still in 1582, in the possession of more than one million guilders in unpaid 'obligations' of Holland, issued during the years 1572–6, including 368,465 guilders still owed on the spectacular 500,000 guilders obligation of August 1572.[64] Secondly, he found examples of high officials in Holland who had felt forced to lend sums for the continuation of the war in exchange for obligations, and also examples of merchants who had accepted obligations in payment for deliveries, and who were later allowed to use these obligations to pay taxes.

Thirdly, the most important source of the creation of new 'obligations' were the 'repartitions' of sums for the war across the cities, based on a division made by the Prince. Until the end of the 1580s, it was as hard for the cities as for the States of Holland to get voluntary loans subscribed,[65] because not only the revenue of provincial excises, but even that of urban excises, out of which in normal times interests on urban loans were paid, was now partly used directly for the war, and no longer available for debt service.[66] The sums repartitioned

---

63 Tracy, *The founding of the Dutch Republic*, p. 102.

64 J. Tracy, 'Holland's New Fiscal Regime, 1572–1576', *The Political Economy of the Dutch Republic*, ed. O. Gelderblom (Ashgate, Surrey, 2009) pp. 41–55, pp. 47–48.

65 In Delft, then a city of about 16,000 inhabitants, burghers provided 106,131 pounds (guilders) for the cause between August 1572 and April 1574. Only two times the city government tried a voluntary loan of 10,000 pound and both times it was not fully subscribed (a loan of February 1573 furnished 8,843 guilders, the next one in April 1573 8,335) guilders. Tracy, *The founding of the Dutch Republic*, p. 106, based on Van Dijk, 'De geldelijke druk op de Delftse burgerij', pp. 48–52.

66 The account of the receiver-general (*'ontfanger-generaal van de gemeenelandtspenningen'*) Nicolaes van der Laen for the year 1573/4 contained an amount in 'urban excises' of 105,038 pounds (=guilders) on top of 27,373 pounds in provincial excises.

across the cities were mostly realized, therefore, by means of forced loans apportioned by the city governments to inhabitants above a certain amount of wealth, by way of personal registers. The debt paper they received was called an 'obligation' as well.

A difference with the individual obligations was that they were not made out on name, but 'on bearer', and that these obligations were as a rule interest bearing, at the high rate of 12 percent until at least 1595.[67] Forced loans were of course preferable for citizens to direct tax levies. They were intended to be short-term loans to be repaid as soon as possible from future provincial tax receipts just like other obligations. In fact, however, a large amount of them remained in circulation for a very long time.

Tracy found about 600,000 guilders in – mainly forced – loans issued by the cities between August 1572 and November 1575, not only resulting from decisions for '*repartities*' by the States of Holland, but also from local decisions.[68] For the next period a rather detailed contemporary overview of Holland's war expenditure and revenue between 1577 and 1586 was found in the archive of Van Oldenbarnevelt (1547–1619), - who was a member of the financial commission of the States of Holland since 1579, a confidant of the Prince of Orange since 1582, and Holland's main political leader since 1586. He mentions an amount of 900,000 guilders 'raised by the cities on interest' in the years 1583 and 1584.[69] So, in the period 1572–1586 the States of Holland had been dependent for an amount of at least 1.5 million guilders on the ability of the individual cities to realize revenues by means of (mainly) forced loans, a sizeable proportion of total revenue during the earliest years of the Revolt.[70] These urban

67 This percentage is mentioned for the forced loan of 120,000 guilders in 1574 (*GFH*, p. 178) and it is in conformity with the increase in the interest burden and the estimate on the amounts in forced loans (*GFH*, p. 181); the *'Memorie van 1755'*, f20v-21r mentions that levies on personal registers were sometimes *'geevensgeld'* (money that had to be given) sometimes loans resulting in obligations on *ordinary* (my italics WF) interest (*'obligatien lopende op ordinaris interest'*); also Tracy, *The founding of the Dutch Republic*, p. 250.

68 Ibidem, p. 106; my earlier estimates based on less primary data than Tracy's research amounted to even more than 1 million guilders for the years 1572–1575, *GFH*, 160, 177–179.

69 *GFH*, p. 499 (f3r2), 501–502 (f5r1); the complete text (in French) is published (with a translation in Dutch) in *GFH* pp. 497–509.

70 Tracy's, *The founding of the Dutch Republic,* emphasizes Holland's financial dependence on the individual cities during the early years of the revolt; it is valid for this part of public revenue, however after about 1578 no longer for the 'common means', the most important part of public revenue.

debts would come to be recognized by the States of Holland as provincial debt in 1587.

A fourth and last way by means of which 'obligations' came into existence is mentioned in another memo found in the personal archives of Oldenbarnevelt dating from 1589. It mentions the amounts in 'money raised during the last years upon the common means by the receivers of the common means', a capital of about 500,000 pounds (=guilders) in total,[71] less than the 900,000 guilders 'by the cities on interest', during only the two years 1583–4, but still a not inconsiderable amount of money. The receivers of the common means could apparently be used by the States of Holland, already in the 1580s, as 'bankers' for short-term loans,[72] a function fulfilled by Antwerp bankers before the Revolt (see Tables 2.1 and 2.2), although only to a very restricted extent in comparison to the former advances of the Antwerp bankers. Already in one of the very scarcely preserved receivers-accounts of the period, that of Holland's receiver-general Cornelis van Mierop over the years 1581–1583 a distinction was to be found between 'money furnished by the cities (…) by repartition' (an amount of 148,633 guilders), and 'loans on interest' (an amount of 35,000 guilders) which may refer to the money raised in short-term loans by either by himself or by the receivers of the common means. When Holland's tax receivers succeeded in realizing these short-term loans for the States, they were allowed to pay themselves a broker's commission of mostly 1% (in 1586 even 2% is mentioned once) for their efforts to convince people in their surroundings to borrow them money for a short term.

The credit of this 'obligations on interest' sold by the tax receivers must initially have been based on the confidence that the receipts of the common means would enable the receiver to pay interest and to redeem this short-term debt at short notice, indeed. This confidence may have been furthered by the fact that the collection of the 'common means' during a year was auctioned publicly three times a year (each time another group of taxes) in each of Holland's tax districts, which secured a rather regular stream of income from these taxes, the size of which was publicly known. Its credit was most probably also based on the fact that the provincial receivers were part of the urban elite, which was able to invest in these obligations. They formed themselves

71 National Archives 3.01.14, Oldenbarnevelt, inv.nr. 84; *GFH*, 181; to avoid confusion I will always use in this book 'guilders' where sources have Dutch pounds or fl. (=florins).

72 See also: M. 't Hart, 'Mutual Advantages: State Bankers as Brokers between the City of Amsterdam and the Dutch Republic', in: *The Political Economy of the Dutch Republic*, ed. O. Gelderblom (Ashgate 2009) pp. 115–142.

a part of the social group that had to be convinced of the reliability of the interest payments on these obligations, which implied that also their personal respectability was involved in the credibility of these loans.[73] They had also a personal interest therefore in a careful and reliable management of this loan facility.

Lastly, a very essential element of the credit of these short-term loans will have been that the receivers were probably from early on allowed to give absolute priority to the payment of interest. They did not need a separate preceding payment order of the States as was the case for other payments: for interest payments they were automatically 'de-charged'. For later periods we know that the amounts that each receiver was allowed to borrow were carefully divided among them, that they were not allowed to borrow more without explicit permission, and that they had to send monthly reports of all their revenue and expenditure and their cash balance to the States.

In the meantime, Holland struggled to regain the confidence of investors for long-term loans as well. Holland's receiver-general was instructed by the States, in January 1586, to start to pay interest arrears up to 1583 on old annuities, and in November 1586 he was instructed to pay the interest over 1584. It should be added, however, that in the same year it was decided to levy a tax on the value of debt paper, any time when extra direct taxes on land and houses were levied, despite warnings by representatives, especially of the larger cities, that this would harm credit. The possession of public debt was an easily retrievable and extremely easily taxable element of property for the government, as this tax could be 'collected' simply by means of an interest reduction. The result was that the real rate of interest paid on redeemable annuities issued at a rate of 8.3 percent ('the twelfth penny') was already since 1584 mostly only 7.1 percent ('the fourteenth penny') instead, and on life annuities declining from 15.5 to 13.4 percent, instead of the nominal rate of 16.7 percent.[74] (This did not necessarily imply, of course, that they could be sold by the government at these low rates as well.)

When the States repartitioned an amount of 100,000 guilders across the cities, in August 1586, they allowed them the choice to issue the annuities either on their own credit or on the credit of the province, instead of raising the money by means of a forced loan, apparently in an attempt to discover if long-term loans on the credit of the province, instead of that of individual cities, were possible already. It is known that Amsterdam and Delft still preferred the

73 't Hart, 'Mutual advantages', pp. 130–134.

74 *GFH*, p. 363.

first option for their citizens,[75] and that Delft was even still inclined to prefer a forced loan.[76] In Amsterdam voluntary urban loans were certainly possible again since 1587.[77] No indications were found, however, that *provincial* annuities could be sold already in one of the cities.

Probably all remaining interest arrears had been paid by the province in 1587, because that was the year when the States decided to acknowledge all city debts, incurred for the war, as provincial debts. This decision would have been useless and even harmful, if the States would not have expected to be able to pay the interests. As of 1588 the 1.5 million guilders in former city debts were no serviced from provincial taxation, on top of the existing old provincial debt from the time of the Habsburg. The decision must have more than doubled Holland's total long-term debt to about 2.3 million guilders.[78] This decision can be seen as a core-element of the process of state formation that was developing since the start of the Revolt, a resolute step in the attempt to become independent of the credit of the individual cities and in the strengthening of Holland's 'urban system' as the core of its fiscal system.

Yet it was not before July 1594, that the States tried again to sell redeemable annuities at an interest of 8.3 percent on the credit of the province instead of its two alternatives: either repartitioning the amount across the cities in order to use *urban* credit, or instructing the receivers of the common means to try to sell short-term loans in obligations. The attempt was, however, not yet very successful. They decided to try a new loan in May 1595, but they now allowed the receivers to sell life-annuities (at 16.67 percent) as well, because it had proved to be hard to sell enough redeemable annuities in 1594. Houtzager's detailed research on the sale of Holland's annuities showed that, from July 1594 until the start of the Twelve Years' Truce in 1609, the States gave orders eighteen times to the tax receivers in Holland to try to sell annuities for a certain amount of money, mostly allowing them the sale not only of redeemable annuities at 8.3 percent, but also of life annuities at 16.7 percent on one life or at 12.5 percent on two lives.

75 Houtzager, *Hollands lijf- en losrenteleningen vóór 1672* (Schiedam, z.j. (1950)) p. 122, nr. 77.

76 Ibidem, nr. 75; NB the repartitions of 31/1/1586 and 26/8/1586 in nrs. 75 and 77 are not mentioned in Tracy's list of Repartitien, 1583–1588 in Tracy, *Founding*, p. 251-2.

77 M. van den Burg and M. 't Hart, '*Renteniers* and the recovery of Amsterdam's credit', in M. Boone a.o. eds., *Urban public debts* (Turnhout 2003) 197–219, 202–203: about 40,000 guilders in 1587, 90,000 guilders in 1588 and even nearly 200,000 guilders in 1589.

78 The document on Holland's finances between 1577 and 1586 mentions that the interest burden on the old debt had been 120,000 guilders. A contemporary estimate for 1599 sets

However, time and again it proved to remain necessary to allow the receivers to sell obligations as well: investors evidently preferred short-term obligations over long-term redeemable annuities. The remarkable fact was that this remained the case even after the rate of interest on obligations had been reduced from 12 percent to 8 percent in 1597, whereas that on redeemable annuities was still 8.3%. To give one example: the States decided in February 1604, that the tax receivers should try to sell for an amount of 300,000 guilders in annuities (half in redeemable ones at 8.3%, half in life-annuities at 14.2 percent on one, 11.1 percent on two lives); by July 1605 only less than half of the amount had been realized; the States then decided to borrow the rest on obligations at 8% (which cost them in addition a one-time brokers-commission of 1% for the receivers). Houtzager's research leaves no doubt at all, therefore, that it continued to be difficult to find enough investors in the regular types of long-term debt, the annuities, although the interest rate on life-annuities could be reduced to 14.2 and 11.1 percent in 1603: they were evidently easier to sell than the redeemable ones.

Holland's 'Real' Financial Revolution

More remarkable than the preference for life annuities was the preference for the short-term obligations above redeemable annuities, even although they had a slightly lower rate of interest. It may seem obvious that lenders had a preference for obligations on the credit of the receivers, because they could trust their redemption. An interesting element in Oldenbarnevelt's memo of 1589 on the 'money raised upon the common means by the receivers' was, however, a proposal to redeem this short-term debt, from then on, from the revenue of next year's *'verponding'*, in order, as he wrote, 'to liberate the common means'. The proposal to charge their redemption no longer on the receipt of the 'common means', needed for army expenditure, but on that of the *'verponding',* the direct tax on land and houses, would unavoidably keep these obligations longer in circulation, as the collection of the this tax was nearly always in arrears. This tax was received by 'treasurers' completely separate from the provincial receivers of the common means and was transferred in its entirety to Holland's general-receiver in Delft.[79] By 1589 it seemed safe, apparently, to charge the redemption of this short-term paper on a somewhat less reliable

the interest burden at about 400,000 guilders. At an interest rate of on average 12% on obligations between 1572 and 1599 an addition of 280,000 guilders interest implies an addition to the debt of in total about 2.3 million guilders, of which 1.5 million in urban debts taken over by the province.

79 See for a diagram of relations between different types of urban and provincial tax receivers Fritschy, 'Three centuries of urban and provincial public debt: Amsterdam and Holland', p. 89.

source of revenue than the common means. The explanation appears to be that holders of these obligations were not always particularly eager to have their money refunded soon, as long as the interest, of until 1595 12 percent per year and since 1597 of 8%, was paid punctually.[80]

The deputies forming the daily board of the States were, understandably, reluctant to have large amounts in short-term debts circulating.[81] Nevertheless they appear to have often felt forced to allow the sale of this short-term debt paper in order to get loans fully subscribed, as we saw.[82] In July 1606 it was decided to borrow 400,000 guilders, half in redeemable and life-annuities, half in obligations: the annuities at the prevailing rates of interest of 8.3 percent, but the obligations now even at only 7 percent interest plus 0.5 percent broker's commission, instead of 8 percent and 1 percent. It was evidently expected that many possible investors would prefer obligations (without a name!) at 7 percent above redeemable annuities (which were always on name!) at 8.3 percent, although it has to be added, that between 1584 and 1607 interest-reductions often reduced the real interest rate on redeemable annuities already to rates varying from 7.06 to 7.78 percent.[83]

Real changes in the credit of the States of Holland would become visible only after 1606, perhaps because the large increases in the rates of many taxes, as were decided in 1605, had a 'credit-improving' effect. Between 1601 and July 1606 the States were able to negotiate an amount of in total maximally about 1.8 million guilders in annuities and obligations on the free market, i.e. only about 450,000 guilders on average per year at an interest rate of at least 8.3 percent. It should be noticed that this was already much more per year than the c. 185,000 guilders during the 1550s, but still at the rather high rate of interest of 8.3 percent instead of the 6.25% of the 1550s. From July 1606 to December 1607, the tax receivers were asked to negotiate even no less than 2.9 million guilders in public debt, which amounts to on average nearly 2 million guilders per year, and now at an interest rate of only 7%, which does not seem to have been a problem anymore. Probably the interest rate on long-term annuities and 'short' term obligations was identical at that time. The main difference between the two was that the transfer of annuities was subject to a transfer tax

80 See *GFH* pp. 381–382 for a table with nominal rates of interest from 1569–1794 or Fritschy, 'A "financial revolution" reconsidered', p. 64 for 1569–1655.

81 C.M. Reinhart and K.S. Rogoff, *This Time is Different. Eight Centuries of Financial Folly* (Princeton 2009) p. xxv.

82 Houtzager, *Lijf- en losrenteleningen*, pp. 124–126.

83 See *GFH* p. 363 for a table with an overview of these reductions and the (differing) reductions on the interest on life-annuities as well.

existing since 1598, which did not apply to the transfer of obligations, because they could change hands without registering a change in names.

The nominal interest rate was, moreover, voluntarily reduced to 6.25 percent after the start of the Twelve Years' Truce: the annuities of holders that would not accept the announced interest reduction would be redeemed. It was apparently expected that most holders would prefer the lower interest to losing this investment possibility, the more so, because in 1607 an interest reduction of 12.5 percent did already reduce the real interest rate on redeemable annuities to 7.1 percent. Since then, Holland would be able to let its public debt continuously increase, while, nevertheless, its nominal interest rate would yet decline to 4 percent, during the next decades. By then, therefore a 'financial revolution' had occurred.

At the same time 'obligations' appeared to become the most common long-term loan format, despite several attempts of the States to convince holders that they had to convert them into long-term annuities. In contrast to what modern economists would tend to expect, Holland's increasing short-term debt did not 'need to be constantly refinanced' to avoid a crisis of confidence.[84] The explanation must be, that they were, in contrast to the annuities, not on name, which made them much more easily – and tax-free – transferable than annuities.

This second 'financial revolution' that Holland experienced between about 1606 and 1610, might perhaps rather be called its 'real' financial revolution, in view of the much higher amounts in loans on average per year than during the 1550s, and in view of the fact that no redemptions were felt to be necessary any longer, in contrast to the 1560s (see Table 2.1).

One of the most remarkable aspects of Holland's 'second financial revolution' was that it was built on 'obligations', an originally short-term debt paper, and that it was realized without the institutional help of a central bank. In Britain it would be the establishment of the Bank of England, trusted by London's merchant community, that would offer the British government the facilities to negotiate long-term loans and to convert high renting short-term debt into low renting long-term debt (see also Chapter 5). In Holland it was the network of tax receivers, grafted onto its urban system that not only supplied Holland's government with loans, but also allowed apparently the gradual change of obligations from a short-term into a long-term debt paper.

In 1609 Amsterdam's city government established the famous Amsterdam's Exchange Bank, which offered international merchants the possibility to

84 Reinhart and Rogoff, *This Time is Different*, p. xxv.

change the different coins of often uncertain intrinsic value that came into their possession into a bank account, and to receive and effectuate future payments by means of transfers to other accountholders. This Exchange Bank would never become a credit-institution for the States of Holland, however. Although the East India Company would be allowed to use it as such, and sometimes also Amsterdam's city government, the States of Holland would never even *try* to make use of this bank for Holland's public finance before the 1790s.

We may conclude, that the importance of the network of the sixteen (later eighteen) provincial receivers for Holland's fiscal system shows that the 'embodiment' of Holland's 'urban system' by then consisted of more than of the available infrastructure for common decisions on taxation in the States of Holland, and the economic integration of this territory that had allowed the introduction of very remunerative of 'common means'. The role of Holland's urban system in its fiscal system became manifest also, in the widespread and easy access to large amounts of cheap credit in the form of easy investment possibilities in public debt for large numbers of people by means of this network of tax receivers in a very large number of its cities. Or, in the terminology of 'institutional economists': the existence of a fiscal system based upon an urban system largely decreased the 'transaction costs' of this fiscal system.

Holland's Fiscal System at the Start of the Twelve Years' Truce

Table 2.4 summarizes the main characteristics of the structure of Holland's fiscal system during the last decade of the period under discussion in this chapter.

A comparison with Tables 2.1–2.3 highlights the revolutionary change in the totals. On the left side, it shows the dominance of war expenditure, which had become about fifteen times as high as during the 1550s. On the revenue side, it shows the importance of the 'common means', nearly eight times as much as in the 1550s and still more than double the amount in 1586. The high percentage for these 'common means' was the result of what may be called a process of 'provincial centralization', not based on the power of an absolutist ruler, but on the availability of an 'urban system'.

The table shows also, that the total tax increase was not only the result of indirect, price-increasing taxes, involving less 'coercion' – to use Tilly's terminology – than direct taxes. Not only did the common means consist partly of direct taxes themselves, especially the rather important tax on cattle; in addition, nearly a quarter of Holland's annual public revenue in this decade consisted of direct taxes on property. It consisted by then for nearly a quarter of loans.

TABLE 2.4 *The structure of Holland's public finance in the decade before the Truce, 1600–1609 (million guilders).*

Average annual expenditure 1600–1609			Average annual revenue 1600–1609		
on war	4.6	74%	from the 'common means'	3.4	55%
on interest payments	1.0	16%	from direct taxes on property	1.4	23%
other	0.6	10%	from loans	1.4	23%
total	6.2	100%	total	6.2	100%

Source: *GFH* pp. 160–161.

It can be seen on the expenditure side that the amount spent in interest on average per year was by that time already not much lower than the amounts realized on average per year by means of loans. It is noticeable, however, that this does not necessarily imply that the fiscal system of the Dutch Republic was more 'capital-intensive' than coercion-intensive. Dormans appeared to have assumed in his study on the debts of the Dutch Republic that the increase in Holland's debt from 3.6 million guilders in 1599 to 17.5 million in 1610 had been completely the result of the sale of redeemable annuities. The earlier in-depth research in Holland's annuities by Houtzager made it very unlikely, however, that more than about 4.9 million was raised as *voluntary* loans on the free market – partly annuities, partly obligations – as we saw. This means that an amount of about 9 million guilders must have been the result of *forced* loans, on average c. 0.9 million on average per year, still in this first decade of the seventeenth century. The conclusion is that 'coercion' had been much more important than 'capital' – to use Tilly's terms – during the formation period of the Dutch fiscal system in the important province of Holland.

It is of course very impressive that by then no less than about 4.6 million could be spent on war, but it should be immediately added that Spain send no less than on average c. 7.8 million guilders per year as subsidies to the army in Flanders during this same decade.[85] This calls for the question how

85 G. Parker, *The army of Flanders and the Spanish Road, 1567–1659* (Cambridge 2004), p. 225.

and to what extent the other provinces were able to contribute their shares in the war expenditure of the Dutch Republic and, if so, how and why, they were able to attain increases in their public revenue to this end between 1579 and 1609.

2.3 The Other Provinces

From the start to the end of the Dutch Republic Holland's fiscal system would remain always the most important element of its public finance, but the sum of public revenue of the other ones was by no means negligible. What were the implications of the revolt against Spain for the fiscal systems of the other provinces? The province of Zeeland, directly south of Holland, deserves special attention, not only because it was Holland's first ally, but also because it accepted in 1574 the same system of 'common means' as it was accepted in Holland in that year. It will be argued in what follows that it was its economic development that made it impossible for Zeeland to keep pace with Holland in contributing to the required increases in public revenue, rather than a tendency to 'free ride' on its richer ally.

The next sub-section in this section on 'the other provinces' will describe the failed attempts to realize 'general means' similar to the 'common means' in Holland and Zeeland in *all* provinces on the same footing, attempts that were started in fact already before the Union of Utrecht, when the States General of all the Netherlands convened for the first time autonomously in 1576. The failure to realize centralized 'general means' would exclude the 'political body' of the States General for some time from the possibility to obtain loans on its own credit.

The third subsection describes the toilsome process of the acceptance of 'general means' in the other provinces of the northern union, although at conditions that maintained provincial autonomy as to their number and rates. Just like in Holland and Zeeland the revolt resulted in an increase of urban political influence in the provincial states assemblies also in the other provinces. Urban elites in all provinces became willy-nilly convinced that they had to accept the *provincial* fiscal centralization, required for the introduction of 'general means', which implied a considerable decrease in urban fiscal autonomy. When they were convinced of the usefulness of belonging to the Union they had to be able to contribute to the required increases in public revenue. It proved to be unavoidable to use to this end the fiscal potentialities of the commercial integration that had resulted from urbanization, also in the territories of the Netherlands outside Holland and Zeeland.

The fourth and last sub-section describes the '*quoten* (=quotas)-system' that would be used for 'general' expenditure by the members of the Union of Utrecht instead of fiscal unification. It ends with an attempt to assess to what extent the new Republic suffered from 'free riding' by the provinces outside Holland as a consequence of the failed centralization of its fiscal system on the level of the state as a whole.

The Importance of Zeeland

In the province of Zeeland some cities had been involved in the Revolt already right from the start. The Prince of Orange, who had also been stadholder of Zeeland and Utrecht before Alva's arrival, succeeded in convincing Zeeland's rebellious cities to start to convene, in March 1574, as 'free' States of Zeeland.[86] Like the 'free' States of Holland, they accepted him again as their stadholder and as the representative of the nobility in their province. Orange even convinced them to join Holland in levying 'common means' for the war.[87]

Until 1574 Zeeland's financial contribution to the Revolt had consisted of the booty of privateering and the levying of customs in the rebellious port cities of Veere and Vlissingen, which financed the war at sea.[88] In contrast to its acceptance of 'common means' Zeeland would initially not accept that customs revenue had to be left to centralized control. In this respect, it would submit only in 1598, and it would in fact continue its attempts to maintain provincial authority over this source of public revenue as much as possible.[89] Customs as a revenue source of the Dutch Republic will be further discussed in Chapter 3. Here the focus will be upon Zeeland's 'domestic' taxation.

Zeeland consisted of a number of islands south of Holland of which Walcheren with its main city Middelburg, was the most important. Its territory was much smaller than that of Holland (see the map on p. XVII) and also the level of urbanization was lower. In Holland the number of cities with more than 10,000 inhabitants had increased from eight in 1550 to twelve in 1600 and the

86 Swart, *William of Orange*, p. 44.

87 Zeeland's rates for the important beer excise were indeed similar to those in Holland at least in 1578; for the other taxes the rates seem to have remained quite different in practice and even for beer they were not identical; GFZ (=W. Veenstra, *Gewestelijke financien ten tijde van de Republiek der Verenigde Nederlanden. Deel VII Zeeland, 1573–1795* (Den Haag, 2009)), pp. 156–157, *GFH*, pp. 306–307.

88 Enthoven, *Zeeland en de opkomst van de Republiek*.

89 W. Veenstra, *Tussen gewest en generaliteit. Staatsvorming en financiering van de oorlog te water in de Republiek der Verenigde Nederlanden, in het bijzonder Zeeland (1586–1795)* (Amsterdam diss. VU 2014).

number of cities with voting rights in the Provincial States assembly became no less than sixteen after the Revolt. The population of Middelburg on Walcheren of about 7,000 in 1550 increased largely after the Revolt to about 20,000 in 1600, but among Zeeland's seven cities it would remain the only one with more than 10,000 inhabitants during the period of the Dutch Republic.

Like in Holland, urban influence became more prominent in Zeeland's new States-assembly, however, than in the old one before the Revolt, when nobility, church and cities had one vote each. Now Zeeland's three main commercial cities, Middelburg, Veere and Vlissingen, all on the island of Walcheren, obtained each one vote. Two other urban votes – one of the city of Goes on the island of Beveland and the city of Tholen on the island of Tholen – represented, in fact, mainly agrarian interests, whereas the vote of the city of Zierikzee on the island of Schouwen-Duiveland represented a combination of commercial and agrarian interests.[90] Like in Holland the acceptance of 'common means' therefore implied the constitution of an 'urban system', in which individual cities, that since about the thirteenth century had developed their own urban fiscal systems,[91] accepted the loss of an important part of their fiscal autonomy by accepting provincial fiscal authority. In the States of Zeeland, contrary to Holland, the stadholder – or his representative – was allowed the right to be the first voter, which gave him some influence on voting behaviour, and the acceptance of his leadership will certainly have contributed to an easy acceptance of the 'common means' in Zeeland. However, the number of six votes of Zeeland's cities largely outweighed that of its 'First Nobleman' (*Eerste Edele*). So, as in Holland, fiscal decisions were now primarily made by a collectivity of cities.

In 1575 the two provinces decided that they would jointly provide the Prince with the 100,000 guilders per month needed for the army, 22.5 percent of which would be paid by Zeeland. The percentages to be paid by each of the two provinces seem to have been based on the yields of the 'common means' during 1574/5.[92] As 22.5 percent of the total came down to 29 percent of Holland's contribution Zeeland's part may seem high: under Alva Zeeland only paid 'a quarter of Holland'. At that time Amsterdam did not yet participate in the Revolt, however, and Haarlem, another of Holland's six largest cities, had not yet

90 *GFZ*, p. 12.

91 Dirksen, 'Stedelijke heffingen in Middelburg', p. 15.

92 This assumption was confirmed for later years (see below); common means revenue in Zeeland was in 1574/5 64,449 guilders (10,742 Flemish pounds), this would mean about 220,000 guilders for Holland, which seems acceptable in view of the estimates in Table 2.3.

been reconquered on Spain. Zeeland's share would be somewhat diminished later on. In addition the custom duties, a very important source of revenue in Zeeland, were not yet centralized (see Section 2.4 below).

The idea was that the two provinces would realize the required war payments from the revenue of 'common means', to be levied on an equal footing in both provinces. Two representatives from Holland would be allowed to attend the meetings in Zeeland, and vice versa, in order that both could remain convinced that no divergent fiscal decisions would be taken by the other province. By 1583, however, Holland thought further increases in the 'common means' unavoidable. By that time such taxes were not yet in force in most of the other provinces then forming part of the Union of Utrecht of 1579. This must have spurred Zeeland not to join this policy of rate increases automatically, but to regain its fiscal autonomy as well.

What were the consequences for the level of public revenue in Zeeland? In contrast to Holland and most other provinces, detailed information on Zeeland's complete financial administration has been preserved for the whole period of the Dutch Republic, starting with the accounts of Adriaan Manmaker, appointed by William of Orange as Zeeland's general receiver already in September 1573.[93] Figures 2.3a and 2.3b offer a comparison of public revenue in Zeeland during the years 1574–1609, with a reconstruction of public revenue in Holland – complemented with estimates for missing years – in the same period.

The graphs show that until about 1595 the revenues of the 'common means' in Zeeland continuously increased, just like in Holland, and that the resumption of Zeeland's fiscal autonomy in the 1580s did not lead to a decrease in its financial efforts until 1595. In 1585 it was decided that Zeeland had to pay 20.5 percent of what Holland had to pay in the 200,000 guilders per month then required for the war. In 1586 this proportion was increased again to 24.6 percent.[94] These percentages were more or less in conformity to the actual proportions of the 'common means'-revenue of the two provinces, which was on average about 20.5 percent during the period 1574–1584, on average 24.4 percent in 1583–1585. The two provinces kept each other apparently informed of the yields at that time. The procedure of determining the relative contribution to war expenditure by means of the revenue of the common means is reminiscent of the procedure of the royal enquiry on the relative fiscal capacity of the cities in Holland's territory in 1515, which was based on the yields of urban

93 *GFZ*, p. 35.

94 Zwitzer, '*De militie van den staat*', p. 66.

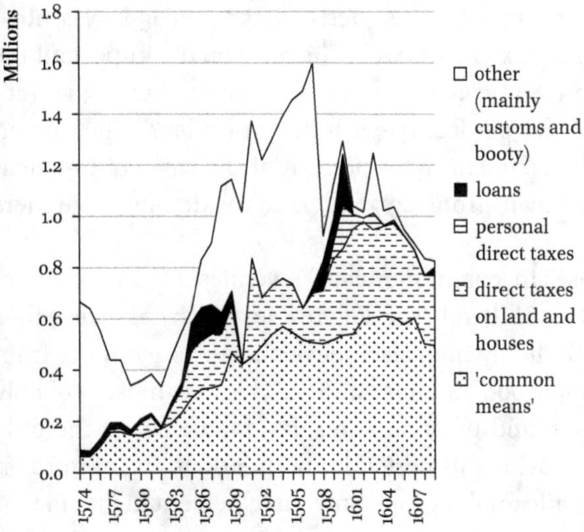

FIGURE 2.3A *Public revenue Zeeland, 1574–1609 (million guilders).*

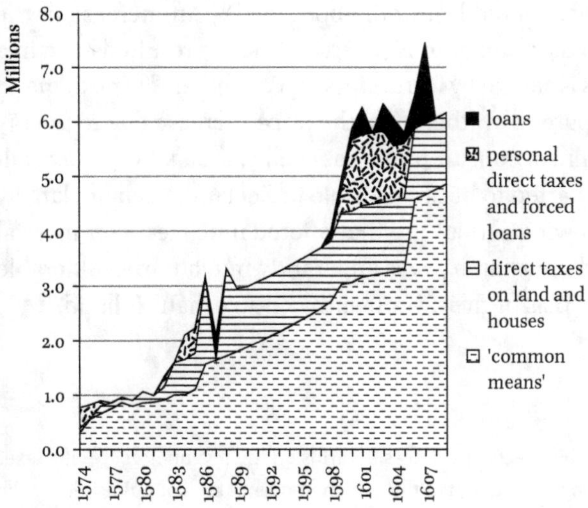

FIGURE 2.3B *Public revenue Holland, 1574–1609 (million guilders).*

indirect taxation. The main difference is of course that now two whole provinces were the fiscal units instead of individual cities.

In view of the population increase experienced in Middelburgs, it seems likely that Zeeland shared, at least temporarily, in Holland's economic boom after the fall of Antwerp in 1585, and that this contributed to the rise in revenues of the 'common means'. The revenue increase between 1583 and 1594 was, however, partly due to increases in tax rates as well. The rates on the important tax on milling of grain were in 1586 twice that of 1576, being by then 0.3 guilder per 'last' wheat and 0.15 guilder per last rye, just like in Holland. The rate on slaughtering increased from 5 percent to 8.3 percent of the value of the meat in 1586, that on beer for publicans from 2.3 guilders to maximally 3.1 guilders per ton beer in 1588.[95]

After 1594 similar increases in 'common means' revenues did no longer occur in Zeeland in contrast to Holland (see Figures 2.3a–2.3b) and revenues declined until 1598. They gradually increased, nevertheless, once more from 503,000 guilders in 1598 to 592,000 guilders in 1604. This was most probably again the result of economic and of population developments, as the only known increase in tax rates during this period is another doubling of rates on the milling of grain which made total revenue only three percent higher in 1601 than in 1599.[96]

After 1604, however, the revenue of the 'common means' started to decrease. Research into its economic history shows, that Zeeland entered a period of economic stagnation which would last until about 1750.[97] An increase in the rate on slaughtering from 8.3 percent to 12.5 percent in 1607 resulted even in a decrease of its revenue, as is shown by its receipts on Walcheren.[98] The demand elasticity of meat was apparently rather high: the price-increase due to the tax increase appeared to diminish consumption noticeably. So, a kind of 'tax ceiling' for indirect taxation started to became visible in Zeeland. Zeeland, largely dependent on a wheat growing agriculture that offered much less commercial possibilities than Holland's husbandry, was apparently much more vulnerable for the general European crisis of the seventeenth century than Holland.[99]

---

95 GFZ, pp. 68–69, 150–181; the effects of changes in tariffs on the revenues of specific taxes are not known, as data on the revenues of the 'common means' are not published for the period since 1604 (and then only for Walcheren).

96 In 1604 the tax on the milling of grain was good for 22% of total revenue of the common means' on Walcheren; figures for each of the 'common means' separately are only available since 1604 and only for Walcheren; GFZ, pp. 102–118.

97 P. Priester, *Geschiedenis van de Zeeuwse landbouw* (Wageningen 1998).

98 GFZ, p. 102; electronic database: choose 'Zeeland', 'Walcheren', 'middelen', 'slachtgeld'; http://www.historici.nl/Onderzoek/Projecten/GewestelijkeFinancien.

99 J. de Vries, *The Economy of Europe in an Age of Crisis, 1600–1750* (Cambridge, CUP, 1996); Priester, *Geschiedenis van de Zeeuwse landbouw*, p. 57, confirms a period of continuing economic stagnation in Zeeland between 1600 and 1750.

Until 1605 the revenue of the common means in Zeeland had been on average still about 20 percent of that in Holland. This percentage declined drastically since 1606 to only about 13 percent during the last years before the Twelve Years' Truce, partly due to considerable increases in Holland's tax rates in 1605, partly due to Zeeland's economic stagnation. The percentage share it had to take officially would be diminished from 24.6 percent of Holland's contribution to 19.2 percent in 1612. So, the other provinces were apparently not completely insensitive to Zeeland's relative economic decline within the Republic. Its 'common means' revenue had by then decreased to less than 12 percent of that in Holland. Zeeland's plea that the revenue of the 'common means' should continue to be taken as the yardstick for its contribution, despite lower rates than in Holland, was dismissed. The other provinces would, nevertheless, agree again to a diminishing of Zeeland's formal share in war expenditure in 1616, now from 19.2 percent to 15.8 percent of that of Holland.

Estimates for the total population of both provinces are only available for the 1620s, when the size of Zeeland's population was probably about 15 percent of that of Holland.[100] In view of the fact that Zeeland's population was evidently much less wealthy than that of Holland the share it had to take in the general expenditure of the Republic remained comparatively pretty high therefore.

Like in Holland, the revenue of the 'common means' had anyhow never been sufficient for Zeeland's total public expenditure, not even before 1595. In 1594 when Zeeland's 'common means'-revenue was at a top, it was able to finance 75 percent of Zeeland's public expenditure, by 1600 this had declined to 56 percent. As Figure 2.3a shows, additional direct taxes *and* loans were levied. Zeeland decided in 1579 to levy a 'hundredth penny' of the value of real property, partly to be paid by owners, partly by tenants, like Holland did since 1576. If necessary, more than one hundredth penny per year was levied. In Zeeland, the yield of this type of taxation rose from about 50,000 guilders in 1580 to on average about 350,000 from 1600–1609, similar to the increase in Holland, from about 200,000 guilders in 1580 to c. 1,3 million guilders on average per year during the period 1600–1609.

---

100 Total population for Zeeland was 110,929 in 1795/6; for the area north of the Westerschelde it was 76,000 in 1626 and 80,000 in 1795/6; if the proportion was similar in 1626 then total population may be estimated at about 105,000 in 1626; Priester, *Geschiedenis van de Zeeuwse landbouw*, p. 55; Holland's total population was about 675,000 in 1622; Vries and van der Woude, *First Modern Economy*, p. 52. The revenue of the common means in the decade before 1584 suggests that Zeeland's population was then more than 20% of that of Holland.

Forced loans, based on assessments of total wealth by local committees, started in Zeeland somewhat later than in Holland, but the conditions of the so called *'capitale impositie'* of 1599 were a copy of a forced loan under the same name in Holland of the same year. It demanded 0.5 percent of the value of all movable and unmovable property worth more than 3000 guilders.[101] Salaries and pensions were 'capitalized', by equating 100 guilders in income to 600 guilders in property, comparable to the interest rate on life annuities. The same was done in 1600 and 1602. No interest rate on these forced 'loans' is mentioned, neither in Zeeland, nor in Holland, and it is doubtful if they were ever redeemed.

Figure 2.3a shows that also modest amounts in other loans were negotiated in Zeeland: from 1574 until 1584 on average about 15,000 guilders per year, in the periods 1585–1589 and 1597–1600 on average about 100,000 guilders per year.[102] Until 1593 these were not yet 'provincial' loans, but, like in Holland, loans negotiated on the credit of the individual cities. Unfortunately, even less details on loan financing are known for Zeeland than for Holland. The receivers-accounts mention varying amounts in 'interests paid to the cities' during some of the years between 1585 and 1592. Since 1593 they started to mention also amounts for the payment of *provincial* 'interests and life annuities'. It is not known exactly since when the province started to try to sell life and redeemable annuities on its own credit, neither at what interest rates.[103] However, Zeeland's last substantial public loan in the period before the Twelve Years' Truce was in 1600, this in sharp contrast to Holland's 'real financial revolution' in the first decade of the seventeenth century.

Debt redemptions are to be found in Zeeland already since 1574. This will most probably indicate that Zeeland's early loans were short-term loans and that Zeeland's general receiver played the same role as Holland's receivers for short-term credit to the provincial government. Did a network of tax receivers exist in Zeeland that facilitated access to the public to sell annuities and pay investors their interests? Zeeland's general receiver received, according to his accounts, not only the direct taxes on property, but also all 'common means' revenues.[104] This in contrast to Holland, where the receipts of, and

---

101 *GFZ*, p. 187; *GFH*, p. 364.

102 *GFZ*, p. 75.

103 Alberto Feenstra (University of Amsterdam) is now working on a PhD-thesis on the capital market for public loans in the provinces outside Holland supervised by J. Jonker and M. 't Hart, which may offer more information in the future.

104 The information for Holland is based on an overview of revenue and expenditure of Holland's receivers for 1665, published in *GFH*, pp. 36–37.

the expenditure from most of the 'common means' was accounted for by the district-receivers. This seems to imply that no network of 'common means' receivers came into existence in Zeeland, that could have reinforced the fiscal possibilities of its 'urban system' by allowing a very efficient access to large numbers of small lenders in the whole province like in Holland.

A contra-indication may be, however, that at least since 1599 a repartition system for loans across Zeeland's cities existed. It showed that it was expected that 33 percent of the required amounts could be sold in Middelburg, 67 percent in the three cities on Walcheren together, and that 35 percent was expected to be invested by inhabitants of the other isles.[105] It seems likely that this implied that part of the revenue of the 'common means' was not physically transferred to Zeeland's receiver general but only accounted for by him, and that the money remained somehow available on the spot to secure easy interest payments to the investors, but how exactly is not known.

What did Zeeland's fiscal performance until 1609, as it is visible in Figure 2.3a, mean for the share Zeeland took in war expenditure? The data on war expenditure in Holland are less reliable than those for Zeeland, but what is available suggests that during the years 1583–1598 Zeeland's war expenditure paid from domestic revenue amounted to on average about 29 percent of Holland's war expenditure, largely because of its contribution to navy expenditure. After it had been forced to keep its customs revenues separate from its provincial fiscal administration, because of the centralization of customs revenue (see Section 2.4 below) this share declined, however, to on average about 17 percent or even less. The official norm, namely that it had to pay 24.6 percent of what Holland paid did not change until 1612, but apparently Zeeland simply paid much less already long before this norm was changed to 19.2%.

Zeeland's decision in 1583 not to join Holland's rate-increases on the 'common means' was evidently not inspired by a tendency to start to 'free-ride' on Holland's fiscal efforts for the war, which is theoretically seen as the main risk of a federal as opposed to centralized states. Rate increases for the 'common means' did not stop in 1583. Additionally, necessary direct taxes were levied indeed, and were even modelled on Holland's examples, as we saw. As to loan financing, its urban system seemed initially to have allowed a similar slow transition from urban to provincial credit as in Holland. No 'financial revolution' is visible however in Zeeland between 1600 and 1609. Loan financing appeared to have come completely to a halt during this decade, when tax revenues decreased. A last strong argument for the view that its decreasing total

105 *GFZ*, p. 18.

fiscal performance was due to economic problems instead of a tendency to 'free ride' is the fact that the other provinces accepted in 1612 a decrease in Zeeland's share in war expenditure and even yet another one in 1616.

Notwithstanding all this, the main conclusion of this paragraph can be, however, that a new fiscal system, similar to that which had resulted from Holland's urban system, came into existence in Zeeland since the first meeting of a 'free' States-assembly in Zeeland, mainly consisting of a collectivity of cities, just like in Holland. By means of this new fiscal system, public revenue increased from less than 100,000 guilders in 1574 to more than 1.2 million guilders in 1600. The decline to about 0.8 million guilders in 1609 does not make the fiscal performance of this new fiscal system less impressive.

The 'General Means' and the States General

The idea of 'general means' for all the Netherlands, in order to be able to realize 'general expenditure' for a collective aim, had been raised already in the States General in 1576, three years before the Union of Utrecht. In that year the States of Brabant, at the time a much more prominent and wealthy province than Holland, took the initiative for a 'free' States General assembly of the fifteen provinces not participating in the Revolt, to be held in Brussels in October 1576. The reason was that Spanish troops had started to mutiny and plunder in the Netherlands, weary of the arrears in their payments, due to the fact that much less money than before had been sent from Spain during the preceding year to pay them (see Figure 2.1).

It was decided, during the first meeting, that Holland and Zeeland had to be invited to come as well. A 'Pacification-treaty' with the two rebellious provinces was signed in the city of Ghent, on 8 November 1576, one day after the atrocious behaviour of unpaid mutinying Spanish troops in Antwerp from 4 to 7 November, during which at least about 8,000 people were killed.[106] The re-entry of Holland and Zeeland in the States General implied the re-entry of the Prince of Orange too. During this meeting it was decided that the financial committee had to draft a 'war list (*"Staat van Oorlog"* = Statement of War) (…) as had been customary in the times of Charles V' to plan the recruitment of troops and to determine the amounts which each province would have to contribute.[107] It was decided that 'general means' would have to be introduced in all provinces to provide the States General with the necessary means to pay for

106 Parker, *The Dutch Revolt.*

107 GFH, p. 387; even after 1595 they would however not be drawn up each year as sometimes the same *'Staat van Oorlog'* was used for more than one year; GFH, p. 387.

troops.[108] This decision in 1576 might very well be seen, therefore, as an initial step into the direction of an independent state consisting of *all* the seventeen provinces of the Netherlands.

To obtain the desired return of rest and order in the country as soon as possible, the money would have to be advanced by means of short-term loans in Antwerp on obligations, to be redeemed subsequently by means of the sale of annuities. Representatives of Brabant, Flanders and Hainault had already in September prepared a proposal to borrow 600,000 guilders by selling long-term annuities at an interest of 6.25 percent 'secured on the common body of the States'.[109] These interest payments would have to be realized from the revenues of the new 'general means'. The access to Antwerp bankers – an integral part of Holland's fiscal system before the Revolt – was hardly ever tried by Holland since the Revolt. The fact that this loan of 600,000 guilders was an initiative of the two economically most powerful provinces of the Netherlands was apparently sufficient for Antwerp's merchants, however, to accept obligations. Maybe the bankers' readiness to cooperate at reasonable conditions was stimulated more specifically by their own fear for mutinying soldiers, a fear that became a reality in Antwerp in November 1576. The interest rate is not mentioned.

The sale of annuities on the 'common body' of the States General in order to redeem the obligations appeared to be not easy, however. Not surprising, as the introduction in the provinces of the 'general means', from which the interests would have to be paid, appeared to be a very slow and toilsome process. In 1577 the States of Utrecht decided to accept 'general means', after they had first decided to join Holland and Zeeland in accepting the Prince of Orange again as their stadholder, but Utrecht's largest city, with the same name as the province, obstructed their actual introduction. The province of Friesland decided to join the three rebellious provinces as well. Friesland accepted the 'general means' in March 1578, but only if the other provinces would do the same. A representative of the States of Holland was sent to Gelderland, Utrecht, Friesland and Overijssel in January 1578, in order to try to convince these provinces of the desirability of the introduction of the general means to support the Prince, but no similar decision came forward from these other provinces.

108 *'que l'on pratiquera par tous les Estatz per moyens généraulx pour trouver l'argent'*; RSG, I, 121; Resoluties Staten Generaal www.inghist.nl/retroboeken/statengeneraal.

109 www.inghist.nl/retroboeken/statengeneraal RSG, I, 112: *'hipothéqué sur le commun corps desdicts éstatz'.*

In April 1578 merchants started to present Generality-obligations to the city government of Antwerp to get them paid. The States General saw no other solution, in September 1578, than to ask the cities to try to sell annuities on their own credit to redeem the obligations that might be presented to them, in order to prevent financial problems. It had evidently been impossible to sell (enough) annuities on the credit of the 'common body' of the States General-assembly as long as it had no regular tax revenues of its own.

At about the same time the new Spanish governor in the Netherlands since 1578, Alexander Farnese, the later duke of Parma, a very capable military leader, was able to convince two southern provinces, Hainault and Artois, where Protestantism had not yet really spread, to achieve a reconciliation with the king and a renewed prohibition of the protestant religion. This led to the so-called Union of Atrecht (=Arras) of these two southern provinces, that was concluded in January 1579. Very different from the Union of Utrecht (realized some days later in Utrecht) this Union of Atrecht was not the start of a new state, but only a united return of these provinces under the authority of the Spanish king. As Spanish subsidies had started to flow again to Flanders since 1577 (see Figure 2.2) this union did not have to develop a new fiscal system and to try to exploit the fiscal possibilities of its many cities.

The centralizing fiscal ambitions, as cherished by Alva, who had left the Netherlands in 1573, in order to make the Netherlands no longer dependent on Spanish subsidies, were abandoned under his successors. In the Southern Netherlands the old royal fiscal system would continue to function, based on expensive short-term advances by Antwerp bankers to the Spanish king. These advances remained secured on the silver revenues from America for war expenditure, and on the *alcabala*-taxes under the control of the Castilian cities for the interest payments on the long-term loans by means of which the obligations had to be redeemed, when the silver revenues did not cover what was needed. The continuation of the Spanish subsidies to Flanders (see Figure 2.1) would keep the tax burden much lower in this part of the Netherlands than it would become in the North. This would keep the urban system in the Southern Netherlands politically underdeveloped. The fiscal potentialities of commercialization and economic integration would not be exploited here, by the introduction of 'general means'. It may be added, that the economic decline in the Southern Netherlands of this period would have made the results probably much less impressive than in the North as well.

The existence of the two unions of Atrecht and Utrecht formed the start of the definitive separation between the northern and the southern Netherlands, which would be further consolidated by Farnese's successful reconquering of the main cities in Flanders and Brabant for Spain during the 1580s, culminating in the fall of Antwerp in 1585. Perhaps he would have been able to reconquer the northern provinces as well, if not the king's order in 1590 to go to France to support the Catholics in their civil war against the protestant Huguenots, had intervened. However, by then the capable military leadership of William of Orange's son, prince Maurice (1567–1625), and the capable political leadership of Holland's 'state-pensionary' Johan van Oldenbarnevelt (1547–1619) contributed to the consolidation of the new Republic in the North.[110]

Joint meetings in the States General of northern and southern provinces under the leadership of William of Orange, now without Artois and Hainault and some southern cities, like Valenciennes, Lille and Doornik, continued. It was this reduced States General that deposed the Spanish king in 1581, after he had outlawed the Prince of Orange in 1580, and after a high reward had been promised by the king to get him murdered. 'Statements of War' issued by this assembly have been preserved for the years 1581 and 1583. The idea of 'general means' was apparently abandoned by then, however. It was decided explicitly, in March 1583, that it should be considered as sufficient for each province to just pay its share in the war expenditure specified on these 'Statements', instead of by means of uniform taxation.[111]

The States General meeting of 1586 would be the first in which only northern provinces were present. Representatives of two Flemish cities, that had still pleaded access, were now refused. It was convened by the Earl of Leicester in the city of Utrecht. The States General had proposed to the queen of Britain to become their new sovereign after Orange had been murdered in 1584, and she had sent Leicester to be their new governor. Leicester tried in vain to effectuate a centralized government in the Northern Netherlands with Utrecht as its governmental centre, and to diminish the power of the province of Holland. As part of his centralization policy he sought again to exact the introduction of 'general means'. However, Holland's political leader Oldenbarnevelt succeeded in getting Leicester dismissed because of his lack of military successes. After this, attempts to realize *centralized* 'general means' in all provinces were nearly completely abandoned.[112]

110 Parker, *The Dutch Revolt*, p. 228.

111 *RSG* IV nr. 43 p. 182; *GFH* 32: on 21 April 1583.

112 In 1608 by the Council of State attempted once more to introduce general means at common rates in all provinces to pay for the war, in order to replace the quotas-system; it was supported by Holland and Zeeland, but not by the other provinces that feared the high tax rates in Holland; *GFZ*, p. 17.

The 'General Means' and the Provinces: Urban Resistance and Urban Acceptance

Although the other provinces of the Dutch Republic were less urbanized than Holland,[113] the influence of cities in all provinces increased after the Revolt. Initially this rendered the acceptation of the 'general means' difficult, because urban elites feared to lose urban autonomy. Gradually they would become convinced, however, that their introduction was unavoidable to realize the required increases in public revenue. The process will be summarized for each of the provinces in what follows.

The States of *Utrecht* was the only States-assembly in the Dutch Republic that had maintained all three estates with each one vote in its assembly after the Revolt, because the rich chapters of its main churches had adopted Protestantism. Nevertheless, like in Zeeland, also in Utrecht the political influence of the five cities in this province increased after the Revolt. They got four of the eight seats in the committee of deputies of the States that formed its daily board since Utrecht had joined the revolt. The city of Utrecht, by far the largest of the five cities in the province of the same name, initially obstructed the actual introduction of 'general means' and continued to pay a contribution by means of taxes levied under urban authority. This changed, however, when in September 1578 a receivers-office for the 'general means' of all the cities of the province was established in this city. Since 1583 taxes on beer and wine became provincial taxes in cities and countryside alike, and in 1601 this became also the case for the important tax on the milling of grain, and in 1602 the taxes on slaughtering, salt and horned cattle were added.[114]

In *Friesland,* the States had consisted of representatives of its three countryside-districts, grouped in three 'chambers' with each one vote. After joining the Revolt Friesland's eleven small cities – of which only Leeuwarden would become a city with more than 10,000 people around 1600 – succeeded in becoming a separate fourth 'chamber' of 22 members, two of each city, in the States. The cities also got two deputies (since 1584 three) in the daily board of deputies of the States, consisting of eight (since 1584 nine) deputies in total. This in exchange for the promise that they would contribute 11.1 percent ('one ninth') in what Friesland had to pay for the war. The representatives in

113 In Holland the number of people living in cities >2,500 increased from 27% in 1525 to 42% in 1675; for other provinces less estimates are available; in Overijssel the population of its three largest cities was 38% of total population in 1475 and 28% in 1675; by then total urban population was 43% of total population; on the Veluwe in Gelderland it was 32% in 1650; De Vries and Van der Woude, *The first modern economy*, pp. 54, 61, 67, 68.

114 *GFU*, p. 16.

the other three 'chambers' consisted of an equal number of nobles and farmers. Decisions on taxes would require the agreement of all four 'chambers'. Friesland was the only of the seven provinces with voting power in the States General in which the cities would remain a clear minority, but even here their influence had increased.

After the Union of Utrecht Friesland's cities would initially no longer consent in general provincial taxes like Holland's 'common means'. Only in 1585 the cities announced that they would agree to general taxes on milling and slaughtering, under the condition that these would be leased in the cities for cities and countryside combined. In addition, they were ready to levy more urban – not provincial – taxes on beer, wine, and salt, in order to pay their 11.1 percent in Friesland's contribution to the war. This would give them, on the one hand, some control over tax collection in the countryside, whereas, on the other hand, possible surpluses would remain under urban, instead of provincial authority. Of course the three countryside districts did not agree.

In 1586 the Earl of Leicester forced Friesland to introduce the general means. Their revenue was very modest, however, and after Leicester's departure the general means gradually disappeared again. In 1600 the country districts threatened to split the States assembly, if the cities would not comply with general means leased by the provincial government. The States General sent a committee of representatives from other provinces to convince Friesland of the urgent need to comply. It proposed concessions to both parties: for the cities the acceptance of the general means would suffice to pay their share in Friesland's contribution to the Union; for the country districts the tax on horned cattle could be replaced by an increase in the tax on lands. This was a very important concession to the representative of the countryside, in a province famous for its husbandry, which reflected the maintenance of their majority position in the States, despite a relatively great number of cities.[115] In this way the introduction of general means in Friesland would become a fact in 1602.[116] Only in 1632 the province felt forced to accept the introduction of the important tax on horned cattle, however, which had been accepted in the other province as part of the 'general means' mostly already three decades earlier, which shows the power of the countryside.[117]

115 H. Spanninga, *Gulden Vrijheid? Politieke cultuur en staatsvorming in Friesland, 1600–1640* (Hilversum, Verloren, 2012) p. 103: in no other province the political influence of the cities was so small, despite the fact that it was more urbanized than most of the other provinces.

116 *GFF*, pp. 13–24 offers much more details on the struggle for the 'general means'.

117 *GFF*, pp. 169–173; not as part of the 'general means', but as part of a number of direct taxes, together with a poll tax, a hearth tax and a tax on horses.

In *Overijssel* the first failed attempt to introduce the general means dated from 1579. Resistance from its main city, Zwolle, postponed a new attempt to 1582, which failed again. All cities now argued that they needed the receipts of the urban taxes on wines, beers, meat, milling, salt and soap for debt service on their urban loans. Despite continuing resistance by Zwolle, the States of Overijssel decided to start the farming of provincial general means in 1600. The cities of Deventer and Kampen refused to cooperate in tax farming on behalf of the province, if not Zwolle would do the same. In 1601 Zwolle submitted and provincial general means could be definitively introduced in Overijssel as well.[118]

The small province of *Drenthe*, which contained no cities and would not obtain voting rights in the States General, had to contribute 1 percent to war expenditure to be protected by the States General. When it remained slack in paying its due, the States General demanded the States of Drenthe to introduce the general means. In 1600 the States of Drenthe, consisting of representatives of the landowning farmers having two votes and the nobility having one vote, decided to yield to the pressure.

Not much information has been preserved on public finance in the province of *Gelderland*, consisting of three fiscally autonomous quarters each dominated by one city. But it is known that 'general means' were leased in the quarter of Nijmegen at least since 1594.[119] Moreover it is known that the States assembly of the quarter of Zutphen after the revolt consisted of five cities with each one vote and the nobility with only one vote, and that half of the six deputies responsible for fiscal affairs were representatives of the cities. The composition of the States assembly of the quarter of Veluwe, also containing five cities, with Arnhem as the main city, was similar. None of the cities in Gelderland counted ever more than 10,000 inhabitants during the time of the Republic, except Nijmegen which had about 12,000 inhabitants since 1550. The general means were probably introduced in all three quarters soon after they were reconquered on the Spanish by the troops of the States General in the course of the 1590s.

Groningen was different from the other provinces, firstly, because there was only one city in this province, no collectivity of cities; secondly, because the States General intervened militarily to force this province to accept a fiscal system producing enough revenue for its contribution. The city had, similar to

118 *GFO*, p. 16.

119 Gelders Archief, arch.nr. 0508, inv.nr. 366 mentions a decision to lease the general means on 16 February 1594; http://www.geldersarchief.nl/. Introduction to the inventories of the archives of each of the three quarters by K.W. Peeneman.

Utrecht, the same name as the province, that was itself often just called *Stad en Lande* (= City and Countryside). Having about 19,000 inhabitants in 1550 as well as in 1600 it was by far the largest city in the whole northern part of the Republic. After the re-conquest of this city on the Spanish in 1594 the province was forced to accept the leasing of the general means by a committee sent by the States General.

After this committee had left, the city government put the tax farmers accepted by the States General in jail and started in 1596 to lease the taxes themselves at their own conditions. Necessary increases were since then realized by just increasing the rates on horned cattle, not on the other general means. Whereas the tax on horned cattle had been good for 30 to 40 percent of the general means revenue in 1594 and 1595, in the next years this increased to 50 to 65 percent.[120] Of course the countryside was furious. It had proposed an increase in the direct tax on land *and* houses instead, which would burden the city as well. When arrears in tax collection started to occur, because of the internal differences between City and Countryside, the States General at last decided to intervene. Troops were sent to the province. A fortress with cannons was built near one of the city gates and new city governors were appointed by the stadholder.[121]

The result was that tax revenues in Groningen increased from about 400,000 guilders in the years 1599 and 1600, to about 550,000 guilders in 1601 and 1602. Payments in its 'generality' expenditure for the war increased from about 350,000 guilders to 460,000 guilders. Direct taxes on land and houses had been introduced to this end, as had been done in all the other provinces when the 'general (common) means' failed to produce enough revenue. The extreme increases in the tax on horned cattle until 1600 were reduced to about 45 percent of the total revenue general means during the next decade.

The internationally famous Dutch political theorist and law scholar, Hugo Grotius (1583–1645), would disqualify this military action against Groningen later as 'bitter and unusual among free people'.[122] From the perspective of the

120 *GFG*, pp. 150–151, Table III.4.1 column (3).

121 *GFG*, p. 15; J.v.d. Broek, *Groningen, een stad apart. Over het verleden van een eigenzinnige stad* (Assen 2007) pp. 154–156.

122 Quoted by Broek, *Groningen*, p. 155 from a Dutch translation of Grotius' *Annales et historiae de rebus Belgicis* (Amsterdam 1657): *Hugo de Groots Nederlandtsche Jaerboeken en Historien, sedert het jaer* MDLV *tot het jaer* MDCIX; *met de belegering der stadt Grol en den aenkleven des jaers* MDCXXVII; *als ook het Tractaet van de Batavische nu Hollandtsche Republyk en de vrye zeevaert* [...] *alles vertaelt door Joan Goris* (Amsterdam 1681) p. 407: *'Om dees tijdt heeft de langduerighe halsterrigheit der stadt Gröninghen, welkers benijders de niet*

process of state formation, it might perhaps be qualified, however, as a successful sanction by the central state organ of the young federal state that was sufficient to end the stalemate between the two parties in the province which prevented the coming into existence of the fiscal system required to increase its public revenue. It sufficed to convince the city of Groningen that it had to resign for the future in what was evidently unavoidable for partners in this federal state. Since then only Drenthe was once threatened by the States General that it would take its governing elite as hostage to enforce the payment of arrears.[123] Among the seven provinces with voting rights persuasion would be the only instrument used to try to convince each other of necessary improvements in payment-behaviour.

We may conclude that in all provinces cities feared the encroachment on their urban fiscal autonomy to be expected from the introduction of 'general means' and that in nearly all provinces the political influence of cities increased since the Revolt. By the early seventeenth century, however, they had become convinced that it was necessary to resign to the introduction of *provincial* 'general means' in the Dutch Republic to exploit the fiscal potentials of its commercialized territory if they wanted the military protection of the Union.

The general means became the most important part of the provincial tax systems in all provinces, with the exception of Friesland. Only in Friesland direct taxes on land and houses remained the largest source of public revenue (70 percent or more during the period until 1609). In all other provinces, the general means yielded more than 50 percent of total revenue both in the decade before and after 1600.[124]

The tax systems of the provinces became far from identical, however. Many taxes were not (yet) levied in all provinces, but only in some; much more taxes would remain levied only in some, or even in only one of them. An Appendix at the end of this book offers an overview of all taxes ever levied during the Dutch Republic showing that the total number of taxes varied in the end from 24 in Drenthe and Gelre to 58 in Holland, showing a number of taxes above

onreghtveerdighe gramschap meerder gaende maekten, d'andere Staeten der Vereenighde Nederlanden bewooghen een seer scherp, en onder vrye volken naeulijx gebruykelijk, besluyt te neemen'. I owe thank to Jan van den Broek for his friendly information.

123 Fritschy, 'Schulden als leerschool?', p. 13.

124 Holland 66% (1578–99) and 56% (1600–09); Zeeland 70% (1578–99) and 53% (1600–09); Groningen 51% (1601–09); Utrecht 60% (1585–95); Overijssel 65% (1604); Drenthe 56% (1603–09).

TABLE 2.5 *Provincial tax rates on domestic beer in pubs, 1583–1609 (guilders per ton).*

	Holland	Zeeland	Utrecht	Friesland	Groningen	Overijssel
1583	2.2	2.2				
1595					1.5	
1597			1.2			
1598						1
1601			1.9			
1602				1	1.6	
1603						0.9
1605	2.7			1.2		

Sources: *GFH* p. 306, *GFZ* p. 156, *GFU* p. 116, *GFF* p. 120, *GFG* p. 210, *GFO* p. 178.

average in Zeeland (43), Utrecht (41) and Friesland (39), and below average in Groningen (33), Brabant (31), and Overijssel (30).

The rates at which taxes were levied could be very different moreover, as shown, for example, in Table 2.5 for the in those years still important tax on beer for publicans (*tappersaccijns*), for the period before 1610.

In Holland and Zeeland the levying of the 'common means' had been a precondition for the additional development of a system of provincial public loans. In the other provinces, however, revenue from loans by means of the sale of provincial annuities does not seem to have been very well possible before 1610. It obviously took some time, after the introduction of the general means, before people trusted their provincial governments as to their ability to pay interests regularly. The decision in 1616 of the States General to redeem a large British loan (to be further discussed in the last section of this chapter) was a main cause to try the realization of domestic provincial loans in many provinces. Until then provincial governments remained dependent for loan revenue on the credit of individual cities in their province. A further discussion of provincial loans in the other province will follow in Chapter 3.

The 'Quotas-system' and the Fiscal Performance of the Provinces

Anyhow, whereas the cities in all provinces had to accept a loss of urban autonomy by the acceptance of provincial 'general means', the provinces succeeded in maintaining their fiscal autonomy. This meant that a distributive key had to be employed to determine the sums each province had to pay in the total sum for war faring thought necessary by the States General. Table 2.6 offers an overview of the varying shares for each of the provinces in the course of time.

TABLE 2.6 *The quotas-system, 1570–1616.*

	1570	1575	1585	1586	1595	1612	1616	1616	1616
							gld-st-p		incl. Drenthe
Holland		77.5%	66.5%	64.3	59.8%	57.1%	58-6-2¼	58.31%	57.73%
Zeeland	1/4 of Holl.	22.5%	13.6%	15.8%	14.7%	11%	9-3-8	9.18%	9.09%
Utrecht	1/10 of Holl.		6.7%	6.7%	6.2%	5.7%	5-16-7½	5.83%	5.77%
Friesland	1/5 of Holl.		13.3%	13.3%	12.4%	11.4%	11-13-2¾	11.66%	11.55%
Stad&Lande (Groningen)	1/10 of Holl.				7.0%	5.7%	5-16-7½	5.83	5.77%
Gelre (Gelderland)						5.5%	5-12-3	5.61%	5.56%
Overijssel						3.5%	3-11-5	3.57%	3.54%
		100%	100%	100%	100%	100%	100-0-0	100%	
Drenthe						1%	1-0-0		0.99%
									100%

Sources: Grapperhaus, *Alva*, 27; NA, Raad van State 1.01.19 inv.nr. 1226; Zwitzer'*De militie van den staat*,' pp. 66–69; *GFZ*, p. 17; *GFO*, pp. 13–14.

The shares were called the 'quotas' (*quoten*), the system as a whole can be called the 'quotas-system'. At the time the quotas were not expressed as percentages, but as an amount in guilders, stivers and pennies, which each of the province would have to pay in each amount of 100 guilders thought necessary for general expenditure. Drenthe had to pay one guilder on top of each 100 guilders, in which the other seven provinces had consented, as is shown in the last column. (This explains why Holland quota is mostly given as 58.3 percent, although it was 57.7 percent if Drenthe is included.)

The table shows that, for Zeeland, Utrecht, Friesland and Groningen, the shares before the Revolt as used by Alva in 1570 were the initial norm. Whereas Zeeland's quota was adapted, in the course of time before 1616, and even between 1621 and 1635, this was not the case for Utrecht, Friesland and Groningen, which after some small changes became again exactly in conformity with the distributive shares used by Alva of resp. 1/10, 1/5 and 1/10 of Holland, in 1616.

The other quotas were, like that of Zeeland, a compromise between what these provinces regarded as reasonable themselves and what the other provinces thought acceptable. Overijssel's share for instance had been a fixed amount per month in 1580, which was increased in 1584 and 1597. In 1602 it wanted to be set at a quota of 2 percent, whereas the other provinces thought

4 percent more reasonable. It paid in fact 2.25 percent during several years, but agreed in 1611 to 3 percent, in 1612 to 3.5 percent. As it suffered relatively heavy under the resumption of the war after the end of the Truce in 1621, a temporary reduction to 2.25 percent was accorded since then until 1635.

Similarly, Zeeland would be allowed a temporary reduction with 2 percent after the end of the Truce. However, since 1635 the quotas-system of 1616 would function again and it would remain unchanged until 1792. To prevent the quotas-system to become a divisive element it was apparently simply avoided to reconsider it again until then. In view of the lack of data on relative wealth and population it is impossible to determine to what extent the quotas were in conformity with the relative tax bearing capacity of the provinces.

One evident conclusion from Table 2.6 is that Holland had always to be by far the most important contributor to common war expenditure. Another evident conclusion is, however, that the 42 percent to be provided by the other provinces was yet by no means negligible. This made their actual 'performance' an important element of the fiscal system of the Dutch Republic.

The quotas-system did not imply that the provinces transferred the total amounts of the amounts they were supposed to contribute to the general treasury of the Republic. Right from the start in 1579 the 'Statements of War' contained lists of infantry and cavalry per province, specifying exactly which companies had to be paid by which province, naming the captain and the number of men, and the required amounts of money.[125] Army captains received payment ordnances assigned to tax receivers in the different provinces in conformity to the repartition of war expenditure across the provinces.[126] During peace years the garrisons were largely garrisoned in the provinces that paid them. The treasurer-general of the Generality had to keep track of the degree to which the war expenditure in which the provinces had consented was actually realized,[127] but the most important payments were not done from the treasury of the Generality, but by the provincial tax-receivers.

125 NA, Raad van State 1.01.19 inv.nr. 1226: *'Staet int corte van het voetvolck ende paertvolck mitsgaders de repartitie van deselvige op de provincien'* voor het jaar 1579; Holland 80,000 pounds (=guilders), Zeeland, 20,000, Friesland 24,000, Utrecht 12,000, Ommelanden (=countryside of Groningen) 16,000, de stad Groningen 2,000, het land van Wedde 6000, and Gelderland 40,000 in a total of 200,000 guilders.

126 Zwitzer, *'De militie van den staat'*, p. 206 shows a copy of such an ordnance dating from 1773 in which Zeeland's provincial government orders Zeeland's general receiver in Middelburg to hand over the pay for one month of 42 days to a certain captain for the 55 heads of his company in exchange for a quittance.

127 R. Sprenger, 'De thesaurier-generaal aan zijn bureau en op dienstreis', in: *Van tresorier tot thesaurier-generaal. Zes eeuwen financieel beleid in handen van een hoge Nederlandse ambtsdrager*, ed. J. de Smidt e.a. (Hilversum, Verloren, 1996) pp. 137–222,p. 156.

TABLE 2.7 *Contribution of the other provinces to war expenditure compared to Holland and the quotas, 1586–1609.*

Periods for which data were available	Average annual amount spent on war (glds)	Average annual amount spent on war (glds)	Column c as % of column b	Quota as % of Holland's quota	Column d as % of column e
a	b	c	d	e	f
	Holland	Zeeland			
1586–1599	2,444,120	672,898	27.5%	24.6%	112%
1600–1609	4,948,222	832,932	16.8%	24.6%	68%
		Groningen			
1596–1599	3,263,537	308,731	9.5%	11.7%	81%
1600–1609	4,948,222	464,717	9.3%	11.7%	79%
		Friesland			
1593–1596	2,444,870	697,606	28.5%	20.7%	138%
1604–1605	5,182,289	805,313	15.5%	20.7%	75%
		Utrecht			
1589–1592	1,723,879	143,645	8.3%	10.4%	80%
1594–1597	2,650,648	190,066	7.2%	10.4%	69%

Table 2.7 offers an attempt to evaluate to what degree the provinces lived up to what was expected of them in comparison to Holland. For an answer to this question no estimates of war expenditure could be used of course. The table had to be restricted to the provinces and the years for which archival data were available on the amounts really spent on war before the Truce of 1609, and preferably for a continuous number of years, to enable an elimination of accidental fluctuations on a year to year basis as much as possible.

Column f in Table 2.7 shows that Zeeland and Friesland actually contributed more than they had to (>100 percent) before 1600, but that this markedly changed after 1600. The table also shows that this was not due to the fact that they started to pay less than before (see column c), but to the even larger increases in war expenditure in Holland (column b). According to Holland's own calculations it paid on average about 4 percent more than it had promised to the States General, during the years 1595–99, 5.5 percent more during the years 1600–1609.[128] The other provinces seem to have paid increasingly less than they were supposed to.

128 *GFH*, pp. 192, 390 Tabel IV column a and f.

The decreasing percentages paid by the other provinces in proportion to Holland (column f) despite the increasing absolute amounts (column c) are a second sign that a Truce was becoming desirable for financial reasons in 1609, just like the decreasing distance between the amount Holland borrowed per year and the amount of its interest burden per year (Table 2.4).

2.4 The Financial Scope of the 'Generality'

As a result of the fiscal autonomy of the provinces and the maintenance of a quotas-system for war finance the central level of the new state – the 'Generality' – was primarily important for the planning and coordination of war expenditure. However, apart from the taxes and loans realized by the provinces to fulfil their quotas, also some central sources of public revenue that contributed to the high level of Dutch public finance became available during the formation period of the fiscal system of the Dutch Republic. They consisted at the start of the Revolt of (1) the confiscation of royal domains and the confiscation of ecclesiastical and other property in the Netherlands, (2) foreign subsidies, (3) some Generality-taxes (4) loans issued by the General Receiver of the Generality; n addition, (5) customs were introduced as a new form of centralized public revenue, collected and administered by five admiralties spread over three provinces (Zeeland, Holland and Friesland) that were accountable to the Generality.

Figure 2.4 offers an impression of the relative importance of the main central sources of revenue in comparison to the revenues of the provinces, based on a limited amount of data complemented with estimates.

It shows that, far from counteracting the disquieting tendencies in the public finance of the provinces, the importance of centralized sources of public revenue decreased during the first decades. Besides, it offers yet another indication that the start of the Twelve Years' Truce can be seen as the end of the formation period of the fiscal system of the Dutch Republic. By 1609 not only 'common' or 'general means' are accepted in all provinces, and by then Holland's provincial credit was restored, but also foreign subsidies, that were until then a rather important part of the centralized revenue-sources, came to an end. Each of the main different elements of Generality revenue will be shortly discussed in what follows.

Former Royal Domains and Other Confiscated Property as Sources of Public Revenue

Article v of the Union of Utrecht not only mentioned the introduction of 'general means' for the financing of wars. Also the revenue of the former royal

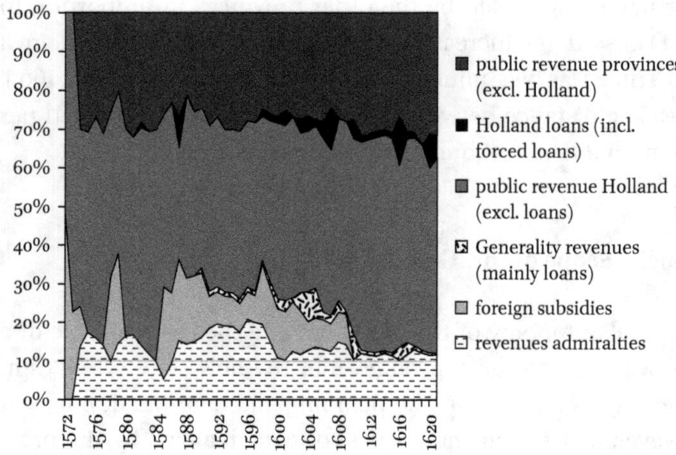

FIGURE 2.4 *Relative importance of centralized and provincial sources of public revenue in the Dutch Republic, 1572–1621.*

domains, after deduction of expenses charged on them, should accrue to the Generality to this end, according to the same article.[129] The drafters of the Union may not yet have been aware of the fact that this source of public revenue was no longer really significant in the Habsburg Netherlands during the years before the Revolt. This was partly due to sales of domain lands, partly to the fact that loans had been negotiated on their security, resulting in debt service that had to be deducted from total domain revenue to arrive at the net revenue for the general treasury. Their declining relative importance was related to the general tendency in West-European state finance in the early modern period, towards a much larger importance for tax and loan revenue when total amounts increased.[130] Table 2.8 shows that the amounts for domain surpluses for the years 1567 and 1569 constituted 12 to 14 percent of the sum of the ordinary revenues of *beden* and domains in those years (column a). In 1570 and 1571 this was reduced to no more than about 3 percent due to the large increases in *beden* revenues by means of taxes and loans realized by Alva. As a percentage of total public finance the share of the domains in total was already even only 3 percent since 1567.

129 '(…) *dat men oock hier toe imployeeren sal den incomen vande domainen van Concklicke Majesteyt die lasten daer op staende afgetogen*'; Groenveld, *De Unie van Utrecht*, p. 32; https://nl.wikisource.org/wiki/Unie_van_Utrecht#V.

130 Ormrod, Bonney and Bonney, 'Introduction', in: *Crises, Revolutions and Self-Sustained Growth*, pp. 4–8.

TABLE 2.8 *Revenue of the royal central treasury in Brussels, 1566-1576.*

	Domains	***beden***		**Sale of domains and annuities**	**Remaining revenue**	**Total received from the Netherlands**	**Spanish subsidies for the army in Flanders**	
	a	b	c = a/ (a + b)	d	e = f – (a + b + d)	f	g	h = a/ (f + g)
1566						618,192	8,86,162	
1567	75,845	450,432	14%	103,094	221,931	851,302	1,596,620	3%
1568							3,673,615	
1569	118,432	838,879	12%	50,094	1,171,189	2,178,594	3,462,208	2%
1570	121,479	3,610,065	3%	16,032	124,289	3,871,865	881,379	3%
1571	121,479	3,610,065	3%	16,032	1,190,351	4,937,927	229,999	2%
1572		443,211		12,334	379,237	834,782	3,419,042	
1573						980,813	3,491,196	
1574						1,300,430	7,357,730	
1575						2,226,764	4,957,661	
1576						1,819,284	1,679,249	

Sources: Columns a,b,d: Grapperhaus, *Alva*, p. 122; columns f,g: Parker, *Army of Flanders*, p. 250. (Grapperhaus' data are based on Craeybeckx who used Flemish sources; Parker used also Spanish sources).

Not only interests on old debts hypothecated on the domains, but also salaries of provincial juridical offices that continued to exist, had to be paid from the revenues of the domains.[131] This will have been an important reason why their management was in practice taken over by the provincial governments after the Revolt, despite article V of the Union of Utrecht.[132]

The confiscation of the property of catholic churches and monasteries during the early phases of the Revolt created new forms of revenue-generating

131 W. Fritschy, 'Domeinen en financieel beleid in Overijssel', in: *Doel en middel : aspecten van financieel overheidsbeleid in de Nederlanden van de zestiende eeuw tot heden*, eds. W. Fritschy, J.K.T. Postma & J. Roelevink shows attempts to improve the fiscal performance of the domains during the second half of the seventeen the century in Overijssel.

132 These forms of public revenue were in fact part of the provincial financial administrations, therefore (they are subsumed in the database under 'other revenue'); it has been preferred to discuss them in this chapter, however; the royal domains, because of their origin, the other forms of confiscated property, because of their similar character.

public property. The new States of Holland started to sell gold and silver chalices from catholic churches to contribute to the payment of the prince's army immediately in July 1572,[133] and explicitly prohibited the looting of catholic churches and houses of those loyal to the king of Spain in August 1572, in order to preserve them for the financial needs of the province.[134] According to K. Swart the income of Catholic landed property was to a large extent used to finance the war from 1572 to 1576.[135] Also property of wealthy persons loyal to Spain who had fled the country was confiscated. In November 1574 sale of 'annotated property', the term that referred to confiscated property of private persons, was suggested in the States as a possibility to cover deficits as an alternative for raising the rates of taxes.[136] Tracy even suggested once that 'emigré and ecclesiastical property' played possibly 'an important if not precisely quantifiable' role as 'the sheet-anchor of Holland's public finance' during the years 1572–1584.[137] He suggested that the disposal of this property prevented Holland's unpaid debts from mounting to an 'unmanageable level' and mentions examples of the redemption of debts from this revenue source, however only for relatively small amounts, like 10,000 and 50,000 guilders.[138]

In 1582 the States of Holland handed over some confiscated real property, belonging to a noble woman who had fled to Spain, indeed, to the family of Ernst van Mandersloo, one of the army enterprisers that had put faith in the obligation of the States of Holland of 500,000 guilders of 4 August 1572. We also saw, however, in Chapter 1 that the final settlement of still more than 100,000 guilders of the debt to Mandersloo had to be postponed to as late as 1599. It took then the form of a payment in annuities, which may indicate that there was not enough confiscated property to redeem even this first debt contracted by Holland's new 'free' States.[139]

133 According to Swart, *Willem van Oranje*, p. 44 this was done in July 1572.

134 Tracy, J.D., 'Emigré and ecclesiastical property as the sheet-anchor of Holland's finance, 1572–1584', in P. Benedict et al., eds., *Reformation, revolt and civil war in France and the Netherlands, 1555–1585* (Amsterdam, 1999) 255–266.

135 Swart, *William of Orange*, 37 referring to Res. Holland 1572–4, pp. 20–22 (edict of 10 Febr. 1573), J.F. van Beeck Calkoen, *Onderzoek naar de rechtstoestand der geestelijke en kerkelijke goederen in Holland na de reformatie* (Amsterdam 1910), 41 223–224 and De Jonge van Ellemeet, *Geschiedkundig onderzoek.*

136 Memorie1755, f17r; http://www.historici.nl/Onderzoek/Projecten/GewestelijkeFinancien/memorie.

137 Tracy, 'Emigré and ecclesiastical property'.

138 Tracy, *The founding of the Dutch* Republic, p. 109.

139 Fritschy, 'A "financial revolution" reconsidered', p. 62; already on 11-7-1568 Mandersloo had offered his services to the prince of Orange; in a letter of 14-7-1571 he warned him that Alva

Most ecclesiastical property was probably just left to the cities to compensate them for their financial sacrifices during the early stages of the Revolt,[140] although a formal resolution to this end was only taken on 23 May 1577. A famous example, which was effectuated already somewhat earlier, is the city of Leyden, where a university was established in 1575. The buildings in which it was housed in the first years of its existence, first the cloister of St. Barbara, later one of the White Nuns in this city, were both given to the city by the prince of Orange to this end, who was apparently seen as entitled to do so as the leader of the victorious army. He allowed the city, moreover, to finance the functioning of the new university by means of the revenues of the rich abbey of Egmond in North-Holland. Other early examples of leaving confiscated property to the cities are the monasteries that were changed into 'court buildings' for the prince of Orange, where he could be housed with his court during a stay in these cities. They became what is called a *Prinsenhof*. Buildings bearing this name can still be found in cities like Delft, Rotterdam, Amsterdam, but also outside Holland in Leeuwarden, Groningen and Middelburg.

Curious examples are, lastly, the *'Haagse Bos'* (= The Hague's Wood) and the 'Malieveld' in The Hague. When it became known in 1576 that the States of Holland intended to sell these terrains to use the receipt to make up for army deficits, the inhabitants of The Hague objected. William of Orange came to their help and was able to enact a formal decision prohibiting their sale forever, a decision that would yet in 2010 prevent an attempt by the Dutch government to sell them.[141] In short, the literature seems to offer at least as much examples of ecclesiastical and émigré property in Holland that could *not* be used to finance the war, as the reverse.

Regarding ecclesiastical and monastery estates the general decision was in all provinces that they had to be used for pious uses (*ad pios usos*): mainly for salaries to Calvinist ministers and schoolmasters and for poor relief, but also for the livelihood of remaining monastics, and even for allowances to unmarried noble ladies who were now deprived of their possibility to enter a monastery. The revenues do not seem to have been really abundant anyhow. In Holland the office in Delft that was established to administer the former ecclesiastical

---

was recruiting cavalerists; on 26-6-1572 he asked Orange money for the cavalerists he recruited for him; on 27-7-1572 he informed him that Alva had placed orders in Neurenberg for the equipment of 6,000 men; he suggested to confiscate it during its river transport.

140 Also Tracy, *The Founding of the Dutch Republic*, p. 111.

141 Daily newspaper *Trouw* on 30. October 2010: *'Willem van Oranje dwarsboomt natuurplan Rutte'.*

TABLE 2.9 *Role of sales of ecclesiastical and other property in public revenue, 1574–1609 (average amount in guilders and as % total provincial revenue).*

	Zeeland	%	Friesland	%	Overijssel	%
1574–79	96,941	20%				
1589/90	6,641	5%	60,054	8%		
1593–96	2,255	2%	60,560	8%		
1604–05			20,000	2%		
1617–18					21,945	7%
1619–21			272,553	19%		

and monastery properties in this province had from the very beginning to be subsidized to be able to do the necessary payments to Calvinist ministers. This was done by granting it half of the so-called 'ration money' (*rantsoenpenningen*) on the 'common means': a surcharge of 5 percent to be paid by the tax farmers on the lease sum, earmarked for this kind of expenditure.[142] In 1656 this subsidy furnished nearly half, in 1790 more than three quarters of the revenue of this office. This underlines again the lack of importance of ecclesiastical properties as a source of revenue for public expenditure in Holland.

Somewhat more quantitative information is available for the other provinces than for Holland, on the role of the sale of immoveable property for war financing during the first decades of the Revolt. Table 2.9 shows that this role could be incidentally relatively important indeed (at least in proportion to provincial totals), more specifically in Zeeland during the 1570s, and in Friesland in the years just before the end of the Twelve Years' Truce.

Nevertheless, also in Zeeland and Friesland, most former Roman Catholic properties became a source of revenue to pay the ministers in the Calvinist churches salaries instead of being sold for war financing.[143]

In the course of the seventeenth and eighteenth century, domains and former ecclesiastical properties would be sold on a somewhat larger scale. As far as we know the financial results were only really impressive in Friesland. In 1644 the complete Frisian provincial debt could be redeemed after a series of sales of former monastery properties in 1639, 1640 and 1644 which provided a

142 The other half was earmarked for the expenses of tax leasing and as the 'penny for the poor' to be spent locally.

143 Enthoven, *Zeeland en de opkomst van de Republiek*, pp. 35–36.

TABLE 2.10 *Revenue of domains and former ecclesiastical goods before deduction of expenditure, 1600–1790 (a: glds; b: % of total provincial revenue).*

a	Holland	Zeeland	Utrecht	Groningen	Friesland	Overijssel	Drente
ca. 1600		207,000		94,000	98,000	57,000	
ca. 1650	530,000*	225,000	200,000	187,000			28,000
ca. 1700		228,000		94,000		80,000	
ca. 1750		191,000	112,000	91,000	46,000		
ca. 1790	400,000*	178,000		32,000	93,000	77,000	17,000
b	**Holland**	**Zeeland**	**Utrecht**	**Groningen**	**Friesland**	**Overijssel**	**Drente**
ca. 1600		14%		11%	7%	13%	
ca. 1650	5%	16%	17%	11%			15%
ca. 1700		10%		5%		9%	
ca. 1750		6%	7%	6%	2%		
ca. 1790	2%	6%		1%	3%	9%	6%

* After deduction of provincial subsidy out of 'ration-money'.
Sources: *GFH* p. 56; *GFZ* p. 26, *GFU* pp. 22–23, *GFG* p. 30, *GFF* p. 32, *GFO* p. 57, *GFD* p. 29.

total amount of no less than about six million guilders.[144] In the years 1752–1765 sales for another amount of about 1.8 million guilders in total would be realized. In Holland results of sales during the 1720s appeared in the provincial administration in 1731–35 for a total amount of 2.3 million guilders, in Overijssel in 1711–18 for about 0.2 million guilders.

Table 2.10 gives an impression of the amounts of the revenues of this type of public properties before deduction of the expenditures with which they were charged, during the seventeenth and eighteenth centuries.[145]

It shows that in provinces outside Holland this type of public revenue was certainly of some importance during most of the seventeenth century, although decreasingly so in the course of time. In Holland this was apparently less the case. As Holland's public finance amounted to at least about 60 percent

144 Spanninga, *Gulden vrijheid?*, pp. 357, 364; 4,295,020 goldguilders = about 6 million (Carolus)guilders.

145 In Holland in 1710 about 35% of the 401,615 guilders in revenues from former royal domains had to be spent on interests, about 30% on salaries to provincial juridical officials; *GFH*, p. 52.

of the public finance of the Dutch Republic as a whole, the conclusion can be, that, at least since 1577, real property acquired by the provinces after the start of the Revolt by means of confiscation did not play an important part, neither in the financing of the Dutch war against Spain nor in the revenue system of the Dutch Republic as a whole.

Foreign Financial Support

The Prince of Orange had been very well aware of the fact that it would be hard to compete with the Spanish army on the basis of only Holland's tax revenue and that of confiscated real property, without external financial help. He succeeded in convincing the Queen of Britain to provide an amount of about 300,000 guilders for his war against Spain already in 1572. The Queen withdrew this early support, however, because of the complaints of British merchants about the activities of Dutch privateers.[146]

Parker found indications that moreover 'possibly as much as 200,000 florins a month' reached Orange from France throughout 1573 and the early months of 1574. He also mentioned other information, however, suggesting a total from France of no more than about 250,000 to 300,000 guilders in all during these years.[147] This seems more likely in view of the fact that Holland had felt forced to devalue its money in 1573 to obtain funds to pay Orange's soldiers. Swart reports in his biography of William of Orange that France remitted 180,000 guilders to Louis of Nassau in 1573 and he makes no further mention of French subsidies in these early years. Between 1598 and 1610, however, more than 10 million guilders – perhaps even more than 12 million guilders – came from France to support the Dutch Revolt against the common enemy Spain.[148]

146 Glawischnig, R., *Niederlande, Kalvinismus und Reichsgrafenstand : 1559–1584 : Nassau-Dillenburg unter Graf Johann VI* (Marburg 1973).94; Parker, *The Dutch Revolt,* 148 even has an amount of 0.6 millions guilders; according to Glawischnig this was the debt including accumulated interest arrears during the following decade.

147 Parker, *Dutch Revolt,* p. 149 mentions 0.1 million écus; according to Posthumus, N.W., *Inquiry into the history of prices in Holland. I. Wholesale prices at the Exchange of Amsterdam, 1585–1914, rates of exchange at Amsterdam, 1609–1914* (Leiden, Brill, 1964) p. 583, 1 écu = 100 'groten' and 1 'groot' = 0.025 guilder; however he also mentions a rate of 125 groten in 1619 and of 104 groten in 1648 (pp. 585 and 590).

148 Parker, *The Dutch Revolt*, p. 217; idem, *The emergence of modern finance in Europe 1500–1730* (London, Collins, 1973)p. 565; A. van der Woude, 'De Staten, Leicester en Elizabeth in financiële verwikkelingen', *Tijdschrift voor Geschiedenis*, 74 (1961), pp. 64–82, p. 71n39; W.A. Shaw, *Report on the manuscripts of Lord De Lisle and Dudley preserved at Penshurst Place* (Hist. MSS. Comm., Rep. No. 77), III (1936), p. XLV.

In 1578–9 Elizabeth I of England became again convinced of the usefulness of support to the Dutch Revolt against Spain and supplied the significant amount of one million guilders. Between 1585 and 1603 she provided support for in total nearly fifteen million guilders in loans, the annual average in the period 1585–90 being 1.2 million guilders per year, in the period 1591–1603 about 0.6 million guilders per year. The Prince had been obliged to give the Queen the port cities of Vlissingen, Brielle and Breskens in pawn for the loans from Britain.[149] About 4.4 million guilders of these loans was redeemed during the years 1599–1601 and 1611–1615. In 1616/7 the last 6.2 million to redeem these cities was repaid by the States General, mostly financed by the sale of annuities on the domestic capital market in all provinces.[150]

The average amount in foreign loans and subsidies had been probably about as much as 23 percent of estimated average war expenditure of the Dutch Republic during the years 1585–1590 and about 10 percent on average during the years 1591–1610: a very welcome, but in comparison to other sources of revenue for war expenditure a rather modest addition all the same.

Generality Taxes

Some Generality taxes were introduced during the 1580s to guarantee the interest payment on the British loan, to be levied in all provinces. A 'Generality-tax' on salt, used to this end until 1616, existed until 1640. In 1622 Holland announced that it would no longer hand over the revenue of this to the Receiver General of the Union if not all other provinces did so.[151] It was officially changed by Holland into a provincial tax in 1640, and was no longer levied in other provinces already before.[152] In addition 'Generality taxes' on beer and soap were levied for debt service on the British loans since the 1580s until 1616.

In view of the size of the British loan of about 15 million guilders the amounts involved in the taxes earmarked for the interest payments must have

149 Fritschy, 'A "financial revolution" reconsidered', p. 67 note 43.

150 National Archives, Raad van State, 1.01.10, inv.nr. 2115I ('Liquidatie met de provintien ter saeke van de versogte consenten') redemption-payments to Britain are to be found for the years 1599–1601 and 1611–1617 for a total amount of 10.581.928 guilders; 6.157.300 guilders in total in the years 1616/7.

151 M. 't Hart, 'Salt tax and salt trade in the Low Countries', in: *Le roi, le marchand et le sel*, J.C. Hocquet ed. (Lille 1987) pp. 293–315, pp. 302–303.

152 A.Th. van Deursen, 'Tussen eenheid en zelfstandigheid', in: *De Unie van Utrecht*, ed. Groenveld, pp. 136–154, p. 146; according to F. Sickenga, *Bijdrage tot de geschiedenis der belastingen* (Amsterdam 1864) p. 114 it had been only levied in fact in Holland, Friesland, Overijssel en Groningen.

been rather considerable; the interest rate on this loan is not known, however. These revenues were probably administered as part of the public finance of the provinces before they were transferred to the Receiver-General of the Generality. No estimate for these revenues has been added, therefore, to that of the Generality to avoid double counting. This foreign loan was, as far as known, the only loan, for the interest payments on which special taxes were explicitly earmarked, whereas the credit of domestic provincial loans, was always based on the total revenue of the provincial tax receivers

Since 1635 a Generality stamp tax would be levied, probably because by then stamp taxes were levied in some provinces as well, in Holland already since 1624, and because it seemed unreasonable to leave Generality-documents tax free. Its revenue, as far as known, was very insignificant: about 12,000 guilders on average per year between 1635 and 1650 nearly 30,000 guilders in the 1790s.[153] The issue of passports by the Generality yielded an additional amount, which was about 48,000 guilders in 1639.[154]

The most important tax revenues that would accrue to the 'Generality' in the course of time were the tax revenues from conquered territory. No data are available on these revenues before 1639, when their total amount was 855.150 guilders. By far the most important of these territories would become the northern part of Brabant. After cities like Den Bosch (Bois-le-Duc) and Breda had been re-conquered on the Spanish in respectively 1629 and 1637 it was in 1639 good for 73% of this amount.[155] In 1648 the Generality would introduce a fiscal system in 'Staats-Brabant' similar to that in Holland.[156]

Generality-loans

Yet another source of Generality revenue were loans negotiated by the Generality. The start of a Generality debt dates from 1596.[157] No annuities were issued by the Receiver General of the Generality, only obligations. Although this was originally a short-term debt paper, Generality obligations, just like Holland's obligations, were to a large extent prolonged for many years and had, just like in Holland, a clear tendency to become a permanent debt. The first loans

---

153 't Hart, *The making of a bourgeois state*, pp. 93–94; NA, Generaliteitsrekenkamer, inv.nr. 101.

154 *Ibidem*, p. 94.

155 For the 1790s some accounts of the Receiver-General of the Union have been preserved; NA, Generaliteitsrekenkamer, inv.nr. 101; in 1790 about 1.5 million guilders came from taxes in Generality territories, c. 80% of which from Brabant; the quota of the Generality territories, when they became part of the quotensystem in 1792 was 4.4% (see Table 2.7).

156 Kappelhof, *Belastingheffing in de Meijerij van Den Bosch*, 79–80.

157 't Hart, *The making of a bourgeois state*, pp. 166–167.

were probably redeemed rather soon, but at least since 1599 there was a steady rise in the debt of the Generality from 100,000 guilders in that year to nearly 4.5 million in 1610; by that time Holland's debt amounted already to nearly 18 million guilders.[158] The Generality loans allowed the Republic for instance to pay more troops than had been 'repartiated' on the provinces on the 'Statements of War'.[159] In the course of time Generality loans would increasingly function, however, as a 'safety valve' in case of arrears in payments by the provinces.[160] Another institution, important to this end would become that of the *'solliciteurs-militairs'*, to be further discussed in the next chapter.

That the Generality could issue obligations, despite the fact that it did not redeem them, must have been due to punctual interest payments. How was this possible in view of the lack of Generality taxes to this end before 1648? The answer to this question is that interest payments on Generality debt were always 'repartiated' on Holland's quota in military expenditure on the 'Statements of War' until 1648.[161] So until then, the loans were in fact raised on Holland's credit, but in a way that secured the involvement of the other provinces in the debt service, because Holland's quota in 'general expediture' did not change of course. Any time when the Receiver-General of the Generality was ordered by the Council of State of the Union to try to negotiate a loan, it just charged Holland with the required amount of interest on the next 'Statement of War' (*Staat van Oorlog*), which would lead to a decrease in the share Holland had to take in military payments, which was transferred to the other provinces in the next 'Statement of War'.

A noticeable aspect of the Generality loans was that the tight control on Holland's receivers, as implied by the required monthly reports to the financial committee of the States on revenue and expenditure in their offices, and by the direct link between tax revenues and interest payments, was missing in the case of the Receiver-General of the Generality. After the death of the first Receiver-General of the Generality, Philips Doubleth, in 1612, there were misgivings about the way he had performed his duties. His accounts appeared to be in great disorder and gave rise to many questions. Had he done all the

---

158 Dormans, *Het tekort*, pp. 139, 65.

159 NA, Archief Johan van Oldenbarnevelt, toeg.nr. 3.01.14 inv.nr. 2811 'Lijsten van betalingen in de soldij door Philips Doubleth, ontvanger-generaal van de Generaliteit, van 22 november 1599, en 14 september 1600 aan ongerepatrieerde compagnies, 1599 en 1600; afschriften (eind 16e eeuw)'.

160 Fritschy, 'Schulden als leerschool?', pp. 15–7.

161 E. Dormans, *Het tekort: staatsschuld in de tijd der Republiek* (Amsterdam, NEHA, 1991) pp. 139–140 has a list of the Generality debt per year for 1599–1670.

payments as he was supposed to do them? Had he charged discounts to creditors when they wanted priority? Had he duly administered debt redemptions by the provinces? Had he already charged interest payments before obligations were sold in fact? Anyhow, he had evidently preferred the continuance of the circulation of obligations above actively pursuing the amounts to be received from the provinces after they had given their consent in war expenditure, in order to be able to pocket his commission-percentage on the interest payments. The Receiver General of the Union received a broker's commission of 0.5 percent, not only, like Holland's receivers, in recompense for the negotiation of loans, but even, unlike Holland's receivers, continuously on the payment of the interest. Moreover, he had evidently used funds under his control also for personal ends, and he and his heirs were, as was the case with all tax receivers at the time, personally responsible for deficits.

Because the financial administration of the Generality was very complicated, his son Johan who succeeded him was allowed a delay in getting the accounts in order until 1618. By that time the mess had not yet been cleared, however. The settling of the accounts was again postponed to 1628, and by that time, Johan was succeeded by his younger brother, Philip. Philip junior agreed in 1642 to pay 242,441 guilders for deficits he had not been able to account for in the accounts of his father, but legal proceedings against the Doubleth family continued. In 1673 the Council of State claimed no less than 5.6 million guilders from the family. In the end the family was 'only' sentenced, however, to another payment of 259,107 guilders, which was paid indeed.[162] 't Hart, who researched the case of the Doubleths, found yet one other example of failing control in the case of the Generality finance: a tax-farmer of the Generality salt tax in Hoorn, who left a debt of 35,000 guilders to the Generality at his death in 1634 of which only 800 guilders could be recovered.[163] For Holland similar cases are not known.

The most important increases in Generality debt occurred in the years 1603 (565,000 guilders), 1604 and 1605 (both nearly 950,000 guilders).[164] As the Generality loans depended on Holland's credit this confirms that the breakthrough in Holland's credit, that announced its 'second financial revolution', had taken place by then. The total amount issued in obligations by the Generality of 4.5 million was not very different from the total amount in voluntary

162 M. 't Hart, 'Staatsfinanciën als familiezaak tijdens de Republiek: de ontvangers-generaal Doubleth', in *Fiscaliteit in Nederland*, eds. J.Th. de Smidt a.o. (Deventer, Walburg Pers, 1987) pp. 57–67, p. 63.

163 't Hart, *The making of a bourgeois state*, p. 194.

164 Dormans, *Het tekort*, p. 139.

loans – obligations and annuities – in Holland of probably about 5.2 million guilders during the first decade of the seventeenth century. These were important and attractive additional amounts,of course, for a state at war that was intent on paying its soldiers in time to prevent the feared mutinies of unpaid soldiers. The total amount of 9.7 million guilders was, however, less than 10 percent of total 'general' (=war-)expenditure by the provinces and the Generality in the period 1600–1609.

During the last three years of this period, when the war still continued, the extra revenue from Generality-loans became even less than about 120,000 guilders per year. Such modest extra amounts cannot have been helpful any longer. It was even less than the interest burden of by then of more than 300,000 guilders per year resulting from former loans.[165] This discrepancy makes one wonder if and to what degree Generality loans would be able to resume a function for war financing after the Truce.

Privateers Booty and Customs ('convooien en licenten')

The last and most important structural addition to the public revenue of the Dutch Republic on the central level was the revenue of the so called 'admiralties', established in order to maintain a navy for the war at sea. Booty from privateering was one source of revenue for the admiralties. Several kinds of customs duties soon became a second, more reliable, revenue source.

After Brielle in Holland had been conquered by Orange's privateers on 1 April 1572, port cities in Zeeland like Veere, Vlissingen and Zierikzee, had been among the first to go over to the Prince, providing him with a number of suitable naval bases for the war at sea. Veere had been the seat of the Admiralty of the Netherlands during the Burgundian and Habsburg periods before this seat had been transferred to Ghent in 1560. The Prince of Orange was appointed admiral-general of Holland and Zeeland in July 1572. The admirals whom the provinces appointed to serve under him continued and expanded their lucrative privateering activities from these ports in Zeeland.

An early extraordinary windfall came from a Portuguese fleet which sailed unsuspectingly into Vlissingen harbour in June 1572, not yet informed that Vlissingen had gone over to the Prince of Orange. On board were valuable spices from Asia and 600,000 ducats in cash, worth no less than about 1.2 million guilders.[166] Between 1573 and 1576, privateers' booty provided on average nearly 150,000 guilders a year for the war, much less spectacular than the big

---

165 Dormans, *Het tekort*, p. 139.

166 Tracy, *The founding of the Dutch* Republic, p. 84; Parker, *The Dutch Revolt*, p. 11: there were two florins to the ducat until 1578.

haul in 1572,[167] but nonetheless a very useful addition to war expenditure, at a time when the revenue from taxes still amounted to probably less than about 600,000 guilders on average per year for Holland and Zeeland together.

The more regular sources of revenue to finance the navy, the so called *convooien* (convoy-money) and *licenten* (license-money) soon became much more lucrative than booty.[168] Already in the fourteenth century groups of merchants in the Netherlands, or also city governments, financed warships by getting merchants to pay 'convoy-money' on imports in order to finance escorts for voyages on dangerous routes. It was levied from all imports from neutral and enemy territory. License-money had to be paid for export to the enemy, a policy that was mostly preferred to just forbidding this trade.[169] Also the license money had incidentally existed already in the form of urban duties before it became a provincial tax.

A common regulation for convoy- and license-money was initiated by a number of cities in Zeeland: Vlissingen, Veere and Zierikzee in 1572, joined in 1574 by Middelburg. Its revenue was at that time still seen as part of Zeeland's provincial revenue.[170] The seat of Zeeland's admiralty, initially in Veere, was transferred by the province to Middelburg, to the same locality where the deputies forming the daily board of Zeeland's States met.[171] In Holland, however, it was not the province, but the Prince of Orange who sanctioned the introduction of convoy- and license-moneys in 1573. An admiralty was established in Rotterdam in the province of Holland in 1575, when Amsterdam did not yet take part in the Revolt. It had authority for the whole territory of Holland's so called Southern Quarter as far as this was loyal to the prince, and this admiralty functioned from the start under the Council of State of the Prince, not under Holland's provincial government.[172]

---

167 Enthoven, *Zeeland en de opkomst van de Republiek*, pp. 64, 401; the amounts reported by Veenstra are even somewhat lower: 3.6 million guilders, nearly 120,000 guilders per year; GFZ, p. 137.

168 GFZ, p. 137.

169 Licence-money had already been among the revenue sources of the admiral of Veere in 1550; Korvezee, 'Belastingen in Noord-Brabant vóór 1648', p. 131.

170 F. Grapperhaus, *Convoyen en licenten* (Zutphen, Walburg Pers, 1986) 16 note; Enthoven, *Zeeland en de opkomst*, p. 400.

171 W. Veenstra, 'Geld is de zenuw van de oorlog; de financiën van de Zeeuwse Admiraliteit in de achttiende eeuw' (1698–1795), *Archief. Mededelingen van het Koninklijk Zeeuwsch Genootschap der Wetenschappen* (2008) pp. 91–121, p. 95.

172 GFZ, p. 285; Korvezee, 'De belastingen in Noord-Brabant', p. 151.

Like the issue of 'letters of marque' the levying of customs was at the time quite generally seen as a princely prerogative. In Zeeland, the most important source for customs revenues until about 1600, this revenue source had a more 'republican' origin, however, that was comparable to the introduction of the 'common means'. Here the initiative of a collectivity of cities had been decisive for the change in the customs from an urban to a provincial revenue source. The States of Holland and Zeeland decided to equalize their custom-tariffs in 1575, as they had done with the common means. The so called Pacification of Ghent of 1576, which had temporarily restored the unity of the seventeen Netherlands provinces, led to an agreement on a general list of custom tariffs for the whole territory of the Netherlands. Three years later the idea was taken over, as we saw, in article XVIII of the Union of Utrecht of 1579.

The license-money levied by Holland and Zeeland on exports to hostile territory in the Netherlands, was temporarily abolished as a result of the peace of Ghent of 1576, but was reintroduced again after the Union of Utrecht.[173] Between 1580 and 1587, there were many discussions regarding the permission to trade with the enemy. A prohibition would lead to a loss of trade as well as to a decrease in the revenues that were necessary to finance the navy. The States General decided in 1583 to forbid the export of ammunition and articles of food, but the States of Holland highhandedly decided to exempt Amsterdam's grain trade from the prohibition, to the disapproval of the other provinces.[174] Leicester issued an embargo on all trade with the enemy, when he became the governor of the Republic in 1585. After his departure in 1587, the embargo was cancelled again and the license-money reintroduced.[175] In 1581 a first list with tariffs for the convoy- and license-money for the Republic was made, which was revised in 1584. Divergent provincial tariffs were yet tolerated, however.

Amsterdam's admiralty came into existence in August 1586, despite the fact that the Earl of Leicester had appointed the city of Hoorn as the admiralty for Holland's Northern Quarter, to curtail Amsterdam's increasing power. Hoorn had not accepted the admiralty board appointed by the States of Holland, as it wanted to appoint the members of the admiralty board itself. The board appointed by the States then decided to start its activities in Amsterdam. In 1589, when Leicester was gone, the conflict between Hoorn and the States was appeased by granting the Northern Quarter a separate admiralty as well, the board of which would meet alternately in Hoorn and Enkhuizen. In March 1596

173 Korvezee, 'Belastingen in Noord-Brabant vóór 1648', p. 146; Kernkamp, *De handel op de vijand*, p. 188.

174 Grapperhaus, *Convoyen en licenten*, p. 18.

175 Korvezee, 'De belastingen in Noord-Brabant', p. 149.

a fifth admiralty of the Dutch Republic was erected in Dokkum in Friesland (which would in 1645 be moved to Harlingen). The five boards supervised each a great number offices spread all over the Dutch Republic to levy customs not only on the trade over sea, but also over land and on the river trade.

In 1597 the States General centralized the organization of the admiralties more strictly. Since then the admiralties had to send the accounts of their revenue and expenditure to the Audit Chamber of Accounts of the Generality and regularly convened in The Hague. The seven to twelve members of each of the admiralty boards were appointed by the States General and in each board some members from another province were appointed to prevent departures from the unified tariffs for particularistic interests. Historians on the Dutch admiralties are unanimous, nevertheless, on the fraudulent practices in all of the admiralties attempting to benefit their own trade. After 1597, when Zeeland was forced to accept central authority on admiralty finances, especially the admiralty of Middelburg has been believed to become notorious for its fraudulence.[176] More recent literature is less pertinent as to the degree of fraudulence, however.[177]

Between 1587 and 1599 the admiralty of Zeeland was good for on average about 40 percent of customs revenue, Amsterdam for about 30 percent, Rotterdam for about 25 percent. The revenues of the admiralty of Middelburg in Zeeland decreased sharply after 1599, partly perhaps because of increasing fraudulence, mainly, however, due to the prohibition of trade with the enemy in the Southern Netherlands, which put an end to revenue from the license money, although the name convoy- and license money was always maintained.[178] After 1599 the admiralty of Amsterdam became by far the most important of the five admiralties.

The development of total customs revenue during the first decades of the war with Spain, as visible in Figure 2.4, was partly the result of tariff policy, partly of economic developments. Since the reorganization of the admiralties and the establishment of a new general tariff list in 1597 provincial tariffs for convoy and license money were no longer allowed. Tariffs increased steadily, which will have been a main cause of the rise until 1599. The following decline was due to the abolition of the license money, because trade with the enemy was completely forbidden again. In 1603 a new tariff list was introduced,

---

176 Johan de Vries, 'De ontduiking der convooien en licten in de Republiek tijdens de achttiende eeuw', *Tijdschrift voor Geschiedenis* (1958) pp. 349–361, p. 359.

177 Veenstra 'Geld is de zenuw van de oorlog', pp. 99–100; Veenstra, *Tussen gewest en Generaliteit*, 177–180; Brandon, *War, capital and the Dutch state*, p. 125.

178 Grapperhaus, *Convoyen en licenten*, p. 34.

but the Twelve Years' Truce (1609–1621) led to a reduction in all tariffs, which caused an immediate decline in revenue from about 1.8 million guilders in 1608 to about 1.2 million guilders in 1610. The continued increase since then until about 1.7 million in 1621 has to be fully explained by the increase in trade during the Truce.

Figure 2.4 showed, that, although total customs revenue increased appreciably before the Truce from about 0.25 million guilders per year in the 1570s to about 1.6 million guilders per year in 1609, the relative importance of customs for total revenue, during the decades preceding the Truce, declined from on average 18 percent in the 1590s, to on average only 13 percent between 1600 and 1610.

In sum: the introduction of centralized custom duties, to be collected by five admiralties responsible for the maintenance of the navy, was an important novelty in the Northern Netherlands in comparison with the period of the Habsburgs, but their declining importance in total revenue calls for the question to what extent customs revenue would be able to contribute to the increase in public revenue that would become necessary in the period after the Truce.

2.5 Conclusion

Alva's attempt to introduce a centralized VAT-like 'tenth penny' in all provinces in the Netherlands is often said to have been inspired by Castile's tax system. Castile's system appeared to have been, in one important respect, in fact quite similar, however, to the one that had developed in Holland in the decades *before* the Revolt, when common taxes of a collectivity of cities had come to be earmarked for interest payments, by a provincial instead of a royal reciver, on common loans needed for war faring realized by means of the sale of annuities to the public. Castilian cities had the power to earmark their *alcabala* for interest payments on annuities already long before. Alva's new fiscal system, in contrast, would have seriously undermined the increasing financial power of Dutch provinces to determine to which ends its public revenue had to be used. In this sense it was quite different from that in Castile.

Alva succeeded impressively in his attempt to increase public revenue during his first two years as governor of the Netherlands as a result of his negotiations with the Provincial States, although he had felt forced to shelve his original plan for a 'tenth penny'. His threat to billet unpaid Spanish troops on the cities had no doubt helped in this success. He failed to realize his centralized 'tenth penny', when he tried to enforce it by means of an 'absolutist' top down decision after these two years had ended. By then Holland's cities decided to support the Prince of Orange in his Revolt, partly stimulated no doubt by the severe economic depression of the years 1569–1573. The attempt to introduce 'general means' on an equal footing in all the Netherlands as the result of a decision of an autonomous meeting of the States General, four years later in order to get rid of the Spanish troops, would fail as well, however. It was only on the provincial level that a centralization of an important part of the Dutch tax system Netherlands would turn out to be successful. Collectivities of cities, with their increased power in the Provincial States-assemblies, gradually and reluctantly became aware that a provincial centralization and expansion of what formerly had been typically 'urban taxes' was unavoidable in order to realize the increasing revenues necessary for the war.

Between the start of the Revolt in Holland in 1572 and the start of the Twelve Years' Truce in 1609 new fiscal systems gradually developed in all provinces of the emerging federal Dutch Republic. The systems had in common that they were everywhere the result of decisions in – already long existing – representative institutions, in which, as a result of the Revolt, the influence of cities had largely increased. The most important element of these new fiscal systems was in all provinces the introduction of what were still called 'general means', which exploited the fiscal possibilities of the commercialized economies of these provinces and which encroached on urban fiscal autonomy. It resulted in revolutionary larger amounts in tax revenue than before. The provinces remained autonomous, however, in the actual number of these 'general' means and in the tax rates, as a result of which they became adapted to differing economic conditions.

The Dutch state developed in this way into a federal, not into a centralized state, as the result of the requirements of early modern war faring. The 'tax revolution' that started in Holland and Zeeland already in 1574, was supported by the economic recovery that started in the same year, after four years of deep economic crisis. Rising real wages since then contributed to the broad acceptance of the large number of price-increasing taxes. Less economic development or even economic stagnation made the developments in Zeeland and the other provinces slower. It was only reluctantly that all provinces became convinced that they would have to exploit the fiscal possibilities of the 'urban system' of the Dutch Republic each in its own territory to finance the war in the course of time. It would take until the beginning of the seventeenth century until all provinces had introduced 'general means' taxing commercial assets and activities like production, distribution and consumption.

Contrary to what is often thought, the negotiation of voluntary loans on the capital market did hardly belong to the fiscal possibilities of the provinces during the first decades of the Eighty Years War. Even in Holland loan financing on a voluntary basis was only possible on a very modest scale until c. 1600, despite its 'financial revolution' in the 1540s and 1550s, simply because war payments had priority above interest payments for many years. Not this old 'financial revolution', but the 'tax revolution' of the 'common means', in combination with a large increase in the burden of direct taxes and forced loans was the 'secret' of the fiscal system of the early Dutch Republic, or, in other words: 'coercion', rather than 'capital' between c. 1575 and the first decade of the seventeenth century. Even in 1575, however, the emergency measure of a currency debasement had yet been felt as unavoidable to pay the army as had been the case already in 1573.

In contrast to the Spanish king Holland's States were not able to make use of the services of foreign bankers for short-term loans. It was its new network of provincial 'common means'-receivers in the cities, that would gradually be able to fulfil this function. After the interest payments on the existing public debt were gradually resumed, it was this network that would also start to offer a wide and easy access to potential domestic investors in public debt, in the course of time. During the first decade of the seventeenth century, this would result in what may be called Holland's 'second', or even its 'real', 'financial revolution', allowing much larger public loans than ever during the 1550s, and allowing an increasing long-term public debt, that no longer was redeemed – in contrast to the debt redemption of the 1550s – and, nevertheless, at gradually decreasing rates of interest during the next decades. Taxation in all the provinces remained, however, by far the most important source for war financing during the first decades of the Eighty Years War with Spain, in contrast to Holland's fiscal system under the Habsburgs.

The quantitative importance of centralized public revenue in the Dutch Republic, in addition to the revenue of the provinces, appeared to be certainly not negligible in the period until 1609, approaching sometimes no less than nearly one third of the sum of the various sources of public revenue of the Republic. This importance would decrease largely when loans and subsidies granted to the States General by England and France stopped after the start of the Truce. It was the novelty of customs duties earmarked for navy expenditure, with centralized tariffs and collected and spent by the new institutional feature of five admiralties under the authority of the States General, that offered the most important structural addition to the 'centralized' part of the public finance of the Dutch Republic (Figure 2.4). As a percentage of total revenue its importance soon declined as well however. The amounts involved in the sale of Generality obligations since the 1590s were probably very important to keep army payments going, but their contribution to total public revenue remained

TABLE 2.11 *War expenditure in the Dutch Republic and the Spanish subsidies to the army in Flanders, 1571–1610 (annual averages in million glds).*

	Estimated war expenditure Dutch Republic	Estimated war expenditure Dutch Republic excl. navy	Available for the royal army in Flanders from Spanish subsidies
1571–1580	?	?	3.2
1575–1580	1.6	1.3	?
1581–1590	3.4	2.5	6
1591–1600	6.7	5.0	9
1601–1610	9.5	7.5	7.8

Sources: http://resources.huygens.knaw.nl/gewestelijkefinancien/en; Parker, *The army of Flanders*, p. 225.

modest in the period until the start of the Truce. Abuse of the possibility to sell obligations instead of raising taxes, and to use part of such revenues to private instead of public purposes, appeared to be remarkably easier on the level of the Generality than within Holland. The mutual control inherent in a fiscal system grafted onto an urban system largely prevented such practices among Holland's tax receivers.[179]

The results of the new fiscal system of the federal Republic of the Seven United Provinces as a whole were really impressive, during the first half of the war against Spain between 1572 and 1609. A comparison of the amounts for war expenditure in the Dutch Republic with the amounts of the Spanish subsidies to the Spanish government in Brussels, as visible in Table 2.11, shows, that during the first decade of the seventeenth century the Dutch republic became gradually able to spend nearly as much on its army as the royal army in Flanders received in subsidies from Spain.

The decreased amount in Spanish subsidies in this decade, as visible in the table, reflects the increasing financial problems in Spain, which led to the Twelve-Years Truce. During the same decade, however, tensions in the Dutch fiscal system started to become visible as well. The Generality seemed to have

179 The tax receiver Coenraad Ellents of the small province of Drenthe who appeared to have a debt of 382,181 guilders to the States of the province in 1737, claimed that he had never received the instruction that forbade the negotiation of loans on his own authority and the lending of money to the public from his funds. His property was confiscated (its sale yielded about 300,000 guilders); *GFD*, p. 34.

lost its function as a source of loans during the last years before the Truce, and the relative importance of the revenue of customs duties started to decline (Figure 2.4). The war expenditure paid by the other provinces started to lag behind to what they were supposed to pay (Table 2.7). The amount to be paid in interest per year in Holland began to approach the amount borrowed per year in the preceding years (Table 2.4).

Oldenbarnevelt held the Republic's financial position for no longer tenable already in September 1606.[180] 'Holland regents (...) needed little convincing that Generality finances were insufficient for the war to continue without major tax increases and this they deemed unadvisable', Israel wrote in his magnum opus on the Dutch Republic. He added that there were doubts whether the Republic would ever be able to survive without British and French help and subsidies.[181] It was not only because of the increasing financial problems of the king of Spain, that the Truce of 1609 became a possibility.

---

180 Israel, *The Dutch Republic*, p. 401.

181 Israel, *The Dutch Republic*, pp. 404–405 in the section named 'The pressure to negotiate'; also Parker, *The Dutch Revolt*, pp. 238, 261.

CHAPTER 3

Public Finance of the Dutch Republic in the 17th and 18th Centuries

The amounts needed for war faring after the Truce would become much larger than they had ever been before. Chapter 2 answered the question how the fiscal system of the Dutch Republic emerged between 1572 and 1609, and why it was able to raise the unheard of amounts of public revenue required to persevere in its war against Spain. It showed moreover what potential 'weaknesses' became apparent. Chapter 3 will focus on the questions why, to what ends, the increasingly higher amounts in public expenditure were necessary after the Truce and how the required revenues were raised during the remaining period of the Republic's history, despite the fact that the four detected 'weaknesses' of the system just continued to exist. The 'elasticity' of the federal fiscal system that had emerged in the decades before the Truce would prove to be much larger than had seemed likely by 1609, despite these weaknesses.

In the first section the public expenditure of the Dutch Republic since the end of the Truce until the fall of the old Republic in January 1795 is analysed, this in order to determine to what extent changes in public expenditure after the end of the Twelve Years' Truce were caused by the requirements of land wars and naval wars and to what extent by non-military public tasks. The degree to which the provinces outside Holland actually paid their part in war expenditure according to their quotas since 1621 will be examined again. Special attention will be paid to attempts to contain the increasing interest burden on public debts.

The second section discusses public revenue. On the one hand, what is called its 'institutional structure' is examined: the extent to which revenue increases were realized by the central and by the federal institutional elements of the Dutch Republic in the course of time. On the other hand, what will be called the 'social-economic structure' of public revenue will be discussed: the extent to which increasing revenues were the result of price-increasing indirect taxes hitting mainly the less well-to-do, or of direct taxes hitting the (somewhat) more well-to-do, and the extent to which they were the result of loans. In this context also the relatively small role of tax riots in the Dutch Republic and the 'tax morale' of the more well-to-do will be discussed, and the differences in the tax burden between Holland and other provinces. Moreover, the relative

 | DOI 10.1163/9789004341289_006

importance of 'capital' and 'coercion' in the increases in public revenue in the period after the Truce will be examined.

Whereas Chapter 2 started with a comparison of Holland's tax system before and since the Revolt, Chapter 3 will end with a comparison between the fiscal system of the federal Republic at the end of the eighteenth century and the centralized tax system realized in 1806 after the 'Batavian Revolution' of 1795, by means of which a spectacular growth in tax revenue was realized again. It will be argued that the much less spectacular growth in public expenditure in the eighteenth century than in the seventeenth century was, nevertheless, not due to the federal structure of the Dutch state.

3.1 The Increasing Public Expenditure of the Dutch Republic

After the end of the 'Twelve Years' Truce' the Republic had to continue the war with Spain from 1621 until the Peace of Munster in 1648. It would become involved in many new wars since then. Four of the wars after 1621 were naval wars with Britain; four were land wars with France that mostly involved also other states. More than forty percent of the years from 1621 until the end of the Dutch Republic in 1795 were war years, if restricted to the seventeenth century even more than sixty percent. Public expenditure had to increase tremendously after the Truce during each of these wars, and it mostly remained higher after each war than it had been before (Figure 3.1).

It had not only to increase at the start of each war; it had, moreover, to increase more for each next war until 1713. Figure 3.1 shows, moreover, that these increases may have been determined by price developments only to a rather limited extent. It may be added that it is even doubtful to what extent price corrections are needed in the case of public finance, during the seventeenth and eighteenth century. Military pays were by far the most important element in public expenditure, and nominal military payments in the Republic did hardly change between 1599 and 1766/1792.[1] It has been argued that even naval expenditure was not very much subject to increasing costs due to price fluctuations, because of the use of cheaper building materials in the course of time.[2]

1 Zwitzer, *'De militia van den staat'*, pp. 200–203; the amounts in military pays he mentioned are on average 6% higher for 1792 than for 1766; most infantry amounts remained the same from 1599–1766; for cavalerists the amounts mentioned for 1766 are even 9% lower than the one for 1599, because the number of horses per lieutenant or commander was reduced.

2 Brandon, *War, capital and the Dutch state*, p. 133; this result is not completely supported, however, by data (of a very different, more general, character) in Fritschy, *De patriotten en de financien van de Bataafse Republiek*, p. 64.

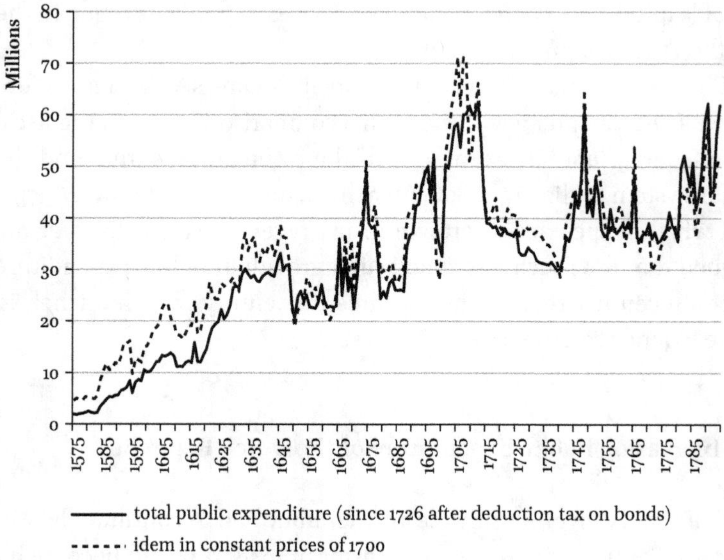

FIGURE 3.1 *Total public expenditure of the Dutch Republic in current guilders and after correction for price fluctuations, 1575–1794 (guilders of 1700).*
Source: index consumption prices: Van Zanden, http://www.iisg.nl/hpw/data.php#netherlands.

Developments in the structure of public expenditure are made visible in Figure 3.2. In what follows the main elements of this structure will be discussed starting with war expenditure (land and naval wars), then debt service (interest payments and debt redemption) and lastly 'other provincial expenditure' than that for war and debt service.

War Expenditure

War was, no doubt, the main cause of the rises in public expenditure visible in Figures 3.1–3.2, which was primarily due to increasing sizes of the army. Troop payments fluctuated mostly between 60 and 80 percent of total military expenditure between 1640 and 1795, most of it for infantry.[3] The decreased relative importance of war expenditure after 1713 was the result of a conscious political choice to avoid further involvements in war as much as possible in order to be able to continue debt service as much as possible without too many increases in taxation.[4] This choice does not necessarily have to be interpreted as an

3 Brandon, *War, capital and the Dutch state*, pp. 213–215; his Chart 4.1 suggests that 50 percent or more of troop payments went to the infantry.

4 *'Memorie van 1755'*, (http://resources.huygens.knaw.nl/gewestelijkefinancien/memorie.pdf); for an introduction to this important contemporary document see *GFH*, pp. 122–129.

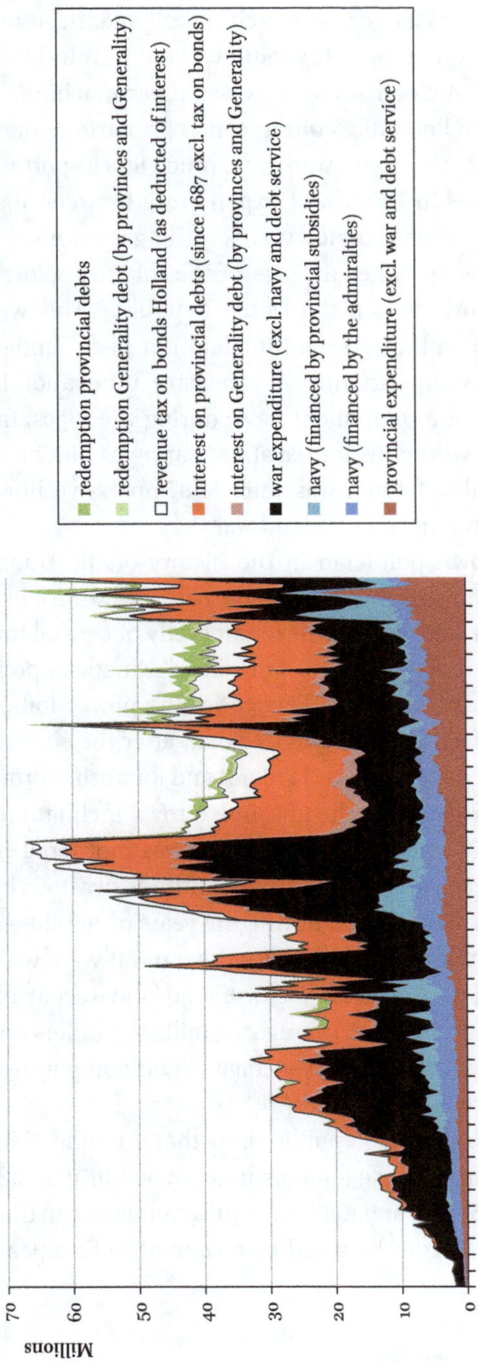

FIGURE 3.2 *Development and structure of the public expenditure of the Dutch Republic, 1575–1794 (current guilders).*

indication of the *inability* of this federal state to exploit its fiscal potential more efficiently to generate more war expenditure. It should be kept in mind that the Dutch state was, from early on, not conceived of as just a 'war-machine'.

In view of the fact that the Dutch Republic is often seen as primarily a maritime state, it may come as a surprise that naval wars were much less important for the explanation of the increases in Dutch war expenditure between 1621 and 1795 than land wars. The early modern period was, regarding the amounts in money and in men involved, really rather the 'age of the infantry-soldier' than that of the 'merchant-warrior', even in the Dutch Republic.[5] This was the case despite the fact that the 'military revolution' had not been limited to changes in war faring on land. An important, and expensive, innovation in naval warfare was the realization of a permanent navy, during the 1650s, instead of the use of merchantmen with guns for naval war faring as had been customary before. Its impact on public finance was much less impressive, however, than the required increases in army size for land wars.[6]

During 1653–1672 the best known politician in the history of the Dutch Republic, Holland's so-called 'state pensionary' Johan de Witt – who was, like his earlier famous colleague Johan van Oldenbarnevelt not only of central importance in the Republic's foreign policy, but also in Holland's financial policy – gave as much priority as possible to naval defence for the protection of Holland's foreign trade. This was facilitated by the fact that, after the sudden death of stadholder William II of Orange in 1650, Holland and four other provinces preferred to do for the future without the absolutist, royal inclinations of a stadholder demanding priority for the army. De Witt was murdered in 1672, because the Republic then nearly succumbed under military invasions by German and French armies. Nevertheless, even during the years of his statesmanship, when moreover two of the increasingly expensive naval wars with Britain were fought successfully (1652–54 and 1665–67), and no land wars at all, the average amount in navy expenditure of on average 6.3 million guilders per year between 1653 and 1672, was less than the on average 8.6 million guilders per year spent on army expenditure in that period.

The available figures on army size in the Republic show that it intended its army to amount to about 37,000 men in 1595–1609, about 49,000 in 1621–48, about 83,000 in the wars between 1671–78 and 1688–97, and about 112,000 in that of 1701–1713.[7] After 1713 the Republic tried to avoid involvement in European

5 This qualification in Brandon, *War, capital and the Dutch state,* p. 83.

6 J. Glete, *Navies and nations. Warhsips, navies and state building in Europe and America 1500–1860* (Stockholm 1993); Brandon, *War, capital and the Dutch state,* p. 86.

7 Zwitzer, *'De militia van den staat'*, pp. 175–176.

war faring as much as possible.[8] However, when it was forced to participate in the War of Austrian Succession in 1741–48, the intended size of the army was again about 85,000 men.[9] It should be added that the actual numbers were often much lower, in 1671 for instance only 53,000 men instead of the nearly 65,000 planned for that year, but even then the numbers remained relatively very large. France, the Republic's main enemy after the end of the Eighty Years War with Spain, with a population of about ten times that of the Republic, had a (real) army size less than five times as large at the start of the war of in 1672: probably 253,000 (on paper 267,600 men).[10]

Figure 3.2 shows that the most remarkable increase in public expenditure since the end of the war with Spain occurred in the year 1672, known as the 'Year of Disaster' in Dutch historiography, and mentioned with awe and abhorrence in European historiography too.[11] In that year the Republic was attacked by France, Britain, and two German aggressors simultaneously. Voltaire wrote in his famous *The age of Louis XIV* that

> the history of mankind scarcely furnishes us with another instance of such formidable preparations being made for so small an expedition; of all the different conquerors who have invaded any part of the world, no one ever began the career of conquest with so many regular troops and so much money as Louis employed in subduing the petty State of the United Provinces (...) No one of all the enemies who combined to sink this little state could allege the least pretence for war.[12]

The provinces Overijssel, Gelderland and Utrecht surrendered already in 1672 and were temporarily integrated into the Holy Roman Empire. Only thanks to the support of allies interested in curbing French expansionist aggression (Spain and Brandenburg), the re-conquest of the three provinces was possible in 1674. The Third Naval War with Britain, starting in the Year of Disaster, was successfully ended in 1674, despite a lower total number of guns on the Dutch fleet, so probably as a result of the qualities of the famous admiral Michiel de

8 See the 'Memorie of 1755'.

9 The actual size was estimated by van Nimwegen at about 70,000 men.

10 J.A. Lynn, 'Recalculating French army growth during the *Grand Siècle*, 1610–1715', in: *The Military Revolution Debate* ed. C.J. Rogers (Oxford 1995) p. 125.

11 L. Panhuysen, *Rampjaar 1672. Hoe de Republiek aan de ondergang ontsnapte* (Amsterdam 2009).

12 *The Works of Voltaire. A Contemporary Version.* A Critique and Biography by John Morley, notes by Tobias Smollett, trans. William F. Fleming (New York: E.R. DuMont, 1901). In 21 vols. Vol. XII. http://oll.libertyfund.org/index.php?option=com_staticxt&staticfile=show.php%3Ftitle=2132&Itemid=27.

Ruyter. It is very doubtful, however, whether the Dutch Republic would ever have been able to survive the war – even despite the large increase in army-expenditure visible in Figures 3.2 –, if the French army would not have had to fight on multiple fronts.

During the 1670s and the 1680s, the necessary increase in the number of soldiers was not only realized by means of more expenditure, but also by greater efficiency. A so-called 'second military revolution' required a dramatic increase in the size of the Dutch army.[13] An increase in government involvement in war financing facilitated the increases in real army size since the 1670s, because it diminished the difference between army strength on paper and in reality. An important element was the regulation of the functioning of the '*solliciteurs militairs*'.[14] Such 'solicitors' had to collect the military payments for the army captains from the tax receivers' offices in the Republic unto which these payments were assigned and to travel to the companies in the field to pay them.

These 'military solicitors' had often to act as 'bankers' for short-term loans to the state to secure regular payments, especially during military campaigns. Captains paid them their wages and the interest on their loans by reducing the number of soldiers in their pay, due to which the real number of soldiers was often much smaller than the number on paper. The States General decided in 1681 not only to set limits to the number of *solliciteurs* (28 for the Republic, 14 of which for Holland)[15] and to demand higher requirements as to their creditworthiness. They also set a limit to the interest rates for their important banking services, thus diminishing the possibility for frauds as to the real number of soldiers in the field. In the 1620s the solicitors often asked 12 percent for their 'banking services', in 1681 the maximum they were allowed to charge was set at 5.2 percent per year.[16] This implies that the real size of the army increased not only due to more money furnished by the provinces, but also thanks to better management at the central level of the Dutch state.

During the next two great wars visible in Figure 3.2 the Dutch Republic was right from the start a partner in coalitions. Its participation in the war of 1701–1713 has to be explained by the fact that it was widely felt to be in the interest

---

13 O. van Nimwegen, *The Dutch army and the Military Revolutions, 1588–1688* (Woodbridge, Boydell, 2010).

14 Brandon, *War, capital and the Dutch state*, offers a nice study of these solicitors in Chapter 4: 'Troop payments, military soliciting and the world of finance', pp. 210–263.

15 Van Nimwegen, *The Dutch army and the Military Revolutions*, p. 518.

16 W. Fritschy, and R. Liesker, 'Overheidsfinanciën, kapitaalmarkt en "institutionele context" in Holland en Overijssel tijdens en na de Spaanse Successie-oorlog', in: *Kapitaal, ondernemerschap en beleid*, red. C.A. Davids e.a. (Amsterdam 1996) 165–197, p. 180.

of Dutch trade to prevent the expansion of French power. The peace treaty did no longer give the Republic the commercial advantages it had hoped for, however. This contributed to a change in foreign policy, in combination with the fact that the largely increased interest burden made a reduction in military expenditure and an avoidance of further involvements in international war faring very desirable. Bound by its alliance with Britain the Republic had nevertheless yet to participate in the international War of the Austrian Succession (1740–1748), which led to an invasion by France in 1747, but it managed to keep out of the Seven Years War (1756–1763) between France and England. A last naval war with Britain in 1780–1784 made it evident that the Dutch state was really too small to win wars without allies against much larger states (see also Chapter 5). It succumbed to the third French invasion of January 1795.

War expenditure in the Dutch Republic during the eighteenth century has often been denounced as insufficient, due to the federal structure of the Republic that allowed the provinces to pay less than might have been expected according to the quotas-system.[17] To examine the degree to which the provinces outside Holland contributed to war faring Figure 3.3 gives an overview, in seven periods for which enough reliable data were available, of the *de facto* payment

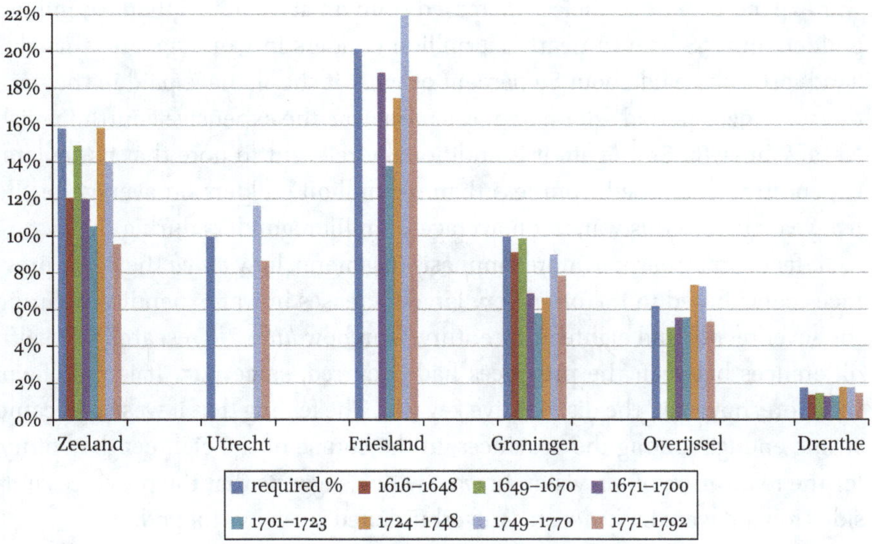

FIGURE 3.3 *Average war expenditure in six provinces as % of what Holland paid, compared to the required percentage according to the quotas-system, 1616–1792.*

17 Van Zanden and Van Riel, *Nederland 1780–1914* (transl. *The strictures of inheritance*), pp. 49–50.

behaviour of five such provinces with sufficient data, and of the small province of Drenthe, fiscally autonomous and having to contribute to the Union, although it did not belong to the seven with voting rights in the States General.

As the use of estimates had of course to be avoided as much as possible in this case, Figure 3.3 had to be based on available data, or on contemporary estimates directly based on available data, which explains the choice of the periods and which explains why the graph does not show data for all periods in some provinces,[18] and no data at all for the province Gelderland. What Holland paid in fact is taken in this graph as the yardstick for the payment behaviour of the other provinces, for instance: as Groningen's quota was 5.8 percent and that of Holland 58.3 percent, Groningen should have paid 10 percent of what Holland paid in war expenditure. This is the height of the first bar for each of the provinces in Figure 3.3. The following bars show to what extent the province paid conform this norm, or not, in different periods.

The graph shows that, especially during the period 1701–1723, the provinces outside Holland often paid less, indeed, than what could have been expected on the basis of the distributive key of the quota-system, Groningen for instance paid in this period only 6 percent instead of 10 percent of what Holland paid. It should be noted, however, that Groningen's absolute amount in war expenditure nevertheless increased from on average less than 0.9 million guilders in 1698–1701 to nearly 1.4 million guilders in 1701–1713, and that this 'land'-province paid about 80 percent of what it should have paid in the period 1771–1792, a period dominated by a naval war, the expensive Fourth English Naval War (1781–84). Again it is additionally relevant to note that its 'general expenditure' increased from less than 0.7 million guilders on average in the five years before this war, to on average 1.1 million guilders during this war.

In fact, it may deserve more emphasis in general, how *much* the other provinces contributed to the often very large increases in war expenditure during the seventeenth and eighteenth century, than how *little*. No research in wealth differences between the provinces had occurred, since 1515. It is unknown, therefore, how 'fair' the distributive key was. The feeling that it wasn't, became strong enough among the provinces, in the course of the eighteenth century, for the realization of a revision in 1792, which suggests that the provinces outside Holland were in fact seen as 'overburdened' even by Holland.

Table 3.1 shows the distributive key of the quota-system as it was fixed in 1616, compared to the one agreed to in 1792 (after having remained unchanged

18 The choice of the periods was determined by the wish to use as many of the data as possible and to make the periods not too short because of the unavoidable error margins, as explained in the section on the reliability of the figures.

TABLE 3.1 *Quota-distribution and population distribution, 1616 and 1792.*

	Quotas 1616		Quotas 1792		Population distribution 1795
Holland		57.8%		62.1%	41%
Friesland	11.6%		9.3%		8%
Zeeland	9.1%		3.8%		6%
Utrecht	5.7%		4.5%		5%
Stad en Lande (Groningen)	5.7%		5.4%		6%
Gelderland	5.5%		6.0%		12%
Overijssel	3.6%		3.5%		7%
Drenthe	0.99%		1%		2%
sum excl. Holland		42.2%		33.5%	
Generality (mainly N-Brabant)				4.4%	13%
		100%		100%	100%

Sources: Table 2.6; Zwitzer, *'De militie van den staat'*, p. 71.

until then, with the exception of the years 1621–1634, when some provinces that were extremely plagued by the renewal of the war in 1621, got a temporary reduction). It also offers a comparison with the distribution of the population of the Republic in 1795, the year of the first census in the Northern Netherlands, and as such the first year for which these data are available.

The remarkable outcome of this revision was that the about 42 percent of the war expenditure to be paid by the provinces outside Holland since 1616, was decreased to about 34 percent. This revision was made possible not only by the fact that the tax revenue of the Generalities (until then mainly used for debt service on the Generality-debt) was then incorporated into the quota-system. It was also made possible by the increase of Holland's contribution from 57.7 percent to 62.1 percent. We will come back to this point at the discussion of the tax burden in the next section.

When France declared war on the Dutch Republic in 1793 and the 'general expenditure excl. on naval war' of the Republic increased from on average about 14 million guilders to nearly 23 million guilders, the *de facto* contributions of Holland, Friesland, Overijssel, Groningen and Zeeland during that year were resp. 60%, 10%, 4%, 6% and 4%, which means that the contributions of the provinces outside Holland were then generally even higher than what would have been required according to the new quotas. In 1794 this would no longer be the case, although not only Holland, but also the other the provinces again increased the amounts in war expenditure. The fact that total war expenditure (excl. navy) during that year was nevertheless much higher than ever before in the history of the Dutch Republic could no longer prevent, that the third French invasion in the Dutch Republic – now one supported by a domestic revolution, known as the Batavian Revolution – would put an end to the 'old regime' federal Dutch Republic.

Debt Service

Figure 3.2 shows, that the most important part of public expenditure after 'war' was 'debt service', consisting of the interest payments and debt redemption on the provincial debts and the Generality debt. During most of the eighteenth century this sum was even larger than the amounts for war. Not only in Holland, also in the other provinces loans, either on their own provincial credit or on that of the Generality, became gradually a rather substantial source of public revenue, especially during the very costly War of the Spanish Succession (1701–1713). The possibility to borrow, without having to redeem the resulting debt, is of course a very welcome addition to public revenue, especially in times of war, but the threat of an interest burden increasing faster than tax revenue due to the frequency of wars and their increasing costs, was a source of concern too. This section will focus on attempts to contain the interest burden.

Five ways were possible to achieve this, apart from trying to minimize the need for new loans by avoiding involvement in wars, and apart from choosing for forced loans at a lower interest rate than would have to be paid on voluntary loans, an option to be discussed in the section on public revenue below. Firstly, debt holders could be forced to accept a permanent reduction of the nominal interest rate on the existing public debt. A special form of a forced interest reduction was, secondly, a tax on all bonds – 'obligations' as well as redeemable and life-annuities – that was 'collected' at the source by just diminishing the real amount in interest to be paid by the tax receiver with the amount in tax to be paid by the debtholder. The difference with a forced interest reduction was that a tax could be made undone each next year, whereas an interest conversion was permanent for the public debt accumulated until then. Thirdly, the interest burden could be diminished by means of *voluntary* interest reductions. In that case the provincial government repaid debtholders the capital sum of their investment, if they did not want to accept an interest reduction. Fourthly the interest burden could be restrained by attempts to diminish the proportion sold in expensive debt forms, such as life-annuities. Lastly, it could be done, of course, by means of the burdensome and costly way of debt redemption, feasible in peace periods when war expenditure could be substantially decreased.

a) *Forced Permanent Interest Reductions and the Tax on Bonds*

The easiest way to contain the unavoidable increases in the interest burden during the many years when public debts continuously increased, were forced reductions in the interest rates. One remarkable form of a forced interest reduction, the centralized setting of a maximum interest rate for the services of the military solicitors that guaranteed smooth army payments, was mentioned already in the former section, because such short-term debts to the military solicitors can be considered as part of war expenditure. This section is restricted to debt service on the long-term debts in the Republic.

The gradual decline from 12 percent to 6.25 percent in Holland before the Truce had been completely the result of forced interest reductions. Despite warnings of some representatives in the States, that this could harm provincial credit,[19] new loans proved to be possible at the reduced rate of interest after such reductions. Even the voluntary reduction of the nominal interest rate to 6.25 percent of 1609 was prepared by a forced tax reduction which lowered the nominal interest rate of 7.14 percent in 1606 to 6.21 percent. Between 1609 and 1671, however, no similar forced interest reductions occurred any more.

The instrument of a tax on bonds to diminish the interest burden was used in Holland for the first time in 1673. Until then bonds had only been taxed incidentally as part of taxes on total property that were often felt to be necessary for war financing. The result of the first property taxes after the outbreak of the war of 1672 was disappointing, due to the fact that old registers of taxable persons, dating from 1654, still had to be used as long as the renewal of these registers had not yet been finished. Levying a tax on bonds separately, by just paying less interest, was a very easy and convenient way to have more money available for the war rather soon. During each of the years 1673 and 1674 a tax of 'the 200th penny' (=0.5 percent) on all bonds was levied six times, which implied a reduction of the real interest on obligations and redeemable annuities from nominal 4 to in reality only 1 percent in both years.

Although the new registers for the property tax were completed in the course of 1674, Holland's government decided to continue to keep the tax on bonds separate from the tax on property and to continue to tax bondholders in the same way as in 1672 and 1673 by just withholding part of the interest payments. The rates varied from 2 to 0.5 percent of the nominal value of

19 *GFH*, pp. 363–364.

the bonds during the remaining years of this war and during the next wars. This convenient instrument to contain the interest burden would only be copied by the province of Zeeland.

A reduction to a real interest rate of only one percent did not occur any more in the history of the Dutch Republic. After 1714 the rate of Holland's tax on bonds was nearly permanently 1.5 percent, which made Holland's 'real' rate of interest on 4 percent-bonds 2.5 percent. Only in 1746 and 1747 it would be again reduced temporarily to 2 percent to allow more war expenditure. In 1747 the States decided, however, that the tax on bonds would never increase again to more than 1.5 percent and this promise was kept until the end of the old Republic. The next comparable fiscal measure to reduce the interest burden was only taken after the annexation of the Dutch territory to France: Napoleon decided, in 1810, to reduce all interest payments on a – by then even much larger – public debt with two thirds.

In Figure 3.2 the considerable effect of Holland's tax on bonds on the amounts in interests really paid since 1687 is made visible.[20] The amounts in contemporary financial sources booked as 'paid in interest' were always the amounts that were due *before* taxation. They can be said to have been artificially high, therefore, in periods when a voluntary interest conversion would have been very well possible. The part that was taxed away was accounted for as tax revenue in the financial administration, and tax revenue was, therefore, in fact artificially high as well in that case.[21] Even when in 1741 the '*collectloon*' (= wage for the 'collecting' of) of the '200th, 100th etc. pennies' on bonds for Holland's tax receivers was abolished at last,[22] this did not lead to a change in the way the interest burden and the tax receipts were entered into the accounts, because the transfer by these receivers, of the amounts not paid in interests, to Holland's General Receiver who had to pay most of Holland's military expenditure,

20 The year since which sources were available for the 'revenue' of the tax on bonds separately from the other elements in the taxes on personal wealth (*GFH*, p. 286 and p. 368).

21 In the Tables and Figures in this book 1726 was used, mostly, as the year since which the 'revenue' of the tax on bonds was no longer considered as such, because (1) it may be assumed that at some time during the 1720s a voluntary conversion might have certainly been accepted in Holland, (2) because for the period between 1726–1776 very reliable detailed sources for Holland's public finance are available (see *GFH*, pp. 85–106) and for earlier years estimates had to be used, and (3) because the sharp change in 1726 visible in a graph is a reminder that there is a problem with the data; incidentally it seemed more reasonable to use 1687 instead of 1726; the year used as starting point for a correction of the amounts in the archival source material is always explicitly indicated in the column heading or the legenda.

22 *GFH*, p. 46; the measure would reduce the personal revenue for Holland's new general receiver after 1741 from about fl. 19,000 to about fl. 10,000.

had to remain administratively visible. Theoretically one would expect that a government reducing a promised interest rate at will, when it could not afford to pay what was due, would spoil its credit. In Holland this was evidently not the case. The continual increase in Holland's debt from nearly 131 million guilders in 1673 to nearly 311 million guilders in 1714[23] was mainly a result of *voluntary* loans, despite these taxes on bonds. Only during the 1670s probably about half of the loans were forced loans.

None of the provinces could avoid drastic measures to contain the interest burden after the war of 1701–1713. Investors in public debt in Holland and Zeeland had to accept taxes on bonds that were sold during the war with the explicit promise that they would remain 'tax-free'. Investors in public debt in the other provinces had to accept forced permanent interest conversions on the debt. In Friesland the interest burden would have demanded 75 percent of the amount of tax revenue in 1711, if it had been paid. In Utrecht it would have demanded even more than the total of the provincial tax revenues in 1714. Drastic permanent cuts in the promised interest rates were preferred by most provinces to large increases in taxation, in order to be able to pay debt-holders. Most life-annuity holders in Utrecht, for instance, just received only 3.5 percent interest on their life-annuities since 1715, instead of the promised 9 or 10 percent. Only debt holders older than 40 year were allowed a somewhat smaller reduction and received 7 percent.[24]

The office of the General-Receiver of the Generality had to remain closed for interest payments in 1715 during more than nine months. The receiver was no longer able to pay any interest, due to the many loans negotiated during the war on its credit for the provinces. The provinces had simply stopped to send the contributions required for the interest payments to the Generality, because they gave priority to their own financial problems, and to the loans negotiated on their own provincial credit. The main part of the solution was a forced reduction of the interest rate on the Generality debt as well, from 4 to 3 percent.[25] The payment office of the Generality would again be unable to continue interest payments for some days in 1754, because of renewed arrears in the necessary contributions of the provinces to this end. Its inability to pay interest was an awkward problem when it happened. It cannot be regarded, however, as a 'state bankruptcy', given the limited amount involved in comparison with the provincial debts.

23 Dormans, *Het tekort*, 66 and 81 (Tables 3.9 and 3.18).

24 More details in Fritschy, 'Schulden als leerschool?', pp. 18–20.

25 Dormans, *Het tekort*, pp. 147–148.

The Generality did no longer really fulfil a function in debt financing in the Republic after 1713. Apparently Holland took incidentally over its function, when necessary. In 1745 it lent 2 million guilders at 3 percent to Friesland and in 1757 0.6 million at 3 percent to Zeeland. Interests and redemption on these loans were promptly paid each year to Holland until the loans were completely redeemed after respectively 32 and 37 years. Holland's position in the federation was, in contrast to that of the Generality, obviously powerful enough to prevent arrears in these payments.

b) *Voluntary Interest Conversions*

Voluntary conversions of the nominal interest on existing debt were practiced in Holland three times: in 1609 to 6.25%, in 1640 to 5% and in 1655 to 4%. They were successful, despite a continually increasing debt from 17.5 million guilders in 1609, 23.5 million in 1621 (mainly due to the fact that the English loans had to be redeemed) to more than 130 million guilders in 1652. This possibility of voluntary interest reductions must have been the result of an increasing capital supply, due to increasing wealth, and a wide demand for this investment possibility. The 'second' financial revolution had made provincial public debt again into an appreciated type of investment in Holland's commercialized society: it secured a continuous income during old age – or for widows and orphans – in a way much easier than by means of investments in land or in commercial or industrial enterprises. The amounts in urban loans were by that time evidently no longer sufficiently extensive to meet the demand for this investment opportunity.[26]

The provinces outside Holland were apparently able to follow Holland's voluntary interest reductions in the course of time, although with a distance of several years. The available data show that Overijssel tried to borrow at 6.25 percent in 1616, when it needed a loan to pay for its part in the redemption of the debt to England, but that it still had to pay 8 percent in fact, during that year. In 1625 it paid 6.25 percent on a new loan, since 1640 5 percent (like in Holland) and at least since 1659 4 percent, the same rate as Holland paid since 1655. A small province like Overijssel experienced what may be called a 'financial revolution', too: declining interest rates despite a continuously increasing debt burden resulting from voluntary loans.[27] Friesland had to pay 7 percent

26 The size of Amsterdam's urban debt was in 1680 only about 7 million guilders, Holland's debt was by then 162 million guilders, and Amsterdam started to reduce its urban debt after 1680; Fritschy, 'Urban and provincial public debt', pp. 83–84.

27 It paid 37,000 guilders in interest on long-term provincial debt in 1635, 85,000 guilders in 1658; GFO, p. 306.

in 1618 and even in 1653, but at least since 1664 it could borrow at 4 percent as well. Incidentally provinces tried to negotiate part of a loan in Amsterdam during the years when their own rates were higher than in Holland, but not really often.[28]

In the course of the eighteenth century, after the forced reductions that had followed the war of 1701–1713, the provinces outside Holland and Zeeland became gradually able to reduce the nominal interest rate voluntarily, Overijssel for instance to 3.5 percent in 1732 and to 3 percent in 1744; it was even able to negotiate a loan at an interest rate of only 2.5% in 1777, the same rate, therefore, in fact, as in Holland. In Groningen interest rates on public debt of 3 to 3.5 percent were found for 1744 and varying from 2.5 to 4 percent during the years 1783 to 1790.[29] So, financially the seven provinces seemed to become more integrated, although new loans continued probably to be mostly sold on the domestic provincial market.

c) *Avoiding Loans in Life-Annuities*

The interest rates of life annuities declined in the course of time mostly in tandem with the decline in the interest on redeemable annuities and obligations.[30] It remained always higher than on the redeemable annuities, of course, because the payments on these annuities just stopped when the holder died and they were never redeemed, whereas redeemable annuities were heritable and could be in fact perpetual if they were not redeemed. Life annuities were offered, as a rule, more sparingly to the public, because they were more expensive for the government

Holland's state-pensionary Johan de Witt calculated in 1671 that life-annuities at the prevailing rate of interest of then mostly 8.3% were on balance more expensive for the province than redeemable annuities and obligations, despite the fact that they automatically expired after the death of the holder, because they were often bought on the lives of young people.[31] The next

---

28 For Friesland data are available showing that about ten percent of the 43 million guilders in loans to which the States decided between 1618 and 1715 was offered for sale in Amsterdam; *GFF*, pp. 185–190.

29 For the other provinces similar data are yet hardly available.

30 An overview of nominal interest rates in Holland is to be found in *GFH*, pp. 381–382; an overview of taxes on bonds in *GFH*, pp. 362–375, a summary of the rates is offered in Figures III.5.d.1-2 in *GFH* pp. 372–373 (see the list of Abbreviations for the Internet acces to *GFH*).

31 J. de Witt, *Waerdye van lyf-rente naer proportie van los-renten* (Den Haag 1671) http://www.dbnl.org/tekst/witt001waer01_01/.

year they were sold at 7.1% (which was in fact still too much according to his calculations). For 1632 it is known that 17 percent of Holland's debt was the result of the sale of life annuities, in 1648 only 8 percent, in 1679 only 6 percent. During the next two wars it increased again to 10 percent of the total debt in 1714. Since then it nearly continuously decreased to less than one percent in 1794.[32]

The proportion sold in expensive life annuities had been in the provinces outside Holland always higher than in Holland, and there are indications that this was not only a result of an insufficient demand for redeemable annuities, but incidentally also of yielding to the preference of the investors in an irresponsible way. In Overijssel a pamphlet, printed in the 1660s, accused the official responsible for the sale of annuities to have sold much more in life-annuities than he had been allowed to.[33] In Utrecht about 78 percent of about 20 million guilders in loans between 1694 and 1714 had been in life annuities. It was rather unlikely that this was due to market circumstances, as in Friesland only 27 percent of 23 million guilders was borrowed by means of life-annuities.[34] In Holland this had been only 12 percent of the 111 million in loans during this war. The policy of limiting the sale of expensive life-annuities was followed in the provinces outside Holland in the course of the eighteenth century. In Overijssel in 1715 45 percent of interest payments were on life annuities, in 1794 only 16 percent.[35]

Since 1711 the States of Holland had started to prefer 'term-annuities' above life annuities, when necessary to get enough loans (which was the case during the last years of the war of 1701–1713, because investors in Amsterdam started by then to prefer investments in more attractive English loans). Term-annuities had rather high rates of interest for a restricted time period, varying from 10 to 31 years with lower interest rates of course for longer periods, before they expired without redemption.[36] The policy of selling less life-annuities, and selling term-annuities instead, when necessary, was visible in the other provinces as well.

---

32 Dormans, *Het tekort*, pp. 65, 80, 81, 110, 111 (NB The amounts for *'lijfrenten'* in Holland's Southern Quarter in Dormans' book, are erroneously placed under the column heading *'Noorderkwartier Losrenten'*; the amounts for *'Noorderkwartier losrenten'* are erroneously placed under the column heading *'Rest'* !).

33 Fritschy, 'Domeinen en financieel beleid in Overijssel', p. 87.

34 *GFU*, p. 110; *GFF*, 188–190.

35 Dormans, *Het tekort*, pp. 110–111; GFO, pp. 339–341.

36 Dormans, *Het tekort*, pp. 110, 111, 121, 122; *GFH*, p. 383.

The autonomous development of the public finance of the other provinces did not preclude that their public finance became increasingly comparable to that of Holland. Holland remained financially always by far the strongest link in the federal chain, however, not only in its wealth and the size of its public revenue, but also in the sophistication of its financial policy and the quality and stringency of its financial administration.

d) *Debt Redemption*

The last factor to be discussed among the attempts to contain the size of the interest burden is debt redemption. This also occurred in all provinces during some periods, as is visible at the top of Figure 3.2, although not always simultaneously in all provinces. Friesland's remarkable debt redemption in the early 1640s was mentioned already in Chapter 2.4.

Under Holland's famous state-pensionary Johan de Witt a policy an active policy to achieve a structural containment of the amounts needed for debt service was started in a form similar to what later would be called a 'Sinking Fund'.[37] In 1653 it was decided that for an amount of 4.4 million guilders had to be sold in either life-annuities at an interest of 9.1% or redeemable annuities at a rate of 5% because of the naval war with Britain. This would increase the interest burden with maximally about 400,000 guilders per year (when only life-annuities would be sold). To this end a new annual tax of a 1000th penny of personal wealth was levied from people whose property was valued at more than 2000 guilders in the 'personal registers' made by city governments, that were used for the personal levies of the 200th or 100th penny on property. The result of a levy on these registers in the case of a 1000th penny was also about 400,000 guilders per year. The part not needed for interest payments – in case lower renting redeemable annuities instead of life annuities had been sold, or when the amount needed for the life annuities decreased in the course of time when holders of these annuities died – was earmarked for debt redemption. Even more importantly, it was decided in 1655 that in addition the complete interest reduction from 5 to 4 percent had to be used for debt redemption as well, during the following years. This policy explains how it was possible that Holland's debt did not increase during the First English Naval War.[38] This policy was

---

37 *'Memorie van 1755'*, f27v (http://resources.huygens.knaw.nl/gewestelijkefinancien/memorie.pdf); *GFH*, p. 369.

38 Dormans, *Het tekort*, p. 66: it amounted to 130.5 million guilders in 1652, 130 million guilders in 1654, 128,7 million guilders in 1655; (at variance with Downing's assumption that Dutch naval wars were always financed by loans as mentioned earlier in the General Introduction).

continued until 1663, during which year debt redemption gradually increased from 1.2 million in 1655 to more than 1.6 million guilders in 1663. Holland's debt declined from 130 million guilders in 1653 to 119 million guilders in 1663.[39]

The ingenuity of the first measure was that it made the more well-to-do bear the burden of the increased interest payments that had to be paid to probably about the same social group. In the case of the second measure it is harder to say how wise it was to keep a tax level of – at that time – annually about 12 million guilders, that mostly burdened the common man, more than one million higher than necessary, in order to be able to reduce the interest burden with each year some (ten) thousands of guilders more than the year before.

Debt redemption was resumed after the War of the Spanish Succession reducing the debt in Holland with on average nearly 0.9 million guilders per year from 311 million guilders in 1714 to 295 million in 1732. Between 1750 and 1780 public debts everywhere in the Dutch Republic were reduced with even no less than on average about 3.6 million guilders in total per year, of which on average about 1.2 million guilders by Holland, at least about 1.3 million guilders by other provinces combined, and about 1 million guilders per year by the Generality. Debt redemption was regretted by the public, because it robbed them of an easy, reliable and appreciated investment opportunity and forced to more risky investments abroad (as for instance in the so-called West-Indian plantation loans between 1750 and 1780).[40] Nevertheless Holland's debt was again much higher at the end of the eighteenth century than in 1715, due to the last naval war with Britain and the start of the last war with France in 1793. Figure 3.4 summarizes the development in Holland's public debt in comparison to Holland's GDP.

The size of the debt of the provinces outside Holland is not known before 1796. By then the sum of these debts had become 35 percent of Holland's debt. If the same proportion was valid in 1794 when Holland's debt was 400 million guilders, the debt of the other provinces may have been about 140 million guilders in 1794, about a quarter of the total sum of all provincial debts.

Unlike the debts of the provinces the Generality debt was nearly completely redeemed between 1715 and 1794, from a top of 68 million guilders (22 percent of Holland's debt at the time) in 1715, to only 17.5 million guilders in 1794, mainly by means of the tax revenues of 'Brabant of the States' and the revenues resulting from the introduction of very popular Generality lotteries, once or twice a year since 1726. This debt redemption is more an illustration of the general decrease of the importance of the Generality in the fiscal system of the Dutch Republic than of its strength.

---

39 Dormans, *Het tekort*, p. 66.

40 J.P. van de Voort, *De Westindische plantages van 1720 tot 1795* (Eindhoven 1973).

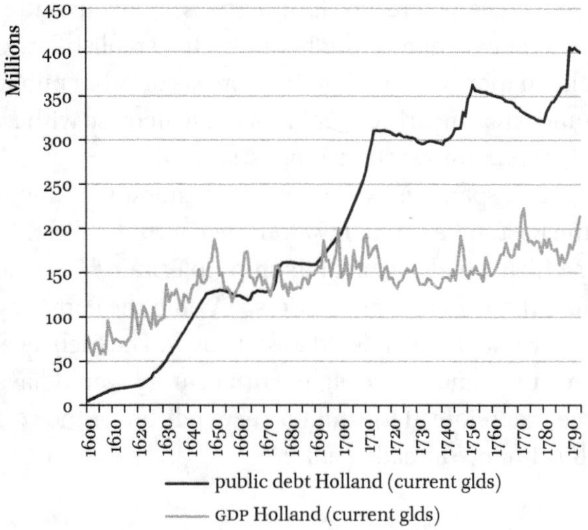

FIGURE 3.4 *Public debt and GDP of Holland, 1600–1794.*
Sources: Dormans, *Het tekort*, pp. 65, 66, 80, 81, 110, 111; http://www.cgeh.nl/reconstruction-national-accounts-holland-1500-1800-0.

Other Public Expenditure

The last element of public expenditure, visible at the bottom of Figure 3.2, can be summarized as 'domestic provincial public expenditure other than war expenditure and debt service'. Not much attention will be paid to this category of public expenditure within the framework of this book. It is not only the smallest, but quantitatively also the least reliable part of public expenditure. Hardly anything is known about this type of expenditure in the finances of the Generality, and about the question to what extent parts of this type of expenditure were charged onto 'domanial' revenues, especially in the provinces outside Holland. It is for this category of public expenditure that the distinction between public finance *of* and public finance *in* the Dutch Republic is moreover especially relevant, of course. Expenditure on public tasks like water management and urban facilities, including schools and poor relief was certainly large in comparison to the amounts for 'other' expenditure visible in Figure 3.2 (see Section 0.3 in the Introduction to Part 1).

The graph shows that its role in total public expenditure, according to the public finance definition used in this book, was certainly modest,[41] but that

41 It was impossible to include the 'other expenditure' of the admiralities and the Generality in this expenditure item (it is part of war expenditure in the Figure), but given the comparatively modest fiscal role of both in total public finance, it is evident that this could hardly have altered this conclusion.

it was increasing. In the provinces where tax farming was abolished after 1748, this increase was to a large part due to the necessity to establish a tax-collection apparatus. In Holland more than half of the increase in 'other public expenditure' between 1730 and 1790 – nearly one million of an increase with 1.7 million guilders – was due to this administrative innovation.[42]

During the later 1780s Holland spent an exceptional high amount of about 21 million guilders to save the East India Company after the Fourth English Naval War (1780–1784), during which it had lost all of its ships to Britain.[43] In 1796 the debt of the VOC was more than 120 million guilders.[44] When the company was abolished in 1798 its debt would be considered as state debt. The high level of Dutch public expenditure at the end of the eighteenth century would have been even significantly higher, therefore, if the military expenditure of the VOC had been covered from public finance already before.

3.2 The Resilience of the Provincial Revenue Systems

It may be expected that developments in the wealth of a state are an important determinant of its ability to raise public revenue. Was the Dutch Republic able to wage wars with much larger states, perhaps simply because its economic development had made it so much richer? Table 3.2 offers an impression of results of economic research on GDP per capita in states with which the Dutch Republic had to wage war in as far as available. Table 3.3 offers estimates of population figures for such states.

Although estimating GDP in early periods of history is still an ongoing process,[45] and although no estimates for GDP in the Dutch Republic as a whole are available already, there is no doubt whatsoever, that the size of GDP per capita in Holland could by far not compensate for the small size of its population

42 *GFH*, p. 426 Table V.2.1.

43 Dormans, *Het tekort,* p. 128 offers a summary of the ways in which the more than 50 million guilders of this forced loan was spent.

44 J.J. Steur, *Herstel of ondergang. De voorstellen tot redres van de Verenigde Oost-Indische Compagnie* (Utrecht 1984) p. 300.

45 For Holland the values in the years in Table 3.2 are moreover very different from the values for nine years averages; in 1800-guilders they would result in the following range for 1600–1650–1700–1750: 108–105–100–111–120 (the much higher values for the years 1600 and 1650 than in Table 3.2 are due to the fact that these were accidentally exceptionally good years for shipping and trade; the rather unexpected increasing trend between 1750 and 1800 remains visible however.).

TABLE 3.2 *Estimates of the development of GDP per capita in the Dutch Republic (Holland), Spain and (Great)Britain, c. 1570–c. 1800 (index numbers; italic my estimates).*

	Holland (Netherlands)	Spain	Britain (Great Britain)
1570	68	43	53
1600	126	42	51
1650	128	33	44
1700	100	39	75 (72)
1750	112	37	*84* (81)
1800	124 (*95?*)	44	*104* (100)
1807	114 (*87?*)		(103)

Source: Table 3.2: J. Bolt and J.L. van Zanden, The First Update of the Maddison Project; Re-Estimating Growth Before 1820. Maddison Project Working Paper 4 (2013); http://www.ggdc.net/maddison/maddison-project/home.htm.

TABLE 3.3 *Population estimates for the main European states involved in wars with the Dutch Republic, 1500–1800 (millions).*

	Holland (Dutch Republic)	Spain	Britain (Great Britain)	France
1500	0.28 (1.0)	5.0	3.5	15.0
1600	0.50 (1.5)	6.8	4.5	18.5
1650	0.81 (1.9)		5.6	
1700	0.84 (2.0)	7.4	5.5	21.5
1750	0.78 (2.0)	9.3	6.3 (7.1)	24.6
1800	0.76 (2.1)	10.5	9.3 (10.9)	29.0

Source: Table 3.3: P. Malanima, *Pre-modern European economy. One thousand years (10th–19th century)* (Leiden, Brill, 2009) p. 9; M. Flinn, *Scottish population history from the 17th century to the 1930s* (Cambridge: Cambridge University Press, 1973) pp. 198–199.

in comparison to its enemies, to explain its ability to realize the necessary public revenue. Between 1500 and 1600 Spain's population was about five times larger than that of the Dutch Republic, whereas the Republic's estimated wealth per capita was probably no more than about 50 percent higher than

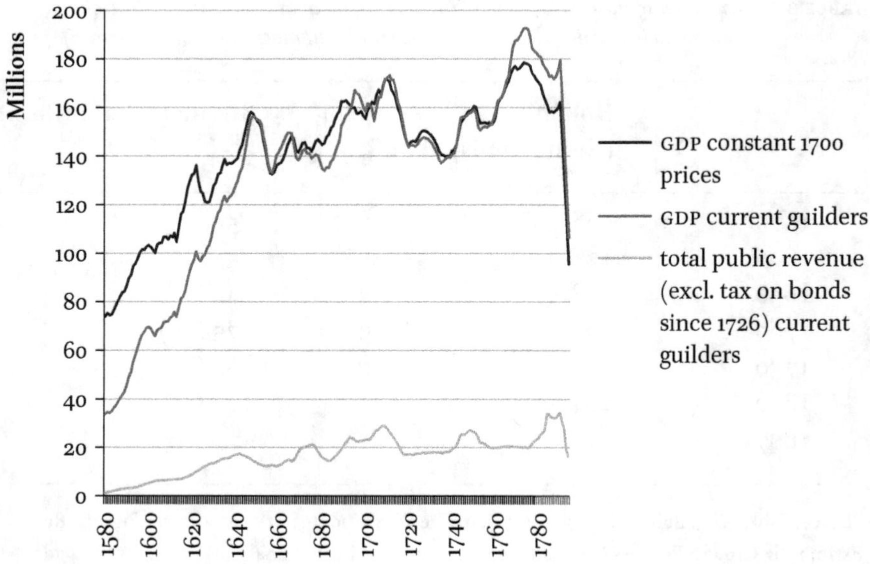

FIGURE 3.5 *GDP and total public revenue in Holland, 1580–1790 (9 years averages).*

that of Spain around 1570. Around 1700 Britain's population was nearly three times as large as that of the Republic, the Republic's wealth per capita was probably only about 25 percent higher than that of England, and less thereafter. These data make the question the more intriguing therefore, how exactly the Dutch Republic was able to finance the hugely increasing amounts in public expenditure in the course of its history.

For the province of Holland it is possible to give an impression of the role of economic development in public revenue, because for this province estimates are available on the development of its GDP for all years of the existence of the Dutch Republic. Figure 3.5 gives a comparative summary of the development of this GDP and Holland's total public revenue in nine years averages. It shows that the increase in Holland's public revenue until the first decade of the eighteenth century was evidently to a large extent made possible by the increase in its GDP.

The differences in the fluctuations of the two graphs in this Figure indicate also, however, that the percentage of GDP that was extracted from Holland's GDP as public revenue fluctuated in the course of time. Table 3.4 offers a summarizing view of this percentage in five periods: (1) the period of the formation of Holland's fiscal system before the Truce, (2) the period after the Truce before the 'second military revolution', (3) the period of the involvement of the Republic as a 'Great Power' in the increasingly expensive international wars

TABLE 3.4 *Holland's total public revenue (excl. tax on bonds since 1726) as % of Holland's GDP averages, in five periods, 1572–1794.*

1572–1620	7%
1621–1671	11%
1672–1713	13%
1714–1780	13%
1781–1794	18%

of the years 1672–1713, (4) the periods in which the Republic tried to avoid involvement in wars as much as possible, and (5) the last period characterized by the disaster of the Fourth English Naval War, with the huge financial problems of the VOC in its aftermath, which ended with the French invasion and the Batavian Revolution that brought the Republic to an end.

Table 3.4 confirms that the developments in Holland's public revenue were not only a result of Holland's economic development. Continuously new political decisions were necessary to make it possible to extract increasing percentages of Holland's GDP as public revenue. The next section will analyse how exactly this was done, not only for Holland, but for the whole Republic.

The public revenue increases in the Dutch Republic can be analysed from two points of view, that of what will be called its 'institutional structure', which refers to the centralized and the federal parts of the fiscal system, and that what will be called its 'social-economic structure', which refers to the proportion of taxes and loans in total revenue, and to the role of indirect taxes, the direct taxes on real estate and the personal direct taxes on total personal wealth, and therefore to the proportion of taxes mainly burdening the less well-to-do and burdening the more well-to-do.

The 'Institutional Structure' of the Public Revenue of the Republic

The main point to be made regarding the 'institutional structure' is that the necessary large increases in public revenue since 1621, resulting from the increases in public expenditure discussed in the former section, did *not* lead to an increasing financial role of the centralized institutions in the course of the existence of the Dutch Republic. The fiscal contribution of the own revenues of the Generality, mainly consisting of the taxes in the Generality territories, as well as the customs revenues of the admiralties, remained always relatively rather small and even decreased during the eighteenth century (see Figure 3.6).

In 1648 a tax system similar to that in the other provinces was introduced in 'Staats-Brabant' (= 'Brabant of the States (General)'), which would become the most important source of revenue for the Generality. Nevertheless, revenues generated by the Generality, including loans, would not become more than on average only about six percent of total public revenue of the Republic between this year and the year 1713 including long-term Generality loans, although during the war of 1701–1713 Generality-loans were still used rather frequently as an additional source of public revenue. During the rest of the eighteenth century Generality-revenues would become on average only about four percent of the Republic's total public revenue. Although one might be inclined to expect that 'Staats-Brabant', as conquered territory, was fiscally plundered as much as possible, this was in fact not the case.[46] The rates of the 'common means' in Staats-Brabant were, on the contrary, low in comparison to other provinces, and taxes on property like Holland's '200th and 100th etc. pennies' were probably even never levied in Generality territories.

The relative importance of customs revenue, the tariffs of which were centrally determined as well, was also rather small, although it absolutely increased during the seventeenth century partly due to the development of international trade, partly due to decisions to increase rates.[47] Customs revenues amounted to on average about eleven percent of total public revenue in the Republic during the seventeenth century (2.7 million guilders) and about seven percent during the eighteenth century (2.8 million guilders). In the course of this last century customs revenues decreased even absolutely. As it is often assumed that foreign trade – and especially the VOC – must have been important for the explanation of the large and increasing public revenue of the Republic, this result seems surprising and makes it worthwhile to have a closer look at the position of the VOC in relation to the Dutch fiscal system.

As was mentioned, the VOC had to pay for war faring and its protection in the Indies from its own revenues, albeit after an initial period of incidental support from the Generality during the first decades after its establishment in 1602. This did not mean, however, that it did not have to pay customs (apart from incidental dispensation). A change occurred in 1690, when all VOC-trade was freed from custom duties in exchange for the payment of a fixed amount of 364,000 guilders per year, to be divided among the admiralties according to a fixed key. The question should be raised, therefore, if the declining importance

46 Kappelhof, *Belastingheffing in de Meijerij*, p. 331.

47 J.F. Meijer, 'Voorstellen tot herziening van de heffing van convooien en licenten', in *Doel en middel. Aspecten van financieel overheidsbeleid in de Nederlanden van de zestiende tot heden*, eds. W. Fritschy, J.K.T. Postma and J. Roelevink (Amsterdam 1995) pp. 97–115, p. 101.

of customs revenue in the Dutch fiscal system might be due to the fact that this amount of 364,000 guilders was much too low in comparison to the – increasing – importance of the VOC-trade in the course of the eighteenth century.

The VOC-contribution amounted to 14 percent of the total of customs revenue of the admiralties during the 1680s. During the 1770s it amounted to 19 percent. Surprisingly there are indications that this percentage was not lower, but even somewhat higher than what could have been expected if incoming VOC-ships would have paid customs revenues on the same footing as other ships. De Vries and Van der Woude estimated the value of imported VOC goods between 1750 and 1780 at 18 to 21 million guilders. This would imply that the value of VOC-imports was only 13 to 15 percent of the estimated value of all imports, as this was estimated by them at 143 million guilders.

The amount of 18 to 21 million seemed surprisingly little in comparison to the total value of imported colonial goods in the 1770s of no less than 63 million guilders. Estimates of the value of traded goods based on the number of ships by Van Zanden and Van Leeuwen resulted in an amount of on average even only 17 million guilders for the eighteenth century, however. De Vries and Van der Woude saw the percentage of the East Indies in the value of total trade confirmed, moreover, by a well-informed contemporary, the VOC-director Van der Oudermeulen, who in 1785 estimated the foreign trade turnover (imports plus re-exports) accounted for by the VOC during the 1770s, at 13 percent of the total value of Dutch foreign trade, imports plus (re-)exports.[48] This low percentage was accepted by VOC-specialist Gaastra, too, and again in Brandon's recent study, which pays special attention to the role of the VOC in the character of the Dutch state.[49] The available information makes it unlikely therefore that the relatively low contribution of customs to the total public revenue of the Dutch Republic can be explained by a privileged position of the VOC as to customs.

Anyhow, the governing elites of the Dutch Republic had evidently no inclination at all to use just any part of foreign trade as a really important source for increases in public revenue, especially during the eighteenth century. During the seventeenth century tariff increases had several times led to attractive revenue increases, but a reform in 1725 leading to a new simplified tariff-list aimed at a more efficient functioning of the admiralties, not at raising tariffs. A proposal during the preparation of the reform of 1725 to re-introduce tax farming for customs, as a more efficient system than collection, foundered on the resistance of merchants in Amsterdam as well as of admiralty-officials themselves.

48 De Vries and Van der Woude, *The first modern economy*, pp. 457, 499.

49 Brandon, *War, capital and the Dutch state*, p. 104 referring to Gaastra (1994) pp. 25–26.

During the years 1687–1690 half of the customs revenues had been leased, which may have contributed to an increase of total customs revenue from 3 million guilders in 1687 to 3.6 million in 1688, although it has to be added that it decreased again to only 3.2 million, already in 1689, when it was still leased. In 1690 tax farming was abolished again and the revenues declined to 2.8 million in that year, to which it should be added, however, that in 1691 revenue was again 3.6 million, and that customs revenue could also in general fluctuate rather strongly from year to year. This makes it not easy to determine the effects of reform-measures, although it is certain that the reform of 1725 did not lead to a revenue-increase.[50] Even in this case, however, it is not sure if this was due to the inefficacy of the measures resulting from the reform or to economic developments. The decentralized structure of customs collection, without strong central management, may have had a negative impact on customs revenue, by allowing customs evasion, as contemporaries strongly suspected. Van Leeuwen and Van Zanden found a negative growth rate for GDP in trade between 1720 and 1800 as well, however (and their estimates were not based on customs revenues).[51]

Anyhow, when it was necessary to raise public revenue, it appears to have been always preferred to exploit fiscally the domestic economy and domestic wealth, the flourishing of which partly depended, of course, on foreign trade, rather than to increase the tariffs on foreign trade itself. Although the provinces outside Holland were slow and negligent in paying their dues in subsidies to the navy (see Figure 3.2), they apparently yet preferred having to contribute to these subsidies above insisting on attempts to increase the revenue from this centralized element of the public finance of the Dutch Republic. Elites in all provinces may have been very well aware how much their consumption pattern was dependent on foreign imports.

A summarizing 'institutional analysis' of the developments in the Republic's public revenue is offered by Figure 3.6. It shows the relatively very small size of the contributions of the Generality and the admiralties, and it shows that Holland's public revenue formed always by far the largest part of the total public revenue of the Dutch Republic. The extreme peak in 1788 is due to a

50 It was on average 4.1 million guilders in 1721–25, about 3.8 million guilders in 1726–30, about 3.2 million guilders in 1731–6; W. Veenstra, *Tussen gewest en Generaliteit. Staatsvorming en financiering van de oorlog te water in de Republiek der Verenigde Nedrlanden in het bijzonder Zeeland (1586–1795)* (diss. VU Amsterdam 2014) p. 242.

51 Van Zanden and Van Leeuwen, and 'Persistent but not Consistent', Table 4; the data on http://www.cgeh.nl/reconstruction-national-accounts-holland-1500-1800-0.

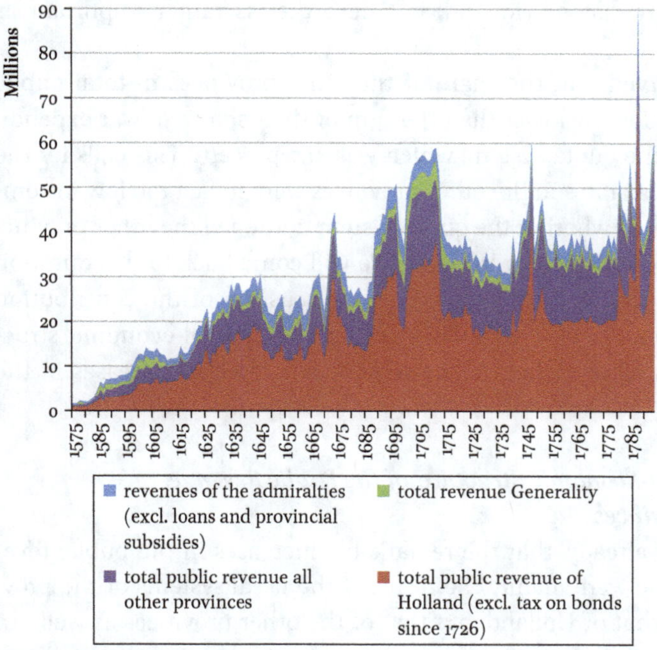

FIGURE 3.6 *Total public revenue of the Dutch Republic: Holland, the other provinces, the Generality and the admiralties, 1575–1794.*

forced loan only in Holland of no less than 4% of the value of property mainly destined to save the VOC after the Fourth English Naval War, with a net result of nearly 45.3 million guilders.[52] The peak in 1748 was mainly due to a direct tax of 2% of property, called 'the Liberal Gift', which will be further discussed below.

Holland's share in total public revenue was on average 59 percent during the seventeenth century since 1621, 58 percent during the eighteenth century. (If the forced loan of 1788 with a result of about 50 million guilders is excluded its share would have been only 56 percent in the eighteenth century.) The part played by the other provinces was on average 28 percent since 1621 during the seventeenth century and 33 percent during the eighteenth. It was

52 Dormans, *Het tekort*, pp. 127–128; 21,150,000 for the VOC, 8 million for the admiralties; the total result was according to p. 128 53 million guilders; for this graph the 7,7 million guilders used to redeem obligations was removed from the total in this graph; NB in *GFH* p. 240 the 53 million have been counted as a levy on property.

much smaller than that of Holland, but nevertheless rather important as well.

It may be observed that the share of the other provinces in total public revenue was considerably lower than the sum of their shares in war expenditure according to the quota system, which was 41.7 percent. This calls for the question whether tax rates in the other provinces were in fact too low in comparison to Holland, or whether the quota-system burdened the other provinces too heavily in comparison to Holland. We will come back to this question at the end of this section after first a general discussion of the contribution of the different elements of – what will be called – the 'social-economic structure' of the Dutch fiscal system to the remarkable revenue-increases in the Republic.

The 'Social-Economic Structure' of the Public Revenue of the Provinces

Figure 3.6 showed already, that the remarkable increases in the public revenue of the Republic were mainly the result of the fiscal systems of the provinces, not only of that of Holland, but that of the other provinces as well. An analysis of the social-economic structure of provincial public revenue shows by what means more specifically the provinces realized the required public revenue-increases.

Figures 3.7a–3.7b illustrate the differences and similarities in this respect between Holland and four provinces for which enough data were available.[53] They show that the importance of indirect taxes[54] was relatively highest in Holland. In the other provinces direct taxes, especially on land, were relatively more important. In all provinces 'other direct taxes' – consisting of direct taxes on elements of personal wealth, transfer taxes, and direct taxes in the 'common' or 'general means' (for instance on cattle, horses, servants, coaches etc.) – were additionally important. Remarkable is the increasing importance of loans in the fiscal systems of the provinces also outside Holland. Also in this respect the provinces became more similar. The 'fabric' of the total of public revenue was 'stretched' from on average nearly 17 million guilders between 1621 and 1700, to on average about 24 million guilders between 1700 and 1794

53 Figure 3.7b is restricted to the four provinces, for which enough detailed data were available or could be estimated in a rather reliable way; for the absolute amounts in guilders of the different elements see the tables in *GFH*, GFZ, GFF, GFG, GFO (electroniscally accessible see the list of Abbreviations).

54 For an overview of all taxes levied in all provinces based on the categories used in these graphs during the Dutch Republic see the Appendix at the end of this book.

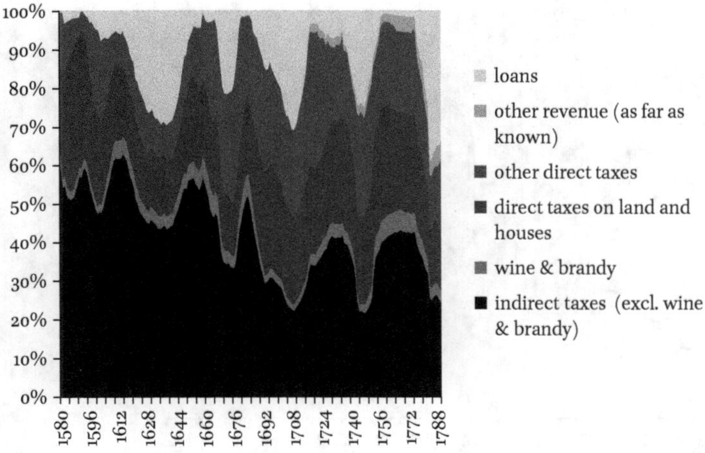

FIGURE 3.7A *Structure of provincial revenue in Holland, 1580–1790 (nine years averages).*

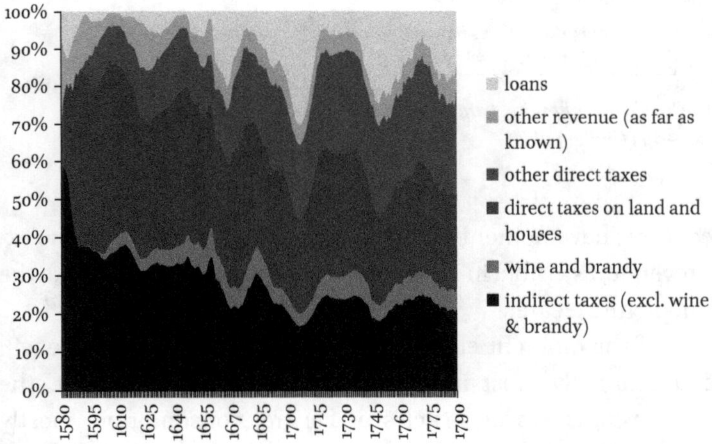

FIGURE 3.7B *Idem in four other provinces (Zeeland, Friesland, Groningen, Overijssel).*

in Holland,[55] and from on average about 5 million guilders to about 9 million guilders during the same two periods in the other four provinces.

Figure 3.7c shows that the three main tax categories all continued to contribute to the necessary rises in public revenue, although indirect taxation more so than the other two until about 1650 and less so between 1700 and 1715, the period in which Van Zanden GDP-estimates (that are based on production data, not on fiscal data!) sharply decline (Figure 3.5). It shows the important

55 For 1700–1787 (excluding the extreme peak in 1788) it would have been 23.2 million guilders.

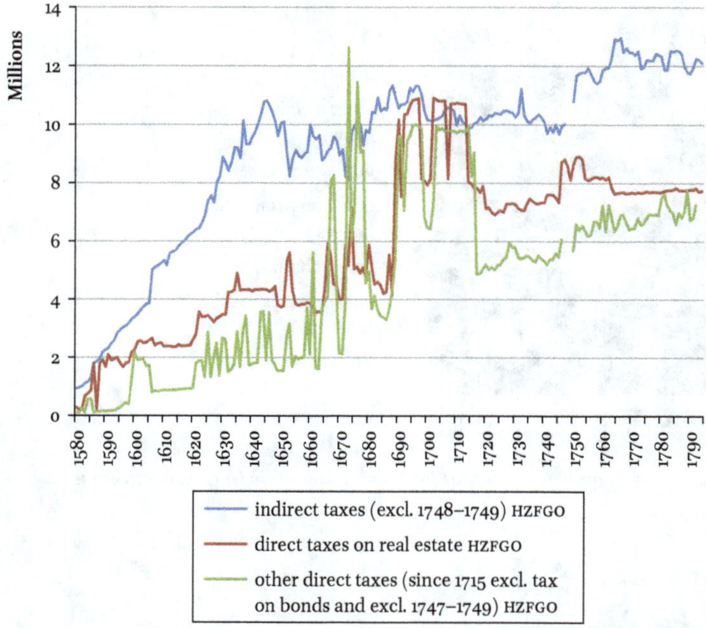

FIGURE 3.7C *The 'resilience' of indirect and direct taxation in five provinces (HZFGO), 1580–1794 (million glds).*

influence of economic development on this part of taxation. Note that the extreme peaks in revenue, as visible in Figure 3.6, have been omitted to make the overall long-term picture clearer.

The discussion of the different elements of provincial public revenue will start with the traditionally most important social-economic element, the indirect price-increasing taxes on articles of general consumption, mostly burdening the less well-to-do, and then examine successively the other elements visible in Figures 3.7a–3.7b. The extreme values omitted from Figure 3.7c will receive due attention as well in this discussion.

Price-Increasing Taxes on General Consumption and Tax Riots

The first decade after the Truce can be seen as the baptism of fire for Holland's fiscal system. Table 3.5 shows that the revenues of indirect taxes, the price-increasing taxes on products of general consumption, increased significantly during that decade (column a), and this occurred in a situation of fiercely declining real wages (column g), not only in absolute terms, but – despite population increases (column b) – also per capita (column c).[56] No wonder, therefore, that

56 http://www.iisg.nl/hpw/data.php#netherlands.

this was the period in which a first 'wave' of tax riots occurred in many cities in Holland (in Haarlem, Leiden, Amsterdam, Geertruidenberg, Den Haag and Delft).[57] A new tax on butter in 1624 was the immediate cause of the riots. The rioters were severely punished, but the intended tax rate was diminished somewhat, too, after which the riots ended. The riots of 1624 did not prevent the revenues of the 'indirect taxes on general consumption' to be about 20 percent higher during the 1630s than in the 1620s, whereas the estimated average of the population size was only about 5 percent higher.[58]

The expansion of the burden of general indirect taxation continued without further tax riots, during the next decades until the end of the Eighty Years War in 1648. It seems likely that especially the continuously rising nominal wages (column d) will have given Holland's tax system sufficient 'elasticity' to get the tax increases accepted during these decades, despite a probably again slightly declining real wage during 1642–1651. Tax rates did not decline after the Eighty Years War. The remarkably lower revenue in the period 1652–1661 was mainly due to a dramatic decline in revenues during the First English Naval War and on the other hand to a structural decline in the beer-production in the Netherlands.[59]

Holland's fiscal resilience became clearly visible again in a range of clever political fiscal decisions after the end of the war of 1672–1678. The rates on the most remunerative indirect price-increasing tax, like the milling of grain and that on peat and coal, were raised, the first one even with one third, but at the same time many other indirect taxes on general consumption (on shoes, candles, oil, fish etc.) were abolished. These were in fact the ones that were simply not very remunerative. In this way the revenue of indirect taxes on general consumption was increased with more than ten percent (column a), without causing disruptive social unrest.[60] Renewed increases in the rates of indirect taxes in later years, like especially the flat ten percent increase on the tax rates of all 'common means' in the 1680s, may again have been facilitated by the

57 R. Dekker, *Holland in beroering. Oproeren in de 17de en 18de eeuw* (Baarn 1982) pp. 30–31.

58 Van Zanden, http://www.cgeh.nl/reconstruction-national-accounts-holland-1500-1800-0 (column EB) [last access 2016-08-27].

59 Total revenue of the common means (excl. 5% 'ration-money') declined from 8.4 million guilders in 1651 to 7.8 million guilders in 1652 and 7.1 million guilders in 1653 and only slowly recoverd to a next top of 8.1 million guilders in 1663. (*GFH*, p. 162); the sum of the revenue on beer taxes declined from 2.43 million in 1650 gradually to 2.05 million guilders in 1661 (*GFH* p. 246).

60 W. Fritschy, 'The efficiency of taxation in Holland', in: *The Political Economy of the Dutch Republic*, ed. O. Gelderblom (Farnham, Ashgate, 2009) pp. 55–85.

TABLE 3.5 *Indirect taxes on general consumption and real wages in Holland, 1600–1790 (ten years averages).*

Holland	Revenue general indirect taxes (mill. glds)	Estimated population (*1000)	General indirect taxes p.c. p.yr. (glds)	Average nominal wage of a journeyman for 300 days (glds)	Consumption price index (1700 =100)	Real wage of journeyman if working 300 days a year (in glds of 1700)	Difference with real wage in the period before
	a	b	c=a/b*1000	d	e	f=d/e*100	g
1600–1609	3.2	537	5.96	264	62	426	
1610–1621	4.4	622	7.07	284	65	437	3%
1622–1631	**5.6**	**675**	**8.30**	**303**	**85**	**356**	**-19%**
1632–1641	6.8	704	9.66	321	85	378	6%
1642–1651	7.9	773	10.22	339	93	365	-3%
1652–1661	6.9	822	8.39	361	99	365	0%
1662–1671	6.9	869	7.94	371	94	395	8%
1672–1681	7.1	874	8.12	368	91	404	2%
1682–1691	7.9	861	9.18	364	90	404	0%
1692–1701	**8**	**848**	**9.43**	**359**	**105**	**342**	**-15%**
1702–1713	7.5	834	8.99	358	94	381	11%
1714–1722	7.3	821	8.89	361	94	384	1%
1723–1731	7.4	810	9.14	363	90	403	5%

1732–1740	7.4	799	9.26	373	91	410	2%
1741–1750*	**5.8(7.0)**	**788**	**8.88(7.36)**	**369**	**95**	**388**	**–5%**
1751–1760	8	783	10.22	374	96	390	1%
1761–1770	8.6	783	10.98	368	100	368	–6%
1771–1780	8.5	783	10.86	369	107	345	–6%
1781–1790	8.4	783	10.73	373	111	336	–3%

NB Rows in bold font indicate periods with tax riots.

* In 1748/9 the indirect 'common means' were abolished and temporarily replaced by direct taxation; the amounts between brackets are the averages without the years 1748 and 1749.

Sources: (b) my estimates, based on determining the growth percentage between the years for which estimates were available in De Vries and Van der Woude, *The first modern economy*, p. 512 (d) *ibidem*, pp. 610–611; (e) Van Zanden, http://www.iisg.nl/hpw/data.php.

fact that they do not seem to have caused declining real wages. They increased from 5.6 million in the 1620s to 8 million guilders during the 1690s.

The historian Rudolf Dekker found only a few other – and less widespread – tax riots in Holland between that of 1624 and the second and last real 'wave' of tax riots of 1747/8. One in 1678 in the Zaanstreek, an industrial region north of Amsterdam, was directed against a new way of measuring peat (used as fuel), that was to the advantage of the peat-tax farmers. One in 1690 in Rotterdam was directed against a tax farmer of wine, and one in 1696 in Amsterdam against the introduction of a provincial tax on burials. One of the slogans of this riot was, however, that *all* new taxes introduced during the last twenty years, had to be abolished. Especially in the last case it will not have been a coincidence, therefore, that the 1690s, showed again the concurrence of an increase in taxation (not only on burials, but also on marriages, and, already in 1691, on coffee and tea) with a fierce decrease in real wages of about 15 percent.

The other 'wave' of tax riots was in 1747/8, again in a decade of decreased real wages. The riots were directed against many of the increasingly wealthy farmers of the 'common' and the 'general means' and were much more widespread, also in the provinces outside Holland, than the butter riots of the 1620s. They would lead to the abolition of tax farming in most – but not all – of the provinces. After two years, in which the collection of the amounts formerly produced by the common means was 'outsourced' to the cities with very disappointing results, Holland started in 1750 to have the 'common means' collected by provincial public servants instead of leasing them out to tax farmers. At their reintroduction the rates on the milling of grains and the slaughtering of cattle became higher.[61] This must have increased prices, but it did not cause disruptive social unrest. It is probably not irrelevant that, by that time, not only nominal wages, but even real wages seem to have been rising again (Table 3.5).

It has often been thought that the increase in the revenue of the common means in the 1750s in comparison with the years before 1748 – from ca. 8.5 million to nearly 11 million guilders – was due to the change from tax farming to tax collection. In fact, however, it was partly simply the result of increased tax rates. Moreover, the revenue from the additional 5 percent for the

61 *GFH*, pp. 320, 324. The tax on brandy in Holland showed a remarkable revenue-increase, as well, from less than 40,000 guilders per year before 1748 to on average about 450,000 guilders in the years since 1750 (*GFH*, p. 248, 250); the incidentally sharp fluctuations in the revenue displayed by this tax also in other periods were probably caused by not always leasing it to tax farmers, but using another tax method like for instance the selling of a monopoly for a certain period of time in certain places; in those years the revenue was no longer part of the administration of the common means.

'*rantsoenpenningen*' to be paid by the tax farmers was not part of the revenue-figures in Holland's printed overviews of the revenues of the common means before 1750, which made these revenues higher in fact than the available figures suggest.[62] Lastly, an amount of nearly one million in 'collection costs' is to be found on the expenditure side of Holland's public finance after 1750, as was mentioned already. This was an expenditure item that was absent for taxes that were leased, and which in fact should be deducted from the revenue increase, of course, for a fair comparison with the earlier period.[63]

In general, it can be said, that the fiscal 'elasticity' in Holland regarding the increase in tax rates on items of general consumption was certainly partly due to rather clever political decisions of the States and the general administrative capability of the Finance Office of the States of Holland,[64] but very probably also to economic circumstances regarding the wage level, that facilitated the acceptance of price-increasing indirect taxes without many tax riots.

Price-Increasing Taxes on 'Luxury' Consumption

The relatively low importance of the taxes on the luxury (or unnecessary) consumption goods wine and brandy, the second element visible in Figure 3.7a–3.7b, may have been partly related to the much higher elasticity of the demand for such products, implying that a higher price due to a tax-increase – or a decrease in income or wealth – might easily result in a decrease in demand.

In Holland the yearly revenues of all 'common means' could be monitored by the representatives of the cities in the Provincial States Assembly, because, since 1650, they were made each year available in print by Holland's Finance Office, for each tax and for each tax district. The representatives in the States must have been aware, therefore, that the revenue of the wine tax had declined from about 400,000 guilders in 1672, to about 329,000 guilders in 1673, and that this might have been partly a side effect of the long range of levies and forced loans on property during the same years.[65] This makes it understandable that

62 In the database 5 percent was added to the revenues of Holland's common means (and to provincial expenditure) to correct for this administrative characteristic.

63 The costs of the auctions were paid from a quarter of the revenue of the '*rantsoenpenningen*'('ration-money'), the rest of which had to be used for payments to the ministers of the Calvinist churches and to subsidize urban poor relief; as the revenue of the common means in Holland was about 9 million guilders in the years before 1747/8 the amount for the lease-costs will not have been more than about 100,000 guilders per year.

64 For more details on this office see Fritschy, 'The efficiency of taxation in Holland'.

65 The decrease from nearly 560,000 guilders in 1671, to 400,000 guilders in 1672 was due however to a change to a direct levying of this tax by means of 'quotisation' in Amsterdam,

it was preferred to increase the rate of the peat-tax to realize more revenue in 1674.

In 1679/80, two years after the war, it was expected that the revenue increase resulting from an increase in the wine tax rate in Holland (in addition to the increases in that on the milling of grain and on peat and coal mentioned above) would be ca. 400,000 guilders. In fact it would be less than 200,000 guilders.[66] It is not certain however to what extent this was a result of decreasing demand or of increasing tax fraud.

During the first years of the War of the Spanish Succession, when taxes on property increased from on average 2.5 million guilders per year to on average about 5.1 million guilders per year, a decrease in the revenues from the tax on wines was to be observed from on average about 420,000 guilders in the years before the war to on average about 370,000 guilders from 1702–1706.[67] No wonder that again the tax on peat, widely used as fuel in households as well as in industries, was preferred in 1707 to realize an increase in revenue, necessary for the increasing interest burden during the war. During the eighteenth century further increases in the tax on wine were simply no longer attempted, only that on brandy was increased once, in 1786 (with hardly any visible effect on its revenue).[68]

Nevertheless, much more revenue from this type of taxes appeared not to have been impossible. After the Batavian Revolution of 1795, that ended the old Dutch republic, a new unified tax system would be introduced in the Northern Netherlands. The then Minister of Finance Alexander Gogel, an enthusiast for the principles of 'freedom, equality and brotherhood', wanted explicitly to shift the tax burden resulting from price-increasing taxes to the more well-to-do. He succeeded in the realization of taxes on wine and brandy that would yield 3.2 million guilders in the province of Holland, while in the 1790s this had been no more than one million guilders in this province, about half for brandy, about half for wine. Theoretically it is possible that the elasticity of the demand for these alcoholic beverages had decreased by that time. More probably, however, it was the determination of this minister to get more revenue from luxury consumption and the absence of this determination among the ruling elite of Holland before the Batavian Revolution of 1795 that made the difference. A full comparison of the main aspects of Gogel's new tax system with the old system will be offered at the end of this section.

---

due to this the revenue was not entered in the administration of the farmed common means of that year (*GFH* p. 312).

66 Fritschy, 'The efficiency of taxation in Holland', p. 67.

67 *GFH*, pp. 238, 246.

68 *GFH*, pp. 250, 315.

The Increasing Role of Direct Taxation

Much more important than indirect, price-increasing taxes for the realization of the necessary huge increases in public revenue since 1672, was, however, direct taxation, in Holland as well as in the other provinces. Table 3.6 illustrates this for the five provinces for which sufficient data were available.

Although the amounts in price-increasing general taxes still grew until 1702 and would grow again after 1750(see Table 3.5), the lower half of Table 3.6 shows a clear shift from indirect price increasing taxes to 'coercive' direct taxation in the tax system, especially since the 'second military revolution' of the 1670s. The part of indirect taxes on general consumption in the total of taxes changed from on average about 53 percent before 1672 to on average about 38 percent since then. Direct taxation consisted not only of the tax on land and houses, but also of other forms of direct taxation: on the one hand direct taxes belonging to the 'common means' on cattle, servants in households, the possession of coaches and yachts, and on forms of 'consumption' that were estimated in personal tax-registers for the more wealthy people – like on coffee and tea since the end of the seventeenth century, (sometimes) on wine, and (during a certain period) on soap and salt –, and, on the other hand, of personal taxes on assessed property in general, including on having an income from offices. The importance of the taxes on land and houses was especially large in the period of the great international wars between 1672 and 1713, but decreased again since then.[69] The importance of 'other direct taxes', was smaller, but increased more markedly from on average about 15 percent before 1672 to on average about 26 percent since then. Personal direct taxes on total property, in addition to the 'ordinary' direct taxes on real estate, were considered originally as 'extraordinary taxes' to be abolished again as soon as possible. In practice they became in the course of time as ordinary as the 'ordinary' direct taxes.

It should be noted that the tax on bonds – which was in fact an interest-reduction as was explained above – is not considered as tax-revenue under 'other direct taxes' already as of 1687 in Table 3.6. It can be argued, quite correctly, that it should be still considered as a tax during most of the years between 1687 and 1726, because a voluntary interest conversion cannot be expected to have been possible during most of these years. If this had been done, the shift to direct taxes on more wealthy people as visible in Table 3.6

---

69 The decrease in the periode 1621–1671 to 22% (Table 3.6) may be due to too low estimates in the case of missing data. Because the main focus of the book is on an explanation of the high level of public revenue, lower revenue estimates were always preferred to higher ones in case of uncertainty.

TABLE 3.6 *Structure of public revenue in five provinces (HZFGO) in four periods, 1575–1794.*

	Indirect taxes on general consumption	Wine and brandy	Direct taxes on land and houses	Other direct taxes (excl. on bonds since 1687)	Other revenue	Loans (forced and voluntary)		Average total amount (mill. glds.)
1575–1620	51%	3%	28%	11%	2%	4%	100%	6.1
1621–1671	44%	4%	22%	14%	2%	14%	100%	18.5
1672–1713	31%	3%	26%	18%	1%	20%	100%	30.3
1714–1794	31%	4%	24%	23%	4%	13%	100%	31.7
1575–1620	55%	3%	30%	12%			100%	5.7
1621–1671	52%	5%	26%	17%			100%	15.7
1672–1713	39%	4%	34%	23%			100%	23.7
1714–1794	37%	5%	29%	28%			100%	26.2

would have been even more remarkable during the last decades of the seventeenth and the first decades of the eighteenth century.[70]

The threat of a continuously increasing interest burden as a result of the virtual permanency of most of the public loans was presented in Chapter 2 as a main 'weakness' in the Dutch fiscal system since the 'second' financial revolution in Holland. This makes it interesting to compare the interest burden – as it resulted from the attempts of the provinces to contain it – to the structure of the tax system. This might be done by asking to what extent the revenue of the 'common' ('general') means, mainly burdening the 'common man', had to be used to realize the interest payments to the bondholders.

The revenues of the 'common' and 'general' means were not at all earmarked for the interest burden on the public debts, however. In Holland more than one third of the interest payments were done by Holland's receiver-general, whose main revenues were direct taxes.[71] His office was initially in Delft, later in The Hague and the large number of interest payments assigned on his office is probably to be explained by the fact that many public debt holders lived in The Hague, the government centre of the Republic and of Holland.

A preserved account of 1764 of this receiver (one of the very few accounts that were preserved in fact for Holland) shows that 4.8 million guilders of a total of 13.3 million guilders of his expenditure consisted of interest payments (the main entry was 5.4 million guilders for 'generality expenditure'). The original core of the revenues of Holland's general receiver was Holland's tax on land and houses, good for 2.3 million guilders in 1764. Among his revenues was only one tax belonging to the 'common means', the tax on peat and coal in Holland's Southern Quarter, which amounted then to 1.8 million guilders. More than half of his revenue, however, consisted by that time of the revenues of the 'extraordinary' '200th, 100th etc. pennies', amounting to about 7.5 million guilders, which mainly consisted of the 'tax' on bonds.

We may conclude that the eighteen district receivers of Holland's 'common means' had to transfer to Holland's general receiver the amounts that they were not allowed to pay to the bondholders the nominal amount in interest assigned on their office, because of the tax on bonds. The Hague housed no district-receiver of the common means. So it was de facto the interest reduction to be realized by the tax offices of the 'common means' that enabled the

70 In 1672–1713 'general indirect taxes' would have been only 29 percent in this case, 'direct taxes on real estate' 25 percent and 'other direct taxes' 24 percent.

71 This was the case in 1651 and in 1665, see *GFH*, p. 40; in fact he was only the receiver general of Holland's 'Southern Quarter', receiving as such about 90% of Holland's public revenue, however (ibidem, pp. 267, 289).

receiver-general to pay the interest to bondholders in The Hague and surroundings (of course also after deduction of the tax on bonds). This makes it at least as logical, therefore, to ask the question to what extent the interest payments were met by direct taxes, and to see what the more well-to-do – who may often have been bondholders as well as persons assessed in direct taxes – contributed 'on balance' to the fiscal system of the Republic.

Figures 3.8a–3.8b show that most of the time more in direct taxes was paid than was received in interest, certainly so in the provinces outside Holland. (Note that the upper graph, on Holland's total tax revenue, offers an indication how much in promised interest was not paid due to the tax on bonds between 1687 and 1726 and that both direct taxes and the interest burden would have been higher between 1687 and 1726, if the tax on bonds would have been omitted only since 1726).

In as far as owners of real estate were able to rent their property to others, they will have been able to transfer at least part of the direct tax burden on real estate to tenants, which may not at all have belonged to the more-well-to-do. More relevant is, therefore, the conclusion that the amounts paid

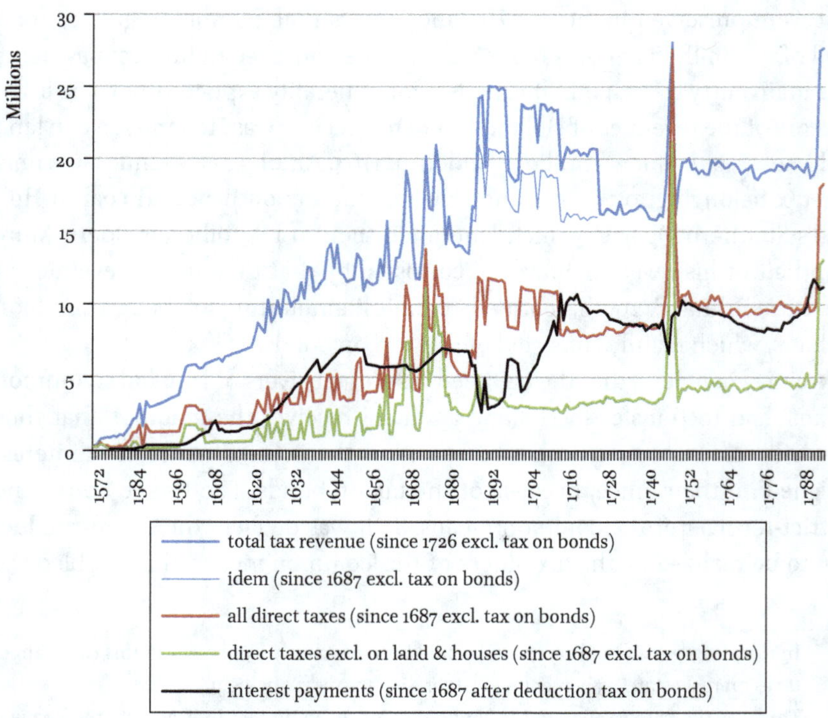

FIGURE 3.8A *Direct taxation and the size of the interest payments in Holland, 1572–1794 (million guilders).*

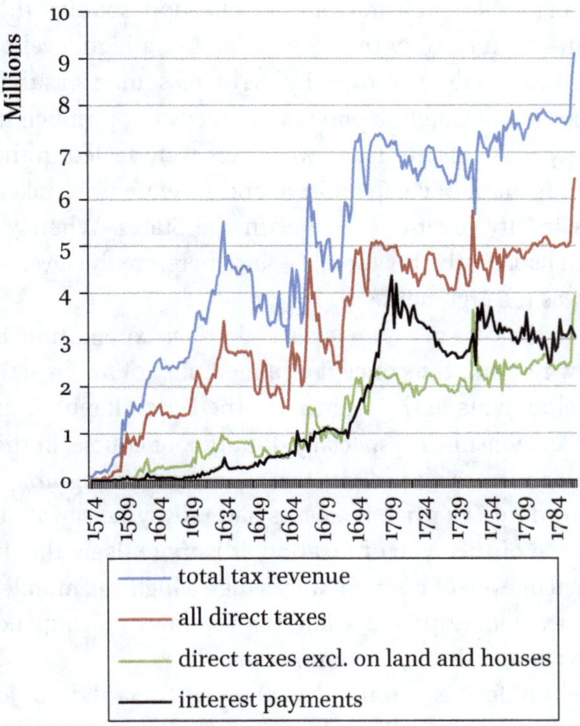

FIGURE 3.8B *Direct taxes and the size of the interest payments in four provinces outside Holland* (ZFGO)*, 1574–1794.*

by the provincial governments to its bondholders were in Holland nearly always higher than the amounts to be paid in *personal* direct taxes which certainly burdened the more well-to-do.

In the other provinces this became the case as well in the eighteenth century, but the difference between Holland and the other provinces is also evident in Figure 3.8. If it may be assumed that people assessed in more direct taxes than only those on land and houses, were about the same social group as the people who had invested in public debt, then the proportion of what was 'left' to bondholders in interests after having paid direct taxation, was clearly higher in Holland than in the other provinces in the eighteenth century. This difference can be seen as an indication that especially the rentiers among the more well-to-do in the other provinces were, on balance, fiscally less well off than those in Holland.

The 'Tax Morale' of Dutch Citizens

Given the increasing importance of direct taxation in the Dutch fiscal system it is understandable, that it has been suggested that the Dutch Republic was characterized by a high 'tax morale'. Prak and Van Zanden supposed that this was the result of a 'citizenship' mentality that contributed to a high level of public revenue, in addition to economic prosperity.[72] The reasoning was that the inhabitants of the cities in the Dutch Republic were ready to pay much in taxes, because they actively participated in the way taxes were levied in the cities, and because decisions on public expenditure and revenue were taken by urban representatives in city-governments and in the States. Wherever citizenship is organized 'transparently', tax morale – and therefore the level of public revenue – is high, was the argument.[73]

The idea seems logical in the case of *urban* taxes and *urban* expenditure. It is debatable, however, how relevant the concept of a mentality of *urban* 'citizenship' is to explain developments in the finances of the Dutch Republic as a whole. The relevance of 'citizenship' is especially doubtful, of course, in the case of the important price-increasing *indirect* taxes, even regarding *urban* public finance. People confronted by price-increases had mostly no say at all in public finance. In the case of this type of taxation, it is more likely that it was the development of real or even of nominal wages than a high 'tax morale', that kept the number of tax riots restricted – and tax revenues flowing and increasing – than the high tax morale of the common people.

Regarding the more well-to-do it is certain, that many of them did not at all appreciate 'transparency' regarding direct taxation. The very successful republic-wide direct tax known as the *Liberal Gift* of 1747/8, which was offered as proof by the authors for the existence of a high tax morale in the Republic, had only been accepted by the provincial elites in the States-General under the condition that it would be based on 'self-assessment' and that the revenues would be kept strictly secret, a promise that was kept.[74]

The Liberal Gift of 1747, that demanded in Holland 2 percent from people with a property worth more than 2000 guilders and 1 percent from people with a property worth between 1000 and 2000 guilders, produced in this province more than twenty million guilders.[75] Similar surprisingly high results for this 'Liberal Gift' are reported for the other provinces. When a tax of 0,5 percent

---

72 Prak and Van Zanden, 'Towards an economic interpretation of citizenship', p. 163; Prak and Van Zanden, 'Tax morale and citizenship in the Dutch Republic, in; *The political economy of the Dutch Republic* ed. O. Gelderblom (Farnham 2009) pp. 143–167; J.L. van Zanden, *The long road to the Industrial Revolution. The European economy in a global perspective, 1000–1800* (Leiden 2009), Chapter 7 (with M. Prak). 'State formation and citizenship: the Dutch Republic between medieval communes and modern nation states', pp. 205–233.

73 Van Zanden and Prak, 'Towards an economic interpretation of citizenship', p. 144.

74 *GFH*, p. 104.

75 *GFH*, p. 149 shows the archival document mentioning the revenue in Holland's Southern Quarter of 18.8 million guilders.

was levied on the personal tax registers of all persons with an assessed property of more than one thousand guilders in Holland, the revenue result to be expected was about 2.2 million guilders in 1674.[76] At a rate of two percent this would be less than nine million guilders, much less, therefore than the 'Liberal Gift'.[77] The 'tax morale' of the more well-to-do appeared to be much less praiseworthy, therefore, in the case of the regular taxes on wealth than in the – very exceptional – case of the Liberal Gift. The large degree of tax evasion in the case of the regular taxes on property was one of the reasons why Holland's property taxes remained, since 1723, mostly restricted to easily retrievable wealth in land and houses, bonds and offices, and were no longer levied from everyone's total wealth as assessed by urban committees, as had been the case until 1723.

A much more likely explanation for the exceptional success of the once-only levy of the 'Liberal Gift' than the involvement of urban 'common councillors' in its collection put forward by Prak and Van Zanden,[78] was that it was levied on the occasion of the return of a prince of Orange as stadholder in all the provinces of the Netherlands in 1747, after a 'stadholderless period' of 45 years, in most of the provinces, caused by the invasion of Brabant by the French army in that year. It was thought desirable to enable Willem IV 'to defeat the enemy and save the Republic, just like earlier stadholders of the House of Orange did', as was explained in the long propaganda-text accompanying a beautiful engraving commemorating this very unusual levy.[79] Nation-wide 'Orangist enthusiasm' seems a much more convincing explanation for the success of this once-only levy, therefore, than 'urban citizenship'.

On the one hand, the huge revenue of this republic-wide direct tax to support William IV can be seen as another proof of the remarkable fiscal 'elasticity' of the Dutch Republic, in cases in which the expenditure to be realized by the revenue was considered worthwhile. It was in this sense comparable to the success of the forced loan of no less than 4% of wealth in Holland in 1788 in order to save the VOC and the admiralties, mentioned already above, of the desirability of which most people were apparently convinced as well. On the other hand, however, the extremely high yields of these two levies can be

76 *GFH*, p. 367.

77 It is evident that a difference of this size cannot be the result of an overall wealth increase (GDP in Holland in 1674 is estimated at 154 million guilders (9 years average 143 million guilders), in 1747 at 181 million guilders (9 years average even only 158 million guilders)).

78 Prak and Van Zanden, 'Tax Morale and Citizenship', pp. 154–155.

79 *GFH*, p. 151.

seen as proof that the revenues of the *regular* direct taxes on personal property were much too low, notwithstanding the shift, in the course of time, to direct taxes burdening the somewhat more well-to-do.

A more plausible relevant factor in the high level of Dutch public revenue is the existing infrastructure of an 'urban system' of mutually dependent cities jealously guarding each other, in order to ensure that they produced each a fair share in the continuously needed increases in taxation. It is more probable that this contributed to the high levels of public revenue in the Dutch Republic, than a mentality of urban citizenship among individual taxpayers.

The Tax Burden in Holland and in Overijssel

A question yet to be addressed is, if the defective performance of the other provinces in war expenditure implied that Holland was 'overburdened' or, in contrast, that the quotas of the other provinces were perhaps in fact too high.

A comparison of the tax burden in Holland with that in other provinces proved to be only more or less possible for the province of Overijssel, one of the so-called 'land-provinces' in the eastern part of the country, due to a lack of the required combination of data on tax revenue and population size to calculate the tax burden per capita for other provinces. The revenue of 'general indirect taxes' per capita in c. 1790 appeared to amount to 1.3 daily wages per year for a journeyman in Overijssel, and 7.7 daily wages in Holland, a really high difference proportion of no less than nearly 6 : 1, therefore. If a journeyman is assumed to have had to pay the land- and house tax, too, the difference would be less, but it is hard to estimate the amount of land- and house tax per capita, because the percentage of the population who had to pay this tax is not known. If it would have been 50 percent of the population in both provinces, the difference in tax burden on journeymen in Overijssel and Holland would have been 5.4 and 18.2 daily wages per year, still a proportion of 3.4 : 1.

It is not that easy, however, to say what such proportions meant, because the weight of the tax burden depends, of course, also on the price and wage levels in both provinces. As to differences in prices between the two it is known that the price of 100 kg rye bread was three times as high in Holland as in Overijssel in c. 1790 – including the important tax on the milling of bread grains of 8.21 guilders in Overijssel and 11.50 guilders in Holland. This meant that – at a daily wage of 0.92 guilders in Overijssel and of 1.26 guilders in Holland – a journeyman in Overijssel would have been able to buy 11.2 kg for one daily wage and a journeyman in Holland only 11 kg. This makes it likely, therefore, that ordinary people in Holland were indeed less well off as to their standard of living – due to the higher level of 'general indirect taxes' – than in Overijssel, despite higher wages in Holland, and that the large differences in the rates of these indirect price-increasing taxes mainly burdening the 'common man' resulted in Holland being relatively 'overburdened'.

A different picture emerges, however, regarding the taxes on the more well-to-do in both provinces. If the revenue of the 'Liberal Gift' is considered as having been two percent of the wealth of the people who had to contribute to it in 1747/8, this offers a possibility to calculate the total wealth of the contributors in this tax. The percentage of wealth received from the *regular* taxes on the (somewhat) more well-to-do (all direct taxes and the taxes on wine and brandy) in both provinces can then be calculated and compared. It appeared to be 1.8 percent for Overijssel and for Holland only 1.2 percent at that time, 30 percent more in Overijssel than in Holland, therefore. To this can yet be added that in Overijssel the people who had to contribute in personal taxes on property were those with property worth more than hundred guilders. In Holland the contributors were people with property worth more than one thousand guilders; and in Holland owners of property between 1,000 and 2,000 guilders had to pay, in fact, only one percent in the Liberal Gift instead of two percent. This means that the discrepancy in the tax burden resulting from this type of taxes between the two provinces was in fact probably yet considerably larger than 1.8 and 1.2 percent. It means that the more well-to-do in Holland were far from 'overburdened' in comparison to Overijssel in c. 1750.

A last argument that the distributive key of the quotas-system of 1616 'overburdened' the other provinces given the differences in wealth with Holland was the revised quotas-system of 1792. A general feeling appears to have existed, in the later eighteenth century – even among Holland's urban elites – that Holland should pay more. The new distributive key increased Holland's contribution from 58.3 to 62.1 percent as we saw (see Table 3.1). This increased quota was in line with the already longer existing – and no doubt only grudgingly accepted – awareness, that increases in tax revenue required more direct taxation burdening the more well-to-do.

'Capital' or 'Coercion': The Role of Loans in Dutch War Finance

The last element of the revenue system of the Dutch Republic to be discussed is the contribution of public loans to public finance. Table 3.6 above suggested that this contribution was rather modest in comparison to that of taxes, especially during the seventeenth century, despite the common assumption that the Republic was primarily a 'capital-intensive' state. However, the most important function of loans was of course that they facilitated the raising of large sums of additional revenue during *war* years. A more relevant question than their average contribution to total public revenue in periods also including peace years is, therefore, how much loans contributed to the increases in revenue necessitated by wars. This has been made visible in Table 3.7.

For the wars since 1621 until 1697 (51 war years in total) the (weighted) average of this contribution turned out to have been about 46 percent. It may yet be added that it is known that about half of the loans in Holland for the war of the 1670s were forced loans, more fitting in with what may be called a 'coercive' than a 'capital-intensive' fiscal system. Without these forced loans the mentioned percentage would have been only 42 percent, and it may have been even lower yet, because for the other wars during the seventeenth century the part taken by forced loans is not known. Only the very modest increase necessary for the First English Naval War was for 90 percent financed by borrowing, the second half of the Eighty Years War after the Truce only for 39 percent, the Nine Years War of 1688–1697 only for 36 percent.

For the three wars between 1700 and 1785 (in total 25 war years), however, the contribution of loans to the necessary increases in revenue in comparison to the average of some preceding peace years became on average even 111 percent in 1701–1713, 79 percent in 1741–48 and again 111 percent in 1781–84. These loans were, moreover, always voluntary loans on the free market. We may conclude that, in contrast to what most authors since Tilly's study on 'Coercion, capital and European states' inclined to expect, the Dutch Republic only started to be a state in which war financing was fully based on its 'capital-intensity', during the eighteenth century, when its successful involvement in European war faring was decreasing.

During the last two years of its existence the Republic was, moreover, forced to return again to a mix of voluntary and forced loans and forced levies in public finance, as had been the case in the 'Year of Disaster' 1672 and at the start of the Revolt. The forced loan of 4% of property of 1788 necessary to save the VOC and the admiralties after the disastrous Fourth English Naval War, that yielded the extreme amount of 53 million,[80] was mentioned already. When the French armies had occupied Antwerp and Brussels in 1792 and the Republic had to prepare for war as well, a voluntary loan was issued at an interest rate of 4%. It did by far not bring in the nearly 16 million in extra public revenue thought to be necessary. When it was made more attractive with additional lottery-like advantages, it resulted in nearly 8 million guilders in cash in the course of 1794.[81]

When the French declared war on the Republic, indeed, in 1793, a 'Liberal Gift' of 2% of property was asked in addition from the more-well-to-do in

80 A. van der Meulen, *Studies over het ministerie van Van de Spiegel* (Leiden, Kooyker, 1905) p. 351.

81 Dormans, *Het tekort*, pp. 128, 131.

TABLE 3.7 *Percentage of revenue increases in war years financed by loans, 1621–1794.*

Start war	End war	Total public revenue on average pyr (mill. glds.)	Annual average of tot. publ. rev. in 3 or 5 preceding years (mill. glds.)	Revenue increase due to war on av. pyr (mill. glds.)	Financed by loans on av. pyr (mill. glds)	% of rev. increase financed by loans	Nr. of war years
a	*b*	*c*	*d*	*e = c–d*	*f*	*g = f/e*	*h = b–a+1*
1621	1648	24.4	13.5	10.9	4.2	39%	28
1652	1654	24.5	21.6	2.9	2.6	90%	3
1665	1667	28.3	23.2	5.1	3.2	63%	3
1672	1678	35.8	26.8	9.0	6.0	67%	7
1688	1697	43.7	26.6	17.1	6.1	36%	10
1621	1697						51
weighted average for all war years in 1621–1697						**46%**	
1701	1713	54.3	39.2	15.0	16.6	111%	13
1741	1748	42.7	31.3	11.4	9.0	79%	8
1781	1784	45.7	37.3	8.4	9.3	111%	4
1701	1784						25
weighted average for all war years in 1701–1784						**101%**	
1793	1794	57.8	41.6	16.2	4.0	25%	2

Holland. It did not yield 25 million guilders as was hoped for, but nonetheless still 19.5 million guilders. In 1794 a fourth '*ambtgeld*' (forced loans on officials) was levied, at an interest of 5 percent and for a total amount of 3.3 million guilders.[82] It was the resumption of a practice used incidentally already earlier during the eighteenth century, yielding 1.5 million guilders in 1717, 2.2 million guilders loans in 1726 and the same amount again in 1744. So, although far from easily and smoothly, Holland alone had yet been able to realize in total nearly 31 million guilders extra on the eve of the French invasion in January 1795, by means of (mainly forced) loans and extraordinary direct taxation on top of the revenue of the more than 19 million guilders in regular taxes at that time, much less than was thought necessary, but more than the extra revenue raised at the start of any of the other wars during the eighteenth century.

At the start of the Fourth English Naval War the other provinces had still joined Holland in negotiating loans on behalf of the war, for an amount of about 3.5 million guilders (Holland for an amount of 11.8 million guilders). They appeared to have felt no longer any urgency to do the same in 1793/4. It is unlikely, however, that it would have helped to stop the French invasion of January 1795, supported by domestic Patriots (and facilitated by frozen rivers), if the other provinces had again displayed a comparable financial effort to raise loans on the eve of this invasion, despite the disastrous outcome of the former war.

The problem of the Republic in the year of its downfall was not that it had a federal system of public revenue. Its problem was, firstly, that it was too small to be able to survive without the support of allies. Secondly it was too small to finance a huge monopolistic state-like body like the VOC without an intense fiscal colonial exploitation as would only start during the nineteenth century. Thirdly, the Republic had become too politically divided between pro-English conservative 'Orangists' supporting stadholder, William V of Orange, on the one hand, and pro-French 'Patriots' striving for changes inspired by the new ideals of the Enlightenment and the restauration of Dutch international prestige, and criticizing the lack of access to many social and political functions for men not belonging to the ruling protestant families, on the other hand.

Conservative 'Orangists', had felt forced, in 1787, to accept Prussian military support to oust the 'Patriot' party that had come to power in 1785, and to secure

82 As the result of a curious bargain with the States of Holland it was the VOC, not the province, that paid the interests on these '*ambtgelden*' to holders, in exchange for the promise that Holland's 'tax on bonds' had to be paid on a fixed amount of the value of VOC-bonds, not on their real value on the market.

the position of the Prince of Orange and his Prussian wife. The exiled radical 'Patriots', who had fled to France, who embraced the new ideals of 'freedom, equality and brotherhood' and who despised the weakness of Prince William V, returned to the Republic with French revolutionary troops in 1795, to realize a 'Batavian Revolution'.

A Comparison with the Centralized Tax System of 1807

In Chapter 2 the new fiscal system of Holland emerging since 1572 was compared to the preceding system under the Habsburgs. To conclude Chapter 3, the tax system of the Dutch Republic at the end of the eighteenth century will be compared to the first centralized tax system after the collapse of the old Republic, a system realized in 1806, when Napoleon's brother Louis Napoleon had become the first king of the northern Netherlands (called at that time the 'Kingdom Holland').[83]

This new tax system was the achievement of the first national Dutch Minister of Finance, Alexander Gogel.[84] It increased total Dutch tax revenue from on average 33.3 million guilders (excl. Holland's tax on bonds, excl. customs, and excl. loans) in c. 1790, to 43.6 million guilders in 1807 (see Table 3.8).[85] In the historiography on the Dutch Republic this increase in tax revenue of more than 10 million guilders, is usually put forward as an important argument for the view that it was the federal character of the Dutch Republic that diminished its ability to realize sufficient public revenue to survive further wars during the eighteenth century. The realized revenue increase was no doubt a very remarkable, administrative achievement, indeed. It is debatable, nevertheless, to what extent this administrative masterpiece should be considered as proof of the incompetence of the ruling elites of the old Republic to realize a fiscal system yielding more revenue, due to its federal character.

---

83 For a more general comparison between Dutch public finance in the eighteenth and nineteenth century see: W. Fritschy and R. van der Voort, 'From fragmentation to unification, 1700–1914', in: *A financial history of the Netherlands* eds. M. 't Hart, J. Jonker and J.L. van Zanden (Cambridge 1997) pp. 64–93.

84 Much information on Gogel and the fiscal history of his time can be found in the publication of his correspondence with tax specialist Elias Canneman by M. van Leeuwen-Canneman, *Een vriendschap in het teken van 's lands financien. Briefwisseling tussen Elias Canneman en Isaac Jan Alexander Gogel 1799*–1813 (Den Haag 2009); J.K.T. Postma, *Alexander Gogel (1765–1821). Grondlegger van de Nederlandse staat* (Hilversum 2017).

85 The average in 1790–94 was 38.9 million guilders (exclusive 2.3 million guilders in customs, 6.9 million guilders in long-term loans, and the tax on bonds in Holland amounting to 6 million guilders on average per year). The year 1790 was chosen to emphasize the size of the difference between the old and the new system.

The most important objection to this analysis is the fact that this new tax system was primarily meant to make the Dutch state part of a large imperial 'war-machine'. The realized increase in public revenue resulted primarily from the extravagant demands made by the absolutist, 'predatory' ruler (to borrow Margaret Levi's term), Napoleon Bonaparte, on his brother Louis Napoleon, whom he had made king of the northern Netherlands. About three million per year of the realized permanent tax increase of 10.3 million guilders had to be spent on the new royal court of Louis Napoleon (whereas the last stadholder of the old Republic had cost the provinces in total about 350,000 guilders per year);[86] the rest was meant to allow the new Kingdom – called the 'Kingdom Holland' although it contained all provinces – to spend permanently seven millions more per year for war in order to support Napoleon's expansion policy.

The main explanation for the sharp contrast with the tax system of the eighteenth century Republic is not an 'institutional incompetence' of the federal Republic to increase public revenue, therefore, but a deeply felt conviction among the old urban elites then in power, that it was not at all desirable to realize a permanent increase in war expenditure, firstly, because war had simply to be avoided as much as possible, secondly, because the normal way to realize extra revenue in the face of unavoidable imminent war was to decide ad hoc for extraordinary direct taxes and loans, voluntary if possible, forced if necessary, not the permanent maximization of public revenue in peace years.

In other words: the ruling elites in the eighteenth century Dutch Republic were not 'predatory rulers', continuously focusing on revenue maximization, despite Levi's theoretical assumption that this is always the case in any state. Although the seventeenth century Dutch fiscal state had been – to a large extent willy-nilly – mainly a 'war-machine', indeed, this was no longer the case after 1713. Especially between 1714 and 1733 and between 1752 and 1780 there had been no necessity at all to increase public expenditure in the Republic. On the contrary, surpluses resulting from existing tax revenues allowed large scale debt redemptions, for an amount of on average 2.6 million guilders per year, as we saw, to the sorrow of the Republic's *rentiers*.

It is true that this was no longer the case during the aftermath of the disastrous Fourth English Naval War. By then public finance continued to be burdened with deficits. Holland was forced to negotiate about on average four million guilders in loans per year for structural deficits, also after the war, and even after the huge forced loan of 1788, during the peace years 1789–1792. This

86 W. Fritschy, 'De financien van de Oranjes tussen revolutie en restauratie', *Jaarboek Oranje-Nassau museum 1996* (Rotterdam 1996) 35–67, pp. 35–36.

was partly due to the continuing financial problems of the VOC,[87] partly however to the maintenance of a much higher level of military expenditure after the end of the Fourth English Naval War than during the 1770s.

A more adequate remedy to the problem of the continuous deficits of these years than an attempt to permanently increase public revenue, in the situation of that period, was a decision to *reduce* ordinary military expenditure. This decision was actually taken by the States General at last, in 1792. Military expenditure in peace years was then reduced from respectively 13.2 million for army and fortifications and 3.2 million guilders in naval subsidies (as had been spent on average per year between 1788 and 1792) to 11 million guilders for the army and a – from then on fixed – annual amount of 2.5 million guilders for the navy.[88] This reduction of military expenditure with about three million guilders may be considered as a more sensible alternative for the deficits of these years than an attempt to put an end to the federal structure of the Dutch Republic by the introduction of a unified tax system to enable a permanent increase in military expenditure.

It should not be left unmentioned, that Gogel was a remarkably clever, very hard working and incorruptible politician, not particularly interested in personal gains, and cherishing the social ideals of the French Revolution. In fact, he wanted mainly to use the unification of the Dutch tax system to decrease the burden of taxation on the poor and to increase that on the rich in the province of Holland. In this aim he succeeded, indeed, not only by increasing the tax on wine and brandy, as was mentioned already, but also by reducing the amount paid in indirect price-increasing taxes in Holland from 8.2 million guilders to 7.2 million guilders, despite a total increase in tax revenue of 10.3 million guilders. Table 3.8 offers an overview of the changes realized by Gogel's new tax system, for Holland and for the other provinces.

It shows that Gogel increased the 'taxes on the more well-to-do', in line with his social ideals, not only by increasing the taxes on wine and brandy (row 5), but also by means of the '*personeel*'. This was a 'personal' tax, which added a tax based on house rents to the old direct taxes in Holland's 'common means' (row 3). It had to be paid by all heads of families who lived in a house with a rental value of more than 30 guilders per year, which appeared to be in 1808 a

87 Van der Meulen, *Ministerie van de Spiegel*, pp. 351–410 called the VOC after the Fourth English Naval War a 'pump continuously draining Holland's treasury', but paid no attention to the structural higher military expenditure as another cause of Holland's gigantic financial problems from 1788–1794.

88 In fact naval subsidies amounted to only resp. 2.6 and 2.3 million guilders already in 1790 and 1791, and would increase again to on average 4.1 million guilders in 1792–94.

TABLE 3.8 *A comparison of the federal Dutch tax system c. 1790 with the centralized tax system in 1807 (million glds).*

		c.1790		1807					changes			
		Province Holland	**Rest Dutch Rep.**	**Dutch Republic**	**Province Holland**	**Other provinces**	**Total 'Kingdom Holland'**	**Contribution province Holland**	**In-crease**	**Contribution to total increase**	**Contribu-tion of Holland**	**Contribution of other provinces**
1	direct taxes on land and houses	5.2	4.8	10.0	4.6	6.4	11.0	42%	1.0	10%	–60%	160%
2	direct tax on trades, enterprises and professions (*'patent'*)				2.5	1.5	4.0	63%	4.0	39%	63%	38%
3	direct taxes on the more well-to-do (incl. the *'personeel'*, stamp taxes and inheritance)	4.6	4.6	9.2	6.1	5.4	11.5	53%	2.3	22%	65%	35%
4	taxes on wine and brandy	1.0	0.9	1.9	3.2	0.8	4.0	80%	2.1	20%	105%	–5%

5	all indirect taxes excl. on wine and brandy	8.2	4.0	12.2	7.2	5.9	13.1	55%	0.9	9%	−111%	211%
6	all taxes	19.0	14.3	33.3	23.6	20.0	43.6		10.3	100%	45%	55%
7	proportion Holland/other provinces	57%	43%		54%	46%						

Source: Fritschy, *De patriotten en de financiën van de Bataafse Republiek*, pp. 303–304.

number of 150,749 houses on a total of perhaps about 500,000 houses in the whole kingdom.[89] The revenue of all taxes on the more well-to-do, which continued to include the old taxes on cattle, servants and horses – and which, in Table 3.8, also includes the tax on inheritance in the side-line and some stamp taxes – increased from 4.6 million to 6.1 million guilders in Holland, and from 9.2 million to 11.5 million guilders in total.

The main innovation in the new system was a tax on trades, enterprises and professions, called the '*patent*', mainly burdening not the rich, therefore, but the urban middle class (row 2). It contributed nearly 40 percent to the increase of 12.2 million guilders (see Table 3.7). Holland's urban population was in the Batavian-French period about 56 percent of total urban population in the northern Netherlands.[90] That the revenue of the '*patent*' in Holland was nevertheless 63 percent of the total revenue of the '*patent*' may be seen as an indication for a somewhat higher level of industrial and commercial activity and of wealth among the middle classes in Holland than in the other provinces. Given this fact it is remarkable that the effect of the tax reform was that Holland's contribution to total tax revenue *decreased* from 57 to 54 percent. This in remarkable contrast to the revision of the quotas system of 1792 which had, on the contrary, increased Holland's quota from 58.3 to 62.1 percent. It is possible however, that this difference resulted at least partly from the fact that especially Holland's economy suffered from Napoleon's 'Continental System' (1806–1814) that forbade all trade with Britain.

The revenue increases from the indirect taxes burdening the common people (row 6) and also that from the tax on land and houses (row 1) – together contributing 30 percent to the total revenue increase of 10.3 million guilders – were completely contributed by the other provinces, whereas in Holland the revenue from these tax categories decreased. The nominal amount per capita on the 'common man' of these taxes remained much higher in Holland with a population of about 750,000 than in the other provinces (with a population of about 1,250,000) respectively 15.70 guilders and 9.84 guilders.

The main objection to the new system is, however, that Gogel's diligence and astuteness mainly served Napoleon's lust for power. It earned him the Legion of Honour, presented to him in Paris by Napoleon personally. It did not prevent the formal annexing of the northern Netherlands to the French Empire in

89 Fritschy, *De patriotten en de financiën*, p. 138; total population of the Netherlands was about 2.2 million in 1808; if the household size was on average 4 persons the total number of households was 550,000.

90 De Vries and Van der Woude, *The first modern economy*, p. 58.

1810, which was according to Gogel and other intellectuals of the time by then anyhow inevitable, and perhaps even desirable. The fact that the introduction of a unified tax system replacing the old federal tax system coincided with a large increase in tax revenue does not at all 'prove' an 'institutional incapacity' to realize a similar structural increase in public revenue in the old Republic, due to its federal structure. It shows other choices as to the desirability and usefulness of a continuously extremely high level of military expenditure in a small state.

The cuts in military expenditure, which the old ruling elites had envisaged in 1792, can in fact be considered, therefore, as a rational approach to the financial predicament of the years following the Fourth Naval War. The comparison of the Dutch Republic with Britain in Chapter 5 will further corroborate this. It is not very likely that a tax system regularly producing ten million guilders (thirty per cent) more per year than the old one at the end of the old Republic, would have been able to maintain a navy of the size of that of Britain by that time or to stop the French invasion of January 1795, an invasion that was facilitated not only by frozen rivers but also by enthusiastic domestic support of adherents of the ideals of the French Revolution.

Apart from its small size it was a republic-wide antagonism between the *ancien-régime* mentality of the governing elites that accepted Prussian support to maintain the Prince of Orange, on the one hand, and the enthusiasm of the political movement of the 'Patriots' for support from revolutionary France, on the other hand, that sealed the end of the Dutch Republic, not the inefficiency of its federal structure.

3.3 Conclusion

The main 'secret' of the high level of public revenue in the Dutch Republic before the Truce had been a 'tax revolution' in all provinces, based on the character of the 'urban system' in the territory of the Republic, reinforced by economic growth (certainly in Holland), and supported by Holland's 'second financial revolution' since the first decade of the seventeenth century. The main 'secret' of the even much higher levels of public revenue after the Truce appeared to be the 'resilience' of the tax systems in all the provinces, now supported by an expansion of the ability to create long-term public debts at low rates of interest to the provinces outside Holland as well. The ability of the federal Republic to raise total public revenue was certainly supported by its 'capital-intensity' but the role of the provincial tax systems was quantitatively much more important.

The even much larger increases in public finance after the end of the 'Twelve Years' Truce' than before, that were due to continuously renewed involvements in the international wars of the early modern period, did not lead to an increasing financial centralization in the Dutch Republic. The federal elements of its institutional structure continued to be by far the most important parts of its fiscal system. The role of the customs and other Generality-revenues remained rather marginal. On the one hand the failure of the provinces to pay for war expenditure conform the quotas-system – a phenomenon visible already in the first decade of the seventeenth century – continued to manifest itself. On the other hand, the degree to which not only Holland, but also the other provinces continued to contribute ever larger sums, by continually increasing all main elements of public revenue, was actually more remarkable.

It is true that the ability to pay ever more soldiers resulted for a small part from increasing efficiency, due to centralized government intervention, in the way army payment was organized by means of the 'military solicitors'. More important for the ability to spend as much as possible of the realized revenue increases on war, was the ability of all provinces to contain the provincial interest burdens, resulting from former wars, by decreasing rates of interest. A remarkable aspect of this policy in Holland and Zeeland was that the low real rate of interest on public debt was to a large extent not a result of a 'credible commitment' to pay promised interests. States-assemblies simply decided to pay (much) less interest, when this was required for war expenditure, initially by means of forced interest conversion, later, more elegantly, by means of an – in the first instance temporary – tax on bonds. That interest rates on new loans continued to decline – and that voluntary interest conversions appeared to be possible as well – should mainly be explained, therefore, by a continuing capital abundance, and the continuing large demand-that could be expected in a commercialized urbanized society-for easy investment possibilities in the form of bonds, a demand, that could no longer be satisfied by the size of the public debts of each of the cities separately.

After the war of 1701–1713 very drastic forced measures to reduce the hugely increased interest burden were unavoidable in all provinces. Nevertheless market rates of interest for public debt started to decrease again in all provinces in the course of the eighteenth century. The fact that the office of the Generality could no longer pay the interests on its loans two times during the eighteenth century was not a case of '*state* bankruptcy'. It was just a symptom of the decreasing fiscal importance of the central institution of the Dutch Republic and the self-evident priority of provincial public finance.

Until the 'second military revolution' of the 1670s the price-increasing indirect taxes in Holland had been the most important element in the fiscal system of the Republic. Economic developments contributed to their acceptance. Since the 1670s direct taxation became increasingly important in all provinces, although until the end of the century also the revenue of indirect price increasing taxes continued to grow. Indirect taxes even resumed their increase again after 1750, despite republic-wide riots against the farmers of the 'common' and the 'general' means in 1748. Tax rates were increased again after 1748. The increased revenues were only very partially a result of the abolition of tax farming. The collection by public officials, since 1748, resulted moreover in a considerable increase of public expenditure for the collection costs.

After 1672 'coercive' direct taxation became on average by far the most important element in the fiscal system of the Dutch Republic (Table 3.6), much more so than loans. During the seventeenth century even the increases in military expenditure needed during war years were for less than fifty percent financed by loans. Only during the three wars of the eighteenth century before the 1790s the 'capital intensity' of the Dutch Republic was the only source for the realization of extra revenue for a war.

It was not a remarkable 'tax morality' among its wealthy citizens, but rather the lack of a strong central authority that contributed to the high level of its public revenue. The lack of a strong central authority forced the many cities and the small numbers of remaining nobles in the States to collective decisions on indirect taxes, mutual control, the negotiation of public loans if necessary, decreases in the interest burden and increases in direct taxes burdening the more well-to-do to.

The Provincial States remained the basic 'political infrastructure' of the 'urban system', which made the high amounts in tax revenue possible. They allowed the required communication on common fiscal policy, felt as necessary despite an inclination of the cities to serve primarily particularistic interests and allowed an efficient exploitation of the economic characteristics of the urban system. The federal structure of the Republic allowed, in addition, a diversification in fiscal systems adapted to the economic differences between the provinces.

It was not 'citizenship' that explained the remarkable high revenue of the 'Liberal Gift' of 1747, the first 'national tax' in the history of the Dutch Republic, but rather 'Orangism', a collective feeling that the Republic needed the return of a Prince of Orange, after a long stadholderless period, and that the Prince needed the money to save the country. Even if his successor William V had been a much stronger ruler than this stadholder was, the Dutch Republic would never have been able, however, to regain its status as a Great Power within the changed international political constellation of the eighteenth century. The increasing economic development and internal stability of much larger states like Britain and France had made the Republic's 'tax base' simply too small to win a naval war with Britain. The only realistic fiscal policy for a small state like the Dutch Republic was to avoid war, not to try to raise permanent war expenditure.

The radical Patriot Gogel was able to realize a tax system that raised Dutch tax revenues to a level about 30 percent higher than had been reached at the end of the eighteenth century. The answer on the question 'why' is not that the Dutch state was by then at last no longer a federal state. The main answer is that the 'predatory' ruler Napoleon was powerful enough to force the new centralized Dutch kingdom to contribute to his imperial 'war machine'. For the old Dutch elites the Dutch Republic was not 'made' to make war for territorial gains. An earlier introduction of a centralized fiscal system, permanently producing ten million guilders more in public revenue than the federal one, would not have allowed a victory on the navy of powerful Britain or on the French army at the end of the eighteenth century. The Dutch Republic had become too internally divided for a consistent foreign policy of alliances to maintain its independence.

PART 2

The Fiscal System of the Dutch Republic in International Comparative Perspective

Introduction to Part 2

When the French historian Fernand Braudel shortly discussed 'the state' in the introduction to the third part of his famous *Civilization and capitalism, 15th–18th century*, he highlighted three states in particular: the Venetian Republic in the fifteenth century, the Dutch Republic in the seventeenth and Great Britain in the eighteenth and nineteenth centuries.[1] In his footsteps other historians have approached the Dutch union of seven provinces as a stage in between that of the medieval Italian city-states and that of the British national state in the eighteenth century.[2] The Venetian Republic and Britain have been chosen as points of comparison for this study as well. The comparisons will not focus, however, on the Venetian fiscal system in the fifteenth, the Dutch in the seventeenth and the British in the eighteenth century. They will be approached here as states contemporaneous with the Dutch Republic in the seventeenth and eighteenth century but with different preceding historical developments determining their fiscal systems in the early modern period.

What makes these two states interesting cases within the framework of this book is that their economic development made them sufficiently comparable and that the Venetian Republic and Britain would both develop into rather centralized fiscal states, in contrast to the federal state of the Dutch Republic. They all became more urbanized than most other European states but with differing kinds of 'urban systems' and, for all three, trade oversea was so important for their economy that they are often designated as 'maritime states'. The Dutch Republic shared, moreover, its republican constitution with Venice, and although Britain was a monarchy, the strong political influence of a national parliament in Britain especially since 1688 was comparable to the influence of representational institutions in the two republics. Additionally, it was of course important that relatively much data on both their fiscal systems have been made available in the last two decades. Chapter 4 is dedicated to the comparison with the Venetian Republic, Chapter 5 to that with Britain.

In Chapter 6 the comparison will be expanded to a very different state, the Ottoman Empire. The choice for the Ottoman Empire seemed interesting, because there is a European tradition since Macchiavelli, later followed

---

1 F. Braudel, *Capitalism and material life Part III* (1974; orig. French ed. 1967).

2 *A miracle mirrored. The Dutch Republic in European perspective*, eds. K. Davids and J. Lucassen (Cambridge 1995); L. Pezzolo, *Il fisco dei Veneziani. Finanza pubblica ed economie tra XV e XVII secolo* (Verona 2003) p. 153; S.R. Epstein, *Freedom and Growth. The rise of states and markets in Europe, 1300–1750* (London/New York 2000) p. 12.

 | DOI 10.1163/9789004341289_007

by authors like Bodin and Montesqieu, and more recently mainly by Perry Anderson[3] and Timur Kuran,[4] to present the Ottoman state as the antithesis of European states. There is also a tendency, however, among modern historians to emphasize increasing economic similarities between the Ottoman state and Western-European states especially in the course of the eighteenth century.[5] Also for the Ottoman Empire much more quantitative material on public finance has become available in recent years, in contrast to that for other parts of the world in the early modern period.[6]

As finance is the nerve of war and of the state, and as military inferiority would be felt as a key problem of 'the world of Islam' in the Near-East and North-Africa in the nineteenth century, a comparison of the fiscal systems of both these parts of the world seemed promising in order to better understand their differing history. It will be argued that striking differences of the Dutch fiscal system with the fiscal system of the Ottoman Empire were determined in large part by specific historical trajectories of urbanization. To discuss the relative importance of on the one hand social-economic and political factors, and on the other hand a historical and institutional factor like the degree of centralization of their fiscal system for their fiscal performance, a long-term time perspective will again be used.

The method chosen for the comparison is not the strict, econometric one of the comparative history of public finance of some recent authors in the field,[7] but a descriptive, historical approach. Attempts to compare the fiscal systems of a large number of states unavoidably have to treat history as a kind of laboratory in which social-economic and political-institutional 'experiments' were repeated with variations to allow general conclusions. A less rigorous comparison of a smaller number of states may be better able to account for the problem that the 'experiments' were of course never repeated under constant conditions. The approach chosen in this book implies an argument that a description of long-term similarities and differences in historical trajectories may be as helpful to understand fiscal systems, as a statistical analysis based on 'measurable' abstracted social-economic and political-institutional differences.

3 T. Kuran, *The long divergence: how Islamic law held back the Middle East* (Princeton 2011).

4 P. Anderson, *Lineages of the absolutist state* (London 1979) p. 361.

5 S. Pamuk, 'Institutional change and the longevity of the Ottoman Empire, 1500–1800', *Journal of Interdisciplinary* History 35 (2004) pp. 225–247, p. 232; S. Faroqi, 'The ruling elite between politics and "the economy"', in: *An economic and social history of the Ottoman Empire. Volume 2; 1600–1914* (Cambridge, 1997),pp. 545–576, p. 573.

6 M. Genç and E. Özvar eds., *Osmanlı maliyesi: kurumlar ve bütçeler* (*Ottoman financial institutions and budgets*) 2 vols. (Istanbul 2006).

7 M. Dincecco, *Political Transformations and Public Finances: Europe, 1650–1913* (Cambridge f.c.); K. Karaman and S. Pamuk, 'Different paths to the modern state in Europe'.

CHAPTER 4

A Comparison with the Venetian Republic

In several aspects, the Dutch and the Venetian Republic were rather comparable states. Nevertheless, some remarkable differences existed in the character of their public finance. The Venetian Republic was much more a 'maritime state' than the Dutch Republic, as a comparison of public expenditure as well as of public revenue of the two states will show. Military historians are inclined to ask why the Republic did not spend more on army and navy to prevent its downfall and tend to blame the federal structure of the Republic. A comparison with the much more centralized Venetian Republic rather raises the question why Dutch military expenditure continued to remain so high during the eighteenth century.

Differences between the two republics in the relative contributions of 'centre' and 'periphery' to public revenue cast doubt on the advantages of a centralized above a federal state for the realization of increases in public revenue. Differences in long-term history and in the character of their 'urban systems' led also to some remarkable differences in the history of their public debt.

The first section of this chapter will offer a discussion of general similarities, on the one hand, and diverging preceding domestic developments and histories of power expansion, on the other hand. This section forms the background for the comparisons of public expenditure, public revenue and public debt in the early modern period in the next three sections.

4.1 Common Characteristics but Long-Term Differences

Much in Common

The most obvious similarity between Venetian and the Dutch Republic is of course the republican form of government that made them different from most other European states arising in the early modern period.[1] Their maritime and their urban character, and their role in international trade, made them moreover more comparable to each other than to the Swiss republican state, that originated, at the end of the thirteenth century, in three rural cantons instead

1 E.O.G. Haitsma Mulier, *The myth of Venice and Dutch republican thought in the seventeenth century* (Assen 1980) p. 3.

 | DOI 10.1163/9789004341289_008

of in cities, and that lacked any access to maritime trade. Both the small Dutch Republic and the small Venetian Republic found their end after an invasion of armies of the much larger French state, the Dutch Republic in 1795, the Venetian Republic in 1797.

The size of the Dutch and Venetian territories and their European historical context made them much more comparable to each other than to the large republican federation of American states that came into existence at the end of the eighteenth century. They had roughly the same population size, the Dutch Republic about 1.5 million in 1600 and 2.1 million at the end of the eighteenth century, the Venetian Republic about 1.5 million in 1550 and 2.3 million in 1770. The city of Venice was larger than Amsterdam until the beginning of the seventeenth century, about 190,000 inhabitants in 1607, against in Amsterdam about 65,000 in 1600. Venice's population decreased since then, while that of Amsterdam increased. Both cities were, nevertheless, of a similar kind of magnitude in comparison to cities like London and Paris. Venice had a population of about 102,000 in 1633[2] growing again to about 140,000 in 1800; that of Amsterdam grew from about 105,000 in 1623 to about 220,000 in 1800. London's population in contrast increased from about 200,000 in 1600 to nearly 900,000 in 1800, Paris' population from about more than 200,000 in 1600 to nearly 600,000 in 1800.[3]

Although their most important cities were not really large, the territories of both republics as a whole were more urbanized than that of other European states. The percentage of people, that lived in the eight cities with more than 10,000 inhabitants in the Venetian Republic – Bergamo, Brescia, Chioggia, Crema, Padua, Treviso, Udine, Verona and Vicenza – was in 1550 higher than that of the nineteen such cities in the territory of the later Dutch Republic, resp. about 23 percent and 15 percent. In the seventeenth and eighteenth centuries it became lower than in the Dutch Republic, resp. about 15 percent and 29 percent, but in both states the urbanization percentage was always much higher than the only 6 to 10 percent percentage on average for Europe as a whole between 1550 and 1800.[4] In the course of the eighteenth century the importance of the cities in Venice's *hinterland* increased in comparison to that of Venice.[5]

2 Venice was hit severely by the plague in 1630.

3 F. Lane, *Venice: a maritime republic* (Baltimore 1973) 18; De Vries and Van der Woude, *The first modern economy,* pp. 50, 64; L. Pezzolo, *Una finanza d'ancien régime. La Reppublica Veneta tra XV e XVIII secolo* (Roma 2006) 55; De Vries, *Urbanization,* pp. 218, 235, 271, 276; Amsterdam 1622/3: Noordegraaf and Valk, *De Gave Gods,* p. 234.

4 De Vries, *Urbanization,* p. 39.

5 De Vries, *Urbanization,* p. 30 and p. 36.

Both republics were able to reclaim about 70,000 to 80,000 hectares land from water to increase their agricultural area. In addition, grain trade played a very important role in the economic development of both states.[6] Both Venice and Amsterdam became moreover world centres of commercial and industrial leadership, in large part as a result of the necessity of trade. Both lost their central position in world trade in the course of time.[7]

The Dutch Republic succeeded the Venetian Republic in assuming an intermediary role in the Atlantic world trade, comparable to Venice's role in the Mediterranean international trade before. Since the emergence of the Atlantic economy with its sea routes to Asia, and the subsequent decline of the Mediterranean economy that had connected Europe with the rich Arab trade overland with Asia, before the discovery of the sea routes to Asia, Venice lost its international economic importance for the trade in luxury products from the East, first to the Portuguese, then to the Dutch and the British. This was even the case in the Mediterranean, as the British and Dutch started to build cheaper ships and were able to operate them more efficiently. Like Venice the Dutch would lose economic importance in the course of time, too, not only because of the increasing protectionism of other states with larger interior markets, but also due to major changes in the character of world trade as a result of the Industrial Revolution and the rise of the British economy.

For Venice, the seventeenth century was the main century of economic decline, for Holland the first half of the eighteenth, but the same general characterizations apply to both: loss of export markets resulting in reduction of employment in major manufacturing industries and in output,[8] and both lost their position of industrial innovator.[9] In the economy of both, the export of primary materials from their *hinterland* would become more important since then, than that of industrial products. The Venetian Republic exported since the seventeenth century increasingly raw materials (silk) and unfinished products (thread) instead of finished cloth.[10] The Dutch Republic became a major exporter of agricultural products in the course of time.[11]

---

6 S. Ciriacono, 'The Venetian economy and the world system of the semi-periphery', in: H.J. Nitz ed., *The early modern world system in geographical perspective* (Stuttgart 1993) pp. 120–136, p. 129.

7 C.A. Davids, *The rise and decline of Dutch technological leadership. Technology, economy and culture in the Netherlands 1350–1800* (Leiden 2008) p. 2.

8 R.T. Rapp, *Industry and economic decline in seventeenth century Venice* (Harvard 1976).

9 Davids, *The rise and decline of Dutch technological leadership*, p. 2.

10 Ciriacono, 'The Venetian Economy', p. 127.

11 De Vries and Van der Woude, *The first modern economy*, p. 503.

For both the term 'relative decline' has been proposed, as wealth does on average not seem to have decreased significantly.[12] However, while the silver value of the nominal daily wage of a day labourer in Venice was somewhat higher than in the Western Netherlands in 1623, in 1770 it was less than half that level. Although there are no figures to compare overall economic wealth in both republics in the course of time, the silver value of their wage levels suggests that the Venetian Republic had become much less wealthy than the Dutch Republic in the eighteenth century. In 1623 the value of the daily wage of a day labourer in Venice was about 8 grams of silver, in the Western Netherlands about 7.5 grams silver. In 1770 it was somewhat less than 4 grams of silver in Venice and somewhat more than 8 grams of silver in the Western Netherlands.[13]

Differing Long-Term Domestic Developments

Both states were republics, their population size and degree of urbanization were comparable and they more or less resembled each other social-economically. The character of their historical development was in many respects quite different, however. A first difference was of course that the timespan of Venice's survival as an independent state was much longer. As the population in the boggy area at the north end of the Adriatic Sea increased during the early Middle Ages, parishes on the isles in the Venetian lagoon became united by ferries, footpaths and bridges. Gradually this agglomeration of isles would become an increasingly impressive city, over which a *dux* or doge started to rule already in 697. Until the conquest of Constantinople by crusaders supported by Venice in 1204, Venice was formally part of the Byzantine Empire, but already the first doge was probably chosen by the male members of the important families on the isles.[14]

A feeling of common identity among the population of the isles forming the city was stimulated by the legend and the cult of the apostle Saint Mark, originating in the ninth century, and strongly supported by the doges. Unlike the Low Countries, and despite clashes with the Papal State, the Venetian Republic would never be confronted with problems of religious diversity, nor with other forms of disruptive social unrest like tax riots.

---

12 Rapp, *Industry and economic decline*; J. de Vries, *De economische achteruitgang der Republiek in de achttiende eeuw* (Leiden 1968); Ciriacono, 'The Venetian economy', p. 120.

13 Pezzolo, *Una finanza*, p. 55; De Vries and Van der Woude, *The first modern economy*, pp. 610–611; silver values Venetian ducat Pezzolo, *Una finanza*, p. 12; silver values Dutch guilder www.iisg.nl/hpw/brenv/php.

14 F. Lane, *Venice, a maritime republic* (Baltimore 1973).

The Low Countries had become part of the German Empire after the death of Charlemagne. Its feudal lords, counts, dukes and bishops became, like the Venetian doge, de facto independent of the emperor, but in contrast to the Venetian ruler, they were never chosen. In Holland, the heartland of the later Dutch Republic, cities came into existence only since the early thirteenth century, much later than in the territory of the emerging Venetian Republic. The agglomeration of new settlers in the boggy grounds between the rivers Amstel and Y near the Zuiderzee, that built a dam in the Amstel to force ships to offer their merchandise for sale, became only at the start of the fourteenth century the city of 'Amstelredam'.

Like in Spain and France – and unlike in Italy – *provincial* representative institutions came into existence in the Low Countries, allowing lords to address representatives of a number of cities in his territory combined, and together with representatives of nobility and church. Moreover, contrary to Venice and its surrounding territory, Holland and the other provinces of the Low Countries became in the later Middle Ages, part of new much larger political entities, comprising many provinces, first under the dukes of Burgundy, then under the Habsburgs.

In the twelfth century Venice had been part of the Lombard League of north-Italian cities that was established to resist the power claims of the German emperor Frederick Barbarossa. He was 'the first ruler of a modern type, aiming at the complete destruction of the feudal state making the people profitable in the utmost degree to the exchequer', as Burckhardt described the early 'fiscal-military state' of this ruler in one of his famous studies on Italy long ago.[15] The Lombard League, however, did never develop into a federal state. It ended when Barbarossa died. The Venetian Republic did not originate in a meeting of representatives of cities and regional nobles, jointly defending 'liberties' against an oppressive, centralizing ruler.

The largest Italian municipalities 'displayed that force which transforms a *city* (my italics WF) into a state'; the more powerful Italian cities 'shrank so little from extreme measures to damage their competitors, in their commercial dealings with each other, that the end was always usurpation instead of cooperation', as Burckhardt wrote.[16] Venice simply subjected the cities in its *hinterland* to its power, as soon as political and economic developments made this opportune. The cities in its mainland territory – called *Terraferma* to distinguish it from the numerous isles in the lagoon on which the city of Venice was built – were allowed to retain their communal institutions, but taxes came

15 J. Burckhardt, *The state as a work of art* (London 2010; originally 1860; transl. 1878).

16 Burckhardt, *The state*, pp. 61–62.

to be levied by Venice, and were spent as Venice thought best, without any consultation of other city governments. In 1554 74 percent of the total expenditure of eighteen subjected cities consisted in transfers to the city of Venice, perhaps only about 12 percent was spent locally.[17]

The structure of the Venetian Republic was quite different, therefore, from that of the federation of autonomous provinces of the later Dutch Republic, in which in most provinces more than one city – in Holland at last even eighteen – sent representatives to meetings of Provincial States, having the right to vote together with members of a mostly non-urban nobility. The Venetian Republic, in contrast, was governed by only one city, and in this sense it was a centralized state right to the end in 1797. After their conquest by Venice the governor (*podesta*) and the top military and financial officials of the cities in Venice's *hinterland*, were appointed by, and came from Venice. Nobles of the cities subject to Venice were not given any part in the Venetian government, and remained restricted to subordinate roles in their own cities. In the Dutch Republic Amsterdam was incidentally accused of wanting to subjugate the rest of the Dutch Republic as Venice had done.[18] However, although Amsterdam was no doubt the most powerful city in the Dutch Republic, its power was much more limited than that of the city of Venice in the Venetian Republic.

By the end of the fourteenth century a so-called Great Council consisting of about 2,500 members, originating in about 150 patrician families,[19] elected the more than 800 officials necessary for all the state organs by means of a very complicated system of secret balloting: more than 500 for the city, the rest for its maritime territories or *Stato da Mar*, and its mainland territory or *Terraferma*. Nothing comparable existed in the Dutch Republic. The Great Council elected the 200 to 300 members of the 'Senate', which took decisions over most proposals on domestic, foreign and financial affairs that were prepared by the *Collegio*.[20] The tasks of Senate and Collegio are in some respects comparable to that of the Dutch States General, but the States General consisted of representatives of all the Provincial Estates, and only inhabitants of the city of Venice could be members of the Great Council and the Senate.

---

17 Pezzolo, *Una finanza*, p. 35 Tab. 2; the character of 14 percent of public expenditure was uncertain.

18 Haitsma Mulier, *The myth of Venice*, p. 61.

19 Haitsma Mulier, *The myth of Venice*, p. 12; Finer, *The history of government. II*, Chpt. 7. 'The republican alternative: Florence and Venice 950–1051', p. 985: in 1380 1,200 members, in the seventeenth and eighteenth century 2,300 members.

20 Haitsma Mulier, *The myth of Venice*, p. 13.

The Venetian state was led in fact by the *Collegio*. It consisted of three committees of *savi* (wise men). The *savi grandi*, the six inner counsellors of the doge, were perhaps best comparable to the Dutch 'Council of State', which was, however, much less powerful than this committee of *savi*. A committee of five *savi di mare*, managed the affairs of Venice's overseas territory, and five *savi di terra ferma* that of its conquered mainland territory. A 'Council of Forty' looked after judicial affairs, and a powerful and feared 'Council of Ten' guarded internal political security. The tasks of these committees were in the Dutch Republic mainly fulfilled by the boards of the admiralties and the colleges of the 'Commissioners of the Provincial States', rather than on the central level of the state.

In both republics the power was in the hands of a restricted number of rich urban patrician families. The rules for the election of Venice's many offices, in which appointment by lot played an important role, restrained rivalries between these aristocratic families, while the amount of conspicuous expenditure expected from persons in office in Venice, diminished the attraction of public functions for the poorer part of the nobility. In the Dutch Republic the families of the 'patriciate' increasingly succeeded in excluding the offices to a small circle of Protestant families by exchanging written contracts on their voting behaviour for appointments in offices, in this way restraining rivalries as well. The difference between the two republics was again that members of patrician families also of other cities and other provinces than only Holland took part in the network of urban elites that met in the States General in the Dutch Republic, not only that of its largest city.

Venice's doge was the only official who held office for life after his election. He had been powerful until about the twelfth century, but had lost most of his power to his councillors since then.[21] The famous Dutch political thinker Hugo Grotius (1583–1645) liked to compare the position of the doge to the position of the prince-stadholder in the Dutch Republic, which in fact mainly reflected his view on the desirability of an only marginal influence for stadholders in Dutch politics.[22] William of Orange's son prince Maurice, who was stadholder from 1584–1625 and as such captain-general of the Dutch army and admiral of the navy which the doge was not, once said, however, that he would prefer the existence of a galley slave to that of the doge of Venice.[23] The Venetian political system did not experience the political antagonism perceptible in these two views. The question if this may have influenced the difference in the size of military expenditure between the two will be shortly addressed in the next section.

21 Haitsma Mulier, *The myth of Venice*, p. 76.
22 Haitsma Mulier, *The myth of Venice*, p. 70.
23 Haitsma Mulier, *The myth of Venice*, p. 13.

Another Maritime State and Its 'Year of Disaster'

In contrast to the Dutch Republic Venice's power expansion over sea had preceded its development as a territorial republic. Already since c. 1100 Venetian fleets made their power felt all over the Eastern Mediterranean. To realize its geopolitical maritime aims the Venetian Republic developed in many senses into a much more centralized and interfering state than the Dutch Republic. Like the Dutch Republic during the first stadholderless period under Johan de Witt, it would be confronted with the question if the international political situation allowed more priority for the navy than for the army. Much more than in the Dutch Republic the choice seemed evident for a very long time.

Already in the thirteenth century the city of Venice possessed an overseas empire, its *Stato da Mar*, also denoted as *Levante*,[24] consisting of coastal territories and isles east of Italy.[25] Venice considered the Adriatic Sea as '*mare nostrum*' (='our sea'). All cargos entering this sea had to be unloaded in Venice.[26] Its expansion had started in the eleventh century with the conquest of parts of the Dalmatian coast, and in the course of time it included, during varying time periods, also important isles like Crete, Corfu, and Cyprus. Due to the scant space for provisions in the Venetian galleys, the ports in Venice's territory *da Mar* were of vital importance for victualling. Venice needed them also as strategic bases to give credibility to its maritime claims. Last but not least it needed the *hinterland* of those ports as recruiting areas for mariners.[27] The Dutch Republic did never try to conquer nearby territories oversea.

When the Byzantine Empire had proved to be no longer able to provide protection on Venetian trade routes, the Venetian government had built, already in 1104, an Arsenal for the production of arms and ships to this end. All ships in the Venetian Republic were subject to regulation by Venice's city government. In contrast, initiatives for trade regulation and protection in the Low Countries were initiated mostly by groups of merchants, and were only gradually seen as a task of city governments. Only since the Revolt protection of Dutch international trade was seen as a responsibility of the States General to be financed

24 An old meaning of the term Levant is: the coast territories and isles east of Italy.

25 For a good map of the Venetian state at the start of the sixteenth century see for instance: upload.wikimedia.org/wikipedia/commons/0/09/Repubblica_di_Venezia.png [last access 28/08/2016] offers; for a map with information on territorial losses in the course of time see for instance https://en.wikipedia.org/wiki/Domini_di_Terraferma#/media/File:Venezianische_Kolonien.png.

26 Lane, *Venice*, p. 3; most of this section stems from Lane's admirable study of Venice.

27 M. Mallett and J. Hale, *The military organisation of a Renaissance state. Venice c. 1400–1617* (Cambridge 1984) pp. 429, 435.

from customs collected by the admiralties. The granting of a monopoly for the trade in the East Indies to the VOC had implied, that the VOC had to finance from its own revenues the protection of its trade routes outside Europe as well as the maintenance of its position in an immensely much larger colonial world than Venice's *Stato da Mar*.[28] This made the relation of the Dutch Republic to its overseas empire very different from that in Venice. The Venetian state maintained troops in garrisons overseas already since the thirteenth century.

In the thirteenth and fourteenth centuries, the Venetians found their strongest commercial rival in Genoa, with which four costly naval wars were fought, ending in Venice's triumph in 1380. Venice had a very strong position in the profitable spice trade with the East, after this last war, which it would only lose again, first to Lisbon and then to Amsterdam, after the discovery of the Atlantic sea route to the East. After Constantinople had been conquered by the Ottomans in 1453, the Ottomans became the main enemy of the Venetians. Seven Ottoman-Venetian wars were fought between 1463 and 1718. Venice was therefore much more a maritime republic during many centuries, than the Dutch Republic, where already the Eighty Years War against Spain – the first major war in which it was involved – was predominantly land based. Land wars to contain French expansion continued to demand much more of Dutch public finance than the four naval wars with Britain. Venice's maritime power would gradually diminish since the middle of the seventeenth century.[29]

During the later Middle Ages, incidental wars over territories and cities in its *hinterland*, had mostly been won by Venice, too, and in the fifteenth century its mainland territory became increasingly important, on the one hand for the safety of its trade routes overland, on the other hand for the supply of food, and of raw materials for shipbuilding and the recruitment of mariners. The navy would not have remained able to defend the republic's possessions without the manpower of its *Terraferma*. In addition, *Terraferma* would turn out to provide agricultural and industrial compensation for Venice's decreasing income from trade with the Ottoman Empire since the development of the Atlantic trade of other European powers.[30] The result of Venice's expansion into its *hinterland* was also, however, that it became an element in the emerging Italian five powers state system, consisting of Venice, Milan, Florence, the Papal States and Naples, and their Spanish and French connections, in the fifteenth century.

28 For a map of the area involved see https://upload.wikimedia.org/wikipedia/commons/c/c7/VOC_Octrooigebied_2.jpg

29 Mallett and Hale, *The military organization*, p. 4.

30 Mallett and Hale, *The military organization*, pp. 212–213.

In 1508 a league, consisting of France, that ruled Milan, Spain, ruler in Naples, and the Papal State, was signed in Cambrai in France with the aim to force back Venice's power expansion. Troops of the French king, the German emperor and the Pope invaded Venice's *Terraferma* and after the battle of Agnadello in 1509 Venice had to leave Bergamo, Brescia, Crema and Cremona to the French, Verona, Vicenza and Padua to the German Emperor and its possessions in the Romagna to the Pope. It had not been prepared for the defence of its own increased land territory and 'lost in one day what it had taken them eight hundred years exertion to conquer', as Macchiavelli wrote.[31]

The year 1509 in the history of the Venetian Republic, can be compared therefore to 1672, the 'Year of Disaster', in the history of the Dutch Republic, as was done, in fact, for instance by Voltaire.[32] For both republics these were the years when they threatened to fall apart. The cities in the *Terraferma* accepted the king of France and the German emperor as their new rulers, just as the Dutch provinces of Overijssel and Gelderland in 1672 would declare for the bishops of Munster and Cologne and for the German Empire, after they had been invaded by German troops.

This situation was even more threatening for Venice than for the Dutch Republic, because it had come to depend, economically and financially, much more on its *Terraferma* than the Dutch Republic on these conquered provinces. Probably about 35 percent of total tax revenue of the Venetian Republic came by then from its mainland territory outside Venice.[33] The provinces Overijssel, Gelderland and Utrecht, that were temporary lost in 1672, contributed less than 15 percent to the general public expenditure of the Dutch Republic.

Eight years of warfare, from 1509 to 1517, were needed for Venice to regain its former possessions. It succeeded in this only thanks to the collapse of the League of Cambrai in 1510, and the subsequent support, first of France, and later of the Pope. The loyalty of the *Terraferma* cities could be taken for granted again, only after 1517. After this war Venice decided to maintain, apart from its

31 Mallett and Hale refer to Chapter 12 of Macchiavelli's, 'The Prince'.

32 In his famous *The Age of Louis XIV* (1751); see *The Works of Voltaire. A Contemporary Version.* A Critique and Biography by John Morley, notes by Tobias Smollett, trans. William F. Fleming (New York: E.R. DuMont, 1901). In 21 vols. Vol. XII. http://oll.libertyfund.org/index.php?option=com_staticxt&staticfile=show.phppercent3Ftitle=2132&Itemid=27,137.

33 In 1490 38 percent, in 1550 48 percent; Pezzolo, *Una finanza,* 47; a remarkably low percentage given the fact that the population of the total Venetian Republic was about ten times the population of the city of Venice.

navy, also a standing army of about 9,000 men.[34] Mallett and Hale concluded that '1509' had made Venice's patriciate aware, at last, of the importance of the *Terraferma,* and that since then it could in fact no longer be termed 'A Maritime Republic'.[35]

At the same time, however, Venice started to prefer the acceptance of humiliating treaties above increasing military efforts to win a war, when help from allies was not to be expected. In 1540 it agreed to pay the Turks 300,000 ducats in order to end a war, a 'very painful' amount of money, according to one specialist on Venice's military history.[36] This seems to be an exaggeration, however, as Venice could at that time dispose of a total tax revenue per year of about 1.5 million ducats per year and moreover of a developed capital market.[37] Its new foreign policy was not restricted to war faring on land, but was also extended to naval wars.

In 1571 a league with Spain and the Papacy was signed to stop the Turks who had occupied Cyprus in 1570. Despite the successful naval battle of Lepanto in 1571 during this 'War of Cyprus' or 'Fourth Ottoman-Venetian War', the Venetian Senate began to notify its allies already in 1573, without even having regained Cyprus, that it was quitting the league for financial reasons. Venice's ambassadors were instructed to argue that 'we have spent on this war up till now over twelve millions of gold – a fact that amazes even us as to how and whence we have been able to extract it'.[38] A unilateral withdrawal from a league was an offence in international law, but Spain and the new pope Gregory XIII did not object to Venice's move, as they had already come to regret their investment in an area of the Mediterranean from which Venice alone would reap the major benefit.[39]

Venice's early retreat from this war reminds of that of the Dutch Republic in 1678, which was enforced by Holland in the States General despite resistance of the stadholder. According to Jonathan Israel, the unilateral ending of the war with France in 1678 burdened the Dutch Republic for years afterwards with the reputation of being an untrustworthy ally, concerned only with its commercial

---

34 Mallett and Hale, *The military organization,* p. 220.

35 Referring to the title of Lane's famous study from 1965; Mallett and Hale, *The military organization,* pp. 1 and 227.

36 Total tax revenue in Pezzolo, *Una finanza;* qualification 'very painful' in Mallett and Hale, *The military organization,* p. 239.

37 In 1532 a voluntary loan at 6 percent had been completely subscribed in one day, see the section on public debt below.

38 Mallett and Hale, *The military organization,* p. 240.

39 Mallett and Hale, *The military organization,* p. 241.

interests.[40] The unprecedented height of Dutch war expenditure during this war makes it plausible that the state of its public finance was decisive in the Dutch case as well like in Venice. The decision of 1678 did not yet withhold the Dutch Republic, however, to spend even much more on the two next international wars against France. In contrast, the Venetian patriciate's instinct became – as historians of its military history put it – 'to survive and prosper on the cheap', since the last decades of the sixteenth century, although it would have to fight three more wars with its main enemy as well.[41]

What were the consequences for public finance in the Venetian Republic of the backgrounds sketched in this section in comparison to the Dutch Republic since the 1570s?

4.2 'Survive and Prosper on the Cheap'

For the period since 1579 until 1736 more or less detailed data on Venice's public finance are available for 21 years,[42] showing that total public expenditure in the Venetian Republic became soon much lower than that in the Dutch Republic at the end of the sixteenth century (Figure 4.1). Figures on public finance for a single year are, of course, rather unreliable as they may be accidentally much higher or lower in a specific year than in other years in the same time period for a wide variety of reasons. Figure 4.1 shows, however, that the differences between the two states are too consistent – and too large since the renewal of the Dutch War with Spain after 1621 – to allow any doubt on this point. In comparison with the Dutch Republic the Venetian Republic did succeed, indeed, in 'surviving on the cheap' since the end of the sixteenth century.

The years for which Venetian data are available for the seventeenth century and 1710 were all peace years for Venice and all war years for the Dutch Republic, which makes the higher level of Dutch expenditure in this period self-evident. The years in the graph since 1736, however, were peace years in both republics. This calls for the question why during these years, Dutch public

40 Israel, *The Dutch Republic*, p. 825.

41 Mallett and Hale, *The military organization*, p. 217.

42 Pezzolo, *Una finanza*, p. 77: details on the structure of public finance are only published for the years visible in Figure 4.2a; totals are available for all years since 1736: ibidem, pp. 38–40, fluctuating from 4.9 million ducats in 1737 to 7.1 million ducats in 1788; the five-years averages around the years 1740, 1750, 1760, 1770, 1780, were rather constant resp. 5.6 milllion, 5.6 million, 5.4 million, 5.8 million, 5.8 million ducats, rising to 7.2 million ducats around 1790 (the silver value of the ducat was always 14,97 gr between 1733 and 1797).

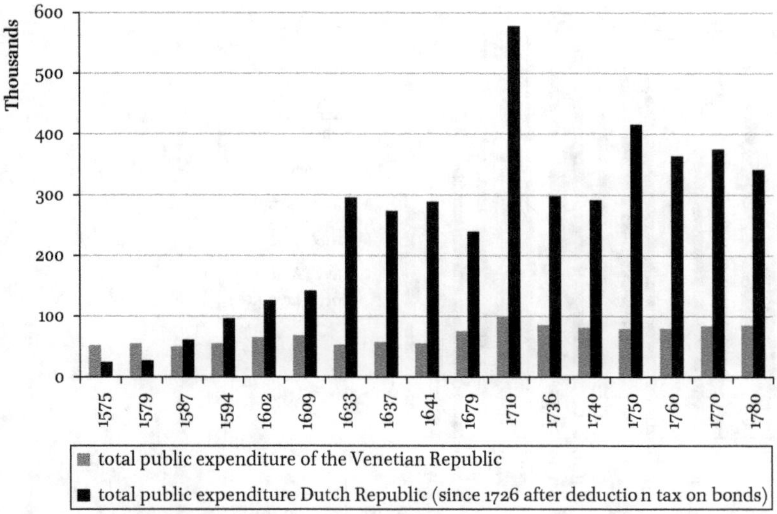

FIGURE 4.1 *Total public expenditure of the Venetian and the Dutch Republic, 1575–1780 (kg silver).* Sources: Pezzolo, *La finanza*, pp. 12 and 38–40; grams silver per guilder: Van Zanden, http://www.iisg.nl/hpw/brenv.php.

expenditure continued to be so much higher. We will first discuss the structure of public expenditure and then come back to this question.

The Structure of Public Expenditure

The structure of Venetian's public expenditure shows, firstly, that the proportion of 'other expenditure' in total public expenditure was always higher in the Venetian Republic than in the Dutch Republic for the years for which data are available. It was often more than 30 percent of total public expenditure against mostly less than 15 percent in the Dutch Republic. One remarkable reason for this was the formation of a 'war chest' since the 1580s, filled – apparently each year and probably until the War of Gradisca (1615–1617) – with about 500,000 ducats, which was about 20 to 25 percent of total public expenditure in the years for which data were available.[43]

Another reason for the high Venetian percentage was that 'other expenditure' sometimes consisted of large amounts for water management ('*acque*') as for instance in 1679, or for 'poor patricians', as for instance in 1780. In the Dutch Republic, such types of expenditure belonged to the tasks of waterboards, and urban governments. This means that in fact the differences in total

43 The so-called '*Deposito Grande*' (this detailed information stems from a spreadsheet with research data kindly put at my disposal by L. Pezzolo).

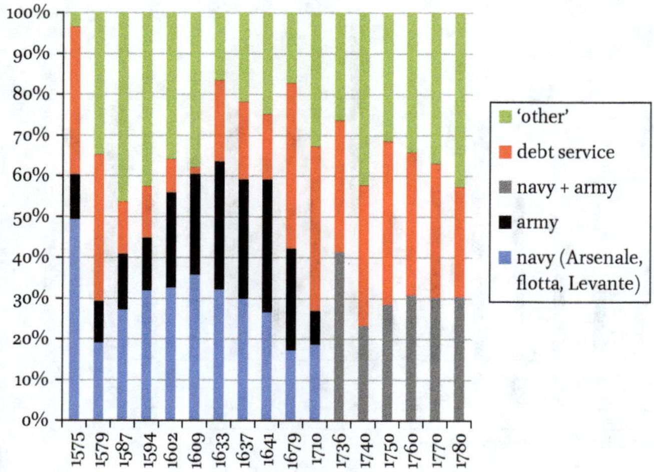

FIGURE 4.2A *Structure of public expenditure in the Venetian Republic for available years, 1575–1780.*

expenditure between the two republics were even much larger than Figure 4.1 suggested, because these types of expenditure are not included in the 'public finance *of* the Dutch Republic' according to the definition used in this book (see the third section of the Introduction to Part One).

Figure 4.2 shows, secondly, that not only total expenditure in the Venetian Republic was much less than in the Dutch Republic (Figure 4.1), but that war expenditure was, in addition, a much smaller part of total expenditure. A third evident difference is, that Dutch naval expenditure was mostly a much lower percentage of military expenditure than in the Venetian Republic – on average 26 percent in the years from 1579 to 1679 for which also Venetian data were available, against on average 58 percent in Venice – this despite the experience of '1509', after which Venice was no longer really a maritime state according to its military historians.[44] Even when an estimate is added for war expenditure by the VOC – as was done in Figure 4.2b – it is evident that the Venetian Republic remained a 'maritime' state at least to a larger extent than the Dutch Republic. In the Dutch Republic, naval expenditure was only near or more than fifty percent of military expenditure in years of major naval wars (not visible in Figure 4.2; see Figure 3.2).

It should be added, perhaps, that the distinction between naval and land wars was not always clear cut. Venice's two wars in the sixteenth century after the war of the League of Cambrai were against the Ottomans,[45] for whom

44 Mallett and Hale, *The military organization,* pp. 1, 227.

45 The Third and the Fourth Venetian-Ottoman Wars, resp. 1537–1540 and 1570–1573.

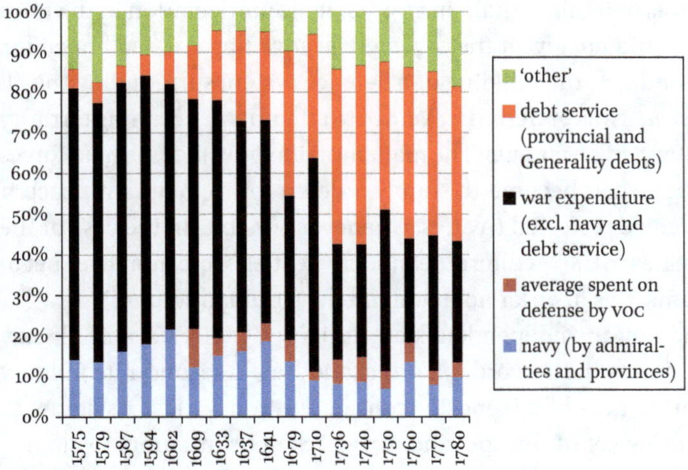

FIGURE 4.2B *Idem for the Dutch Republic for the same years as for Venice.*
Sources: L. Pezzolo, *Una finanza d'ancien regime. La Repubblica Veneta tra XV e XVIII secolo* (Napoli 2006) p. 77; a spreadsheet with a further breakdown of military expenditure for 1575–1679 was kindly put at my disposal by L. Pezzolo.

territorial gains were in fact much more important than commercial rivalry. This meant that sometimes also land forces of the Venetian Republic, as garrisoned in its *Stato da Mar*, had to play an important part in these wars. During the war in which the famous battle of Lepanto was won (1570–73) Venice paid nearly 36,000 soldiers, a number even somewhat larger than the 31,000 to 35,000 (on paper) of the Dutch army at the end of the sixteenth century.

The War of Gradisca (1615–17) was for the Venetian Republic the last land war fought against European enemies – in this case Austria and Naples. Even this war was partly a war against Dalmatian corsairs supported by Austria to undermine Venice's position in the Adriatic Sea. Venice had still to fight three wars with the Ottomans during the next century.[46] Since 1644 the Ottomans tried to conquer Crete, in which they succeeded at last in 1669. In 1683 the Venetians yet conquered Morea (the Peloponnesus) on the Ottoman Empire, which re-conquered this territory however in 1714. Austria, its ally in Venice's seventh and last war with the Ottoman Empire between 1714 and 1718, forced Venice to accept the loss of Morea. So, Venice's 'overseas empire' became reduced to the Dalmatian coast and the Ionian islands during the eighteenth century. Venice felt cheated by its ally in 1714, but was by then as powerless to Austria as the

46 The Fifth, Sixth and Seventh Venetian-Ottoman Wars, resp. 1645–1669, 1684–1699 and 1714–1718.

Dutch Republic was to its ally Britain in 1713, when its participation in the huge war against France did not give it the commercial advantages it had hoped for.

Between 1744 and 1782 the building of a defence system surrounding the lagoon (not *Terraferma*) was preferred by Venice to attempts at regaining territory by means of military involvements. The main function of Venice's armed forces and its fortifications had become to supply a deterrent to maintain peace.[47] Since the 1760s Venice preferred treaties, whenever possible. In the case of the Barbary corsair states in the Mediterranean such 'treaties' were moreover negotiated by merchants, this in order not to offend the Ottoman sultan.[48]

Although remaining an independent state until 1797, Venice became already in the sixteenth century in the words of Mallet and Hale 'a second-rate military power'.[49] The Dutch Republic is mostly considered to have lost its status as one of the Great Powers of Europe since 1713.[50] Serious attempts to survive in a cheaper way than before started here after 1713, in order to cope with the dramatic increase in debt service after the war of 1701–1713. The army was reduced from 119,000 men during 1708–1713 to only 34,000 men in 1718 as it had been in 1669. Total military expenditure (incl. the navy) had amounted to on average about 200 tons silver in the three peace years preceding 1701 and would become about only 144 ton silver on average during the peace years 1717–1740. Nevertheless this was still a much larger amount than the 35 tons silver in the Venetian Republic in 1735 and the even only 19 tons silver by 1740.

Although the Venetian Republic must have become poorer than the Dutch Republic in the eighteenth century, judging from the fact that the silver wage of a Venetian day labourer was probably more than two times smaller than that in the Western Netherlands in 1770, the difference in military expenditure was much larger, than can be explained by this difference. This calls for the question why the Dutch level of public finance remained that high after 1713. Why did it not follow the Venetian example 'to survive on the cheap' more intensively during the eighteenth century?

A 'Peaceful Republic' and an 'Expenditure Bottom'

According to the early seventeenth century author Boccalini, Venice had not undergone the expansion normally to be expected from such a powerful republic, because it sought peace.[51] Already in the sixteenth century one of

---

47 Mallett and Hale, *The military organization*, p. 214.

48 Lane, *Venice*, p. 419.

49 Mallett and Hale, *The military organization.*

50 According to Van Nimwegen, *De Republiek der Verenigde Nederlanden als grote mogendheid,* only in 1748.

51 Mallett and Hale, *The military organization*, p. 34.

Venice's influential patricians had written a treatise stating that enlargement of frontiers cannot lead to well-being and that peace should be the main aim of political activity.[52] The peace-aspiring Venetian Republic was in the seventeenth century seen by some other states with republican aspirations as a model, as for instance by Naples in 1647, by Britain after the execution of king Charles I at the start of the Cromwellian republic, and more than a century later also by the new republic in America.[53] In his 'The history of government' (1997) the political and military historian Finer devoted no less than about forty pages to Venice's government system (and no one at all to the Dutch Republic). He evaluated it as 'the best in the world', whereas earlier military historians like Mallett and Hale (1984) had preferred the qualification of 'second rate power' for the early-modern Venetian state, as we saw.[54]

Venice was also praised by Dutch writers since the end of the sixteenth century, for its statesmanship and avoidance of war.[55] Like the Englishman Harrington some Dutch writers saw in Venice the ideal example of a 'mixed government' of monarchic, aristocratic and democratic elements (although others, like the sixteenth century French political philosopher Jean Bodin, saw it – more realistically – as mainly an aristocracy). According to Haitsma Mulier who researched the influence of 'the myth of Venice' in the Dutch Republic, references to Venice in the Dutch Republic became much less frequent, during the stadholderate of William II (1647–1650): the stadholder, who married the eldest daughter of the king of Britain, and committed a (failed) assault on Amsterdam in 1650 in an attempt to force the province of Holland to accept less cuts military expenditure after the end of the Eighty Years War against Spain than its urban elites wished.[56]

There are no indications that the resumption of cuts on the army after the death of William II in 1650, from nearly 35,000 men in 1648 to less than 25,000 in 1661 during the first 'stadholderless period', were due to an influence of the Venetian example. Nevertheless, the cutbacks on the army that were realized at that time can be very well seen as a typically 'republican' fiscal policy, characterized by a relatively low level of military expenditure due to the absence of a prince.

It seems logical to expect that the amounts voted for war in the Dutch Republic were a compromise between what the provinces thought useful and

52 Paolo Paruta, *Della perfettione della vita politica*, quoted in Lane, *Venice*, pp. 392–393.

53 Lane, *Venice*, p. 405.

54 Finer, *History of government*, p. 1016.

55 Haitsma Mulier, *The myth of Venice*, p. 200.

56 Haitsma Mulier, *The myth of Venice*, p. 209.

what the Council of State – that prepared the financial decisions of the States General in the presence of the prince-stadholder – thought necessary. However, in 1688 and in 1701, the merchants of Amsterdam appeared to be in fact as eager to curb the increasing French power in Europe for commercial reasons, as the son of stadholder William II – Holland's stadholder since 1672 and king of Britain since 1688 – for political reasons. So, although most Dutch provinces decided to do without a stadholder again after the death of William III in 1702, they would continue their involvement in the costly war of 1701–1713. The peace negotiations at the end of this war made it clear that the Dutch hopes to gain commercial advantages from the war were in vain and that the Dutch Republic was no longer treated by Britain as an equal ally. Due to the increasing strength of the larger states, after civil war faring in Britain and France had ended, the Dutch Republic had become a really small, much more powerless, state by 1713.

After 1713 the main explanation for the continuously remarkably high amounts in military expenditure in the Dutch Republic in comparison to Venice seems to be that it had a history in which rather high amounts in military expenditure were normal already since the end of the sixteenth century, because of the costliness of land wars in comparison with maritime wars. After the extremely expensive war of 1701–1713 the army was reduced, but it did not become lower than the number of about 34,000 men (on paper) that had been customary at the end of the period before the three wars against France. Between 1752 and 1793 it was still thought as self-evident that the Dutch Republic should have an army of more than 40,000 men in peacetime, implying about 20 soldiers per 1000 inhabitants.[57] During the years 1815–1830 this would become only about ten soldiers per thousand inhabitants, when the Southern and Northern Netherlands combined had an army of about 50,000 men.[58] Even this was still much in comparison to for instance France at that time, where it was only about 7 soldiers per thousand inhabitants (200,000 men).

The development of public expenditure in the Dutch Republic during the eighteenth century suggests the idea of the existence of an historically determined 'expenditure bottom' : war expenditure was lowered after a war, but not much more than to what was felt as a more or less 'usual' size. Contrary to what might have been expected, the absence or presence of a stadholder did not determine the size of the army in peace periods. The intended average army size of about 44,000 men during the 'stadholderless' peace years 1714–1740 was

57 Zwitzer, *'De militie van den staat'*, p. 176.

58 W. Fritschy, 'Staatsvorming en financieel beleid onder Willem I', in: *Staats- en natievorming in Willem I's koninkrijk (1815–1830)* eds. C.A. Tamse and E. Witte (Brussel 1992) pp. 215–237, p. 229.

about equal to that during the peace-years after the return of a stadholder in all provinces during 1748–1792.

Yet one wonders if not the federal character of the Dutch Republic may have functioned as a brake on the realization of more cuts on military expenditure. The views of stadholders found generally more support in the other provinces than in Holland. The – in comparison with the Venetian Republic – relatively high level of Dutch public expenditure may have resulted from a tendency to avoid disruptive discussions on changes in expenditure norms for which agreement had been possible in the past, a tendency which was not operative in the centralized Venetian Republic.

4.3 Taxation in a Centralized and in a Federal Urbanized Republic

The level of Venice's *total revenue* was very high in international comparative perspective during the fifteenth century. In 1464 the amount was equal to c. 46 ton silver, about the same as in France at that time.[59] British state revenue was less than 20 tons silver on average per year from 1462 to 1486, and Castilian state revenue on average less than 15 tons silver per year between 1405 and 1475.[60]

In 1590 Venetian public revenue amounted to 55 tons silver, in 1609 about 66 tons silver.[61] By then, the amount in public revenue in the Republic was already worth 119 tons silver, however. By 1700 Venetian *total* annual public revenue was already lower than in eight other of the ten states compared by Karaman and Pamuk regarding their public revenue.

Like public expenditure (Figure 4.1) also public revenue would, of course, remain much lower in the Venetian Republic than in the Dutch Republic during the seventeenth and eighteenth century, although Venetian annual public revenue *per capita* was not yet really low in international comparative perspective. Around 1700 it was still higher than in France and seven other states of the ten states, the public expenditure of which was examined by Karaman and Pamuk, and only lower than in Britain and in the Dutch Republic.[62]

59 In the decades after 1460 France's revenue would increase from about 49 tons silver to about 95 tons in 1483; W. Ormrod, 'The West European monarchies in the Later Middle Ages', in R. Bonney ed., *Economic systems and state finance* (Oxford 1996), p. 142.

60 Ormrod, 'The West European monarchies in the Later Middle Ages', pp. 123–163, pp. 151, 153.

61 Pezzolo, *Una finanza*, p. 38, p. 12.

62 Karaman and Pamuk, 'Ottoman state finances', pp. 610–611.

Differences in Public Revenue and in Wealth

Their commercial character allowed both republics to obtain a relatively large part of tax revenues from indirect domestic taxes and customs revenue. A difference between both was the initially much larger role of customs than of domestic indirect taxes. 'Foreign purchasers were major contributors to the Venetian state budget through tariffs', as Rapp concluded in a study on Venice's economy in the seventeenth century. Although quantitative data are only scarcely available they show the contrast to the Dutch Republic clearly enough (Figure 4.3).

About one third of the public revenue of the Venetian Republic came from trade still in 1609,[63] but the proportion declined in the course of the century to less than 15 percent in 1670, due to Venice's commercial decline. Details on the role of different categories of taxation in Venetian public revenue are even scarcer, but Figure 4.4 makes it nevertheless evident that direct taxation was much less important in the revenue structure of the Venetian Republic than in the Dutch Republic, due to its much lower level of total tax revenue.

As no separate data were available on the relative importance of long-term loans in Venice's public revenue structure loans, loans will be mainly discussed

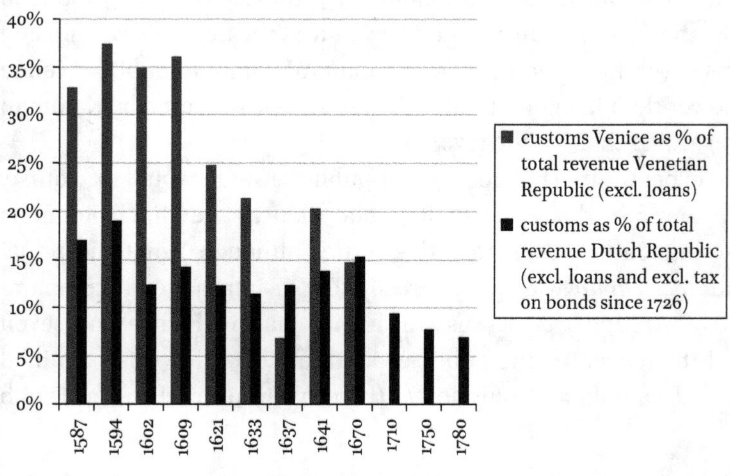

FIGURE 4.3 *Customs as % of total public revenue (excl. loans) in the Venetian and the Dutch Republic for available years, 1587–1780.*
Sources: Rapp, *Industry and economic decline in seventeenth century Venice,* Table 5.1; Pezzolo, *Una finanza*, pp. 38–40.

63 Rapp, *Industry and economic decline, p.* 139; I owe thanks to Luciano Pezzolo for the reference.

64 Pezzolo, *Una finanza*, pp. 38–39.

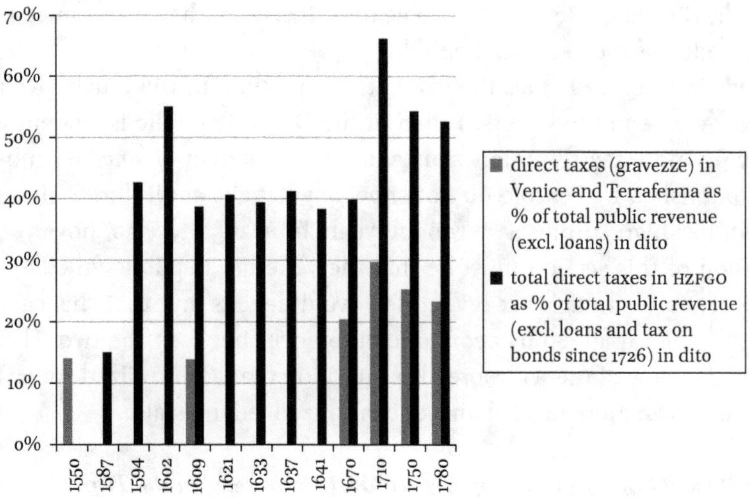

FIGURE 4.4 *The percentage of direct taxation in total public revenue (excl. loans) in the Venetian and the Dutch Republic for available years, 1550–1780.* Sources: Pezzolo, *Una finanza,* tab. 6, p. 47.

in the fourth section of this chapter, on public debt. It is certain, that since the 1580s loans were for many years simply not needed, as Venice was then even able to form a war chest, as we saw. During the period from 1600 to 1641 still six of the seven years for which data were available showed surpluses of revenue over expenditure,[64] only the year 1621 had a small deficit.

Between about 1650 and 1750, however, eighteen out of the twenty years for which data were available showed – often large – deficits, only one of which was a year of war. Venice was apparently no longer able, during this period, to realize sufficient tax revenue for public expenditure even during peace-years. The Venetian Republic was apparently not able to attain a level higher than 90 tons silver in taxes per year, whereas Dutch annual public revenue exclusive loans amounted in the early 1740s to nearly 300 tons silver.

It is not likely that this very large difference was due to the difference in wealth between the two republics. If wage differences in 1770 may be seen as a rough indicator for differences in wealth, the Dutch population was on average not much more than two times as wealthy: in 1770 the wage of a Venetian day labourer amounted to about 0.26 ducats (3.9 gr silver),[65] that of Dutch unskilled day labourers to about 0.89 guilders (8.6 gr silver). This cannot explain,

65 Sources: Pezzolo, *Una finanza,* 55 (see also L. Pezzolo,, 'Republics and principalities in Italy', in *The rise of fiscal states. A global history,* p. 283); De Vries and Van der Woude, *The first modern economy,* pp. 50, 610, 200.

therefore, why the Dutch Republic was able to realize more than *three* times as much tax revenue as the Venetian Republic.

For the 1770s, 1780s and 1790s the evident explanation for the much lower level of tax revenue in the Venetian than in the Dutch Republic is evidently that simply no more tax revenue was needed. The Venetian '*Bilanci*' of public finance published by Pezzolo do not show any deficits at all during these years, but rather high surpluses.[66] For the years from 1650 to 1750, however, the conclusion of this section must be that the Venetian Republic failed apparently to generate enough tax revenue to avoid deficits and that this cannot sufficiently be explained by economic differences between the two. This is remarkable in view of the widespread assumption that a centralized state is better able to realize more taxes than a decentralized federal state.

The Fiscal Contributions of 'Centre' and 'Periphery' in the Two Republics

In a study of the effects of political regimes on the performance of states Epstein was convinced that the Italian *republican* city-states disproportionally taxed the territories outside the main city. 'Disproportionately' means here, most probably, that the tax burden per capita outside the central city was heavier than inside it. He found support for this view in early modern authors like Guicciardini and Hume, who were convinced that 'whereas sovereigns maximize revenue by taxing everyone proportionally, republics maximize

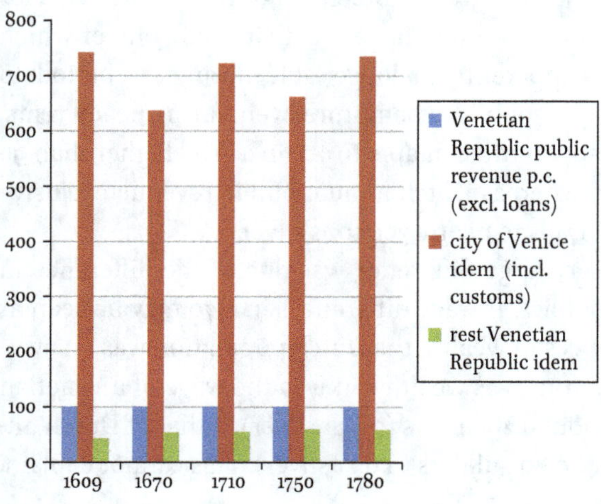

FIGURE 4.5A
Differences in public revenue (excl. loans) per capita in the Venetian Republic in some years, 1609–1780 (index numbers; public revenue p.c. in Venetian Republic = 100).

66 Pezzolo, *Una finanza*, pp. 39–40.

revenue by taxing some disproportionally'.[67] A comparison of the relative contributions of the 'centre' and the 'periphery' of the Venetian and the Dutch Republic to public revenue gives reason for doubt, however, on the correctness of this expectation as regards the Venetian city-state.

Figure 4.5a gives an impression of the differences in the average amount in public revenue per capita realized from the less than 200,000 inhabitants of the city of Venice, and the average amount per capita for the rest of the about two million inhabitants of the whole republic. Figure 4.5b does the same for Amsterdam, Holland, and the Dutch Republic. Because the figures for Venice included customs revenue, the total amounts in customs revenue in the Dutch Republic have been added to the amounts for Amsterdam and Holland to make the graphs more comparable. A comparison with Holland has been

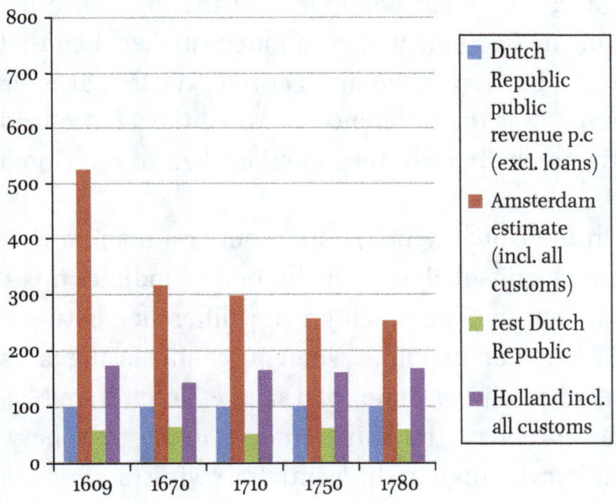

FIGURE 4.5B *Idem in the Dutch Republic (index numbers; revenue p.c. in Dutch Republic = 100).*
Sources: Pezzolo, *Una finanza*, pp. 47, 55; De Vries and Van der Woude, *The first modern economy*, p. 50 (missing population data were constructed by interpolations assuming a constant percentage growth or decrease in between two known figures; Amsterdam estimated).[68]

67 Epstein, *Freedom and growth*, p. 33.

68 The revenue of the common means in the tax district of Amsterdam was mostly about 35 percent of that in Holland (see spreadsheet 'Gemeenelandsmiddelen' on http://www.iisg.nl/hpw/data.php#netherlands). Of the personal direct tax of 1654, too, 35 percent came from Amsterdam (*GFH* p. 25); for 1609 the estimate was reduced to 23 percent of Holland, because at that time Amsterdam's population was probably only 14 percent of Holland, and in 1670 probably about 21 percent.

added, because in fact Holland's urban system, rather than Amsterdam, should be seen as the fiscal 'centre' of the Dutch Republic.

The amounts in public revenue per capita realized in the cities of Venice and Amsterdam were on average much higher, of course, than the average in the 'periphery' of the two republics, because of the much larger wealth in these cities and the much wider fiscal possibilities offered by a large urban economy. Because the customs revenue was in the Venetian Republic part of the revenue of Venice and because no breakdown of indirect taxation (*dazi*) in domestic indirect taxes and customs was possible for most of the years, the customs of the Dutch Republic were completely added to Amsterdam. The graphs show that tax revenue per capita was in the city of Venice six to seven times as large as in the Republic as a whole, in Amsterdam provincial tax revenue plus customs was in the course of time only five times as large as on average in the Dutch Republic, and the difference between *Holland* and the rest of the Republic was even much smaller than that between the city of Venice and its *Terraferma* and *Levante*. What is at issue in this comparison is, however, that the difference between the 'centre' and the 'periphery' was evidently much larger in the Venetian than in the Dutch Republic.

Chapter 3.3 argued that in the Dutch Republic the 'common man' in Holland was less well off than in Overijssel, due to the burden of indirect taxes, at the end of the eighteenth century. The much greater difference between 'centre' and 'periphery' in the Venetian Republic, where price-increasing taxes were a more important part of public revenue than in the Dutch Republic, makes it unlikely, that the tax burden on the 'common man' in the 'periphery' of the Venetian Republic was heavier than in the 'centre', notwithstanding the expectations of Guicciardini, Hume and in their wake Epstein.

The graphs suggest, therefore, that an 'urban system' dominated by one powerful city, did enforce not *more*, but in fact relatively *less* in fiscal contributions from the population outside the centre, than an 'urban system' in which collective decisions on fiscal policy were necessary.

The character of the Dutch 'urban system' contributed apparently to a fiscal burden spread out somewhat more evenly across its whole territory than the Venetian urban system in which power was centralized in only one city. The situation in the Venetian Republic is actually reminiscent of the fact that the centrally determined tax rates in the conquered part of the former province of Brabant were in the eighteenth century lower than that of the economically comparable province of Overijssel. It may have been in fact rather a contribution to the fiscal strength of the federal Dutch Republic, therefore, that it was a federal instead of a centralized republic, than a source of weakness.

4.4 Differing Debt Developments

Long-term public debts started in continental Europe often as *urban* debts during the processes of urbanization and state formation in the later Middle Ages. In many Italian cities urban debts started in the twelfth century, in France and the Netherlands in the thirteenth.[69] A first difference in the history of public debt in the Venetian Republic, in contrast to that of the Dutch Republic, was a preference for forced loans during nearly three centuries, before voluntary loans became common practice since the early sixteenth century. A second difference was that the Venetian debt always remained the debt of the city of Venice alone, whereas Holland's debt became a provincial debt originating in the urban debts of a great number of cities, while that of the Dutch Republic consisted in many provincial debts plus that of the Generality. A third difference between the two states was that the Venetian *Banco del Giro* became an important instrument of the Venetian government in the realization of voluntary public loans, a function that the Amsterdam Exchange Bank never had to perform. This last section offers a more detailed description of the developments in public debt formation between the two republics in relation to their different 'urban systems'.

'Mountains of Debt', Forced Loans and 'Citizenship'

The first known loan to the Venetian government was a voluntary loan supplied in 1164 by twelve rich individuals. In return they received the city's rental income from the Rialto market for a period of eleven years. This loan format started under the name *compera* in Genoa already in 1149 and it remained in existence there until 1408. In Venice, however, 'this dangerous path' – by which parts of public revenue were ceded for some periods of time to private consortia of lenders – 'was soon abandoned in favour of a system of forced loans', as Luzzatto wrote in his study on Venice's loans.[70]

The first known forced loans in Venice, raised to finance a war against the Byzantine Empire, date from the early thirteenth century. They were realized by means of individual assessments of rich citizens according to the value of their property in real estate, and were characterized by low rates of interest varying from only 2 to 4 percent. Short-term voluntary loans to finance wars, supplied by merchants at interest rates varying from 12 to 20 percent,

69 J. Tracy, 'On the dual origins of long-term urban debt in medieval Europe', in: *Urban public debts. Urban government and the market for annuities in Western Europe (14th–18th centuries* eds. M. Boone, K. Davids and P. Janssens (Turnhout 2003) pp. 13–27, pp. 16, 20.

70 Gino Luzzatto (1929) as cited by Tracy, 'On the dual origins', p. 21.

continued to exist besides. Lane dates the start of Venice's long-term public debt in 1262, when the government decided to consolidate all existing short-term loans at high interest rates forcibly into a long-term debt at 5 percent interest.[71] A board of *Ufficiali dei Prestiti* (Officials of the Loans) was established that was allowed to collect certain urban revenues for the service of this debt.[72] This institutionalization facilitated the emergence of a market in public debt, as debt-holders needing liquidity could now sell it by having a transfer registered in the books of the *Ufficiali* for which they paid a small transfer tax. The prices at which public debt was sold to third parties at that time appeared to vary from 60 to 102 percent of their original value between 1285 and 1344.[73] There are indications that the government sometimes redeemed some debt to support the price.[74]

In Italy, it were, according to Mueller, especially city-*republics* that chose a system of forced loans at low rates of interest, whereas Italian cities ruled by *princes* used the system of voluntary short-term loans from merchant-bankers.[75] In the Netherlands a third system existed during the late Middle Ages: that of a ruler asking (or forcing) a collectivity of cities to guarantee the interest payments on annuities to be sold to their citizens in order to finance his wars. The count of Holland and Zeeland, William IV, asked a collectivity of six cities in his territory already in 1345 to stand surety for the interest payments on an amount to be sold in life annuities.[76] Exact interest rates on these early life annuities are not known. They were anyhow certainly higher than the interest rate on redeemable annuities that were sold as well, since at least since the end of the thirteenth century, and these bore an interest of ten percent, much higher than that on Venice's early forced loans.

The sale of long-term annuities at rather high rates of interests, but less than that of short-term loans by merchants, was evidently more convenient for rulers over a territory with many cities, than forced loans at low interest rates. Such loans would certainly have made a ruler unpopular. An urban government consisting of members of the same type of rich families as were assessed in the forced loans, in contrast, could appeal to feelings of 'citizenship' to make

71 Lane, *Venice*, 150; Mueller agrees with Lane that Venice 'consolidated its debts in a single and lasting fund in 1262', Mueller, *Money and banking*, p. 457.

72 Tracy, 'On the dual origins', p. 21.

73 Mueller, *The Venetian money market*, p. 462.

74 Lane, *Venice*, p. 184.

75 Tracy, 'On the dual origins', p. 23 ; Pezzolo, 'Republics and principalities', p. 277.

76 Zuijderduijn, *Medieval Capital Markets*, p. 85.

them acceptable, or even to a direct personal economic interest of their fellow citizens, in wars to be financed with such loans.

Venice's public debt of 1262 grew by the addition of new forced loans. Contemporaries report that Venice's 'Loan Office' that organized the issue of new loans and the debt service, was valued at the time as 'the life and health of this blessed Signoria' and 'the main foundation of our existence'.[77] According to Mueller the citizens of Venice, Genoa and Florence 'were happy to contribute to the functioning of the state, on the single condition that their support took the form of interest bearing loans'.[78] An important part of the explanation for the easy acceptance of forced loans was of course that the rich assessed in them could subsequently sell their debt holdings if necessary. Forced interest reductions – the first one from 5 to 4 percent in 1423, followed in the 1430s by a reduction to 3 percent – reduced the market value of the debt to only 20 percent by 1445, however, and it never regained a level higher than 30 percent any more since then.[79]

As a remedy to this unpleasant development the rich governing elite proposed to start a '*Monte Nuovo*', a new 'debt mountain', at again 5 percent interest, in 1482, when new loans were needed for a war with the city of Ferrara. In this way a new, more valuable asset for their fellow rich citizens was created. The promise was added, that no taxes on the interest revenues or the possession of this new debt would ever be allowed. Those who had to pay more than eight ducats in a tax of a tenth of income from houses, land, loan interests, merchandise etc., that was regularly levied two times a year already since 1463, would have to lend the state an amount equal to their assessment in three of such 'tenths'. Those who paid less than 8 ducats in the income tax – and were, therefore, not assessed in the forced loan – would have to pay a permanent extra amount in income tax of one percent to secure the interest of 27,500 ducats on this loan, a procedure comparable to the way in which Johan de Witt tried to limit the increase in the tax burden due to public loans to the social group assessed in taxes on personal wealth. Venice's Great Council agreed in 1482 with 992 out of 1211 votes with the proposal.[80]

Like the *Monte Vecchio*, the 'old debt mountain', that still amounted to more than 8 million ducats at 3 percent interest at that time,[81] the *Monte Nuovo*,

77 Respectively in 1384 and 1434; Mueller, *The Venetian money market*, p. 457.

78 Mueller, *The Venetian money market*, p. 457.

79 Pezzolo, 'The Venetian government debt', p. 65 (graph).

80 Chambers and Pullan, *Venice*, p. 160.

81 Pezzolo, 'The Venetian government debt', p. 64.

of originally 550,000 ducats, increased in size during the next years as a result of new loans. A remarkable new step during these years was that the government now decided to try to obtain *voluntary* loans as well at these new conditions, and with success.[82] 'People were eager to invest in public debt, because they knew not what to do with all their money', wrote a contemporary.[83]

In the case of voluntary loans the government felt forced to sell the debt sometimes at prices below their nominal value to keep the nominal interest rate on public loans at the promised level of 5 percent, especially during war years, when people became more aloof. In December 1494, for instance, new debt had to be sold at 75 percent,[84] which implied a real rate of interest of in fact 6.7 percent. However, when war had ended, the *Monte Nuovo*-debt recovered its value, and it traded in 1505/6 even above par. Until 1509 the *Monte Nuovo* remained to be seen by Venetians as a generally very safe and attractive investment opportunity, often preferred above laborious investments in landed estates outside the city, by charitable funds as well as by merchants, because of its convenience.[85]

During the disastrous war of Venice with the League of Cambrai starting in 1509 all public revenue had to be spent on military expenditure for the sheer preservation of the Venetian Republic. No interest at all could be paid for the time being. The value of the *Monte Nuovo* sank to 40 percent and that of the *Monte Vecchio* to 25 percent, and both soon even further. So, when the war to reconquer the *Terraferma* made new forced loans necessary, the rich families in power decided again to just start a new 'mountain', the *Monte Novissimo,* to make the new debt an attractive form of property again. Apparently however the confidence of the public in the reliability of interest payments on such 'mountains' of forced loans now started to wane. The new debt sold at only 25 percent of its nominal value already in 1529. A fourth *Monte,* the *Monte del Sussidio,* which was started in the meantime already in 1526, suffered a similar fate. Pezzolo concluded that by then such successive *monti* of forced loans had become 'a worn-out and inefficient debt instrument'.[86]

82 Ibidem.
83 Chambers and Pullan, *Venice*, p. 160.
84 Pezzolo, 'The Venetian government debt', p. 66.
85 L. Pezzolo, *Il fisco dei veneziani. Finanza pubblica ed economia tra XV e XVII secolo* (Verona 2003) p. 35 Tabella I.4.
86 Pezzolo, 'The Venetian government debt', p. 67.

Voluntary Loans Based on Trust and Private Interest

In the 1520s a new series of now voluntary loans started under the name *Depositi in Zecca* (= deposits in the Mint), at an initially higher interest than the forced loans. It would become the most important and powerful tool for state financing for the next centuries.[87] The fact that the interests on this debt were paid out directly at the Mint in Venice, will have made the public confident that interest payments on this debt were now first priority for the government. After the undesirability of a continuation of '*monti*' of forced loans had become evident, the dependence on voluntary loans compelled the Venetian government to avoid interest reductions as much as possible to maintain its credit.

In 1532 a voluntary loan of 50,000 ducats at an interest of 6 percent was subscribed in only one day, indicating that by then the government's credit debt would probably already have allowed a lower interest rate. Pezzolo sees the loan format of the *Depositi in Zecca* as the start in Venice of a public debt funded that was based on trust in the government. New loan formats were tried as well. In 1538 the first life annuities in Venice were sold at an interest rate of 14 percent. Venice's fiscal policy was thus since about 1530 no longer characterized by a preference for a 'republican' policy of relying on forced loans at low rates of interest, but by dependence on – and active exploration of – the market for voluntary loans. The interest rates of 6 and 14 percent of the 1530s were already lower than in Holland under the Habsburgs in the 1540s, which were then either 8.3 percent or 6.25 percent on redeemable, and 16.7 percent on life annuities, a difference no doubt related to the greater wealth in Venice at that time. During the War of Cyprus with the Turks (1570–73) Venice continued to be able to finance the extra amounts needed by means of voluntary loans, although at slightly higher costs, resp. 7 percent, 7.5 percent and 8 percent on perpetual, but still 14 percent on life annuities.

Holland did not have much other choice than to rely on forced loans, as the main alternative for further increases in taxation, during the first decades after the start of the Revolt in 1572, as we saw in Chapter 2. Until ca. 1600 Holland was not able any longer to sell annuities guaranteed by a collective of cities, as had been customary during the wars between its Habsburg ruler and France during the 1550s. Holland's forced loans, in contrast to that of Venice had the form of 'repartitions' across its many cities according to a distributive key and the States mostly left the cities the choice to realize the required sum from its citizens by means of a forced or a voluntary loan.

At first sight one may be inclined to qualify Holland's policy of forced loans in this period as a typically 'republican' policy similar to that in Venice until

87 Pezzolo, 'The Venetian government debt', pp. 67–68.

about 1500. However, the interest rates on Holland's forced loans were much less 'republican' than in Venice. The meeting of the Provincial States allowed the cities in Holland in 1574 to promise no less than 12 percent interest on a forced loan,[88] a remarkably high percentage compared to the 5 percent interest which had always been deemed sufficient by Venice's Great Council. Higher interest rates of course implied heavier taxes, constituting a heavier burden for the less well-to-do, in order to secure the revenues for bondholders that consisted of course mainly of more wealthy people.

It shows that the historical differences between a republic like Venice, governed by one powerful wealthy city, on the one hand, and a confederation of cities historically used to the presence of a ruler that forced them to a collective responsibility for voluntary loans, on the other hand, could have important consequences for public finance.

A history of voluntary loans before the Revolt, the interest rate of which was determined by the market, made it evidently unthinkable for Holland's Provincial States to offer on forced loans much less interest than what buyers on the market would have perceived as more or less reasonable. The same approach can be perceived in Holland's urban governments. Rather than being dependent on a 'republican' approach of extracting forced loans at a low interest rate of its citizens, also the city of Delft tried in 1576 primarily a voluntary loan at an interest rate of no less than 15 percent to increase the financial support for the prince of Orange. As it was not fully subscribed, however, it saw no other way than to have recourse to forced loans since then until about 1587.[89]

In Amsterdam, that joined the revolt against Spain in 1578, urban loans on the free market, instead of forced loans became possible again since 1585 at an interest rate of 8.3 percent,[90] in other cities probably somewhat later. Holland's provincial government, however, remained forced to pay Amsterdam 12 percent interest at that time, if it wanted to borrow from this city for urgent payments during the decades before 1600.[91] Provincial credit was only restored sufficiently to allow loans at 8.3 percent in the course of the first decade of the seventeenth century. Holland's ruling elites appeared to have strongly preferred the resumption of a policy of voluntary loans to forced loans at low rates of interest as soon as possible. Only if really necessary, as would become the

88 *GFH*, p. 178.

89 *GFH*, p. 179; Tracy, *The founding of the Dutch Republic*, p. 106; Fritschy, 'A "financial revolution" reconsidered', p. 75.

90 Van de Burg and 't Hart, '*Renteniers* and the recovery of Amsterdam's credit', in *Urban public debts*, pp. 197–219, p. 204.

91 Fritschy, 'A "financial revolution" reconsidered, p. 76.

case in the 1670s, when its credit had sunk dramatically in the 'Year of Disaster', the States of Holland had recourse to forced loans again, and these took again the form of repartitions across the cities, to be organized by the city governments themselves.

It was probably of course just easier for a large political body of only one city like Venice to convince its citizens of the desirability of forced loans at low rates of interest for public expenditure in the interest of the city, than for a small number of representatives of many cities to convince the citizens of their own city of the desirability of compulsory measures for a collective interest. Since the 1520s, however, the Venetians had felt forced to accept a rate of interest determined by market conditions, as well, as we saw. By then private interest seems to have become a stronger social force than a 'citizenship-mentality', also in Venice. What did this mean for the participation in public loans outside the city of Venice?

Information as to the degree in which inhabitants of *Terraferma* participated in Venice's voluntary loans is missing. When the interest rate in the 1620s had to rise to 6 percent in order to persuade investors, 7 percent was offered in outer areas of the Venetian Republic.[92] The government expected, apparently, that capital was available, but that it would have to offer a higher interest to persuade investors outside the centre to invest as well. A reason may have been that they would have to travel to the city to get their interest paid or to sell their bonds. In 1645 only seven percent of the capital of forced loans realized was owned by inhabitants of the *Terraferma*, despite the fact that this was the century of the economic decline of the city and of economic development in the *Terraferma*, and despite the fact that more than ninety percent of the population of the Venetian Republic lived outside the city of Venice. It is more probable therefore that this low percentage is indicative of a failing ability of a centralized urban republic to tap the capital market outside its centre.

For Holland we know exactly how the investment in government debt was spread over all its cities for the years 1651 and the 1667. In 1667 27 percent appeared to be owned by people in the government centre The Hague, 11 percent in Amsterdam, the remaining 62 percent was spread over 15 other cities in proportions varying from 6 percent to 1 percent.[93] For the federal Dutch Republic as a whole we know for the 1790s that the largest part of the total public debt (74 percent), was Holland's debt (at an effective interest rate of only 2.5 percent since about 1720 until the war of 1780–84). This implies that about 26 percent consisted in the public debts of the other provinces (at interest rates of mostly

92 Pezzolo, 'The Venetian government debt', p. 69.

93 *GFH*, p. 44.

about 3 percent since the 1730s until 1780), a much higher percentage than the seven percent in the Venetian Republic in 1645. In the decentralized Dutch Republic even the very small and poor province of Drenthe had its own public debt. We do not have enough quantitative information for reliable conclusions, but what we know indicates nonetheless that its decentralized structure seems to have given the Dutch Republic a better access to potential investors in public debt than the centralized Venetian Republic.

Debt Sizes, Interest Burdens and Interest Rates

Figure 4.6 offers a long-term overview of the available data on total amounts of public debt in tons silver in the Venetian and the Dutch Republic. It shows how much larger the public debt became in the Dutch Republic in the course of time than in the Venetian Republic, as could be expected, of course, because of its much higher war expenditure. It also shows that Venice started already in the sixteenth century with a policy of debt redemption.

Figure 4.7 shows what is known on the development of debt service in Venice compared to the Dutch Republic, or in fact to Holland, and that it was evidently the fact that debt service required about forty percent of public revenue in 1554 that led to the start of the policy of debt redemption visible in Figure 4.6. It was interrupted during the War of Cyprus with the Turks (1570–73), but resumed again afterwards. It now started with the most expensive part of the debt, the 14 percent-life-annuities by just appointing the ones to be redeemed each year by lot. This policy was no doubt not very appreciated by the holders of these annuities. It was – as far as I know – never practiced in the

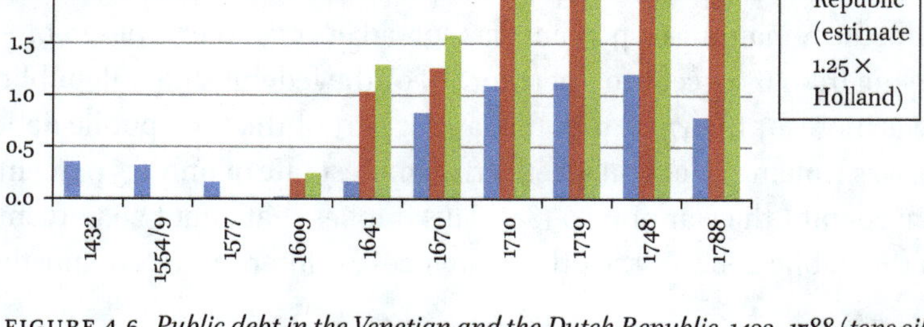

FIGURE 4.6 *Public debt in the Venetian and the Dutch Republic, 1432–1788 (tons silver).* Sources: Pezzolo, 'The Venetian government debt', 66; idem, *Una finanza*, 88, 101, 107; Dormans, *Het tekort*, 65, 80, 110–111.

Dutch Republic, where debt redemption remained always restricted to that of redeemable annuities.

The amounts in interest payments saved in Venice as a result of the redemption were added to the amount for redemption in the next year. The same would be done in the following years until the whole debt would be redeemed: an early example of a so-called 'sinking fund'.[94] An additional measure was the sale of publicly owned estates to reduce the debt. In these ways the Venetian public debt of more than 6 million ducats after the War of Cyprus was completely redeemed already in 1584, a situation that would never be achieved by Holland in the whole course of its existence.[95] In the Dutch Republic only the province of Friesland was temporarily able to redeem its complete debt by means of the sale of expropriated monastery estates in 1644.

When between 1653 and 1663 a 'sinking fund policy' was pursued in Holland by Johan de Witt, it was self-evident for him that this could only be done with redeemable annuities not with life-annuities. Due to the much larger size of Holland's debt in 1653 his redemption policy led to a reduction in the debt with only about ten percent after eleven years. The two debt redemption periods in Holland in the eighteenth century reduced the debt with 16 percent in 26 years and with 15 percent in 25 years. In Venice the sinking fund resulted in a sudden surplus of 550,000 ducats per year as of 1584, which was used during

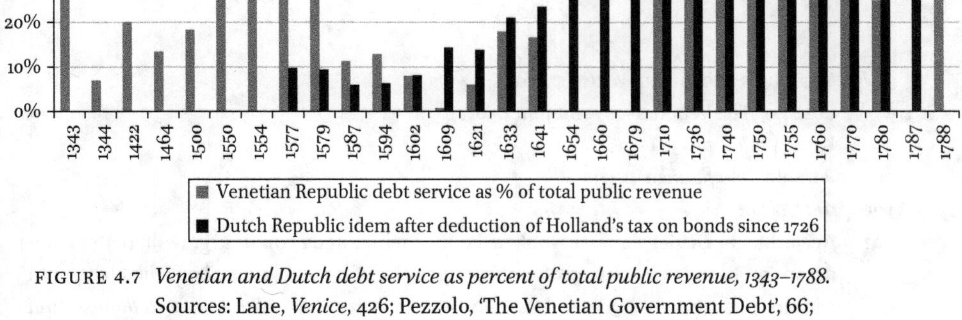

FIGURE 4.7 *Venetian and Dutch debt service as percent of total public revenue, 1343–1788.* Sources: Lane, *Venice*, 426; Pezzolo, 'The Venetian Government Debt', 66; idem, *Una finanza*, 77.

94 Lane, *Venice*, p. 326.

95 Pezzolo, 'The Venetian government debt', p. 72.

the following years for a reserve chest for war, as was mentioned already.[96] In the Dutch Republic debt redemption simply had to stop when the money was needed for new wars.

The implication of debt reduction was, that the more well-to-do were deprived of an attractive easy investment opportunity and had to find other outlets for their capital. Pezzolo mentions that the government of Genoa met so much opposition within the patriciate, when it attempted at the end of the sixteenth century a similar debt redemption policy as in Venice, that it did not succeed in its aims. He concluded that in Venice, contrary to Genoa, public interest still prevailed over private interest.[97] Doubts must have risen in Venice, too, however, as to the desirability of its extreme debt redemption policy. The fact that charitable foundations now lacked suitable securities in which to invest their funds, led to the decision to allow them 'deposits in the Mint' at an interest of 4 per cent, although no new loans were needed for the government.[98] These new investments in public debt in Venice led to a modest debt of about 0.9 million ducats in 1616.

The war of 1615–7 did not result in renewed alarming indebtedness thanks to the war chest. In 1619 the Senate felt forced to yield to pressure to give investors the opportunity to invest in 10 percent life annuities and 5 percent redeemable annuities,[99] although the government did not need the money. These interest rates were low in comparison to Holland, which had yet to pay 11.1 percent on life annuities and 6.25 percent on redeemable annuities at that time.[100] In later years, complaints by the rich about decreasing investment opportunities in safe government debt in periods of debt redemption are documented for Holland as well,[101] but there are hardly any indications that this led to the issue of debt paper without necessity, at least not for Holland.[102]

---

96 Chambers and Pullan, *Venice,* p. 162.

97 Pezzolo, 'The Venetian government debt', p. 72.

98 Lane, *Venice,* pp. 324–326.

99 Pezzolo, *Una finanza,* p. 93.

100 *GFH*, p. 382.

101 According to Gelderblom and Jonker, 'Public finance and economic growth', p. 16 the redemption in the 1650s was 'profoundly unpopular'; for complaints about the eighteenth century debt redemption see M. Prak, *Gezeten burgers. De elite in een Hollandse stad 1700–1780* (Amsterdam 1985).

102 In Overijssel a pamphlet was published in the 1667 accusing the government of issuing high amounts in 10 percent life-annuities in 1665–7 (apart from 4 percent redeemable annuities) without necessity (Fritschy, 'Domeinen en financieel beleid, pp. 87–88), in Utrecht the percentage of government debt issued in life annuities seemed irresponsibly high between 1702 and 1713.

Venice started since 1625 with the sale of life annuities at interest rates that varied according to the age of the person on whose life it was bought, a remarkably sophisticated approach.[103] A similar example for the Dutch Republic is known for the province of Groningen, that was able in 1672 to sell for 0.6 million guilders in life-annuities in Amsterdam, that paid an interest of 10 percent on lives of 1–20 years old, increasing to 33.33 percent on lives of >75 years old, which were eagerly bought.[104] In Holland Johan de Witt's famous study of 1671 into the value of life-annuities resulted in a reduction of their interest rate from 8.3 percent to 7.1 percent, although according to De Witt, even 6 per cent would have been enough in comparison with the interest on redeemable annuities, in view of the fact that life-annuities were mostly bought on the lives of young children.[105] In Venice the interest on life annuities seems never to have declined below 10 percent, which made them rather expensive, therefore, for the government in comparison to the Dutch Republic by then.[106]

In 1670 about 18 percent of Venice's debt consisted in the capital of life annuities, 90 percent of which still paid an interest of 14 percent,[107] in Holland in 1670 only 8 percent of the debt consisted of the capital in life annuities and at much lower rates of interest, probably varying from 11 percent to 7 percent. In view of the earlier readiness of Venice to yield to social-political pressure to make life-annuities available it is likely that this difference in interest rates was not the result of a difference in market conditions, but of the wish of the Venetian governing elites to keep this interest rate high.

When extra money was needed for the War of Candia (1645–1667), the Venetian government decided again to *forced* loans at an interest rate of 5 percent. Even guilds, charitable institutions and subject cities, were forced to lend the government money.[108] New kinds of voluntary loans were issued as well, however. Since 1648 it was successfully tried to attract money by means of lottery loans, which offered, apart from interest, a chance on prizes, an initiative, which was, after some initial hesitance, very much welcomed by investors.[109] This rather expensive type of loans was introduced in Holland only in 1711, under pressure of British competition on the international capital market (see Chapter 3).

103 Pezzolo, *Una finanza*, pp. 94–95.

104 *GFG*, p. 285.

105 Dormans, *Het tekort*, p. 59.

106 Pezzolo, *Una finanza*, p. 100.

107 Pezzolo, *Una finanza*, p. 101.

108 Pezzolo, 'The Venetian government debt', p. 69.

109 Pezzolo, *Una finanza*, pp. 99, 100.

Because of the increased interest burden it was thought desirable in Venice in 1672 to forcibly reduce all *depositi in Zecca* of 5 percent to an interest rate of only 3 percent, as had often been done with public debt in the course of its history. The important difference of this Venetian interest reduction with the four interest reductions in Holland of 1609, 1640 and 1655, from 8.3 percent to 6.25 percent to 5 percent to 4 percent was, of course, that by that time the conversions in Holland were voluntary. They were based on the expectation that debt holders were aware of the fact that the market rate of interest had declined and that debt paper would keep its value despite the interest reduction. The debt of holders in Holland who did not want to accept the lower interest was redeemed, but most holders indeed preferred to keep their bonds at the reduced interest.

In the course of time, however, Holland increasingly used, if necessary, the instrument of a temporary tax on the nominal value of bonds instead of a voluntary interest conversion, by just paying less than the promised interest, as we saw in Part 1. In 1673, when this tax reduced the interest actually paid on Holland's 4 percent bonds to in the end only 1 percent, the price of these bonds dropped to 70 percent in the city of Gouda,[110] which implied a yield of 2.86 percent for the holder who had paid this price, which will have reflected the prevailing market rate of interest. It may at least partly also have reflected, however, the expectation that the tax would be temporary. The decline in the price of government debt paper in Venice after the forced interest reduction to 3 percent, resulted in a yield for new buyers of about 4.2 percent in 1688/9, which will have reflected the real market rate of interest. The temporary character of the interest reductions in Holland by means of taxes on the value of bonds may have mitigated the declining effect on bond prices and the advantages for new buyers of old debt.

Venetian government debt remained an appreciated type of property as well, however. Pezzolo emphasizes that trade in debt paper in Venice was quite lively. He found that nearly 30 percent of the *depositi in Zecca* negotiated between 1645 and 1671 changed owner.[111] He also found that by 1673 about 30 percent of the 3 percent-*depositi* were owned by Genovesi, an indication that they remained to be seen as sufficiently attractive and reliable, despite forced interest reductions.[112] In 1710 the Venetian debt had risen again to an unprecedented nearly 68 million ducats, the service of which required again more

110 Data were found only for the city of Gouda; Gelderblom and Jonker, 'Public finance and Economic Growth', p. 15 (fig 5).

111 Pezzolo, *Una finanza*, p. 102 (Table 17).

112 Pezzolo, *Una finanza*, p. 103.

than 40 percent of public revenue (see Figure 4.6). The government decided in 1714/5 again to reduce the interest rate on all redeemable annuities to now only 2 percent and on all life-annuities to 6 percent.[113] When between 1716 and 1720 new loans were offered at 4 percent, these were no longer administered by the Mint like the *depositi in Zecca*, but by the tax offices for the taxes on oil and milling of grain. After 1739 interests were forcibly reduced again.

Forced interest reductions had been resorted to in the whole Dutch Republic as well, after 1713, as we saw, but a difference with Venice remained that forced measures to reduce the interest burden were resorted to more frequently and more easily. The most likely explanation remains that it was easier for just one city to appeal to a citizenship susceptible for urban public interest in its representative institutions than for a provincial government consisting of a collectivity of cities.

Figures 4.8a–b offer overviews of the developments in the resulting interest rates in both republics. Figure 4.8a shows a comparison of nominal interest rates on the Venetian voluntary *depositi in Zecca* and on Holland's 'obligations'. Figure 4.8b offers for the period after 1700 for the Venetian debt not only nominal interest rates, but also some actual yields for buyers in years for which data were available. Because Venice sold debt, if necessary, at prices below *par*, to keep the interest rate fixed, these yields were often higher than the nominal interest rate. For Holland the rates in Figure 4.8b are those actually paid by the government, after the tax on bonds had been deducted. Only for a short period yields for new buyers, resulting from market-prices deviating from par, as found by Gelderblom and Jonker, could be added for the Dutch Republic as well.

One may conclude that while Holland experienced a rather steady decline in interest rates after the high levels in the first decades after the Revolt in 1572, 'real' interest rates in Venice seem to have been always more volatile. Despite a nominal interest rate in Venice of only 2 percent between 1715 and 1740, lower than the real interest rate in Holland of 2.5 percent, loan financing was in the period after 1700 overall more expensive for the Venetian government than for Holland, due to the sale of debt at prices below par, until the 1770s. Then a policy of debt redemption became possible again, which diminished the interest rates to not much more than 2 percent, as public debt remained an appreciated investment opportunity and no new loans were needed. In the Dutch Republic interest rates would start to rise since the 1780s, until no loan was possible any more in 1794 even at 5 percent, because by then adherents to the 'Patriot' movement refused to support the government with loans, while

113 Pezzolo, *Una finanza*, p. 106.

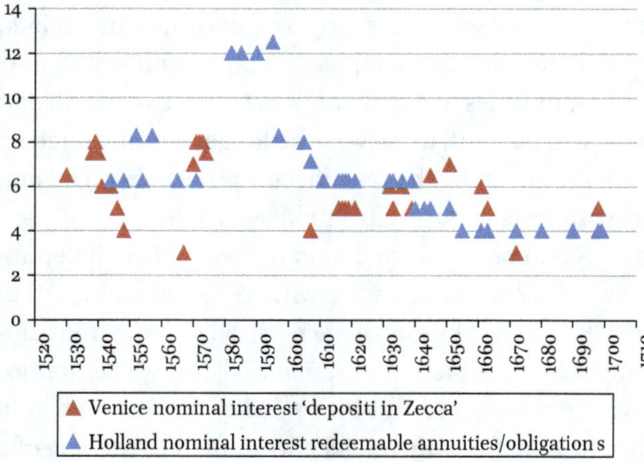

FIGURE 4.8A *Nominal interest rates in Venice and Holland, 1520–1710.*

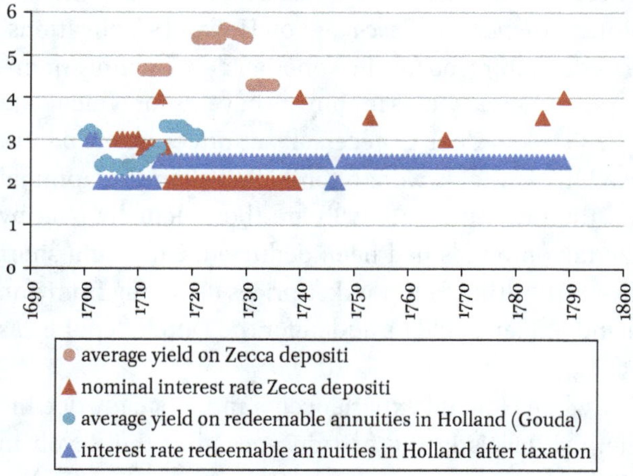

FIGURE 4.8B *Yields on bonds in Venice and Holland compared to nominal interest rates in Venice and interest rates after taxation in Holland, 1690–1790.* Sources: (a) Pezzolo *Una finanza*, 90–91; GFH, 381–382; (b) Pezzolo, *Una finanza*, 105; *GFH*, 372–373, 381–382; Gelderblom and Jonker, 'Public finance and economic growth', 23.

others may have lost trust not only in the government, but also in the survival of the Dutch Republic.[114]

In general, however, the real interest rate to be paid by the government in the centralized urban Venetian Republic on voluntary loans was higher than that in Holland, where fiscal policy had to be determined by a collectivity of

114 Van der Meulen, *Ministerie van der Spiegel*, pp. 351–380.

cities. It shows the importance of the character of an 'urban system' for public finance.

Public Banks and Public Loans in Both Republics

The Venetian government had used in the sixteenth century the private Pisani bank for short-term loans, a large bank used by merchants having an account for mutual payments by means of transfers in the books. The cash deposited by the merchants for their account was used by the bank for short-term loans to the government and to other merchants, as had always been done by private banks. It had resulted in bank failures more than once, when such loans appeared to have been less safe than was thought. In contrast to other European cities, which had established public banks to prevent such harmful failures controlled by the urban government already in the early fifteenth century (Genoa, Barcelona, Frankfurt), Venice had not given in to pressure to do the same before the dramatic failure of the large Pisani-bank in 1584. In 1587 the government created the *Banco della Piazza di Rialto*, a public bank with a monopoly for three years for payments by means of transfers in bank accounts, which was not allowed to give loans at all; its cover ratio had to be maintained at 100 percent. This was the bank that became the model for the famous Exchange Bank in Amsterdam established in 1609.

The Venetian Rialto-bank was gradually replaced since 1619, however, by a new public bank, the *Banco del Giro*. The government paid the merchant Giovanni Vendramin for a huge amount of silver with government debt in the form of a large credit on the books of a new bank. The debt would be gradually repaid with coined silver, and Vendramin was allowed to pay his creditors by transferring parts of this credit to accounts in their name, which they could use in their turn to pay each other. In contrast to the Rialto-bank this government controlled bank was allowed to issue loans, to the government as well as to private persons. Merchants soon came to prefer this bank to the Rialto bank, which closed in 1637, whereas the Banco del Giro remained in existence until 1811. One element in which this bank remained similar to the Amsterdam Exchange Bank was that large bills of exchange would be only recognized in law courts, if drawn on accounts in this bank, which forced all important merchants in Venice to open an account in this bank. It was very different from the Amsterdam Exchange Bank, however, because this *Banco del Giro* continued to provide the Venetian government with loan facilities.

In principle the cash/deposits ration of the Amsterdam Exchange Bank had to remain 100 percent, although in practice it provided sometimes loans to Amsterdam's Lombard (*Stadsbank van Leening*), that were backed by goods pledged to it by small debtors, when this Lombard had a temporary shortage of liquid means. Moreover the Exchange Bank used to provide credit to the VOC to equip outbound ships, which were repaid out of the profits when the VOC-fleet had returned. In this way the cash/deposits ration of the Exchange Bank declined in practice from on average more than 90 percent in the seventeenth century to less than 80 percent in the middle of the eighteenth century, and its downfall would be mainly due to the VOC's loss of ships during the Fourth English Naval War, which made its cash/deposits ratio decline to 36 percent in the 1790s.[115]

Although the amount of VOC-debt that had replaced cash reserves in the vaults of the bank was not known, merchants in Amsterdam very well guessed what was going on. The number of accountholders sharply dropped in this period, never to recover again, although the bank was able to continue its existence as a much smaller bank until 1820.[116] However, neither Holland's provincial government, nor the States General, had ever been allowed or been able to deposit public debt in the bank in exchange for cash. A central bank, lending to the government like the Venetian *Banco del Giro,* never existed in the Dutch Republic. Here it was the decentralized network of provincial tax receivers in Holland that functioned as brokers for government loans in an, until 1794, apparently satisfactory way.

4.5 Conclusion

The Venetian Republic was the result of aggressive wars of just one city expanding its power over sea and over the cities in its hinterland. This in contrast to the Dutch Republic, which was the result of a defensive war against a powerful empire, of a federation in which many cities had political influence. The level of public expenditure in the Dutch Republic started to surpass that of the Venetian Republic, already very soon after the start of the Dutch Revolt. Unlike the Dutch Republic the Venetian Republic was hardly involved in the expensive wars between the Great European Powers during the seventeenth and eighteenth century. Its main war faring was with the Ottoman Empire. Much more than the Dutch Republic the Venetian Republic remained for many centuries primarily a 'maritime republic'.

115 P. Dehing and M. 't Hart, 'Linking the fortunes: currency and banking, 1550–1800', *A financial history of the Netherlands,* eds. M. 't Hart, J. Jonker and J.L. van Zanden (Cambridge 1997) pp. 37–64, p. 46, p. 49, p. 47.

116 Dehing and 't Hart, 'Linking the fortunes', pp. 46–47, figs. 3.2 and 3.3.

From an earlier date and to a larger degree than the Dutch Republic the Venetian Republic started to try to 'survive on the cheap' and to avoid expensive war faring as much as possible. In comparison with the Venetian Republic it was remarkable how much was still spent on the army in the Dutch Republic after 1713. The federal character of the Dutch Republic has often been blamed for its incapacity to realize more public revenue for military expenditure in order to prevent its downfall at the end of the eighteenth century. The comparison with the Venetian Republic suggested that its federal character may rather have been a brake on realizing really drastic cuts in military expenditure in the preceding peace years.

Venice's much lower level of public expenditure resulted in much lower amounts in total public revenue than in the Dutch Republic, already since about 1590. The result was that Venice could continue to depend to a much larger extent than the Dutch Republic on indirect taxation, the easiest – although of course not unlimited – source of public revenue for commercial states. A remarkable difference was moreover that the revenues from indirect taxation were to a much larger degree than in the Dutch Republic the result of customs paid by foreign merchants. The Venetians had apparently less to fear from retaliation by trade partners. The decline of its trade in the course of time was due to the increasing importance of Atlantic trade and the declining importance of the Mediterranean trade in general, rather than to the level of its custom duties.

Between the middle of the seventeenth and the middle of the eighteenth century, during which period yet three of its seven wars with the Ottomans had to be fought, the Venetian Republic proved not to be able to raise tax revenue sufficiently to prevent large deficits. As the difference in the tax burden per capita between the two republics was much larger than the difference in wage levels, it is unlikely that the wealth difference between the Dutch and the Venetian Republic of that period was large enough to explain the difference in fiscal performance.

It is in fact more likely that it was due to the difference in the character of their 'urban systems'. The Venetian Republic appeared to have been relatively less able to extract tax revenues from the territory outside its centre than the Dutch Republic. The difference in tax burden between centre and surrounding territory was much larger in the Venetian than in the Dutch Republic. This was still the case in the eighteenth century, when the economic development in its *Terraferma* improved. Although the provinces outside Holland often did not pay in war expenditure what they had to according to the quota-system, the federal Dutch Republic was not *less*, but evidently *more* able to generate tax revenues in cities and provinces outside its centre than the centralized Venetian Republic.

The same turned out to be true for public loans. They had been common in the Venetian Republic already since the thirteenth century. A remarkable difference with the Dutch Republic was that forced loans and forced interest reductions played a much larger role in the history of the Venetian than in that of the Dutch public debt. A likely explanation is that it was easier to convince the council of one city of the desirability of compulsion, than the representatives of a larger number of cities. The compulsory lowering of interest rates led to a declining value of Venice's public debt, however, which stimulated a change from a 'republican' loan policy based on 'citizenship' to voluntary loans based on private interest in the sixteenth century. When necessary the Venetian Republic did not hesitate, however, to return to a policy of forced interest conversion, a policy used in the Dutch Republic only in the wake of the extremely expensive War of the Spanish Succession (1701–1713) and then only for the Generality debt and some provincial loans outside Holland.

Another remarkable feature of the Venetian public debt in the course of this century was its complete redemption in 1584. This would led to a pressure, in the seventeenth century, to give charity institutions the possibility to buy *Depositi in Zecca,* and to give citizens opportunities to invest in life annuities, even although the Venetian government did not need the loans for its public expenditure until about 1650. When the Venetian Republic needed loans again for the three last Ottoman-Venetian Wars, its centralized government, completely controlled by one city, was able to keep the nominal interest rate artificially low by selling debt beneath par if necessary. Holland's collectivity of cities, in contrast, kept Holland's nominal interest rate artificially high, by preferring a temporary tax on bonds, at variable rates, to forced permanent interest reductions. The fact that the much higher and nearly continuously increasing public debt in the Dutch Republic was much more the result of voluntary loans than in the centralized Venetian Republic controlled by one city did not prevent the Dutch market rate of interest to be mostly lower than the Venetian interest rate for public loans.

The fact that the public debt of the provinces outside Holland was about a quarter of the sum of the provincial public debts in the Republic, while only about seven percent of the Venetian public debt had been invested from outside the city of Venice, is another indication that a rather integrated urban system within a federal republic was fiscally more efficient than a centralized republic, where all political power was concentrated in only one of its cities.

CHAPTER 5

A Comparison with Britain

Comparisons between Britain[1] and the Netherlands have a rather long and widespread historiography.[2] A stubborn tradition even assumes that the British fiscal system was heavily influenced by the Dutch example, since the Glorious Revolution of 1688 which brought the Dutch stadholder William III to the British throne.[3] An important institutional similarity since 1688 was no doubt the complete control of Parliament over fiscal policy, comparable to – concededly not that of the States General – but certainly to that of the Provincial States-assemblies in the Dutch Republic. This chapter will mainly highlight some remarkable fiscal differences between the two, however, resulting from long-term historical differences.

Britain's geographical position as an island led to remarkable differences in the development and structure of public expenditure. Differences in the size of total population would become increasingly important in the course of time for the size of public revenue. Long-term historical differences in the urbanization process of the two states led to differences in their public revenue systems, especially as to excise revenues and the public debt.

The main institutional difference between the two states before 1688 is, of course, that Britain, apart from the years 1649 to 1660 under the dictatorship

---

1 The term 'Britain' will be used when only 'England and Wales' are meant; when 'England, Wales and Scotland' are meant 'Great Britain' will be used.

2 Between 1964 and 2003 fourteen Anglo Dutch historical conferences resulted in the series *Britain and the Netherlands*; examples of more recent studies are D. Ormrod, *The Rise of Commercial Empires: Britain and the Netherlands in the Age of Mercantilism, 1650–1770* (Cambridge 2003) on the period 1477–1559: S. Gunn, D. Grummit and H. Cools, *War, state and society in Britain and the Netherlands* (Oxford 2007); De Vries and van der Woude, *The first modern economy*, pp. 631, 707.

3 Recently summarized in L. Jardine, *Going Dutch. How Britain plundered Holland's glory* (New York 2008); specifically on fiscal policy: J. Scott, '"Good Night Amsterdam". Sir George Downing and Anglo-Dutch State Building', *English Historical Review* 118 (2003) pp. 334–356; Brewer, *The sinews of power*, pp. 24, 133; Dickson, *The financial revolution in Britain*, p. 17; the idea is criticized in M. 't Hart, ''The devil or the Dutch': Holland's Impact on the Financial Revolution in Britain, 1643–1694', *Parliaments, Estates and Representations* 11 (1991)1, pp. 39–52; M.J. Braddick, *The nerves of state : taxation and the financing of the English state, 1558–1714* (Manchester: Manchester University Press, 1996); Braddick, *State formation in early modern Britain*; P.K. O'Brien, 'The nature and historical evolution of an exceptional fiscal state etc.', *Economic History Review*, 64,2 (2011) pp. 408–446.

 | DOI 10.1163/9789004341289_009

of Oliver Cromwell was not a republic but a monarchy. It used to be seen in older historiography as one of Europe's 'new monarchies', comparable to Portugal, France and Spain rather than to the Dutch Republic.[4] An institutional difference between the two remained the centralized character of British public finance since 1688, which is supposed to have been an advantage in comparison to the Dutch Republic in order to realize increases in public revenue. It is in particular the comparison with Britain that leaves no doubt at all that it was not due to the weakness of its decentralized federal fiscal system, that the Dutch Republic could not raise sufficient public revenue to defeat this state in the Fourth English Naval War.

The first section of this chapter reviews the general comparability of the two states. The second section describes the coming into existence of Britain's national fiscal system in a long-term historical perspective. The third section compares the public expenditure of the two states in the course of time, the fourth section does the same for public revenue, and the last section discusses the developments in the public debt of both states. In the second and third section special attention will be paid to the importance of differences in the 'urbanization trajectory' in the two states for an understanding of differences in the development of public finance.

5.1 The Comparability of Britain and the Netherlands

At the end of the eighteenth century Great Britain succeeded the Dutch Republic as the leading nation in world trade and finance and as the industrially most advanced economy of the early modern period in Europe.[5] Both became since the early seventeenth century colonial empires with monopolistic access to highly valued Asian products on behalf of chartered companies. The large East India companies of both states had far reaching state-like military powers in colonial territory unequalled by other European states. No wonder, that both states are often characterized, like the Venetian Republic, as 'maritime states'.

An important difference between the two states was, of course, that Britain's total population was much larger than that of the Dutch Republic. It grew from 4.4 million to 5.4 million to 9.2 million people in respectively 1600, 1700 and

4 *The New Monarchies and representative assemblies*, ed. A. Slavin (Boston: Houghton Mifflin, 1964).

5 R. Allen, *The British Industrial Revolution in global perspective* (Cambridge: Cambridge University Press, 2009) p. 20.

1800 in Britain (England and Wales).[6] The Dutch Republic had a population of about only 1.5 million, 2 million and 2.1 million in 1600, 1700 and 1795 and the province of Holland even only 0.6, 0.9 and 0.8 million in the same years.[7]

Another difference was its urbanization trajectory. Apart from London, Britain's urbanization had been rather late, also in comparison with other territories in Europe. For a long time it consisted mainly in the very early development of its huge metropolis. Roman London had been practically abandoned by the end of the fifth century, but the city became a trading settlement incorporated into an East Saxon kingdom in the early seventh century. In 1100, at a time when the territory where Amsterdam would arise was yet hardly inhabited, its population was already about 15,000. It grew from about 200,000 in 1600 to about 900,000 in 1800, against 65,000 and 217,000 for Amsterdam in those years.

Around 1600 Britain had, apart from London, not more than five cities with more than 10,000 inhabitants, the Dutch Republic apart from Amsterdam eighteen. In 1700 there were still only ten such cities in Britain with an average population of less than 15,000, while in the small Dutch Republic the average population of nineteen such cities was then about 24,000. No dense network of middle sized cities comparable to that in the territories of the Venetian and the Dutch Republic had yet developed.[8]

At the end of the eighteenth century, however, the territories of both states were more urbanized than any other territory in Europe. At that time about 20 percent of the population of England and Wales lived in cities of more than

---

6 In Great Britain (incl. Scotland) it grew from 6.7 million to 10.8 million between 1707 and 1800. Sources: E. Wrigley and R. Schofield, *The population history of Britain, 1541–1871 : a reconstruction* (Cambridge 1981) pp. 528–529, 566; J. Thirsk, *The agrarian history of Britain and Wales* (Cambridge: Cambridge University Press, 1967; 2011) p. 143; M. Flinn, *Scottish population history from the 17th century to the 1930s* (Cambridge: Cambridge University Press, 1973) pp. 198–199; B. Mitchell and Ph. Deane, *Abstract of British historical statistics* (Cambridge: Cambridge University Press, 1971) p. 5; Vries, *European Urbanization*, 36,39; P. Malanima, *Premodern European Economy* (Leiden: Brill, 2009) p. 9. In what follows the (lower) data of P.K. O'Brien and Ph. Hunt, 'The Rise of a fiscal state in Britain, 1485–1815', *Historical Research. The Bulletin of the Institute of Historical Research* 66 (1993) pp. 129–176, p. 176 were often preferred, because they are more recent and because in per capita comparisons with the Dutch Republic the emphasis is on the high Dutch level.

7 De Vries and Van der Woude, *The first modern economy*, p. 50.

8 Only around 1750 the number of cities in Britain outside London started to become comparable to that of the Dutch Republic. By then 20 cities had about 10,000 or more inhabitants, but the average was still only about 17,000, and the cities were spread out over a much larger territory than in the Dutch Republic; De Vries, *European Urbanization*, pp. 270–271.

10,000 inhabitants, less than the 29 percent in the Dutch Republic, but much more than the on average 10 percent in Europe as a whole at the time.[9]

For a long time Britain's territory remained an agrarian based economy, much more so than that of the Netherlands. It shared with Holland a substantial rise in productivity per head in the agricultural sector in the early modern period, in contrast to Holland no grain imports were needed, however. Apart from grain production, England had a remarkable comparative advantage in raising sheep. Its wool exports fed the development of medieval textile industries in Italy and the Netherlands in the thirteenth century, but already since the end of the fourteenth century an indigenous textile production developed in Britain, which was increasingly exported as well.[10] The relatively very large importance of the service sector in the Dutch economy was an important factor in its wealth. Britain's role in international shipping services was smaller than that of the Dutch Republic until the end of the seventeenth century, but by the end of the eighteenth century the ratio had become two to one.

Dutch national income per head has been said to be about 30 percent to 40 percent higher than that in Britain at the end of the seventeenth century.[11] According to more recent estimates, a difference of 40 percent was valid for the about 45 percent of the population living in the rich province of Holland.[12] On average the Dutch Republic was richer as to average wealth per capita, probably until about the last quarter of the eighteenth century. In Holland GDP per capita was even in 1800 still about 20 percent higher than in Britain according to these estimates. Real wages of craftsmen in Southern Britain were less than half that in the Western Netherlands around 1600 and still around 1700, but in the course of the eighteenth century they became on average nearly similar to the Western Netherlands at the end of this century.[13]

Economic similarities between the two states appear to have obscured sometimes the importance of apparent differences: total population and the very limited British involvement in European war faring before the end of the seventeenth century. In an in many ways excellent comparison of the two 'commercial empires' the 'striking speed' of the 'enormous tax increases'

---

9 De Vries, *European Urbanization,*, p. 71.

10 Allen, *The British Industrial Revolution*, p. 19.

11 De Vries and Van der Woude, *The first modern economy*, p. 710.

12 J. Bolt and J.L. van Zanden (2013). The First Update of the Maddison Project; Re-Estimating Growth Before 1820. Maddison Project Working Paper 4; http://www.ggdc.net/maddison/maddison-project/home.htm; GDP p.c. in international dollars of 1990 in Holland of $2.105 and in Britain of $1.513 in 1700, and resp. $2.609 and $2.097 in 1800 (see also Figure 3.1 above).

13 De Vries and van der Woude, *The first modern economy*, p. 631 fig. 12.6.

in Britain between the 1670s and 1720 is attributed, for instance, to the taxation policies of a central state able to promote commercial growth by means of a centralized national fiscal policy, and the author emphasizes the contrast with the inability of the Dutch to realize similar increases in tax revenues since the end of the seventeenth century, which he blamed to 'the disadvantages of weak federal government'.[14]

The high speed and the huge size of the tax increases in Britain at the end of the seventeenth century were mainly a function, however, of its – in a European perspective – very low level of total public revenue in the preceding centuries, due to the lack of involvement in European land wars until then. The total level of British public revenue resulting from its 'enormous tax increases' was in fact still rather low in comparison to what was realized inside the 'weak' federal Republic, if the difference in total population between the two is taken into account. The failing awareness of the importance of such obvious facts in a comparison of the public finance of both states is an indication for the relevance of a longer-term time perspective for an adequate 'comparative history of fiscal arrangements'.[15] The next section will pay some attention to such a long-term perspective, therefore, preceding the quantitative comparison of Dutch and British public finance in the early modern period.

5.2 National Public Finance: A Long-Term Perspective

Like in the case of Venice, state formation started much earlier in British territory than in that of the later Dutch Republic. After the disintegration of the Roman Empire, indigenous Anglo Saxon kingdoms in Britain unified their forces since the ninth century to withstand Viking invasions. General public taxation was introduced under the name of '*danegeld*', to this end, and this national direct tax remained in force after Britain's conquest by William the Conqueror, a Viking who had become duke of Normandy in 1035, and who was crowned as the new English king in 1066. Hence the claim that Britain had 'the first system of national taxation to appear in Western Europe',[16] whereas a Dutch 'system of national taxation' had to await the year 1806, after the territory of the Dutch Republic had become a unitary kingdom under a brother of Napoleon as its

14 Ormrod, *The Rise of Commercial Empires*, pp. 21–23.

15 Ormrod, *The Rise of Commercial Empires*, p. 22 uses this term.

16 W.M. Ormrod and J. Barta, 'The feudal structure and the beginnings of state finance' in R. Bonney (ed.) *Economic systems and state finance* (Oxford: Oxford University Press, 1995), pp. 53–81, pp. 57–58.

first king. The only 'national' direct tax during the Dutch Republic was the so-called 'Liberal Gift' of 1747 levied to enable the newly appointed stadholder William IV of Orange 'to save the country' from the threat of French expansionary ambitions.[17]

England's conquest by William of Normandy in 1066 made it into a kingdom with large fiefs overseas in France. In this way it became temporarily part of a fragmentized feudal Europe. From the very start, however, the political importance of counties and cities in Britain was much less than that of provinces and cities on the Continent. A centralized system of royal administration developed very soon. Already at the end of the twelfth century England can be described as 'a united and coherently administered polity'.[18] Contrary to continental European states like France and Spain, and later the Low Countries, regionalism and particularism were weak in Britain. No representative institutions on county level came into existence, apart from the king's central advisory council of nobles.

The British king would become much more dependent on taxation than before due to his loss of Normandy to the French king in 1203, as this implied a sensitive loss of royal demesne revenue. This made the British nobles relatively more powerful. In 1215 they were able to force their king to sign a *Magna Charta Libertatum* establishing that he would need the consent of his royal council for important decisions. The charter was confirmed in 1225 as part of a negotiation about the national imposition of a fifteenth penny (6.6 percent) on the value of movable property and revenue. All those who had at least 40 shillings per year income from their land were taxed. In addition, they were obliged to possess a bow for military service in case of necessity. They got in exchange the right to vote for a representative in the council that came to be called the Parliament.[19]

In this way a rather powerful 'national' parliament developed, dominated by the high nobility, although since 1337 also urban representatives were present in a separate national meeting of lesser nobility.[20] In the history of the provincial 'States of Holland' the oldest preserved document – dating from 1276 – was

17 *Eereprent ter gedachtenisse voor de inwoonders van gantsch Nederlandt over het geven hunner liberale giften van den 50. penning ten dienste van den landen, in het jaar 1747*, published a.o. in R. Liesker and W. Fritschy, *Gewestelijke financien ten tijde van de Republiek der Verenigde Nederlanden. Deel IV Holland (1572–1795)* (The Hague: Instituut voor Nederlandse Geschiedenis, 2004) [hereafter: GFH], p. 150.

18 Brewer, *Sinews of power*, p. 3.

19 C.J. Rogers, 'The military revolution of the Hundred Years War', in: *The military revolution debate* ed. C.J. Rogers (Oxford 1995) pp. 55–93, p. 62.

20 Ormrod, 'The West European monarchies in the Later Middle Ages', p. 129.

already about the granting of privileges by the count of Holland, not to nobles, but to cities.[21] The county of Holland became part of the rising Burgundian state in 1433, but its provincial states assembly that formally existed since 1428 continued to exist. The first 'States General'-meeting of a number of provinces of the Netherlands was convened by Philip the Fair of Burgundy only in 1464. States General-meetings, bringing together representatives of several provincial states, tended to be avoided by rulers on the Continent.[22] In Britain Parliament often met already in early periods sometimes even more than once a year, although also British kings tried to restrict their dependence from parliament.

In each of the provinces of the later Dutch Republic the subsidy (*bede*) for the Burgundian duke, and later the Habsburg monarch, was a quota tax: a fixed amount was granted by the States and subdivided across the cities and the countryside, an arrangement which was – on a provincial level – comparable to the British national direct taxation, therefore. In addition, however, cities in the provinces in the Netherlands could be the count's guarantors for extra revenues by means of a loan.[23] In Britain only London fulfilled a function for 'loans' to the king, in ways, different from that of the cities in the Netherlands, that will be discussed in the section on public debt. Another important difference with Britain was, moreover, that the cities in the Netherlands were allowed and able to sell annuities to pay extraordinary *bedes* and to levy and increase indirect urban taxation for interest payments and debt redemption, which was never the case in Britain. As we saw in Part 2 Holland developed already shortly before the Revolt common *provincial* indirect taxation that for a large part consisted of formerly typically *urban* excises. No urban excise taxation existed in Britain and national excise taxation would only start to develop since the 1640s.

The first indirect tax in Britain was an export tax on wool, wool fells and hides, the so-called 'ancient' or 'great' customs. This first British export tax on wool was negotiated by the Crown in 1275, not with the parliament or with urban governments, but directly with a group of London merchants. Customs

---

21 *Bronnen voor de geschiedenis der dagvaarten van de Staten en steden van Holland voor 1544. Deel I 1276–1433. Tweede stuk: teksten*, eds. W. Prevenier and J.G. Smit (Den Haag 1987) p. 1.

22 R.H. Long, 'Parliamentary Monarchy', in: *The 'New Monarchies' and Representative Assemblies. Medieval Constitutionlism or Modern Absolutism?*, ed. J. Slavin (Boston 1964) pp. 67–77, p. 69: 'the crown continued in most countries occasionally to prefer the method of treating with each local community or with each class separately, for taxation specially'.

23 The first case mentioned was on 6. April 1291: Floris V borrowed 12,000 Dutch pounds from a nobleman, a rich burgher of the city of Utrecht and a squire for which the cities of Dordrecht, Middelburg, Zierikzee, Delft, Leiden, Haarlem and Alkmaar stood surety; ibidem, p. 4.

were originally seen in Britain – as in many other states in world history – as a royal privilege. The early British customs did not require parliamentary consent and were meant to be permanent. Gradually the king widened the range of goods to be taxed on export, and increased the tariffs. After protests in 1362 against a rate-increase to no less than 40 percent the king promised a reduction of the rate in peace time, which seems to indicate that the Commons gained some control over the important wool customs.[24] In practice customs were granted by parliament to a new king for his lifetime at the start of his reign, but remained for the rest of the time a royal prerogative. New rates generally continued to be negotiated with groups of merchants directly not with Parliament. Like Venice, and unlike later the Dutch Republic, Britain could obviously relatively easily afford to shift part of the burden of public finance unto foreigners without fear for losing trade. Taxes on foreign trade developed in the territory of the Netherlands only since the Dutch Revolt, as we saw in Chapter 2.

As to direct taxation, the assessment of taxable estate and goods consented by the British parliament was administered centrally until 1332.[25] Since then, however, this aspect of centralization weakened. The crown negotiated block payments with towns and villages based on one fifteenth of the value of 'movable property' in rural areas and one tenth for urban areas and the royal demesne to them. The British king was dependent on the cooperation of local officeholders and the country gentry for the assessment of individual tax payers and for the collection of this type of public revenue, but no provincial or regional power centres developed with their own representative institutions to discuss taxation. From 1334 onwards the sums required from each community were fixed at the amounts that had been levied in 1332, although the tax remained known as the 'fifteenths and tenths' until its abolition in the 17th century. Other direct taxes had to be added in the course of time with the consent of parliament, the main of which was called the 'subsidy' for the king.[26] Direct taxes and customs revenues were the main forms of public revenue by means of which the Hundred Years War (1337–1453) between England and France was financed.

The first British participation in a major European conflict after the Hundred Years War was in the 1540s, when Henry VIII participated in the Italian Wars (1542–1546), by means of which he hoped in vain to acquire again a

24 Ormrod, 'The West European Monarchies in the Later Middle Ages', p. 135; already in 1351 according to Rogers, 'The military revolution of the Hundred Year War', p. 62.

25 Ormrod and Barta, 'The feudal structure and the beginnings of state finance', pp. 57–58.

26 A useful overview is provided on http://en.wikipedia.org/wiki/History_of_the_English_fiscal_system.

foothold in France.[27] For this war the king had to hire European mercenaries for the first time. This did not yet lead to the rise of a fiscal-military state in Britain, however, because the king was able to finance these troops partly by the sale of expropriated monastic lands instead of by tax increases, partly also by devaluing the currency.[28] In the Dutch Republic a devaluation of the currency was also used as a means of war financing during the 1570s (see Chapter 1), but most ecclesiastical properties would be handed over to the cities to compensate them for their role in financing the earliest phase of the war with Spain (Chapter 2).

Until Parliament allowed the Puritan army-leader Cromwell to deploy, since 1645, his nationwide professional 'New Model Army', wars and rebellions on the British Isles culminating in the civil 'Wars of the Three Kingdoms' (1639–1651), were fought with locally raised companies.[29] Military service was obligatory, and the principal defensive duty of the militia was against internal subversion, not foreign invasion.[30] Even until 1660 'not inconsiderable' amounts of military expenditure in Britain were still allocated to cities, boroughs and shires.[31] According to Brewer, Britain's militia-army showed real vigour in preserving domestic order until the Civil War, implying that no necessity was felt by the state to have a standing army before that time.[32]

5.3 Public Expenditure in Two 'Maritime States'

Total Public Expenditure before and after c. 1690

A quantitative comparison of total public expenditure for Britain and the Dutch Republic is for the period before about 1690 only possible, if figures for public revenue as made available by O'Brien and Hunt are accepted as an indication for public expenditure. They found that in the mid sixteenth century some seventeen percent of total national tax receipts may have been spent

27 Brewer, *Sinews*, p. 7.

28 Brewer, *Sinews*, p. 21. According to the data collected by O'Brien and Hunt 43 percent of the increase that was on average necessary during this war on average resulted from additional (direct) taxation, 20 percent from increases in the sale of lands, 31 percent from revenue from the Mint, 6 percent from increases in Crown revenue (mainly customs).

29 Braddick, *State formation*, p. 279.

30 Braddick, *State formation*, p. 227, p. 229.

31 S. Gunn, D. Grummit and H. Cools, *War, state and society in Britain and the Netherlands* (Oxford 2007) p. 54; in fact still in 1763 there were about 28,000 men militia, in 1778/9 even about 40,000: Brewer, *Sinews*, p. 33.

32 Brewer, *Sinews*, p. 10.

locally and between 1598 and 1602 still about eight percent. They found also, however, that the amounts spent locally were administered centrally by means of 'tallies' and that the amounts on these tallies were counted as part of central revenue. They are confident therefore that, since 1559, their figures display total public revenue, including central public revenue locally spent.[33]

Their figures exclude public loans, which in the Dutch Republic were an important source for war finance. In Britain loans to the king were mostly short-term loans of modest size, before 1694, repaid (at least partly) from public revenue within three to five years.[34] Although public expenditure will in fact have been somewhat higher, especially during war years,[35] this makes a comparison of public expenditure that is partly based on their figures for public revenue acceptable (see Figure 5.1).[36] The figures are certainly not reliable on a year to year basis, however, but this is a *caveat* which the British data have in common with Dutch public finance data.

Figure 5.1, which compares total public expenditure for the two states between 1575 and 1795, lacks data for most years of the period of the Civil War in Britain and for some other years. It illustrates for the remaining years that the total amount in public expenditure of this much larger state was nearly always less than in the Dutch Republic until 1688, as a result of its lack of participation in the European land wars of the period, which was no doubt partly due to its relative geographical isolation as an island.

As a result, the British did not yet experience the fiscal consequences of the 'military revolution' until then, and during the eighteenth century naval expenditure would remain a much more important part of British military expenditure than in the Dutch Republic.

In 1688, however, war against France was felt to be a necessity, not only by Britain's new Dutch protestant king, but also by a parliament increasingly concerned about commercial interests. 'The domestic price of French hegemony in Europe was obviously too great for even the most isolationist MP', as Brewer

33 O'Brien and Hunt, 'The rise of a fiscal state', pp. 141–142.

34 O'Brien and Hunt, 'Britain 1485–1815', p. 55.

35 O'Brien and Hunt, 'The rise of a fiscal state', p. 133 'Medium or long-term borrowing by the Crown occurred intermittently between 1485 and 1688, (…) usually in wartime'; the section on public debt below suggests, however, that the amounts involved cannot have been very large.

36 S.M. Healy, *Crown revenue and the political culture of early Stuart Britain*, P(hD thesis, Birkbeck, University of London, 2015) Table 1.1 p. 34 has an amount of £669,243 in total for 'crownloans of the City of London', which was therefore £12,393 on average per year, which was 2.4% of total public revenue on average per year in this period.

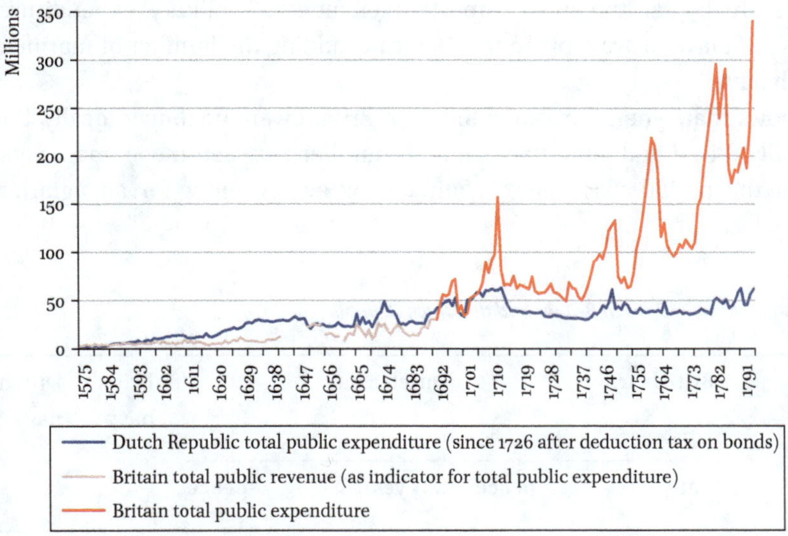

FIGURE 5.1 *Dutch and British total public expenditure, 1575–1794 (guilders).*
Sources: Data prepared on English revenues, 1485–1815, by Professor P.K. O'Brien and Mr P.A. Hunt http://esfdb.websites.bta.com [last access 27-08-2016]; Mitchell and Deane, *British historical statistics*, 389–391; exchange rates: N.W. Posthumus, *Nederlandsche Prijsgeschiedenis. I Goederenprijzen op de beurs van Amsterdam 1585–1914. Wisselkoersen te Amsterdam 1609–1914* (Leiden 1943) 583–612 (interpolation for missing years; until 1609 estimated at fl. 10.40 as in 1609 in order to have at least a rough comparison).

wrote.[37] Only since then total British public expenditure became larger than that of the Dutch Republic and increasingly so in the course of time. A comparison per capita will be given in the section on public revenue.

Data for a breakdown of British public expenditure are not available for the period before c. 1690. In the first of the two subsections below, British and Dutch military expenditure for this period will be compared by means of other data, especially the number of soldiers for the army and the number of ships for the navy. Subsequently the total structure of public expenditure of the two states can be compared for the period since c. 1690.

A Comparison of Military Expenditure before 1688

A comparison with the Dutch Republic of military expenditure for the period until 1688 is to some extent possible by means of the number of soldiers that had to be paid by both states in the course of time, because the payments to

37 Brewer, *Sinews*, p. 171.

soldiers are by far the most important element of military expenditure. Table 5.1 offers data available in the literature, adding the number of mariners on both navies.

It shows that, when the armed forces in Britain were no longer locally, but nationally raised and paid, they came to number between 11,000 and 47,000 men in the period 1647–1660, 'a miraculous achievement for an agrarian

TABLE 5.1 *Armed forces in Britain and the Dutch Republic, 1633–1784.*

	British army		**Dutch army**		**British navy**	**Dutch navy**
	war years	**peace**	**war years**	**peace**		
1633					*9,000*	
1643			60,000			
1648				35,000		
1646–1660	11,000–47,000					
1660/1661				24,000	*20,000*	
1673/4			93,000			*17,000*
1676					*30,000*	
1686				40,000		
1688					*42,000*	
1688–1697	76,000		65,000–102,000		*40,000*	*25,000*
1700						*23,000*
1702–1714	93,000		108,000–119,000		*42,000*	
1715					*13,000*	
1739–1748	62,000	35,000	95,000	43,000	*50,000*	*15,000*
1756–1763	93,000			41,000	*75,000*	
1750–1800		45,000				
1775–1784	108,000			42,000	*82,000*	

Sources: Brewer, *The sinews of power*, 30, 32; H. Zwitzer, '*De militie van de staat*'. *Het leger van de Republiek* der *Verenigde Nederlanden* (Amsterdam: Van Soeren, 1991) 175–176; R. Prud'homme van Reine, 'De Republiek als grote en kleine mogendheid ter zee (1648–1763)' in: J. Bruijn and C. Wels (eds.) *Met man en macht, De militarie geschiedenis van Nederland, 1550–2000* (Amsterdam: Balans 2003) 105–139, 109; Bruijn, 'States and navies', 89; Braddick, *The nerves of state*, p. 31; D. Chandler and I. Beckett (eds.) *The Oxford history of the British Army* (Oxford: Oxford University Press, 2003) 132.

economy', as public finance historian Michael Braddick wrote.[38] By then its size became comparable, therefore, to that of a European power like the Dutch Republic as was suggested by the available figures for total public expenditure for this period (Figure 5.1). In the absence of an integrated urban system in seventeenth century Britain, this miracle was no doubt a result of the 'coercive' fiscal abilities of a central administration. It should be added, however, that the expansion of the Civil War to Ireland is reported to have enabled Cromwell to pay 12,000 men of his troops by means of confiscated Irish catholic properties, instead of by increased taxation in Britain.[39]

After the Restoration of 1660 the central state would continue to assume nearly complete responsibility for defence expenditure. An attenuated standing army was now retained.[40] Its internal wars and rebellions did not yet result for Britain in the astonishing increase in the size of national armies as experienced by other states in Europe in the period of the early modern military revolution, this in contrast to the Dutch Republic, that emerged in the middle of these developments.[41] I found no data on army size between 1660 and 1688. It was probably only after 1688, however, – when Britain became involved in what is often called its Second Hundred Years War against France – that British armed forces increased to about 76,000 men during the Nine Years War.

This did not mean that Britain had no interest in the world outside the British Isles before 1688. Whereas a standing army had been slow to develop because the water offered a natural barrier against the invasion of foreign armies, the safety of its sea lanes was increasingly seen as significant for Britain's foreign trade already in the first half of the sixteenth century. In Britain with its centralized administration it was the crown that established the infrastructure of a national navy by building thirty royal ships at that time from revenues that did not require parliamentary assent. This in contrast to the Netherlands, where it were rather city governments who started to support merchants in protecting their ships from privateers and war enemies.[42]

38 Braddick, *State formation*, p. 214.

39 http://en.wikipedia.org/wiki/New_Model_Army referring to I. Gentles, *The New Model Army in Britain, Ireland and Scotland 1645–53* (Oxford 1994) and M. O'Siochru, *God's Executioner. Oliver Cromwell and the Conquest of Ireland* (London 2008).

40 P.K. O'Brien and Ph. Hunt, 'Britain 1485–1815', in R. Bonney (ed.), *The rise of the fiscal state in Europe, c.1200–1815* (Oxford: Oxford University Press, 1999) pp. 53–100, p. 54.

41 Brewer, *Sinews*, p. 8; reference to Parker, New Cambridge Modern History vol 12 (1979) p. 5; Erik Swart, *Krijgsvolk, professionalisering en het ontstaan van het Staatse leger 1568–1590* (Amsterdam 2006).

42 Sicking, *Neptune and the Netherlands.*

In the Dutch Republic it would be the Earl of Leicester who would try to organize a centralized Dutch navy financed by national customs revenues, by means of three admiralties under the direct supervision of the Council of State, after he had been sent to the young Republic in 1585 by the British queen Elizabeth as governor, when the States General were looking for a new lord after their abjuration of the Spanish king. His attempt at centralization during the short period of his stay in the Republic (1585–87) largely failed, however. Whereas Britain provides us with an example of a highly centralized naval organization with London as its heart,[43] the Dutch Republic would become a leading maritime and naval power with a naval organization decentralized over five cities.

In Britain private ships used for war ends had still far outnumbered royal ships during the Elizabethan war with Spain (1585–1604), and privateering was still one of the main forms of British maritime activity.[44] The decisive change came, like so many other fiscal changes, in the 1640s. By 1640 the king's navy consisted of only 40 ships,[45] in the period 1643–5 it would consist of 164 state ships and pinnacles, to which 124 hired merchant men were added.[46] As Figure 5.3 below shows the British government spent more on its navy than the Dutch already during the early 1650s, when they had to fight the Dutch in the First British-Dutch naval War that resulted from Cromwell's mercantilist Navigation Acts. According to the data in Table 5.1 the navy continued to expand between 1660 and 1702 more than the Dutch navy. According to Braddick the navy was the biggest spending department of the British state by 1688.[47]

Another and probably more adequate way to compare naval strength than by the number of men involved as in Table 5.1, is, the available number of ships of the line, adding the number of merchant vessels armed with at least 30 guns (since 1670 at least 40 guns, and since 1690 at least 50 guns) hired by the state, as was done in a study by Modelski and Thompson.[48]

---

43 Bruijn, 'States and navies', p. 83.

44 Braddick, *State formation*, pp. 202–203.

45 Braddick, *State formation*, p. 211.

46 Braddick, *State formation*, p. 219 citing Capp, *Cromwell's navy*, pp. 6, 9–10.

47 Braddick, *State formation*, pp. 222–224.

48 J. Glete, *Swedish naval administration* (Leiden: Brill, 2009) p. 395 offers a table of the amount of tons per country of sailing warship of 100 tons displacement and larger for 1620–1640–1660–1680, and of 300 tons displacement and larger for 1700 and 1720, based on data in his *Navies and nations: warships, navies and state building in Europe and America, 1500–1860* (Stockholm, 1993); according to this table the Dutch navy was only slightly larger than the English navy in 1640, about 75 percent of the English navy in 1660 and only

Whereas Table 5.1 suggested that British naval power superseded that of the Dutch Republic already by the last quarter of the seventeenth century Table 5.2 shows that it is more likely that this was only definitely the case by 1700. (It also suggests that France was in fact a more powerful maritime power at the start of the eighteenth century than Britain.)

Dutch maritime historians are convinced of the inefficiency and the disadvantages of the lack of naval centralization of the Dutch navy. They point for instance to the fact that between 1631 and 1657 the States General had still to accept the existence of private local navies for the purpose of escorting shipping to and from the Baltic, paid for from special duties placed on the merchantmen involved. Beyond the Cape of Good Hope the Dutch state even simply delegated all military activities to the VOC until 1783.[49] In comparison to the Dutch navy in later times there may be good reasons for their criticisms. Nevertheless during most of the seventeenth century the strength of the navy of the small federal Dutch Republic seems to have been either larger or not much less than that of the British monarchy despite the fact that Britain spent more on its navy already in the 1650s and despite the fact that the Dutch had to finance a much larger army than the British as well.

TABLE 5.2 *Naval strength in ships in Britain, the Dutch Republic and France, 1585–1790.*

	Britain	Dutch Republic	France
1585	30	37	2
1600	34	38	0
1625	40	114	15
1650	80	70	35
1675	60	63	90
1700	115	86	118
1725	120	42	36
1750	116	33	53
1775	108	11	75
1790	137	34	90

Source: Bruijn, 'States and their navies', p. 71.

about half the English navy in 1680; Bruijn chose for Modelski and Thompson, however, because the number of guns was more decisive in naval strength than the amount of tons.

49 Bruijn, 'States and their navies', p. 81.

The Structure of Dutch and British Public Expenditure since c. 1690

Figures 5.2a–b offer a comparison of the structure of public expenditure in both states by means of nine years averages for the years since c. 1690. For the Dutch Republic the data for the period before c. 1690 have been added. This addition shows the even greater dominance of the army in Dutch military expenditure during the period before than after c. 1690, despite the fact that during this period three of the four naval wars with Britain were fought. This refutes the common assumption that, like the British, the Dutch 'always devoted a high proportion of its expenditure to a floating force'.[50] The data used for Figure 5.2a indicate that – between 1575 and 1690 – this proportion was in fact on average only 17 percent of total public expenditure (25 percent of total military expenditure) in the Dutch Republic.

In the period since c. 1690 total military expenditure was on average 49 percent of total expenditure in the Dutch case and 55 percent in Britain, not really very different, therefore. The main difference remains the continuously much lower percentage spent on the navy in the Dutch Republic, in this period on average only 12 percent of total expenditure (a quarter of military expenditure) against on average about 25 percent of total in the British case (nearly half of military expenditure).

An element of the structure of military expenditure not visible in the graph is yet that British attempts to stop French power expansion were not only realized by increasing the amount spent on the British army and navy, but also by means of subsidies to allies. Brewer mentions that in Britain between 1702 and 1713 seven million pounds, which was about 25 percent of the money voted for the army, went to foreign subsidies, and between 1702 and 1763 in total 24,5 million pound, which according to Mitchell and Deane's figures amounted to about 17 percent of army expenditure in that period.[51] The decentralized state structure of the Dutch Republic did not prevent it from voting for subsidies to allies as well, but the degree to which this alternative was used by the Dutch was much smaller than in Britain: in the period 1702–1713 only about 7 percent of the army expenditure of the five provinces for which relevant data are available was spent on subsidies to allies, in the period 1742–1750 about 5 percent, in all other periods less or nothing. The explanation may be that the risk of invasions during a war was much smaller in the British than in the Dutch case.

For navy expenditure data were available for a longer period than for the rest of British public expenditure. Figure 5.3 shows that British public expenditure on the navy was more than in the Dutch Republic already in the 1650s. It

50 Brewer, *Sinews*, p. 29.

51 Brewer, *Sinews*, p. 32.

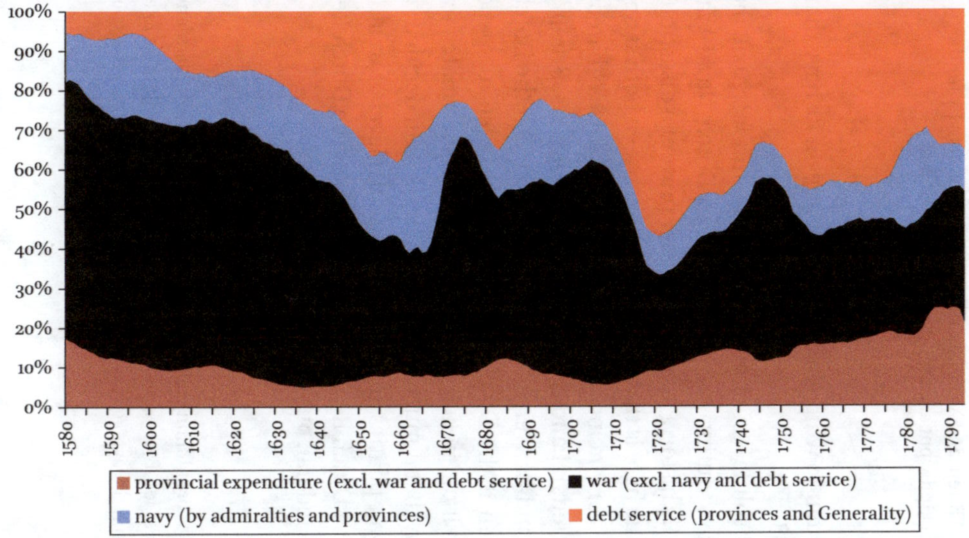

FIGURE 5.2A *Structure of Dutch public expenditure, 1575–1794 (9 years averages).*

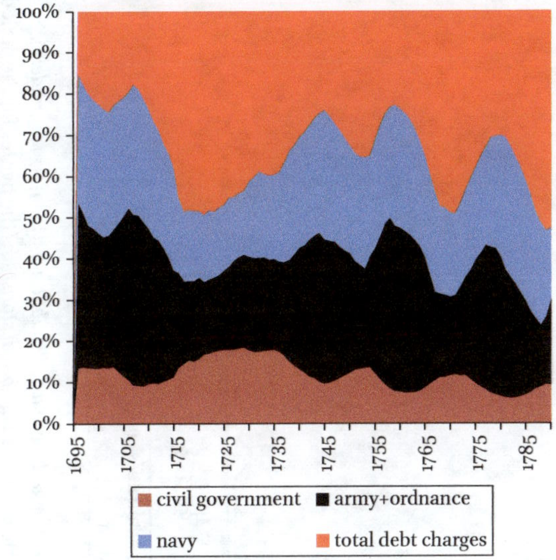

FIGURE 5.2B *Structure of British public expenditure, 1692–1794 (9-years averages).*

Sources: Mitchell and Deane, *British historical statistics*, pp. 389–391; Posthumus, *Nederlandsche Prijsgeschiedenis*, pp. 583–612.

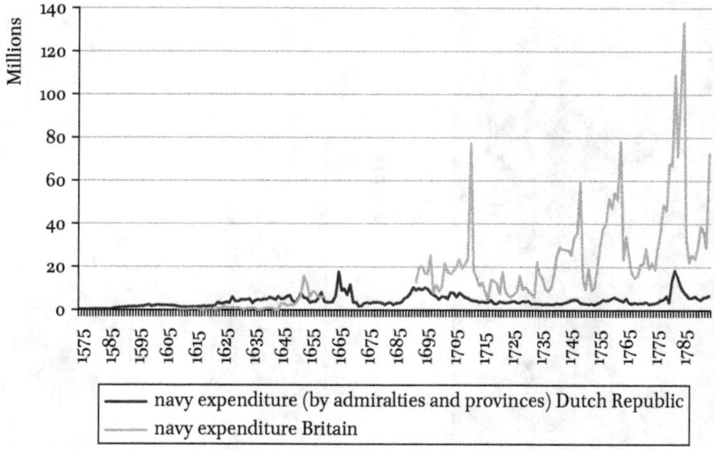

FIGURE 5.3 *Naval expenditure in Britain and the Dutch Republic, 1575(1609)–1794 (guilders).* Sources: Mitchell and Deane, *British historical statistics*; (the figures for the period before 1688 used in P. O'Brien, and X. Duran, 'Total Factor Productivity for the Royal Navy' (2011) were kindly put at my disposal by the authors).

shows moreover, the huge extent to which Britain spent more on its navy than the Dutch Republic since 1688.

The huge difference in absolute amounts explains why the fact that the Dutch spent more on its navy during the Fourth British-Dutch Naval War (1781–84) than ever before in its history,[52] could no longer prevent a disastrous Dutch defeat. The point at issue here is that the difference between both states can be explained much more convincingly by their relative 'tax bases' than by the difference between their federal and centralized state structures. Britain's population was much larger and its average wealth started to reach the Dutch level by then (Table 3.2). Even if the Dutch Republic had decided to spend twice as much on the navy as it did in fact, it could not have been a match for Britain. From the moment on that a much larger state like Britain decided to get involved in European power politics and started to attain a level of wealth per capita similar to that in the Dutch Republic, the problem of the Dutch Republic was not that it was too federal, but that it was too small.

52 On average per year in 1652–54 6.3 million guilders, in 1665–67 12.0 million guilders, and in 1781–84 14.6 million guilders (for 1672–74 not enough data were available; data on Zeeland's contribution suggest that the average amount per year was certainly much less in 1672–74 than in 1665–67).

As to the other two expenditure categories Figures 5.2a–b show that the relative importance of debt service was rather similar in the two states during the eighteenth century. It required on average 38 percent of Dutch and 35 percent of British public expenditure between 1690 and 1794, in the last case increasing from on average 32 percent in the first half to on average 37 percent in the last half of the period. Debt service will be further discussed in the section on public debt at the end of this chapter.

'Other' public expenditure was good for respectively on average 13 percent in the Dutch and 10 percent in the British case, decreasing from on average 14 to 9 percent in the British case and increasing from on average 9 percent in the first half of the eighteenth century to 17 percent in the second half in the Dutch case. This increase was mainly due to Holland's huge financial support for the VOC after 1784. It is likely that the rest of the difference in the relative importance of this category may be seen as an indication of the larger efficiency of a centralized state for this type of expenditure.

5.4 Public Revenue in Two 'Commercial States'

Total Public Revenue Compared

Total tax revenue in constant prices in Britain remained more or less constant since already about 1350 until as late as 1640: public revenue increases were always followed by decreases to about the same level as before and the next revenue peak was not really higher than the former after correction for price increases.[53] Also after the start of Britain's involvement in early modern European power politics with the Anglo-Spanish war (1585–1604) under Queen Elizabeth I, the same pattern continued to exist. This in sharp contrast, therefore, to the 'tax revolution' in Holland since the start of its revolt against Spain in 1572, followed in the next decades by remarkable increases in tax revenues in all provinces and the emergence of a permanent public debt.

It is possible that the restrictive role of parliament and the cumbersome machinery of tax assessment, necessitated by the absence of domestic indirect taxation, contributed to the modest level of British public revenue in this period. The large difference with the Dutch Republic was evidently mainly due, however, to the fact that war faring on land was simply much more expensive than Elizabeth's naval war faring with Spain. When Spain tried an invasion of Spanish troops in 1588, by means of its powerful brand-new 'Armada', it was sufficient for Britain to have a navy (although stormy weather, some Dutch

53 O'Brien and Hunt, 'The rise of a fiscal state', p. 161; on p. 150 a graph with deflated figures.

support and the relative incompetence of the enemy seem to have been helpful as well).[54]

Figure 5.1 on public expenditure gave already an impression of the differences with the Dutch Republic in the development of *total* public revenue, showing that even total public revenue was higher in the Dutch Republic than in Britain until 1688. Figure 5.4 shows that tax revenue *per capita* remained still higher in the Dutch Republic until as late as about 1780 (even although Scotland was not included in the calculation of the per capita figures since the Union of 1707.)[55] Public revenue per capita became incidentally already much higher than in the Dutch Republic due to loans in some war years, starting with the last years of the big international war of the Spanish Succession (1701–1713).

That Britain seemed better able to realise increases in tax revenue than the Dutch Republic cannot be attributed to the centralized character of its parliamentary system of government. It was evidently a result of the comparatively very low level of tax revenue per capita in the period before 1688, due to its late entry in the land wars of the European power struggle. Table 5.3 gives a

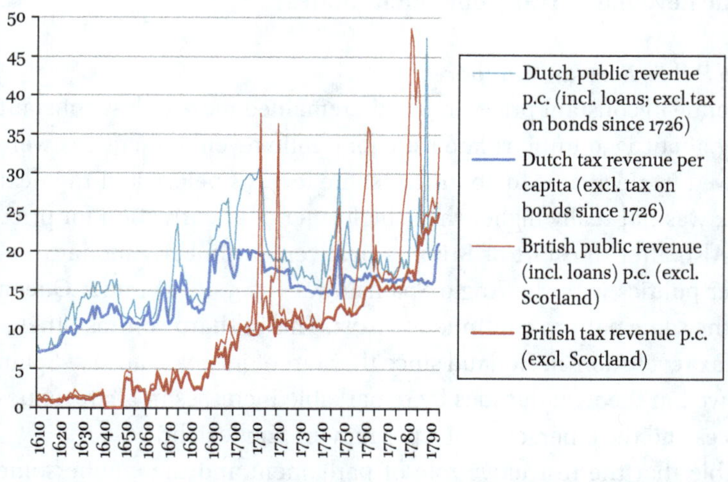

FIGURE 5.4 *Public revenue and tax revenue per capita in Britain and the Dutch Republic, 1690–1794 (glds).*
Sources: same as for Figure 5.1; population: O'Brien and Hunt, 'England 1485–1815', p. 176.

54 Ibidem, p. 161.

55 No clear increase in tax revenue was visible in the available data since the Union of 1707: public revenue in Scotland was probably spent locally. A restriction to England and Wales was, of course, anyhow preferable, as the argumentation of this chapter focuses on the centralized character of British public finance.

TABLE 5.3 *Public revenue as a percentage of national income in Britain and the Dutch Republic, 1700, 1750, 1790.*

	Britain	[Britain]	Dutch Republic
1700	6.8 to 7.7%	[7.3–9.5%]	11 to 13%
1750	8.8%	[8–10%]	12 to 14%
1790	11.6 to 11.7%	[12%]	13 to 15%

Sources: O'Brien&Hunt, 'Rise of a fiscal state', p. 175; the alternative estimates for Britain between square brackets in: M. Daunton, 'The politics of British taxation', in *The rise of fiscal states. A global history,* (2012) pp. 111–145, p. 112; De Vries&Van der Woude, *The first modern economy*, p. 707.

rough impression of the probable differences in the tax burden as a percentage of national income during the eighteenth century between the two states, which suggests that this percentage remained higher in the Dutch Republic even right until the end of the eighteenth century.

National income estimates for this period are rather uncertain, of course. It seems nevertheless safe to conclude that a small decentralized federal Republic remained during most of the time able to extract a larger percentage of national income as public revenue than a large centralized state like Britain.

Figures 5.5a–b offer an overview of the development and the structure of public revenue in both states (in pounds for Britain and in guilders for the Dutch Republic). Figure 5.5a shows the still modest extent to which the Civil War (1642–1651), and the revolutionary extent to which Britain's involvement in international land wars since the Glorious Revolution, required a rise in public revenue. It also shows that the relatively high level during the early 1650s of on average about c. 2.3 million pound was for a large part not due to tax increases, but to 'other' public revenue, in this case the sale of confiscated royal and royalist property, that provided about 20 percent of total revenue in these years.[56]

For the period since 1688 the graphs show the huge increase in the importance of excises in Britain after 1688 and their decreasing relative importance in the Dutch Republic. Excises were introduced in Britain already in the 1640s, but no separate data on domestic indirect taxation were available before c. 1690. Figures 5.5a–b also show the large weight of direct taxation in the Dutch Republic in comparison to Britain in the eighteenth century, and the increasing

56 'Data prepared on English revenues, 1485–1815, by Professor P.K. O'Brien and Mr P.A. Hunt' accessible on http://esfdb.websites.bta.com.

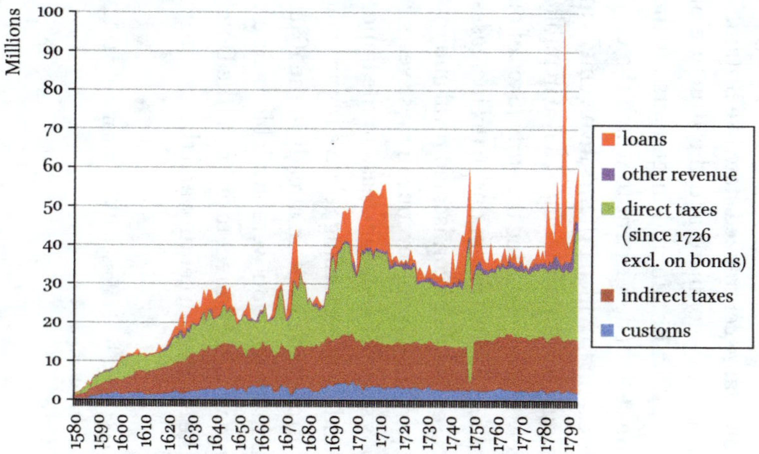

FIGURE 5.5A *Development and structure of public revenue in the Dutch Republic 1580–1794 (glds).*

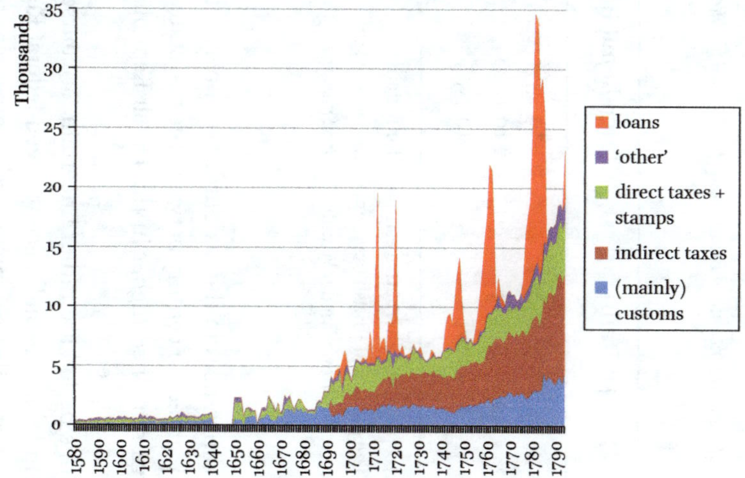

FIGURE 5.5B *Idem in Britain, 1580–1794 (British pounds).*

Sources: Britain 1580–1692: Data prepared on English revenues, 1485–1815, by Professor P.K. O'Brien and Mr P.A. Hunt http://esfdb.websites.bta.com/Database.aspx (nb 1643–1692 '(mainly)customs' includes (domestic) indirect taxation); 1692–1794: Mitchell and Deane, *British historical statistics*, 386–388, 404 ('loans' = increases in public debt).

TABLE 5.4 *Structure of British and Dutch public revenue before and after 1688.*

	Dutch Republic		(Great) Britain	
	1575–1688	1689–1794	1575–1688	1689–1794
customs	12%	7%	35%	19%
indirect taxes	40%	28%	11%	36%
direct taxes	36%	49%	37%	22%
'other revenue'	2%	3%	17%	2%
loans	10%	13%	-	21%
	100%	100%	100%	100%

importance of customs in Britain in contrast to the Dutch Republic. It shows also the much larger importance of loans in Britain in the eighteenth century than in the whole period of the Dutch Republic.

Table 5.4 offers a summary of the main differences in the structure of public revenue before and after 1688 in percentages, in which the differences in the relative importance of loans and direct taxation in both states stand out even more clearly. The comparison with Britain again confirms therefore the relatively low extent to which the Dutch Republic can be called a 'capital-intensive' state in the early-modern period.

The next subsections on public revenue will offer a discussion of the different elements of the structure for British public revenue and the differences between the two states.

Non-parliamentary and Parliamentary Taxation

A remarkable characteristic in the structure of the early revenue system of the British monarchy in comparison to that of the Dutch Republic was the distinction between 'parliamentary' and 'non-parliamentary' state revenue. In the period from 1560–1640 about 73 to 76 percent of revenue was the result of 'non-parliamentary' state revenue (consisting of customs and 'other revenue', mainly Crown revenue and the Mint), only 24 to 27 percent of 'parliamentary' taxation (consisting of the direct taxes).[57]

In 1629 the announcement by Parliament of the intention to grant the new king Charles I the customs revenue for only one year instead of for the duration of his reign – attempting, therefore, to make it into parliamentary

57 Braddick, *The nerves of state*, p. 10, 12 Tables 1.3 and 1.1.

taxation – made the king decide to reign without parliament. Until 1640 he met extra military costs on the one hand by demanding localities the presentation of trained men rather than the money to recruit them. On the other hand he tried to revive old rights to sources of income that did not require parliamentary consent.[58] This resulted in the so-called 'Ship Money'.

It had long been customary to augment the navy in times of emergency with vessels owned by the king's subjects, similar to the use of armed merchantmen for naval wars by the Dutch. In the 1620s however merchant ships design had started to diverge from that of warships, making them more efficient for trade, but much less useful for war aims.[59] The new design allowed no longer enough place for the desirable number of guns per ship, especially when this number had to increase due to increasing naval competition.[60] Such merchant ships had to be protected, therefore, by specialized naval convoys. As international trade was not only important for public revenue, but also for the welfare of the country as a whole, the king started to introduce the notion that all taxpayers should pay for the upkeep of the royal fleet to protect international trade as a source of national wealth. Until then a 'Ship Money' could only be levied by the king in times of war and only from the coastal counties. The king maintained that he had the right to act as he did, as the wellbeing of the British people required it.[61]

Centrally appointed sheriffs instead of local commissions assessed the rates for this new direct tax, thanks to which this Ship Money became a real success, at least financially, during the first years of its existence between 1634 and 1638.[62] It was seen as illegal, however, by many people, because it was felt that – as a direct tax levied in peace time – it required the consent and constant control of parliament. Its revenues started to decrease, when opposition among the wealthy against this direct tax increased. When Charles needed more money to suppress a rebellion in Scotland, he needed again a Parliament, after eleven years of 'personal rule' without one. The so-called Long Parliament, starting in November 1640 and lasting to 1660, put an end to the Ship

58 Braddick, *State formation*, p. 284.

59 Braddick, *State formation*, p. 285.

60 Bruijn, 'States and their navies', p. 83.

61 Braddick, *State formation*, p. 242 sees the decrease in the king's dependency upon merchantmen as the start of the 'impersonal state' in Britain, legitimized by necessity and national interest; medievalists like M. Ormrod, however, tend to emphasize that already in medieval law taxation by a prince had to be justified by 'necessity' in P. Hoppenbrouwers (ed.) *Power and persuasion : essays on the art of state building in honour of W.P. Blockmans* (Turnhout: Brepols, 2010).

62 Braddick, *State formation*, pp. 243–244.

Money. Since that time direct taxation was again completely under the control of Parliament.

The introduction of a range of excises in Britain needed for the civil war against the king and his adherents that would end in the decapitation of Charles I in 1649, was a decision of this Long Parliament as well. All new taxation in Britain had to be approved by Parliament in practice already since the 1640s, although this would only legally be the case since the Glorious Revolution of 1688.

Customs in a Large Monarchy and a Small Republic

Customs were a much more important part of public revenue in the British monarchy than in the Dutch Republic (see Figures 5.5a–b), where customs had not been a source of state revenue before the Revolt. The very widespread notion that it is a prerogative of kings to tax foreign trade was only once and only for one year (1543) put in practice in the Netherlands before the Revolt as we saw. Until then only city governments in the Netherlands taxed imports sometimes, in order to be able to finance the protection of maritime trade (see Chapter 2).

A characteristic aspect of British custom revenues was that they were partly used by the king as a security for loans already in the thirteenth century. London merchants who supplied loans to the king got the right to farm part of the customs for a certain time.[63] Leasing part of the customs gave certainty about the amount of money to be expected for the period of the lease, but also allowed the Crown to realize advances on tax revenues. In Holland, in contrast, it was a collectivity of cities, instead of a private syndicate of merchants, that got the right to farm not customs, but excises under their own control as a security for common loans to Charles V. This option was not available to the English king. Britain's different trajectory of urbanization made him dependent on the powerful group of merchant in just one city.

The use of tax farming for the customs in Britain implied that it were the tax farmers who profited from increases in trade during the lease period, which could last several years, in contrast to the Dutch Republic, where tax farms were auctioned anew each year. To become better informed on the profits realized by the British tax farmers their books had to be handed in to the government from 1585 onwards, to provide a reliable basis for the next lease-negotiations.[64] The wish to avoid that farmers made unjustifiable profits brought customs farming to an end for the first time in the 1640s. In 1662 there was a temporary

---

63 Braddick, *State formation*, p. 251.

64 Braddick, *The nerves of state*, p. 61.

return to farming, when receipts turned out to be 25 percent lower than expected after the introduction of new rates. When negotiations for new leases failed in 1671, the farming of the customs was cancelled again, never to return. Improved administration in combination with increasing commerce now led to constantly increasing yields.[65]

It was the absence of an 'urban system' which made the British crown dependent on the eagerness of private syndicates in London to obtain customs farms. The abolition of tax farming and the establishment of a well-managed centralized administration for the levying of customs were imperative to obtain better revenue results. In Holland an urban system, in which cities jealously guarded each other's auctions of domestic 'common means' to prevent too low amounts for the leases, was sufficient to this end. The competitiveness of great numbers of small tax farms with a duration of only one year further contributed to auction results that were advantageous for the government.

Tax farming had not been the regular form of raising revenue for customs in the Dutch Republic. Most of the time customs were collected by the five admiralties under the final responsibility of the States General. It is likely that the weak central control of the States General facilitated fraud. From 1625 to 1637 the States General attempted to improve revenues by means of a partial form of tax farming, allowing farmers the right to a quarter of total revenue part of customs, thus giving them an interest in preventing frauds to the advantage of the remaining three quarters of revenue as well. Between 1687 and 1690 the same attempt was resumed for half of the custom revenues. Both times the attempts did not lead to revenue increases, however.

Table 5.5 contains an attempt to compare tax evasion in both states by juxtaposing the estimated average level of the percentage of custom rates to customs revenues as a percentage of the value of foreign trade. (The same is done for the value of imports as tariffs tended to be highest on imports.) In Britain the General or Great Statute of 1660 regarding the customs had provided a scale of duties of 5 percent on imports and exports.[66] Custom tariffs in the Dutch Republic were different for different goods, but the available information suggests that at that time they may have amounted to on average about the same percentage and the extremely long list of goods suggest that on everything that was imported or exported customs had to be paid.[67] Custom rates were much

---

65 Chandaman, *The English public revenue 1660–1688*, p. 24, p. 27.

66 http://en.wikipedia.org/wiki/History_of_the_English_fiscal_system; this percentage is also mentioned by Brewer, *Sinews*, p. 211.

67 Sources see under Table 5.5; 't Hart, *The making of a bourgeois state*, p. 103 estimates the average rate until the 1650s at about 5 percent in war time, 3 percent in peace time.

TABLE 5.5 *Customs revenue as % of value of trade compared to customs tariffs in Britain and the Dutch Republic, 1650s–1770s.*

	Britain				Dutch Republic			
	average value foreign trade (mill. glds)	customs as % of value of trade	customs as % of value of imports	average of tariffs	average value foreign trade (mill. glds)	customs as % of value of trade	customs as % of value of imports	average of tariffs
1650s				5%	260	1.1%	2.1%	5–6%?
1699–1701	125	12%	26%	15%?				
1722–1724	152	11%	23%	15%				
1720s					198	1.2%	2.3%	c. 3%
1752–1754	213	8%	20%	20%				
1772–1774	303	9%	20%	25%				
1770s					243	0.8%	1.4%	c. 3%

Sources: R. Davis, 'British Foreign Trade 1700–1774', *Economic History Review* 15 (1962) 285–303, 300, 302; exchange rates in Posthumus, *Price History*, 583–612; Dutch trade estimates in: De Vries and van der Woude, *The first modern economy*, 499; British tariffs: Braddick, *The nerves of state*, p. 54; Brewer, *Sinews of power*, 211; estimate average Dutch tariff: the tariff of the '*Last- en Veilgeld*' was 1 percent on exports, 2 percent on imports; the receipts were in the 1650s 27 percent of total customs receipt; J. Hovy, *Het voorstel van 1751 tot instelling van een beperkt vrijhavenstelsel in de Republiek* (Groningen: Wolters, 1966) 482–493 (tariffs when mentioned amount to 0.5 percent to 2 percent for export, 0.5 percent to 10 percent for imports).

higher in Britain after 1688; in the Dutch Republic they became lower during the eighteenth century than during the seventeenth.

Table 5.5 suggests that the difference between revenue as a percentage of the value of trade and especially that of imports, on the one hand, and the average percentage of the tariffs, on the other hand, in the eighteenth century tended to be lower in Britain than in the Dutch Republic, which makes it probable that higher custom revenues in Britain were, at least partly, due to less evasion of the customs than in the Dutch Republic. It is very well probable that this was related to the centralization of the custom organization after the abolition of customs farming in Britain. Suppressing smuggling became in Britain one of the main tasks of the peacetime standing army, that consisted mainly of horse regiments widely dispersed throughout the country.[68]

Although a recent overview of the politics of British taxation emphasizes, that the customs service was an inefficient part of the British state during the eighteenth century and that the British coastline made it extremely hard to prevent smuggling,[69] the situation in the Dutch Republic was probably worse. In the Dutch Republic where five admiralties were responsible for the customs, the cities which housed them competed for trade. As the personnel of the Dutch admiralties was not appointed and controlled centrally but locally, evasion was most probably largely tolerated to attract trade. Dutch cities had more reason to fear that foreigners would steer clear of ports with high and strictly controlled import duties, than reason to fear decreases in domestic consumption due to higher prices resulting from increases in the rates of excises among the 'common (or general) means', because so much of these excises were levied from primary necessities.

Although – or perhaps in fact: because – foreign trade was a more important part of the Dutch than of the British economy, customs were consistently much less important in the structure of Dutch public revenue than in that of Britain (see Figures 5.5a–b). The provincial governments in the Dutch Republic preferred to tax domestic trade by exploiting the fiscal possibilities of its urban network. The long dominance of customs in British indirect taxation can be explained by the old historical right of the Crown to customs revenue from foreign trade, by the dependence of the Crown on the merchants of just one very large city for loans, by the long absence of the financial requirements of the 'military revolution', and by the absence of a political structure requiring

68 Brewer, *Sinews*, pp. 51–52.

69 M. Daunton, 'The politics of British taxation', in B. Yun-Casalilla and P.K. O'Brien (eds.) *The rise of fiscal states. A global history, 1500–1914* (Cambridge 2012) pp. 111–145, p. 119.

collectively felt political responsibilities by its cities. Collective urban excises did not have to develop, because the king had the right to levy customs.

It is evident that the relatively small importance of customs revenue in Dutch public finance resulted primarily, not from the weak centralization of the Dutch admiralties, but from much lower Dutch customs tariffs in combination with a – certainly since the 1770s but probably during most of the eighteenth century – lower value of the total volume of trade than in Britain. It is not very likely that custom tariffs could have been raised substantially in the Dutch Republic without a serious loss of trade given the much smaller domestic market and the existence of competitors like London and Hamburg.

Even if the Dutch Republic had been able to realize, just like Britain, 9 percent instead of only 0.8 percent of the total value of its trade as customs revenue during the 1770s, however, its total level of public revenue would have been still only about half of total public revenue in Britain. This confirms again that the disastrous outcome of the Fourth English Naval War was not due to a lack of centralization frustrating the realization of substantial rises in public revenue, but to the much smaller size of the Dutch Republic. Changes in its institutional structure would not have been very helpful to strengthen the international position of the Dutch Republic. A policy of avoidance of involvement in international conflicts was the only option.

Indirect Taxation, Urbanization and Centralization

In Britain excises were introduced by Parliament in 1643 after a decision to raise an army against the king, because of his absolutist leanings and Roman Catholic sympathies. It was a decision comparable therefore to what had happened at the start of the Dutch Revolt against the Catholic Spanish king in the sixteenth century. It did not at all result, however, in a similar predominance of domestic indirect taxes in public revenue in Britain, as in the Dutch Republic during the seventeenth century.[70] Only during the eighteenth century indirect domestic taxation became the largest part of Britain's fiscal system. In the Dutch Republic, in contrast, direct taxation became predominant during the eighteenth century.

In Britain a proposal for excises in the Commons to increase public revenue had still met with extreme hostility among the population in the 1620s.[71] Figures on British public revenue in the 1640s are not available, but most probably the bulk of the increase in total revenue was still due to direct taxation during

70 W.J. Ashworth, *Customs and excise. Trade, production and consumption in Britain, 1640–1845* (Oxford 2003) p. 6.

71 Braddick, *The nerves of state*, pp. 96–97.

these years, despite the start of excise taxation in 1643. Whereas the number of excises in the Dutch Republic constantly increased between 1572 and 1679, excises on salt and meat, that were in the Dutch Republic among the most remunerative excises, were dropped in Britain already in 1647 and pamphleteers continued to agitate against excises during the years thereafter.[72]

A difference with the Dutch Republic was moreover that since 1657 all remaining excises were levied from the producer rather than from the retailer or the consumer, this in an attempt to make them less visible to the British consumers.[73] The most important Dutch excises, like those on beer, bread grains, peat (the main fuel in the Netherlands), soap and salt were levied in different ways: from retail sale and consumption as well as from wholesale traders, transporters and incidentally producers. The restriction in Britain to producers may have facilitated a taxpayers' strike in 1659 during which no excises were paid any longer.[74] The Restoration of the monarchy in 1660 brought a restriction of excises to only beer and liquors,[75] at a time, therefore, when the Republic's richest province Holland levied already about forty different excise taxes.[76] Although the Dutch excises were seen by some as an example, their number and their characteristics were actually very different from Britain in the seventeenth century, and British Parliament kept a preference for direct taxes. It was preferred to avoid the risk that the king would become too independent from parliament by means of invisible revenue increases in indirect taxation not under their control, either resulting from economic development or from unauthorized increases in the tariffs.[77]

This difference with the Dutch Republic can, of course, partly be explained by the less extreme need for continuing increases in public revenue in Britain because of the absence of the necessity of a 'military revolution'. It is no doubt also related, however, to a difference in the urbanization trajectory of the two countries. In the Dutch Republic the important provincial excises, which, as the main part of the 'general means', formed the backbone of the fiscal system of the Dutch Republic, had been amply prepared by the existence of urban excises. Already long before the emergence of the Dutch Republic, cities in the

72 Ashworth, *Customs and Excises*, p. 102 mentions for instance a pamphlet from 1653 titled *A Condemnation of the Dutch Devil Excise*.

73 Ashworth, *Customs and excise*, pp. 56, 101 (until 1653 still many excises on the retailer).

74 Braddick, *State formation*, p. 276.

75 Braddick, *The nerves of state*, p. 10.

76 A chronological survey in Fritschy, 'The efficiency of taxation in Holland', pp. 68–69; a survey for the Republic in the Appendix at the end of this book.

77 Brewer, *The sinews of power*, p. 147.

Netherlands had a much more prominent political existence than in Britain, and this required the realization of urban public revenue. Urban indirect taxes had developed already since at least the thirteenth century. Receipts from urban excises were even used to pay interest on urban loans already in the fourteenth century.[78]

A remarkable aspect of the British fiscal system was, in contrast, 'the fragility of municipal finances' in the early modern period.[79] No urban excises and no urban loans developed in British towns. Even in seigniorial towns with some self-government around 1540 the level of urban revenue was very low. Examples available in the literature suggest how much lower, indeed, than in provincial towns in the Netherlands.[80] The large urbanized area of London outside its City did not even have a centralized governing body. It were the guilds, the companies and the parishes that performed and financed a multitude of social and economic tasks, that were organized and financed by means of urban governments in the Netherlands, like the solving of disputes, poor relief, providing granaries, or even being a source of troops and weapons in emergencies.[81] In Britain the largest source of income of city-corporations was rental income from property, while dues, tolls and fines were the other, less important, income sources.[82] Even in London other indirect taxes than tolls were in 1584/5 not mentioned among the main revenue sources of the city.[83] Urban tolls existed in the Dutch Republic as well, but among the urban taxes they were not a very important source of revenue.

78 Zuijderduijn, *Medieval Capital Markets*.

79 Ian Archer, 'Politics and government 1540–1700', in: *Cambridge Urban History* Cambridge Histories Online (Cambridge 2008) pp. 235–262, p. 246.

80 Archer, 'Politics and government 1540–1700', p. 246: urban revenue was 40 to 80 pounds per annum for provincial towns with a population of 2,500 to 5,000; as 1 pound contained in 1540 153,4 gr silver and 1 guilder 19,15 gr silver (http://www.iisg.nl/hpw/data.php) this equaled maximally about 640 guilders per year; annual urban revenue in Zwolle, a Dutch town with a population of 6,500 in 1599 and probably less in 1540/50 was in 1550 about 15,000 guilders, 35% of which came from excises; annual urban revenue in Dordrecht with a population of 11,700 in 1514 and perhaps about 15,000 in 1540/50, was about 9,000 guilders about 45% of which from excises (Van der Heijden, *Geldschieters*, pp. 270, 274).

81 Ibidem, p. 333.

82 J. Innes and N. Rogers, 'Politics and government 1700–1840', in: *Cambridge Urban History II* (Cambridge 2008), p. 548 Cambridge Histories Online.

83 V. Harding, 'The crown, the city and the orphans: the city of London and its finances, 1400–1700' in M. Boone, K. Davids and P. Janssens (eds.) *Urban public debts. Urban government and the market for annuities in Western Europa (14th–18th centuries)* (Trunhout: Brepols, 2003) pp. 51–61, p. 56.

The oldest form of domestic indirect taxation in Britain, apart from urban tolls, was the granting of royal monopolies to wholesale producers in exchange for a certain sum. A group of soap makers paid the crown, for instance, 8 pounds per ton for a monopoly on the sale of soap in the 1630s. Like the customs this kind of taxation was seen by the king as a prerogative of the crown. Monopolies also consisted for salt, starch and coal. The profits to monopolists are reported to have been exorbitant in comparison to the advantage for the crown.[84] In the Dutch Republic monopolies remained an exception. They were granted only incidentally to producers of certain products like brandy and tobacco. It is known that the introduction of a monopoly on brandy in the province of Overijssel caused a revolt in the city of Zwolle in 1726 and that the revenues from the brandy-tax doubled at the same tax rate after the abolition of the monopoly in 1729.[85]

Excises came to be mostly leased to tax farmers in Britain, although tax farming of the customs was abolished already in the period between 1640 and 1662. An important reason for this was that the government continued, of course, to need credit. Cromwell, Britain's dictator after the decapitation of Charles I, as well as, later, Charles II remained to a large degree dependent on private financiers to finance short-term deficits in their war expenditure. The leasing of excise-revenue was eagerly accepted as the security for loans by financiers, since the farming of the customs had been abolished. Not only the London leases, but even the more cumbersome country leases of excises were increasingly taken up by wealthy London merchants and financiers. The West-Indian shipper and City of London alderman Martin Noell, for instance, leased excises on glass, copperas and alum, and, when tax farming was temporarily reintroduced for customs as well, in 1662, Charles II allowed him in addition the customs on wine, linen, silks and tobacco.[86] In 1671, when the king, needed a very large amount of money for the navy, the increased British excises were leased in their totality to a group of financiers, supported by a large conglomerate of London brewers and subsequently subcontracted by them to smaller collectors.

In the Dutch Republic, most indirect taxes were also farmed until 1748 as we saw. A difference between the two systems was, however, that in the Dutch

84 For the 1630s the total costs to consumers of the monopolies was £750,000, the total profit to the crown only £100,000, whereas the farming of the customs cost £420,000 and provided a net revenue of £350,000; Braddick, *The nerves of state,* p. 78.

85 S. Elte, 'Het monopolie-oproer in Zwolle in mei 1726', *Tijdschrift voor Geschiedenis* 68(1955) pp. 224–237.

86 Ashworth, *Customs and excises*, pp. 100–101.

Republic tax farming was not used for public borrowing. This made it easier to sustain competition between a rather large number of small farmers. Only during the first half of the eighteenth century larger farms came to be preferred by the provincial governments, because they were less prone to failure, which would contribute to the tax riots directed against the increasingly wealthy tax farmers of 1747/8. In Britain, the complete abolition of tax farming already in 1683 would require new methods of loan financing which will be discussed and compared to those in the Dutch Republic in the last section of this chapter.

Already before 1683 the whole excise administration was centralized and regularized by the British government to increase excise revenue.[87] Since 1674 the farmers had to hand over their account books to inform the government about their costs and profits, as had been done with the customs farms before they were abolished.[88] In 1676/7 out of a gross revenue amount of £710,000 nearly 9 percent turned out to have gone to administrative costs. This was the same percentage as the collection costs for the common means in Holland after the abolition of tax farming in 1748. As tax farmers had, of course, a personal interest in keeping the costs of administration as low as possible to increase their profit margin, this can be seen as an indication of the remarkable efficiency of Holland's tax administration. This profit margin appeared to have been no less than on average nearly 20 percent in Britain in the 1670s. In the Dutch Republic, the competition between a large number of rather small tax farmers, will have made their profit margins smaller, certainly so during the seventeenth century.

As the British excise receivership had in fact become a credit agency, it was hard to abolish the tax farming system as long as the government was dependent on loans and as long as the loans from farmers had not yet been totally redeemed. In 1683 at last, however, after some years of peace and of revenue increases, and thanks to a general increase in trade and welfare, all outstanding loans from tax farmers could be redeemed indeed, and tax farming, which for the customs had been permanently abolished already in 1671, could be abolished for the excises as well. Subsequently an aggressive campaign for fiscal reform started under James II (1685–1688), in order to secure maximum tax extraction, by means of regular inspection circuits and standardized instruction to gauge and to measure taxable goods.[89]

87 Brewer, *Sinews*, p. 221: 'Since the end of the seventeenth century the governmnt grew ever more eager for detailed and precise information to be more effective in its fiscal policy. The most effective example was the administration of the excise'.

88 Ashworth, *Customs and excises*, p. 108.

89 Brewer, *Sinews*, p. 94.

By then the British population will have gradually become more or less accustomed to the inevitability of excises. Probably even more important to explain the improved acceptance of excises was that real wages had entered a period of continuous increases since c. 1650,[90] which will have made price-increases resulting from indirect taxation less troublesome. The price increasing effect of excises was of course more of a burden to the 'common man' in periods when real wages were continuously declining, which was the case in Britain during the first half of the seventeenth century.[91]

The importance of indirect taxes in British increased from on average 18 percent of total public revenue during the years 1661–1674 to on average 32 percent already during the years 1675–1687. This makes it unlikely that the increasing importance of domestic indirect taxation was due to the influence of the new Dutch King who only entered Britain in 1688, although it is true that revenue from excises grew from on average 530,000 pounds in the last period to on average 980,000 pounds during the decade after the Glorious Revolution. The relative importance of domestic indirect taxation decreased to 22 percent in this decade, however.[92]

Parliament did still not like excises even after the Glorious Revolution, until 1702. Many members of parliament continued to argue that the Land tax was a tax that could much more easily be controlled by Parliament than excises, and that excises were, moreover, harsh on the poor.[93] The years 1692–1697 even saw a decrease again in excise revenues, from 1,214,000 to 919,000 pounds.[94] A small body of new excise legislation was accepted at the end of the 1690s, mainly additional duties on beer, wine and spirits, resulting in a remarkable increase to 1,413,000 pounds in 1699, but there was again a decrease to 986,000 pounds in 1701. Between 1688 and 1714 the bulk of tax increases was still borne by means of the land tax. It was apparently the increasing burden of direct taxes during the very expensive War of the Spanish Succession that contributed to the final acceptance of indirect taxation.

After 1702 fiscal policy was almost never again stopped by parliamentary opposition.[95] Already since 1688 there was an extraordinary lack of popular resistance to excise taxation, except for some riots against the malt tax in Scotland in 1725 and, more important, the so-called Excise Crisis of 1733. Under Prime

90 Allen, *The British Industrial Revolution*, p. 123 fig. 5.6.
91 Allen, *The British Industrial Revolution*, p. 123 fig. 5.6.
92 Figures for 1661–1688 in Chandaman, *English public revenue*, pp. 24–27.
93 Brewer, *Sinews*, pp. 147–148.
94 Mitchell and Deane, *British historical statistics*, p. 386.
95 Brewer, *Sinews*, p. 149.

Minister Walpole new excises on tea, chocolate and coffee had been introduced in 1724 without problems, and even on salt in 1732. When he proposed in 1733, however, to replace the customs duties on wine and tobacco – goods very prone to smuggling – by excise duties, as one of the measures to allow a reduction in the land tax from 4 shillings to 1 shilling in the pound, a press campaign against this change and against the increasing expansion of government bureaucracy started. Parliament received a flood of petitions of shopkeepers and tradesmen from all over the country against the exclusive powers of search of the excise-men, and in London demonstrations against Walpole were organized. The proposal was withdrawn.[96]

Brewer described convincingly the increased skill and efficiency in the levying of excises after the abolition of tax farming.[97] The most important factors in the explanation of the impressive and relatively trouble-free growth in total excise revenues in Great Britain, as visible in Figure 5.5a, were, however, no doubt the introduction of more excises and population growth and economic growth during the eighteenth century. A kind of 'tax ceiling' seems to have been reached for indirect taxation in the Dutch Republic during the first half of the eighteenth century related to the economic stagnation of the period. Excise revenue *per capita* remained higher, nevertheless, in the federal Dutch Republic than in centralized Britain until about 1760, with the exception of the years 1748/9, when they were temporarily abolished as a result of tax riots (see Figure 5.6).

During the later decades of the eighteenth century, Britain was evidently better able to obtain increasing amounts of tax revenue per capita from price increasing indirect taxes mainly burdening the 'common man' than the Dutch Republic. As total tax revenue remained higher in the Dutch Republic until at least about 1780 (see Figure 5.4), the Provincial States of the small federal Republic were apparently sooner inclined to a relatively large degree of direct taxation (Figure 5.7) than the national parliament of the much larger state of Britain.

The EIC, the VOC and Public Revenue

Already since the 1580s–90s public pressure developed in Britain for the idea that Britain's future survival and greatness as a nation lay in developing

96 P. Langford, *A Polite and Commercial People: England 1727–1783* (Oxford 1989); J. Cannon, 'Excise crisis.' *The Oxford Companion to British History* (2002) Encyclopedia.com (September 13, 2011), http://www.encyclopedia.com/doc/1O110-Excisecrisis.html.

97 Brewer, *Sinews*, pp. 100–101.

FIGURE 5.6 *Domestic indirect taxes per capita in Britain and the Dutch Republic, 1690–1794 (guilders).*

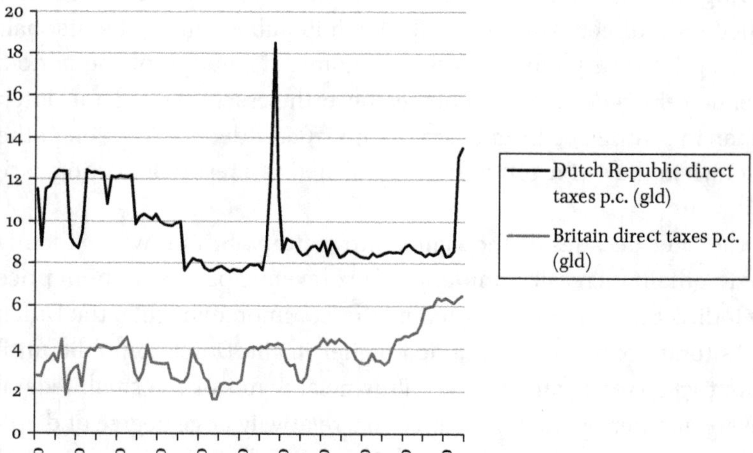

FIGURE 5.7 *Direct taxes per capita in Britain and the Dutch Republic, 1690–1794 (guilders).*

a colonial and trading empire overseas.[98] British traders in the Levant were alarmed by the success of Dutch ships to reach East-India over sea in 1599. In reaction to this a charter was granted by the government, already in 1600, to an East India Company with the task to gain markets in the East for British merchants to be able to avoid the high prices of spices and other products

98 Ph. Lawson, *The East India Company: a* history (London: Longman, 1993) p. 3.

from the Indies that had to be paid to Spanish, Portuguese and Dutch traders. Contrary to the VOC (established two years later), the original intention of the EIC was to focus entirely on trade and profit, not on conquest and colonization. Unlike the Dutch East India Company, the EIC did not start, as a form of planned armed expansionism, a national endeavour explicitly related to defence and war faring. A main argument for the Crown to lend the initiative its support was that it was seen as a promising new source of state revenue as well.[99]

In 1621 customs revenue from the EIC was £20,000 per annum, nearly 10% of total annual customs revenue, which was in fact seen as disappointing. The Dutch VOC, however, was exempted from paying customs during the first ten years of its existence,[100] and did not produce any addition to customs revenue until 1623.[101] Between 1623 and 1637 its contribution to Dutch customs revenue amounted to not much more than about 130,000 guilders, less than 6 percent of average total customs revenue in the Republic in that period, and equalling no more than about £12,000, despite a probably higher volume of Indian trade than that of the EIC at that time. I found no data on the contribution of the EIC to customs revenue in Britain in later periods.

For British public finance, it turned out to be very important already in the 1640s, that parliament was able to exploit the EIC for forced loans.[102] The EIC also offered the government an amount of £170,000 in loans on the occasion of the restauration of the monarchy in 1660, after having first honoured the king and his brother with presents and after having purged all republicans on its board.

The EIC would continue to be an important source of credit for the British government since then.[103] It was seen by the States of Holland as a very exceptional demarche to beg the VOC for a loan of two million guilders (less than 200,000 pounds) in 1672, the 'Year of Disaster' when the Dutch Republic was attacked from four sides.[104] The main explanation is probably that the VOC had

99 Lawson, *The East India Company*, pp. 20, 23, 29.

100 P. van Dam, *Beschryvinge van de Oostindische Compagnie. Eerste boek, deel II* ed. F.W. Stapel (The Hague 1929) p. 485.

101 V. Enthoven, 'Van steunpilaar tot blok aan het been. De Verenigde Oostindische Compagnie en de Unie', in: *De Verenigde Oostindische Compagnie tussen oorlog en diplomatie* eds. G.v.d. Knaap en G. Teitler (Leiden 2002) pp. 35–59, p. 41, p. 48.

102 Lawson, *The East India Company*, p. 38.

103 Ibidem, Chapter 4.3.b.

104 C. Hop and N. Vivien, *Notulen gehouden ter Staten-vergadering van Holland (1671–1675)*, ed. N. Japikse (Amsterdam: J. Müller, 1903) 309–314; van Dam, *Beschryvinge etc. Boek 1, deel 2*, p. 501.

to pay for its own protection and for military activities, whereas the EIC enjoyed the protection of the British navy. The relevant conclusion for our comparison is that the level of public finance in the decentralized Dutch Republic was higher than that in Britain despite the fact that its large East Indian Company was much less integrated in its public finance than that of the British EIC.

The last section of this chapter will discuss the remaining part of public revenue, that of long-term loans, since Dickson's study on Britain's 'Financial Revolution' (1688–1756) seen as an element that was at least as crucial in British superiority in public finance above its main rival France, as taxation, and since then a more important part of its public revenue than in the Dutch Republic, indeed, as we saw (Table 5.4).[105]

5.5 A Comparison of Loan Financing and Public Debt

Foreign Merchants and the King's Subjects versus Cities and Citizens

British Parliament functioned mostly as a brake on the ambitions of kings, during the centuries before the large-scale involvement of Britain in international war faring. In 1275 already, the British king tried to make himself less dependent on Parliament by negotiating a loan with Florentine merchant-bankers with the revenues of the new customs duty as their security. Until 1294 the Ricciardi family lent the crown 307,000 pounds, equalling about 13,000 pounds on average per year, a very important addition to the king's revenue, which is known to have totalled about 33,000 pounds in 1280.[106] In the second half of the fourteenth century the king turned increasingly to his own wealthy subjects for loans, directly, without involving parliament.[107] In fact he often just forced them to lend him sums, justifying this by the long-established traditional obligation to aid the sovereign in the defence of the realm in case of necessity. The forced loans were very controversial, the more so as they were in fact often not repaid.[108]

Loans to the Count of Holland were already in the thirteenth century guaranteed by the revenues of city governments. Here the Count was able in the fourteenth century to force city governments, instead of individual wealthy

105 See also, Daunton, 'The politics of British taxation', pp. 120–126.

106 N. Barratt, 'English royal revenue in the early thirteenth century and its wider context, 1130–1330', in *Crises, revolutions and self-sustained growth*, pp. 59–96, p. 70.

107 Ibidem, p. 75.

108 Ormrod, 'The West-European monarchies in the later Middle Ages', p. 128; the deposition of Richard II in 1399 was partly due to non-repayment of forced loans.

people, to lend him money for his wars, which they did by selling annuities for him, the first such sale being mentioned in 1345.[109] Urban magistrates in Holland always preferred selling annuities in the capital market above forcing their citizens, already in the late Middle Ages. City governments levied forced loans only very incidentally.[110]

In Britain London was a main source not only of tax revenue, but also of loans – and gifts – to the king. It was the only British city in which the king could find large sums within short periods. London's citizens were very often coerced to provide forced loans, often even without interest. The City of London was during the Middle Ages in fact known as 'the king's chamber', a kind of treasury of reserve for funding central government.[111] Forced loans were often raised by assessing the guilds or companies, which subsequently assessed their own members. Braddick mentions sixteen forced loans from 1557 to 1626. Of an amount of 461,000 pounds borrowed between 1574 and 1603 only 85,000 pounds bore interest.[112] Between 1625 and 1635 290,365 pounds was raised in loans on which no interest was paid, 177,192 pounds of which was still owed in July 1635.[113]

During the first decades after the Dutch Revolt, forced loans decided by Holland's Provincial States, and organized by city governments, were an important means of war financing as well. However, in contrast to Britain, interest was always promised on such loans, and also paid. Debt paper was issued on forced loans, which did not mention the name of the creditor which made it easily transferable. It could be sold or used as collateral for cash loans between private persons. Forced loans were felt as an unpleasant burden in the Dutch Republic no less than in Britain at the moment that they were levied. Nevertheless public debt redemption would not always be appreciated in the course of time, because it deprived people of a reliable source of interest income.[114]

---

109 June 1345: the cities of Dordrecht, Zierikzee, Middelburg, Delft, Leiden and Haarlem sold life-annuities for count William IV of Holland and Hainault to finance his wars against Utrecht and Frisia; Prevenier and Smit (eds.) *Bronnen voor de geschiedenis der dagvaarten in Holland, p.* 39 [nr. 72].

110 Zuijderduijn, *Medieval capital markets,* pp. 154, 274.

111 Harding, 'The Crown, the city and the orphans', p. 53.

112 Braddick, *The nerves of state,* p. 36.

113 Braddick, *State formation,* p. 24; Braddick, *The nerves of state,* pp. 85–86.

114 Sir William Temple, Britain's ambassador to the Netherlands in 1668–1670, wrote in 1676: '(…) when they pay off any part of the principal, those it belongs to receive it with tears, not knowing how to dispose of it to interest with such safety and ease'; cited in 't Hart, 'The Devil or the Dutch', p. 49.

As an alternative to raising forced credit through the Corporation of London on behalf of the guilds, the British crown also turned to the rising class of London capitalists for *voluntary* loans since the end of the fourteenth century. But until the 1660s no market existed in Britain where lenders could sell their claims on the state.[115] London's money market was aimed at short-term lending to traders, until then, and poorly suited to the provision of government loans.[116] In the early decades of the seventeenth century borrowing still depended on the security of the word of the monarch, whose reputation was bad, which made interest rates on royal loans high.

London's city elite appreciated, however, personal lending to the crown in exchange for the right to farm taxes, which was evidently a very attractive security.[117] London tax farmers became willing creditors to the monarchy, anxious to secure renewals of their profitable leases. Although tax farming became a criticized source of corruption and favouritism, government felt increasingly forced to fall back on customs farmers since the late 1620s and since the 1640s merchants could lease excises as well in exchange for loans. Loans funded on tax farming were short-term loans and they were pretty costly to the government given the high profits enjoyed by British tax farmers, known to be about 20 percent in the 1660s and most likely even higher in earlier periods.

In Holland even the 'obligations' on short-term loans became in practice long-term loans, as we saw in Chapter 2, and the interest on annuities and obligations decreased from about 12 percent in the 1580s to only 4 percent in 1655. This historical differences in raising loans for public expenditure, that were strongly related to a difference in the character of urbanization in both states, would have much more influence on the course of subsequent developments in loan financing in Britain, than what the famous seventeenth century Finance Minister George Downing would call the 'Dutch example'.

Downing and the Dutch Example

During the turmoil of the 1640s and 1650s institutions as the Corporation of London and the Livery Companies appeared to be very unwilling to act as intermediaries for public borrowing any longer. War expenditure in Britain in this period was mainly financed by a huge increase in direct taxation and by the sale of seized assets of enemies of the revolution.[118] Prominent merchants

115 Dickson, *The Financial Revolution in Britain*, pp. 39, 43.

116 Braddick, *The nerves of state*, p. 35.

117 London yielded 50 to 75 percent of total customs revenue between 1558 and 1714; Braddick, *The nerves of state*, p. 65.

118 Braddick, *The nerves of state*, p. 16.

still remained government creditors as farmers of the excise taxes,[119] but customs farming had been abolished in 1640s and the revenue from excises was much less than that of the customs.

Since the 1660s the city of London, when providing a loan, took over the tax from which it had to be serviced, and interests on such loans were paid from then on by the Guildhall.[120] Although this resembles the way in which Charles v had been able to secure loans from the cities in the Netherlands since the 1540s, an important difference was of course that the British king remained dependent on just one, instead of on a network of cities that collectively discussed the necessity of loans. Britain's lack of an urban network and of urban financial development did not allow the kind of 'financial revolution' that was described by J. Tracy for sixteenth century Holland: large common loans based on a collectivity of cities, to be served by common taxation handed over to a provincial receiver.

Since the Restoration of 1660 government borrowing became mainly monopolized by a group of so-called 'goldsmith bankers' in London. They were ready to receive foreign money and to credit their customers with the equivalent in British currency on their account.[121] Already at least since about 1610 goldsmiths often functioned as 'scriveners' or cashiers for merchants, who deposited their money with them at an interest.[122] They could draw on these accounts by means of 'cashier notes'. This allowed payments among merchants by means of circulating 'cashier notes'. It also allowed the goldsmith to extend credit to merchants at of course higher interest rates than on the deposits. The goldsmith bankers discounted commercial bills as well as all kinds of government paper.

King Charles had an account at the leading London goldsmith Backwell, too, since 1660. The concept of '*public* credit' did in fact not yet exist in Britain, as loans, also for the Commonwealth, were at that time still negotiated on the personal credit of the king. A widespread idea seemed to have existed that an official public bank was out of place in a monarchy, and could only exist in republics.[123]

---

119 Braddick, *The nerves of state*, pp. 38–39; custom farming was abolished between 1640 and 1662; Chandaman, *The English public revenue*, p. 21.

120 Braddick, *The nerves of state*, p. 40.

121 Clapham, *The Bank of England*, pp. 7–9.

122 According to Clapham, *Bank of England*, p. 10 they paid in the 1660s 6 percent on deposits.

123 Clapham, *Bank of England*, p. 10; also S. Pincus, *The first modern revolution*, (New Haven: Yale University Press, 2009) p. 395; for a general discussion of 'princely' versus 'republican' fiscal policy see also L. Pezzolo, 'Republics and principalities in Italy', in: *The rise of fiscal states*, pp. 267–285, p. 278.

Goldsmith bankers enjoyed returns of 10 or even 12 percent on advances to the government, at a time when Holland's provincial government paid already only 4 percent on its debts.[124] The goldsmith bankers paid the wide circle of private lenders to which they had access, much lower interest rates than they received from the state, the legal maximum interest rate in Britain for private persons being 6 percent.[125]

Since 1665 the new Secretary of the Treasury George Downing (1623–1684), who had been the king's representative at The Hague in the Dutch Republic before this appointment, started to develop a consistent policy to improve the credit of his government. He wanted the Treasury to be able to address the public directly to subscribe state loans, as was done in the Dutch Republic by means of the provincial receivers, and thus to undercut the bankers. Downing is thought to have been the author of the 'Additional Aid Act', the first attempt at a public loan of £1.25 million to be levied in 24 monthly instalments, asked from parliament in 1665 for the second naval war against the Dutch.

The clauses of this Act can be viewed as the start of a change of mentality in governmental circles, that prepared the ground for the 'Financial Revolution' that would gradually unroll between 1688 and 1756, and that would result in a permanent debt at low rates of interest, as it can be said to have developed in the Dutch Republic since the first decade of the seventeenth century culminating in the voluntary interest conversion to only 4 percent in 1655. Downing can be seen as an early example of a new political elite that took pride in engaging a struggle with private financial power to command more financial resources for the public cause in a clever and efficient way. The 'Additional Aid Act' of 1665 shows a beginning awareness that a powerful efficient government, able to raise enough money for a military power strong enough for wars with other European powers, required public support in parliament as well as strict procedures in financial affairs. That's why these clauses will be discussed in some more detail in comparison with practices in the Dutch Republic, which will turn out to have been quite different in several aspects.

Firstly, to the annoyance of the king the notion of 'audit' – a retrospective check if expenditure was used to the purpose intended – became a norm with this act. Auditing had been normal for provincial administrations in the Netherlands already since the late medieval Burgundian administration. The registers in which in Britain the monthly revenues of the Additional Aid of

124 H. Roseveare, *The Treasury 1660–1870. The foundations of control* (New York: Columbia University Press, 1973) pp. 23–25.

125 Braddick, *The nerves of state*, pp. 39, 41; Dickson, *Financial Revolution*, p. 46.

1665 would be recorded, and those for the recording of the war expenditure for which it was granted, would be open to *public* inspection, however.[126] This suggests that in principle just everyone was allowed to see the records, a remarkable requirement, which was definitely not a feature of the Dutch fiscal system before the 'Batavian Revolution' of 1795. During his period as British ambassador in the Netherlands Downing may have seen the printed overviews of the revenues of all the different 'common means' of the province of Holland, from which a large part of Holland's interest burden had to be paid, and that were produced each year since 1650 by its Finance Office, neatly specified for each of the sixteen tax districts. These supplied the Provincial States with information on the maximum amounts available for interest payments at the provincial receivers in Holland's cities. There is no indication, however, that these overviews enjoyed in general a wider circulation than among city governments and their representatives in the Provincial States alone.[127] A long-time experience with reliable interest payments had been, quite probably, much more important for public credit in the Republic than this, rather restricted, 'transparency'.

Secondly, the 'Additional Aid Act' required payments to be done in a strictly predetermined numbered order in order to prevent corruption and favouritism in payment priorities. The payment orders issued by the Treasury would be numbered accordingly and the numbers to be redeemed were to be announced in the public press,[128] an idea that was not borrowed from Dutch practices either. In the Dutch Republic each provincial government made written lists of the payments to be done by each of the tax receiver's offices, which were never published in print. The receivers had to send monthly reports to the provincial government to inform it of the state of their coffers to enable them to keep payments going as smoothly as possible. They were not allowed to effectuate any payments without having received the related written order, with the exception of interest payments, for which receivers were automatically discharged beforehand, which implied that they were seen as first priority. No mention at all has been found in Dutch archives of numbered payment orders to ensure people that they would be paid when it was their turn. Public credit in the Netherlands was built but on the long-term experience of investors that interest payments enjoyed high priority.

The new procedure in Britain was an important improvement in comparison with the loans in the form of advances by tax farmers, who had the power to

126 Roseveare, *The Treasury*, p. 24.

127 W. Fritschy, 'The efficiency of taxation in Holland'.

128 Roseveare, *The Treasury*, p. 33.

withhold tax receipts not only for interest payments, but also for redemption, thus jeopardizing other payments.[129] Payment orders on the Additional Aid of 1665 were decided to be of three kinds: those to department officials such as the Paymaster of the Forces, and those to suppliers of goods and services for the war; these would both be paid as soon as the necessary amounts in the monthly instalments of the loan would allow payment and they would both bear no interest. The third kind of payment orders were those to repay individuals who lent the king money on the credit of the tax receipts, called 'Treasury Bills'. Only these received an interest rate of 6 percent.

A difference with the Dutch Republic remained, however, that the Treasury bills had still to be redeemed within 24 months and were not yet long-term (permanent) loans as Holland's 'obligations' had (gradually) become. It was an additional difference that in the Dutch Republic interest was also paid on short-term military debts due to the system of the 'military solicitors' that had developed in the Dutch Republic since the end of the sixteenth century (see Chapter 3). Since 1676 this was limited to a maximum of 6.95 percent per year (gradually to be reduced to 3.48 percent at the end of the Dutch Republic).[130] The solicitors in their turn borrowed money from private persons at rates of mostly 3.5 to 4 percent. The short-term loan facility offered by the military solicitors contributed to the possibility to keep interest payments by tax receivers a priority in the Dutch Republic.

The third novelty introduced by the Act for the Additional Aid of 1665 was that it would be legally allowed for all three kinds of payment orders to be transferred to third parties by written endorsement with notification to the Exchequer. They could be used to raise cash with bankers, or even as means of payment among private parties. This allowed private economic transactions to continue, therefore despite the huge money transfers necessary for the war. By issuing transferable payment orders, the Treasury became in fact a kind of bank itself. Initially it seemed a success indeed, and the orders of payment began to circulate. This implied at the same time, of course, a risk of overdrawing, when government needs were acute and Treasury management was not firm, which was exactly what would happen. In the Netherlands over-issue of debt paper was prevented by the system of strictly controlled provincial tax receivers in a network of cities. The most spectacular example of a fraud that had partially existed in negotiating money instead of collecting arrears in the tax on real estate, was that of the receiver-general of the Generality Doubleth

129 Roseveare, *The Treasury*, p. 25.

130 Zwitzer, *De militie*, p. 93.

in the 1620s, whose office was not part of Holland's strictly controlled urban network (see Chapter 2.4).[131]

An important fourth novelty of the Act of 1665 was of course that the interest on the British interest bearing debt paper was not only much lower than what the king was forced to pay to the goldsmith bankers for loans, or what he lost in taxes due to the profits of the tax farmers, but that the debt service was now guaranteed by Parliament instead of by the King, because the clauses were part of a Parliamentary Act. Especially this was similar, indeed, to the Dutch Republic, where loans and their conditions were always the result of decisions by the Provincial States. An important difference with Britain remained, however, that in the Dutch Republic redeemable annuities and Holland's 'obligations' were in practice long-term loans.

In short, the main aim of the clauses for Additional Aid of 1665 was to attract money from small lenders at a moderate rate of interest to undercut in this way the group of goldsmith-bankers with their near monopoly on government short-term lending at high interest rates. This aim was evidently inspired by the Dutch example, but the way in which it was realized can only very partly be said to have been modelled on Dutch examples.

Two last points have to be made as to the supposed influence of the Dutch example on Downing. Firstly, Downing had become convinced that to exceed the Dutch in creditworthiness each new government loan should be funded on a specific part of revenue. Secondly, he was convinced that all revenues should be placed under the centralized control of a powerful Treasury.[132] These two requirements were never features of the financial system of the Dutch Republic. Loans were nearly always funded on *all* the tax revenues of a province, not each loan on a specific part of revenue. In Holland it was even not only funded on the 'common means'. Holland's 'General Receiver', whose main revenue consisted of ordinary and extraordinary taxes on property, paid in 1651 nearly 40% of Holland's interest burden.[133] The experience that the tax receiver in their city that sold Holland's 'obligations', enjoyed enough tax revenue to pay the interests due on what he had sold (after deduction of the taxation thought necessary by the Provincial States) appeared to be in practice at least as effective to maintain creditworthiness, as 'transparency' by means of centralized earmarking of the revenues of a specific tax for the interest payments on a specific loan.

---

131 Hart, 'Staatsfinancien als familiezaak', pp. 57–67.

132 Roseveare, *Treasury*, p. 23; R. Bonney, 'Revenues', in idem (ed.) *Economic systems and state finance*, pp. 423–507, p. 444.

133 *GFH*, p. 40; Fritschy, 'A "financial revolution" reconsidered', p. 77.

Centralized control in the Dutch Republic over the tax receivers that had to sell annuities and obligations existed only on the provincial level. In case of a loan annuities had to be sold by Holland's tax receivers according to a distributive key, that was determined by the amount in taxes each of them could be expected to receive and their other expenditure obligations, in order to safeguard a smooth payment of interest. Tax receivers did take care not to exceed the amount that they were allowed to borrow by means of the sale of annuities and obligations.[134] The fact that the actual implementation of provincial financial policy was decentralized across many tax receivers appeared to be a better check against an over-issue of obligations than the centralized procedure in Britain, which would not be able to prevent the 'Stop of the Exchequer' that had to be proclaimed in 1672. A national bank, that could take decisions independently from the government, would, after 1694, become the main check in Britain, on an over-issue of short-term debt paper not covered by additional parliamentary tax grants, as the one that led to the Stop of the Exchequer in 1672. The establishment of the Bank of England in 1694 would be a crucial element of Britain's 'Financial Revolution', that was not required in Holland's fiscal system, based as it was on a network of tax receivers grafted upon its 'urban system'.

As regards Downing's preference for a centralization of interest payments in the Treasury, it may be noticed that it was in fact rather one of the strengths of the system of the Dutch Republic, that they were done *de*centralized by the tax-receivers of the 'common (general) means' who had sold the loans in all tax districts and who were allowed to give absolute priority to interest payments from the receipts of *all* the 'common (general) means' in their tax district. This system made it much less easy to divert the money necessary for interest payments to other aims than in the case of a completely centralized treasury, not only because of the intensive control by Holland's Finance Office on their financial management, but also because of the likeliness of personal ties of the tax receivers with investors in public debt in the same city.

Direct access to a large public of small long-term lenders, instead of a dependency upon a small group of large financiers, was what Downing rightly

134 The correspondence of Holland's state pensionary with tax receivers as cited in Fritschy, 'The poor, the rich and the taxes', p. 251, shows examples of Amsterdam's receiver Scott receiving, in January 1710, explicit permission from the state pensionary to sell more than his share, and reports by the receivers of Haarlem and The Hague informing the state pensionary that the same was possible in their cities.

envied in the Dutch fiscal system.[135] A really widespread access to small lenders was much harder to realize in Britain, however, than in the Dutch Republic, because of the lack of an urban network of cities and the lack of a long history of urban long-term public debts.

'1672' in Britain

After the end of the Dutch Naval War in 1667 the British government continued to issue 'Treasury Bills', now no longer on the credit of an earmarked tax, but on public revenue in general, and in round sums of 100 or 1000 pounds with no reference to the expenditure for which it was meant. Downing's carefully devised provisions were abandoned. London's goldsmith 'bankers' in Lombard Street continued, nevertheless, to accept this paper from holders – at unknown discount rates – with the result that, by 1672, the government was in debt to them for about one million pound,[136] while total public revenue in the five preceding years had been not more than on average about 1.3 million pounds per annum.[137]

The goldsmith bankers started to refuse the king loans, however, when he badly needed much more money for the Third Naval War with the Dutch as part of the common attack with France and some German states on the Republic in 1672. That's why the Crown decided in January 1672 to lease all the excises together to one group of financiers (as was the custom in France) to be able to borrow a great amount of money at once. It was also decided, however, to stop to redeem the bills charged on general tax revenues, a decision that came to be known as 'the Stop of the Exchequer of 1672'. It put bankers that had accepted such paper as a security for loans and that relied on their redemption on the promised date, into serious trouble, as it was evident to the merchant community that this 'Stop' meant that the large amounts in circulating 'cashier notes' were now to a much smaller amount backed by cash money than before.

Continental commercial city governments had perceived already earlier the risks of an uncontrolled increase in the credit possibilities of circulating cashier notes, and the benefits for trade, when the urban government would offer a possibility to guarantee the security of money transfers among merchants

---

135 Roseveare, *The Treasury*, p. 25: 'it was the small investor whom Downing hoped to attract, anxious as he was to undercut the group of goldsmith bankers, who, since the Restoration had monopolized government borrowing with a return of 10 or even 12 per cent'.

136 Clapham, *The Bank of England*, p. 12.

137 http://esfdb.websites.bta.com; Data prepared on English revenues, 1485–1815, by Professor P.K. O'Brien and Mr P.A. Hunt.

without cash, as was discussed in Chapter 4. In the Dutch Republic Amsterdam established an urban exchange bank (*Wisselbank*) controlled by the urban government in 1609, inspired by earlier initiatives elsewhere, and the same was done later in the cities of Rotterdam and Middelburg. The Exchange Bank exchanged foreign coins according to their real silver or gold value and credited merchants for the sums involved on an account in their name in the bank, which they could use for payments, and it accepted deposits to enable merchants to make payments to each other by means of transfers to each other's accounts. It was made obligatory also for foreigners to use the Exchange Bank for all commercial payments larger than 300 guilders in Amsterdam.[138]

Amsterdam's famous urban Exchange Bank was not allowed to discount bills of exchange or to extend other forms of credit to merchants. The extension of credit remained the activity of private bankers. Neither did this bank ever, as was emphasized already in the chapter on the comparison with Venice, issue loans to provincial governments. Brewer thought that the Dutch governments 'were able to borrow heavily without insolvency' because of 'their sophisticated banking system'.[139] In fact however, it was the decentralized system of tax receivers that fulfilled these 'banking' functions for the provincial governments in all the provinces, not the private bankers or the urban 'exchange banks'.

The decision in 1672 by the British government to stop repayments of short term credit paper realized since 1665, was in fact only a partial 'stop of the exchequer', as the interest of 6 percent on this paper continued to be paid (until 1680).[140] Bankers just had to except new annuities without a redemption date in exchange for the old ones, which were comparable therefore to Holland's 'obligations'. Due to the 'Stop' bankers holding this debt paper had much less cash available in 1672 than they could have expected and were forced, therefore, to refuse to honour obligations to third parties, which caused a shock. Especially the two largest bankers, that had been able to act, if necessary, as bankers' bankers before 1672, were hit hard, and lost many customers. Although they were able to continue their existence, they were no longer able to fulfil this 'central bank' function since then. Nevertheless, the continuation of the interest payments ensured that a lively market in the new annuities emerged immediately as well.[141] An important difference with Holland's 'obligations' was of course,

138 Dehing and 't Hart, 'Linking the fortunes, p. 46.

139 Brewer, *Sinews*, p. 24.

140 J. Keith Horsefield, 'The "Stop of the Exchequer" Revisited', *The Economic History Review* 35, 4 (1982) pp. 511–528.

141 Braddick, *The nerves of state*, p. 42; Braddick, *State formation*, p. 259.

that these obligations had *gradually* developed from a short-term into a long-term paper, instead of by a sudden government decision to stop redemption.[142]

I found no mentioning of prices of the new 1672 annuities without redemption date in Britain, but as long as loans remained a royal affair, without parliamentary involvement, King Charles II and his government will not have enjoyed much credit. After 1680 interest arrears on these debts that had not been tied to specific parts of state revenue, as would again be the case with subsequent public loans began to accumulate. At their final settlement in 1705 both the principal and the interest debt on these old loans were halved.[143] In contrast, provincial governmental in the Dutch Republic did not have to be concerned about final settlements to redeem debts, which of course largely eased accurate interest payments.

Voluntary public loans became impossible for the British government in the 1670s due to the 'Stop of the Exchequer'; neither could the king hope for cooperation in London for forced loans any longer at the time.[144] This meant that the British government had – to a much larger degree than the Dutch – to resort mainly to huge increases in direct taxes. French subsidies, received secretly by the British king for his support in the attack on the Dutch republic in 1672, were good for no more than about 10 percent of total revenue in the top-years 1671/2–1673/4.[145] After mistrust of their French ally had begun to increase, and after the British fleet had suffered much damage in four battles with the Dutch under Admiral De Ruyter – and had lost, moreover, hundreds of merchantmen to Dutch corsairs – Britain hastily concluded peace with the Dutch in 1674 due to sheer lack of money.

In Holland the prices of public debt paper plummeted in the 'Year of Disaster', because many feared that this massive attack would be the end of the Republic. Gelderblom and Jonker found prices as low as 30 percent in the urban archives of Gouda, one of Holland's cities. Early 1673 the price of Holland's 'obligations' had recovered again to 76 percent, however. About half of the debt increase during the war between 1672 and 1678 took the form of forced loans by the common decisions of the cities (and the nobility) in the Provincial States, and the States of Holland had to pay 6 percent on short-term voluntary advances on the revenue of the forced loans. Nevertheless, long-term voluntary

142 W. Fritschy, 'A "financial revolution" reconsidered: public finance in Holland during the Dutch Revolt', *Economic History Review* 56 (2003) pp. 57–89.

143 Dickson, *Financial Revolution*, p. 44.

144 Ashworth, *Customs and excise*, p. 18.

145 Chandaman, *The English public revenue*, pp. 324, 333.

loans continued to be possible as well, although as late as 1678 an interest of 5% instead of 4%, had to be offered.[146]

During the years between 1674 and 1688 Britain was no longer involved in wars on the continent and hardly in domestic military affairs (except for two short lived rebellions in Scotland and southern Britain when the Roman-Catholic James II succeeded in 1685 his brother Charles II). This gave it a breathing space to reorganize part of its state finance. The increase in total public revenue since about 1680 allowed the repayment of all advances to excise farmers and the abolition of tax farming in 1683, resulting subsequently in large increases in excise revenue as well.

The abolition of tax farming did not yet mean, moreover, that short-term borrowing on the credit of excises had had to end. 'Monied men' were appointed as cashiers in the excise departments with easy access to funds in the private money market. They appeared to be able to lend short-term sums of 150,000 to 250,000 pounds per year to the monarch on the security of the constant flow of revenues in their offices.[147] This strongly reminds one, of course, of the provincial receivers of the 'common means' fulfilling a similar function for the provincial governments in the Dutch Republic. The difference remained again, however, firstly that the loans in Britain still remained short-term loans, and secondly that provincial governments in the Dutch Republic were not dependent on the contacts of their officials in just one city, but had a very wide and fine-meshed direct access to capital available among the public at large by means of their tax receivers in many cities. Contrary to Dutch tax receivers, individual financiers in London were able to secure considerable political influence in exchange for their services to the king, which was a source of concern to many contemporaries.[148]

The need for a better banking system was felt and voiced in London, where private bankers continued to issue bank notes which circulated without any regulation.[149] However an attempt for a 'City of London Bank' like the public banks in many continental commercial cities proved yet a failure in 1682.[150] In Britain it would be government's financial needs that gave the decisive push for the successful establishment of a 'Bank of England' in 1694 as a major step in its 'Financial Revolution'. As William Petty wrote in 1681: 'what remedy is

146 Gelderblom and Jonker, 'Public Finance and Economic Growth', p. 20; Fritschy, 'Efficiency', p. 64.

147 Brewer, *Sinews*, p. 94.

148 Braddick, *The nerves of state*, p. 18.

149 Dickson, *Financial revolution*, pp. 5–6.

150 Clapham, *Bank of England*, p. 13.

there if we have too little money? We must erect a Bank which well computed doth almost double the effect of our coined money'.[151]

Long-term instruments of private finance such as annuities, insurances and mortgages in the private financial sector started to develop in Britain in the 1670s. The first long-term loan on life annuities was floated in London in 1674.[152] Long-term investments in canal digging promoted internal trade. More joint stock companies, requiring long-term investment, came into existence. These new developments contributed to the development of a stock market.[153] So people became more accustomed to the idea of long-term investments. It would yet take some decades after the establishment of the Bank of England, however, for public finance, to reach the stable possibility of long-term loans at declining rates of interest, that had been in existence in the Dutch Republic since about 1600.

The Long Road of Britain's 'Financial Revolution'

The Glorious Revolution brought the start of Britain's involvement in European war faring, requiring huge sums of money. Its new Dutch king was the first to be completely dependent on Parliament to get the necessary sums. The time was obviously not yet ripe, however, for a change in fiscal policy towards a long-term debt, despite increases in long-term investments in the private sector and despite the increase in the revenues of excise taxation as a possible fund for interest payments on long-term loans. Until 1693 the war was mainly financed by short-term loans at rather high interest rates, and by large increases in direct taxation: direct taxation, which yielded less than 0.2 million pounds on average per year in the 1680s, provided more than 1.3 million pounds in 1689–91 and on average more than 2 million pounds per year in 1692–7.[154] In addition on average about 3 million pounds per year was raised in short-term debts during the years 1688–1694. These debts had usually to be redeemed within 3 to 5 years at interest rates of 7 to 8 percent.[155] The emergence of a sustainable long term public debt required evidently more than an increased power of Parliament. Apart from institutional change and appropriate economic conditions it required experimenting, and much time.

151 Clapham, *Bank of England*, p. 4.

152 Dickson, *Financial revolution*, p. 41.

153 Anne L. Murphy *The origins of English financial markets : investment and speculation before the South Sea Bubble* (Cambridge 2009); Braddick, *State formation*, p. 266.

154 Hunt and O'Brien; http://esfdb.websites.bta.com.

155 Dickson, *Financial revolution*, p. 344 Table 53; O'Brien and Hunt, 'The rise of a fiscal state', p. 55.

It was not before January 1693 that Parliament decided for the first time to sell life annuities as a modest additional source of finance for the war. It was hoped to raise 1 million pounds by means of tontine life-annuities – a very uncommon loan format in the Dutch Republic, only very incidentally used by urban governments and never used by provincial governments for state finance – which offered a group of subscribers a revenue of 10 percent per year, on the security of the revenue of new excises on beer, vinegar, imported beer, cider and brandy for a period of 99 years. The interest due would be divided among the group, which increased the interest per person if someone of the group died, and interest payments stopped after the last one had died. Not much more than 108,000 pounds could be raised in this way, however.[156] The subsequent sale of life annuities on the life of only one person, paying 14 percent per year as long as he or she lived, was more successful, although the invitation to subscription had yet to be renewed a year later to raise the last 118,506 pounds to complete the intended amount of one million pounds.

In the Dutch Republic, life annuities on one or two lives were already at the end of the sixteenth century seen as the least preferred way for raising long-term money by provincial governments, because they were much more expensive than redeemable annuities. Holland's state pensionary De Witt calculated in 1671 that at an interest rate of more than 6 percent life annuities were more expensive for the government than 4 percent redeemable annuities, due to the fact that they were often bought on the lives of new born children. They were, as a rule, only sold when it was feared that the market would not want to take enough 'obligations' or redeemable annuities. Between 1688 and 1700 only 23 percent of the increase of Holland's debt was due to the sale of life annuities at interest rates of 8 to 9 percent, much lower, therefore, than the 14 percent that was offered in Britain in 1693.[157]

In an attempt to raise money in a somewhat less expensive way the British government subsequently tried a lottery loan, hoping to profit of the increased public interest in lotteries in the private sector.[158] 14 percent interest during 16 years was promised on this loan, on the security of half of the revenue of new duties on beer, vinegar, cider and brandy, and buyers had the chance to receive an amount of maximally 1000 pounds and minimally 1 pound per year extra in a lottery in addition. All payments would stop after 16 years. Probably this loan

156 Dickson, *Financial revolution,* p. 48.

157 Dormans, *Het tekort,* pp. 80–81; NB there is a mistake in the headings of two of Dormans' columns '*Noorderkwartier Losrenten*' should be '*Zuiderkwartier Lijfrenten*'; '*Noorderkwartier Rest*' should be '*Noorderwkartiern Losrenten*.'

158 Dickson, *Financial revolution,* pp. 45–46.

was a success. It was decided to further explore the preferences of the market by trying, only a month later, yet another, somewhat less expensive loan format by now selling 0.3 million pounds in life annuities at 14 percent on one life, 12 percent on two and 10 percent on three lives, on the security of 2/7 of the other half of the revenue mentioned above; the second variant turned out to be the most attractive of the three: 60 percent of the sales was on two lives, 35 percent on one.[159] However by the same Act of Parliament of 24 April 1694 it was decided to start a third way of raising money, different from addressing the public directly with sales of annuities.

The government had been approached by a group of London merchants that was ready to lend the state 1.2 million pounds at a rate of 8 percent on the security of the remaining 5/7 of the other half of the new duties just mentioned and a parliamentary decision for new customs duties. They asked in exchange to be incorporated as the 'Bank of England' with the right to give out bank-notes 'payable to bearer' to facilitate the payment traffic among merchants in the City of London.[160] The government, and in its wake Parliament, decided to agree, on the condition that at least half of the loan would be available by the first of August. The initial subscription to the bank, enabling it to the loan to the government, was completed in about ten days.[161] So this proved to be a much easier as well as a cheaper way to raise money for the war than the sale of life annuities directly by the government, but a way very different from that in the Dutch Republic.

The explanation for this success was that in this period in which national and international trade increased much faster than the available means of cash payment there was a real need among British merchants for a bank with a right to issue bank notes backed by governmental support. It allowed merchants having an account in this bank to pay each other without fear about the safety of the bank. Banknotes were in fact Britain's contribution to the evolution of European banking.[162] Neither the Exchange Bank in Amsterdam, nor that in Venice, or in other important commercial cities on the Continent had the right to issue bank notes. Payments were done by such banks by means of transfers in accounts. Holland's obligations were valued by Amsterdam's merchants mainly because they could be used as a widely-appreciated collateral, or as a temporary store of value that could easily be sold or purchased. Their format can hardly have allowed an easy use as a means of payment.

---

159 Dickson, *Financial revolution*, p. 48.

160 http://www.bankofBritain.co.uk/about/legislation/1694act.pdf; 5 & 6 Will. & Mar. c. 20.

161 Pincus, *The first modern revolution*, p. 390.

162 Clapham, *The Bank of England*, p. 5.

The new Bank of England with its credit facilities for merchants as well as for the government, which was so very different from Amsterdam's Exchange Bank, appeared to have been rather deeply mistrusted in Amsterdam during the first years of its existence, judging from the development of the exchange course made visible in Figure 5.8. This despite the fact that the Bank remained independent and could be expected never to agree to loans not backed by parliamentary decisions for new taxation. Only by 1700 the guilder course of the pound had returned to its customary level.

The idea that British credit structures were 'imitations' of those in the Dutch Republic, is evidently mistaken, therefore.[163] The accession of a Dutch Stadholder to the British thrones after 1688–9 did not at all lead to the adoption in Britain of 'financial techniques' developed in the Dutch Republic.[164] The

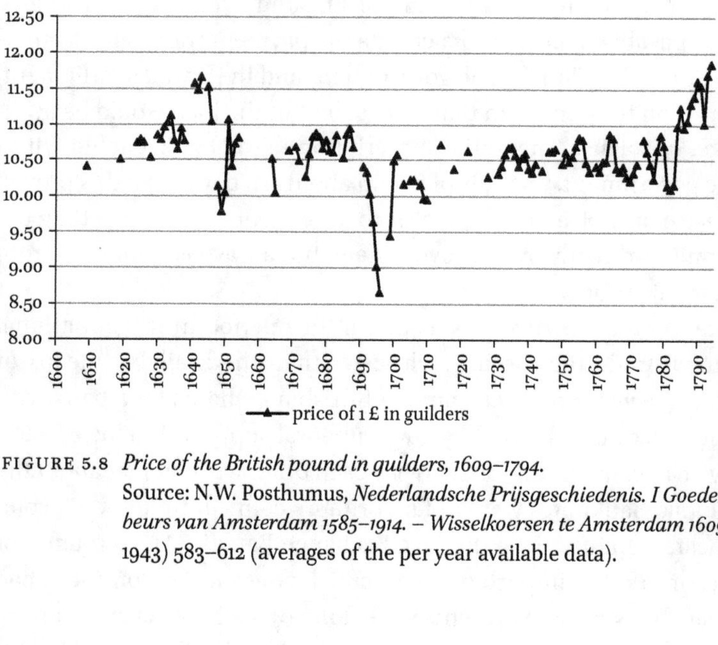

FIGURE 5.8 *Price of the British pound in guilders, 1609–1794.*
Source: N.W. Posthumus, *Nederlandsche Prijsgeschiedenis. I Goederenprijzen op de beurs van Amsterdam 1585–1914. – Wisselkoersen te Amsterdam 1609–1914* (Leiden 1943) 583–612 (averages of the per year available data).

163 Dickson, *Financial revolution*, p. 50; Scott, '"Good Night Amsterdam." Sir George Downing and Anglo-Duch Statebuilding', p. 337; see also the literature mentioned in footnote 40 in H. Scott, 'The Fiscal-Military State and International Rivalry during the Long Eighteenth Century', in: *The fiscal-military state in eighteenth century Europe: essays in honour of P.G.M. Dickson* ed. Chr. Storrs (Farnham: Ashgate 2009) pp. 23–53, p. 32.

164 In fact king William would have preferred a Land Bank to outdo the influence of the London business community; an initiative to this end would however become a failure; see 't Hart, 'The Devil or the Dutch', p. 51, referring to D. Rubini, 'Politics and the battle for banks, 1688–1697', *English Historical Review* 85 (1970) pp. 693–714.

establishment of the Bank of England rather fitted into a long tradition in Britain of dependence on direct contacts of the government with merchants for loans. The British merchant community disposed in this new bank of an intermediate institution independent from, but backed by the government, useful for themselves, and useful for the government, to obtain voluntary loans in an easy way. In the Dutch Republic, the function of intermediary, when the government needed loans, was fulfilled by provincial tax officials, with informal contacts with the economic elites of its main cities, never by public banking institutions like the Exchange Banks in Amsterdam and some other cities in the Dutch Republic.

The economists Sussman and Yafeh did point out already that, contrary to what earlier institutional economists thought, the increased parliamentary control on fiscal policy in Britain after the Glorious Revolution did not automatically result in low rates of interest very soon.[165] Until October 1710, during the last phase of the extremely expensive international War of the Spanish Succession, Holland had still been able to borrow at 4 percent, although it had been felt necessary to promise investors that the new loans during the war would be tax-free. Britain had to offer 9 percent interest on a new loan in January 1710.

In March 1711 Amsterdam's 'city-pensionary' Buys wrote to Holland's 'state pensionary' Heinsius, that he had received reports from London that about two million guilders had been invested by Dutchmen in a British lottery loan in March 1711.[166] This loan guaranteed investors a minimum yield of 6 percent and a chance on much more by means of the lottery part of the loan. It cost the British government about 10 percent, because of the prizes in the accompanying lottery. An emerging integration of the markets for public debts in London and Amsterdam forced Holland to start with a similar type of expensive loans as well in 1711, to prevent that capital flight would jeopardize the continuation of its own war efforts.

The different character of the development of the financial revolution in Britain is also apparent in the way in which the very high interest burden resulting from the War of Spanish Succession was reduced after the war. Whereas in the Republic governmental decisions to reduce interests were the main instrument to this end, in Britain it was a new private intermediary institution that played a central role to achieve this, without 'coercion'. It was the South Sea Company, which was founded in 1711 that would lure British holders in to

---

165 N. Sussman and Y. Yafeh, 'Institutional Reforms, Financial Development and Sovereign Debt: Britain 1690–1790', *Journal of Economic History* 66, 5 (2006) pp. 906–935.

166 Fritschy, 'The poor, the rich and the taxes in Heinsius' times', p. 250.

voluntary financial decisions that would led to important interest reductions for the government, and often to more severe losses for the private persons involved than the forced interest reductions as practiced in the provinces of the Dutch Republic.

In exchange for a monopoly on trade in the South Sea the South Sea Company had agreed to accept government debt paper as payment for its shares. In this way, the part of the British government debt that was short-term, could be consolidated into long-term debt. It was agreed that the government would have to pay the Company an interest of only 6 percent on the debt in the possession of the South Sea Company, at a time when the interest on its usual annuities was still 7 percent.[167] In 1718 the British government allowed the company the sale of new shares that could be paid with all types of government debt, now under the condition that the government would have to pay only 5 percent interest on debt paper in the possession of the South Sea Company, and after seven years only 4 percent. The prices at which the Company was able to sell its shares increased from on average about 113 percent of their nominal value in 1718 to 950 percent in June 1720.[168] By 1720 the Company was in the possession of 26 million pounds of the British public debt of then about 50 million pounds in exchange for no more than nominally 8.5 million in South Sea stock, that appeared to have been sold, therefore, at an average price of about 300 percent.[169]

The bubble burst after June 1721, when too ambitious initiatives of the Company had brought it into payments problems. The price of its shares declined to about 97 percent during the last four months of 1721.[170] The Company could be saved with the help of the Bank of England, that had avoided involvement in the speculative mania. It became an institution that mainly managed a large part of Britain's public debt. Former British holders of government debt, who had been lured into buying South Sea-shares at high prices in exchange for their government paper, will often have had greater losses than holders of Dutch public debts, confronted with forced interest reductions. The operations had evidently been to the advantage of the British government, however, as it had led to a considerable reduction in the interest rate to be paid on this debt.

167 Dickson, *Financial Revolution*, p. 86.

168 L. Neal, *The Rise of Financial Capitalism. International Markets in the Age of Reason* (Cambridge 1990).

169 Dickson, *Financial Revolution*, p. 122.

170 L. Neal, *The Rise of Financial Capitalism. International Markets in the Age of Reason* (Cambridge 1990).

The much earlier history of the establishment of a long-term public debt in the Dutch Republic, where the public was more accustomed to the fact that either an interest reduction, or (increased) taxes on bonds, were sometimes inevitable, and where differing decentralized collective decisions to this end could be taken in the provinces (see Chapter 3), had made the intermediary role of risky private initiatives as the South Sea Company, and its French parallel the Mississippi Company, unnecessary in the Dutch Republic.

Sussman and Yafeh's conclusion, that the cost of the public debt in Britain became lower than in Holland since 1728 was based on the amounts in interest payments in Holland before the deduction of the tax on bonds, due to which the real rate of interest on Holland's 4 percent-obligations and redeemable annuities was most of the time in fact only 2.5 percent. A voluntary interest conversion would certainly have been successful in Holland in peace years, but just continuing of the tax on bonds was evidently felt to be a preferable alternative. In fact the interest rate on government debt was in 1728 still clearly higher than in Holland therefore. The interest rates in most provinces in the Dutch Republic fluctuated between 4% and 3% since about 1730, according to the scarce available evidence, incidentally even decreasing to 2.5% like in Holland.

It should be added, on the one hand, that the increase in public debt in Holland with 67 million guilders (from 295 million to 362 million guilders) between 1740 and 1752 was by then for only about 30 percent the result of the sale of the ordinary 'obligations', it consisted for nearly 70 percent of much more expensive lottery loans. On the other hand, it may be added, however, that in Great Britain the total amount in new long-term loans realized between 1739 and 1748 amounted to only about 4.80 guilders on average per capita per year, whereas in Holland the amount invested in new loans amounted to 6.60 guilders on average per capita per year between 1740 and 1752.[171] After the war Holland's government was able to convert the expensive war loans into loans with the usual low rates of interest now on a voluntary basis.

Not only the cost of the British pubic debt remained higher than in the Dutch Republic for a long time during the eighteenth century, it would also last until the war of 1739–1748 before all long-term loans in Britain took the form of ordinary long-term debt which *could* be paid off, but need not be,[172] as was the case with public debts in the Dutch Republic already since the early

171 The average amount per investor per year was, of course, much higher, but I do not know of data that would allow an estimate of the total number of investors in public debt in both states.

172 Dickson, *Financial Revolution*, p. 244.

seventeenth century. For Dickson, the main historian of Britain's 'Financial Revolution', it was in fact even only Pelham's gradual reduction of the interest rate of 4 percent on by far the largest part of the public debt to only 3% between 1748 and 1756, that brought its completion.

5.6 Conclusion

Despite the persistent view that the Dutch and the British fiscal system came to resemble each other largely, especially after the Glorious Revolution, the differences between the two turned out to be at least as remarkable. Firstly, Britain had a very long history of forms of national taxation. Already in the Middle Ages voting for direct taxes became a national affair in contrast to the regionalized representative systems in the Netherlands. In addition, the structure of Britain's fiscal system was mainly determined by the distinction between non-parliamentary revenue – then good for about 75 percent of total revenue and largely consisting of customs revenue – and parliamentary revenue, largely consisting of direct taxation until the 1640s.

Secondly, a large difference between the two states was of course that until the last decade of the seventeenth century Britain was hardly involved in European land wars and did not yet experience until then the expensive financial consequences of the 'military revolution'. The total amount in public revenue remained lower than that in the Dutch Republic until nearly the end of the seventeenth century. Naval wars were much less costly than land wars and naval expenditure was a much larger proportion of military expenditure in Britain than in the Dutch Republic. During the Second English Naval War (1665–1667) British naval expenditure started to outreach that of the Dutch Republic. Despite yet remarkably large increases in Dutch naval expenditure during the Fourth English Naval War (1780–1784) its navy was by then no longer a match for that of Britain.

British commercial interests started to call for participation in warfare in Europe after the Glorious Revolution. The necessary rise in tax revenue would now become in much larger part realized by means of increases in indirect than in direct taxation, a development that continued during the eighteenth century. The Dutch Republic, in contrast, felt forced to diminish its military involvements after 1713, and to increase direct taxation much more than indirect taxation, whenever revenue increases were yet unavoidable. In addition, customs had always been a much less important part of Dutch than of British public revenue. Although Dutch per capita total taxation remained higher than in Britain for most of the eighteenth century, the probably still higher wealth of

Dutch taxpayers until far in the eighteenth century could no longer compensate their much lower number. The Dutch Republic was too *small* – rather than too *decentralized* – to be able to operate any longer as a Great Power internationally in the new historical situation in Europe: other states were no longer plagued by the internal religious turmoils of the two preceding centuries, and increased colonial competiton became an exclusive British-French affair in the course of the eighteenth century.

A third characteristic difference was the role for public finance of the East Indian chartered companies in the two states: important customs revenues as well as loans to the government in Britain were provided by the EIC, this in sharp contrast to the Dutch VOC. This implied that the difference in the amounts of public revenue per capita between the two states would have been even larger if the VOC would not have been expected to pay for its own defence and military activities outside Europe.

The fourth difference to be emphasized was Britain's long-term history of 'fragile municipal finance', visible in the absence of urban indirect taxes and urban public debts even in London. This may on the one hand have accounted for the slow and toilsome introduction of national excises in Britain during the seventeenth century. It meant on the other hand, that the British king had never been able, in contrast to rulers in the Netherlands, to rely on a network of city governments to get loans. London merchants were able to continue to claim customs and excise tax farms in exchange for loans until 1683. A dense urban network facilitating fiscal developments did not develop in Britain before the second half of the eighteenth century.

Extra public revenue for war faring by means of loans was needed in Britain as well as in the Dutch Republic and increasingly so in the course of time. George Downing had claimed that the way in which he tried to improve the credit of the British government to this end, already in the 1660s, was inspired by the Dutch Republic. This was true to the extent that he started to fund public credit on an Act of Parliament instead of remaining dependent on the king's credit with private bankers in London. In contrast to the Dutch Republic, however, he tried to realize his aim by emphasizing the importance of a powerful *central* Treasury and the funding of each public loan on a specific part of tax revenue. The strength of credit in the Dutch Republic had in fact consisted, however, in the *decentralization* of interest payments across the tax receivers in Holland, who were allowed, moreover, to give priority to interest payments loans from *all* the taxes they had to receive, and who were not allowed to issue more in loans than the amounts decided for by the Provincial States.

The 'Stop of the Exchequer' in Britain in 1672 showed that this decentralized structure was at that time safer than the availability of a central powerful

Treasury. Only a strong central bank, independent from the government, but with strong ties to the important merchants in the City of London and having been granted a monopoly on the issue of paper money, would make possible the issue of long-term loans at declining rates of interest, and an easy supply of short-term advances to the government at moderate interest rates in Britain as well. The increased transparency of public borrowing based on Acts of Parliament in combination with the establishment of a powerful bank regulated and backed by, but in its functioning independent from the government, were important preconditions of Britain's Financial Revolution. This was not the same as a public credit based on a long-term experience with the reliability of interest payments by means of a network of provincial tax receivers grafted upon the existence of a politically and economically rather integrated urban network.

The last difference between the two states was the trajectory along which Britian's Financial revolution was realised in the course of time. It would take several decades yet before public credit in Britain was more or less comparable to that in the Dutch Republic. Most of the time the real interest rate was, at least in Holland, but incidentally also in other provinces, still lower than in Britain even during the second half of the eighteenth century.

In sum: the comparison between the fiscal systems of Britain and the Dutch Republic did not support the idea that a centralized state with a national parliament and a central bank was fiscally more efficient than a decentralized federal state without a similar bank like the Dutch Republic. The comparison reinforced the conclusion of the fiscal viability of a federal state, where urbanization had resulted in the coming into being of a relatively intensely integrated urban system.

CHAPTER 6

A Comparison with the Ottoman Empire

6.1 Two Incomparable States

The last chapter of this book ventures a comparison of two extremely different states arisen from extremely different circumstances: the very large agrarian Ottoman Empire with its central bureaucracy, and the very small commercial, federal Dutch Republic.[1] During the sixteenth century the Ottoman Empire had developed into a feared neighbour and opponent of Venice and the Habsburg Empire and an ally of France against the Habsburgs. It came to be valued as a commercial relation not only by Venice and France, but also by Britain and the Dutch Republic. A comparison with the Ottoman Empire seemed interesting, not only because it was to a certain extent part of the European power struggle, but also because already contemporaries were fascinated by comparisons between the Ottoman Empire and West-European states.[2] A comparison has become more or less possible, as many research results on public finance in the Ottoman Empire became available during the last decades, including an important publication with many quantitative data.[3]

Already Montesquieu compared in his 'The Spirit of Laws' the fiscal system in the Ottoman Empire to that in West European states. During the Middle Ages people had come to prefer 'Mahometan' rule to the former Byzantine rule, he wrote, because under Islamic rule 'they were subjected to a simple tribute which was paid and collected with ease',[4] a view confirmed in modern

1 This chapter is a revised version of W. Fritschy, 'State formation and urbanization trajectories: state finance in the Ottoman Empire before 1800, as seen from a Dutch perspective', *Journal of Global History* 4 (2009) pp. 405–428 and idem, 'Indirect taxes and public debt in "the world of Islam" before 1800', in *La fiscalità nell'economia europea secc. XIII–XVIII* (Firenze University Press 2008) Vol. I, pp. 51–75.

2 D. Goffman, *The Ottoman Empire and Early Modern Europe* (Cambridge: Cambridge University Press; 2003) p. 4.

3 M. Genç & Erol Özvar, eds., *Osmanlı maliyesi: kurumlar ve bütçeler*, Istanbul: Osmanlı Bankası Arsiv ve Arastırma Merkezi, 2006; I am grateful for help in using this publication to Ismael Hakkı Kadı and Asim Han.

4 Ch. De Secondat, baron de Montesquieu, *The Spirit of Laws* (1748; transl. T. Nugent 1752; publ. Kitchener, Canada, 2001)) accessible on http://socserv.mcmaster.ca/econ/ugcm/3ll3/montesquieu/spiritoflaws.pdf; Book XIII, Chapter 16.

 | DOI 10.1163/9789004341289_010

research.[5] For his own time he observed that 'one can raise higher taxes in proportion to the liberty of subjects', Britain and Holland being for him the states where liberty was highest, 'Turkey' where it was lowest.[6] This emphasis on an institutional feature like 'liberty' is remarkable because the main thesis of his 'The Spirit of Laws' was that this 'spirit' differed among countries according to climatic and geographical conditions.[7] The more 'institutional' approach focusing on 'liberty' resembles, as we will see, some modern answers to the question why the big Ottoman Empire at the end of the eighteenth century was no longer able to generate enough money to defend itself against the growing military power of Europe.[8]

Montesquieu's primary fascination for a geographically determined 'spirit' of laws has received later on much less attention than his doctrine of the desirability of separate law giving, executive and judicial institutions as important for 'liberty'. This chapter will argue that differences between the Ottoman fiscal system and that of other European states, and especially the Dutch Republic, can be partly understood by the influence of differences in geographical and ecological conditions on processes of urbanization. When useful or necessary, comparisons with the fiscal systems of other states than the Dutch Republic have been added.

Why was Ottoman Public Revenue so Low?

An impressive comparison of Ottoman public revenue with that of ten other countries, based on ten-year averages of the relevant data, was realized by Ş. Pamuk and K. Kivanç Karaman.[9] It showed the extremely high level of public revenue per capita in the Dutch Republic as well as the extremely low level in the Ottoman Empire. The authors attempted to answer the question why the level of state revenues in the Ottoman Empire came to lag so much behind that of European states between 1500 and 1800. After having pointed at the difference in population development, stagnant in the Ottoman case, doubling in

5 H.W. Lowry, *The nature of the early Ottoman state* (New York 2003) p. 103; K. Fleet, 'The Turkish economy, 1071–1453', in idem ed., The Cambridge History of Turkey Volume 3. Byzantium to Turkey, 1071–1453' (Cambridge: CUP, 2009) pp. 227–266, p. 237.

6 Montesquieu, *The Spirit of Laws,* Book XIII, Chapter 12 on http://socserv.mcmaster.ca/econ/ugcm/3ll3/montesquieu/spiritoflaws.pdf.

7 *The Spirit of Laws* http://socserv2.socsci.mcmaster.ca/econ/ugcm/3ll3/montesquieu/spiritoflaws.pdf, Books XIV–XVIII.

8 D. Acemoglu and J.A. Robinson, *Why nations fail. The origins of power, prosperity and poverty* (London, 2012) p. 56.

9 Karaman and Pamuk, 'Ottoman state finances'; based on data for the Ottoman Empire, Britain, Dutch Republic, France, Spain, Venice, Austria, Prussia, Poland, Sweden, and Russia.

Europe, and at the more densely populated urbanized territories in Europe that simplified tax collection, they mainly discussed the role of economic factors.

Price-levels in silver in Europe increased faster than in the Ottoman Empire, especially in North-Western Europe, they argued, which resulted in a price-level twice as low in the Ottoman Empire in the second half of the eighteenth century, implying that the Ottoman Empire needed less silver for its military expenditure than states with a higher price level. The silver supply in the Ottoman Empire may have been insufficient due to a policy of preferring imports and preventing exports, in contrast to the export-promoting mercantilist policies of many European states. This made it difficult for the Ottoman state to increase the silver value of its tax revenues.

Rising gross domestic product in Western Europe must also have contributed to the increasing gap in state revenues between the Ottoman Empire and other states, especially in the case of Britain and the Dutch Republic, they added. An increasingly higher percentage of gross domestic product (GDP) was extracted in tax revenue in these states, moreover, whereas this percentage remained low in the Ottoman Empire. Here it was probably never higher than 4 to 6 percent of GDP[10] and declining in the eighteenth century, while it became 5 to 10 percent in many European countries and more than 10 percent in Britain and the Netherlands in the course of the eighteenth century.[11]

Increases in the level of the average amount in state revenue per head in the Dutch republic, as well as in other states, cannot solely be accounted for by increasing price levels and a higher GDP per capita. Decisions had to be taken to augment the rates and number of taxes. Pamuk and Karaman suppose that 'a significant part' of European tax increases was related to the centralization of tax systems, making decisions to increase taxation more effective. They contrast this with an 'Ottoman pattern of control over provincial violence (…) through negotiated, selective and short term co-optation of an evolving array of semi-autonomous military formations and contractors, since mid-seventeenth century, but without a long-term and stable political deal with well-defined obligations and privileges'.[12]

They refer in this context to estimates that in 1527/8 only 46 percent of the tax amounts paid by the population reached the central treasury, in 1661/2 even only 25 percent, and during the eighteenth century only 33 percent of net

10 Ş. Pamuk, 'The evolution of fiscal institutions in the Ottoman Empire', in *The rise of fiscal states. A global history*, pp. 304–335, p. 321.

11 Karaman and Pamuk, 'Ottoman state finances', pp. 608, 614: 6 percent; Pamuk, 'The evolution of fiscal institutions', pp. 321–322: 4 percent.

12 Karaman and Pamuk, 'Ottoman state finances', p. 618.

tax revenues after deduction of collection expenses estimates to which we will return in Section 7.4 on public debt.[13] They mention for Britain an estimate of 90 percent of gross tax collection that made it into the central treasury in the eighteenth century, for France of 40 percent.[14] They point to the fact that Ottoman provincial governors increasingly financed the troops that they had to keep available for the sultan directly, maybe for an amount of about a third of total imperial revenue.[15]

Karaman and Pamuk's publication suggests in addition that the 'geographical compactness of European states' in comparison to the Ottoman Empire may in the end have been more important to understand the differences in their fiscal systems than decentralization as such'. This important difference, made it, in their words, 'perhaps even inappropriate' to compare the Ottoman Empire with other European states.[16] They remained nevertheless sufficiently intrigued by the possibilities for comparison to continue their comparative project. Their conclusion was that the main handicap of Ottoman state finance in the seventeenth and eighteenth century was a combination of decentralizing tendencies and a lack of representative government.

In a paper on 'Different Paths to the Modern State' based on similar data they primarily pointed to the fact that Europe was unique in terms of the intensity and spread of interstate warfare.[17] The Ottoman Empire waged wars as well in the early modern period, mainly with Persia, Venice and the Habsburgs, and was moreover plagued by internal revolts. However, especially for the period at the end of the sixteenth century and the first decades of the seventeenth century, the relative peace in comparison with European states prevailing in most of Ottoman territory for most of the time, is emphasized.[18] This suggests that war faring in the Ottoman Empire did not require the remarkable rise in public revenue visible in West European states: its war faring was less costly, because it was less intensive. It should be noticed, however, that the fact remains, that, in the course of the eighteenth century, the Ottoman state struggled less successfully than many European states to obtain more revenue, which may at least partly explain an increasing lack of success in military competition.

13 Ibidem, p. 609.

14 Ibidem, p. 616.

15 Ibidem, pp. 605–606.

16 Ibidem, p. 625.

17 Karaman and Pamuk, 'Different Paths to the Modern State' (2011), p. 38.

18 Also S.N. Faroqhi, 'Introduction', in idem ed., *The Cambridge History of Turkey. Volume 3* (Cambridge: CUP 2006) pp. 3–17, p. 3.

On behalf of an elaborate econometric statistical analysis Karaman and Pamuk concluded in this paper that 'urban economies with representative regimes (...) tended to better withstand war pressure and to translate it into building a centralized state apparatus'[19] than the Ottoman Empire. They related the fiscal capacity of European states, enabling them to wage so many wars, to 'economic structure' now operationalized as 'urbanization'.

The comparison between the public finance of the Dutch Republic and that of the Ottoman Empire in the last chapter of this book will be more in line with the changed focus on differences in urbanization than with the emphasis on decentralization in their former publication. The aim of this chapter is not to deny that decentralizing tendencies can be considered as a problem for the public finance of the very large Ottoman Empire in the course of the eighteenth century. Nor does it want to deny that in long-term comparisons there is always more than just one relevant explanation for differences, and that, of course, the degree to which states were involved in war faring is important in understanding differences in the total level of state revenue.

The main objective of this chapter is to ask more attention for the influence of long-term geographic characteristics and historical developments on the character of urbanization in this part of the world, as a relevant background to understand differences in fiscal systems and in the ability to generate more revenue when necessary. This will be done by looking not only at the *level* of public revenue, which was the focus of Pamuk's and Karaman's research, but also at its *structure*: the proportion of indirect and direct taxation and the proportion of tax revenue and revenue from what may be called 'advances on tax revenue', that may be compared to the sale of annuities in European states.

Some authors consider the lack of the development of a national debt in Ottoman state finance as 'one of the most obvious departures from what could be considered a rather similar path of modern state building with most European states during the seventeenth century'.[20] According to Pamuk, however, the Ottoman fiscal system became in fact more similar to European systems of state finance in the course of the eighteenth century, because of its ability to generate money for wars in addition to taxes, on behalf of the so-called *malikane*-system of tax farming and the subsequent *esham*-system – to be explained in

19 Karaman and Pamuk, 'Different Paths (2011), p. 38; in the later version of this article(2013) p. 22 the conclusion was generalized into: 'it was authoritarian regimes in more rural economies and representative regimes in more urban economies that tended to better translate war into state-building'.

20 E. Eldem, 'Istanbul: from imperial to peripheralized capital', in *The Ottoman City*, pp. 135–207, p. 176 n101.

the fourth section of this chapter – that showed resemblances to the European sale of life annuities. Çizakça, another important economic historian of the Ottoman Empire with a special interest in state finance, maintains however – on behalf of an analysis of the same *malikane*-system – that the Ottoman fiscal system remained different, because state objectives in the Ottoman Empire were fundamentally different from those in Western European states. To explain the low level of public revenue he pointed especially to the empire's 'risk averseness', a tendency to prefer certainty in the amounts of public revenue.[21]

A comparison of the fiscal system of the Ottoman Empire with that of the Dutch Republic and that of other West-European states not only allows to put the Dutch fiscal system in a wider, more global perspective, but may also offer a contribution to this discussion.

The next section of this chapter offers an overview of relevant long-term developments. It focuses on demographic differences resulting from geographic and ecological factors that resulted in specific 'urbanization-trajectories', as decisive elements in the development of the 'tax base'. The third section offers a quantitative comparison of the size and structure of state revenue in the Ottoman Empire and the Dutch Republic, as far as allowed by the available figures. In the fourth section the relation between the tax farming system and the development of public debt in the Ottoman Empire will be discussed and compared to that in other West-European states. The conclusion will return to the connection between differences in fiscal systems and in the character of urbanization resulting from geographic and ecological factors.

6.2 Contrastive Long-Term Trajectories of State Formation

The Ottoman Empire was the result of a long history of Turkish migratory and expansionist movements. In the last decades of the eleventh century Turkish bands had started to flood Asia Minor from the eastern steppes as part of the disintegration of the Abbasid Empire since c. 975. The Byzantine emperor was defeated by Seljuq Turks, already in 1071, to the dismay of medieval Europe, but the Byzantine Empire would still continue to exist for nearly four centuries. Mongol invasions put an end to the Seljuq Empire, but would be followed by further Turkish invasions. Osman, the leader of a small Turkish warrior state that had developed south of Constantinople, conquered a large part of Anatolia and he established a foothold in Europe by crossing the straits to Gallipoli

21 M. Çizakça, *A comparative evolution of business partnerships. The Islamic world and Europe with specific reference to the Ottoman archives* (Leiden: Brill, 1996) pp. 142–143.

in 1345. Thereafter masses of Turkish warriors established themselves on farming lands in Greece, Macedonia and Bulgaria. Invading the Balkans became a deliberate state enterprise, which brought the Ottoman state not only an immense wealth in booty, but also many new taxpayers. In addition, it stimulated the establishment of a navy for raids in these territories. By 1475 81 percent of total Ottoman tax revenue in cash came from Rumeli (the Balkans) a proportion which only would change when wealthy Egypt became part of the empire in 1517.[22]

A coalition organized by Venice and the papacy to check Ottoman expansion was defeated in 1396 at Nicopolis. In 1453 the Ottoman leader Mehmed II (1432–1481) succeeded in conquering Constantinople, which gradually came to be called Istanbul.[23] His followers, especially Selim I the Conqueror (1456–1520), expanded the new Ottoman Empire to the Middle East and to the frontiers of the Persian Savafid Empire. The result was an empire, containing large parts of South-Eastern Europe, West Asia and Northern-Africa, which by 1683 stretched roughly from Budapest to the Caspian Sea, from the Persian Gulf to Damascus, from the mouth of the Red Sea to Algiers and from there to Athens, with Istanbul as its centre and heart.[24]

This section will show that state formation in the Ottoman Empire during most of the period between 1000 and 1800, occurred largely in a territory with a more or less stagnating population, this in contrast to impressive population growth in Europe. This was due to geographic and ecological characteristics in the Middle Eastern and North-African parts of its territory which made it extremely sensitive to a continuing occurrence of disasters. The result was 'land abundance' and 'population scarcity', which contributed to a 'state-driven' 'urbanization-trajectory' in the Ottoman Empire in contrast to much more 'economy-driven' urbanization-trajectories in Europe with important consequences for its fiscal system.

Contrasting Population Developments

According to the available estimates Ottoman population-development displayed a remarkable contrast with the part of Europe designated in the

---

22 H. Inalcik, 'The Ottoman state: economy and society, 1300–1600', in: *An economic and social history of the Ottoman Empire. Part 1*, ed. H. Inalcik (Cambridge: CUP, 1997) pp. 1–380, p. 55.

23 I. Lapidus, *A history of Islamic societies* (Cambridge: Cambridge University Press, 2005) pp. 112, 248–251.

24 http://europelostandfound.net/node/1073 offers a map of the development of the Ottoman Empire since 1300 until 1683.

TABLE 6.1 *Estimated population in parts of the territory of the Ottoman empire and the 'Latin West', 1000–1800 (millions).*

	Middle East & North Africa	Balkans	'Latin West'	Low countries	(territory of the) Dutch Republic
1000	22	5	29	0.7	
1300	21	6	66	(2.2)2.1	0.8
1400	17	5	48	(1.8)1.4	0.6
1500	17	6	65	2.2	1.0
1600	22*	(7)8**	83	(2.8)3.0	1.5
1700	21*	(9)8	94	3.8	2.0
1800	22*	(12)15***	137	(5.0)5.3	2.1

* Estimates for the population in the area of present-day Balkans, present day Turkey, greater Syria and present-day Iraq and Egypt in: 1550: 19.0 million; 1600: 21.3 million; 1650: 20.2 million; 1700: 20.4 million; 1750: 19.8 million; 1800: 21.5 million (in Karaman and Pamuk, 'Ottoman state finances', pp. 606–607 note 34, based on Jones & McEvedy, Malanima and Palairet)
** 8 million already in the late sixteenth century according to B. McGowan, *Economic life in Ottoman Europe. Taxation, trade and the struggle for land, 1600–1800* (Cambridge UP, 1981), p. 85
*** 12 million is more likely than 15 million (cf. McGowan, *Economic life in Ottoman Europe*, p. 82)
Sources: Calculated on behalf of the data in Table 1 and Table 2 in M. Bosker, E. Buringh and J.L. van Zanden, 'From Baghdad to London. The dynamics of urban growth in Europe and the Arab world, 800–1800', *Centre of Economic Policy Research Publications* (2008) http://www.cepr.org/meets/wkcn/1/1699/papers/Bosker.pdf [last access 2016-07-22] based on data in P. Bairoch, J. Batou and P. Chèvre, *Population des villes européennes de 800 à 1850* (Droz, 1988)); data between brackets: P. Malanima, *Pre-Modern European Economy One Thousand Years (10th–19th centuries)* (Leiden: Brill, 2009) p. 9.

literature as the 'Latin West',[25] especially the non-European territory of the later Ottoman Empire. Population decreased rather dramatically between 1000 and 1500 in the Asian and North-African part of the later Ottoman Empire (Table 6.1). This in sharp contrast to the 'Latin West' where population more than doubled in the same period, despite the fact that the demographic effects of the Great Plague of 1347 had been disastrous not only in the Middle East and North Africa, but in Europe as well. Population development in the Balkans,

25 This term, used in the article on which Table 6.1 is based, refers to Europe exclusive the territories dominated by the eastern orthodox churches which were, on the one hand, Russia, on the other hand the most important European parts of the Ottoman Empire.

the European part of the later Ottoman Empire, was alternately stagnating and growing slowly between 1000 and 1500. In the Low Countries, in contrast, population may even have tripled between 1000 and 1500.

In the 'Latin West' population more than doubled gradually between 1500 and 1800, and it was especially fast in the Dutch Republic between 1500 and 1700. In the Ottoman Empire it increased probably between 1500 and 1600, like in Europe, but then stagnated.

An explanation for the remarkable lack of population growth in the Ottoman Empire in comparison with the Latin West may be found in the continuous occurrence of a number of disasters, afflicting this part of the world to a much larger degree than the 'Latin West'. White argued in a recent study that the arid and semi-arid regions of the territory of the Ottoman Empire are especially vulnerable to periodic fluctuations in climate and most of all to severe droughts, obstructing the recovery of agriculture and population sometimes for generations or centuries to follow.[26] He offers detailed examples for the period 1600–1800. Especially between 1590 and 1620 he found extreme climate events and devastating setbacks for the Ottoman Empire. For the seventeenth century as a whole, he found 'frequent and extreme cold-events' and several significant periods of droughts, and during the 1680s and 1690s again severe weather conditions with a long-term impact.[27] Of course the so-called 'Little Ice Age' is also well known for Europe in this period, but there are no reports of similar long-term impact as described by White for the Ottoman Empire. Research on the Dead Sea level has shown moreover a long-term drop in rainfall after the sixteenth century in this part of the world, occasioning famines due to drought in wide areas of the Middle East in the seventeenth and eighteenth century. This downward trend was only reversed in the second half of the nineteenth century.[28]

Invasions of locusts, recurring every few years, were always a serious danger in Mesopotamia, Syria, Cyprus and Anatolia and sometimes even in the European parts of the Empire.[29] Earthquakes and epidemics should yet be added to this combination of disasters that continuously had ravaging effects

---

26 S. White, *The climate of rebellion in the Early Modern Ottoman Empire* (Cambridge: CUP, 2011) p. 11.

27 S. White, 'Climate change and crisis in Ottoman Turkey and the Balkans 1590–1710', conference-paper http://sci.martinkoechy.de/Climate_Change_and_the_Middle_East_2006_Proceedings/07_the_past_as_a_key_for_the_future.pdf, pp. 394, 393.

28 H. Gerber, *The social origins of the Middle East* (London, 1994) p. 16.

29 W. Hütteroth, 'Ecology of the Ottoman lands', in ed. S.N. Faroqhi, *The Cambridge History of Turkey Volume 3* (Cambridge: CUP 2006) pp. 18–41, p. 36.

in this part of the world.[30] A study of Izmir relates that the earthquake which completely destroyed the city in 1688 was yet followed by two more centuries of earth tremors, fires and plagues. 'Villages, towns and cities, that had experienced devastating earthquakes, cluttered the Ottoman domain', this study noted.[31]

Forms of the plague continued to reappear in the 'Latin West' as well as in the Ottoman Empire, but much more so in the Ottoman Empire. It may even have been the most important factor in the deviating demographic history of the Ottoman Empire. The plague has been documented 19 times in Amsterdam, between 1450 and its last occurrence in 1668, in total in 37 years of the 218 years of this period.[32] In Izmir, however, the bubonic plague returned almost every spring and summer.[33] It remained a major event in the non-European parts of the Ottoman Empire until the second half of the nineteenth century, whereas the last outbreak in Europe dates from 1720 in Marseille.[34] According to White 'the ravages of plague and other epidemics have afflicted the Near East more than perhaps any other part of the world'.[35]

Population growth in the Latin West since 1000 would make land increasingly scarce relative to people, and this would contribute to an intensification of land use and agrarian specialization and commercialization especially in the Netherlands.[36] In the Ottoman Empire, however, people would remain scarce relative to land.[37]

---

30 S. Faroqhi, 'Plagues, famines and earthquakes', in eds. S. Faroqhi, B. McGowan, D. Quataert, S. Pamuk, *Economic and social history of the Ottoman Empire. Part II* (Cambridge: CUP 1997) 441; D. Quataert, *The Ottoman Empire 1700–1922* (Cambridge: CUP, 2005) pp. 114–115.

31 D. Goffman, 'Izmir: from village to colonial port city', in *The Ottoman City*, pp. 83–160, 115–117.

32 L. Noordegraaf and G. Valk, *De Gave Gods. De pest in Holland vanaf de late Middeleeuwen* (Bergen: Octavo, 1988) 230; it lasted often more than one year, up to six consecutive years from 1652–1657; however, it appears to have accounted for only 10 percent of all the deaths between 1620 and 1670 (with serious epidemics in 1624–5, 1635–6, 1654–6 and 1664–7) and afterwards the general death rate remained large because of the increase in other illnesses; De Vries and van der Woude, *The first modern economy*, 48–49.

33 Goffman, 'Izmir: from village to colonial port city', pp. 115–117.

34 D. Panzac, *La peste dans l'Empire Ottoman 1700–1850* (Louvain, 1985), pp. 30–35, 605–609.

35 White, *The Climate of rebellion*, p. 11.

36 Malanima, *Pre-Modern European Economy*, pp. 100, 104, 120–121; the point is also made by McGowan, *Economic life in Ottoman Europe*, pp. 2–5.

37 See also McGowan, *Economic life in Ottoman Europ*, pp. 2–5.

Contrasting Patterns of Land Use

In the territory of the Low Countries, where population increase was no less than about threefold between 1000 and 1500, people were forced to land reclamation wherever possible, and to an intensification of land use by means of specialization and commercialization of primary activities, agriculture as well as fisheries. It has been calculated that in Europe a peasant family of five members needed between 5 and 10 ha of reasonably fertile flat land to survive. In West-Flanders, however, more than 75 percent of the population had less than 5 ha, and the majority of them less than 3 ha, already in the thirteenth century. In the late 14th century about 1000 out of 1250 peasants in a sandy, not very fertile, region in Flanders owned fewer than 5 hectares.[38] This required intensification of agriculture in order to feed the increasing population, and as a precondition for an increase in urbanization.

Between 1500 and 1800 land productivity increased indeed in most parts of Europe, whereas agricultural labour productivity mostly declined due to population growth.[39] Geographical factors, like a territory decreasingly fit for grain production, stimulated specialization in the Netherlands and an increase in industries and commerce and urbanization, which further stimulated population growth and urbanization in its turn.[40] For their fiscal systems this meant that the general demographic development in Western Europe would increase possibilities to levy indirect tax revenues based on consumption, industrial production and trade, much more so than in the Ottoman Empire where population stagnation and relative land abundance prevailed.

A remarkable aspect of the early land reclamation process in the Low Countries was that cultivated areas became the private property of the cultivators. They were no longer held as part of domain property within a context of feudal serfdom. Feudal lords, especially in the Western part of Europe, perceived that property rights or lease rights for farmers were a better guarantee to increase production than a continuance of feudal relations. Increased production was the main way in which they strengthened the 'tax-base' in their territories, not territorial expansion as was the case in the Ottoman Empire until the end of

38 Malanima, *Pre-Modern Economy*, pp. 106, 110; T. Soens, *De spade in de dijk? Waterbeheer en rurale samenleving in de Vlaamse kustvlakte (1280–1580)* (Gent, Academia Press, 2009) pp. 74–76 has data for West-Flanders in 1227, 1292, 1388, 1398.

39 Ibidem, 149, 150; research on the developments in land productivity was only available for Italy and Holland.

40 W. Blockmans, *Metropolen aan de Noordzee* (Amsterdam: Prometheus, 2010) B. van Bavel, *Manors and markets. Economy and society in the Low Countries* (Oxford: Oxford University Press, 2010).

the sixteenth century, resulting in 'booty' as a main source of public revenue. In a later phase city inhabitants in European cities would buy land in the countryside, which would further stimulate the use of production-increasing technology and profit-increasing land use.[41]

The bulk of the lands in the territory of the Ottoman Empire outside Europe had been state owned already well before the Ottomans and this would continue to be the case. The only exceptions were lands used for horticulture around the cities, and lands permanently handed over as a source of revenue to *waqfs*, religious and charitable institutions (also: *awqaf, evkaf, or habous*). Conquered territory was given in usufruct to warriors. Military commanders received the right to collect taxes on a certain piece of territory – first called *iqta'*, later, in the period of the Ottoman Empire, *timar* – sufficient to maintain themselves and a specified number of cavalries under their command. Although such *timars* became often hereditary, they always could be – and often were – withdrawn by the sultan again. In regions conquered in Europe by the Ottomans where feudalism had prevailed, feudal relations were wiped out by the *timars*. Territories in the Balkans were integrated in the *timar* system in order to finance increased armies. Indigenous local lords could become *timar*-holders under central state control as well.[42]

In the Ottoman Empire land taxes were not only a main source of public revenue, but also a stimulus for peasant flight, either to mountainous areas that were less accessible for tax collectors than the plains, or to big cities. In South-Eastern Europe and the whole Middle East an opposition developed between empty plains and relatively densely populated mountains.[43] In a fascinating overview of ecological developments in the Ottoman Empire Hütteroth has pointed to the increasingly *extensive* use of agriculturally optimal areas in the plains. Many fertile plains came to be used for herds instead of arable farming, which lead to soil deterioration and further depopulation of large parts of the countryside.[44] Also fear for bands roaming the countryside led to peasant flight. Especially during the years 1596–1610 dismissed soldiers that had been paid in devalued money were roaming a countryside that was

41 A. Verhulst, *The rise of cities in North-West Europe*, Cambridge: Cambridge UP, 1999, p. 142; B. van Bavel, 'Rural development and landownership in Holland, c. 1400–1650', in ed. O. Gelderblom, *The political economy of the Dutch Republic* (Farnham: Ashgate, 2009) pp. 167–197, 184.

42 Ibidem, pp. 15, 150, 17.

43 W. Hütteroth, 'Ecology of the Ottoman lands', in ed. S.N. Faroqhi, *The Cambridge History of Turkey Volume 3* (Cambridge: CUP 2006) pp. 18–41, p. 31.

44 Hütteroth, 'Ecology of the Ottoman lands', p. 31.

moreover plagued by extreme weather conditions. Of course it was an urgent problem in a state dependent on taxes from land, that peasants fled the countryside. 'Since the peasants did not own the land, and as there were moreover always other lands available, flight from their tract was frequently resorted to', wrote Inalcik.[45] Deserted villages became an ever more pressing problem for the state nearly everywhere in the Ottoman Empire, when the possibilities to acquire new rich territories began to reach their limits. The government took drastic measures attempting to repopulate abandoned villages in Anatolia.[46]

In the conditions of decreasing population, prevailing in most of the territory of the Ottoman Empire before the sixteenth century – and of population stagnation after the sixteenth century as shown in Table 6.1 – processes of intensification of agriculture and other forms of economic specialization could not be expected to occur on a scale comparable to that in Western Europe, although agricultural innovations were not absent in the Ottoman Empire. Especially the sixteenth century was a period, not only of population growth, but also of extension of arable land, and of specialization, productivity growth and trade. The earliest information on silk-worm breeding, leading to a Turkish silk industry dates even already from the fifteenth century. The use of abandoned agricultural lands for sheep was not only a symptom of an increasingly extensive agriculture; it also stimulated the trade in wool and meat allowing urbanization. It should be noted however that this obstructed repopulation of the countryside as well.[47] Rice, another innovation, was probably introduced in south-eastern Europe by the Turks during the last decades of the fifteenth century. However, until the eighteenth century this was usually a kind of state enterprise with special labourers irrigating and draining the fields, not primarily an 'economy-driven' development.[48] According to a land tax register of 1572 only 60 percent of the cultivable lands in the fertile Cilicia flood plain were used for regular agricultural exploitations even during the sixteenth century, when population increased. The rest remained cultivated only on a temporary basis by nomadic groups.[49]

45 Hütteroth, 'Ecology of the Ottoman lands', pp. 161, 165.

46 Inalcik, *Economic and social history of the Ottoman Empire, p.* 32; McGowan, *Economic life*, p. 57.

47 McGowan, *Economic life in Ottoman Europe*, p. 65: it was discovered 'how sheep's foot turns sand to gold'.

48 Hütteroth, 'Ecology of the Ottoman lands', pp. 38–39; for 'economy-driven' (my wording) as opposed to 'state-driven' development see the next section.

49 Ş. Pamuk, *A monetary history of the Ottoman Empire* (Cambridge: Cambridge UP, 2001) p. 20.

'State-Driven' Versus 'Economy-Driven' Urbanization Trajectories[50]

That land was much more abundant in the Ottoman Empire than in the Latin West, did not imply, remarkably enough, that a much smaller percentage of the population was urban. Table 6.2 displays the percentage of people living in cities with more than 10,000 inhabitants for the same territories and the same periods as in Table 6.1. It shows that the percentage of people living in cities of more than 10,000 inhabitants in the non-European part of the later Ottoman Empire, although much lower than in the territory of the later Dutch Republic, was until the end of the eighteenth century probably not very different from that in the 'Latin West' in general.

In view of these figures it may seem reasonable to expect that the possibilities to realize tax revenue by means of taxes on domestic commercial activities and assets in the form of indirect, price-increasing taxes were comparable to

TABLE 6.2 *Percentage of population in cities > 10,000 in the Ottoman empire and the 'Latin West' (a) and the number of such cities (b), 1000–1800.*

	Middle East & North Africa		'Latin West'		Low Countries		Dutch Republic	
	a	b	a	b	a	b	a	b
1000	8%	31	5%	74	3%			
1300	7%		6%		12%	11		
1400	9%		7%		23%	9		
1500	9%	26	7%	178	19%	23		
1600	10%		8%				24%	19
1700	11%		9%				33%	19
1800	10%	24	11%	522			30%	18

Sources: Bosker, M., 'From Baghdad to London. The dynamics of urban growth in Europe and the Arab world, 800–1800' (2008); http://xinkaishi.typepad.com/files/bosker_baghdad-to-london.pdf, Tables 1 and 2; De Vries, *European Urbanization*, Appendix 1.

50 The relation between geographic and institutional developments to explain long-term differences in urban development in Europe and the Islamic world has recently been explored in an innovative statistical way in M. Bosker, E. Buringh and J.L. van Zanden, 'From Baghdad to London. Unraveling urban development in Europe, the Middle East and North Africa, 800–1800', *Review of Economics and Statistics* 95,4 (2013) pp. 1418–1437.

those in states in the Latin West. In fact this was not the case, as we will see, and the question why will be addressed in the course of this chapter.

An important difference in the urbanization-trajectories in both these parts of the world was that the relatively high urbanization percentage in the Middle East and North Africa was largely due to a small number of huge cities like Istanbul and Alexandria. The number of cities with more than 10,000 inhabitants decreased in the Middle East and North Africa between 1000 and 1800, whereas it increased considerably, not only in the Low Countries and the Dutch Republic until the seventeenth century, but also in the whole 'Latin West' during the whole period. The small number of cities in its relatively large territory hindered, of course, the formation of an 'urban system' as part of the process of state formation. The huge increase in the number of cities of some importance in the 'Latin West' is an indication for the much larger importance of economically interdependent 'urban systems'.

Not only the number of cities was relatively small in the Ottoman Empire, also their historical development and their character were different from that in the 'Latin West'. A remarkable aspect of urbanization in the Ottoman Empire was the phenomenon of forced migration, known as *sürgün*.[51] When Mehmed II had conquered Istanbul in 1453, he started a policy of forcibly importing individuals with professional skills and experience to Istanbul, to bring about an economic revival.[52] The re-population of Istanbul through forced migration was not an isolated phenomenon. Already in 1331 about 25,000 people were snatched from the Aegean isles and brought to Anatolia as slaves.[53] Already even earlier Osman had repopulated the empty town of Karaca Hisar. Murad II had settled people in Thessaloniki after its conquest in 1430.[54] Under Mehmed II forced migration was an overall policy throughout his reign of thirty years as a means urbanization and sedentarization.[55] The well-known *devşirme,* or tribute of Christian children, mainly from the Balkan countryside to Istanbul,

---

51 F. Acun, 'A portrait of the Ottoman Cities', *The Muslim World,* 92 (2002) pp. 255–285, p. 263 ; S. Faroqhi, 'Taxation and urban activities in sixteenth century Anatolia', *Journal of Turkish* Studies, 1, 1, 1979/80, p. 19 mentions studies in Turkish by Ö. Barkan et al. on the forces transplantations of population known as sűrgűn (there are also examples in Leo Africanus for Morocco in the 16. century).

52 In about 1550 it had become a city of about 400,000 people It is said to have been a city of only about 30,000–50,000 inhabitants. Inalcik, *Economic and social history of the Ottoman Empire,* pp. 18, 32.

53 Fleet, 'The Turkish Economy, 1071–1453', p. 233.

54 Fleet, 'The Turkish economy, 1071–1453', p. 244.

55 Acun, 'A portrait of the Ottoman Cities', pp. 262–263; K. Hayashi, ' Turkey', in: *Islamic urban studies.: historical review and perspective,* ed. M. Haneda, New York: Columbia

between about 1350 and 1650 though decreasing in the course of time, may be seen as an aspect of this forced migration as well.

State initiative was also important in attempts to create *new* urban centres. Complexes of soup kitchens (*imaret*) and hospitals and other facilities (*külliyes*) were often founded by the state, in cooperation with sheikhs of religious brotherhoods or individuals bequeathing their property to *waqfs*, charity institutions, attempting to induce a nomadic population to settlement to facilitate and protect the caravan trade.[56] The presence of an *imaret* is even considered as the main characteristic of Ottoman cities in Anatolia and the Balkans.[57] The expenditure on infrastructure and the welfare demands required by urban settlements were mostly financed by state tax revenues from lands that were handed by the state over to *waqfs*, not financed by urban taxes.

The relation between cities and rulers in the Low Countries would develop in a way very different from that in the Ottoman Empire. For the early centuries, the focus of our comparison will be not on the territory of the later Dutch Republic alone, but on the Low Countries as a whole, as urbanization in the Southern Netherlands can be seen as a precursor and part of that in the Northern Netherlands. Already in the tenth century many small new markets, often fish markets, were established without the mediation of the counts governing in these regions. They emerged autonomously as the start of urban conglomerations. Also Amsterdam would start in the thirteenth century as a village of fishers and peasants and achieve a large degree of urban autonomy in the course of time at the initiative of the community.[58]

Forced migration to cities did never occur in this part of the world, and welfare arrangements were the result of initiatives inside the city and of demographically and economically determined processes of urbanization, not arranged by the central state in an attempt to promote urbanization. Flemish counts consciously furthered the development of existing cities, as they

---

University Press, 1994, 194, referring to O. Barkan, 'Forced migration (sürgün) as the means of sedentarization and settlement in the Ottoman Empire', 1949–54.

56 Lowry, *The nature of the early Ottoman state*, p. 73 mentions the establishment by Osman of the town of Mekece in Bithynia, in order to feed and house traveling poor, strangers, mendicants, dervishes and knowledge seekers roaming the countryside as the first initiative of this kind by a ruler.

57 Hayashi, 'Turkey', p. 195.

58 B. Speet, 'Een kleine nederzetting in het veen', and E. Dijkhof, 'Op weg naar autonomie', in: *Geschiedenis van Amsterdam tot 1578. Een stad uit het niets, ed. M. Carasso-Kok* (Amsterdam 2004) resp. pp. 21–63 and pp. 63–75; M. Prak, 'The Dutch Republic as a bourgeois society', in eds. K. van Berkel and L. de Goei, *The international relevance of Dutch history* (The Hague: *The Low Countries Historical Review* 25 (2010)) pp. 107–141, p. 111.

wanted to be able to profit fiscally from their autonomous economic dynamics, but urbanization in the 'Latin West' was much more 'economy-driven', much less 'state-driven' than in the Ottoman Empire.

According to Verhulst, specialist on the rise of cities in north-west Europe, the rise of international trade in this part of the world was grafted onto new regional market functions, made necessary and feasible due to population growth. Due to the autonomous 'economy-driven' character of urbanization, the resulting development of trade and industry in this part of the world came to be in the hands of an indigenous bourgeoisie, whose wealth would enable them to maintain a great measure of autonomy. The urban economy of cities in the Ottoman Empire, in contrast, would remain in large part determined by the state, and by urban officials appointed by the state, whose wealth would come to depend mainly on their involvement in tax collection for the state, instead of an involvement in industry and commerce.

In the Southern Netherlands guilds assumed already in the eleventh century responsibilities in city administration resulting in a *de facto* near-autonomy of cities in the twelfth century.[59] An important effect was that urban taxes were levied, not only for the ruling count, but also to finance urban expenditure as deemed necessary by city administrations. In the Ottoman Empire guilds were an important feature of urban life as well, but it was the central government that took the initiatives for urban development. These initiatives were mostly financed from the revenues of land tax, not by autonomous forms of urban public finance. In Flanders, the count forced the city governments already since 1280 to keep books on their city finances, which kept him informed on urban revenue potentials from taxes on urban production and consumption.[60] The autonomous development of industry and commerce in urban concentrations offered the count possibilities to get other sources of tax revenue than land alone to rule the area.

The three largest cities In Flanders would be responsible for about half the tax revenue of this county already in the middle of the fourteenth century.[61] In exchange for financial support from cities new counts and dukes had, since 1312, always to confirm privileges of the cities in the region. Rulers in the Netherlands remained in large part dependent on the consent of regional states assemblies to obtain money for war faring, in which the economically

59 Verhulst, *The rise of cities*, p. 152.

60 Blockmans, W., 'De vorming van een politieke unie (veertiende-zestiende eeuw)', in: *Geschiedenis van de Nederlanden*, eds. J.C.H. Blom and E. Lamberts (Rijswijk, s.a.) pp. 45–117, pp. 50–52.

61 Blockmans, 'De vorming van een politieke unie', p. 57.

so important cities were represented, together with the landed classes of the nobility and the church. This in sharp contrast to the Ottoman Empire where urban development had to be assisted by the revenue of land taxes handed over by the state to state-appointed city officials. Here war faring was mainly financed by taxes on land, either or not within the *timar*-system, or by capital taxes on special parts of the population, Christians and Jews, in exchange for their protection.

In the Ottoman Empire, it had been the expansion of the central treasury by means of booty and additional taxpayers, resulting from a policy of territorial expansion, that not only enabled to increase army-expenditure, but also to build big new war ships. No interdependent relationships developed between sultan and cities realizing public revenue in exchange for protection. In Holland the protection of commerce at sea by convoy was originally organized by merchants themselves, as we saw, and would subsequently become a task of city governments. The duties needed to finance the protection of international commerce and shipping started locally and got earmarked for the protection of the fleet on a *local* level. Before the Revolt they did not become an independent source of income or credit for a *central* ruler. Attempts at centralization of these means of public revenue by the Burgundian dukes in the fifteenth century failed completely.[62] Only after the Revolt some degree of centralization of this revenue source was achieved in the Dutch Republic, although still in the form of five admiralties in different cities, each of them eager to primarily protect its own commerce.

The development of trade in the 'Latin West' had been largely dependent on waterways, with the simultaneous advantage that trade could increasingly become more cost-efficient by means of technological improvements, an advantage that the Ottoman Empire missed, dependent as it was for the rich international trades on transport over land with camels.[63] No impulse to try to participate in the nascent Atlantic trade developed in the Ottoman Empire, because of its already long-established contacts with the rich trades of the Far East by means of the caravan trade. The development of the navy in

62 Sicking, *Neptune and the Netherlands*; L. Sicking, 'De integratie van Holland : Politiek en bestuur in de Bourgondisch-Habsburgse tijd' in *Geschiedenis van Holland. Deel1: tot 1572* (2002) pp. 259–290.

63 According to Bosker, Buringh and Van Zanden, 'From Baghdad to London', it was a different choice of main transport mode (camel versus ship) and the development of forms of local participative government in Europe that made cities less dependent on the state are the main factors that explain why Europe's urban development eventually outpaced that in the Islamic world.

the Ottoman Empire had primarily been motivated by the interests of territorial expansion. When commercial interests became important in the Ottoman Empire as well – the Portuguese had to be fought in the Indian Ocean to secure the supply for the important overland trade – the expansion of the navy was centrally financed not by merchants or cities. The Dutch East India Company largely financed itself the protection of its conquests in the East.

In the late-medieval Low Countries a relationship of mutual dependency developed between cities and rulers. On the one hand, rulers promoted urban development because they were eager to maintain access to the developing urban finances. On the other hand, the existence of a strong ruler was mostly perceived as necessary by city governments for an undisturbed economic development increasing the wealth of the inhabitants.[64] When the city of Ghent revolted against the fiscal policy of the Burgundian duke in 1447, it hardly received any support of other Flemish cities. Amsterdam entered the Dutch Revolt only hesitantly, not immediately at its start in 1572, but only in 1578.

For the Ottoman government urbanization was a source of central concern rather than a source of fiscal dynamism, because of the large number of mouths to be fed. Istanbul was basically 'a parasitic giant, which sucked in large proportions of the production of the Empire',[65] not leaving very much for export. Merchants, especially in Istanbul, far from becoming virtually autonomous urban rulers as in the 'Latin West' and especially in the Netherlands, often functioned in a 'command economy' organized by the state to ensure the provisioning of the city.[66] What has been called the 'provisionism'-principle[67] of Ottoman economic policy implied a very restrictive regulation of export and the advancement of imports, the opposite of the export-oriented mercantilist policies that would develop in West European states. The wealth of important cities, like Istanbul, Alexandria or Aleppo, was at least partly related to trade, of course, not only to caravan trade over land, but also to that across the Mediterranean Sea. But even in these cities merchants, dependent as many of them

64 Blockmans, 'De vorming van een politieke unie', pp. 81–83.

65 E. Eldem, 'Istanbul from imperial to peripheralized capital', in *The Ottoman City*, pp. 135–207, p. 162; McGowan, *Economic life in Ottoman Europe*, pp. 12–15, 35.

66 Traian Stoianovich, "Cities, Capital Accumulation and the Ottoman Balkan Command Economy, 1500–1800" in C. Tilly and W. Blockmans (eds.), *Cities and the rise of states in Europe,* Boulder: Westview Press, 1994.

67 M. Genç, 'The role of the state on the private capital accumulation in Ottoman economy before the nineteenth century', unpublished paper for a colloquium at Leiden University 3-12-2008, based on Turkish publications; I. Hakkı Kadı, *Natives and interlopers. Competition between Ottoman and Dutch merchants in the 18th century*, diss. Leiden, 2008, pp. 12–13; Pamuk, 'The evolution of fiscal institutions', pp. 312–313.

were on the economic policy of the government, never became a dominant social class. Military and religious elites involved in the government apparatus, remained always richer and more influential than merchants, even in the most commercial Ottoman cities.

The intense interference of the state with the process of urbanization and of urban development in the Ottoman Empire had important consequences for what Raymond called 'the management of the city', rightly avoiding the term 'government'. Even major cities in the Ottoman Empire functioned in the absence of a true urban administration and were 'bereft of any homogeneity and any juridical and regulatory cloak'.[68] With approval Raymond cited Sauvaget who wrote already in 1934 that 'The status of Islamic] cities is the subject of no specific provision on the part of Islamic law. There are thus no (...) municipal institutions (...). The city is not (...) regarded (...) as an entity, as something having its own existence (...) (it is) an inconsistent and inorganic assemblage of quarters.'[69]

Cities in the Ottoman Empire were governed by centrally appointed officials, the three main city officials being the *amir* for military affairs, the *muhtassib* for economic affairs and the *qadi* for juridical and religious affairs. Although political intervention by local powers, especially guilds, was less absent in cities than often was supposed,[70] also the heads of the guilds were appointed by the central government. Even when persons from the local upper class and their sons succeeded in being appointed as the city's *qadi, amir* or *muhtassib* for longer periods, as was increasingly the case in provinces like Egypt, they did not constitute a city government keen on protecting its economic sources of wealth against the fiscal greediness of the state, and levying urban taxes and negotiating urban loans to finance urban development itself. In the Ottoman Empire wealth was on the contrary the result of the relation of city officials with the central government. They were the ones that levied the taxes for the sultan, partly to be transferred to Istanbul, partly to be spent locally and partly for their personal income.[71]

For the old city of Damascus it has been observed that the fact that during the eighteenth century the members of the Damascene 'Azm-family were retained in office for relatively long periods does not have to be seen as a sign

68 A. Raymond, 'The management of the city', in: *The city in the Islamic world*, ds. S.K. Jayyusi a.o., Leiden, 2008, pp. 775–795, p. 792.

69 Ibidem, p. 775.

70 Hakkı Kadı, *Natives and interlopers*, pp. 36–39, 37n6.

71 S.J. Shaw, *The financial and administrative organization and development of Ottoman Egypt, 1517–1798* (Princeton UP 1962).

of an increasing autonomy of the city, but rather as a sign that tax dues were regularly remitted by them to Istanbul indeed.[72] In Damascus, like in other cities, it was, moreover, the central imperial authorities that coordinated the urban *waqf*-system to support policies directed at economic development,[73] and there were strong ties between the Damascene *'ulama'*, the religious authorities, and Istanbul.

Aleppo, although already a commercial centre in the second millennium BC and situated at the end of the famous Silk Road, had no urban government during the Ottoman Empire, but was placed by the sultan under the governor of Damascus after Syria had been conquered in the fifteenth century. In the sixteenth century janissaries – the feared Ottoman infantrymen – were garrisoned here to collect taxes. It was control of the revenues of Aleppo's agricultural hinterlands that was the source of economic power among city elites, not urban revenues. An in-depth study of Aleppo notes on the one hand, that military forces located in Syria were increasingly of local origins, albeit rather of tribal and rural than of urban origins, and that important administrative positions in the city came in the hands of the local elite. On the other hand, top-officials continued to be sent from Istanbul. The city elite remained divided and could thus be manipulated by the representatives of Istanbul. 'Not perceiving a community of interests, individual elite families wielded little direct political power', was the author's conclusion.[74]

In Izmir, having come to prominence as a commercial city since the thirteenth century and exceptional in the Ottoman Empire because 'it operated almost as an independent city state',[75] sultan Murad II had not hesitated in the fifteenth century to encroach on its international commercial position. He made the city into Istanbul's 'fruit-basket' by earmarking much of the harvests in the surrounding countryside for Istanbul's consumption as part of a general policy to secure the capital of food at centrally determined prices.[76] In the seventeenth century it had been again Istanbul in the person of Koprülü Fazıl Ahmed Paşa that ordered the building of a castle that could seal Izmir's harbour to secure an easy collection of customs, and who used the revenue to build an aqueduct, a *bedestan* (covered market), public baths, a custom house

72 Ibidem, p. 140.

73 R. van Leeuwen, *Waqfs and urban structure. The Case of Ottoman Damascus* (Leiden: Brill, 1999) pp. 118–119.

74 B. Masters, 'Aleppo: the Ottoman Empire's caravan city', in Eldem, Goffman and Masters, *The Ottoman City*, pp. 19–79, 21, 25, 51–52.

75 Goffman, 'Izmir: from village to colonial port city', p. 86.

76 Ibidem, p. 86.

and new thorough fares, to give the city the essential infrastructure for a leading commercial city.[77] There was no urban government which identified and satisfied urban needs by realizing urban revenues.

The 'state-driven' character of urbanization in the Ottoman Empire that would make cities dominated by centrally appointed religious and military, rather than by local economic elites – entailed that no autonomous urban finance developed. In the absence of an urban government and urban finance it was the – mostly state-controlled – *waqf*-system that performed an integrating function in the domains of economy, social structure and administration in the Ottoman Empire.[78] The absence of the development of urban finances managed by an urban government became in this way a very characteristic difference between large parts of Europe on the one hand, and the Ottoman Empire on the other hand, and very important to understand differences in their fiscal systems.[79]

The Consequences for Public Finance of Different Urbanization Trajectories

In the 'Latin West' the existence of urban public finance in combination with administrative autonomy implied the possibility not only of levying urban taxes, but also of issuing urban loans for instance for investments in city improvements, as well as to support rulers in war faring. The commercial town of Bruges had a capital debt due to the sale of life-annuities and perpetual annuities amounting to more than six times the city's annual income already by 1283. The wealth of the urban bourgeoisie in combination with the demand for possibilities to secure revenues during old age and for widows and orphans had created the necessary capital supply. This enabled the count of Flanders to appeal to other forms of financial support than taxation alone to finance

77 Ibidem, p. 105.

78 Van Leeuwen, *Waqfs and urban structure*, p. 197; the author discusses the question if the *waqf*-system should be considered an 'essential' characteristic of society in the Ottoman Empire; although he concedes that the *waqf* should not be treated 'as something which is determined by its "essential nature" *only*' [my italics WF]. He emphasizes that its integrating function in cities should at least be considered as a pattern with a remarkable continuity; the book does not explicitly mention the absence of urban finance as 'a pattern with a remarkable continuity'.

79 M. Prak, 'Citizenship in pre-modern Eurasia: a comparison between China, the Near East and Europe' presented at 'Modern and comparative economic history seminar, 24th November 2011, London School of Economics and Political Science'; version of November 2011 available at: http://eprints.lse.ac.uk/39751/ summarizes the discussion on the 'essentialism' of the concept of 'the Islamic city'.

war faring. He could ask city governments to negotiate loans for him by means of the sale of life annuities or perpetual heritable annuities, to enable him to wage wars that might increase the safety of their commerce.

This development did not remain limited to Flemish towns. Tracy found sales of *rentes viagères* in cities also in Northern France already in the thirteenth century and the same can be said for south German towns.[80] In Catalonia in Spain cities preferred to sell life annuities and heritable perpetual annuities to provide the king with money already in the fourteenth century above increased taxation.[81] The contracts between the king and the communities stipulated that the local authorities themselves were authorized to collect the taxes for the interests and to pay them, which made public debts a rather safe investment, the same as what would later happen in Holland in the sixteenth century, when Charles V convinced its six biggest cities to negotiate large amounts in loans on their common credit.[82]

To explain why the sale of life annuities developed in some parts of Europe and not in others Tracy pointed to the establishing by royal jurists in this part of Europe of the principle that urban communes were one of the few forms of association privileged by the king to act as 'moral persons', and therefore capable of owning property and swearing oaths.[83] This made it possible for them to be debtors as a 'corporate body', which, he argued, greatly increased the legal security of creditors. It can be debated, whether indeed royal privilege or rather the 'economy-driven' character of urbanization was the decisive factor in the development of urban credit. In Italy it could apparently be also the city government itself, instead of a juridical guarantee offered by a king, that was considered sufficiently trustworthy: in the case of cities like Genoa and Venice there was no doubt that the city-'state' had the power to rule and to effectuate financial policies in the interest of the wealthy creditors of the city. The same would become true in the Netherlands. In Holland even villages turned out to have enough credit to issue loans on the 'corpus' of the village, probably already since the fifteenth century, for instance to build mills for water management and industrial applications.[84] The fact that cities in the Latin

80 Tracy, *Urban public debts*, p. 197.

81 M. Sanchez Martines, 'Dette publique, autorités princières et villes dans les Pays de la Couronne d'Aragon (14e–15e siècles)', in *Urban public debts* (2003) pp. 27–51, pp. 37, 42.

82 Tracy, *A financial revolution in the Habsburg Netherlands*.

83 Tracy, 'On the dual orignis of long-term urban public debt', p. 20.

84 C.J. Zuijderduijn, *Medieval capital markets. Markets for renten between state formation and private investment in Holland (1300–1550)*, PhD-thesis, Utrecht, 2007; NB McGowan, *Economic life*, p. 158 mentions that 'to a degree' villages in Ottoman Europe 'were fiscal

West were 'corporate institutions' with an independent political existence and urban fiscal systems was, however, a very important difference with cities in the Ottoman Empire, indeed.

As we saw in Part 1 of this book the development of the public credit of the provinces in the Dutch Republic was based on the introduction of provincial taxes on domestic commercial activities and assets, partly originating in forms of urban indirect taxation, partly in the commercialization of agriculture. Provincial public credit could be established in most provinces only after a period in which provincial governments had yet been forced to rely on the credit of individual cities to realize loans. In France an important part of the state debt remained dependent on urban credit until the end of the eighteenth century, as is shown by the name of its most important debt paper, the *obligations sur l'Hôtel de Ville de Paris* (= bonds on the Town Hall of Paris).[85] Similar annuities came into existence in other French cities like Reims, Marseille, Provins, Moulins, but an urban network similar to that in the Dutch Republic did not develop.[86] Kings had less credit than cities and had to pay higher rates of interest as their reliability in debt service was much more doubted. Kings could only make use of the credit of cities, if they left them enough taxing power – or priority access to tax revenues – to secure the interest payments.

Unlike in most states of the 'Latin West', in the Ottoman Empire there was no institutional development towards cities as 'corporate bodies', to political entities separate from monarchical power. Nor did Ottoman cities see the development of a merchant class that assumed urban government. Cities in the Middle East and North Africa were often physically centred round a mosque, a public bath house and a *suq*, but remained institutionally a collection of separate quarters often separating ethnic and religious groups, without common urban institutions. One building that was always missing in Ottoman cities was a town hall, the natural heart of so many Western European cities. In Ottoman cities urban economic and social tasks were fulfilled by a scattered number of *waqfs* (or *awqaf, evkaf, habous*) which were charity institutions, either initiated by the rich to circumvent the inheritance laws in Islam, or by the central state to stimulate settlement of nomadic parts of its population.[87] Already by the end of the 16th century it was the Ottoman central state that had taken almost

---

collectivities, as we see from the fact that they took loans as collectivities' without further details.

85 D. Stasavage, *States of credit. Size, power and the development of European polities* (Princeton UP 2011). pp. 133–142.

86 M. Körner, 'Public credit', in: *Economic systems and state finance*, pp. 507–539, pp. 515–517.

87 T. Kuran, *The long divergence: how Islamic law held back the Middle East* (Princeton 2011).

total control of the field of the *waqf*.[88] In Ottoman cities there was no urban public finance, no urban taxation to finance urban public expenditure. This implied that there was no basis for the establishment of urban credit and for the urban loans that had been so crucial for the development of state debts in Western European countries.

In the 'Latin West' Britain seems to have been a remarkable exception to the rule that public credit for long-term loans at moderate rates of interest can be traced back to urban credit. Here the credit of public loans came to be based on the one hand on the introduction of *national* excise taxation without comparable pre-existing *urban* taxes.[89] On the other hand the breakthrough of its 'financial revolution' had required the establishment of the Bank of England. The credit of this bank was not based on the taxing power of London's chosen Lord Mayor and its Common Council. It was based on the fact that the members of the board of the Bank of England formed part of what in Britain has always been called the City, the inner part of 'Greater London'. In the context of the Latin West the history of Britain's public finance was that of an 'exceptional state',[90] indeed, not only due to the fact that it was an island, much less threatened by land wars than other parts of the Latin West, but also due to its divergent extremely London-centred urbanization pattern until the second half of the eighteenth century. Nevertheless, also in Britain the development of the national public debt was based on the independent financial-economic power of the merchant elite of the City of London.

Remarkably the legal characteristics of British philanthropic foundations turned out to be rather different from those in other parts of the Latin West as well. The use of their legal form is believed to have been introduced in Britain by British Franciscan friars and Templars, who were active in the Middle East. In his history of philanthropic foundations in the Islamic world Çizakça supports the thesis of two authors who found the origins of British philanthropic trusts in Islamic *waqfs*. This would – in a rather unexpected way – again underline the exceptionality of the history of public finance in the case of the British state.[91]

---

88 Van Leeuwen, *Waqfs and urban structure*, p. 117.

89 See Chapter III.8.

90 P. O'Brien, 'The nature and historical evolution of an exceptional fiscal state and its possible significance for the precocious commercialization and industrialization of the British economy from Cromwell to Nelson', *Economic History Review* 64, 2 (2011) pp. 408–446.

91 M. Çizakça, *A History of philanthropic foundations. The Islamic world from the seventh century to the present* (Istanbul Bogazicki University Press, 2000) 8–10.

Concepts like 'the Islamic city' or 'the Ottoman city', as formulated in the work of Max Weber,[92] are nowadays mostly rejected.[93] It has nevertheless been sensibly argued by one author that, if a similar concept would ever be revived, the extent to which urban structures are shaped by *waqfs* might be an important criterion.[94] We may conclude this section with the suggestion that the absence of the development of urban public credit as a source of state credit due to the absence of the development of autonomous urban public finance might qualify as a distinguishing criterion perhaps even better.

Long-term historical differences between 'state-driven' and 'economy-driven' trajectories of urbanization, related to the demographic consequences of geographical and ecological differences between the Latin West and the Ottoman Empire, resulted in the lack of a development of more or less integrated 'urban systems' in the Ottoman Empire. An awareness of such long-term historical differences will be helpful to understand the results of the quantitative comparison between the fiscal systems of the Ottoman Empire and the Dutch Republic, which will be presented in the next section.

6.3 A Comparison of Public Revenue

The Extremely Low Level of State Revenue in the Ottoman Empire

Figure 6.1 offers a comparison of total revenue of the Ottoman Empire with that in the Dutch Republic from the last decades of the sixteenth to the end of the eighteenth century, on behalf of published figures converted in tons of silver. Published amounts in Ottoman state revenue per year – designated as 'budgets' although they were produced *ex post*[95] – are only available for a limited number of years in the period until 1790.[96] The amount of archival material on state finance in the centralized bureaucratic Ottoman Empire is very large. However, most of it has been preserved in the form of series of *daily* accounts

92 Max Weber, *The City* (Munich, 1921) reprinted in Max Weber, *Economy and Society*, eds. G. Roth and C. Wittich, Berkeley: University of California Press, 1978, pp. 1233–1234.

93 Eldem, Goffman, Masters, *The Ottoman City*, pp. 207–214; Prak, 'Citizenship in pre-modern Eurasia', http://eprints.lse.ac.uk/39751/.

94 Van Leeuwen, *Waqfs and urban structure*, p. 208.

95 L. Darling, 'Ottoman fiscal administration: decline or adaptation?' *Journal of European Economic History* 26, 1 (1997) p. 166.

96 Genç and Özvar eds., *Osmanlı maliyesi: kurumlar ve bütçeler*, Volume 1, provides comparisons across time for components of revenue and expenditure for twenty-four years between 1653 and 1786. Volume 2 gives all the components of revenue and expenditure and totals per year for eleven years between 1509/10 and 1761/2.

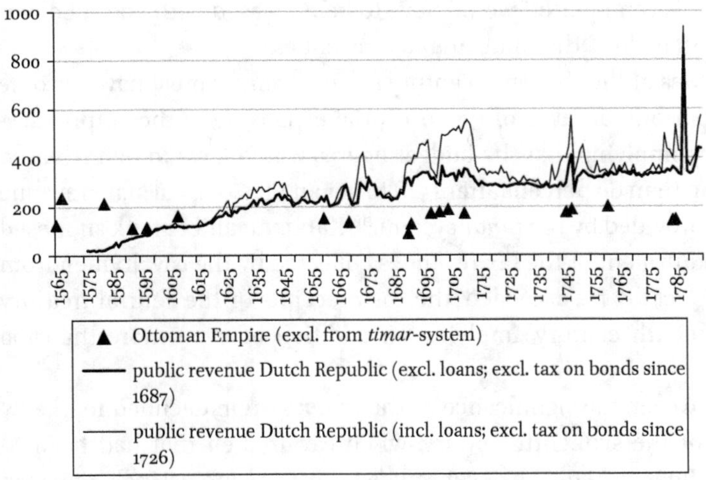

FIGURE 6.1 *Total public revenue of the Ottoman empire and the Dutch Republic, 1565(1575)–1794 (tons of silver).*
Sources: M. Çizakça, *A comparative evolution of business partnerships*, Leiden: Brill, 1996, p. 144, McGowan, *Economic and social history of the Ottoman Empire*, p. 717; M. Genç and E. Özvar eds., *Osmanlı maliyesi: kurumlar ve bütçeler* = Ottoman financial institutions and budgets], 2 vols, Istanbul: Osmanlı Bankası Arsiv ve Araslırma Merkezi =Archive and Research Centre of the Ottoman Bank] 2006; electronic database; for silver values of the akçe see Ş. Pamuk on http://www.iisg.nl/hpw/data.php.

of state revenue and expenditure, and of registers of *daily* totals, being apparently rather unmanageable even for Turkish historians.

The Ottoman figures need some elucidation and qualification, before conclusions can be drawn from Figure 6.1. Firstly, the 'budget'-figures in the graph do not include revenues from the so-called *timar* system. It is known that in 1527/8 out of a total revenue of nearly 538 million *akçe*, no less than about 200 million was that of *timar* holders.[97] For this year the *timars* were explicitly accounted for not only in the number of men, goods and services they had to provide, but also in amounts in *akçe*.[98] This implies that the 'normal' budget-figure for 1527/8 was only 338 million *akçe* or, in other words, that budget-figures for

97 Inalcik, 'The Ottoman state': economy and society', pp. 81, 90.

98 McGowan, *Economic life in Ottoman Europe,* 47 offers an example from the fifteenth century.

other years in this time-period would have to be increased with about 60 percent (200/338) to include the value of *timar*-revenues.

In later decades of the sixteenth century *timar*-revenues must have become even more important, because of the territorial expansion of the empire during this century, implying that the budget figures would have to be increased by (much) more than 60 percent after 1528 to get an idea of total state revenue including that provided by the *timar* system.[99] Karaman and Pamuk supposed that the cash equivalent of the tax revenues collected by the cavalrymen from their *timars* in fact 'by far exceeded' the cash receipts of the central treasury during the sixteenth century, implying an addition of even more than 100 percent.[100]

Secondly, however, the significance of the *timar* system declined markedly since the end of the sixteenth century, when cavalrymen that had been financed by the timar-system in a decentralized way were increasingly replaced by large numbers of infantrymen, centrally paid in cash.[101] Since then there was a sharp increase in centrally organized tax farming (*iltizam*), necessary to obtain cash for restructuring and modernizing the army.[102] According to Barkan the number of *timar* cavalry fell from 87,000 in the 1560s to 8,000 in 1630, while *janissaries* and palace *sipahis* (cavalrymen) that had to be paid in cash, increased from 12,900 to 67,500.[103] In Anatolia even all remaining *timar* land had been usurped by fiscal entrepreneurs by 1760.[104]

---

99 According to Omer Lutfi Barkan and Enver Mericli, *Hudavendigar Livasi Tahrir Defterler* (Ankara: Turk Tarih Kurumu Basimevi, 1988) p. 5 the possessors of timars (about 37,000 persons) were allocated 'nearly half' of the taxes levied in the territories of the Empire at the beginning of the sixteenth century [cited in a review by Y. Terzibasoglu Bogazici University Istanbul of D. Kolodziejczyk, *The Ottoman Survey Register of Podalia* (Cambridge: Harvard University Press 2004) on http://h-net.msu.edu (http://www.h-net.org/reviews/showrev.php?id=11048) [14-08-2012].

100 Karaman and Pamuk, 'Ottoman state finances', p. 604 Figure 1.

101 According to Barkan cited by J. Goldstone, 'East and West in the seventeenth century: political crises in Stuart Britain, Ottoman Turkey and Ming China', in *Comparative Studies in Society and History*, 30, 1991, p. 111n, the number of timar cavalry even fell from 87,000 in the 1560s to 8,000 in 1630 and that of janissaries plus palace sipahis increased from 12,900 to 67,500.

102 Faroqhi, *Economic and social history of the Ottoman Empire*, p. 568.

103 Goldstone, 'East and West in the seventeenth century', p. 111 (he refers to Barkan); also Faroqhi, *Economic and social history*, pp. 434, 568; according to Hakkı Kadı, *Natives and interlopers*, 26 (no further reference) the number of cavalry-men amounted to 20,000 during the campaigns against Russia in 1787–1792 (only part of which were still timar-holders), while their number had been 200,000 during the reign of Suleiman (I (1520–1566).

104 McGowan, *Economic and social history*, p. 670; Quataert, ibidem, p. 711.

Thirdly it should be repeated that, similar to the Dutch Republic, an important part of what was received in the provinces of the Ottoman Empire was spent in these provinces themselves. From the tax revenue in Egypt at the end of the eighteenth century, for instance, 75 percent had to be spent in Egypt, only 25 percent came at the disposal of the central treasury, and even this amount became subject to an increasing burden of deductions to meet obligations imposed on the Porte in Egypt, so that by that time very little was sent to the Porte itself.[105] One may wonder if this does not make the figures for state finance of the Dutch Republic, which consist in the combined figures for provincial finance as was explained in Part 1 of this book, utterly incomparable to the Ottoman budget-figures. However, the Ottoman central government is reported to have had constant supervision over provincial financial activities. It received each year balance sheets with detailed provincial accounts. According to Sahillioğlu only Wallachia, Moldavia and Dubrovnik enjoyed complete autonomy, being obliged only to send an annual tribute at a fixed amount to the sultan.[106] He could demonstrate – at least for the years after 1698/9 – that the totals of the published 'budget' figures are comparable to the *sum* of figures in the *ruznamce*, the daily accounts of revenue and expenditure at the centre, and the *mahsub*, specifying revenue and expenditure in the provinces including the amounts that never reached the treasury.[107] This must imply that the Ottoman 'budget-figures' included provincially spent tax revenues, just like the constructed figures for the Dutch Republic.

Fourthly, Faroqhi points to services to the army required from peasants and nomads for transport, that are not accounted for,[108] and to the fact that the prices they received in payment for what they had to deliver in goods to the army were set low by the government.[109] Pamuk and Karaman supposed

---

105 Total revenue in the Imperial Treasury from the rich province of Egypt in 1798 was nearly 120 million *para*, which amounts to 9.5 ton silver (Shaw *The financial and administrative organization and development of Ottoman Egypt*, pp. 304–305; Pamuk in OE II 958). In 1671 it had been 95.8 million para, this was probably between 52 and 67 ton silver. Total revenue of the Ottoman Empire in 1669 had been 273 ton silver.

106 Inalcik, *Social and Economic History*, 84.

107 H. Sahillioğlu, '1683–1740 Yıllarında osmanlı imparatorluğun hazine gelir ve gider' [=Yearly revenue and expenditure of the Ottoman Imperial Treasury, 1683–1740'] in Genç and Özvar, *Osmanlı maliyesi*, Vol. 1, p. 156, Table 30: of the total revenue of 1.1 million akçe in 1691/2 0.54 million was found in the *ruznamce* and had been received at the central treasury, 0,51million akçe was found in de *mahsub*, specifying what had been received and spent in the provinces.

108 Faroqhi, *Economic and social history*, p. 536.

109 McGowan, *Economic life*, 154–155.

moreover that in the course of the eighteenth century allowances should yet be made for soldiers provided by provincial notables to the army and for other indirect contributions.[110] For the end of the eighteenth century they estimate the necessary addition at about 30 percent of the 'budget'-amounts.[111] As was mentioned they supposed that total state revenue including that from the *timar*-system was around 1600 somewhat more than double the 'budget'-amounts. For the period since about 1650 they suggested the desirability of a revision of the revenue amounts to somewhat less than double the amounts in the budgets.

Lastly it should be mentioned, that of the 538 million in 1527/8, about 11 percent came from *waqfs*, the religious endowments, originating in gifts by the state or by private persons, by means of which social and economic forms of public expenditure – such as poor relief, schools, hospitals and other, mostly urban, facilities – were financed. These *waqfs* (or *awqaf, evkaf, habous*) could be a source of revenue as well, revenues that remained earmarked for religious and charitable expenditure.[112] The kind of services these *waqfs* provided, and the revenues they generated, were in the Dutch Republic often part of *urban* public finance, and not included in the data for *provincial* finance that were the main foundation for the figures for the Dutch Republic in Figure 6.1. It might be argued therefore that for a comparison with the Dutch Republic the *waqf*-part of Ottoman state revenue, which also appears in the 'budgets', should be excluded.

Karaman and Pamuk decided eventually to use just the published 'budget'-figures, not their own revised estimates, for their comparisons with the revenue of other states, because the results would not have been much different.[113] Likewise we may safely conclude from Figure 6.1 that there needs to be no doubt whatsoever, that *total* tax revenue in the very small Dutch Republic was either (much) higher, or in any case not very different from that in the huge Ottoman Empire, even when the 'budget'-figures for the Ottoman Empire would in fact have to be doubled for the whole period to include revenues that were not accounted for by the central treasury. This despite the fact that population

110 Karaman and Pamuk, 'Ottoman state finances', 602, 605; McGowan, *Economic life*, decribes the attempts of the central government to curb tendencies to additional provincial and local taxation in Rumeli in 1729, 1740, 1779 and 1781 and assumes that it became increasingly easy for kadis to disguise their manipulations.

111 Karaman and Pamuk, 'Ottoman state finances', p. 604 Figure 1, the graph called 'Ottoman II'.

112 Darling, 'Ottoman fiscal administration', p. 165.

113 Karaman and Pamuk, 'Ottoman state finances', pp. 605–606.

in the Dutch Republic was not more than about 1.5 million in 1600 and about 2.1 million in 1800, while the population in those parts of the Ottoman Empire that contributed to its central treasury, was more than about ten times as large.[114] Figure 6.1 shows that state revenue in the Ottoman Empire even decreased, at least in tons of silver, despite some indications for economic growth in the course of the eighteenth century.[115]

Already contemporary foreigners noted with surprise the relatively very small amounts in public expenditure in the Ottoman Empire in comparison with other states at the end of the eighteenth century.[116] Genç has argued that tax revenues worth some 3.4 million British pounds might be more probable for the Ottoman Empire than the 2.25 million pounds in 1789 mentioned in a foreign estimate. However, this would still be less than the public revenue of the small state of the Dutch Republic at the end of the eighteenth century (worth about 3.5 million pounds). In both Britain and the Dutch Republic tax revenue has been estimated by then at about 10 percent or more of the value of Gross Domestic Product, in the Ottoman Empire at certainly less than 6 percent at that time.[117]

Wages and soldiers' payments, as well as the general price level, were much lower in the Ottoman Empire than in the Dutch Republic, however. Despite its low level of public finance the Ottoman Empire had an army of about 130,000 men in 1700 against 90,000 in the Dutch Republic and 62,000 in Austria, its main European enemy at that time.[118] Therefore the tax revenues received per capita in Figure 6.2 are expressed in the number of days that unskilled urban labourers would have to work to earn these amounts. The graph shows that the number of daily wages received by the government in taxes per capita in the Ottoman Empire was comparatively really very low.

It should be noted that the average tax revenue per capita received by the state is not identical to the average tax *burden* per capita. It has been estimated that in the case of tax revenues farmed under the *malikane* system (to be discussed in the next section of this chapter) even no more than 'only one third of the net tax receipts ended in the central treasury'.[119] There are reasons to

114 Around 22 million; Karaman and Pamuk, 'Ottoman state finances', pp. 606–607 note 34.

115 M. Genç, 'A study of the feasibility of using eighteenth-century Ottoman financial records as an indicator of economic activity', in: *The Ottoman Empire and the world economy*, ed. H. Islamoglu-Inan, Cambridge: Cambridge UP, 1987, pp. 345–373.

116 Quataert, *Economic and social history of the Ottoman Empire,* p. 714.

117 W. Fritschy, 'Taxation in Britain, France and the Netherlands in the eighteenth century', in *Economic and social history in the Netherlands* 2, 1990, pp. 57–81; Pamuk and Karaman.

118 Karaman and Pamuk, 'Ottoman state finances', p. 612.

119 Karaman and Pamuk, 'Ottoman state finances', p. 609.

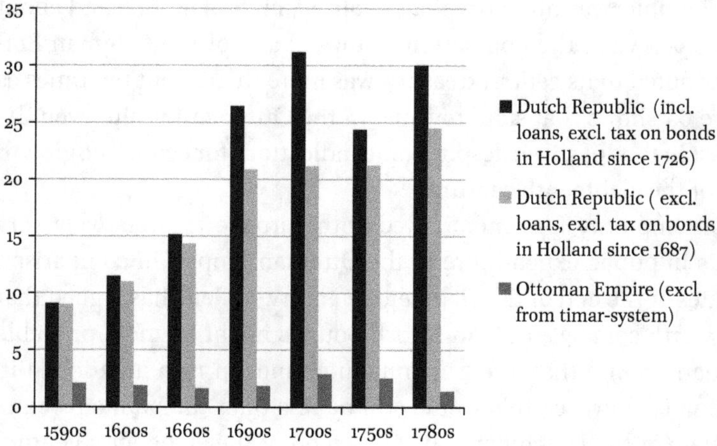

FIGURE 6.2 *Number of daily wages of urban skilled workers received on average per capita in public revenue in the Dutch Republic and the Ottoman empire (1590s–1780s).*
Sources: for tax revenue: see sources Figure 6.1; population and wages Dutch Republic result from interpolation of the estimates in De Vries and van der Woude, *The first modern economy*, pp. 50, 85, 610–611; for population in Ottoman Empire: the estimates in K. Kivanç Karaman and S. Pamuk, 'Ottoman State Finances in European perspective', *Journal of Economic History* (2010) 592–629, 606–607 note 34 were used, which excluded the parts of the Empire not sending any tax revenue to the central treasury; for wages in silver in Istanbul: see http://www.iisg.nl/hpw/data.php.

dispute this extreme estimate, as will be shown in Section 6.4 below. However, even if the amount paid per capita in the Ottoman Empire would have been in fact three times the level indicated in Figure 6.2 this would have been still much less per capita than in the Dutch Republic. Karaman and Pamuk have shown that the same is true for a comparison with most other European states as well.[120]

The Marginal Importance of Domestic Indirect Taxation

Although the break-downs used in the available Ottoman 'budgets' do not allow a systematic division of Ottoman state revenue in direct taxes on real estate or persons and price-increasing indirect taxes, it can be argued that the

120 Karaman and Pamuk, 'Ottoman state finances', fig. 6 p. 615.

TABLE 6.3 *Percentage breakdown of Ottoman state revenue, 1650–1788.*

	mukataa	*cizye*	*avariz*	**% of total revenue that could be assigned to these categories**
1650–1700	53%	26%	17%	96%
1700–1750	48%	40%	11%	99%
1750–1788w	52%	40%	8%	100%

Source: B. Çakir, 'geleneksel dönem (tanzimat öncesi) osmanlı bütçe gelirleri', in Osmanlı Maliyesi I, pp. 167–197, pp. 184–185.

part played by domestic indirect taxation must have been very small in the Ottoman fiscal system, despite the fact that the percentage of people living in cities was not lower than that in Europe.

Subdivisions in the Ottoman 'budgets' are partly geographical, partly according to the way in which taxes were levied. This subdivision consisted of the *mukataa* (farmed direct and indirect taxes), the *cizye* (= *jizya*: a direct tax on Jews and Christians[121]) and the *avariz* (direct extraordinary taxes, which became part of the regular Ottoman tax system in the eighteenth century). What is known on the subdivision into these three categories is summarized in Table 6.3. It shows that the direct *cizye* and *avariz* revenues alone amounted already to about half of tax revenue.

Hardly any quantitative information is available on the composition of the *mukataa*. It is very likely, however, that they consisted, since the start of the decline of the *timar*-system, for the largest part of the land-tax, because – as one author put it – 'the old tendency to tax the countryside and favour the

121 A similar tax was missing in the Dutch Republic. It was not really exclusive for the Ottoman Empire, however. A special tax on Jews existed in The Holy Roman Empire since 1241 and during the fourteenth century the amounts received from Jews varied from 2 to 15 percent of the total amounts paid by cities to the German emperor. In Altona Jews had to pay a tax in exchange for the right to have a synagogue from 1641 until 1842, and a tax on Jews is known for at least some places in Poland and Russia, and since 1747 also for Hungary under the Austrian Empire (see H. Pathe, *Judenschutzsteuern in Altona (1641–1842)* diss. Hamburg, 2007; http://ediss.sub.uni-hamburg.de/volltexte/2007/3395/pdf/Pathe.pdf). The overall quantitative importance in state revenue of taxes on Jews in these Middle and Eastern European regions will have been certainly much lower than that of the *cizye* on Jews plus Christians, as their proportion in the – partly European – Ottoman Empire was certainly much higher than that of Jews in the 'Latin West'.

towns always prevailed', also during the eighteenth century.[122] The land tax, which had to be paid by Muslims as well as Jews and Christians, was paid in cash in Egypt and other southern parts of the Ottoman Empire already before 1660. This means, that the combined amount of the main forms of direct taxation, the land tax, the *cizye*, and the *avariz*, cannot have left much for the part played by indirect taxes. Moreover, the largest part of the indirect taxes in the *mukataa* consisted probably on that on foreign trade.

That the part played by indirect domestic taxes was really very small is confirmed by the scarcely available estimates found in the literature as summarized in Table 6.4. The percentages for indirect taxation in Egypt consisted for by far the largest part of taxes on foreign trade. Percentages of only 6 percent in 1595 and 4 percent in 1671/2 for domestic indirect taxation, despite the existence of large cities like Alexandria and Cairo, can be called really very low, not only in comparison to 'commercial states' like Britain and the Dutch Republic, but also in comparison to other European states.

Ir was the high amount in *total* taxes per capita which made the part played by indirect taxation in the Dutch Republic in the course of the eighteenth century lower than in other West-European states (Chapter 3). Here additional direct taxes – not only on land, but also on houses, cattle, servants and coaches, and on the estimated consumption of salt, soap, coffee and tea of the middle classes, and personal taxes on general wealth and income sources – had become increasingly unavoidable, as we saw. The importance of indirect taxation remained nevertheless much higher than in the Ottoman Empire.

German states have not been included, because they deviated from the states mentioned in the table by very large amounts in non-tax revenues (from domains, mines, forests, postal services and other monopolies), supplying no less than on average about 40 percent of Prussian public revenues in the second half of the eighteenth century (whereas non-tax revenues in states like France, Britain Sweden and the Dutch Republic supplied certainly less than 8 percent). Nevertheless, also in German states indirect taxes were much more important than in the Ottoman Empire: in Brandenburg-Prussia indirect 'urban' taxes

122 S. Özbaran criticized L. Darling, *Revenue-raising and Legitimacy: Tax Collection and Finance Administration in the Ottoman Empire, 1560–1660* (Leiden: Brill 1996) in *Journal of Islamic Studies* 11 (2000) 238–240, p. 239 for not discussing the *kharadj* (the land-tax), which 'should certainly have figured prominently in (her) book'; for the eighteenth century see McGowan, 'The age of the ayans', in: *Economic and social history of the Ottoman Empire*, p. 711.

TABLE 6.4 *Revenues from indirect taxation incl. customs (and between brackets excl. customs) as % of total public revenue excl. loans in the Ottoman empire and some states in the 'Latin West', c. 1500–1800.*

	Ottoman Empire	Egypt	Dutch Republic	Britain	France	Spain
1475	10%					
c. 1550						66%
1595		26 (6)%				
c. 1600			50 (37)%			
c. 1650			63 (50)%			
1671/2		20 (4)%	50 (37)%	(20%)		
c. 1700	12 (3?)%		47 (36)%	62 (24)%		
1725					50%	70–90%
c. 1750	10%		36 (29)%	69 (46)%		70–90%
1774	12%					
c. 1790			43 (37)%	76 (45)%	57%	70–90%

Sources: H. Inalcik a.o., *Economic and social history of the Ottoman Empire*, I, 55–56, 86–87, II, 711; S. Shaw, *The financial and administrative organization and development of Ottoman Egypt, 1517–1798*, Princeton Univ. Press, 1962; electronic database; Mitchell and Deane, *British historical statistics*, 386–388; R. Bonney, 'The rise of the fiscal state in France, 1500–1914', in *The rise of fiscal states. A global history*, pp. 93–111, p. 103; J. Gelabert, 'The King's expenses: the asientos of Philip III and Philip IV of Spain, 1598–1650', in: *Crises, revolutions and self-sustained growth*, pp. 224–249, p. 228; idem, 'Castile, 1504–1808' in *The rise of the fiscal state in Europe*, ed. R. Bonney, pp. 201–243, p. 235; 1774: data in Section 6.4 for the so-called *malikane-mukataas*.

supplied in 1778 27 percent of total revenue, 55 percent of tax revenue; these percentages were in Saxony in 1767 resp. 27 percent and 35 percent.[123]

It may be asked if an explanation for this remarkable difference in the role of 'urban' indirect taxes between the 'Latin West' and the Ottoman Empire, despite rather similar overall urbanization percentages (see Table 6.2) should be found in the fact that indirect taxes (called *maks*, plur. *mukus*) were generally viewed as illegal by Muslim religious legal scholars, although no outright

123 M. Spoerer, 'The revenue structures of Brandenburg-Prussia, Saxony and Bavaria (Fifteenth to Nineteenth Centuries): Are they compatible with the Bonney-Ormrod model?' *La fiscalità nell'economia europea secc. XIII–XVIII* (Firenze 2008).

prohibition is to be found in the Qur'an. Their illegality could be deduced from the fact that the Qur'an only obliges Muslims to pay the *zakat*: a yearly tax, mostly set at 10 percent of agrarian revenues and 2.5 percent of the value of all property that has been in one's possession (except the value of one's house, normal household furniture and belongings, and ordinary personal assets) during the whole year.

On the one hand, it should be emphasized, that, nevertheless, indirect taxes were levied everywhere in the world of Islam, from very early on, as Muslim conquerors often just kept existing fiscal systems intact in conquered areas. Literature on Islamic cities in the later Middle Ages abounds in references to indirect taxes, and also Muslims had to pay them.[124] On the other hand, the idea that they were in fact illegal never disappeared, not only in the minds of legal Muslim scholars, but also in those of contemporary rulers and taxpayers. It was in general even often one of the first public acts of a newly enthroned ruler in Islamic countries to abolish all taxes on trade that were considered illegal and oppressive, at least temporarily.[125] Lapidus points explicitly to 'the frequency with which illegal taxes were denounced and abolished' in Muslim cities.[126] According to Inalcik market dues in the Ottoman Empire were mostly set at a modest rate of only 2.5 percent to make them look like the *zakat*, the only tax acceptable for Muslims according to the Qur'an. It cannot be completely excluded therefore, that the cultural factor of a deep-rooted religiously motivated aversion against indirect taxation may have contributed to their relatively small role in the fiscal system.

However, the specific 'state-driven' urbanization-trajectory, related to specific geographic and ecological circumstances in the Ottoman Empire, and resulting in a lack of urban public finance, is obviously also an important factor in an explanation of this remarkable difference. The same is valid for the last important difference between state revenue in the Ottoman Empire and the Dutch Republic: the absence of long-term public loans in state revenue. Before this aspect of Ottoman public finance will further be discussed in the last section of this chapter, yet one other form of 'revenue raising' will shortly be discussed at the end of this section: diminishing the silver content of the currency.

---

124 I. Lapidus, *Muslim cities in the later Middle Ages* (Cambridge: CUP, 1984) pp. 35, 40, 96, 99, 172, 173, 203, 274, 276.

125 Inalcik, *Economic and social history of the Ottoman Empire*, I, pp. 53, 202.

126 Lapidus, *Muslim cities*, pp. 252, 254.

'Coin Clipping' as a Source of Public Revenue

In order to be able to pay the largely increased numbers of infantry necessary for early modern war faring, the Ottoman government decided in 1585 to lower the silver content of the *akçe* to 0.34 grs, nearly half of its long-lasting content of 0.66 grs silver since 1481 (reduced only once, in 1566, to 0.61 grs).[127] The Ottoman Empire was not unique in using 'coin clipping' to finance a state deficit. It was also used in Holland in 1573 and 1575, when a large amount of money at once was needed for the war against Spain, which could not be raised soon enough in other ways (Chapter 1). The same was true for Britain in the 1540s, when Henry VIII decided to get involved in international war faring (Chapter 5).

It should be noted, in addition, that a decision to reduce the silver content of a local currency could very well result from other causes than the needs of state finance. It could be enforced by rising silver-prices, or by an increased circulation of similar coins with a lower value, causing 'good money' to be melted down and to be replaced by 'bad money'. Reductions in the silver content of currency are not necessarily an indication of a deteriorating budgetary situation, therefore. They could help, as well, to keep enough means of payment in circulation, when the supply of silver or gold was deficient. Sudden large changes, however, like the ones in Britain in the 1540s, in the Dutch Republic in the 1570s and in the Ottoman Empire in the last decades of the sixteenth century could be very disruptive socio-economically, when rising prices resulting from the devaluation, did not lead to rising earnings for people dependent on money-incomes.

Figure 6.4 offers a comparison of changes in the silver content of several currencies. It shows that the change in silver content of the currency in the Ottoman Empire in 1585 with 44 percent at once was more drastic than that in Britain in the 1540s (25 percent in ten years) and in the Dutch Republic in the 1570s (27 percent in three years). It was moreover followed by yet another one in 1595.

Because the devaluation led to rising prices, soldiers started to rebel. Plundering soldiers roaming the countryside became endemic in this period,

127 Figures in three decimals for all years were found in 'Ottoman exchange rates-2' on the web site of the Ataturk Institute of Modern History (www.ata.boun.edu.tr) accessible by searching Google for 'silver content akce' (no author mentioned); a somewhat less detailed file is available on http://www.iisg.nl/hpw/data.php (data not given for all years separately, only in two decimals and some slight differences: 1489-90 0.68, not 0.657; decline to 0.34 in 1586, not in 1585); for Figure 6.4 I used the last data file as this is part of a larger international dataset and mentions its author (Ş. Pamuk).

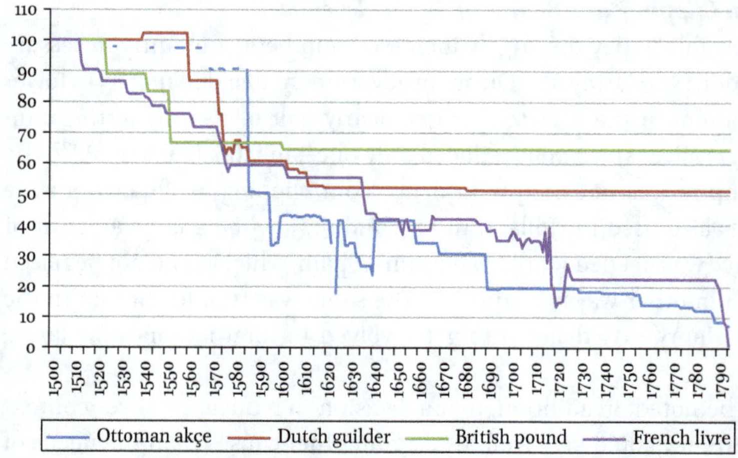

FIGURE 6.3 *Changes in the silver content of the Ottoman* akçe, *the Dutch guilder, the British pound and the French livre, 1500–1800 (Y-axis log scale; index 1500=100).*
Sources: Pamuk, Van Zanden, G. Clark, Ph. Hoffmann on http://www.iisg.nl/hpw/data.php.

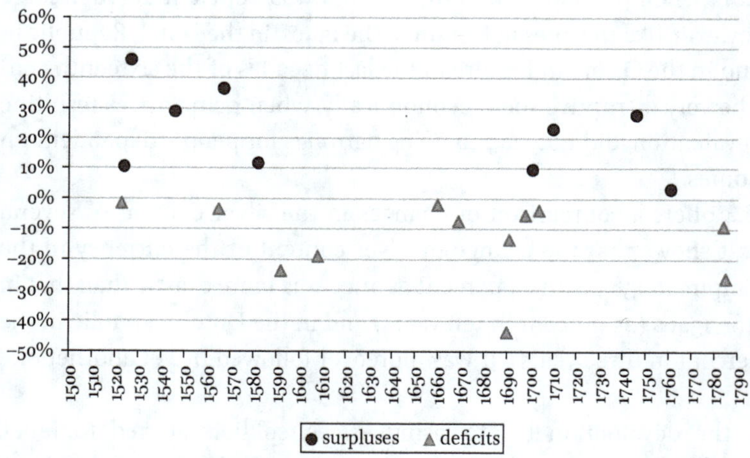

FIGURE 6.4 *Difference between Ottoman imperial revenue and expenditure as % of revenue 1520–1790.*
NB A deficit of 200 percent in 1597 has been omitted to enhance the visibility of surpluses and deficits in other years.
Source: Genç and Özvar, *Osmanlı Maliyesi.*

contributing to a flight of peasants to the cities. In the longer run, soldiers in the Ottoman Empire seem to have adapted to the risk of devaluations by developing economic connections in the cities which they had to guard, in order to secure their livelihood.

Figure 6.4 shows that Britain and the Dutch Republic started to avoid reductions in the silver value of their currencies since resp. about 1600 and 1620, which will have been related to the importance of international trade in their economies.[128] Much larger states like France and the Ottoman Empire, with much larger domestic economies, will have been less vulnerable than Britain and the Dutch Republic in this respect. It is evident, however, that drastic currency devaluation was a risky means to finance deficits, and that it was preferable for a state to dispose of other possibilities to this end.

6.4 Deficits, 'Advance Payments', Advances and Debt

The amounts of total Ottoman state revenue were far from identical to state expenditure in the years for which 'budget'-figures were published, as is shown in Figure 6.4. Conclusions based on public finance data for single years are never very reliable, of course. As regards the occurrence of deficits in Ottoman public finance, a pattern seems to be discernible, however, of periods with relatively many, and with hardly any deficits. It is a pattern that fits into general historical information on the occurrence of fiscal problems in Ottoman history.[129]

No comparative discussion of the structure of Ottoman state expenditure will be offered in this chapter, as a subdivision in categories of expenditure is only published for the 'budget' of the (peace) year 1669/70. This shows about 50 percent for the army, 7 percent for the navy, 30 percent for the sultan's person and upkeep of his palaces, 6 percent for other officials and religion-related expenditure, and a deficit of 7 percent.[130] There is no doubt at all, however, that the main difference with the Dutch Republic and other West-European states in the structure of public expenditure in the early modern period is the lack of debt service.

For most of the sixteenth century the simple explanation is, that long-term loans were not yet needed. Five of the seven years for which data are available between 1520 and 1585 show surpluses, and the deficits in the remaining two years were relatively small (Figure 6.4). Until 1585 revenue surpluses resulting

128 Even although local currency was not used in international trade: in the Dutch Republic special so-called *'negotie-penningen'* were in use in international trade, when payment by means of bills of exchange was not possible, but foreign traders had to use local currency of course during a stay in Amsterdam or London, and it will no doubt have increased the attractiveness of and the trust in a city, when the local currency was stable as well.

129 Pamuk, 'Institutional change and the longevity of the Ottoman Empire', offers a periodization.

130 S. Faroqhi, 'Finances', in: *Social and economic history of the Ottoman Empire* Part II (Cambridge 1997) p. 541.

from conquests were used to fill the 'sultan's treasury' or 'inner treasury', which functioned as a reserve bank for the main or 'current treasury'.[131] It had been the continuous addition of new territories with tax payers to the empire that had made the period 1477–1585 into a period of fiscal strength.[132] In the year 1585, however, a devaluation of the *akçe* had been felt necessary to pay the army, as we saw.

The eight years between 1585 and 1700 in Figure 6.3 show all large deficits. The first available year 1592 shows a deficit of 24 percent. An extremely large deficit in 1597 of 200 percent has even been omitted in order to improve the visibility of surpluses and deficits in other years in the graph. Especially the seventeenth century seems to have known many deficits. The eighteenth century suggests some fiscal improvement until about 1765, as four out of five of the available years between 1700 and 1767 show surpluses again. No information at all is available, however, for the war years 1714–1718, when the Ottoman Empire won from Venice, but lost from Austria, and for the years of the lost war of 1730–1735 against Persia. The peace after the lost war against Russia from 1768 to 1774 required a heavy war compensation to be paid by the Ottoman Empire.

How were deficits handled? Forced loans from the wealthy bearing no interest, like in medieval Britain, are mentioned incidentally since 1460.[133] The terms of repayment do not seem to have been very reliable, again like in Britain at the time. Around 1600 large non-interest-bearing sums, borrowed from high-level bureaucrats, were 'repaid' by giving the lenders the right to collect tax-arrears.[134] No wonder that these loans were resisted by elites.[135] The method of 'coin clipping' to pay the army was mentioned already.

Short-term borrowing from Jewish financiers is known, as well, since the end of the sixteenth century, which will no doubt have required interest payments. Such transactions are not to be found in the 'budgets' however. Borrowing from pious foundations with surplus funds occurred, too,[136] but the amounts that

131 Inalcik, *Economic and social history of the Ottoman Empire*, pp. 77–78; A. Salzmann, *Tocquevile in the Ottoman Empire: rival paths to the modern state* (Leiden, Brill, 2004) p. 86.

132 Ş. Pamuk, *A monetary history of the Ottoman Empire*, Cambridge 2001, p. 20; Inalcik, *Economic and social history of the Ottoman Empire*, I, p. 100.

133 Lapidus, *Muslim cities in the later Middle Ages*, pp. 57, 122.

134 Pamuk, *Monetary history*, p. 85.

135 A. Salzman, 'An ancient régime revisited': 'privatization'and political economy in the eighteenth century Ottoman Empire', *Politics and Scoiety* 21, 4 (1972) pp. 393–423, p. 401.

136 Darling, *Revenue raising and Legitimacy*, p. 8.

could be borrowed from so-called 'cash-*waqfs*' were very modest in comparison to what was needed during war years.[137]

More taxes and higher tax rates were introduced in the Ottoman Empire as well, of course, in attempts to overcome financial problems. The flexibility and adaptability of Ottoman fiscal administration, especially in the course of the seventeenth century, have been emphasized in the literature.[138] The positive effect on the level of total public revenue of the doubling of the *cizye*-tax in the early eighteenth century is clearly visible in the available figures (see Table 6.3 and Figure 6.1).

In addition, however, demanding large advances as part of the system of tax farming would become an important part of public finance in the Ottoman Empire until the end of the eighteenth century. Like in Britain until 1683 this became a preferred alternative to forced loans from subjects, or expensive loans from merchants. In France, the link between tax farming and state borrowing would remain in existence until the French Revolution, alongside an already long existing public debt in the form of 'obligations' and life-annuities. Tax farming did not involve such advances in the Dutch Republic. The network of tax receivers in the Dutch urban system provided a more efficient and convenient alternative.

Developments in the relation between tax farming and advances on tax revenue in the Ottoman Empire show also important differences with Britain and France. Although the gradual replacement of '*iltizam*', the old form of tax farming, by *malikane* tax farms, is sometimes characterized as 'an important shift towards longer-term borrowing by the state',[139] the most important difference with European states would become that the advances on tax revenues asked from Ottoman tax farmers would develop into very large 'advance *payments*' to the government instead of loans, under the *malikane*-system that started in 1695.

The evolution from the *malikane*-system to the *esham*-system has even been said to show 'striking parallels' with the evolution of European public finance,[140] although the *differences* in the evolution of tax farming and in the ability to realize advances on tax revenue were much more striking on fact. The in itself very impressive 'advance payments' were a much more expensive – as well as a much less important – source of additional revenue in the Ottoman

137 Çizakça, *A comparative evolution of business partnerships*, p. 144.

138 Darling. 'Ottoman fiscal administration', pp. 172–173; Pamuk, 'The evolution of fiscal institutions', p. 305.

139 Genç, 'A study of the feasibility', p. 348; Pamuk, *Monetary History*, p. 190.

140 Pamuk, *Monetary History*, p. 190.

fiscal system, than the long-term public debts in the fiscal systems of Western European states.

After a further comparative discussion and explanation of *iltizam*, the *malikane*-system and the *esham*-system this section will mainly argue that a convincing explanation for the extremely slow development of a large public debt at low rates of interest in this part of the world can be found in the difference in 'urbanization-trajectories' in the Ottoman Empire and the 'Latin West'.

Iltizam

Iltizam – an originally Arabic term for tax farming – had been in use in the territory of the Ottoman Empire already long before the sixteenth century, for indirect taxes and revenues from mines and salt works as well as for the land tax. In Western-Europe, too, tax farming occurred already in the Middle Ages, although here mostly restricted to indirect taxes. An Ottoman tax farm was called a *mukataa*, meaning 'section' or 'district', referring to a tax in a certain geographical part of the Empire, leased as a tax farm. A tax farmer was called a *mültezim*.[141]

Under *iltizam* the bids during the auctions in which taxes were leased, were on the tax amount that a *mültezim* would have to cede annually to the government, when granted the right to collect a certain tax – or number of taxes – in a certain district during a certain period of time, at tax rates and other conditions determined by the government, just like in Western Europe. Tax farmers had to pay the state an amount in advance, in addition to the annual instalments, and they had to find guarantors who promised to compensate the government in case they would fail to meet their annual obligations, as was the case in states in Europe.

The guarantors took probably also a share in pre-financing the advances and must of course have shared in the profits of the tax farm. Most tax farmers operated alone or in partnerships of two, sometimes three or four, persons. A tax farmer could also subcontract his tax farm to sub-tax-farmers. Under the system of *iltizam* the profit of a tax farm consisted in the surplus collected above the fixed amounts of the tax revenue that had to be paid to the government during the period of the lease-contract after deduction of the costs (including the costs of the advancement), just like in West Europe. Taxes that

141 A detailed and lucid summary of the main aspects of tax farming in the Ottoman Empire and its historiography is to be found in Çizakça, *A Comparative evolution of business partnerships*, pp. 146–159; on the *malikane*-system pp. 159–179, on the *esham* system pp. 179–192.

could not be leased, because of a lack of sufficient bids during the auction, became the responsibility of salaried government officials (*emins*).

When the profits for tax farmers turned out to be immoderately large the Ottoman government could break off the lease period, and renegotiate the contract. Çizakça showed that between 1550 and 1650 the actual duration of the lease of no less than about two thirds of the 134 tax farms for which he had data, differed from the originally intended duration. The many cases in which the new lease sum was higher than the old one, suggest that the ending was mostly not caused by failures of the tax farmers, but by the premature realization of a higher bid by the government. In the course of the period, however, many tax farms tended to become 'frozen'.[142] In the Dutch Republic and Britain lease terms were not changed prematurely by the government. In France, however, before the coming into existence of the powerful 'Company of the General Farms' in 1661, many examples exist of tax farmers who were confronted by alterations in the number of the taxes they leased or the rates at which they had to be collected,[143] or who were forced to sell their contracts before the end of its duration, when larger bids were made by others in the meantime.

So Ottoman tax farming in the period of *iltizam* was in many respects similar to tax farming systems in West-European states, which differed among themselves from one another in several respects, anyhow. In the Dutch Republic leases were as a rule for one year only, like in the case of many Ottoman tax farms. Britain had in the 1660s and 1670s lease periods of three, four or five years.[144] In France tax farms had since 1726 a lease period of six years. Despite these differences the lengths of the lease-periods in the 'Latin West' fell all of them within the range of one to nine years that has been observed for the Ottoman Empire before 1695.

In France and Britain tax farming came to be concentrated in large organizations of big tax farmers in the course of the seventeenth century. In the Ottoman Empire tax farms remained relatively small, like Dutch tax farms, and the total number of tax farmers remained large, although mergers between Ottoman tax farms did occur and were appreciated by the government, as they

---

142 Çizakça, *A comparative evolution of business partnership*, p. 143.

143 N.D. Johnson, 'Banking on the king: the evolution of the royal revenue farms in Old Regime France', *Journal of Economic History* 66,4 (2006) pp. 963–991, p. 978: 63.2 percent; the publication with Balla in JEH (2009) 818 mentions that 64.7 percent of contracts on the aides were broken and that 26 of the 68 largest farms had their leases broken between 1598 and 1655.

144 Chandaman, *English public revenue*, pp. 23, 24, 57.

were considered as more reliable than small farms.[145] Similarly, a preference for financially more powerful tax farmers did develop in the Dutch Republic in the eighteenth century.

Like in the Ottoman Empire it had been common in Britain and France to ask amounts in advance from the tax farmers, but there were large differences in the extent to which governments became dependent on these loans. The British government was able to abolish the farming of customs in 1671 and of excises in 1683 as we saw in Chapter 5, thanks to the small amount of outstanding debts to tax farmers at that moment and the absence of war.[146] In France, however, the government became increasingly dependent on tax farming, although here, in contrast to Britain, the sale of annuities for public finance, resulting in long-term debts, existed in its cities already during the Middle Ages. The French central government often needed more money, and at shorter notice, than could be realized by means of the sale of annuities or obligations, however. Its increasing dependence on the 'Company of General Farms' would obstruct the abolition of tax farming until the French Revolution. In the Dutch Republic tax farms were never used as a means to get loans in advance of tax revenue, because annuities and obligations were directly sold to the public at large by the tax receivers in all the cities of its 'urban system', when necessary.

The development of the *malikane*-system allowed the Ottoman government much larger advances on tax revenue than ever were realized by means of tax farming in West European states, but at the cost of a much smaller percentage of tax revenue reaching the treasury. As such it was an expensive alternative for the European sale of annuities. The introduction of the *esham*-system in the 1770s would offer a less costly alternative for the malikane-system and led to a diminishing dependence on the tax farming inherent to the malikane-system. The similarity of the *esham*-system to the sale of life-annuities in Western-Europe continued to make it a very expensive form of realising extra public revenue in advance of tax revenues, however, in comparison to the sale of redeemable annuities and 'obligations' with much lower rates of interest and which both did neither have to be redeemed in fact.

The Malikane-*System*

The old *iltizam*-system of tax farming started to be transformed, partly, and gradually, into the *malikane* system since 1695.[147] The word *malikane* is derived

145 Çizakça, *A comparative evolution of business partnerships*, p. 150.

146 Chandaman, *English public revenue*, p. 72.

147 The initial payments already tended to increase under the old *iltizam* system; Çizakça, *A comparative evolution of business partnership*, p. 161, referring to Genç forthcoming.

from the Arabic verb for 'to own' or 'to possess', in contrast to the word *iltizam* that refers to 'having a contract'. The novelty of the *malikane* system was, that it offered investors (called *malikaneci*) lifelong tax farms with a relatively low annual transfer of tax revenues to the government, called the *mal* (the Arabic word for 'money') in exchange for a comparatively very large initial payment, called the *muaccele* (= 'advance payment').

The lifelong duration of the *malikanes* was a remarkable difference with English, French and Dutch fiscal systems, which never knew lifelong tax farms. Another important difference was that the bids in the auctions were now on the size of the initial payment, the *muaccele*. The amounts of *mal* that had to be paid to the government annually were now fixed beforehand by the government. A third important difference with the West European states was that the *muaccele* was a payment, not an interest bearing short-term loan, as was mentioned already. A fourth difference was the very large size of these 'advance payments' in comparison to the advances demanded from West-European tax farmers.

This system to obtain advances on tax revenue was a rather costly one for the government. This can to a large extent be explained by the fact that the actual tax collection was not organized by the *malikanecis* themselves, but by *mültezims*, to whom the tax collection was leased and who wanted to enjoy an attractive profit as well, of course, after having paid the actual tax collectors. In addition, the large size of the advance payments mostly required pre-financing by Greek and Armenian bankers (*sarrafs*), which of course further increased the costs of the system. In the course of time the government was able to increase the cost effectiveness of the system, however, as will be shown.

In the first years after the start 150 to 300 tax farms were auctioned annually under the new *malikane* conditions.[148] In 1714 the state decided to retract the then existing *malikanes* in most provinces, as they appeared to be disproportionately advantageous for the holders, and to start to collect the taxes by means of governmental officials instead.[149] The *malikanes* were reinstituted to their former holders, however, in 1717, when the Empire was at war with Venice and Austria, and large sums at once were needed. By then m*uaccele*-amounts nearly 50 percent over and above the originally accepted bids were realized, in some cases with a considerable upward adjustment to the *mal* as well.

148 McGowan, 'The age of the ayans', p. 713.

149 Çizakça, *Evolution of business partnerships*, p. 184; evidently not all malikanes, however, as the first auction of the important 'customs of Salonica was in 1707, the second in 1722 see Genç, 'The feasibility', p. 362 Table 16.2.

No more system-wide renegotiations of existing *malikane*-contracts during the life time of *malikaneci* occurred after 1717,[150] but it is remarkable how much the size of the *muaccele* – the initial payments of the *malikane*-contracts – could increase *each* time that a tax was auctioned anew after the death of the holder, and how much the *muaccele* increased in proportion to the *mal*, the annual payment to the government. Table 6.5 shows in column *a* an example of this increase – taken from a publication by Mehmet Genç – for one *malikane*.

a) *Muacceles and Their Profit Rates Compared to Public Debts and Their Interest Rates*

Genç published 21 examples of *malikanes* from the hundreds of *malikanes* that came to exist in the course of the eighteenth century.[151] The example in Table 6.5, for the customs in Salonica, was chosen here, because it contained data from a relatively early date and over a rather long period, and because it is one of only two of his examples for which also data on the development of the taxed economic activity were published.

Table 6.5 column *a* shows the changing size of the *muaccele* at each new auction after the death of the *malikane*-holder(s). The *muaccele* was evidently the main objective of the government, not the *mal*, which was also already apparent from the fact that the bids in the auctions were on the *muaccele,* not on the *mal*, in contrast to European states, where maximization of the tax revenues always remained the primary objective of the government.

It has to be added that the development in the *muaccele* of this specific *malikane* is rather extreme. In the eleven *malikanes* with data for a rather long period (from about 1730 to about 1790) of the 21 published by Genç, the average *muaccele* amount in the earliest period was about 10,000 *kuruş*, the maximum average *muaccele* amount reached in the course of time was on average about 80,000 *kuruş*. The lowest *muaccele* amount in Genç' total sample was 100 *kuruş* for a cotton-textiles stamp tax in Şumnu which became a *malikane* in 1752, the highest the 300,000 *kuruş* on the customs-tax farm of Table 6.5 in 1774. The *mals* in the same eleven examples increased from on average about 6,000 to on

---

150 Salzman, 'An ancient régime revisited', p. 417n55, until the 1790s; he refers to a Turkish publication by Genç.

151 According to Genç, 'The feasibility', p. 349 in Istanbul, where about 90 percent of the *malikane* auctions were held, were about 1,000 *malikane*-holders throughout the eighteenth century; according to Salzman 'over the course of the eighteenth century 1,000 to 2,000 Istanbul-based individuals and some 5,000 to 10,000 individuals based in the provinces' were involved (apart from 'innumerable contractors, agents, financiers, accountants, managers'), Salzman, 'An ancient regime revisited', p. 402.

TABLE 6.5 *Results of the auctions of the* malikane-*tax farm of the customs of Salonica, 1707–1774* (kuruş).

	initial payment (muaccele)	(probable) profit rate (= % of a)	estimated annual profit	annual payment to Treasury (mal)	estimated 'gross yearly revenu'	index of column e		value of trade in Salonica (index)
year	a	b	c=a*b	d	e=c+d	f	period	g
1707	3,500	36.1%	1,264	16,500	17,764	72	1700–18	82
1722	7,000	33.3%	2,331	22,500	24,831	100	1722–37	100
1739	66,000	29.8%	19,668	22,600	42,268	170	1738–43	145
1746	80,000	28.3%	22,640	22,600	45,240	182	1744–49	132
1774	300,000	22.7%	68,100	49,000	117,100	472	1771–77	546

Source: Genç, 'A study of the feasibility', p. 362 (Table 16.2; column g: Table 16.2a; column e is my addition).

average about 11,000 *kuruş* per year in this period. The *malikane* of the Salonica customs was evidently a very attractive one for the government, partly as a result of the prosperous development of trade in this port as visible in column g.

The highest *muacceles* and *mals* in Genç' sample were to be found in the nine *malikanes* on foreign trade. Much lower and sometimes even stagnating *muaccele*-amounts prevailed in the twelve *malikanes* on domestic industrial activities, which is of course an indication of the difference in the economic importance of commercial and industrial activities in the Ottoman Empire. After 1775 the average amounts became lower than in the years before, because since 1776 the most remunerative *malikanes* were changed into *esham*-tax farms (to be discussed in the next sub-section) that were much more advantageous for the state.

The advances on tax revenues by European tax farmers never displayed the proportions as visible between *muaccele* and *mal* in the *malikanes*. In Britain the size of the advances had varied from only 25 percent to 50 percent of the annual amounts to be paid to the government in tax revenue.[152] On these advances they could charge the British government an interest of 6 percent as long as they were not yet redeemed.[153] For France it is known that the amount in advances asked from the farmers of the *aides* (indirect sales taxes and excises) was in 1623 nearly 60 percent of their annual tax revenues, a somewhat larger percentage than in Britain, but again much less than in the Ottoman Empire.[154] Loans by the 'Company of General Farms' in advance of the annual payments from tax revenues would become since 1726 a fixed amount of eight million *livres* at the start of a new six year lease, which was in 1726 only 10 percent – and later even less – of the annual tax amounts to be handed over to the government that increased with each new lease. The advanced sum was in principle repaid from the tax revenues before the end of the lease-term, and bore an interest of 4 percent per year in the meantime.

It should be added, however, that the advances on the tax farms in France not only became larger than before since 1750, starting to vary from 15 percent to more than 35 percent of the annual tax amount for the government. It was yet another important novelty since then that they were no longer redeemed, but became part of France's long-term debts.[155] On top of these – now

152 Chandaman, *English public revenue*, pp. 24, 54, 57, 63, 67.

153 Ibidem, p. 63.

154 E. Balla, and N.D. Johnson, 'Fiscal crisis and institutional change in the Ottoman Empire and France', *Journal of Economic History* 69, 3 (2009) pp. 809–845, p. 818.

155 In France no long-term advances were asked from the Company of General Farmers before 1750; the largest long-term advance was 70 percent of the annual amount in tax

long-term – advances, amounts in short-term debt, issued in the form of interest bearing *billets des fermes* ('tax farming bills'), started to circulate, moreover, since 1756, the issue of which did not even have to await the next auction of the tax farms. Although issued as a form of *short-term* debt granted by the Company to the government, they could in practice remain in circulation for a long time, as they could also be used as a convenient security in commercial transactions, comparable to the Dutch 'obligations'. It was the financial power of the large 'Company of the General Farms' that made these *billets des fermes* into a trusted value-paper. The *billets* were used for payments by the government and could be traded by holders to third parties without losses, but only as long as they were trusted, of course. These developments made it impossible for the French government to abolish tax farming as long as it wanted to avoid a financial chaos.

It is known that in 1762 and in 1770 an amount of 60 million *livres* in *billets des fermes* was in circulation. The annual amount in farmed taxes was resp. 110 million and 132 million *livres* in those years. Total tax revenue was about 320 million livres.[156] So even this debt in *billets de fermes* was again not at all as large in proportion to the tax-amounts, as the Ottoman *muacceles*. In France, the total amount in long-term loans of 92 million *livres* realized by means of the Company of General Farmers since 1750 was, moreover, no more than about 5 percent of the total increase in public debt since 1750. The *muacceles*, however, were until the introduction of the *esham*-system in 1776, the *only* possibility for the Ottoman government to realize advances on tax revenue, and in addition a much costlier possibility.

Table 6.5 shows in column b the trend in the 'profit rate' of *malikanes*, as it was reconstructed by Genç on the basis of data for 150–200 *malikanes* sold in Istanbul between 1700 and 1820.[157] Assuming that this 'profit rate trend' must

---

revenue for the government in 1771: G.T. Matthews, *The Royal General Farms in Eighteenth Century France* (New York. Columbia University Press, 1958) pp. 50, 76, 82, 83, 285). In Britain advances were intended for the short term, but could become longer in practice, and were typically about 50 percent of the annual amount in tax revenue for the government. Under the *malikane* system *muacceles* could easily become as large as three or four times the *mal*.

156 R. Bonney, 'The Eighteenth Century II. The struggle for Great Power status and the end of the old fiscal regime', in Bonney ed., *Economic systems and state finance*, pp. 315–393, p. 337.

157 Genç, 'A study of the feasibility', p. 350; fig. 16.1 shows the variations around the trend, for instance: in 1735 when the profit according to the trend was about 27 percent, also a profit of about 40 percent was found; in 1765 when the profit according to the trend was about 22 percent, also a profit of 15 percent was found.

have been more or less valid for most tax farms, Genç could deduct a probable annual profit (column c) and the probable (what he called) 'gross yearly revenue' (column e) of Salonica's customs. That the average 'profit rate' of 36 percent in 1707 decreased to less than 23 percent in 1774 implies that the successful attempts of the state to realize higher 'advance payments' were accompanied by increasing cost-efficiency. The authorities provided potential bidders on the *muacceles* with information on former net profits of *malikanes*,[158] a transparency that must have improved the competitiveness of the bidding process. Bidders will have been inclined to make higher bids – and thus to be content with lower profits – when uncertainty about the profit to be expected was diminished. So, the 'profit rate' is not the net revenue for the *malikane*-holder as a percentage of the total gross revenue of the tax, but the return on his or her investment in a *muaccele*.

The decline in the 'profit rate' may be compared, therefore, to a decline in the interest rate on life annuities, which makes it interesting to make a comparison with the interest rates on life annuities in the Dutch Republic and other European states. In the Dutch Republic annuities on one life had been sold at an interest rate of 16.7 percent in the sixteenth century, lower already at that time, therefore, than the average profit rate on *muacceles* of 22.7 percent in 1774. Life annuities were still incidentally sold in the Dutch Republic in the eighteenth century, now at rates varying from only 5 percent to 10 percent. By far the largest part of the Dutch public debts consisted of heritable, redeemable annuities and 'obligations', however at even much lower interest rates. During the eighteenth century, the amount in capital resulting from life annuities on which interest was still due, was in Holland at its top in 1713, and even then it was only about 9 percent of total public debt. It declined to less than one percent in 1790.[159]

In Britain life annuities on one life had been sold at an interest of 14% in 1694, but also in Britain the bulk of the public debt came to exist, as a result of its 'Financial Revolution', in low renting long-term debt at 3 to 3.5 percent during the eighteenth century. In France fiscal problems had forced Finance Ministers between 1740 and 1787 to raise nearly 60 percent of the large net sums they had to borrow in life-annuities. Their yields varied from about 5 percent to 11 percent, again much lower than the profit rate of nearly 23 percent on the Ottoman *muacceles* in 1774. The yield on the other loan types in France during this period (mostly term annuities with terms varying from 8 to 30 years) varied between 5 percent and 9.5 percent and was on average nearly

158 Genç, 'A study of the feasibility', p. 347.

159 Dormans, *Het tekort*, pp. 110–111.

7 percent.[160] And even in France a large part of the state debt still consisted of lower renting paper from earlier dates, mostly 'obligations' on the *Hôtel de Ville de Paris* at 5 percent.

b) *Ottoman* 'Mals' *Compared to European 'Tax Revenues Minus Debt Service'*

What is called 'gross yearly revenue' by Genç (column e in Table 6.5), was the sum of the profit of the *malikane*-holder (column c) and the mal for the government (column d), or, in other words, the revenue of the *malikane*-owner before the payment of the *mal* to the government, but *after* deduction of the costs made in the process of realizing the tax revenues and the costs to get the *muacceles* pre-financed. The tax revenue *before* the deduction of the costs is called by Genç '*total* gross yearly revenue'. He suggested that the costs may have been between 30 and 50% of 'total gross revenue' and concluded that such margins are too wide for reliable estimates of this total gross revenue of *malikanes*.[161]

He suggested in a later publication, that the division of *total* gross tax revenue across all the parties involved in *malikanes*, may have been about as follows: 14 percent to the *sarrafs*, 17 percent to the *mültezim*, 15 percent for actual collection expenses, 30 percent to the *malikaneci*,[162] 24 percent to the state (= *mal*).[163]

This estimate for the *mal*, of only about 24 percent of total gross revenue for the state, seems at first sight even more ominous than the earlier mentioned estimate of only one third of gross tax revenue reaching the Ottoman treasury. It has to be kept in mind, however, firstly, that the costs of 17 percent for the tax

160 François R. Velde and David R. Weir 'The financial market and government debt policy in France, 1746–1793', *The Journal of Economic History*, Vol. 52, No. 1 (Mar., 1992), pp. 1–39, Table 1, p. 14.

161 Ibidem, p. 350.

162 Note that this is the profit as a percentage of total gross tax revenue, not the *profit-rate* which is a percentage of the muaccele-amount!

163 Mentioned in Çizakça, *The evolution of business partnerships*, p. 166. NB In the case of the malikane of the customs of Salonica of Table 6.5 this would imply that, in 1774, either the profit rate for the malikaneci was in fact even somewhat lower than 22.7 percent, or that the *mal* was even somewhat lower than 24 percent, or both: if the profit-amount in 1774 was 30% of total gross tax revenue, tax revenue would have been 227,000; this would make the *mal* of 49,000 21.6% of tax revenue instead of 24%; if the mal was 24%, total gross tax revenue would have been 204.167 and if the profit was 30% of this tax revenue it would be 61,250 instead of 68.100; this would amount to a profit rate of only 20 percent of the *muaccele* instead of 22.7%.

farmers and 15 percent for the actual tax collection are only somewhat higher than the 20 percent for tax farmers and 9 percent for collection in Britain in the decade before 1683 (see Chapter 6.4), and, secondly, that the parts of the tax revenue spent on the *sarrafs* and on the profit for the *malikaneci* (together 44 percent of tax revenue under the *malikane*-system) was the part of tax revenue necessary to acquire the *muacceles*.

If the investment in *muacceles* is compared to the buying of life annuities, the 44 percent for the *sarrafs* and the *malikanecis* together should be compared, of course, to the percentage of tax revenue required for debt service in Western Europe. Loan financing in the Dutch Republic resulted in amounts for debt service of about 43 percent of total public revenue by the early 1790s. In Britain and France this was then about 50 percent.[164] The main differences with Ottoman Empire were, 1) that the costs for debt service in the European states were annual costs, and those for the muacceles 'once only' costs at the moment that a malikane was leased anew, 2) that in the Ottoman Empire only a small part of the tax revenues was realized by means of *malikanes* and 3) that in the European states the amounts in loans that the governments had enjoyed were much higher and were obtained at much lower costs than in the Ottoman Empire, because the (annual) 'profit rates' for the malikanecis of in the end still nearly 23 percent were much higher than the interest rate on loans in Europe.

It is not realistic, however, to say that a sharp contrast between European states and the Ottoman Empire consists in the fact that only one third, or even only 24% of tax revenues under the malikane-system reached the Treasury, because this ignores that part of the Ottoman tax revenue that did not reach the Treasury had been used to provide the government with increasingly attractive amounts in *muacceles* at decreasing costs.

It has to be added that especially for the land taxes the *iltizam* system, in which taxes were directly leased from the central government, remained important. These *mültezims* were often called *ayans*. They not only performed the task of tax collecting for the central government (or of sub-leasing, like what was done by the Company of the General Farms in France), but often also that of recruiting soldiers. In this way they often became increasingly powerful and independent from the central government and as such will often have been able to withhold more and more of the tax revenue from the central treasury. The soldiers they recruited were paid, of course, from the tax revenues in their territory, and only the remaining tax amounts would reach the treasury. This reminds one of course of the fact that the provinces in the Dutch Republic

164 F. Braesch, *Les recettes et les dépenses du trésor pendant l'année 1789: le compte rendu au roi de mars 1788* (Paris, Maison du Livre français, 1936).

often had to pay for companies garrisoned in their own province and that provincial tax revenues did not reach the central treasury of the Generality in the Dutch Republic either. Two major differences are of course (1) that the fiscal autonomy the Dutch Provincial States with common interests because of their economic interdependency, was less likely to be harmful for the state, than a (relative) fiscal *and* (possible) economic autonomy of *ayan*s in the large Ottoman Empire, and (2) that this extremely large size of the Ottoman Empire made the risk of decentralising tendencies with harmful effects for the state as a whole much larger.

c) *The Quantitative Importance of the* Malikanes *for the Ottoman Fiscal System*

Information on the quantitative importance of the *malikanes* within the fiscal system of the Ottoman Empire is very scarce. According to Genç the total outstanding investment in *malikane-muacceles* can be estimated at about 10 million kuruş in 1774. At a profit rate of 22.7 percent this would imply that *malikaneci* enjoyed about 2.27 million *kuruş* in profits in that year. If profits were 30 percent of total gross tax revenue, this would mean that total gross tax revenue from *malikanes* in 1774 was 7.57 million *kuruş*. If the *mal* was 24 percent of total gross revenue, the part of tax revenue accruing to the state amounted to 1.81 million *kuruş*. This would be about 12 percent of total public revenue of 15 million *kuruş* in that year according to the 'budget'-figures (see Table 6.3).

In this period about 52% of total public revenue consisted of *mukataa* revenues (Table 6.2). This would imply that, in 1774, less than a quarter of the amount realized by means of tax farming was the result from a conversion of *mukataas* into *malikanes.* Genç discusses only *malikanes* on indirect taxes on foreign trade and on industrial production (and his small sample contains even *malikanes* with very small *muacceles* and a *mal* of for instance not more than 110 *kuruş* per year,[165] which suggests that by that time all the more or less important indirect taxes were changed into *malikanes*). This would strongly confirm the earlier conclusion that indirect domestic taxation was only a very small part of Ottoman public revenue, despite the fact that the urbanization rate was not lower than in 'the Latin West'. If also land tax districts were changed into *malikanes*, this would make the role of indirect taxes (most of which were on foreign trade) in the Ottoman fiscal system even smaller than 12 percent. It is very probable therefore that, eighty years after the introduction of

165 Genç, 'The feasibility', p. 369, Table 16.17: the Şumnu cotton-textiles stamp tax, introduced in 1752; the muaccele was 100 *kuruş* in 1752, it was raised to 710 *kuruş* in 1782, but had to be auctioned anew already in 1785 for only 130 *kuruş*.

the *malikane*-system, its quantitative importance for Ottoman public finance was relatively still very small.

Why was it so difficult for the Ottoman government to raise more money at lower costs? The – in comparison to West European public debts – extremely small importance and extremely high costs of *muacceles* resulted of course for a large part from the market conditions under which they had to be raised. Large amounts of money could only be raised at moderate costs in cities with sufficient capital supply and with reliable institutions to create an effective demand for them. The declining trend in the profit rate suggests that the auctions of the *malikanes* were competitive, but the lack of a long-term history of urban public loans from the public at large, and the relatively small capital supply in cities in which the merchant class was financially much less strong than in West-European cities, made it much harder to realize large amounts of money at low costs than in West Europe.

The *malikaneci* were a privileged group in Ottoman society. They were in fact, apart from high bureaucrats and some women at the court, mainly military men and religious officials.[166] It was the specific connection of such people with the central state, that guaranteed their wealth, which made them trustworthy in the eyes of the *sarrafs*, a situation completely different therefore from cities in Western Europe, where people could trust that their urban governments – mostly consisting of economically powerful people – were able and inclined to realize enough public revenue in urban taxes to pay the interest, when issuing loans in which its members invested themselves.

A last important difference between the Ottoman Empire and West-European states was, therefore that West-European state debt, in the form of not only life annuities, but mainly of redeemable heritable annuities and obligations could be bought directly by large sections of the general public. Amsterdam had a number of nearly 4,000 identifiable investors in public debt already in the period 1584 to 1604, when it was a city of only about 65,000 inhabitants. Only 782 of them had been able to buy high renting life-annuities, the majority held other lower renting forms of debt.[167] Istanbul, a city of 400,000 people had in the period 1745–1750 only 795 *malikane*-owners.[168] Investors often bought shares in more than one *malikane*, to diversify their risks, but even the fact that *malikanes* appeared to have been increasingly sold in shares did not make them into an investment opportunity for large sections of the population.[169]

166 Çizakça, *Evolution of business partnerships*, pp. 174–175.

167 Van de Burg and 't Hart, '*Renteniers* and the recovery of Amsterdam's credit', p. 206.

168 Çizakça, *Evolution of business partnerships*, p. 171.

169 Çizakça, *Evolution of business partnerships*, p. 181; shares in the important tobacco customs *malikane*, for instance, could become as small as only 1/128.

The Esham-*System*

The major novelty of the *esham* system, introduced in 1774 was that it significantly improved the conditions at which the Ottoman government realized large amounts in advance of specific tax revenues by directly accessing a much broader group of investors by removing the *malikanecis* and *sarrafs* as intermediaries. In addition, tax farming was abolished for those taxes for which the *esham*-system was adopted. It enabled people to buy shares (*esham* is the plural of *sehm*, which means 'share') in a lifelong *fixed* annual net payment from the revenues of a specific tax. This system was, therefore, much more so than the *malikane*-system, really similar to the sale of life annuities. That the revenues of one specific and very remunerative tax formed the security for the annual payments made it comparable to the British public debt system of earmarking a specific tax for debt service, and different from the French and the Dutch debt, where the reliability of interest payments for investors mostly consisted in guaranteeing the priority of interest payments from the revenues of a great number of taxes collected in the city where the interests were paid.

A first step into the direction of a new system was taken already in 1759, when the state decided to exploit the very lucrative Istanbul tobacco customs from then on by itself. At its last auction as a *malikane* in 1739 a *muaccele* of nearly 250,000 *kuruş* had been realized, at a *mal* of nearly 111,000 *kuruş*.[170] It had at that time been sold to 11 owners, implying an amount of on average about 22,000 *kuruş* per owner at a time when a skilled construction worker did not earn more than about 117 *kuruş* per year.[171] In 1759 the state returned the *muaccele* to the – by then – 22 owners. The smallest share in this tobacco tax farm had by then become 1/128, nearly 2,000 *kuruş*, which shows that shares in *malikanes* changed hands during the lifetime of *malikane*-holders and could become smaller.[172]

It was the first time since 1714 that a *malikane* was ended prematurely by repaying the *muaccele* in order to stop the large losses in tax revenue due to the *malikane*-system.[173] If the *mal* of 111,000 kuruş was 24 percent of total gross revenue, total gross revenue of this tax was about 462,500 *kuruş* in 1739. If the collection costs were 15%, net revenue may have been nearly 400,000 *kuruş* in

170 Çizakça, *Evolution of business partnerships*, p. 181; the table mentions this *muaccele* for 1759, but the text on p. 183 says that this was the *muaccele* 20 years prior to 1759, which is much more likely in view of the still relatively small muaccele.

171 http://www.iisg.nl/hpw/data.php#ottoman: in 1739 44.8 akçe per day (1 *kuruş* = 120 *akçe*).

172 According to Çizakça, *Evolution of business partnerships*, p. 182, ten owners had bought their shares only two years previously.

173 Çizakça, *Evolution of business partnerships*, p. 184.

1739. It had no doubt yet increased considerably since then, given the general increases in world trade and a renewed reduction in the silver content of the currency (Figure 6.3).

In 1774, when 7.5 million *kuruş* at once was needed for war compensation to Russia, at a time when total annual public revenue was probably no more than about 15 million *kuruş*, it was decided to sell 400,000 *kuruş* of the annual revenue of this tobacco customs tax in Istanbul to the public at a price of 2 million *kuruş*, in the form of 160 shares (*esham*) of 2,500 *kuruş* each. The shares could, if necessary, yet be further subdivided into amounts as low as 400 or 500 *kuruş* to make their saleability easier. This meant that the possession of a share of for instance 1000 *kuruş* would entitle the holder to an annual income of 200 *kuruş* for the rest of his or her life, at a time when a skilled construction worker could earn about 200 *kuruş* per year.[174] This shows that under the *esham*-system the Ottoman government now actively sought to involve broader layers of the population in its attempts to realize an extremely large sum at once in advance on tax revenues.

A sale of 400,000 *kuruş* of the annual revenue of a certain tax to the public for a total price of 2,000,000 *kuruş* is financially identical to the sale of two million in annuities at an interest rate of 20 percent on the security of the revenue of a certain tax for the duration of the life of the holder. The sale was a success and in subsequent years more shares in the annual revenue of tobacco customs were sold, also in other ports. The twenty percent rate was of course also attractive for the government in comparison to the costs involved in realizing the *muacceles*. Later, *esham* in reliable tax revenues even sold for six to seven times the offered annual net payments, implying a decrease in the rate of return to about 16.67 percent or even only 14.3 percent.

The introduction of the *esham*-system consisted therefore in the possibility for the Ottoman government of realizing much larger amounts at once in advance of tax revenues, than had been possible by means of the *muacceles* under the *malikane*-system and at an interest rate lower than the profit rate of the malikanecis and with a much smaller loss of tax revenue to intermediaries.

In 1793 the Ottoman government decided that all *malikanes* offering a profit of more than 5,000 *kuruş* per year to their holders – or in other words the *malikanes* with the highest tax revenues – would end at the death of one of the holders, under compensation of the remaining holders. By 1800 the amounts outstanding in *esham* had risen to 12.6 million *kuruş*. Notwithstanding this relatively fast development, the outstanding amount in *malikane-muacceles* was

174 http://www.iisg.nl/hpw/data.php#ottoman: in 1774 79.9 *akçe* per day (1 *kuruş* = 120 *akçe*).

with 12.46 million, also higher in 1800 than in 1774.[175] Evidently new *malikanes* were still added. It was apparently expected that the market would not yet allow the sale of *esham*-shares for all kind of taxes.

A serious draw back of the *esham* system for the Ottoman government was that the smaller sizes and the greater number of holders of the *esham*-shares made it more difficult to track the death of the holders than in the case of the *malikane-muacceles*. This jeopardized the – for the state attractive – possibility to sell part of the annual revenue of the tax in question anew after the death of one of the holders. The government tried to compensate for this not only by offering rewards for reporting the death of *esham*-holders, but also by allowing sales and inheriting of *esham*-shares on the condition of a transfer tax of 10 percent.[176] It should be noted that the fact that the *esham* could in this way become heritable, instead of keeping the character of a life annuities, implied of course that their interest rate should since then in fact no longer be compared to that of West-European life annuities, but to that of the much lower renting West-European heritable annuities.

Public Debts and the Interest Prohibition

We may conclude that there were remarkable differences between the Ottoman Empire and West European states in the development of possibilities to realize advances on tax revenue. The ingenuous *malikane* system made tax farming in the Ottoman Empire, in sharp contrast to tax farming in the Latin West, into a very important, although rather expensive instrument for the realization of large advances on tax revenues. It allowed large, although declining profit rates to a relatively very small number of privileged investors, and it was also an attractive source of income for bankers and tax farmers. The *esham*-system was a very clever improvement of the most remunerative parts of the *malikane*-system. It implied not only the start of the abolition of tax farming, it also allowed the state to realize even much larger sums at once at much lower costs than under the *malikane*-system by now addressing a much larger group of possible investors more directly.

However, not only the *malikane*-system, also the *esham*-system remained still very expensive for the state in comparison to the costs of long-term borrowing in West-European states. Moreover, the introduction of *esham* appears to have been restricted to the most reliable tax revenues, mainly important sectors of foreign trade that could convince investors of the reliability of the annual income to be realized from their investment. Lastly the contribution

175 Çizakça, *Comparative evolution*, p. 185.

176 Çizakça, *Comparative evolution*, p. 160.

of the Ottoman advances on tax revenue to total public revenue was much smaller than that of long-term public debts to total public revenue in the discussed European states.

On the one hand the development from *iltizam* to *malikane*-system, and then to the *esham*-system, supports Darling's thesis of the adaptability and the flexibility of the Ottoman fiscal system.[177] On the other hand, the question remains why a system of public debts really similar to that in West-European states did not develop in the Ottoman Empire. Despite the so-called 'interest prohibition' in Islam, payments on loans had become *de facto* accepted in Ottoman commercial life, although banking remained in practice largely the realm of Christian Greeks and Armenians, and of Jews. Given the important role of secular laws (*kanun*) instead of the Islamic *sharia* – in all fields of law except family law – the Ottoman Empire cannot be called an 'Islamic state'. Why then would a long-term interest bearing debt not have developed in the Ottoman Empire?

A similar taboo on interest bearing loans had prevailed in Western Europe during the Middle Ages. It began to be circumvented through the sale of life annuities entitling their owners to a fixed interest income by urban governments, in French cities already since the thirteenth century, in Dutch and German cities since the fourteenth century. Life-annuities were not considered as interest bearing loans, but as the purchase of a source of income, because they expired on the death of the owner and did not have to be redeemed. The step to the sale of lower renting heritable annuities was not large, especially not for city governments consisting of an economic elite, keen on rational calculating. They could be sold at lower annual costs for city governments because they kept their value after the death of the buyers. Rational calculating will have stimulated repurchasing the annuities from the holders in case of surpluses in public revenue. No wonder that the 'interest prohibition' came gradually to be ignored. State debts in European states like the Spanish Empire, the Dutch Republic, and France were largely based on the credit of cities in large urban networks. City governments dominated by merchants were missing in the Ottoman Empire. This makes the difference in urbanization-trajectories a very likely cause of the difference with Western Europe in the development of a public debt at low rates of interest. It cannot be excluded, of course, that the interest prohibition was felt more as a problem in governmental circles and at the court in the Ottoman Empire than among merchants. This increases the importance of this difference in urbanization-trajectories for an understanding of the differences in fiscal systems.

177 Darling, 'Ottoman fiscal administration: decline or adaptation?'.

The long maintenance of *iltizam* and the costly *malikane*-system, even after the introduction of the *esham*-system, can on the one hand be explained by what Çizakça called the 'risk-averseness' of the Ottoman government, a risk-averseness that was rational in view of the population stagnation and the much slower economic development than in Western Europe. Tax farming guaranteed the government a certain amount of revenue for the duration of the tax farm. The uncertainties as to the realization of enough tax revenue in a very large territory with a stagnating population and a rather restricted economic development were of course much larger than in the West-European territories with increasing populations and a much faster and more widespread economic development. It is evident, on the other hand, that a similar early sale of life annuities and their development into long-term annuities at low rates of interest, as had turned out to be possible in cities in many European states, was precluded in the Ottoman Empire due to its very different 'urban system' resulting from a 'state-driven instead' of an 'economy-driven urbanization trajectory'.

6.5 Conclusion

In comparison to public finance in Western European states, and especially to that of the small Dutch Republic, the level of state revenue of the large Ottoman Empire was remarkably low, not only per capita, but even in total amounts. Its character was different as well: a very low level of domestic indirect taxation, a remarkably intensive – and expensive – use of tax farming to realize advances on tax revenue, and a very late start of the development of a long-term domestic public debt. This chapter has argued that long-term geographic factors, influencing the character of urbanization, may contribute to an understanding of the low level and the different character of state revenue. As such this chapter forms the counterpart to the explanation of the remarkably high level of public revenue in the Dutch Republic in the rest of this book.

More droughts, more voracious, harvest-destroying insects and thus more famines, more earthquakes and a much greater intensity of plague-epidemics, resulted in a declining population between 1000 and 1500 and a stagnating population in the Ottoman Empire between 1600 and 1800. This in sharp contrast to the 'Latin West', and especially the Low Countries, where population more than doubled between 1000 and 1500, despite the Great Plague of the fourteenth century, and again more than doubled between 1500 and 1800. These factors induced a more 'state-driven' urbanization in the Ottoman Empire, consisting of the phenomenon of *sürgün,* the forced migration to cities, and state-initiatives to establish urban centres by means of the creation of welfare facilities.

The continuing population growth in the 'Latin West' since 1000 made fertile land increasingly scarce relative to people, which stimulated an increase in specialization, commercialization and industrialization in the countryside and an 'economy-driven' type of urbanization. In the Ottoman territory, with its stagnating population, people would, in contrast, become scarce relative to land.[178] In the course of time a greater vulnerability of the countryside in large parts of the Ottoman Empire to nomadic people and brigands forced many people to leave the fertile plains either for large cities, or for less fertile regions in the mountains, which were not only less easily accessible for robbers, but also for tax-collectors. Urbanization in the Ottoman Empire led to a small number of large cities in a very large territory.

An important second aspect of the 'state-driven' character of Ottoman urbanization consisted in the intensive central interference to safeguard the food provision of the large cities, which kept merchants dependent on rulers, rather than the other way round. It also consisted in the fact that high urban functionaries were appointed by the central government to supervise the maintenance of public order and law and economic development in cities, and that these officials never constituted urban governments. This in sharp contrast to cities in the Latin West that developed as 'political bodies' with semi-autonomous urban governments consisting of members of the economic elites, discussing the best ways to finance urban interests by means of urban taxes and urban loans. No urban fiscal systems developed in the Ottoman Empire due to a lack of urban governments: no urban public loans and no taxes to service these loans. No wonder that direct taxes were much more important in the Ottoman tax system than indirect taxes, not only on land, but also personal direct taxes, with the *cizye* on Christians and Jews as a very important element. The most important element in indirect taxation was not domestic indirect taxation, but the taxation of foreign trade.

Tax farming had always been used to reduce the uncertainty of tax revenues in ways similar to tax farming in the 'Latin West', for direct as well as indirect taxation. Since the end of the seventeenth century the development of the *malikane*-system of lifelong tax farming, enabled the Ottoman state, to realize very large advance payments on tax revenues, that did not have to be redeemed and on which no interest had to be paid, a development very different from

178 The point is also made in B. McGowan, *Economic life in Ottoman Europe. Taxation, trade and the struggle for land, 1600–1800* (Cambridge: CUP, 1981) pp. 2–5, p. 70, p. 72, his focus is on 'labour hunger', and 'shortage of people to work the land'.

that in the 'Latin West'. It has been argued that the *malikane*-system implied that only a third or less of gross tax revenue reached the treasury. In fact, a large part of tax revenue not reaching the treasury was used for the realization of the large 'advance-payments' which makes this 'invisible' part comparable to debt service in West-European states. Another part remained with the *ayans* and was used to pay soldiers in their own territory. The raising of public revenue, taxes as well as the 'advance-payments' comparable to public debts, was costlier in the Ottoman Empire than in Western Europe, but not as dramatically as the common estimate of two thirds of tax revenue suggests.

The evident growth of foreign trade during the second half of the eighteenth century allowed the abolition of the *malikane*-system of tax farming for the most profitable taxes on foreign trade and the introduction of the much cheaper *esham* system. It allowed advances on tax revenues from larger sections of the population, because of the reliability of the fixed incomes investors derived from their purchase of such *esham*. In comparison to the long-term loans in West European states, the costs of the *esham*-system remained still rather high for the state, however. Despite the ingenuity of its tax farming systems, the addition to public revenue from the large advances on tax revenue by means of the *malikane* and the *esham* remained modest in comparison to the importance of public loans in West-European states, where the character of urbanization had been different. 'Risk-averseness' on the side of the government required the maintenance of tax farming in less dynamic sectors of the economy.

Urban loans, serviced from urban taxes, had already much earlier become an appreciated investment possibility, when wealth increased in cities in the 'Latin West', thanks to the 'economy-driven' development of such cities. They were seen as rather reliable, because the economic elites determining urban fiscal policy were also investors in urban loans themselves. The resulting large demand for this kind of investment possibility diminished interest rates. The importance of the '*obligations sur l'Hôtel de Ville de Paris*' in the French state debt shows the importance of the ability to realize *urban* loans for the emergence of state debts, also in other Western-European states than the Dutch Republic. The same is true for the readiness of the Castilian cities to increase taxes to safeguard the interest payments on the *juros* during the financial crises in the Spanish Empire (see Chapter 2.1) The interests on these European debts were considerably lower than the rates of return on *malikanes* and *esham*.

The state-appointed urban officials in the Ottoman Empire did never form urban governments devising urban fiscal policies. Their tasks and their salaries were financed from parts of the land tax assigned to them by the central government. In the Ottoman Empire, urban economic development, which created the need to provide the cities with enough agricultural products for their large populations, was a source of concern for the central government rather than a source of fiscal strength, for a long time. The large differences in the urbanization-trajectories of the Ottoman Empire and the Dutch Republic offer an important contribution, therefore, to an understanding of the large differences in their fiscal performance.

General Conclusion

The Republic of the Seven United Provinces emerged in a period of increasingly expensive war faring in Europe. It became one of Europe's 'Great Powers' in the course of the seventeenth century, although it remained an only weakly centralized state. Larger amounts of public revenue per capita were realized in the Dutch Republic than in any other contemporary state at the time, much larger than could be explained by its greater wealth. This book showed how the remarkable success of the Dutch Republic in exploiting the new fiscal opportunities of the period can be explained by the character of its 'urban system', resulting from, on the one hand, its preceding economic development and its preceding institutional history, on the other hand, from a new perception of common, instead of merely particularistic urban interests since the start of its revolt against Spain.

Europe's population had doubled already between 1000 and 1500 and doubled again between 1500 and 1800, which contributed to urbanization, economic specialization and commercialization in many regions of Europe. This fuelled not only commercial expansion overseas, but also the development of domestic networks of cities with increasing common interests. Fiscal changes in European states were answers to the new challenges and the new chances that confronted European rulers as a result of these developments. Not only military and commercial expansionist ambitions, but also the need to maintain internal order in a period of religious turmoil, the need to protect foreign commerce, and the need for protection against external threats, had to be met by increases in public finance involving new developments in state formation. Attempts at absolutistic centralization appeared not to be the only or even the best option to these ends.

It was the common decision in 1572 of a large number of cities in the province of Holland to support a war against Spain that was decisive for the successful emergence of the Dutch Republic as a fiscal state. The cities in the provinces Holland and Zeeland were forced to accept a 'tax revolution' – a huge expansion of *common* provincial taxation on commercial urban as well as agrarian activities, products and assets – that restricted urban fiscal autonomy. Holland's *tax* revolution would be followed by what may be called its real *financial* revolution during the first decade of the seventeenth century, although it was prepared by fiscal changes on a much smaller scale already in the Habsburg period, and partly even already earlier. Similar changes had also occurred in Castile's cities already before. Revolutionary new was that Holland's new network of tax receivers, grafted onto its dense urban network, appeared

 | DOI 10.1163/9789004341289_011

to allow a gradual transition from increasing amounts in originally short-term debts to a *de facto* long-term public debt, without the help of the intermediary institution of a strong bank. This network, that was coordinated by the Finance Office of Holland's provincial government, offered the 'infrastructure' for a broad, direct access to investors among the public at large, allowing the development of a long-term debt at declining rates of interests that no longer had to be redeemed.

The formative phase of the new fiscal system was completed in the years shortly before the start of the Twelve Years' Truce. In all provinces, the 'representation' in the States-assemblies that took fiscal decisions, became more based on the geographic reality of an increased number of cities, and no longer primarily on a social ordering of society in three estates. In all provinces, the cities had to resign to the introduction of provincial 'general means' that were more or less similar to Holland's 'common means', implying a loss of urban autonomy in order to serve common interests. Gradually all provincial governments would prove to be able to develop provincial public debts at declining rates of interest without banking institutions. These provincial debts were welcomed by the public as they offered a safe investment opportunity, at a much larger scale than the urban debts of individual cities.

After the Truce the new 'fiscal-military' Dutch state had to share fully in the fiscal consequences of increasing army sizes in Europe – especially in the period of the 'second military revolution' since the 1670s – notwithstanding a relatively small 'tax base' in comparison to its main enemies. Despite the 'maritime' character of the Dutch Republic – and despite the prominence of the four naval wars with Britain in Dutch historical memory – the military costs for land wars appeared to have been much more important in the large increases in its public expenditure than that of naval wars.

The weaknesses becoming visible in the Dutch fiscal system already at the end of its formative phase, did not lead to more centralization after the Truce, as theoretically might have been expected in a 'fiscal-military state'. The available quantitative data left no doubt as to the continuing declining relative importance of the existing centralized sources of public revenue. In absolute amounts Generality loans, as an alternative for provincial loans, increased still for some decades since the middle of the seventeenth century. After the Generality had been forced, however, to stop interest payments temporarily after the expensive war of 1702–1713 (and again in 1754) – 'central' loans were apparently no longer tried as a 'safety valve' for arrears in war payments. Likewise, the revenue of customs still increased, temporarily, in absolute amounts, but not in relative importance, during the seventeenth century, but during the eighteenth century it started to decline in absolute terms. Due to its comparatively very low customs duties Dutch public finance scarcely profited from the value of its rich colonial trade. In addition, the VOC was hardly ever used as a source of loans to the government. Instead it was supposed to finance the expenditure for military colonial expansion and defence in Asia to a very large extent from its own revenues, which started to become impossible in the last decades of the eighteenth century.

It was the fiscal 'resilience' of the provinces that was the main 'secret' of the Dutch fiscal system after the Truce. Not only Holland, all provinces were able to stretch the total 'fabric' of their revenue structure during the seventeenth and eighteenth centuries to meet increasing expenditure. The revenue of indirect taxes on daily necessities in the 'common' and 'general' means, as well as direct taxes hitting the more well-to-do, increased until the end of the seventeenth century. Direct taxation would everywhere become the most important element in the fiscal system, since the 'second military revolution' of the 1670s. After a period of stagnation between the end of the seventeenth and the middle of the eighteenth century even indirect taxation increased again, despite the republic-wide tax riots of 1748.

Like Holland also the other provinces were, moreover, increasingly able to use the capital market to obtain additional revenue by means of loans, not only on the credit of the office of the Generality, but also, and increasingly so, on their own provincial credit, at declining rates of interest. The sum of the public debts of the provinces outside Holland, negotiated on their own credit instead of that of the Generality, became a larger percentage of the sum of the public debts of the Dutch Republic than the debt of the Generality had ever been. 'Coercive' forms of public revenue, like direct taxation and forced loans, appeared to have played generally a more important role in the Dutch fiscal system, however, than a 'capital-intensity' allowing voluntary loans. Not more than on average about 13 percent of total public revenue in the Dutch Republic between 1572 and 1794 was the result of loans. During the seventeenth century, even the extra revenue needed in war years was still for less than 50 percent the result of loans.

As loan financing was, nevertheless, an intrinsic element of the 'fiscal resilience' of the provinces, this made the containment of the debt burden a primary concern of fiscal policy, especially between 1713 and 1780. Comparable measures were taken in all provinces to this end. The most important among them implied that holders of Dutch government could not be as confident that promised interests would be really paid, as is often supposed.

Holland's contribution to the total public revenue of the Dutch Republic always remained larger than that of all other provinces combined, but its share in the total public revenue of the Dutch Republic became in the eighteenth century on average somewhat lower than in the seventeenth century. It remained a fact, nevertheless, that the other provinces paid less than they were supposed to do according to their official quotas.

The answer to the question if this led to a fiscal system in which Holland was 'overburdened' appeared to have two sides. For the 'common man' in Holland the tax burden was probably heavier than for the 'common man' in a province like Overijssel, also after correction for differences in wage- and price levels. The burden from direct taxes hitting the more well-to-do appeared to be relatively lower in Holland, however, than in a province like Overijssel. The 'tax morale' of the more well to do, especially in Holland, was in general certainly not as impressive as has sometimes been supposed. Remarkably enough Holland's ruling elite appeared to be convinced itself, by 1792, that the remedy for the insufficient fiscal performance of the other provinces regarding their quota-contributions to general expenditure, had to be found in increasing Holland's formal quota and in decreasing that of most other provinces.

In view of the available quantitative data it proved to be utterly unlikely, that a 'state reform' could have converted the small Dutch Republic into a state that 'matched the demands of late-eighteenth century power struggle',[1] or in other words: that an earlier abolition of the federal structure of the Republic would have enabled it to win the Fourth English Naval War. Even if its population would have been on average twice as rich as that in Britain – where wealth per capita in fact began to approach the Dutch level – this would not have been sufficient to compensate for the large difference in population size in the two states. Similarly, it was an illusion to expect that a unitary instead of a federal Dutch Republic would have been able to keep the French troops out of the country, especially not in the prevailing situation of growing republic-wide political antagonism and support for the French Revolution among the 'Patriot party'.

After larger European states had been able to shift their attention from domestic religious and political turmoil to economic development and global power struggle, during the eighteenth century, the old Dutch state had become simply much too small to participate in this struggle on an equal footing any longer. The first unified tax system of the Dutch state after the Batavian Revolution was an in several respects very impressive achievement of its first Finance Minister Alexander Gogel. The answer to the question why an increase in public revenue of about thirty percent was possible only after the downfall of the old federal Republic is not, however, that the Dutch state had, at last, got rid of its federal structure. The answer is that Napoleon was powerful enough to force the Dutch state to contribute to his imperial 'war machine'. The Dutch

1 Brandon, *War, capital and the Dutch state*, p. 37.

governmental elites between 1713 and 1780 had been realistic enough to avoid war as much as possible. 'War' had made the Dutch state, but the Dutch state was not 'made' to wage war.

Part 2 reinforced the conclusion of the importance of the character of the Dutch urban system in order to understand its remarkable fiscal performance. The main difference between the urban systems of the Dutch and the Venetian Republic was that in the Venetian Republic fiscal power was centralized in the city of Venice. On the one hand, the much lower level of public revenue per capita in the Venetian than in the Dutch Republic could be attributed to the fact that the Venetian Republic more than the Dutch Republic practiced a policy of 'survival on the cheap'. On the other hand, Venetian public finance was nevertheless characterized by deficits – even in years of peace – between 1650 and 1750, and the difference in wealth between the two was not sufficient to explain the much lower level of tax revenues during this period than in the Dutch Republic.

Remarkably, the difference between the tax burden in the central city of Venice and the surrounding cities and territories was much larger than that between Holland and the provinces outside Holland, despite Venice's centralized fiscal system. The Venetian Republic felt apparently unable to increase tax revenues in the conquered cities and countryside of its surrounding territory, even when economic developments outside Venice improved in the eighteenth century. In the case of the Venetian Republic 'free-riding' appeared to have been easier in a centralized than in a federal fiscal system. Perhaps this was partly also due, however, to the fact that Venice was more inclined than the States of Holland to continue to allow the rich in its central city to invest in public debt in order to have an easy and reliable source of income.

Yet another characteristic difference in the public finance of the two republics was that the powerful central government of Venice had relied much longer on 'republican' forced loans, at low interest rates, but quickly declining in value, before it started to prefer voluntary loans and to end its policy of successive 'mountains of debt' at ever faster declining values. A comparable policy had never been followed in the Dutch Republic, where many provinces and cities had a say in financial policy. Here voluntary loans, with interest rates determined by the market, were always preferred, if possible, and the value of the public debt remained much more stable. When a capital market for voluntary loans developed in the Venetian Republic, the access to (and the accessibility for) investors in the whole territory of the republic was less widespread than in the Dutch Republic, most likely due to the centralized character of its financial policy.

As in the case of Venice, long-term historical differences turned out to be important to understand the large differences between the fiscal systems of

Britain and the Dutch Republic. Until the Glorious Revolution it was mainly its late involvement in European land wars that kept the level of public revenue in Britain relatively low. The early 'national' character of taxation, with its distinction between 'royal' and 'parliamentary' sources of public revenue, and the different character of Britain's urbanization, explain the small role of indirect price-increasing taxation and the late and only very gradual development of a long-term public debt at low rates of interest.

Only in the course of the eighteenth century an urban network of middle sized cities started to develop in Britain. Urban public finance remained utterly underdeveloped during most of the early modern period. Not even London levied urban indirect taxes, or had a tradition of negotiating urban public loans. For the development of a permanent public debt at low rates of interest in Britain royal loans had to become parliamentary loans, requiring parliamentary approval for increases in revenues from specific indirect taxes earmarked for interest payments. The intermediary function of the central Bank of England initiated by a group of important merchants in the City of London, backed by the government and with the right to issue banknotes 'payable to bearer' to facilitate increasing commerce, turned out to be an additional requirement for England's 'financial revolution'. It was a development very different from the 'financial revolution' in Holland, based upon the early development of a politically and economically rather integrated urban system, where urban debts had been common already long before. Despite the absence of a centralized state with a central bank, public revenue per capita remained higher and the *de facto* interest on public debt in Holland lower than that in Britain during most of the eighteenth century, and Britain's public finance became relatively more dependent on loans than had been the case in the Dutch Republic in the seventeenth and eighteenth centuries.

The comparison with the Ottoman Empire highlighted the importance of geographical differences and their effect on urban development to understand the remarkably low level of public revenue in this large empire. A much larger vulnerability for natural disasters led to a nearly stagnant population and a much more 'state-driven' urbanization. Public finance in the Ottoman Empire remained largely dependent on direct taxes on land, and on a special tax-regime for the large numbers of non-Muslims in the country, instead of on increasing indirect as well as direct taxation, and on the development of a public debt at decreasing rates of interest. Despite the existence of some important and very large urban centres, indirect taxation remained largely restricted to foreign trade. In Western Europe, population growth necessitated an increase in domestic economic activities and in urbanization leading to further population growth. In the Ottoman territory, the growth of cities was not the result of demographic and economic development, but of migration forced by the state in order to increase the economic strength of cities, and of the flight of peasants for brigands and for tax collectors to cities. Ottoman urbanization was characterized by the existence of a small number of rather large cities in a very large territory that were very dependent on the active interference of the central government.

The corollary of this more 'state-driven' urbanization was the lack of a development of (semi-) autonomous urban governments and of urban public finance. The functions of Western-European urban governments were fulfilled in Ottoman cities partly by centrally appointed officials, who did not convene in urban governments to discuss urban interests and who did not develop urban systems of public finance. Urban functions paid for by urban governments in most European states were partly fulfilled in the Ottoman Empire by *evkaf*, charity institutions with economic as well as social tasks that were often financed by private donations and legacies, apart from being financially supported and controlled by the state. The lack of a tradition of urban indirect taxes explains the limited development of indirect domestic taxation in Ottoman state finance, which was such an important element in the increases in public revenue in large parts of Europe.

The lack of urban public finance moreover implied the lack of a development of urban public debts and of negotiations between the central governments and cities to raise public loans. The Ottoman Empire would mainly come to use tax farming as a means to acquire amounts in advance of tax collection. The introduction of the *malikane*-system, with its life-long tax farms, allowed much larger advances on the tax revenues to be realized by the tax farms, than to which West-European tax farmers were obliged by their governments in some states. The development into the *esham*-system at the end of the eighteenth century, allowing even much larger advances than under the *malikane* system, meant the transition to a public 'debt' comparable to the sale of life-annuities in Europe. However the importance of the advances that could be realized by means of the *malikane*- and the *esham*-system compared to the amounts realized by means of taxation, remained much smaller than in the 'Latin West'. Moreover their costs remained much higher than that of the public loans in states in the 'Latin West'.

The character of the urbanization trajectory in the large territory of the Ottoman Empire helps to explain the low level of public revenue in Ottoman state finance. This reinforced the conclusion of the importance of the early development of an urban network of cities in the Dutch case, to explain the success of the federal Dutch Republic as a fiscal state in Early Modern Europe.

Epilogue

The comparisons in this book have remained mainly restricted to, on the one hand, short comparisons with earlier fiscal systems inside the Spanish Empire, and, on the other hand, more elaborate comparisons with contemporary more or less centralized other fiscal states. Only in the General Introduction other *federal* states like the Swiss Republic and the United States of America were shortly mentioned. A focus on states that played a role in the early modern international power struggles, which largely determined public finance in the early modern period, seemed justified as the most adequate choice for a comparative approach of the fiscal performance of the Dutch Republic.

However, some articles of the Union of Utrecht as discussed in the Introduction to Part 1 may have reminded the reader not only of the Confederacy of the thirteen states of America in 1776, as it did Hamilton and Maddison, but even of the European Union nowadays.[2] As this book on the viability of a federal state was written in a period of serious financial problems in the European Union, that intensified discussions on the need for more centralized European institutions, it may be important to end this conclusion by emphasizing once more the importance of the hegemonic position of Holland in the functioning of the federal Dutch Republic.

States like Germany, the United Kingdom, France and Italy, contributed in 2015 respectively 21 percent, 18 percent, 15 percent and 10 percent to the total budget of the European Union, more or less in conformity to their respective gross national incomes.[3] These percentages were, in terms of relative strength more comparable to the relative importance of Virginia, Massachusetts and Pennsylvania in the eighteenth century, than to that of Holland, Friesland and Zeeland in the seventeenth century.[4] The former contributed respectively 19 percent, 19 percent and 16 percent of the soldiers for the Confederacy of the United States around 1780; the latter had to take 'quota' of respectively 58 percent, 11 percent and 9 percent in the Dutch Republic's common war expenditure. It was to a large extent Holland's evident hegemonic position,

2 See also W. Fritschy, 'Schulden als leerschool? De Unie der Zeven Verenigde Provinciën en de Europese Unie', *Tijdschrift voor Sociale en Economische Geschiedenis* 9,2 (2012) pp. 3–29.

3 http://eur-lex.europa.eu/budget/data/DB/2017/en/GenRev.pdf [01-08-2016] Perhaps it should be emphasized in addition, that the contributions to the EU are an incomparably much smaller percentage of the public expenditure of its member states than the 'general expenditure' of the provinces of the Dutch Republic as a percentage of their public expenditure.

4 NB If the contribution of the United Kingdom is excluded, the percentages in 2015 would have been: Germany 26%, France 19%, Italy 12%.

resulting from a much larger economic and financial strength than that of all the other provinces combined, that made the lack of strong central institutions in the federal Dutch Republic much less 'imbecile' than Hamilton and Maddison thought it must have been. The lack of an uncontested position of economic and financial leadership for one of the thirteen states made a federal constitution with much stronger central institutions than in the Dutch Republic no doubt imperative for a successful functioning of the USA since the end of the eighteenth century.

It was the early development of an economically and politically rather integrated 'urban system', resulting from the demographic and economic developments in this part of the world, that had made the fiscal system of the Dutch Republic successful. It was the acceptance by Holland of a federal system with economically weaker partners, and the perception by all provinces of the existence of common interests, that had made the Dutch Republic into a more viable state than Holland would have been on its own. At the end of the eighteenth century the viability of the Dutch Republic had become problematic not because it was federal, but partly because of an intensified political antagonism inside and across all provinces, mainly, however, because it was much too small in the international political situation of the eighteenth century, to be a match for much larger states on its own.

Appendix: The Taxes in the Dutch Republic

NB Further information on each of the taxes in the next table can be found in the electronically accessible volumes *GFD, GFF, GFG, GFH, GFO, GFZ* (see the list of Abbreviations) and for Brabant in Kappelhof (1986). For Holland and Zeeland easily accessible overviews of the periods in which each of these taxes were levied can be found in *GFH*, pp. 220–223 and *GFZ* pp. 68–69. The available data on the revenue of these taxes can be found in the database on http://resources.huygens.knaw.nl/gewestelijkefinancien/OverzichtPosten.

 | DOI 10.1163/9789004341289_012

Taxes in the Dutch Republic (excl. customs)

For details as to periods and revenues of (varieties) of these taxes in primary sources (as far as preserved) see http://www.inghist.nl/Onderzoek/Projecten/Gewestelijke Financien/OverzichtPosten for details on tariffs etc. see the printed volumes accessible on http://www.historici.nl/retroboeken /gewestelijke_financien/.

	(arranged according to the total number of taxes)	**Holland (58)**	**Zeeland (43)**	**Utrecht (41)**	**Friesland (39)**
A Indirect (price-increasing) 'general means' on products for general consumption					
1	*beer (many different taxes)*	bier	bier	bier (*also incl. in* logiesgeld, ketelgruit)	bier (*also in* excijsen)
2	*milling of grain (many different taxes)*	gemaal	gemaal	gemaal	gemaal
3	*slaughtering*	bestiaal	slachtgeld	slagerij *or* geslacht *or* bestiaal (*incl. in* geslacht en hoorngeld)	bestiaal
4	*salt (several taxes)*	zout (1680–1762 in direct taxes)	zout	zout (*also incl. in* zout en hoorngeld)	zout
5	*soap (several taxes)*	zeep (1680–1762 *in direct taxes*)	zeep	zeep (*also incl. in* zeep en buitenedik)	(*incl. in* havenspecien)
6	*vinegar*	(*incl. in wine*)	azijn	edik *or* bieredik (*or incl. in* bier en bierazijn *or in* zeep en buitenedik)	(*incl. in* havenspecien)
7	*tobacco*	tabak	tabak	tabak	tabak (*also incl. in* havenspecien)

Groningen (33)	**Brabant: Meijerij (31) (*no electronic data*)**	**Overijssel (30)**	**Gelderland (24) (*no electronic data*)**	**Drenthe (24)**
bier	bier	bier (*also in* koningsaccijns, opaccijns, verkleining der kannen)	bier	bier
gemaal	gemaal	gemaal	gemaal; bakkers- en tappersneringen	gemaal (*replaced by capital tax*)
bestiaal	bestiaal	geslacht	bestiaal / geslacht	bestiaal en vermangeling van paarden
zout, zeep, (azijn)	zout	(zoutgeld: *direct tax*)	zout	zout, zeep, azijn, lakens
zeep, azijn (*also incl. in* zout, zeep, azijn)	zeep	zeep	zeep	(*incl. in* zout, zeep, azijn, lakens)
(*incl. in* zout, zeep, azijn)	azijn	azijn	azijnen	(*incl. in* zout, zeep, azijn, lakens)
tabak		tabak	tabak	tabak

	(*arranged according to the total number of taxes*)	Holland (58)	Zeeland (43)	Utrecht (41)	Friesland (39)
8	*weighage* (*lists of up to 60 products*)	waag	waag	waag	waagrecht
9	*peat*	turf en kolen	turf	turf en kolen	turf en brandhout
10	*woollen cloth*	wollen lakenen (*or incl. in* wollen en zijden stoffen)	lakenen	wollen (en zijden) lakens	lakenen
11	*stivers on the general means* (*5% or more increase*)	tiende verhoging (=2 stuivers per gulden); rantsoen-gelden	stuivers te ponde Vlaams; rantsoenpenningen, schelling te ponde	rantsoenen verpachting	stuivergelden (= rantsoengelden)
12	*ferry money* (*on wagons and ships*)	veer- of passagegeld	veergeld	veer- en passagegeld, wagens en karren	
13	*peat digging*	ontgronding		ontgronding	
14	*tonnage*	rondemaat	rondemaat	ronde maat	
15	*butter*	boter	boter	boter	
16	*coal*	(*incl. in peat and coal*)	kolen	(*incl. in* turf en kolen)	
17	*firewood*	brandhout	brandhout		(*incl. in* turf en brandhout)
18	*oil,* (*olive-*)*tree and whale*	boom- en traanolie	boomolie		(*incl. in* havenspecien *or in* zoete waren)
19	*building materials*	grove waren		grove waren, bak- en muursteen, cement, pannen, kalk	grove waren (*or incl. in* havenspecien)

Groningen (33)	**Brabant: Meijerij (31) (*no electronic data*)**	**Overijssel (30)**	**Gelderland (24) (*no electronic data*)**	**Drenthe (24)**
waag	waag	waag	waag	
turf	turf	turf(tol)		(*incl. in* havenaccijns, turftollen, marskramers)
wollen lakens	wollen lakenen			(*incl. in* zout, zeep, azijn, lakens)
stuivergeld, rantsoen-penningen		stuivers op de generale middelen		
passagegeld, spilsluizen		passagegeld; Ensergeld, stuiver op de schepen	passagegeld	
ontgronding, extraordinaris turf		roedengeld	ontgronding	
	ronde maat boter			
	steenkolen			
	brandhout			
	olie			
	grove waren			

	(arranged according to the total number of taxes)	**Holland (58)**	**Zeeland (43)**	**Utrecht (41)**	**Friesland (39)**
20	*shoes*	schoengeld	schoengeld		schoenen en muilen
21	*candles and grease*	kaarsen en smeer	kaarsen, roet en smeer		
22	*fruits*	fruiten		fruiten stad Utrecht	
23	*harbour dues (domestic transport)*				havenspecien
24	*herring and salt fish*	haring en zoute vis	haring en vis		
25	*wool*			wolgeld (*on shorn sheep*)	
26	*sweet merchandise*				zoete waren
27	*grains, incoming by river or road*	inkomende granen (*excl. from* Zeeland)			
28	*pipes*	inkomende pijpen			
29	*pitch and tar*	pek en teer			
30	*salmon and sturgeon*	zalm en steur			
31	*play cards*	speelkaarten			
32	*potatoes*				
33	*old clothes, rags*				
B Indirect (price-increasing) taxes on luxury that were part of the 'general means'					
34	*wine (many different taxes)*	wijn (*incl.* azijn)	wijn	wijn (*also incl. in* logiesgeld)	wijn (*also in* excijsen)

Groningen (33)	Brabant: Meijerij (31) (*no electronic data*)	Overijssel (30)	Gelderland (24) (*no electronic data*)	Drenthe (24)
	kaarsen fruit			
		havenaccijns (*on beer, wine, brandy*)		havenaccijns, turftollen, marskramers
				schapen (*shorn sheep*)
zoete en Neurenberger waren (*also incl. in* taxatiegeld)				
aardappelen lompen				
wijnen en brandewijn	wijn	wijn (*also in* opaccijns, verkleining kannen e.d.)	wijn	wijn

	(*arranged according to the total number of taxes*)	Holland (58)	Zeeland (43)	Utrecht (41)	Friesland (39)
35	*brandy*	brandewijn	brandewijn	gebrande (wijnen en) (gedestilleerde) wateren	gebrande wijnen (*also incl. in* havenspecien)
36	*silk cloth*	(*in* wollen en zijden stoffen)		zijde (*also incl. in* wollen en zijden lakenen)	(*incl. in* havenspecien)
37	*gold cloth*	gouden lakenen			(*incl. in* havenspecien)
C Direct taxes on land and houses					
38	*land and houses*	verponding	100e etc. penning (=*1% or more*)		floreenrente
39	*land* (*value*)	(verponding)		oudschildgeld	floreenrente kwartieren
40	*land* (*area measure*)		schelling per gemet (*later part of* 200e penning) *and* verpondingen Committimus	morgengeld, 20 stuivers (*or* 200e penning) per morgen	
41	*houses*	(verponding)	huisschatting Committimus	enkel en dubbel huisgeld	floreenrente steden
42	*additional 0.5% or more on land and houses*	extraordinaris verponding	200e etc. penning (=*0.5% or more*)		reele goedschatting
43	*land for horticulture*	warmoeslanden (*in 'general means'*)		boomgaardgeld	
D1 Direct taxes on hearths, heads and families					
44	*fireplaces*	haardstedegeld or schoorsteengeld	haardstedegeld	haardstedegeld	(*incl. in* vijf specien)

Groningen (33)	Brabant: Meijerij (31) (*no electronic data*)	Overijssel (30)	Gelderland (24) (*no electronic data*)	Drenthe (24)
(*incl. in* wijnen)	brandwijn	brandewijn, gebrande wateren (*also in* opaccijns, verkleining der kannen)	brandewijn, gedestilleerde wateren	brandewijn
	gouden lakenen			
verponding	verponding	verponding, contributie, oosterlening	verponding	omslagen; grondschatting
extraordinaris verponding	extraordinaris verponding	extraordinaris verponding		
haardstedengeld	bede	vuurstedegeld	haardstedegeld	haardstedengeld

	(*arranged according to the total number of taxes*)	Holland (58)	Zeeland (43)	Utrecht (41)	Friesland (39)
45	*poll tax and/or familymoney*	hoofdgeld	hoofd- en familiegeld	hoofd- *of* familiegeld	familiegeld (hoofdgeld *incl. in* vijf specien)
D2a Direct taxes in 'general means': agricultural taxes (incl. horses)					
46	*horned cattle and sown lands*	hoornbeesten en bezaaide landen	hoornbeesten en bezaaide gemeten	hoorngeld (*incl. in* zout en hoorngeld)	(*incl. in* vijf specien)
47	*other animals*				
48	*horses* (*transfer and/or possession*)	paarden	verkoop en mangelen (ruil) van paarden	paardengeld	(*incl. in* vijf specien)
D2b Direct taxes in general means: on consumption and expenditure					
49	*coffee and tea*	koffie en thee	koffie en thee	koffie en thee	koffie en theegeld
50	*servants etc.*	herengeld (zout-, zeep-, heren- en redemptiegeld)	taux op knechten en meiden	dienstbodengeld	
51	*coaches and yachts*	karossen en jachten etc.		schepen en schuiten	pleziergeld
D3a Transfer taxes on inheritance, sales of immoveable property and ships, and public sales					
52	*collateral inheritance tax (and voluntary sales)*	collaterale successie *or* 40e penning	collaterale successie	50e, 40e etc. penning	collaterale successie, 40e penning

Groningen (33)	**Brabant: Meijerij (31)** (*no electronic data*)	**Overijssel (30)**	**Gelderland (24)** (*no electronic data*)	**Drenthe (24)**
capitaal; familiegeld		hoofdgeld	hoofdgeld; familiegeld	hoofdgeld (*replacement of* gemaal), capitaal; familiegeld
hoorngeld	hoorngeld, bezaai	hoorngeld en gezaai	hoorngeld; bezaaide landen	hoornvee en bezaaide landen
		reliqua (*sheep, pigs, bees*)		uitdrift ossen, varkens, schapen (*export oxen, pigs, sheep*); bijen (*bees*)
paardenpacht	oorgeld	paardegeld, paarden en reliqua	oorgeld, paardengeld	(*incl. in* bestiaal en vermangeling van paarden)
koffie en thee (*also incl. in* taxatiegeld)		koffie- en theegeld	koffie en thee	
(*incl. in* hoofdgeld)		dienstbodengeld, zoutgeld, consumptie der edelen	consumptietax	
collaterale successie *and* vrijwillige verkopingen	collateraal, 40e penning	50e penning en collateraal	collateraal	30e, 40e penning, collaterale successie en vrijwillige verkoping

	(arranged according to the total number of taxes)	**Holland (58)**	**Zeeland (43)**	**Utrecht (41)**	**Friesland (39)**
53	*transfer of immoveable property*	40e penning onroerende goederen (*also included in collateral inheritance*)	transport (*or*: penningen op verkoop) onroerende goederen		56e en 40e penning, consentgeld
54	*transfer of ships and moveable property; public sales*	40e penning op de schepen	transport (*or*: penningen op verkoop) roerende goederen en renten	50e etc. penning	

***D3b Taxes on legal actions or documents** [part of the (leased) 'general' or of the* **'collective' (*collected*) *means*]**

55	*stamptax on forms and other printed materials*	klein zegel en gedrukte papieren	klein zegel	klein zegel	(*incl. in* havenspecien)
56	*lawsuits, unfunded*	ongefundeerde processen (*also incl. in* 40e penning)	taux op de processen	impost op de processen	
57	*stamptax on receipts of paid taxes*	collectief zegel	biljetgeld		
58	*marriages*	trouwen	trouwgeld		
59	*burials*	begraven			

E direct taxes on income and property

60	*deduction military payments*	korting soldijordonnanties		4 man korting per compagnie	taux der officieren, heffing militaire officien

Groningen (33)	Brabant: Meijerij (31) (*no electronic data*)	Overijssel (30)	Gelderland (24) (*no electronic data*)	Drenthe (24)
(*incl. in collateral successsion and voluntary sales*)	40e penning	(*incl. in* 50e penning en collateraal)	alienatien, 50e, 40e, 20e penning	(*incl. in collateral successsion and voluntary sales*)
50e or 100e penning, koopschatpenning	schepen			
	klein zegel	klein zegel	kleinzegel	
	ongefundeer-de processen			
100e penning van soldijen, ingehouden soldij, korting		korting soldij-ordonnanties, 100e penning		200e penning *for pensions*

	(arranged according to the total number of taxes)	**Holland (58)**	**Zeeland (43)**	**Utrecht (41)**	**Friesland (39)**
61	*deduction salaries*	korting traktementen			taux der officieren, heffing politieke officien
62	*office-money (forced loan)*	ambtgeld	ambtgeld	ambtgeld	equivalent, opschot nieuw verkoren ambtenaren
63	*0.5% or more on the value of offices*	200e etc. penning op de ambten	(*incl. in* 200e penning op de losse goederen en ambtgeld)	100e penning op de officien	officien, ambachten en neringen
64	*0.1% or more on property*	personele kohieren	1000e etc. penning op het kapitaal van de (losse) goederen	15 stuivers personeel per morgen	500e penning van capitale goederen, personele goedschatting
65	*0.5% or more on the value of bonds*	200e penning op de effecten	200e penningen op de renten		

Groningen (33)	Brabant: Meijerij (31) (*no electronic data*)	Overijssel (30)	Gelderland (24) (*no electronic data*)	Drenthe (24)
equivalent			ambtgeld	aequivalenten, ambtgelden
25e penning tractementen, officiegeld (*in* 'nieuwe middelen')		officiegeld, 20e penning op tractementen		
1000e, 500e, 400e, 100e penning (*incl. in* taxatiegeld)		1000e or 500e penning	pondschatting	goedschatting
5% (10%) cut on (life)annuities (*in* 'nieuwe middelen')	100e penning op renten			

Primary Sources and Databases

Sources and Databases for the Public Finance of the Dutch Republic

The aggregated tables of the dataset that were the starting point for the construction of the tables and graphs in this book and the dataset itself can be found on http://resources.huygens.knaw.nl/gewestelijkefinancien/en.

A list of the 296 primary archival sources used for the construction of the dataset can be found on http://resources.huygens.knaw.nl/gewestelijkefinancien/OverzichtBronnen.

The primary source for each of the 7212 public revenue and public expenditure items in the database of the public finance of the Dutch Republic can be found by clicking on its *'Omschrijving'* (=description) on http://resources.huygens.knaw.nl/gewestelijkefinancien/OverzichtPosten.

'Gemeenelandsmiddelen (= "common means") 1650–1800' on http://www.iisg.nl/hpw/data.php#netherlands [these spreadsheets contain only revenues for 'wines', 'beers' and 'coffee, tea and chocolate'; data for all common means can be found in http://resources.huygens.knaw.nl/gewestelijkefinancien/OverzichtPosten].

Some Other Electronic Sources and Databases (see also under 'References' below)

Data prepared on English revenues, 1485–1815, by Professor P.K. O'Brien and Mr P.A. Hunt http://esfdb.websites.bta.com.

GDP Holland: http://www.cgeh.nl/reconstruction-national-accounts-holland-1500-1800-0.

GDP other countries: The Maddison-Project, http://www.ggdc.net/maddison/maddison-project/home.htm, 2013 version.

Letters of William of Orange: http://resources.huygens.knaw.nl/wvo/brieven?query_reset=1.

Prices and wages: http://www.iisg.nl/hpw/data.php.

Resoluties Staten Generaal: www.inghist.nl/retroboeken/statengeneraal.

Union of Utrecht: http://nl.wikisource.org/wiki/Unie_van_Utrecht.

References

Aalbers, J.A., *De Republiek en de vrede van Europa* (Groningen, 1980).

Acemoglu, D., and J.A. Robinson, *Why nations fail. The origins of power, prosperity and poverty* (London, 2012).

Acun, F., 'A portrait of the Ottoman Cities', *The Muslim World*, 92 (2002) pp. 255–285.

Allen, R., *The British Industrial Revolution in global perspective* (Cambridge: Cambridge University Press, 2009).

Althusius, J., *The Politics of Johannes Althusius. An abridged translation of the Third Edition of Politica Methodice Digesta, atque Exemplis Sacris et Profanis Illustrata*, ed. F.S. Carney (Boston, 1964) accessible on http://www.constitution.org/alth/alth_01 .htm.

Anchor, A.J.M. Brouwer, 'Lijsten van door prins Willem I verpande goederen', Oud Holland (1899), pp. 9–32.

Anderson, P., *Lineages of the absolutist state* (London, 1979).

Archer, I.W., 'The burden of taxation on sixteenth-century London', *The Historical Journal*, 44, 3 (2001), pp. 599–627.

Archer, Ian, 'Politics and government 1540–1700', in: *Cambridge Urban History* Cambridge Histories Online (Cambridge, 2008) 235–262.

Ardant, G., *Histoire de l'impot* (Paris, 1971).

Ashworth, W.J., *Customs and excise. Trade, production and consumption in England, 1640–1845* (Oxford, 2003).

Balla, E., and N.D. Johnson, 'Fiscal crisis and institutional change in the Ottoman Empire and France', *Journal of Economic History* 69,3 (2009) pp. 809–845.

Barkey, Karen, *Empire of differences: The Ottomans in comparative perspective*, (Cambridge, Cambridge University Press, 2008).

Barratt, N., 'English royal revenue in the early thirteenth century and its wider context, 1130–1330', in eds. M. Ormrod, M. Bonney and R. Bonneys (eds.), *Crises, revolutions and self-sustained growth: towards a conceptual model of change in fiscal history* (Oxford: Shaun Tyass, 1999) pp. 59–96.

Bavel, B. van, *Manors and markets. Economy and society in the Low Countries* (Oxford: Oxford University Press, 2010).

Bavel, B. van, 'Rural development and landownership in Holland, c. 1400–1650', in ed. O. Gelderblom, *The political economy of the Dutch Republic* (Farnham: Ashgate, 2009) pp. 167–197.

Becht, H.E., *Statistische gegevens betreffende den handelsomzet van de Republiek der Vereenigde Nederlanden gedurende de 17e eeuw (1579–1715)* (Den Haag, 1908).

Beeck Calkoen, J.F. van, *Onderzoek naar de rechtstoestand der geestelijke en kerkelijke goederen in Hollan na de reformatie* (Amsterdam, 1910).

Black, J., 'Was there a military revolution in early modern Europe?', *History Today* (2008) 58,7, pp. 34–41.

Blockmans, W., 'De vorming van een politieke unie (veertiende-zestiende eeuw)', in: *Geschiedenis van de Nederlanden*, eds. J.C.H. Blom and E. Lamberts (Rijswijk, s.a.) pp. 45–117.

Blockmans, W., *Metropolen aan de Noordzee* (Amsterdam: Prometheus, 2010).

Bodin, J., *On Sovereignty* ed. J.H. Franklin (Cambridge: CUP, 1992); http://classiques.uqac.ca/classiques/bodin_jean/six_livres_republique/bodin_six_livres_republique.pdf.

Bolt, J. and J.L. van Zanden (2013). The First Update of the Maddison Project; Re-Estimating Growth Before 1820. Maddison Project Working Paper 4; http://www.ggdc.net/maddison/maddison-project/home.htm.

Bonney, R., ed., *Economic systems and state finance* (Oxford, 1995).

Bonney, R. 'The Eighteenth Century II. The struggle for Great Power status and the end of the old fiscal regime', in idem ed., *Economic Systems and State Finance*, pp. 315–393.

Bonney, R., 'Revenues', in idem (ed.) *Economic systems and state finance*, pp. 423–507.

Bonney, R., ed., *The rise of the fiscal state in Europe, c. 1200–1815* (Oxford 1999).

Boone, M., K. Davids and P. Janssens (eds.) *Urban public debts. Urban government and the market for annuities in Western Europa (14th-18th centuries)* (Turnhout: Brepols, 2003).

Bor, P., *Oorsprongk, begin en vervolgh der Nederlandsche oorlogen etc.* 4 vols. (Amsterdam 1679).

Bosker, M., 'From Baghdad to London. The dynamics of urban growth in Europe and the Arab world, 800–1800' (2008); http://xinkaishi.typepad.com/files/bosker_baghdad-to-london.pdf.

Bosker, M., E. Buringh and J.L. van Zanden, 'From Baghdad to London. Unraveling urban development in Europe, the Middle East and North Africa, 800–1800', *Review of Economics and Statistics* 95 (2013) pp. 1418–1437.

Braddick, M.J., *The nerves of state: taxation and the financing of the English state, 1558–1714* (Manchester: Manchester University Press, 1996).

Braddick, M.J., *State formation in early modern England, c. 1550–1700* (Cambridge: Cambridge University Press, 2000).

Braesch, F., *Les recettes et les dépenses du trésor pendant l'année 1789: le compte rendu au roi de mars 1788* (Paris, Maison du Livre français, 1936).

Brandon, P., *War, capital, and the Dutch state (1588–1795)* (Leiden: Brill, 2015).

Braudel, F., *Capitalism and material life Part III* (1974; orig. French ed. 1967).

Brewer, J., *The sinews of power. War, money and the English state, 1688–1783* (Cambrigde: Harvard University Press, 1989).

Brieven en onuitgegeven stukken van Jonkheer Arend van Dorp, ed. J.B. van der Schueren (Utrecht 1887–8).

Broek, J.v.d., *Groningen, een stad apart. Over het verleden van een eigenzinnige stad* (Assen 2007).

Bronnen voor de geschiedenis der dagvaarten van de Staten en steden van Holland voor 1544. Deel I 1276–1433. Tweede stuk: teksten, eds. W. Prevenier and J.G. Smit (Den Haag 1987).

Bruijn, J.R., *Varend verleden: de Nederlandse oorlogsvloot in de zeventiende en achttiende eeuw* (Amsterdam, Balans, 1998).

Bruijn, J.R., 'States and their navies from the late sixteenth to the end of the eighteenth century', in: Ph. Contamine (ed.) *War and competition between states* (Oxford: Clarendon Press, 2000) pp. 69–98.

Burckhardt, J., *The state as a work of art* (London 2010; originally 1860; transl. 1878).

Burg, M. van den, and M. 't Hart, 'Renteniers and the recovery of Amsterdam's credit', in M. Boone a.o. eds., *Urban public debts* (Turnhout 2003) 197–219.

Cabral de Mello, E., *De Braziliaanse affaire. Portugal, de Republiek der Verenigde Nederlanden en Noord-Oost Brazilie, 1641–1669* (Zupthen 2005).

Cavanaugh, W.T., *The myth of religious Violence. Secular ideology and the roots of modern conflict* (Oxford 2009).

Chambers, D., and B. Pullan eds, *Venice: a documentary history* (Toronto 2001).

Chandaman, C.D., *The English public revenue 1660–1688* (Oxford 1975).

Ciriacono, S., 'The Venetian economy and the World System of the semi-periphery', in: H.J. Nitz ed., *The early modern world system in geographical perspective* (Stuttgart 1993) pp. 120–136.

Çizakça, M., 'Tax farming and financial decentralization in the Ottoman economy 1520–1697', *Journal of European Economic History* 22, 2 (1993) pp. 219–251.

Çizakça, M., *A Comparative evolution of business* partnerships. *The Islamic world and Europe with specific reference to the Ottoman archives* (Leiden: Brill, 1996).

Çizakça, M., *A history of philanthropic foundations. The Islamic world from the seventh century to the present* (Istanbul Bogazicki University Press, 2000).

Clapham, J., *The Bank of England. A history* (Cambridge 1944).

Comín Comín, F., and B. Yun-Casalilla, 'Spain: from composite monarchy to nation-state, 1492–1914. An exceptional case?', in *The rise of fiscal states. A global history, 1500–1914*, eds. B. Yun-Casalilla ad Patrick K. O'Brien (Cambridge 2012) pp. 233–267.

Crises, revolutions and self-sustained growth. Essays in European fiscal history, 1130–1830, eds. M. Ormrod, M. Bonney and R. Bonney (Stamford, 1999).

Dam, P.J.E.M. van, and M. van Tielhof, 'Losing land, gaining water. Ecological and financial aspects of regional watermanagement in Rhineland, 1200–1800', *Jaarboek voor Ecologisch Geschiedenis* 10 (2006) [special issue: *Water management, communities and environment. The Low Countries in Comparative Perspective, c. 1000–1800*] pp. 63–94.

Dam, Pieter van, *Beschrijvinge van de Oostindische Compagnie 1639–1701, 4 vols,* (manuscript 1701) ed. F.W. Stapel (Den Haag 1927) http://resources.huygens.knaw.nl/retroboeken/vandam/.

Darling, L., *Revenue-raising and Legitimacy: Tax Collection and Finance Administration in the Ottoman Empire, 1560–1660* (Leiden: Brill 1996).

Darling, L., 'Ottoman fiscal administration: decline or adaptation?', *Journal of European Economic History* 26, 1 (1997) pp. 157–199.

Daunton, M., 'The politics of British taxation', in B. Yun-Casalilla and P.K. O'Brien (eds.) *The rise of fiscal states. A global history, 1500–1914* (Cambridge 2012) 111–145.

Davids, C.A., *The rise and decline of Dutch technological leadership. Technology, economy and culture in the Netherlands 1350–1800* (Leiden 2008).

Davids, C.A., and M. 't Hart, 'The navy and the rise of the state. The case of the Netherlands, c. 1570–1810', in: Navies and state formation. The Schumpeter hypothesis revisited and reflected (Zürich 2012) pp. 273–316.

Davis, R., 'English Foreign Trade 1700–1774', *Economic History Review* (1962) 15, pp. 285–303.

Dehing, P., *Geld in Amsterdam. Wisselbank en wisselkoersen, 1650–1725* (Hilversum, Verloren, 2012).

Dehing, P., and M. 't Hart, 'Linking the fortunes: currency and banking, 1550–1800', *A financial history of the Netherlands, eds. M. 't Hart, J. Jonker and J.L. van Zanden* (Cambridge 1997) pp.37–64.

Dekker, R., *Holland in beroering. Oproeren in de 17de en 18de eeuw* (Baarn 1982).

De Vries, J., see: Vries, J. de.

Deursen, A.Th. van, 'Tussen eenheid en zelfstandigheid', in: *De Unie van Utrecht,* ed.Groenveld (1979), pp. 136–154.

Dickson, P.G.M., *The financial revolution in England: a study in the development of public credit, 1688–1756* (London 1967).

Dijk, J.H. van, 'De geldelijke druk op de Delftsche burgerij in de jaren 1572–1576', *Bijdragen voor Vaderlandsche Geschiedenis and Oudheidkunde,* 7, V (1935) pp. 169–186.

Dijkhof, E., 'Op weg naar autonomie', in: *Geschiedenis van Amsterdam tot 1578. Een stad uit het niets,* ed. M. Carasso-Kok (Amsterdam 2004) pp. 63–75.

Dincecco, M., *Political transformations and public finances: Europe, 1650–1913* (Cambridge 2011).

Dirksen, W., 'Enige opmerkingen over de belastingheffing in de Republiek der Verenigde Nederlanden in de 17e en 18e eeuw, in het bijzonder over inkomstenbelastingen in Zeeland', in *L'impôt dans le cadre de la ville et de l'ëtat. Pro Civitate Collection Histoire* 13 (1966).

Dirksen, W., 'Stedelijke heffingen in Middelburg', in: *Steden en dorpen in tal en last*, eds. T. Pfeil e.a., (Amsterdam, NEHA, 1999).

Doel en middel : aspecten van financieel overheidsbeleid in de Nederlanden van de zestiende eeuw tot heden, eds. W. Fritschy, J.K.T. Postma and J. Roelevink (Amsterdam, NEHA, 1999).

Dolfing, B., *Waterbeheer geregeld? Een historisch bestuurskundige analyse van de institutionele ontwikkeling van de hoogheemraadscahppen van Delfland en Rhineland, 1600–1800* (s.l. 2000).

Dormans, E., *Het tekort: staatsschuld in de tijd der Republiek* (Amsterdam, NEHA, 1991).

Dougherty, K.L., 'An empirical test of Federalist and Anti-Federalist theories of state contributions, 1775–1783', *Social Science History* 33, 1 (2009) pp. 47–74.

Downing, B., *The Military Revolution and Political Change. Origins of Democracy and Autocracy in Early Modern Europe* (Princeton 1992).

Drelichman, M., and H.-J. Voth, 'The Sustainable Debts of Philip II: A Reconstruction of Castile's Fiscal Position, 1566–1596', *Journal of Economic History* 70,4 (2010) pp. 813–842.

Dyson, H., *The state tradition in Western Europe. A study of an idea and institution* (Oxford 1980).

Economic and Social History of the Ottoman Empire. Parts I and II, eds. S. Faroqhi, B. McGowan, D. Quataert, S. Pamuk, (Cambridge: CUP 1997).

Economic systems and state finance, ed. R. Bonney (Oxford 1995).

Eldem, E., 'Istanbul: from imperial to peripheralized capital', in *The Ottoman City*, pp. 135–207.

Eldem, E., D. Goffman and B. Masters, *The Ottoman City between East and West. Aleppo, Izmir and Istanbul* (Cambridge: CUP, 1999) pp. 83–160.

Elte, S., 'Het monopolie-oproer in Zwolle in mei 1726', *Tijdschrift voor Geschiedenis* 68 (1955) pp. 224–237.

Ent, L. van der, and V. Enthoven, *Gewestelijke financiën ten tijde van de Republiek der Verenigde Nederlanden: Groningen (1594–1795)* (The Hague 2001).

Ent, L. van der, and W. Fritschy, *Gewestelijke financiën ten tijde van de Republiek der Verenigde Nederlanden: Deel I Drenthe, 1602–1795* (The Hague 1998).

Enthoven, V., *Zeeland en de opkomst van de Republiek: handel en strijd in de Scheldedelta, c. 1550–1621* (Leiden 1996).

Enthoven, V., 'Van steunpilaar tot blok aan het been. De Verenigde Oostindische Compagnie en de Unie', in: *De Verenigde Oostindische Compagnie tussen oorlog en diplomatie*, eds. G.v.d. Knaap en G. Teitler (Leiden 2002).

Epstein, S.R., *Freedom and growth: the rise of states and markets in Europe, 1300–1750* (London/New York, 2000).

Ertman, Th., 'State Formation and State Building in Europe', in: *The Handbook of Political Sociology*, eds. T. Janoski a.o. (Cambridge 2005) pp. 367–383.

Faroqhi, S., 'Taxation and urban activities in sixteenth century Anatolia', *Journal of Turkish Studies*, 1, 1, 1979/80.

Faroqhi, S., 'Finances', in: *Social and economic history of the Ottoman Empire* Part II (Cambridge 1997) 541.

Faroqhi, S., 'The ruling elite between politics and "the economy"', in: *An economic and social history of the Ottoman Empire. Volume 2; 1600–1914* (Cambridge 1997), pp. 545–576.

Faroqhi, S., 'Plagues, famines and earthquakes', in eds. S. Faroqhi, B. McGowan, D. Quataert, S. Pamuk, *Economic and Social History of the Ottoman Empire. Part II* (Cambridge: CUP 1997).

Faroqhi, S.N., 'Introduction', in idem ed., *The Cambridge History of Turkey Volume 3* (Cambridge: CUP 2006) pp. 3–17.

Federalist no. 20, 11. December 1787: http://www.foundingfathers.info/federalistpapers/fed20.htm.

Finer, S.E., *The history of government. II. The intermediate ages* (Oxford 1997).

Fiscal crises, liberty, and representative government, 1450–1789, eds. Ph. Hoffman and K. Norberg (Stanford, Stanford UP, 1994).

Fiscal-military state in eighteenth-century Europe. The -, Essays in honour of P.G.M. Dickson, ed. C. Storrs (Ashgate publishers, Farnham, 2009).

Fleet, K., 'The Turkish Economy, 1071–1453', in idem ed., *The Cambridge History of Europe Volume 1. Byzantium to Turkey 1071–1453* (Cambridge: CUP, 2009) pp. 227–266.

Flinn, M., *Scottish population history from the 17th century to the 1930s* (Cambridge: Cambridge University Press, 1973.

Formation of National States in Western Europe. The -, ed. Ch. Tilly (Princeton 1975).

Formsma, W.J., 'De nieuwe geschiedenis staatkundig beschouwd', in: *Geschiedenis van Overijssel*, eds. B.H. Slicher van Bath a.o., pp. 119–135.

Forsyth, M., *Unions of state. The theory and practice of confederation* (Leicester 1981).

Franklin, J., 'Bodin's doctrine and its limitations', *The Cambridge History of Political Thought, 1450–1700*, (Cambridge, CUP, 1991), pp. 299–309.

Fransen, A., *Een kleine dijk met een groot doel. De financiering van de Diemerdijk, 1591*–1864 (diss. Amsterdam 2009).

Fritschy, J.M.F. [=W.], *De patriotten en de financien van de Bataafse Republiek. Hollands krediet en de smalle marges voor een nieuw beleid (1795–1801)* (Den Haag 1988).

Fritschy, W., 'Taxation in Britain, France and the Netherlands in the eighteenth century', in *Economic and social history in the Netherlands* 2 (1990) pp. 57–81.

Fritschy, W., 'Staatsvorming en financieel beleid onder Willem I', in: *Staats- en natievorming in Willem I's koninkrijk (1815–1830)* eds. C.A. Tamse and E. Witte (Brussel 1992) pp. 215–237.

Fritschy, W., 'Domeinen en financieel beleid in Overijssel', in: *Doel en Middel*, eds. W. Fritschy a.o. (Amsterdam 1995) pp. 75–97.

Fritschy, W., 'Geld en oorlog. Financeel beleid in Holland en Overijssel vergeleken met Groot-Brittani;e en Oostenrijk (1740–1785)', in: *De Republiek tussen zee en vasteland*, eds. K. Davids a.o. (Leuven 1995) pp. 207–225.

Fritschy, W., *Gewestelijke financien ten tijde van de Republiek. Deel I. Overijssel, 1604–1795* (Den Haag 1996).

Fritschy, W., 'Three centuries of urban and provincial public debt: Amsterdam and Holland', in: *Urban public debts* (2003) pp. 75–93.

Fritschy, W., and R. van der Voort, 'From fragmentation to unification, 1700–1914', in: *A financial history of the Netherlands* eds. M. 't Hart, J. Jonker and J.L. van Zanden (Cambridge 1997) pp. 64–93.

Fritschy, W., 'The poor, the rich and the taxes in Heinsius times', in *Anthonie Heinsius and the Dutch Republic 1688–1720, Politics, War and Finance*, eds. J. de Jongste and A. Veenendaal jr. (The Hague, Institute of Netherlands History, 2002) pp. 242–259.

Fritschy, W., 'A "financial revolution" reconsidered: public finance in Holland during the Dutch Revolt, 1568–1648', *Economic History Review* (2003) pp. 57–89.

Fritschy, W., 'Willem van Oranje en de overheidsfinanciën', in: W. Fritschy en G. Zalm, *Willem van Oranje en de overheidsfinanciën* (Delft, Museum Prinsenhof, 2006).

Fritschy, W., 'Holland's public debt and Amsterdam's capital market', in: *Banca, crédito y capital. La Monarquía, Hispánica y los antiguos Países Bajos (1505–1700)* eds. C. Sanz Ayán and B.J. García García (Fundacion Carlos de Amberes, 2006) pp. 39–59.

Fritschy, W.,'Indirect taxes and public debt in "the world of Islam" before 1800', in *La fiscalità nell'economia europea secc. XIII-XVIII* (Firenze University Press 2008) Vol. I, pp. 51–75.

Fritschy, W., 'The efficiency of taxation in Holland', in: *The Political Economy of the Dutch Republic*, ed. O. Gelderblom (Farnham, Ashgate, 2009) pp. 55–85.

Fritschy, W., 'State formation and urbanization trajectories: state finance in the Ottoman Empire before 1800, as seen from a Dutch perspective', *Journal of Global History* 4 (2009) pp. 405–428.

Fritschy, W., 'Schulden als leerschool? De Unie der Zeven Verenigde Provincien en de Europese Unie', *Tijdschrift voor Sociale en Economische Geschiedenis* 92, (2012) pp. 3–29.

Fritschy, W., and R. Liesker, 'Overheidsfinanciën, kapitaalmarkt en "institutionele context" in Holland en Overijssel tijdens en an de Spaanse Successie-oorlog', in: *Kapitaal, ondernemerschap en beleid*, red. C.A. Davids e.a. (Amsterdam 1996) pp. 165–197.

Fruin, R. and H. Colenbrander, *Geschiedenis der staatsinstellingen in Nederland tot den val der Republiek* (Den Haag, Nijhoff, 1922).

Gaastra, F., 'The organization of the VOC', in: *The archives of the Dutch East India Company VOC and the local institutions in Batavia* (Jakarta/Leiden 2007).

Gaastra, F., *De geschiedenis van de VOC* (Zutphen 1991).

Gelabert, J., 'Castile, 1504–1808', in: *The rise of the fiscal state* ed. R. Bonney (Oxford UP 2004; 1999) pp. 210–243.

Gelabert, J., 'The fiscal burden', in *Economic systems and state finance*, pp. 539–577.

Gelder, H.E. van, *De Nederlandse munten* (Utrecht, Spectrum, 2002).

Gelderblom, O., and J. Jonker, 'Public finance and economic growth: the case of Holland in the seventeenth century', *Journal of Economic History* 71 (2011) pp. 1–39.

Genç, M. 'A study of the feasibility of using eighteenth-century Ottoman financial records as an indicator of economic activity', in: *The Ottoman Empire and the world economy*, ed. H. Islamoglu-Inan (Cambridge: Cambridge UP, 1987) pp. 345–373.

Genç, M., and E. Özvar eds., *Osmanlı maliyesi: kurumlar ve bütçeler (Ottoman financial institutions and budgets)* 2 vols. (Istanbul: Osmanlı Bankası Arsiv ve Arastırma Merkezi, 2006).

General Collection of Treaties, manifestos (...) from the Year 1495 to the Year 1712, A, London, 1732 (Google Books).

Gentles, I., *The New Model Army in England, Ireland and Scotland 1645–53* (Oxford, Blackwell Press, 1994).

Gerber, H., *The social origins of the Middle East* (London, 1994).

Glawischnig, R., *Niederlande, Kalvinismus und Reichsgrafenstand : 1559–1584 : Nassau-Dillenburg unter Graf Johann VI* (Marburg 1973).

Glete, J., Navies and nations. Warships, navies and statebuilding in Europe and America, 1500–1860 (Stockholm 1993).

Glete, J., *War and the state in early modern Europe. Spain, the Dutch Republic and Sweden as fiscal-military states, 1500–1660* (London 2002).

Glete, J., *Swedish naval administration* (Leiden: Brill, 2009).

Goffman, D., 'Izmir: from village to colonial port city', in E. Eldem, D. Goffman and B. Masters eds., *The Ottoman City between East and West. Aleppo, Izmir and Istanbul* (Cambridge: CUP, 1999) 83–160.

Goffman, D., *The Ottoman Empire and Early Modern Europe* (Cambridge: Cambridge University Press; 2003).

Goldstone, J., 'East and West in the seventeenth century: political crises in Stuart England, Ottoman Turkey and Ming China', in *Comparative Studies in Society and History*, 30 (1991).

Grapperhaus, F., *Alva en de tiende penning* (Zutphen, Walburg Pers, 1984).

Grapperhaus, F., *Convoyen en licenten* (Zutphen, Walburg Pers, 1986).

Groenevelt, F., *De economische crisis van het jaar 1720* (Groningen, 1940).

Groenveld, S., 'De institutionele en politieke context', in: *Van Tresorier tot Thesauriergeneraal* (Hilversum, Verloren, 1996) pp. 55–89.

Groenveld, S., and H. Leeuwenberg eds., *De Unie van Utrecht* (Den Haag 1979) pp. 101–136.

Gunn, S., D. Grummit and H. Cools, *War, state and society in England and the Netherlands* (Oxford 2007).

Gunn, S., D. Grummitt, and H. Cools, 'War and the State in Early Modern Europe: Widening the Debate', *War in History* 15, 4 (2008) pp. 371–388.

Haitsma Mulier, E.O.G., *The myth of Venice and Dutch republican thought in the seventeenth century* (Assen, 1980).

Hakkı Kadı, I., *Natives and interlopers. Competition between Ottoman and Dutch merchants in the 18th centur*,(diss. Leiden, 2008).

Harding, A., *Medieval law and the foundations of the state* (Oxford, 2002).

Harding, V. 'The crown, the city and the orphans: the city of London and its finances, 1400–1700' in *Urban Public Debts*, 2003) pp. 51–61.

Hart, M. 't, 'Salt tax and salt trade in the Low Countries', in: *Le roi, le marchand et le sel*, J.C. Hocquet ed. (Lille 1987) pp. 293–315.

Hart, M. 't, 'Staatsfinanciën als familiezaak tijdens de Republiek: de ontvangers-generaal Doubleth', in *Fiscaliteit in Nederland*, eds. J.Th. de Smidt a.o. (Deventer, Walburg Pers, 1987) pp. 57–67.

Hart, M. 't, '"The devil or the Dutch": Holland's impact on the Financial Revolution in England, 1643–1694', *Parliaments, Estates and Representations* 11, 1 (1991) pp. 39–52.

Hart, M. 't, *The making of a bourgeois state: war, politics and finance during the Dutch Revolt* (Manchester, 1993).

Hart, M. 't, 'Mutual advantages: state bankers as brokers between the city of Amsterdam and the Dutch Republic', in: *The Political Economy of the Dutch Republic*, ed. O. Gelderblom (Ashgate 2009) pp. 115–142.

Hart, M. 't, *The Dutch Wars of Independence and the Republic's Golden Age, c. 1580-c. 1680* (London 2014).

Hart, M. 't, en M.v.d. Burg, '*Renteniers* and the recovery of Amsterdam's credit', in *Urban public* debts (2003), pp. 197–219.

Hart, M. 't and M. Limberger, 'Staatsmacht en stedelijke autonomie. Het geld van Antwerpen en Amsterdam (1500–1700)', *Tijdschrift voor Sociale en Economische Geschiedenis*, 3, 3 (2006), pp.36–72.

Hayashi, K., 'Turkey', in: *Islamic urban studies: historical review and perspective*, ed. M. Haneda, New York: Columbia University Press, 1994.

Healy, S.M., Crown revenue and the political culture of early Stuart England, PhD thesis, Birkbeck, University of London, 2015[http://bbktheses.da.ulcc.ac.uk/125/1/cp_Healy_thesis_REVISED_V3_FINAL.pdf accessed June 2016].

Heijden, M. van der 'Stadsrekeningen, stedelijke financien en historisch onderzoek', *NEHA-bulletin voor de economisch geschiedenis* 14, 2 (1999).

Heijden, M. van der, 'De kosten van het beleg van Haarlem, 1572–1593', *Holland. Historisch Tijdschrift* 352 (2003) pp. 63–75.

Heijden, M. van der, *Geldschieters van de stad. Financiële relaties tussen stad, burgers en overheden, 1550–1650* (Amsterdam, Bert Bakker, 2006).

Heijden, M. van der, e.a. (eds.), *Serving the Urban Community. The Rise of Public Facilities in the Low Countries* (Amsterdam 2009).

Heijer, H. den, 'Plannen voor de samenvoeging van VOC en WIC', *Tijdschrift voor Zeegschiedenis* 13(1994) 115–130.

Heijer, H. den, *De geschiedenis van de WIC* (Zutphen 2002).

Hirschman, A.O., *The passions and the interests. Political arguments for capitalism before its triumph* (Princeton, Princeton UP, 1977).

Hocquet, J.C., 'City state and market economy', in: *Economic systems and state finance*, ed. R. Bonney, Oxford 1995) 81–100.

Hoffman, Ph.T., *Why did Europe conquer the world?* (Princeton 2015).

Houtzager, D., *Hollands lijf- en losrenteleningen vóór 1672* (Schiedam, s.a. (1950)).

Hovy, J., *Het voorstel van 1751 tot instelling van en beperkt vrijhavenstelsel in de Republiek* (Groningen 1966).

Hueglin, Th., and A. Fenna, *Comparative Federalism. A Systematic Inquiry* (Peterborough, Broadview Press, 2015).

Hütteroth, W., 'Ecology of the Ottoman lands', in ed. S.N. Faroqhi, *The Cambridge History of Turkey Volume 3* (Cambridge: CUP 2006) pp. 18–41.

Inalcik, H. 'The Ottoman State: Economy and Society, 1300–1600', in: *An Economic and Social History of the Ottoman Empire. Part I*, ed. H. Inalcik (Cambridge: CUP, 1997) pp. 1–380.

Informacie 1514: http://www.cgeh.nl/enqueste-en-informacie.

Innes, J., and N. Rogers, 'Politics and government 1700–1840', in: *Cambridge Urban History II* (Cambridge 2008).

Israel, J., *The Dutch Republic: its rise, greatness and fall 1477–1806* (Oxford: Clarendon Press, 1995).

Israel, J., *Monarchy, Orangism and Republicanism in the Later Dutch Golden Age* (Amsterdam 2004).

Israel, Jonathan I., *Dutch primacy in world trade, 1585–1740* (Oxford UP 1990).

Janssen, A.E.M., 'Het verdeelde Huis', in *De Unie van Utrecht*, eds. S. Groenveld and H. Leeuwenberg (1979) pp. 101–136.

Jardine, L., *Going Dutch: How England Plundered Holland's Glory* (London 2008).

Jennings, R.C., 'Loans and credit in early 17th century Ottoman judicial records', in *Journal of the Economic and Social History of the Orient*, 16, 1973, pp. 168–216.

Johnson, N.D., 'Banking on the king: the evolution of the royal revenue farms in Old Regime France', *Journal of Economic History* 66,4 (2006) pp. 963–991.

Jong, M. de, 'Dutch public finance during the Eighty Years' War: the case of the province of Zeeland, 1585–1621', in M. van der Hoeven, ed., *Exercise of arms: warfare in the Netherlands, 1548–1648* (Leiden, 1998), pp. 133–152.

Jonker, J., *Merchants, bankers, middlemen. The Amsterdam money market during the first half of the 19th century* (Amsterdam: NEHA, 1996).

Kappelhof, A.C.M. *De belastingheffing in de Meijerij van Den Bosch gedurende de Generaliteitsperiode (1648–1730)* (Tilburg, 1986).

Karaman, K., and Ş. Pamuk, 'Ottoman State Finances in Comparative European perspective, 1500–1914', *The Journal of Economic History* 70 (2010) pp. 593–629.

Karaman, K. Kivanç and Ş. Pamuk, 'Different paths to the modern state in Europe: the interaction between domestic and political economy and interstate competition', *LSE Europe in Question Discussion Paper Series* 37 (2011).

Karaman, K. Kivanç and Ş. Pamuk, 'Different paths to the modern state in Europe: the interaction between domestic and political economy and interstate competition', *American Political Science Review* (2013) pp. 1–24.

Keith Horsefield, J., 'The "Stop of the Exchequer" Revisited', *The Economic History Review* 35, 4 (1982) pp. 511–528.

Kernkamp, J., *De handel op den vijand: 1572–1609* (Utrecht, Kemink, 1931–1945).

Kluit, A., *Historie der Hollandsche Staatsregering tot aan het jaar 1795*. 5 vols. (Amsterdam, Wouter Brave, 1802–1805).

Koopmans, J.W., *De Staten van Holland en de Opstand : de ontwikkeling van hun functies en organisatie in de periode 1544–1588* (Den Haag 1990).

Körner, M. 'Public credit', in: *Economic Systems and State Finance*, pp. 507–539.

Korvezee, E.H., 'Belastingen in Noord-Brabant vóór 1648', Varia Historica Brabantica (Den Bosch 1975) pp. 97–164.

Kuran, T., *The long divergence: how Islamic law held back the Middle East* (Princeton 2011).

Lane, F., *Venice, a maritime republic* (Baltimore 1973).

Lane, F. 'Public debt and private wealth: particularly in sixteenth-century Venice', in: F.C. Lane, *Proftis from power* (New York 1979) pp. 72–82.

Lapidus, I., *Muslim Cities in the Later Middle Ages* (Cambridge: CUP, 1984).

Lapidus, I., *A history of Islamic societies* (Cambridge: Cambridge University Press, 2005).

Lawson, Ph., *The East India Company: a history* (London: Longman, 1993).

Leeuwen-Canneman, M. van, *Een vriendschap in het teken van 's lands financien. Btiefwisseling tussen Elias Canneman en Isaac Jan Alexander Gogel 1799*–1813 (Den Haag 2009).

Leeuwen, R. van, *Waqfs and Urban Structure. The Case of Ottoman Damascus* (Leiden: Brill, 1999).

Lesger, C., 'Intraregional trade and the port system in Holland, 1400–1700', *Economic and Social History in the Netherlands* 4 (1992) pp. 185–217.

Lesger, C., *The Rise of the Amsterdam Market and Information Exchange. Merchants, Commercial Expansion and Change in the Spatial Economy of the Low Countries, c.1550–1630* (Ashgate, Aldershot, 2006).

Lesger, C., 'De wereld als horizon : de economie tussen 1578 en 1650' in: *Geschiedenis van Amsterdam. Deel 2 Centrum van de wereld* eds. W. Frijhoff, M. Prak and B. Bakker (Amsterdam, SUN, 2004) pp. 103–187.

Levi, M., *Of Rule and Revenue* (Berkeley 1988).

Liesker, R., and W. Fritschy, *Gewestelijke financiën ten tijde van de Republiek der Verenigde Nederlanden. Deel IV Holland (1572–1795)* (Den Haag, ING, 2004).

Long, R.H., 'Parliamentary Monarchy', in: *The 'New Monarchies' and Representative Assemblies. Medieval Constitutionlism or Modern Absolutism?*, ed. J. Slavin (Boston 1964) pp. 67–77.

Lowry, H.W., *The nature of the early Ottoman state* (New York 2003).

Lynn, J.A., 'Recalculating French army growth during the *Grand Siècle*, 1610–1715', in: *The Military Revolution Debate* ed. C.J. Rogers (Oxford 1995).

Maissen, T., 'Inventing the sovereign republic: imperial structure, French challenges, Dutch models and the early modern Swiss Confederation', in: *The Republican Alternative* eds. A. Holenstein, T. Maissen and M. Prak (Amsterdam 2008) pp.125–151.

Malanima, P., *Premodern European Economy* (Leiden: Brill, 2009).

Mallett, M., and J. Hale, *The military organisation of a Renaissance state. Venice c. 1400–1617* (Cambridge 1984).

Man-made Lowlands, History of water management and land reclamation in the Netherlands, ed. G.P. van de Ven (Utrecht, Matrijs, 2004).

Masters, B. 'Aleppo: the Ottoman Empire's caravan city', in Eldem, Goffman and Masters, *The Ottoman City*.

Matthews, G.T., *The Royal General Farms in Eighteenth Century France* (New York. Columbia University Press, 1958).

McGowan, B., *Economic life in Ottoman Europe. Taxation, trade and the struggle for land, 1600–1800* (Cambridge UP, 1981).

McGowan, B., 'The age of the ayans', in: S. Faroqhi a.o., *An economic and social history of the Ottoman Empire. Volume II* (Cambridge UP 1997) pp. 637–759, pp. 713–714.

Memorie ofte verhandeling van het geene omtrent het stuk van de finantie van de provincie van Holland en Westvriesland van tijd tot tijd is voorgevallen (1755) http://www.historici.nl/Onderzoek/Projecten/GewestelijkeFinancien/memorie.

Meulen, A. van der, *Studies over het ministerie van Van de Spiegel* (Leiden, Kooyker, 1905).

Military Revolution Debate. The -, Readings on the Military Transformation of Early Modern Europe, ed. C.J. Rogers (*Boulder, CO and Oxford*, 1995).

Miracle mirrored. A -,The Dutch Republic in European perspective, eds. K. Davids and J. Lucassen (Cambridge 1995).

Mitchell, B.R., and Ph. Deane, *Abstract of British historical statistics* (Cambridge UP, 1971).

Moes, J.K.S., 'Speciale en economische facetten uit de geschiedenis van de Leidse textielnijverheid', in *Stof uit het Leidse verleden,* eds. J.K.S. Moes and B.M.A. de Vries (Leiden, 1991) pp. 7–31.

Montesquieu, Ch. De Secondat, baron de, *The Spirit of Laws* (1748; transl. T. Nugent 1752; publ. Kitchener, Canada, 2001)) accessible on http://socserv.mcmaster.ca/econ/ugcm/3ll3/montesquieu/spiritoflaws.pdf; Book XIII, Chapter 16.

Mortimer, G., 'War by contract, credit and contribution: the Thirty Years War', in: idem ed., *Early Modern Military History, 1450–1815* (New York 2004).

Mueller, R.C., *The Venetian money market. Banks, panics and the public debt (1200–1500)* (Baltimore 1977).

Murphy, Anne L., *The origins of English financial markets : investment and speculation before the South Sea Bubble* (Cambridge 2009).

Muto, G., 'The Spanish system: centre and periphery', in: *Economic Systems and State Finance,* ed. R. Bonney (Oxford 1995) pp.231–253.

Neal, L.,*The rise of financial capitalism. International capital markets in the Age of* Reason (Cambridge 1990).

Nederveen Meerkerk, E. van, *De draad in eigen handen, Vrouwen en loonarbeid in de Nederlandse textielnijverheid 1581–1810* (Amsterdam, Aksant, 2007).

New Monarchies and Representative Assemblies, The-, ed. A. Slavin (Boston: Houghton Mifflin, 1964).

Nimwegen, O. van, *De Republiek der Verenigde Nederlanden ls grote mogendheid. Buitenlandse politiek en oologvoering in de eerste helft van de achttiende eeuw en in het bijzonder tijdens de Oostenrijkse Successie-oorlog (1740–1748)* (Amsterdam, 2002).

Nimwegen, O. van, *The Dutch Army and the Military Revolutions, 1588–1688* (Woodbridge, Boydell, 2010; transl. of the Dutch version of 2006).

Noordegraaf, L., and G. Valk, *De Gave Gods. De pest in Holland vanaf de late Middeleeuwen* (Bergen: Octavo, 1988).

North, D., and B. Weingast, 'Constitutions and commitment: the evolution of institutions governing public choice in seventeenth-century England',*Journal of Economic History* 49 (1989) pp. 803–832.

Oates, W., 'On the evolution of fiscal federalism: theory and institutions', *National Tax Journal* 61, 2 (2008) pp. 313–334.

O'Brien, P.K., 'The nature and historical evolution of an exceptional fiscal state', *Economic History Review,* 64,2 (2011) pp. 408–446.

O'Brien, P., and X. Duran, 'Total Factor Productivity for the Royal Navy from Victory at Texal (1653) to Triumph at Trafalgar (1805)', *London School of Economics, Working Papers No. 134/10,* February 2010.

O'Brien, P.K., and Ph. Hunt, 'The rise of a fiscal state in England, 1485–1815', *Historical Research. The Bulletin of the Institute of Historical Research* 66 (1993) pp. 129–176.

O'Brien, P.K., and Ph. Hunt, 'England 1485–1815', in R. Bonney (ed.), *The rise of the fiscal state in Europe, c.1200–1815* (Oxford: Oxford University Press, 1999) pp. 53–100.

Ormrod, D., *The Rise of Commercial Empires: England and the Netherlands in the Age of Mercantilism, 1650–1770* (Cambridge 2003).

Ormrod, M., Bonney, M., and Bonney, R., eds., *Crises, revolutions and self-sustained growth: essays in European fiscal history, 1130–1830* (Stamford, 1999).

Ormrod, W., 'The West European monarchies in the Later Middle Ages', in R. Bonney ed., *Economic systems and state finance* (Oxford 1996) pp. 123–163.

Ormrod, W.M. and J. Barta, 'The feudal structure and the beginnings of state finance' in R. Bonney (ed.) *Economic systems and state finance* (Oxford: Oxford University Press, 1995), pp. 53–81.

O'Siochru, M., *God's Executioner. Oliver Cromwell and the Conquest of Ireland* (London: Faber & Faber, 2008).

Ottoman City, The-, see: Eldem.

Ottoman Empire and the world economy, The-, ed. H. Islamoglu-Inan (Cambridge: Cambridge UP, 1987).

Pamuk, Ş. 'Prices and wages in Istanbul, 1469–1914', on http://www.iisg.nl/hpw/data .php#ottoman.

Pamuk, Ş., *A monetary history of the Ottoman Empire*,(Cambridge: Cambridge UP, 2001).

Pamuk, Ş., 'Institutional change and the longevity of the Ottoman Empire, 1500–1800', *Journal of Interdisciplinary* History 35 (2004) 225–247.

Pamuk, Ş., 'The evolution of fiscal institutions in the Ottoman Empire', in B. Yun-Casalilla and P. O'Brien eds., *The rise of fiscal states. A global history*, Cambridge, 2012, 304–335.

Pamuk, Ş., and J.L. van Zanden, 'Standards of living', in *The Cambridge economic history of Modern Europe. Volume 1700–1870* (Cambridge: Cambridge University Press 2010).

Panhuysen, L. *Rampjaar 1672. Hoe de Republiek aan de ondergang ontsnapte* (Amsterdam 2009).

Panzac, D., *La peste dans l'Empire Ottoman 1700–1850* (Louvain, 1985).

Parker, G., *The Dutch Revolt* (Harmondsworth 2002).

Parker, G., *The Army of Flanders and the Spanish Road*, 1567–1659 : the logistics of Spanish victory and defeat in the Low Countries' wars (Cambridge, CUP, 2004).

Parker, G., *The emergence of modern finance in Europe 1500–1730* (London, Collins, 1973).

Pathe, H., *Judenschutzsteuern in Altona (1641–1842)* (diss. Hamburg, 2007).

Pezzolo, L., 'The Venetian government debt', in: *Urban public debts* (2003) pp. 61–75.

Pezzolo, L., *Il fisco dei Veneziani. Finanza pubblica ed economie tra XV e XVII secolo* (Verona 2003).

Pezzolo, L., *Una finanza d'ancien régime. La Repubblica Veneta tra XV and VIII secolo* (Napoli/Roma 2006.

Pezzolo, L. 'Republics and principalities in Italy', in: *The Rise of Fiscal States*, pp. 267–285.

Pfeil, T., *'Tot redding van het vaderland'. Het primaat van de Nederlandse overheidsfinancien in de Bataafs-Franse tijd* (Amsterdam NEHA, 1998).

Pincus, S., *The first modern revolution*, (New Haven: Yale University Press, 2009).

Pinto, I. de, Traité de la circulation et du crédit (Amsterdam, 1771).

Posthumus, N.W., *Inquiry into the history of prices in Holland; I: Wholesale prices at the Exchange of Amsterdam, 1585–1914, rates of exchange at Amsterdam, 1609–1914* (Leiden, Brill, 1964).

Postma, J., *Alexander Gogel (1765–1821). Grondlegger van de Nederlandse staat* (Hilversum, 2017).

Power and persuasion : essays on the art of state building in honour of W.P. Blockmans, (ed.) P. Hoppenbrouwers (Turnhout: Brepols, 2010).

Prak, M., *Gezeten burgers. De elite in een Hollandse stad 1700–1780* (Amsterdam 1985).

Prak, M., 'Citizenship in pre-modern Eurasia: a comparison between China, the Near East and Europe' presented at 'Modern and comparative economic history seminar, 24th November 2011, London School of Economics and Political Science'; version of November 2011 available at: http://eprints.lse.ac.uk/39751/.

Prak, M., 'The Dutch Republic as a Bourgeois Society', in eds. K. van Berkel and L. de Goei, *The International Relevance of Dutch History* (The Hague: *The Low Countries Historical Review* 25 (2010)) pp. 107–141.

Prak, M., and J.L. van Zanden, 'Tax morale and citizenship in the Dutch Republic, in; *The political economy of the Dutch Republic* ed. O. Gelderblom (Farnham 2009) 143–167.

Priester, P., *Geschiedenis van de Zeeuwse landbouw* (Wageningen 1998).

Prins, I., *Het faillissement der Hollandsche steden: Amsterdam, Dordrecht, Leiden en Haarlem* (Amsterdam 1922).

Prud'homme van Reine, R., *Admiraal Zilvervloot. Biografie van Piet Hein* (Amsterdam, Arbeiderspers 2003).

Quataert, D., *The Ottoman Empire 1700–1922* (Cambridge: CUP, 2005).

Rapp, R.T., *Industry and economic decline in seventeenth century Venice* (Harvard 1976).

Raymond, A. 'The management of the city', in: *The city in the Islamic world*, ds. S.K. Jayyusi a.o., Leiden, 2008, pp. 775–795.

Republican Alternative. The -, The Netherlands and Switzerland compared, eds. A. Holenstein, T. Maissen and M. Prak (Amsterdam 2008).

Reinhart, C.M.. and K.S. Rogoff, *This Time is Different. Eight Centuries of Financial Folly* (Princeton 2009).

Riker, W., 'Dutch and American Federalism', *Journal of the History of Ideas* 18 (1957) pp. 495–518, p.

Riley, J., *Seven Years War and the Old Regime in France: the economic and financial toll* (Princeton 1986).

Rise of the fiscal state, The-, ed. R. Bonney (Oxford UP 2004; 1999).

Rise of fiscal states. The -, A Global History, 1500–1914,eds. P. O'Brien and B. Yun Casalilla, (Cambridge, CUP, 2012).

Rogers, C.J., 'The military revolution of the Hundred Years War', in: *The military revolution debate* ed. C.J. Rogers (Oxford 1995) pp. 55–93.

Roosbroeck, R. Van, *Willem van Oranje* (Den Haag, Kruseman, 1983).

Roseveare, H., *The Treasury 1660–1870. The foundations of control* (New York: Columbia University Press, 1973).

Sahillioğlu, H. '1683–1740 Yıllarında osmanlı imparatorluğun hazine gelir ve gider' [Yearly revenue and expenditure of the Ottoman Imperial Treasury, 1683–1740'] in Genç and Özvar, *Osmanlı maliyesi*, Vol. 1.

Salzman, A., 'An ancient régime revisited': 'privatization'and political economy in the eighteenth century Ottoman Empire', *Politics and Scoiety* 21, 4 (1972) pp. 393–423.

Salzmann, A., *Tocquevile in the Ottoman Empire: rival paths to the modern state* (Leiden, Brill, 2004).

Sanchez Martines, M., 'Dette publique, autorités princières et villes dans les Pays de la Couronne d'Aragon (14e-15e siècles)', in *Urban Public Debts* (2003) pp. 27–51.

Schepper, H. de, 'Beleid en bestuur inzake de hoge overheidsfinancien in het Bourgondisch-Habsburgse Nederland', in: *Van Tresorier tot Thesaurier-Generaal*, ed. J.Th. de Smidt a.o. (Hilversum 1996).

Schwetsinski, D.M. and L. Schönduve, *De familie Lopes Suasso: financiers van Willem III* (Zwolle 1988).

Scott, H., 'The Fiscal-Military State and International Rivalry during the Long Eighteenth Century', in: *The fiscal-military state in eighteenth century Europe: essays in honour of P.G.M. Dickson* ed. Chr. Storrs (Farnham: Ashgate 2009) 23–53.

Scott, J., '"Good Night Amsterdam". Sir George Downing and Anglo-Dutch State Building', *English Historical Review* 118 (2003) pp. 334–356.

Shaw, S.J., *The financial and administrative organization and development of Ottoman Egypt, 1517–1798* (Princeton UP 1962).

Shaw, W.A., *Report on the manuscripts of Lord De Lisle and Dudley preserved at Penshurst Place* (Hist. MSS. Comm., Rep. No. 77), III (1936).

Sickenga, F.N., *Bijdrage tot de geschiedenis van de belastingen in Nederland* (Leiden, 1864).

Sicking, L., *Neptune and the Netherlands : state, economy, and war at sea in the Renaissance* (Leiden: Brill, 2004).

Smith, C.A., 'Types of City-Size Distribution. A Comparative Analysis', in: *Urbanization in history. A process of dynamic interactions*, eds. A. van der Woude, A. Hayami and J. de Vries, (Oxford 1990) pp. 20–42.

Soens, T., *De spade in de dijk? Waterbeheer en rurale samenleving in de Vlaamse kustvlakte (1280–1580)* (Gent, Academia Press, 2009).

Sommerville, J.P., 'The meaning of absolutism', in: *The Cambridge History of Political Thought, 1450–1700,* (Cambridge, CUP, 1991) pp. 347–350.

Spanninga, H., *Gulden Vrijheid? Politieke cultuur en staatsvorming in Friesland, 1600–1640* (Hilversum, Verloren, 2012).

Speet, B., 'Een kleine nederzetting in het veen', in: *Geschiedenis van Amsterdam tot 1578. Een stad uit het niets*, ed. M. Carasso-Kok (Amsterdam 2004) pp. 21–63.

Spoerer, M., 'The Revenue Structures of Brandenburg-Prussi, Saxony and Bavaria (Fifteenth to Nineteenth Centuries): Are They Compatible with the Bonney-Ormrod Model?', *La fiscalità nell'economia europea secc. XIII–XVIII*(Firenze 2008).

Sprenger, R., 'De thesaurier-generaal aan zijn bureau en op dienstreis', in: *Van tresorier tot thesaurier-generaal. Zes eeuwen financieel beleid in handen van een hoge Nederlandse ambtsdrager*, ed. J. de Smidt e.a. (Hilversum, Verloren, 1996) 137–222.

Spruyt, H., 'Institutional selection in international relations: state anarchy as order', *International organization* 48, 4 (1994) pp. 527–557.

Stasavage, D., *States of credit. Size, power and the development of European polities* (Princeton UP 2011).

Statistical mind in a pre-statistical era: The Netherlands 1750–1850, The -, P. Klep and I. Stamhuis (eds) (Amsterdam, Aksant, 2002).

Steur, J.J., *Herstel of ondergang. De voorstellen tot redres van de Verenigde Oost-Indische Compagnie* (Utrecht 1984).

Stoianovich, Traian, 'Cities, Capital Accumulation and the Ottoman Balkan Command Economy, 1500–1800' in C. Tilly and W. Blockmans (eds.), *Cities and the Rise of States in Europe*, (Boulder: Westview Press, 1994).

Stolleis, M., *Pecunia nervus rerum: Zur Staatsfinanzierung in der frühen Neuzeit*, (Frankfurt am Main, Klostermann, 1983).

Sussman, N., and Y. Yafeh, 'Institutional Reforms, Financial Development and Sovereign Debt: Britain 1690–1790',*Journal of Economic History* 66, 5 (2006) pp. 906–935.

Swart, K.W., *William of Orange and the Revolt of the Netherlands, 1572–1584* (Ashgate 2003).

Tallett, F., *War and society in Early Modern Europe, 1495–1715* (London 1992).

Tervoort, A., 'To the honor of God, for concord and the common good'. Developments in social care and education in Dutch towns (1300–1625) in *Serving the Urban Community. The Rise of Public Facilities in the Low Countries* eds. M. van der Heijden a. o. (Amsterdam, Aksant, 2009) pp. 89–107.

't Hart, M. see Hart, M. 't.

Thirsk, J., *The agrarian history of England and Wales* (Cambridge: Cambridge University Press, 1967.

Thomassen, Th., *Instrumenten van de macht. De Staten-Generaal en hun archieven 1576–1796* (Amsterdam 2009) http://dare.uva.nl/document/159807.

Tielhof, M. van, and P. van Dam, *Waterstaat in stedenland. Het hoogheemraadschap Rhineland voor 1857* (Utrecht 2006).

Tilly, Ch., ed., *The Formation of National States in Western Europe* (Princeton 1975).

Tilly, Ch., *Coercion, Capital and European States. AD 990–1992* (Oxford, Blackwell, 1992).

Tilly, Ch., and W. Blockmans (eds.), *Cities and the Rise of States in Europe*, Boulder: Westview Press, 1994.

Tracy, J., 'The taxation system of the county of Holland', in: *Economisch- en Sociaal Historisch Jaarboek* 48 (1985) pp. 71–118.

Tracy, J., *A financial revolution in the Habsburg Netherlands.* Renten *and* Renteniers *in the County of Holland, 1515–1565* (Berkeley, University of California Press, 1985).

Tracy, J., 'Emigré and ecclesiastical property as the sheet-anchor of Holland's finance, 1572–1584', in P. Benedict et al., eds., *Reformation, revolt and civil war in France and the Netherlands, 1555–1585* (Amsterdam, 1999), pp. 255–66.

Tracy, J., 'Keeping the wheels of war turning: revenues of the province of Holland, 1572–1609', in G. Darby, ed., *New studies on the Dutch Revolt* (2001), pp. 133–50.

Tracy, J., 'On the dual origins of long-term urban debt in medieval Europe', in: *Urban public debts* (2003) pp. 13–27.

Tracy, J., *The Founding of the Dutch Republic: War, Finance and Politics in Holland* (Oxford, Oxford University Press 2008).

Tracy, J., 'Holland's New Fiscal Regime, 1572–1576', *The Political Economy of the Dutch Republic*, ed. O. Gelderblom (Ashgate, Surrey, 2009) pp. 41–55.

Trompetter, C., *Gewestelijke financien ten tijde van de Republiek der Verenigde Nederlanden. Deel VI. Friesland (1587–1795)* (Den Haag 2007).

Ucendo, J.I.A., 'Castile's Tax System in the Seventeenth Century', *The Journal of European Economic History* 30, 3 (2001) pp. 597–617.

Ulloa, M., *La Hacienda Real de Castilla en el Reinado de Felipe II* (Madrid 1977).

Unie van Utrecht, De -, eds. S. Groenveld and H. Leeuwenberg (Den Haag 1979).

Urban public debts. Urban government and the market for annuities in Western Europe (*14th–18th centuries* eds. M. Boone, K. Davids and P. Janssens (Turnhout 2003).

Van Roosbroeck, R., *Willem van Oranje* (Den Haag, Kruseman, 1983).

Van tresorier tot thesaurier-generaal. Zes eeuwen financieel beleid in handen van een hoge Nederlandse ambtsdrager, ed. J. de Smidt e.a. (Hilversum, Verloren, 1996).

Van Zanden, see Zanden.

Veenstra, W., *Gewestelijke financien ten tijde van de Republiek der Verenigde Nederlanden. Deel VII Zeeland, 1573–1795* (Den Haag, 2009).

Veenstra, W., "Geld is de zenuw van de oorlog'; de financiën van de Zeeuwse Admiraliteit in de achttiende eeuw (1698–1795)', *Archief. Mededelingen van het Koninklijk Zeeuwsch Genootschap der Wetenschappen* (2008) pp. 91–121.

Veenstra, W., *Tussen gewest en Generaliteit. Staatsvorming en financiering van de oorlog te water in de Republiek der Verenigde Nederlanden in het bijzonder Zeeland (1586–1795)* (diss. VU Amsterdam 2014).

Velde, F., and D.R. Weir, 'The financial market and government debt policy in France, 1746–1793', *Journal of Economic History* 52, 1 (1992) pp. 1–39.

Verenigde Oostindische Compagnie tussen oorlog en diplomatie, eds. G.v.d. Knaap en G. Teitler (Leiden 2002).

Verhulst, A., *The rise of cities in North-West Europe* (Cambridge: Cambridge UP, 1999).

Verstegen, S.W. *Gewestelijke financiën ten tijde van de Republiek der Verenigde Nederlanden. Deel 5. Utrecht (1579–1798)* (Den Haag 2006).

Voltaire, The Works of -, A Contemporary Version. A Critique and Biography by John Morley, notes by Tobias Smollett, trans. William F. Fleming (New York, E.R. DuMont, 1901). 21 vols. Vol. XII. http://oll.libertyfund.org/index.php?optioncom _staticxt&staticfileshow.php%3Ftitle2132&Itemid27.

Vries, J. de, 'Barges and capitalism. Passenger transportation in the Dutch economy, 1632–1839', *AAG bijdragen*; 21 (1978), pag. 33–398 (also published as monograph Utrecht, Hes, 1981).

Vries, J. de, *The Dutch rural economy in the Golden Age, 1500–1700* (London, 1978).

Vries, J. de, *European Urbanization, 1500–1800* (London, Methuen & Co., 1984).

Vries, J. de, *The Economy of Europe in an Age of Crisis, 1600–1750* (Cambridge, CUP, 1996).

Vries, J. de, 'Introduction', in: *Urbanization in history. A process of dynamic interactions*, eds. A. van der Woude, A. Hayami and J. de Vries, (Oxford 1990) 1–20.

Vries, J. de, and A. van der Woude, *The first modern economy: success, failure and perseverance of the Dutch economy, 1500–1815* (Cambridge, 1997).

Vries, Joh, de, 'De ontduiking der convooien en licten in de Republiek tijdens de achttiende eeuw', *Tijdschrift voor Geschiedenis* (1958) pp. 349–361.

Vries, P., 'Public finance in China and Britain in the long eighteenth century', Working papers, 167/12, The London School of Economics and Political Science, London, UK (2012).

Vu, Tuong, 'Studying the State through State Formation', *World Politics* 62, 1 (2010) pp. 148–175.

Weber, M., *Politik als Beruf* (München 1919).

Weber, M., *The City* (Munich, 1921) reprinted in Max Weber, *Economy and Society*, eds. G. Roth and C. Wittich, Berkeley: University of California Press, 1978, pp. 1233–1234.

Wegener Sleeswijk, A., 'Binnenlandse belastingen en internationale handel. De crisis in de wijnhandel van 1749–1715' in: *Ondernemers en bestuurders*,eds. C. Lesger and L. Noordegraaf (Amsterdam 1999) pp. 557–575.

White, S. *The climate of rebellion in the Early Modern Ottoman Empire* (Cambridge: CUP, 2011).

Wilson, E., *Savage Republic. De Indis of Hugo Grotius, republicanism and Dutch hegemony within the early modern world-system (c. 1600–1619)* (Leiden/Boston 2008).

Witt, J. de, *Waerdye van lyf-rente naer proportie van los-renten* (Den Haag 1671) http://www.dbnl.org/tekst/witt001waer01_01/.

Woude, A. van der 'De Staten, Leicester en Elizabeth in financiële verwikkelingen', *Tijdschrift voor Geschiedenis*, 74 (1961), pp. 64–82.

Woude, A. van der, 'De demografische ontwikkeling van de Noordelijke Nederlanden', in: *Algemene Geschiedenis der Nederlanden. Deel 5* (Bussum 1980) pp. 102–169.

Wrigley, E., and R. Schofield, *The population history of England, 1541–1871: a reconstruction* (Cambridge 1981).

Wuergler, A., '"The League of discordant members" or how the old Swiss confederation operated and how it managed to survive for so long', in: *The Republican Alternative. The Netherlands and Switzerland compared*, eds. A. Holenstein, T. Maissen, M. Prak (Amsterdam 2008) pp. 29–51.

Zanden, J.L. van, (data supplied by J. de Vries, J.P. Smits and A. van Riel) 'The prices of the most important consumer goods, and indices of wages and the cost of living in the western part of the Netherlands, 1450–1800' on http://www.iisg.nl/hpw/data.php#netherlands.

Zanden, J.L.van, 'De opkomst van een eigenerfde boerenklasse in Overijssel, 1750–1830', *AAG-Bijdragen* 24 (1983) 105–130.

Zanden, J.L. van, *The long road to the Industrial Revolution. The European Economy in a global perspective, 1000–1800* (Leiden, Brill, 2009).

Zanden, J.L. van, and A.van Riel, *Nederland 1780–1914. Staat, instituties en economische ontwikkeling* (Amsterdam 2000); translated as *The strictures of inheritance. The Dutch economy in the nineteenth century* (Princeton 2004).

Zanden, J.L. van, and B. van Leeuwen, and 'Persistent but not Consistent: The Growth of National Income in Holland 1347–1807', *Explorations in economic history*, Vol. 49 (2) 2012, pp. 119–130, Table 4; data and titles of the contributing publications of the authors are published on http://www.cgeh.nl/reconstruction-national-accounts-holland-1500-1800-0; see also: http://www.cgeh.nl/sites/default/files/WorkingPapers/CGEH.WP_.No4_.vanZandenvanLeeuwen.mar2011.pdf.

Zanden, J.L. van, E. Buringh and M. Bosker, 'The rise and decline of European parliaments, 1188–1789', *Economic History Review* 65, 3 (2012) pp. 835–861.

Zanden, J.L. van, and M. Prak, 'Towards an economic interpretation of citizenship: the Dutch Republic between medieval communes and modern nation-states', *European Review of Economic History* 10 (2006) pp. 111–145.

Zanden, M. Bosker, E. Buringh and J.L. van 'From Baghdad to London. Unraveling urban development in Europe, the Middle East and North Africa, 800–1800', *Review of Economics and Statistics* 95,4 (2013) pp. 1418–1437.

Zuijderduijn, C.J., *Medieval capital markets. Markets for renten between stateformation and private investment in Holland (1300–1550)* (Leiden, Brill, 2009).

Zwitzer, H.L., *"De militie van den staat": het leger van de Republiek der Verenigde Nederlanden* (Amsterdam, Van Soeren, 1991).

Index

www.ingramcontent.com/pod-product-compliance
Lightning Source LLC
LaVergne TN
LVHW010541300926
849162LV00002B/197